# INDUSTRIAL/ ORGANIZATIONAL PSYCHOLOGY

# INDUSTRIAL/ ORGANIZATIONAL PSYCHOLOGY

## Understanding the Workplace  Fifth Edition

### Paul E. Levy

*The University of Akron*

worth publishers
Macmillan Learning

New York

Vice President, Social Sciences: Charles Linsmeier
Senior Acquisitions Editor: Daniel DeBonis
Development Editor: Andrew Sylvester
Assistant Editor: Katie Pachnos
Executive Marketing Manager: Katherine Nurre
Marketing Assistant: Morgan Ratner
Executive Media Editor: Noel Hohnstine
Associate Media Editor: Anthony Casciano
Director, Content Management Enhancement: Tracey Kuehn
Managing Editor, Sciences and Social Sciences: Lisa Kinne
Senior Project Editor: Kerry O'Shaughnessy
Media Producer: Joseph Tomasso
Senior Photo Editor: Robin Fadool
Photo Research Assistant: Candice Cheesman
Senior Production Manager: Stacey B. Alexander
Director of Design, Content Management: Diana Blume
Cover and Interior Design: Vicki Tomaselli
Art Manager: Matthew McAdams
Composition: MPS Ltd.
Printing and Binding: RR Donnelley
Cover Photos: *top:* Jetta Productions/Iconica/Getty Images; *middle:* Juice Images/Cultura/Getty
     Images; *bottom:* Gallery Stock

Library of Congress Control Number: 2016944022
ISBN-13: 978-1-319-01426-1
ISBN-10: 1-319-01426-7

With Instructor's Resource Manual
ISBN-13: 978-1-319-03296-8
ISBN-10: 1-319-03296-6

Printed in the United States of America

First printing

Worth Publishers
One New York Plaza
Suite 4500
New York, NY 10004-1562
www.macmillanlearning.com

## Dedication

To my brother, Jerry, who was larger than life and always managed to make me feel special. Although I miss him and the pain lingers, I'm blessed that I will always be able to see his smile and hear his voice whenever I summon them.   P.E.L.

# ABOUT THE AUTHOR

Sylvia Chinn-Levy

**Paul E. Levy** was born and raised in Baltimore, Maryland, the youngest of his family's five children. He received his BA in psychology and economics from Washington & Lee University and earned his MA and PhD in industrial/organizational (I/O) psychology from Virginia Tech. A faculty member at The University of Akron since 1989 and Chair of the Department of Psychology since 2005, Dr. Levy has been very involved in the development and training of hundreds of graduate students there. During his tenure, he has also provided many undergraduates with their first exposure to the field of I/O psychology through his Introduction to Industrial/Organizational Psychology course. Dr. Levy's consulting and research interests include performance management, feedback, coaching and development, and organizational justice. He has published his scholarly work in many psychology and management journals, including the *Journal of Applied Psychology, Journal of Personality and Social Psychology, Organizational and Human Decision Processes, Personnel Psychology*, and *Academy of Management Journal*. Dr. Levy is married to Sylvia Chinn-Levy and has three sons—Christopher, Sean, and Jared— who have always managed to keep things interesting. Dr. Levy is an avid baseball and basketball fan, a servant leader at his church, a youth sports coach, a basketball player, and a lifelong fan of the Baltimore Orioles.

# BRIEF CONTENTS

# CONTENTS

# PREFACE

Each edition of *Industrial/Organizational Psychology: Understanding the Workplace* has been a unique experience for me. In the first edition, I made every effort to realize the original goals behind writing the book in the first place. In the second edition, I endeavored to further refine our approach to meet the expectations of instructors. For the third edition, I had the opportunity to work with a new publisher, Worth, and placed a greater emphasis on the changing field of industrial/organizational (I/O) psychology. In the fourth edition, I worked with the publisher to improve the look and design of the text as well as add new features that should benefit both instructor and student. The fifth edition represents a pretty substantial revision with some major in-chapter structural changes and significant content-related updates, adjustments, and additions. Yet the reasons I look forward to each revision mirror the reasons why I originally sat down to write the first edition.

I've been teaching Introduction to Industrial and Organizational Psychology at The University of Akron since 1996 and also taught it for a few years at Virginia Tech. I've always loved teaching the course but was never quite happy with the available textbooks; most tend to be quite dry—and a dry textbook for a technical field is not the best combination. My students always had concerns about the textbooks as well, so I wondered if I might make a meaningful contribution to the I/O textbook market.

Therefore, my primary goal for the first edition was to write a textbook that was more interesting, more accessible to students, and a consistently "better read." I worked very hard to produce a book that would engage students, excite them, and, of course, teach them a great deal about the scope of I/O psychology. From the very beginning, what attracted me to this task was the potential to write a book that would draw students into the story of I/O psychology—and that has been my guiding principle for the subsequent editions as well.

Focusing on writing a student-friendly text would have been difficult enough in and of itself. However, my second goal was to also achieve the highest quality in terms of its research orientation. I have been fortunate enough to be a member of one of the finest I/O programs in the country for 27 years; thus, high-quality I/O research is important to me and to my colleagues. So the real task for me was to maintain the rigorous research focus that is critical to understanding I/O psychology—but to do it in a way that students would find interesting and stimulating.

This book was written to serve as the main text in an Introduction to I/O class, which is usually taught at a sophomore or junior level, but I know of quite a few colleagues who have used it in basic or introductory graduate-level courses. It is also more current than most of the other I/O books on the market. Because I also teach separate graduate courses in industrial psychology and organizational psychology, I have to stay current on the research in both areas.

I held fast to the same overriding principles in the design and writing of the fifth edition—to develop interesting, reader-friendly, current, research-based coverage of I/O psychology. In particular, I revised each chapter based on comments provided informally by colleagues who used previous editions and on formal reviews submitted by a diverse cross section of I/O psychology instructors from community colleges, four-year schools, and universities with graduate programs in I/O psychology, who have used previous editions of this book or competitors' books. I attempted to tighten up the writing, expand on the real-world examples, and broaden the coverage to other areas that have emerged more recently on the I/O scene. One of the newer themes for this edition is an increased focus on technology, which is infused throughout the field and is now better infused throughout the text.

## CONTENT AND ORGANIZATION

*Industrial/Organizational Psychology,* Fifth Edition, is divided into three main sections. The first focuses on the history of I/O psychology (Chapter 1) as well as on the basics of the research process (Chapter 2), including measurement, methods, and statistics. Chapter 1 differs from most other I/O books, however, in its treatment of I/O history because it not only includes history of the development of the field, but also presents important information about how I/O psychologists are trained. Students get a flavor of both how the field develops and how I/O psychologists develop. Chapter 2 is more detailed about the research process than the analogous chapter in other I/O texts. This was a deliberate choice because I believe a basic understanding of correlation, extraneous variables, why they are a problem, and so on, is an essential foundation from which students can build a greater appreciation for more complex topics later in the course.

The second section of the text is built around what we have traditionally called industrial or personnel psychology. The first modification of note here is my emphasis on the importance of job analysis (Chapter 3) throughout. Second, I include a full chapter on criterion measurement (Chapter 4), which most I/O texts roll into the performance appraisal or selection chapters; this material provides the foundation for the rest of the second section and even many elements of the third section. Chapter 5, on performance appraisal, emphasizes the social-contextual approach and has a particular focus on current research in this area.

Another significant modification to the middle section is that the material on selection has been broken down into two chapters. First is a traditional Chapter 6, covering the major predictors used in selection. Chapter 7 focuses on how predictors are used in selection and includes a lengthy discussion of the legal issues involved—an interesting area for students and an important one for the field. Reviewers have always seemed to like this chapter and have noted that I was able to make the difficult material more accessible for students. Finally, the last chapter of this section (Chapter 8) presents a traditional look at training, with an emphasis on issues related to diversity.

The final main section of the text provides an overview of organizational psychology. I strove to make the motivation chapter (Chapter 9) more applied; most other I/O texts tend to present just motivational theories. Chapter 10, on job attitudes, uniquely explores the relationships between predictors (like job satisfaction and organizational commitment) and organizational outcome variables (such as turnover and absence).

The stress chapter (Chapter 11) spends a good deal of time on work–family issues, an extremely important element of work. Violence in the workplace has also become a much-talked-about and examined phenomenon in recent years, and I discuss it within the context of the modern workplace.

Groups and work teams are the focus of Chapter 12, which again starts with basic social psychological work and shows how it has been applied to issues such as self-managing work teams. Leadership is presented in Chapter 13, where theories are categorized as either traditional or contemporary. I also discuss at some length various issues revolving around gender and leadership as well as culture and leadership. The final chapter (Chapter 14) talks about organizational theories and applies these theories, as well as others from earlier chapters, to a discussion of how organizations change and develop. Cutting-edge topics such as knowledge management and continuous learning are also discussed here. This chapter has been commended since the first edition by both instructors and students.

## NEW TO THE FIFTH EDITION

The first four editions were well received by most of the instructors who used them; those instructors, as well as several other reviewers, were kind enough to send me a good deal of very useful feedback. Their comments, along with the dynamic nature of the field and several of my own ideas, provided the blueprint for a thoroughly revised fifth edition. New references have been added to every chapter, reflecting some of the best new research currently available, and the writing has been tightened up throughout.

A few significant changes have been implemented to strengthen the pedagogy as well. The **Technical Tip** marginal feature, which reminds students about technical issues that were introduced earlier in the text, has been carried over from earlier editions. This device allows students to connect concepts introduced in one chapter to the application of those concepts in later chapters. The **Practitioner Forum boxes**, another innovation from previous editions, continues to provide students with insights into how the concepts and theories that they are reading about translate in actual businesses and organizations. As always, I worked diligently to provide up-to-date examples and images, including updated **Closer Look questions** for each photograph.

Critical thinking continues to be a strong emphasis, and in addition to the **Critical Thinking Questions** I have also included **Application Questions** at the end of each chapter. These elements work together to enhance learning at two different levels. And the **Taking It to the Field exercises**, added in the fourth edition and updated in several places in this new edition, provide detailed scenarios requiring students to analyze, evaluate, and problem solve. These exercises can be used for discussion in class or take-home assignments, and will help students gain a better handle on the application of the material. Together, these features allow students to go one step further than just understanding the content by getting some experience problem solving and using the content in an applied situation.

The fifth edition also includes an exciting new feature: **I/O Today**. These boxes, which appear in each chapter, present cutting-edge practices, current controversies, and developing theories that practitioners and researchers are grappling with now and that will continue to influence the field in the coming years. Each box presents a brief essay followed by discussion questions and should provide an interesting jumping-off point for research and debate in your classroom.

Finally, while updates and revisions have been made to most discussions in the text, there are several important changes that I would like to highlight for each chapter:

## Chapter 1

- Presents a reorganized historical survey of I/O psychology with a major section covering developments over the last 15 years, including discussions of globalization, the virtual workforce, innovation and creativity, and coaching and employee development.
- Discusses the growing importance of big data, revolutions in performance appraisals, the use of social media, and global competition as major themes that will influence the field in the coming years.
- Expands the discussion of unemployment and underemployment, diversity, and the role of technology in employee selection as contemporary trends.
- Discusses the scientist/practitioner gap and ways to address it in the I/O Today feature.

## Chapter 2

- Updates the discussion of Technological Advances in Survey Methodology to cover recent research on the differences between pencil-and-paper surveys vs. electronic surveys.
- Addresses new electronic survey methods, experience sampling methodology, online panels, and crowdsourcing.
- Discusses the growing importance of big data in the I/O Today feature.

## Chapter 3

- Updates and expands the discussion of the O*NET.
- Includes a major new section covering an expanded discussion of competency modeling.
- Discusses competency modeling in the context of rapidly and continually changing organizational needs and job descriptions in the I/O Today feature.

## Chapter 4

- Includes major updates to the discussion of contextual performance.
- Presents new research on organizational citizenship behaviors (OCBs), organizational effectiveness, and task performance.
- Updates the discussion of counterproductive work behaviors (CWBs) and stress.
- Discusses the diversity-validity dilemma in the I/O Today feature.

## Chapter 5

- Provides significant updates to the discussion of the effectiveness of 360-degree feedback, including new research on its use in the health and education fields.
- Presents new research on the relationships between telecommuting and performance, including a new discussion of the influence of leader–member exchange (LMX) in this context.
- Updates the coverage of forced distribution and forced ranking, including research on the negative effects of these practices.
- Expands coverage of feedforward interviews (FFIs) and coverage of the role of feedback and emotional intelligence in goal setting.
- Adds new coverage of research on politics, perceptions, and rumination on performance, and on feedback orientation and environment.
- Includes major updates to the discussion of legal issues in performance appraisal.
- Discusses legal and ethical issues around the use of technology in performance appraisal in the I/O Today feature.

## Chapter 6

- Updates coverage of Computer Adaptive Testing, including new research on mobile testing.
- Adds new information on emotional intelligence testing and psychomotor testing.
- Discusses validity issues related to remote assessment practices in the I/O Today feature.

## Chapter 7

- Adds a new discussion of the application of eye-tracking technology to evaluate the effectiveness of online recruiting sites.
- Updates the discussion of cybervetting and legal and ethical issues in this area.
- Updates the discussion of the role diversity plays in recruiting, including a new discussion of the effects of affirmative action plans on evaluation and stereotyping, and an update on recent legal developments related to affirmative action policies.
- Adds new coverage on the impact of *Ricci v. DeStefano* and expanded coverage of bona fide occupational qualification (BFOQ).
- Discusses recent cases involving religion in the workplace in the I/O Today feature.

## Chapter 8

- Adds a new discussion on the use of gamification.
- Presents updated research on distance learning, onboarding, executive coaching, corporate universities, sexual harassment, and diversity management and training.
- Discusses case studies in the use of gamification in job training in the I/O Today feature.

## Chapter 9

- Includes an expanded discussion of self-determination theory.
- Expands the discussion of job crafting, including new research on its application and relationship to work engagement.
- Expands the coverage of idiosyncratic ideals (i-deals), including recent research in this area.
- Discusses issues related to results-only work environments (ROWE) in the I/O Today feature.

## Chapter 10

- Includes a new discussion on the role of guilt as it relates to job attitudes.
- Provides a major expansion of the coverage of withdrawal behaviors, including research on its connection to commitment and turnover intentions.
- Expands the discussion of counterproductive behaviors, including new research on affective commitment.
- Includes a major new section on Organizational Commitment Profiles.
- Expands the discussion of workaholism and perceived organizational support (POS).
- Provides a major expansion of the coverage of emotions in the workplace, including new research on the regulation of emotions.
- Discusses recent research on the relationship between unions and job satisfaction in the I/O Today feature.

## Chapter 11

- Provides a revised discussion on the nature and sources of stress.
- Provides a new discussion of the job-demands resources (JD-R) and conservation of resources (COR) models of stress.
- Provides significant updates to the discussion of work–family conflict (WFC), including new discussions of family supportive supervisor behaviors (FSSB) and several recent intervention studies.
- Updates the discussion of family-leave practices, child-care benefits, elder-care assistance, and dual-earner couples.
- Updates the discussion of the effects of job loss, including the addition of research on PTSD and underemployment.
- Expands the discussion of workplace violence to include recent research and interventions.
- Discusses the impact of PTSD and STSD in various occupations in the I/O Today feature.

## Chapter 12

- Includes a major new section on conflict within teams.
- Includes new research on models of team development.
- Expands the discussion of virtual teams, including a survey of recent research in this area.
- Provides new coverage of the Team Role Experience and Orientation (TREO) test in the discussion of team selection.

- Provides a new major section on multiteam systems.
- Discusses issues related to age diversity within teams in the I/O Today feature.

## Chapter 13

- Updates the discussion of consideration and initiating structure.
- Expands the discussions of leader–member exchange (LMX) theory and transformational leadership theory, including new research on these theories.
- Provides a major new section on authentic and servant leadership.
- Updates the discussions of gender and leadership and of culture and leadership.
- Adds coverage of the Dark Triad in the discussion of emotions and leadership.
- Discusses the romance of leadership (ROL) theory in the context of recent news coverage of CEO compensation in the I/O Today feature.

## Chapter 14

- Introduces the concept of organizational ambidexterity in the discussion of organizational development.
- Updates the discussion of knowledge management and learning companies.
- Discusses the concept of holacracy in the I/O Today feature.

## A STUDENT-FOCUSED TEXT

A series of pedagogical features aim to make the book more accessible to students and to teach the material in an effective and interesting way. For example, each chapter includes a **marginal glossary,** designed to help students highlight and understand the important terms *as they read* through the book rather than having to go to the end of the chapter to see the key terms and formal definitions. An alphabetical list of these key terms with their page reference numbers is provided at the end of each chapter, and a complete glossary for the entire book is also presented at the end of the text.

Each chapter also includes a set of **Learning Objectives, Critical Thinking Questions,** and **Application Questions.** The learning objectives, found at the beginning of the chapter, show students what the goals of the chapter are up front—that is, they highlight what I want students to understand after having worked through the chapter. The Critical Thinking Questions, found at the end of the chapter, are designed to help students study and to encourage them to think about the material at a deeper level rather than just memorize key points. Finally, the Application Questions are designed to encourage students to work with the material and to consider ways in which the material can be applied to real-world situations.

One of the most innovative (and favorite) features I've included since the first edition is what I've called the **Practitioner Forum,** in which an I/O psychologist practitioner provides a bit of his or her insight and experience in an area relevant to that particular chapter. Readers will find a Practitioner Forum in 13 of the 14 chapters; each one is written by a practitioner who has wonderful experiences and information to share. In trying to keep this feature short and concise, the practitioners have done a terrific job tying their experiences and the situation they describe to the content of the chapter. I believe students will continue to find this feature very interesting.

A good understanding of technical issues, such as methods and statistics, is useful to fully comprehending the significance of data presented throughout the text, but I find that students often struggle with these technical concepts. For this reason, I decided to incorporate **Technical Tip** marginal notes in each chapter that follows Chapter 2, Research Methods. **Taking It to the Field,** added in the previous edition, presents real-life scenarios or consulting situations where students are provided with information and asked to play the role of an I/O psychologist to solve the described problem. This provides a great opportunity for students to apply what they learn and get a preview of the kinds of problems that I/O professionals commonly address. These scenarios or situations could be used as the basis for written assignments or as the context for interesting and beneficial class discussions. A new boxed feature, **I/O Today,** presents innovative practices, developing issues, and emerging theories that are of interest to I/O practitioners and researchers working in the field now, and could impact practices and policies in the years to come. The topics presented in these brief essays not only give students a window into the very real issues gripping the field today, but they will also hopefully inspire students to view I/O psychology as a living discipline that is impacted by and influences many aspects of modern life.

As with each new edition, I have continued to revamp the **art program** to ensure relevance and clarity for all figures and photos. New photos have been added to provide visual anchors for the main concepts and aid in students' ability to remember them. **A Closer Look** captions, each in the form of a Critical Thinking Question, further enhance the function of each photo, prompting students to think about the given concept on a deeper—and sometimes more applied—level.

I've also provided a valuable list of **Suggested Readings** at the end of every chapter, along with a very brief summary of each. These readings vary from technical journal articles to very general overviews of the different topics covered in the book. I updated these for the fifth edition where I felt new, important works had been recently published. Complete citations are included to help make it easier for students to pursue additional depth or understanding of I/O information.

Finally, I've also incorporated many **Internet citations,** which provide a wealth of information that would be difficult to access via print media. Each of these sites is an active link as of this writing. Websites like that of the Equal Employment Opportunity Commission (EEOC) and the O★NET, for instance, are great resources for students and serve as a rich source of cutting-edge information.

## SUPPLEMENTS

All the supplements to accompany *Industrial/Organizational Psychology,* Fifth Edition, can be found or requested at http://www.macmillanlearning.com/levy5e.

### Instructor's Resource Manual by Kristie Campana, Minnesota State University—Mankato

The *Instructor's Resource Manual* has been newly updated for the fifth edition. Each chapter begins with Learning Objectives, a Chapter Summary, and a practical overview of Teaching the Chapter. Suggested Exercises and Assignments provide meaningful ways for students to engage with the material and interact during class. The manual also includes rubrics for evaluating the end-of-chapter features Taking It to the Field and Application Questions. Finally, a Highlighted Study for Discussion offers a summary and analysis of a study of particular relevance to one of the core concepts of the chapter. New and experienced instructors alike will find invaluable support in the *Instructor's Resource Manual*. To download the manual in PDF or Microsoft Word Format, visit http://www.macmillanlearning.com/levy5e.

### Diploma Computerized Test Bank by Kristie Campana, Minnesota State University—Mankato

The *Test Bank* is newly revised and has been expanded to include approximately 90 questions per chapter, including multiple-choice, short-answer, and essay questions. The Diploma software allows instructors to add an unlimited number of questions; edit questions; format a test; scramble questions; and include pictures, equations, or multimedia links. With the accompanying gradebook, instructors can record students' grades throughout a course, sort student records, view detailed analyses of test items, curve tests, generate reports, add weights to grades, and more.

### Book-Specific Lecture and Art PowerPoint Slides

To ease your transition to *Industrial/Organizational Psychology*, Fifth Edition, a prepared set of lecture and art slides in easy-to-adopt PowerPoint format is available to download from the instructor's side of the book's catalog page at http://www.macmillanlearning.com/levy5e.

## ACKNOWLEDGMENTS

To describe a text as single-authored leaves out so many people whose help, both directly and indirectly, has been a big part of this book's success. While writing this book has been in many ways a labor of love for me, it would have been completely impossible without the help and support of so many friends, family, and colleagues.

I'll start with my current and former graduate students, who have always provided me with the crystal-clear reason why I am a psychology professor. They have been instrumental in helping to shape my thoughts and ideas over the years, and a few have helped with some of the specific tasks associated with the fifth edition. I thank them all, but especially Lauren Borden and Caitlin Cavanaugh, who were vital to the research process that helped produce the current text. Without their efforts I simply couldn't revise the text effectively—they are bright, motivated doctoral students who make my job so much fun.

Next, I must thank all the undergraduates in my Introduction to Industrial/Organizational Psychology class over the years who have experienced this book, in the sense that they lived through the rough drafts via my lectures over the course of each semester. Without their encouragement and favorable response to the class, I would have never considered writing this text.

Third, my I/O colleagues at The University of Akron, with whom I have been so fortunate to have worked over the last 27 years, have contributed in so many ways—from helpful expertise on certain sections, to ideas about how to present information, to those key cites from their areas of expertise that often just helped bring sections to life, to just plain-old social support. All of my non-I/O colleagues in the Department of Psychology at Akron have been instrumental in this process as well, by helping me think through ideas, providing resources, and encouraging my efforts.

The authors of the Practitioner Forum features were terrific contributors to the book through their expertise and insight, which is reflected not only in their written contributions, but also in their willingness to pitch in and do so on our sometimes tight schedule. I appreciate the efforts of Douglas Klein, John F. Binning, Deirdre J. Knapp, Elaine Pulakos, Matthew O'Connell, Elizabeth Kolmstetter, Eric A. Surface, Anne Herman, Brian Welle, E. Jeffrey Hill, Tom Ruddy, Jamen Graves, and Laura Heft.

The following individuals served as reviewers at various stages of this project—I was amazed at the level of detail and care they invested in this endeavor. Without their ideas, suggestions, and criticisms, the finished product would be considerably "less finished." Those involved in the fifth edition provided great insight, and I am appreciative of their hard work. I can't thank these individuals enough! In particular, I would like to thank Kristie Campana, who has been not only an insightful reviewer over the last couple of editions but also an enthusiastic contributor to the pedagogy and supplements for the book. Kristie has done fabulous work taking my content and developing creative ways to enhance and build on it in our pedagogical features.

Jack Aiello, *Rutgers University—New Brunswick*

Michael Amico, *Housatonic Community—Technical College*

William Attenweiler, *Northern Kentucky University*

Pamela Auburn, *University of Houston—Downtown*

Melinda Blackman, *California State University, Fullerton*

Kristie Campana, *Minnesota State University—Mankato*

Kelly Charlton, *University of North Carolina at Pembroke*

Bryan Dawson, *University of North Georgia*

Patrick Devine, *Kennesaw State University*

David Devonis, *Graceland University*

Donna El-Armale, *California State University—Dominguez Hills*

James Farr, *Pennsylvania State University*

Judith Gebhardt, *University of Maryland*

Jennifer Gonder, *Farmingdale State College—SUNY*

Charles Gorman, *East Tennessee State University*

Kathy Hanisch, *Iowa State University*

Donald Hantula, *Temple University*

Robert Harvey, *Virginia Tech*

Teresa Heckert, *Truman State University*

Paul Herrle, *College of Southern Nevada*

Ann Higgs, *Marist College*

Linda Hoffman, *McKendree University*

Keith James, *Portland State University*

Andrea Lassiter, *Minnesota State University—Mankato*

Wendong Li, *Kansas State University*

Nicolette Lopez, *University of Texas at Arlington*

Debra Major, *Old Dominion University*

Karen Marando, *Argosy University*

Daniel McElwreath, *William Paterson University*

Heather McGee, *Western Michigan University*

Mary Meisenhelter, *York College of Pennsylvania*

John Meyer, *University of Western Ontario*

Simon Moon, *La Salle University*

Bryan Myers, *University of North Carolina—Wilmington*

Joel Nadler, *Southern Illinois University Edwardsville*

Brian O'Leary, *University of Tennessee—Chattanooga*

Joshua Oyekan, *Morris College*

Stephanie Payne, *Texas A&M University, College Station*

Harriet Pila, *San Jose State University*

Erin Richard, *Florida Institute of Technology*

Justin Rueb, *University of Wisconsin—Stevens Point*

Charles Samuelson, *Texas A&M University*

Comila Shahani-Denning, *Hofstra University*

Mark Sibicky, *Marietta College*

Nanette Silverman, *Dowling College*

Robert Sinclair, *Clemson University*

Amie Skattebo, *Pennsylvania State University*

Michael Sliter, *ACT Center of Indiana*

Alice Stuhlmacher, *DePaul University*

Harold Takooshian, *Fordham University*

Holly Traver, *Rensselaer Polytechnic Institute*

Liu-Qin Yang, *Portland State University*

I switched publishers for the third edition and have found Worth to be fabulous to work with. Every single individual who has worked on my book has been professional, competent, and fun to work with. Dan DeBonis has been a wonderful editor, always encouraging and helping me every step of the way. I have worked with a series of terrific developmental editors along the way and was really blessed this time to work with Andrew Sylvester who has demonstrated keen insight and was able to get a great feel for my book and my approach early on in the process. Andrew has raised questions, helped clarify some of my thinking and writing, and has just been a terrific partner in this process. Working with Andrew was very, very easy and I hope (!!) that he feels the same way, even though I'm guessing that he sometimes wanted to tell me to just meet the dang deadline and move on. His expertise and professionalism have been hallmarks of the work of this fifth edition. Finally, my appreciation is extended to my friends in editorial and production—namely, Katie Pachnos, Kerry O'Shaughnessy, Robert Leon, Robin Fadool, Candice Cheesman, Vicki Tomaselli, and Stacey Alexander; the marketing support from Kate Nurre; the guidance of Anthony

Casciano on the supplement program; and the Worth sales force for having so much confidence in this book.

I'd like to thank my extended family, whose faith in me in everything I've ever done has never wavered—that means more to me than they realize. My wife, Sylvia, has continued to put up with me through this long process, as I sometimes juggle more things than seems reasonable—and she has done so with the dignity, class, love, and respect that she has spoiled me with since we first met over 30 years ago. I could not have done this without her and would not have even tried—in fact, there is very little that I'm able to do without her or her support! Our three boys, Christopher, Sean, and Jared, have provided the immeasurable joy in our lives that has made everything else seem not quite as important. There is still nothing I enjoy more than spending time with them and being proud of who they are. One of my graduate students, in the acknowledgments section in her dissertation, thanked me for sharing my family with her for five years—I was touched by that notion because I know that my family is my greatest blessing. I thank God for them and for all that He has provided me as I continue to be amazed by His never-ending grace.

# I/O Psychology: Then and Now

## LEARNING OBJECTIVES

This chapter should help you understand:

- How I/O psychologists are trained
- The work of I/O psychologists and how it benefits organizations and employees alike
- The diverse historical trends associated with the development and growth of I/O psychology
- The very important role currently being played by I/O psychology in the changing workplace, as well as the field's great potential to contribute to organizational functioning in the future

For most of us, who we are is in large part defined by what we do. If you were to ask me to describe myself in a few sentences, I would say something like the following: My name is Paul Levy. I have been fortunate enough to be married to Sylvia Chinn-Levy for 24 years and have three terrific young boys named Christopher, Sean, and Jared. I am a psychology professor and department chair at the University of Akron, where I specialize in industrial/organizational psychology. I teach both undergraduate and graduate students and do research in the areas of performance appraisal and feedback. I'm a big sports fan (particularly of the Baltimore Orioles), a youth sports coach, and I play basketball and run for exercise.

You can see from this simple example how prominent my job is in my self-description, even though I think of myself as a husband, father, and psychology professor (in that order!). Most of us spend over one-third of our day at work, traveling to and from work, or preparing to go to work. Many individuals bring work home with them or are called into work at night, on weekends, or even in the early morning hours. We have cell phones, Androids, and iPhones so that our coworkers can reach us when they need to, even if we are at a ball game or a wedding or a concert. Although most of us would concur that family is the most important element in our lives, work is probably a very close second. In this book, I present the world of work from the perspective of I/O psychology and attempt to provide a better understanding of the complexities that are inherent in the interactions between employees and organizations. This chapter introduces I/O psychology by focusing on its history, implications, and trends.

## WHAT IS I/O PSYCHOLOGY?

**industrial/ organizational (I/O) psychology** The application of psychological principles and theories to the workplace.

**Industrial/organizational (I/O) psychology** is the application of psychological principles and theories to the workplace. I/O psychologists study, among other things, the attitudes and behaviors of employees and employers; interpersonal relationships at work; the structure of organizations and organizational policies; the complex processes of motivation and leadership; both individual and organizational performance; the context, culture, and climate of organizations; and the match between people and jobs.

Traditionally, industrial psychology and organizational psychology have been distinguished from each other based on their respective content areas. *Industrial psychology* (sometimes called *personnel psychology*, which shouldn't be confused with *personal* or *personality psychology*) has long been associated with job analysis, training, selection, and performance measurement/appraisal, whereas *organizational psychology* deals with motivation, work attitudes, and leadership, as well as the structure, culture, and processes of organizations. The topics of industrial psychology have traditionally been more technical, focusing on the assessment, measurement, and selection of people into various jobs; organizational psychology's topics tend to include more of the relational elements of the workplace, such as motivation, leadership, employer–employee relations, and job attitudes. In a sense, however, the dichotomy is a false one given the great overlap among the issues involved in each area. Finally, there is no broad line that divides workplace problems into organizational or industrial ones. For instance, a performance problem that might traditionally be defined within the industrial domain (the term *performance* has always been more closely aligned with industrial psychology) is likely to be caused by attitudinal or motivational factors that are traditionally associated with organizational psychology. In addition, most I/O psychologists are trained as exactly that—I/O psychologists—not as industrial psychologists only or as organizational psychologists only. Nevertheless, I use the distinction here to be consistent with other treatments of the topic and, even more important, to provide a framework for the discussion. I want to reiterate that *I* and *O* are put together into *I/O* for good reason: They are interdependent, related areas that form one applied subspecialty of psychology.

Before tracing the history of I/O psychology, we must consider at length how I/O psychologists are trained and what it is that I/O psychologists do. This background will help you gain a better understanding of what skill sets I/O psychologists possess and what they do in their jobs.

## HOW ARE I/O PSYCHOLOGISTS TRAINED?

*The Society for Industrial and Organizational Psychology (SIOP)*, Division 14 of the American Psychological Association (APA), is the professional association with which most I/O psychologists affiliate. Most I/O psychologists have obtained a PhD (or a PsyD, which is a similar degree with less research emphasis) from one of the 70 or so I/O psychology programs currently available in the United States and Canada, but there are programs elsewhere in the world as well. For a detailed look at these numerous programs, see *Graduate Training Programs in Industrial-Organizational Psychology and Related Fields* (Society for Industrial and Organizational Psychology, n.d.). The work of I/O psychology can also be done by people without PhDs in I/O (e.g., there are many I/O psychologists with master's degrees), as well as by people without specific training in I/O. Many of those without training in I/O receive their instruction in a graduate program housed in a business school. Another professional association that many I/O psychologists belong to is the Society for Human Resource Management [SHRM], which is focused on enhancing the professional practice of human resource management across 160 countries.

SIOP publishes guidelines for doctoral training in I/O psychology, called *Guidelines for Education and Training at the Doctoral Level in Industrial-Organizational Psychology* (Society for Industrial and Organizational Psychology, 1999). These guidelines clearly stipulate that the underlying approach to training I/O psychologists is the scientist/practitioner model, which maintains that I/O psychologists are often both the generators of knowledge (scientists) and the consumers of such knowledge (practitioners). Accordingly, doctoral education in I/O psychology must focus on both the theory and applications associated with the various content areas; the dual emphasis on theory and practice is needed regardless of one's career path. Indeed, to be a strong researcher, one needs to understand both the theory involved in the research and how to apply the knowledge that could potentially come from that research. (These guidelines are in the process of revision with a draft document available on the SIOP website—http://www.siop.org/ProposedGuidelinesChanges.pdf—for those interested; as I write this, the formal vote on them has not occurred.)

To effectively teach future I/O psychologists, one must be able to share insights at both a theoretical and an applied level. Similarly, to apply the knowledge in an organization, one must have a theoretical understanding of I/O issues and practices in order to make them work and to enable other employees to understand the potential benefits of the procedures or interventions being implemented.

**scientist/ practitioner model**
An approach used to train I/O psychologists maintaining that because I/O psychologists are both generators and consumers of knowledge, training must be focused on both theory and application.

## I/O TODAY

### The Scientist/Practitioner Gap

Imagine that you are an I/O practitioner who needs to design a new training program and evaluate its effectiveness. You received a doctorate a long time ago, and you haven't had the time or resources to keep up with the latest research on training evaluation. You know you should take the time to conduct some research and design an effective survey for trainees, but you need to have this ready to go in the next two weeks, and you have plenty of other projects that need your attention. So you do your best, knowing that it probably is not a scientifically-supported measure.

Now imagine that you are a researcher at a university. In order to keep your job, you need to get a certain number of papers published this year. Journals are more likely to publish papers that suggest new theories about training evaluation, even if they aren't particularly applicable to the workplace. You know that it would be beneficial to use training data from an organization for your research, but you are worried that the data will not be high-quality enough to get published. So, you conduct a lab study, knowing your research might not be relevant to an actual organization.

As these two scenarios suggest, the scientist/practitioner gap is difficult to overcome. Fortunately, there are some potential solutions. First, improvements in technology allow practitioners access to large amounts of data—certainly more than they would have time to examine. However, many researchers are interested in these data and have the time and resources to publish the results in a paper. This collaboration is one example of how scientists and practitioners are bridging the scientist/practitioner gap.

Another recent change that can help researchers and practitioners work together is a movement among journals for "open access"—that is, instead of having to have an expensive subscription to obtain scientific articles, many sciences are moving toward posting articles in online depositories so that anyone can read them (Björk et al., 2010). One recent example is the International Personnel Assessment Council (IPAC)'s open-access journal *Personnel Assessment and Decisions*, which started in 2015 as a remedy to the "prohibitive costs associated with traditional journals." While this has caused concerns about the quality of articles and how journals will adapt to this new business model, allowing open access helps practitioners who are not directly involved in research stay up-to-date about new developments. Some journals also encourage writers to avoid complicated jargon and emphasize practical results of studies, so that the findings can more readily be used by practitioners (see *Industrial and Organizational Psychology: Perspectives in Science and Practice*, which was first published in 2008, for an example of a journal that mixes science and practice).

Finally, professional organizations such as SIOP have been finding ways to help scientists and practitioners interact. For example, SIOP has started my.SIOP.org, a social networking site where scientists and practitioners can share ideas, ask questions, and make plans to conduct research together. Other researchers have taken action by creating newsletters, student groups, and online tools that make it easier for practitioners to implement science-based interventions (O'Neill, 2012).

The scientist/practitioner gap is unlikely to disappear anytime soon. However, many I/O psychologists are making use of social media, blogging, online courses, and similar tools to help ensure practitioners are using modern, science-based techniques in the workplace, and to continue to use organizational data to forward theories.

### Discussion Questions

1. As the text explains, though I/O psychologists are trained as scientist/practitioners, most will choose a career that favors either practice or research. How do you think a day in the life of an I/O psychologist might differ if he or she is a scientist versus a practitioner? What types of skills or characteristics should a scientist have? A practitioner?

2. We have discussed some ways to bridge the scientist/practitioner gap. What are some other ways that research psychologists and practicing psychologists can use technology and other resources better share their findings?

### References

Björk, B., Welling, P., Laakso, M., Majlender, P., Hedlund, T., & Guðnason, G. (2010). Open access to the scientific journal literature: Situation 2009. *PLoS ONE, 5*(6). Retrieved from http://journals.plos.org/plosone/article?id=10.1371/journal.pone.0011273

O'Neill, T. (2012). Canadian scholars working to bridge the perceived scientist-practitioner gap. *The Industrial-Organizational Psychologist, 49,* 63–66.

### Additional Readings

Silzer, R., & Parson, C. (2012). Industrial-organizational psychology journals and the science-practice gap. *The Industrial-Organizational Psychologist, 49,* 97–117.

---

These guidelines also maintain that the goal of graduate training in I/O psychology is to develop **competencies**, which are the skills, behaviors, and capabilities that allow employees to effectively perform specific functions—or, in this case, to be effective members of the I/O psychology profession. **Table 1.1** summarizes the competencies that have been identified as important for I/O psychologists. This comprehensive list is, in reality, only a guide to be used by graduate programs in the training of I/O psychologists. It is safe to say that no I/O psychologist graduates from school having attained complete competence in every one of these areas, but certainly most graduates have attained some degree of competence in most.

> **competencies**
> The skills, behaviors, and capabilities that allow employees to perform specific functions.

Another issue addressed by SIOP's guidelines is the importance of *diversity* in the training of I/O psychologists. The guidelines point out that, just as science and practice are inherent in each competency, an appreciation of diversity can be applied to each as well. Diversity in this sense refers to an awareness and understanding not only of ethnic, racial, and cultural differences among employees but also of age and gender differences.

Developing competency in the areas outlined by SIOP and graduating with a PhD in I/O psychology usually require at least four to five years of graduate school (following completion of an undergraduate degree). The last portion of this time is spent on a **dissertation**, which is a unique piece of scholarly research; in I/O psychology, it is usually a piece of empirical research. The doctoral student finds a topic of interest and exhaustively reviews the current literature in that area. The student then decides what needs to be done in that area and designs a study to answer

> **dissertation**
> A unique piece of scholarly research that is usually the last hurdle before obtaining a PhD.

**TABLE 1.1** Areas of Competence to Be Developed in Doctoral-Level I/O Psychology Programs

| Attitude theory, measurement, and change | Job/task analysis and classification |
|---|---|
| Career development | Judgment and decision making |
| Consulting and business skills | Leadership and management |
| Consumer behavior | Organizational development |
| Criterion theory and development | Organizational theory |
| Ethical, legal, and professional contexts of I/O psychology | Performance appraisal and feedback |
| Fields of psychology | Personnel recruitment, selection, and placement |
| Health stress in organizations | Research methods |
| History and systems of psychology | Small-group theory and team processes |
| Human performance/human factors | Statistical methods/data analysis |
| Individual assessment | Training: Theory, program design, and evaluation |
| Individual differences | Work motivation |
| Job evaluation and compensation | |

Source: Information from Society for Industrial and Organizational Psychology (1999).

a series of research questions, working closely with a faculty member who has some degree of expertise in the topic. Some students choose to attain a master's degree in I/O; this is typically a two-year degree with a bit less emphasis on research training. One of the fastest-growing demands in the field of psychology is for individuals with master's degrees in I/O. In fact, in 2014 "industrial-organizational psychologist" was labelled as the fastest growing occupation in the United States, with a projected growth rate of 53% between 2014 and 2022 (Farnham, 2014)! In addition, I/O psychologist is ranked as the 37th best job overall and the #1 best science job on the *U.S. News 100 Best Jobs* list (U.S. News & World Report, 2016).

## WHAT DO I/O PSYCHOLOGISTS DO?

Although I/O psychologists are trained according to the scientist/practitioner model, most choose a career that, in a relative sense, emphasizes either science and research *or* practice. The point here is not that academics don't ever deal with the application of research and theory to the real world, because most do on a regular basis; rather, it's that their emphasis is still on the research and teaching. Similarly, there are practitioners who are also involved in research and establish excellent research reputations by publishing their applied work in scholarly journals, as well as in more practice-oriented journals, but who maintain a focus on the application of I/O to their organizations. **Figure 1.1** categorizes I/O psychologists by the various employment settings in which they work. As you can see, a large percentage of I/O

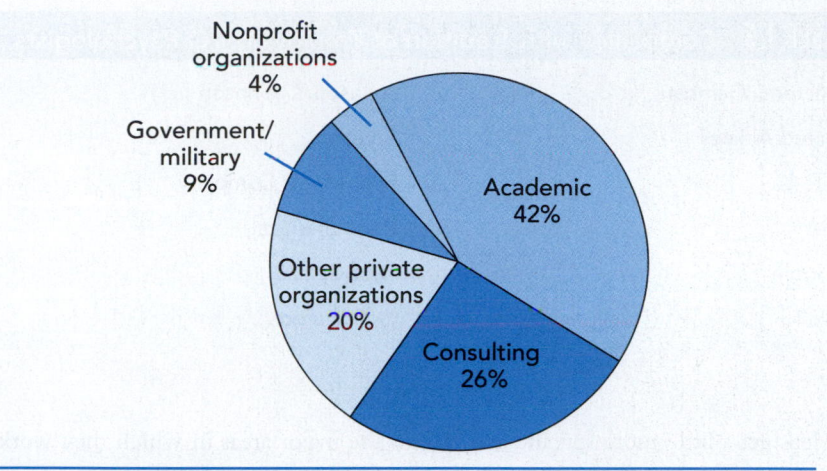

**FIGURE 1.1**   Primary Employment of Doctoral SIOP Members (Information from Khanna, Medsker, & Ginter (2013).)

psychologists—40%—are employed as professors by universities. These individuals typically teach in psychology or business departments, in addition to doing empirical and theoretical research. Other research-oriented I/O psychologists are employed by research consortia or institutes or by public or private organizations.

Those I/O psychologists who do not work in academic settings devote the majority of their time to applying psychology to the workplace, doing so in consulting firms (26%), private organizations (20%), and government and nonprofit organizations (13%). Many of these practitioners work in the human resource departments of companies in the manufacturing, financial services, telecommunications, and consumer products industries, among others. Among those in the public sector, many work in federal, state, and local government, as well as in the military. **Table 1.2** shows a selection of job titles for I/O practitioners and **Table 1.3** shows a sample of companies that have traditionally employed I/O psychologists. But what exactly are these I/O psychologists doing?

You got a sense of what I/O psychologists do from the competencies presented in Table 1.1. From this table, it is clear that I/O psychologists have very broad training,

**TABLE 1.2**   I/O Psychologists in the Workplace: Sample Job Titles

| | |
|---|---|
| Director of personnel | Compensation analyst |
| Vice president of personnel | Project manager |
| Manager of human resources | Senior scientist |
| Organizational development specialist | Management consultant |
| Personnel psychologist | Research scientist |
| Senior consultant | Behavioral scientist |

| TABLE 1.3 Companies with Tradition of Employing I/O Psychologists | |
| --- | --- |
| Procter & Gamble | Johnson & Johnson |
| United Airlines | Amazon |
| Frito-Lay | Ford Motor Company |
| IBM | Dow Chemical |
| Google | PepsiCo |
| AT&T | Wells Fargo |

but let's get a little more specific and discuss the major areas in which they work. In the ensuing chapters, these areas will be examined in greater detail.

SIOP, whose motto is "Science for a Smarter Workplace," publishes a pamphlet called *Building Better Organizations* (Society for Industrial and Organizational Psychology, 2006a) in which major areas are listed; I will highlight the most significant. First, the area in which more I/O psychologists work than any other is *selection*. Here, experts work on the development and administration of tests used for employee hiring (i.e., selection and placement). An important element in this process is the validation of selection instruments to ensure that they adequately predict job performance. Many I/O psychologists spend a lot of time administering tests to applicants and current employees and then relating those test scores to performance on the job as a way of seeing if the test is a good one. A good test is one in which we can predict who becomes an effective employee in a particular job—that's the true bottom-line goal for organizations. We will examine issues of selection in Chapters 6 and 7.

A second area in which many I/O psychologists work is *training and development*. Companies spend a great deal of time and money on training programs that teach new employees how to do their jobs and more established employees how to do new jobs with new equipment. I/O psychologists develop these training programs. First, they carefully analyze the organization and the job; then they conduct the training program with the company's employees to improve performance on the job; and, eventually, they evaluate the effectiveness of the program. Training will be the focus of Chapter 8.

*Organizational development (OD)* is a third area of concentration for many I/O psychologists. Experts in this area analyze organizational structures, cultures, and climates and develop interventions appropriate for a particular organization that might make the organization run more effectively. Organizational change is a large part of OD and one that companies are very interested in, given the many changes that are taking place in organizations of the 21st century. We will discuss organizational development in Chapter 14.

A fourth area of emphasis for I/O psychologists is *performance appraisal* (sometimes also referred to as *performance management*). The emphasis here is on developing both individual and organizational measures of performance and using these measures to improve performance. An I/O psychologist might be responsible for developing an appraisal measure, deciding how to implement it, and overseeing its actual administration. Performance appraisal will be discussed in Chapters 4 and 5.

Zero Creative/Cultura/Getty Images

The last major area I'll mention is what I call *quality of work life*. The chief concerns for people who work in this area are the measurement and improvement of job-related attitudes, such as job satisfaction and organizational commitment. An I/O psychologist might develop and administer an attitude survey to employees in an attempt to understand what employees like and don't like about their jobs. The data from surveys of this kind are often linked to performance; then a plan is devised to improve attitudes by enhancing not only the work climate but also organizational efficiency. Chapter 10 provides a detailed analysis of quality of work life in the context of job attitudes.

**A CLOSER LOOK**
How do you think work setting affects a person's job satisfaction? How might it affect productivity?

Though not mentioned specifically in SIOP's pamphlet, a relatively new and rapidly growing area of focus in I/O psychology is *social justice* and *prosocial work*. SIOP devotes an entire section of their website to the prosocial activities of the society and its members (see http://www.siop.org/prosocial/). This work can be defined as volunteer or extra-role behavior (see Chapter 4 for a discussion of extra-role behavior or OCBs) that makes use of I/O methods and research to benefit society, and is performed in exchange for little or no compensation. An example of a prosocial project that has recently engaged many SIOP members is the Veteran Transition Project, which is aimed at helping veterans as they return home from deployment to reintegrate into their communities and into the workplace. Specific services performed by SIOP members include helping veterans with their resumes, helping employers create policies and cultures that are supportive and welcoming of veterans, and coaching veterans through the job search and interview process. In another example of prosocial work, the Poverty Research Group, made up of SIOP members sponsors Project INCUBATE (International Collaboration Between Universities By Aligning Their Expertise), which seeks to motivate and coordinate antipoverty research globally and locally through interdisciplinary collaboration (http://www.siop.org/Prosocial/Incubate.aspx). Finally, the Volunteer Program Assessment (VPA), which was created and is managed by the Organizational Science Doctoral Program at the University of North Carolina at Charlotte, has as its vision to help nonprofits assess and understand their volunteer workforce better through the use of I/O psychological methods and research. This assessment has been administered to over 100 different organizations since its inception in 2009 (https://vpa.uncc.edu).

Certainly, there are other areas in which I/O psychologists work, such as *consumer psychology and engineering* or *human factors psychology,* but the areas discussed above account for the largest portion of their work. In the remainder of this text, we will take a much more detailed look at what I/O psychologists do; but first we should examine at some length the history of I/O psychology, for nothing is as relevant to the future as the past.

## OVER A CENTURY OF HISTORY

Although I/O psychology is often regarded as a newer branch of psychology, its roots actually go back almost to the founding of psychology itself (Lowman, Kantor, & Perloff, 2007). For those interested in a more detailed history of the field, I refer you to a fine resource by Laura Koppes (2007) on the history of I/O psychology. I will use an organizational structure, which breaks down the last 100-plus years into seven periods (Katzell & Austin, 1992).

### Pre–World War I

The initial phase of this history started around the turn of the 20th century and ended with World War I. In 1901, Walter Dill Scott, a professor at Northwestern University and former student of Wilhelm Wundt, who is one of the founding fathers of modern psychology and the first person to call himself a psychologist, was invited by the western advertising manager of a chain of magazines to give a talk at the Agate Club in Chicago on the psychological aspects of advertising. Because of the content of the talk and the connection of psychology to business, many refer to the date of this talk—December 20, 1901—as the beginning of business and industrial psychology, or what we now call industrial/organizational psychology. Scott published *The Theory of Advertising* in 1903. Twelve years later, in 1915, the Division of Applied Psychology was established at Carnegie Tech (now Carnegie Mellon University), with Walter VanDyke Bingham as its head, and in 1916 Scott became its first professor of applied psychology.

At about the same time, Hugo Munsterberg (another Wundt student) moved to the United States, continued doing the applied work he had begun in Germany, and published his textbook *Psychology and Industrial Efficiency* (Munsterberg, 1913). It's interesting to note that, as virtually all psychologists at this time were trained as experimental psychologists, Scott, Munsterberg, Bingham, and others with applied interests had to fit these interests in amidst their full-time jobs in experimental psychology (Katzell & Austin, 1992).

Koppes and Pickren (2007) note that many assume that all of this early development in the field of I/O psychology was happening in the United States, but, in fact, this is not true. During these early years, there was more financial and governmental support for the development of the field in Europe than in the United States. According to Moore and Hartmann (1931; cited in Koppes & Pickren, 2007), I/O psychology was developing earlier and faster in Europe (England,

Germany, Russia, Italy, etc.), where centers were established to fund research and bring researchers together to collaborate on common interests with particular research objectives. Interestingly, in the United States, the development proceeded in more of an individual researcher paradigm, whereby lone faculty members spent time conducting their own research—there wasn't much of a coordinated effort to move the field along. In some ways, the contrast between how the field developed in the United States and the rest of world is consistent with how individualistic our society is compared with the rest of the world. This important cultural difference will come up many times throughout the rest of this book as we consider cross-cultural issues in the field of I/O psychology.

## World War I Through the 1920s

The second historical phase ranges from the World War I years through the 1920s. This is the period when I/O psychology really came of age and moved out from the hallowed halls of academia into the applied world. This was an intense and busy time for the military as thousands of young men were joining at rates never before seen and they needed to be assessed and evaluated for service. During this time, Scott and Bingham established a psychological program under the army's personnel officer. Their staff was responsible for such things as the development of personnel files for military personnel and the creation of performance rating forms. Another group of psychologists led by Robert Yerkes (at that time the president of the American Psychological Association) worked for the government doing selection and placement of military personnel, using their newly developed tools—the **Army Alpha and Army Beta** mental ability tests. These tests, developed as multiple-choice-based intelligence tests that could be administered in groups, differed from the more typical individually administered intelligence tests that existed at the time. It became very clear during this period that those who studied and practiced I/O psychology had a great deal to offer the military—including the ability to administer these and other tests for the screening and classification of people.

**Army Alpha and Army Beta**
Mental ability tests developed by I/O psychologists during World War I that were used to select and classify army personnel.

It was also at this time that I/O psychology began to expand beyond the academic and military realms into government and private industry. I/O psychologists started consulting firms such as The Scott Company (founded by Walter Dill Scott), which worked in the areas of mental ability testing, personnel planning, training, and personnel administration. The Psychological Corporation, specializing in test development, was founded in 1921 and still exists today as part of Harcourt Assessment.

Also in 1921, Bruce V. Moore received from Carnegie Tech what is believed to have been the first PhD in industrial psychology. His is an interesting story, as he rose from assistant professor to become department chair at Pennsylvania State University (the psychology building at Penn State is named after him) and eventually, in 1945, the first president of Division 14 of the APA, which is the section of APA devoted to I/O psychology. While at Carnegie Tech, he was approached by the Westinghouse Electric and Manufacturing Company with a problem: The company could not distinguish very well between new employees who should be directed toward careers

**A CLOSER LOOK**
Testing for selection and classification was an important part of what psychologists did for the military during World War I and World War II. How might knowing the intelligence of military personnel help military leaders make job placement decisions?

in sales engineering and those who were better suited to design engineering (Gilmer, 1981). Moore and others worked on this problem, discovering that these employees were best differentiated on the basis of items that reflected their interests.

This early work by Moore was expanded in later years by Edward Strong (and eventually David Campbell) in what became the *Strong Vocational Interest Blank for Men* (Strong, 1927). In high school, I took a version of this inventory that told me my interests matched up with the interests of those who like to work with people and that teaching might be a good profession for me! And I'm sure that many of you have taken what is now called the *Campbell Interest and Skill Survey* (CISS, n.d.), which guidance departments commonly administer to high school and college students in an attempt to help students identify what careers they might find stimulating.

Frederick Taylor's approach to work motivation, called Scientific Management, became popular in the late 1800s and early 1900s (see Chapter 14 for more discussion of this work). Taylor argued that employees should be rewarded financially for using the best approach to their work and doing their work most effectively. Lillian and Frank Gilbreth built on some of these ideas but with much greater focus on the workers' well-being, which they believed was ignored by Scientific Management.

Lillian Gilbreth received her PhD in psychology (not applied psychology) from Brown University; her dissertation was published as a book, *The Psychology of Management,* in 1914 (Gilbreth, 1914). She was often called the first lady of management and the mother of Scientific Management (Vinchur & Koppes, 2007). Interestingly, she was also the inventor responsible for refrigerator door shelves and the foot-pedal trashcan. The book *Cheaper by the Dozen* (later made into a series of movies) was written by two of her children about their experiences growing up as 2 of Frank and Lillian Gilbreth's 12 children. It's interesting to note that women played an influential role in the development of I/O psychology during this time but that they did so through their roles in industry rather than academia (Koppes, 1997). Along with Lillian Gilbreth, women like Marion Bills and Elsie Bregman made huge contributions to the field through their work at Aetna Life Insurance and The Psychological Corporation, respectively. Koppes suggests that traditional academic positions were limited for these women because academic psychology departments were male-dominated and that industry provided much better opportunities.

## The 1930s to Pre–World War II

The defining event of the next historical phase of I/O psychology was a series of experiments collectively referred to as the Hawthorne Studies. This period in our history, of course, was marked by the Great Depression, during which unemployment rose to all-time highs and growth in the economy was nonexistent. As a result of these historical trends, our culture became focused less on employee testing and training and more on the human condition (Austin & Davies, 2000).

The Hawthorne Studies were a series of experiments, some of which examined the impact of illumination on productivity (see **Table 1.4**), that were conducted at the Western Electric plant in Hawthorne, Illinois. These experiments highlighted the importance of social relations and employee attitudes, among other things. The remarkable part of the story is that, after observing employees' behaviors, researchers realized that the social and psychological conditions of work were often

**TABLE 1.4** Hawthorne Illumination Study

| Description | Manipulation | Expectation | Results |
|---|---|---|---|
| **Experiment 1** Test group would work under different light intensities, whereas control group would work under constant light. | Test group experienced three different intensities (24-, 46-, and 70-foot candles), whereas control group experienced no change in light intensity. | Test group would show increased productivity, whereas control group's productivity would remain unchanged. | Test group's productivity increased, but control group's productivity increased by about as much. |
| **Experiment 2** Test group would work under less intense light, whereas control group would work under same light intensity. | Test group's lighting was decreased from 10- to 3-foot candles, whereas control group's lighting did not change at all. | Test group would show a decrease in productivity, whereas control group's productivity would remain unchanged. | Test group's productivity still increased, as did control group's productivity. |
| **Experiment 3** Workers' lighting expectations were the focus of this study. | Workers were led to believe that the lighting was being increased, but in fact it was still the same intensity. | Original expectation was that there would be no effect; but if expectations were really important, then they might affect productivity or other variables. | Productivity remained the same, but workers reported favorable reactions to the increase in lighting. (Lighting, of course, did not increase.) |
| **Experiment 4** Workers' lighting expectations were the focus of this study. | Workers were led to believe that the lighting was being decreased, but in fact it was still the same intensity. | Original expectation was that there would be no effect; but if expectations were really important, then they might affect productivity or other variables. | Productivity remained the same, but workers reported unfavorable reactions to the decrease in lighting. (Lighting, of course, did not decrease.) |

more important than the physical conditions, such as the amount of illumination (Roethlisberger & Dickson, 1939). One of the interesting findings was that employees reacted positively to being paid attention to—someone taking an interest in them resulted in positive behavior change. We need to keep in mind that, to this point, the history of I/O had read more like the history of "I" alone! In other words, it wasn't until the Hawthorne Studies that team development, supervision, group process, worker morale, and other organizational phenomena played much of a role in the I/O field. As Haller Gilmer (1981), one of the early I/O psychologists, noted in his later years, "Thinking about industrial-psychology problems changed. Simple answers to simple problems were not enough. Questions about motivation, leadership, supervision, and human relations began to emerge" (p. 13). Many view this time period, and the Hawthorne Studies in particular, as marking the birth of organizational psychology.

## World War II to the Mid-1960s

Like the previous war, World War II was an important and dynamic time for the development of I/O psychology. Bingham, Scott, and Yerkes were brought back to the military to help match recruits to jobs. Selection, placement, evaluation, and appraisal all largely began during the World War I years, whereas World War II saw a great refinement in terms of the knowledge base and how best to apply the existing knowledge to specific situations. Organizational psychology became a more equal partner with industrial psychology and began to emphasize such areas as organizational dynamics, work groups, and employee morale. Whereas much of the military work initiated during World War I was shut down after that war, World War II work continued as the armed services created centers of research such as the Army Research Institute (ARI) and the Air Force Human Resources Laboratory (AFHRL), where studies are conducted to this day. During the 1950s, many companies, including AT&T, General Electric, Metropolitan Life, and Standard Oil of New Jersey, also established large research groups to do I/O work (Dunnette, 1962).

The number and diversity of universities training students in I/O psychology increased during the same period. New programs were developed at the University of Maryland, Michigan State University, and George Washington University. In addition, several university-based programs were developed that emphasized organizational issues (as opposed to industrial ones), such as the Research Center for Group Dynamics established by Kurt Lewin at the Massachusetts Institute of Technology (Katzell & Austin, 1992). Lewin, chiefly considered a social psychologist, was instrumental in developing theory and methodology in the area of work groups and leadership. His early work still influences modern I/O psychology through its impact on more recent motivational theories such as goal setting and expectancy theory (we'll consider these in Chapter 9). Finally, personnel counseling developed during this time as an outgrowth of the Hawthorne Studies. The focus here was on helping employees deal with personal problems that had the potential to affect their work performance (Highhouse, 1999).

## The Mid-1960s to the Mid-1980s

One strong indication of the increasing role of organizational psychology was the fact that, in 1970, Division 14 of the APA changed its name from "the Division of Business and Industrial Psychology" to "the Division of Industrial and Organizational Psychology." Organizational psychology had truly arrived.

On the industrial side, this period saw a great deal of work on selection and performance appraisal. These continue to be two of the largest and most researched topic areas in I/O psychology. One major theme at the time was a concern with ethnic and racial differences on selection tests and the fairness of those tests. This interest emerged as a result of the social, political, and legal climate of the 1960s. As you know, the civil rights movement defined this period; it was a time of great racial tension. Issues of discrimination and fairness permeated society and the workplace. I/O psychology began addressing these issues as well. In Chapter 7, we will discuss Title VII of the Civil Rights Act of 1964, which was the legal framework for much of this work.

Organizational topics of interest during this period included work motivation, job attitudes, and job characteristics. As we will note in Chapter 9, more than a few of the most popular theories of motivation—including goal setting and expectancy theory—came of age during this period. Indeed, Richard Hackman and Greg Oldham's work on the motivating potential of jobs as a result of their characteristics is among the most cited work in the history of I/O psychology (Sackett, 1994). Similarly, much of the work on job attitudes, such as job satisfaction and organizational commitment (see Chapter 10), was conducted during this time.

These two decades were a time of tremendous growth in I/O psychology. New doctoral training programs emerged at such places as Bowling Green State University (1966), North Carolina State University (1966), and the University of Akron (1965). In 1960, there were about 756 members of Division 14; by 1980 they totaled 2,005 (Katzell & Austin, 1992).

## The Mid-1980s to 2000

The field of I/O psychology grew very rapidly toward the end of the 20th century, with more work being done in traditional areas such as selection, performance appraisal, motivation, and leadership, as well as in new domains. For instance, issues of diversity and inclusion as manifested in a focus on the fairness of employment tests—reflecting the legal climate of personnel and labor law—became an even greater focus among I/O psychologists, as demonstrated by the increased frequency of I/O psychologists serving as expert witnesses in discrimination cases. Cognitive processes, too, became the focus of much research in the I/O area, reflecting the emergence of this cognitive framework in all aspects of psychology.

In earlier sections, I highlighted the development of some of the early I/O programs, beginning with Carnegie Tech. The 1980s and 1990s saw a dramatic increase in the number of master's and doctoral programs in I/O psychology or closely allied fields.

Rogelberg and Gill (2004) note that, between 1986 and 2004, there was an increase in I/O doctoral programs of almost 50% and that master's programs increased by over 200%.

## 2000 to Today

The growth continues today, with over 220 programs offering graduate degrees in I/O psychology or closely allied fields and 1,200 new I/O PhDs since 2000 (J. Tegge, personal communication, February 9, 2016). There are more than 1,200 professors of I/O psychology today in both psychology departments and business schools around the globe (Silzer & Parson, 2015).

A recent article on the SIOP website presents some recent trends in I/O psychology research and practice (Society for Industrial and Organizational Psychology, 2015). I'd like to highlight just a few of those to give a feel for what's been happening in the field over the past 10 or 15 years; see **Table 1.5** for the complete list. First on SIOP's list is *globalization* and the *virtual workforce*—two related issues that will come up throughout the rest of the book. Competition among companies is no longer local or interstate, but is increasingly intercountry. As a signal of the importance of globalization, the companies identified in *Fortune*'s Global 500 (their list of the world's largest companies) combined to employ over 65 million people worldwide in 2014 (that's more than the entire population of France). (See Moran, Abramson, & Moran, 2014, for a great overview of globalization in the workplace). The globalization of business has been aided by the emergence of the virtual workplace, which is projected to comprise 1.3 billion people in the next few years. Research has identified three waves of virtual work: (1) virtual freelancers who don't work for a single company, but instead work remotely and provide services to various companies, (2) virtual corporate colleagues who appreciate the collegiality of a stable work group and benefit from companies that also value those connections, and (3) virtual coworkers who take advantage of technology and the virtual work environment, but also connect physically to coworkers through urban hubs or other meeting places (Johns & Gratton, 2013). Virtual work has been the focus of a good bit of research in

| TABLE 1.5 Top 10 Trends in I/O Psychology | |
|---|---|
| 1. Globalization and the Virtual Workplace | 6. Heavy Focus on Developing Top Employees |
| 2. Internet-Based Recruitment and Selection | 7. Increased Coaching in the Workplace |
| 3. Defining Limits for Online Searches of Personal Information | 8. Proactive Approaches to Improve Employee Health |
| 4. Innovation | 9. Facilitating Work-Life Merge |
| 5. Technology-Enabled Training | 10. More Tweeting, Blogging, and Electronic Platforms |

Source: Information from Harris & Hollman. (n.d.). Tip-topics: The top trends in I-O psychology: A graduate student perspective. Retrieved on February 27, 2016, from http://www.siop.org/tip/Apr13/19_TipTopics.aspx.

the last 10 years, such as the recent work of Hoch and Kozlowski (2014) on leading virtual teams, which highlighted both similarities and differences that result from this new approach to work.

We also recognize the growing importance of *innovation* and *creativity* within companies to help them stay competitive and to improve the lives of workers and their families across the globe. In a review of this dynamic research area (2002 to 2013) the authors concluded that creativity research has largely focused on idea generation whereas innovation research has targeted idea implementation (Anderson, Potočnik, & Zhou, 2014). This outstanding review of the literature breaks creative work down by individual factors such as the importance of traits in creativity and innovation, as well as the task and social contexts in which employees live and work.

Finally, I will combine two of the top trends from the SIOP list into one: *coaching* and *development of top employees*. Employee development has been a consistent theme of the last 15 years as employers have realized the importance of training, developing, and preparing their high-potential employees so that they are ready to step into the next position that needs to be filled. Succession planning, as this process is called, now routinely involves coaching employees who are on the fast track to get them ready for their next promotion. Research suggests that it's imperative that the strategic initiatives necessary to create a talent management system include the linking of selection, development, performance management, and succession/career management. Some suggestions for making this work include the creation of a special learning and development track for high potentials; the rotation of employees across functions, divisions, and geographical locations; the development of technology-based learning; and the implementation of coaching/mentoring programs (Fulmer, Stumpf, & Bleak, 2009).

Historians estimate that, in 1939, there were fewer than 100 I/O psychologists in the world (Katzell & Austin, 1992). That estimate grew to 760 by 1960. In 1992, there were about 2,500 members of SIOP and probably a few hundred more I/O psychologists who weren't members, totaling around 3,000 I/O psychologists. The most recent SIOP data indicate that it has about 4,500 professional members and 3,500 student members (J. Tegge, personal communication, February 9, 2016).

## WHERE DOES I/O PSYCHOLOGY GO FROM HERE?

Although the history of I/O psychology presented here seems to reflect a great deal of change over the past century, it is fair to say that this change is just the tip of the iceberg. The 21st century promises to be fast, competitive, and turbulent. Dramatic changes are taking place in the world of work. As American society and the American workplace continue to change, the field of I/O psychology will have potentially more to offer. A content analysis of over 200 dissertations in I/O psychology between 2003 and 2013 confirmed that the traditional areas of interest continue to dominate academic research, but it also revealed some exciting new areas of study including teamwork, counterproductive behaviors, employee well-being, and work–family issues (Piotrowski, 2014). Of course, this movement is in part a function of researcher interest, but it is also a result of practitioner focus and researchers attempting to answer questions posed by today's organizational leaders.

SIOP recently conducted an annual survey of top 10 workplace trends (Society for Industrial and Organizational Psychology, 2015). The survey asked over 700 SIOP members to identify and rank the top trends or needs that businesses will face in 2016 and beyond; the top 10 trends are presented in **Table 1.6**. I will highlight a few that I expect will be addressed by the field through empirical research, theoretical development, and application of knowledge going forward.

*Big Data,* #1 on SIOP's list, has become a huge focus in organizations, universities, hospitals, and so on. The term big data is often used to represent predictive analytics, which is the use of large current and historical data sets to predict future probabilities and outcomes. A great deal of work in recent years has focused on the development of techniques to better use the large data sets that are available to us to improve our understanding of workplace practices and to help us plan and execute new initiatives. Companies have moved toward the use of big data and analytics to make better-informed business decisions. Universities are using analytics to identify courses and other variables that are especially predictive of success. In the years to come, I/O psychologists will be equipped with both the analytics/statistical training and the training in organizational science that will make them particularly competent for this work. (We will look more closely at big data, and some ethical issues around it, when we explore research methods in the next chapter.)

Another trend that emerged from the SIOP survey is continued work to revolutionize *performance appraisals* by using frequent feedback delivered to employees from a variety of

| **TABLE 1.6** SIOP's Top 10 Workplace Trends for 2016 | |
|---|---|
| 1. | Leveraging of big data and analytics when making business decisions |
| 2. | Increasing reliance on technology and automation |
| 3. | Management of virtual teams |
| 4. | Changing approach to performance management to foster employee development rather than competition |
| 5. | Encouraging employee engagement |
| 6. | Focusing on the mental and physical health and well-being of employees |
| 7. | Focusing on agility and flexibility to meet rapidly changing market and customer demands |
| 8. | Balancing of work-life issues across generations |
| 9. | Emphasizing building a workforce that values diversity |
| 10. | Using social media in selection and other employment-related decisions |

Source: Information from Society for Industrial and Organizational Psychology (2015).

sources and by giving employees a larger role in their own evaluations. There has been a great deal of recent controversy in this area: Most practitioners and researchers agree that performance appraisals serve a variety of valuable purposes, but many organizations are finding that the traditional systems don't work as well as they should and both supervisors and subordinates are often displeased with them. Managing performance is critical to organizations, and I expect that we will continue to see research that explores procedures and techniques with the potential to manage performance better. (Chapter 5 is devoted to issues in performance appraisal, including discussion of recent techniques.)

The use of *social media* is another trend that many respondents feel will be influential in the near future. We are just starting to see I/O research in this area, as organizations are increasingly using sites like Facebook and LinkedIn for recruiting and screening of applicants, as well as monitoring and potentially firing employees for behaviors captured on these sites. SIOP believes that I/O psychologists can play a role by helping organizations balance the risks and benefits of the use of social media, and navigate the ethical and legal issues that have already begun to emerge. Research in this area will only grow as the use of social media continues to explode on both the social and organizational scenes. (We'll discuss developments in the use of social media throughout the text, particularly in the discussion of selection decisions in Chapter 7.)

I will close this discussion with some other themes that have begun to emerge in the last few years and are likely to continue drawing the attention of scholars and practitioners alike in the years to come. First, whereas war defined the geopolitical scene of the 20th century, economics will be the defining issue of the 21st century. We discussed *globalization* of the workforce as one of the major hallmarks for the new century, but *global competition* is another aspect of this trend that will continue to be a major focus in the future. Workers and firms in the United States can no longer expect to freely and easily make a profit. Global competition will continue to require us to have a skilled, well-trained, and competent workforce to compare favorably with the many, many countries that are now our competitors. Furthermore, mergers and acquisitions will continue to force companies to bridge cultures as American companies such as Dell, Goodyear, and General Electric operate facilities in many different geopolitical settings. How to merge a production facility in Latin America with a parent company in North America is a complex issue. The collective knowledge of the field of I/O psychology has the potential to help in this transition. (This issue factors heavily into our discussion of training methods in Chapter 8.)

"Three more got laid off today."

Mike Baldwin/Cornered/Cartoonstock.com

**A CLOSER LOOK**
What challenges do I/O psychologists face in helping companies that are going through downsizing?

Second, new technology has transformed the workplace, as we've discussed, but it has also decreased the number of traditional jobs for workers and organizations. At the same time, *downsizing* occurred at an alarming rate in the wake of the 2008 recession, and though the U.S. economy has continued to add jobs at a steady rate in the last few years, many individuals are still struggling with *unemployment* and *underemployment*. We have empathy, and rightfully so, for those who are laid off due to organizational cutbacks; but the rest of the story is that when these individuals are fortunate enough to be reemployed, it is often at a lower wage rate (Cascio, 1995). Further, many of those laid off were approaching retirement age but were not quite there yet. A recent review of the literature has found that age is negatively correlated with speed of reemployment (Wanberg, Kanfer, Hamann, & Zhang, 2015). In other words, older employees who have lost their jobs struggle finding reemployment, and the process, when they do find other employment, takes considerably longer. Companies are always looking to be more competitive, more efficient, and leaner, but the result of massive layoffs is that fewer employees are left to do the work that needs to be done, often being asked to do more for less. I/O psychology is thus important for (1) helping laid-off workers become competitive for other jobs and (2) helping those left behind handle more diverse jobs and sometimes a heavier workload. (We'll revisit these concepts and others related to workplace stress in Chapter 11.)

Third, companies will continue to address the needs of the workforce that is *diverse* in terms of race, gender, age, disability, gender identity, sexual orientation, and ethnicity. This diversity requires much more coordination and sensitivity to "differences" on the part of management and employees. An additional complication is that our workforce is diverse in terms of thoughts, expectations, and culture as well. In fact, some argue that generations develop their own unique cultures such that traditionalists, baby boomers, Gen Xers, and millennials differ significantly in terms of values that develop because of their experiences of different historical events (Doverspike & O'Malley, 2006). Organizations have to recognize and consider how organizational policies and procedures impact these different generations as well as help to ensure reasonable levels of communication between members of these different generations. Education and training regarding diversity among workers have become very important areas for I/O psychologists and will continue to grow in importance in the 21st century. (Legal and ethical issues around diversity and discrimination touch nearly every major topic in this text, including our discussions of selection, performance appraisal, training, teamwork, and leadership.)

Fourth, we already considered issues around virtual work, which became much more prevalent in organizations during the 2000s, but the influx and development of technology goes well beyond virtuality and social media. One area that promises to be a real focal point is the role that technology will play in *employee selection*. The selection process will be more streamlined and make better use of technology in the future. We are already seeing some companies begin to automate the collection/review of resumes, assessments, and interviews. For instance, my son recently completed a virtual interview for an internship with a large Fortune 500 company; he logged in on his computer and was given a question prompt with three minutes to prepare an answer; his response was recorded and then uploaded for the interviewer to view.

Other companies have begun using kiosks located at public places, like shopping malls, where applicants can simply log in to access application materials. Some companies are also doing assessments through these kiosks. I/O psychologists will play a significant role in helping employers implement new technology in useful and reasonable ways that mutually benefit companies and future employees. (The influence of technology in selection and performance prediction is discussed in detail in Chapters 6 and 7.)

Finally, *ethics* in organizations has become an extremely important topic, one commonly addressed in the media since the ethical unraveling of Enron, WorldCom, Pfizer, Arthur Anderson, and other once-respected organizations. A recent review of the literature (Kish-Gephart, Harrison, & Treviño, 2010) proposes and tests a model of unethical choices, with a focus on the antecedents that led to those bad choices. The authors categorize the antecedents according to bad apples (characteristics of people who make poor ethical choices), bad cases (characteristics of the situation surrounding the ethical choice), and bad barrels (organizational climates or cultures that seem defined by poor ethics). The authors provide a great deal of support for the importance of these three types of antecedents and suggest that additional research investigate how the three categories of antecedents interact in affecting ethical intentions and decisions. They conclude by arguing that companies can use many of the tools of I/O psychology, such as assessment, selection, training, and culture change, to avoid the ethical problems that have become so pervasive in today's organizations. A recent conceptualization of ethical leadership relies on what the authors call *moralized leadership,* which is defined as the followers' perceptions of the leader's behaviors as morally right (Fehr, Yam, & Dang, 2015). This recent conceptualization argues that the values that underlie leaders' moralized behavior, such as compassion and loyalty, lead to follower reactions, such as prosocial behavior (see Chapter 4 for more). This is all very new thinking and no empirical work has emerged that has tested these notions, but organizational and leader ethics will be investigated more in the future.

AndreyPopov/Getty Images

**A CLOSER LOOK**
What technological advances will impact interview and selection processes in the coming years? What role do I/O practitioners have to play in this area?

## WHAT DOES I/O PSYCHOLOGY MEAN TO YOU?

As students, you can use much of what you learn about I/O psychology. For instance, what you learn about motivation can not only be applied to your schoolwork; it can also help you understand why you are more motivated to do certain things rather than others and even more motivated in certain situations. In addition, our examination of stress and well-being may shed some valuable light on your own stress levels, the possible root causes of your stress, and, of course, ways to reduce and better deal with stress in your own life.

Many of you are currently working or are about to enter the workforce. The field of I/O has so much to offer you. You should be able to gain something from every chapter in the book that you can apply to your working life. For example, a better understanding of the role that jobs play in our lives should provide you with a better appreciation for work and its effect on you. Further, how performance is measured at work should provide you with a better understanding of the different dimensions of performance, your boss's perspective on these things, and the value that organizations place on different types of performance behaviors. Additionally, a better understanding of leadership might help you in your dealings with the leaders in your organization, and more knowledge about organizational cultures might aid your perspective when thinking about and examining your own organization.

Because I/O psychology is an applied field, you should find the course material and the textbook to be chock-full of information that you can readily apply to all the domains of your life: school, personal, and work.

## Summary

I/O psychology, the application of psychology to the workplace, encompasses such diverse areas as performance appraisal, employment testing, organizational development, and motivation. I/O psychologists receive extensive training in a wide range of areas, but their central approach is based on the scientist/practitioner model, which emphasizes both theory and practice. Most obtain an advanced degree such as a PhD. The training is quite intensive and includes a great deal of coursework, practical experience, and research experience. The culmination of the training is usually the completion of a dissertation.

Over 40% of I/O psychologists work in academic settings such as psychology departments and business schools, where they teach undergraduate and graduate students and conduct research for the purposes of creating and applying knowledge. The majority of I/O psychologists, however, work outside of academia in the public or private sector, applying what they've learned in graduate school to their particular organization. Many of these I/O psychologists also work for consulting firms that provide services to organizations on a project-by-project basis.

I/O psychology has a rich, albeit relatively short, history. Although its beginnings date to around the turn of the 20th century, its growth as a field emerged with World War I, when I/O psychologists were employed by the government to train, test, and measure the performance of soldiers. Other historical hallmarks include World War II, the civil rights movement of the 1960s, the emergence of the global economy in the 2000s, and now the technical revolution of the past 15 years. I/O psychology is positioned to play an ever-increasing role in the constantly changing world of work in the 21st century. In the remainder of this book, we will discuss the various topics and areas in which I/O psychology has, and will continue to have, an impact. You should find a great deal of material that you can apply to your life as a student or employee—the applications of I/O psychology are many, diverse, and useful.

## Key Terms

Army Alpha and Army Beta (p. 11)

competencies (p. 5)

dissertation (p. 5)

industrial/organizational (I/O) psychology (p. 2)

scientist/practitioner model (p. 4)

## TAKING IT TO THE FIELD

One of the more challenging issues facing I/O psychologists is explaining what it is we do. Few people are familiar with the field, and many don't realize how I/O psychology can be useful to a company. Thus, I/O psychologists have to be prepared to educate others in a succinct and polite manner about what I/O psychology is. In addition, I/O psychologists who choose to work in consulting firms have to be persuasive and convince business owners to use their services to help improve their company.

Below is an e-mail from a potential client, Chris. Read the e-mail and then draft a response to Chris that will answer his questions.

Hello—

My name is Chris Covey, and I am the CEO of RainCloud, a tech startup based in Colorado. RainCloud allows users to manage several social media accounts at once, and obtain data about their followers to help them market products. We have recently gone from 12 employees to 130 employees within a few months, and we are having a hard time managing the increased staff. Recently, we've run into some problems. First, because we've grown so quickly, many of our new employees are still waiting to be trained, but we don't really have a program for them that will get them oriented quickly. We also have some problems with our supervisors— many of the people who are currently supervisors have never managed a team before. I'm getting reports that these supervisors spend a lot of time either yelling at their team, or avoiding their teams entirely because they don't want to deal with the problems. Finally, the work that we do at RainCloud requires quick response times, and as a result, many people on my staff work long hours to make sure everything is running smoothly. Employees have begun complaining about stress and exhaustion, and some are starting to call in sick quite frequently.

I was speaking with one of my VPs, and she suggested I contact an I/O psychologist for some help. I looked up your company online, and I am curious about what you do. So, if I hired you, what sorts of things could you help me with?

Thanks for your time.

Chris

Draft a brief, persuasive e-mail to Chris explaining the work your company does and how it might help him with his problems. Keep in mind that this client may not be familiar with technical psychological terms.

## Critical Thinking Questions

**1.** As you probably noticed in reading the chapter, the topics explored by I/O psychology have changed over the years. What topics do you believe are going to be important for I/O psychology to address over the next decade? Why do you think these topics will be so important?

2. You have learned that I/O psychologists can hold a variety of different jobs. Select one of the jobs mentioned in Table 1.2. What knowledge or experience should someone interested in this job seek out in his or her undergraduate or graduate education? What skills might make this person stand out in an interview?

3. The chapter notes that big data and analytic technology are greatly changing the way we do work. In what ways might the availability of big data make the job of an I/O psychologist easier? What challenges might it pose?

## Application Questions

1. Go to http://www.siop.org and find a university that offers an MA, a PsyD, or a PhD in I/O psychology. Visit that university's I/O psychology page and read about the program. What are some aspects of that program that seem appealing to you? What aspects seem unappealing? If you wanted to apply to this school, what would you need to do?

2. The chapter mentions five main topics that I/O psychologists investigate— selection, training, organizational development, performance appraisal, and quality of work life. Which of these topics seems most interesting to you? Write a question about that topic that you think I/O psychology could answer.

3. The chapter discusses the importance of understanding diversity in the workplace. One currently popular topic is the issue of generational differences. How does your attitude toward work differ from that of people who are older or younger than you (e.g., your parents or children)? What kinds of problems might arise out of those differences?

4. The chapter discusses the role that I/O psychology has to play in helping organizations operate in an ethical manner. Consider a current legal battle in the news today, such as a lawsuit or Supreme Court case involving employee rights, affirmative action, or discrimination; a legislative debate on paid leave, fair compensation, or worker rights and safety; or some other newsworthy development. Based on what you've read in this chapter regarding the work of I/O psychology, how would you as a researcher or practitioner address this issue?

5. Consider a problem that you are facing either at work or at school. How might I/O psychology be able to help you solve this problem?

## Suggested Readings

**Arthur, W., Jr., & Benjamin, L. T., Jr.** (1999). Psychology applied to business. In D. A. Bernstein (Ed.), *Psychology: Fields of application* (pp. 98–115). Boston: Houghton Mifflin. A nicely written review of I/O psychology in an interesting book about psychology and its diverse subfields.

**Cooper, C. L., & Locke, E. A.** (2000). *Industrial and organizational psychology: Linking theory with practice.* Malden, MA: Wiley-Blackwell. Leading scholars link the theory underlying core topics in I/O psychology to what happens in "real" organizations.

**Cascio, W. F., & Aguinis, H.** (2008). Research in industrial and organizational psychology from 1963 to 2007: Changes, choices, and trends. *Journal of Applied Psychology, 93*(5), 1062. A nice look at changes in the field with a very clear historical perspective.

**Katzell, R. A., & Austin, J. T.** (1992). From then to now: The development of industrial-organizational psychology in the United States. *Journal of Applied Psychology, 77*(6), 803–835. A thorough history of the I/O field with an emphasis on the role of the people involved in each time period.

**Koppes, L. L. (Ed.).** (2014). *Historical perspectives in industrial and organizational psychology: New York: Psychology Press.* The most comprehensive text ever written on the history of I/O psychology—a must-read for history buffs who are interested in I/O psychology.

**Kuther, T. L.** (2004). *Your career in psychology: Industrial/organizational psychology.* Belmont, CA: Wadsworth. This book profiles psychologists who have chosen various career paths in I/O psychology.

Photo: ultramarine5/iStock/Getty Images

CHAPTER 2

# Research Methods in I/O Psychology

## Measurement
### Reliability
### Validity of Tests, Measures, and Scales

## Ethics

## Statistics
### Measures of Central Tendency
### Measures of Dispersion

Shapes of Distributions
Correlation and Regression
Meta-Analysis

**I/O TODAY** Big Data

## Summary

## LEARNING OBJECTIVES

This chapter should help you understand:

- The scientific method and its goals and assumptions
- The importance of theory to science and psychology
- Internal and external validity
- The complex interplay among experimental variables
- How research is conducted, with an emphasis on induction and deduction as well as the five steps involved in the process
- A variety of measurement issues such as reliability and validity
- Basic-level statistics ranging from descriptive statistics to correlation and regression

Suppose that an organization is having a problem with absenteeism such that, on average, its employees are missing about 15 days of work per year. Absenteeism is a very expensive problem for organizations because it slows down production and it costs additional dollars to replace employees who are missing. Suppose further that this company has hired you as an I/O psychologist to help diagnose the problem, provide a potential solution, and implement and evaluate that solution.

First, then, you have to figure out what the problem is. You might do this by interviewing current plant employees, by talking to managers, and by administering surveys. In addition, you might need to look at the organization's absence data and do some statistical analysis to uncover how frequent the absences are, when they tend to occur (e.g., Mondays and Fridays versus days in the middle of the week), and whether they are occurring in certain departments more than in others. Second, you might need to collect some historical data about the company and its absence policy (usually a written policy in the employee handbook) because this may help you to understand the problem better. Third, you might use this information and your expertise in I/O psychology to develop and implement an approach to remedy the problem.

Furthermore, you will need to look at the absence data again a few months after the new approach is under way to see whether absence has decreased. In addition, you might want to survey and interview employees to see if they have noticed any differences since (and as a result of) the implementation of the new approach. At each of these steps in the process, you will need to gather data in order to understand the problem and to evaluate the solution. In this chapter, I will talk about how I/O psychologists gather data and use it to improve their understanding of organizational functioning.

## WHAT IS SCIENCE?

Science is a process or method for generating a body of knowledge. It's important to note that this term refers not to a body of knowledge but, rather, to the process or method used in producing that body of knowledge. Science represents a *logic of inquiry*—a way of going about doing things to increase our understanding of concepts, processes, and relationships. What makes psychology scientific is that we rely on formal, systematic observation to help us find answers to questions about behavior. Science is not about people in white coats in a laboratory, or brilliant teachers in the thought-provoking world of academia, or mind-boggling technological advances; science is about understanding the world in which we live. But scientists are not satisfied with a superficial understanding; they strive for a complete understanding. For instance, the nonscientist may note that employees seem to be more productive when they are allowed to participate in important organizational decisions. The scientist, on the other hand, works at understanding why this is the case, what kind of participation is most important for employees, when participation might not benefit the organization, why it is that participation seems important for some employees but not for others, and so on. In the next section, we will examine the four major goals of science.

**science**
A process or method for generating a body of knowledge.

### Goals of Science

There are many different lists of the goals or objectives of science, but I will use the list presented by Larry Christensen (1994) because it is most consistent with my thinking on the subject. First, there is *description,* the accurate portrayal or depiction of the phenomenon of interest. In our example, this is the focus of the nonscientist's approach to understanding—simply noting and describing the phenomenon whereby employees are more productive when given some voice by the organization. But the scientist goes further than this—which brings us to the second goal.

In an attempt to better understand the phenomenon, the scientist focuses on an *explanation*—that is, on gathering knowledge about why the phenomenon exists or what causes it. This usually requires the identification of one or more antecedents, which are conditions that occur prior to the phenomenon. Again, in our example, it may be that giving employees the opportunity to participate in decisions makes them feel needed and important, which leads to or causes increased effort. Of course, as scientists, we realize that almost all behaviors are complex and that there tend to be many causes or antecedents for any given behavior.

The third goal of science is *prediction,* which refers to the ability to anticipate an event prior to its actual occurrence. Accurate prediction requires that we have some understanding of the explanation of the phenomenon so that we can anticipate when the phenomenon will occur. In our example, we may be able to predict an increase in effort on the part of the employees if we know that the company just recently sent out a survey asking for their input on important decisions about medical benefits. Without the ability to predict, we have a gap in our knowledge and are left with very little helpful information that we can provide to the company. In other words, if we have described and explained the phenomenon but cannot help the company predict this behavior in the future, our usefulness is somewhat limited.

The last goal of science is *control* of the phenomenon—specifically, the manipulation of antecedent conditions to affect behavior. Ideally, we'd like to have a sufficiently complete understanding of the phenomenon so that we can manipulate or control variables to increase or decrease the occurrences of the phenomenon. In other words, we'd like to be able to help the company provide the appropriate antecedents so that employees will work harder and perform better. Indeed, by providing employees with opportunities for participation throughout the year, the company should be able to maintain high levels of effort and performance.

In sum, we have attained some degree of scientific understanding only when a phenomenon is accurately described, explained, predicted, and able to be controlled.

## Assumptions of Science

In order for scientists to do their work and to make sense of the world, they must have some basic assumptions about the world. First, scientists must believe in *empiricism,* which is the notion that the best way to understand behavior is to generate predictions based on theory, gather data, and use the data to test these predictions. Second, scientists must believe in *determinism,* which suggests that behavior is orderly and systematic and doesn't just happen by chance. Imagine what psychology would be like if its basic assumption was that behavior was a chance occurrence. It would counter what all psychologists believe because it would suggest that we can neither explain nor predict behavior. In effect, if we didn't believe that behavior is orderly, psychology would have nothing to offer society.

The third basic assumption of scientists is *discoverability,* which suggests not only that behavior is orderly but also that this orderliness can be discovered. I'm not suggesting that behavior is so orderly that a psychologist can easily predict what an individual will do at any given moment; if it was that easy, think about how it would change the way you interact with others. For instance, if you knew exactly how a classmate would react to being asked out on a date, you would feel much less stress and be certain that you would never hear the answer "no" (since, in that event, you wouldn't ask the question!). Psychologists do not suggest that behavior is that orderly, only that there is some order to it; so the last major assumption here is that we can experience, examine, and discover—to some extent—that orderliness.

## Theories

**theory**
A set of interrelated constructs (concepts), definitions, and propositions that present a systematic view of a phenomenon by specifying relations among variables, with the purpose of explaining and predicting the phenomenon.

A **theory** is a set of interrelated constructs (concepts), definitions, and propositions that present a systematic view of a phenomenon by specifying relations among variables, with the purpose of explaining and predicting the phenomenon (Kerlinger, 1986). Fred Kerlinger argues that without an emphasis on theory, science would become nothing more than a simple search for answers, lacking any framework or carefully executed process. It is theory and its accompanying propositions, according to Kerlinger, that allow us to describe, explain, predict, and control the phenomenon under investigation. Even though, as I/O practitioners, our focus may be on conducting research that will help us solve an applied problem, that research should be based on a theory, or its results should be used to help develop new theories and alter existing theories. It's important to realize that theories are as important to applied scientific disciplines like I/O psychology as they are to less applied scientific disciplines like microbiology.

**What Makes a Good Theory?** As with everything else in science, there are good theories and bad theories. Scientists generally agree that a good theory should meet certain criteria or standards. First, a theory is of little use if it is not *parsimonious*. In other words, the theory should be able to explain a lot as simply as possible. The fewer statements in a theory, the better. If a theory has to have a proposition or statement for every phenomenon it tries to explain, it will become so big as to be unmanageable. Generally, if two theories make the same predictions, the more parsimonious one is the better theory. After all, if people can't understand the theory or use it in their research, the theory will not help advance science by improving their understanding.

The second criterion for a good theory is *precision*. A theory should be specific and accurate in its wording and conceptual statements so that everyone knows what its propositions and predictions are. You might notice a trade-off here between parsimony and precision, but, in fact, scientists try to develop theories that are both simple and precise: Too much of either is a potential weakness of any theory. If the theory is not very precise but instead is wordy and unclear, scientists will not know how to use the theory or be able to make predictions based on it. They would be left in the position of having to try to interpret the theory based on what *they think* it tries to say.

*Testability* is the third criterion for a theory: If it can't be tested, it can't be useful. Testability means that the propositions presented in the theory must be verifiable by some sort of experimentation. If you have developed a theory that predicts rainfall in inches as a function of the number of Martians that land on the earth per day, you have developed a theory that is untestable (unless you know something I don't know!) and that, therefore, is not a good theory. Notice that I have not said that the theory must be capable of being proven. The reason is that theories are not proven but, rather, are either supported or not supported by the data. We can never prove a theory; we can only gather information that makes us more confident that the theory is accurate or that it is misspecified.

One of the great scientific philosophers, Karl Popper, argued that science is really about ruling out alternative explanations, leaving just one explanation or theory that seems to fit the data (Popper, 1959). He further said that the ultimate goal of a scientific theory is to be "not yet disconfirmed." In making this statement, Popper seemed to realize that most theories are likely to be disconfirmed at some point but that it is in the disconfirmation that science advances.

**A CLOSER LOOK**
A slightly different list of the stages involved in the research process. Why are the steps of the research process so important? What would be the impact of not following these steps?

**induction**
An approach to science that consists of working from data to theory.

**deduction**
An approach to science in which we start with theory and propositions and then collect data to test those propositions—working from theory to data.

Of course, a theory must also be *useful,* such that it is practical and helps in describing, explaining, and predicting an *important* phenomenon. You may be able to generate a theory about how often and when your psychology instructor is likely to walk across the room while lecturing; but I would wonder, even if your theory describes, explains, and predicts this phenomenon pretty well and is testable, whether anyone really cares. The behavior itself is not important enough to make the theory useful. By this criterion of usefulness, it would be a bad theory.

Finally, a theory should possess the quality of *generativity;* it should stimulate research that attempts to support or refute its propositions. We may develop a theory that seems to meet all the other criteria, but if no one ever tests the theory or uses it in any way, then the theory itself would be of little value.

In sum, science is logic of inquiry, and the primary objective of science is theory building. As a set of propositions about relationships among variables, a theory is developed to describe, explain, predict, and control important phenomena. Theories can be evaluated as to their parsimony, precision, testability, usefulness, and generativity. See **Table 2.1** for a useful summary of the characteristics of a good theory. But how do we put all of this together and start to conduct research? That will be the focus of the rest of the chapter. First, however, we need to clarify the relationship between theories and data.

**Which Comes First—Data or Theory?** Theory and data are of the utmost importance to science and can't be overemphasized. Science uses both theory and data, but individual scientists have disagreed about which should come first and which is more important. Empirical observation, referred to as **induction,** involves working from data to theory. Basically, the argument here is that we must collect data, data, and more data until we have enough data to develop a theory. Others, however, take the opposite approach, known as **deduction,** which involves starting with a theory and propositions and then collecting data to test those propositions. In this case, reasoning proceeds from a general theory to data that test particular elements of that theory— working from theory to data.

In their purest forms, there are problems with both the inductive and deductive approaches to research. Collecting data and then generating theories (i.e., induction) is useless unless those theories are tested and modified as a result of additional data. But generating a theory and collecting data to test its propositions (i.e., deduction) is only a partial process, too, unless those data are used to alter or refute those propositions.

| TABLE 2.1 | Characteristics of a Good Theory | |
|---|---|---|
| **Characteristic** | **What Does It Mean?** | **Why Does It Matter?** |
| Parsimony | The theory explains as much as possible, as simply as possible. | Theories that are too complex are unmanageable and, therefore, not very useful. |
| Precision | The theory should be as specific and accurate in its language as possible. | If a theory is wordy and unclear, scientists won't know how to test it. |
| Testability | The propositions in the theory must be verifiable with experimentation. | An untestable theory can't be supported or disconfirmed and is of little use to science. |
| Usefulness | The theory should be practical and describe or predict an *important* phenomenon. | A theory that only predicts or explains something as trivial as the color of the pen in your drawer isn't of any worth. |
| Generativity | The theory should stimulate research aimed at testing it. | If a theory never gets tested—that is, if no research follows from it—the theory has no purpose. |

The approach taken by most distinguished scientists is one that combines inductive and deductive processes.

Both approaches are depicted in **Figure 2.1,** which illustrates the *cyclical inductive–deductive model of research.* Note that it doesn't really matter whether one starts with data (induction) or with a theory (deduction)—neither is used exclusively at the

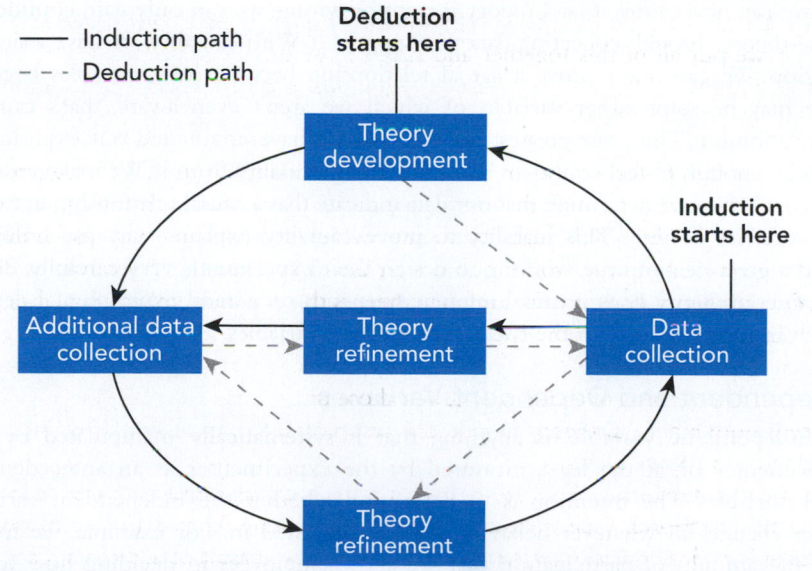

expense of the other. If one starts with a general theory (inside path of the figure), data are collected to test the theory; the data are used to make changes to the theory if necessary; more data are collected; the theory is amended again; and the process continues. If one begins with data collection (outside path of the figure), the data are used to develop a theory; additional data are collected to test this theory; the theory is amended if necessary; even more data are collected; and the process continues.

At least initially, most research tends to be driven by inductive processes. Think about it. Even in research using the deductive approach—theory to data—the original development of the theory was probably based on some data. Hence, induction is an initial part of the process, with an ensuing emphasis on deductive methods. So here, too, we see the cyclical model in action.

By now it should be obvious that there is no perfect way to "do science." However, being aware of the goals of science, the assumptions of scientists, the criteria for good theories, and how induction and deduction feed into each other should help you understand the ways in which the scientific process is best applied. The specific types of research designs and data collection techniques will be discussed soon, but first we need to consider some basic terminology and concepts.

## RESEARCH TERMINOLOGY AND BASIC CONCEPTS

**causal inference**
A conclusion, drawn from research data, about the likelihood of a causal relationship between two variables.

To begin to understand what is involved in conducting experiments, you have to know what is meant by drawing a **causal inference** because this is what we typically want to be able to do at the completion of an experiment. Recall my earlier point that we can never prove that a theory is right or wrong; we can only gain confidence in the theory through collecting data that support it. With causality, we have a similar situation. We can never prove a causal relationship between two variables because there may be some other variable, of which we aren't even aware, that's causing the relationship. Thus, our greatest hope is that we have conducted our experiment carefully enough to feel confident about inferring causality from it. We make a causal inference when we determine that our data indicate that a causal relationship between two variables is *likely*. This inability to prove causality explains why psychologists spend a great deal of time working to design their experiments very carefully. Being able to confidently draw a causal inference depends on careful experimental design, which in turn begins with the two major types of variables.

### Independent and Dependent Variables

**independent variable**
A variable that is systematically manipulated by the experimenter or, at the least, measured by the experimenter as an antecedent to other variables.

An **independent variable** is anything that is systematically manipulated by the experimenter or, at the least, measured by the experimenter as an antecedent to other variables. The intention is to determine whether the independent variable causes changes in whatever behavior we are interested in. For example, we might vary the amount of participation that we allow employees in deciding how to do their work: One group might be given no input and simply told how to do its work, a second group might be given some input in deciding how to accomplish the tasks, and a third group might be given complete control over how to do the job. In this experiment, our independent variable would be the degree of participation granted to employees.

The **dependent variable** is the variable of interest—what we design our experiment to assess. In short, we are usually interested in the effect of the independent variable on the dependent variable. For example, we might predict that participation (the independent variable) will influence employees' job satisfaction (the dependent variable). In other words, the more opportunities employees are given to decide how to do their own work, the more satisfied they will be with their jobs. If we were to find that this is indeed the case, we would conclude that participation causes job satisfaction. Keep in mind, however, that when I say *causes,* I mean that we are making a causal inference, because we can't be certain that participation causes satisfaction. This shortcut in terminology is typically used by psychologists: We talk about causation when we really mean causal inference. In I/O psychology, common dependent variables include performance, profits, costs, job attitudes, salary, promotion, attendance behaviors, and motivation. Usually, we manipulate the independent variable and measure its effect on the dependent variable.

Another type of variable is called an **extraneous variable**. An extraneous variable—also called a *confounding variable*—is anything other than the independent variable that can contaminate the results or be thought of as an alternative to our causal explanation. Extraneous variables get in the way and prevent us from being confident that our independent variable is affecting our dependent variable. In our participation–job satisfaction experiment, for example, performance might be an extraneous variable if better performers were given more opportunity for participation. In this case, they may be more satisfied not because of their participation but, rather, because they are getting more organizational rewards as a result of being better performers.

In I/O psychology, we often refer to independent and dependent variables by other, more specific names. Independent variables are frequently called *predictors, precursors,* or *antecedents,* and dependent variables are often called *criteria, outcomes,* or *consequences.* In the selection context, we often talk of predictors and criteria. We use a predictor variable to forecast an individual's score on a criterion variable. For instance, we might say that intelligence is an important predictor of successful job performance. *Predictors* and *criteria* are discussed in much more detail later in the book, but for now it's important to realize that these terms are often used interchangeably with *independent variable* and *dependent variable,* respectively.

## Control

Control is a very important element of experimental design. To ensure that we can make a causal inference about the effect of our independent variable on our dependent variable—a matter of internal validity—we need to be able to exercise control over the experiment. In order to confidently draw a causal inference, we must eliminate other potential explanations of the effect. One major way of doing this is to control extraneous variables.

**dependent variable**
The variable of interest, or what we design experiments to assess.

**extraneous variable**
Anything other than the independent variable that can contaminate our results or be thought of as an alternative to our causal explanation; also called a *confounding variable.*

Let's say we're interested in the effect of leadership style on employee performance. To examine this relationship, we could use a survey of employees to measure their leaders' style and then match that up with the performance of individuals who work for each leader. We could then look to see if a particular leadership style results in better employee performance. However, there are many potential extraneous variables in this situation, such as employees' ability or experience. It may be that all the employees who work for the leader with the most favorable style also happen to be the employees with the most ability. Therefore, although it looks as though leadership style leads to a particular level of performance, employees who work for a certain leader may actually be performing well because of their own ability rather than because of the leader's style.

There are various ways in which we can attempt to control for extraneous variables. First, the potentially extraneous variable can be *held constant* in our experiment. For instance, if we think that employees' experience might be an extraneous variable in our leadership–job performance study, we could control for this by using as participants only those employees who have the same amount of job experience—exactly 10 years. In other words, rather than allowing experience to confound our results, we hold it constant. Then, if we find that leadership style and employee performance are related, although we cannot say for sure that style causes performance, we *can* be certain that employee experience is not an alternative explanation. Because all the participants in our study have the same amount of experience, any differences in performance must be due to something else.

A second way in which we try to control for extraneous variables is by systematically *manipulating different levels of the variable*. For example, if we think that gender might be a confounding variable in our leadership–job performance study, we might treat gender as an independent variable and use a more complicated experimental design in which we look at the relationship between leadership style and job performance among female leaders versus male leaders. This would be the opposite of holding the variable constant; here, we make the variable *part of the experimental design* and examine whether it plays a role in affecting the dependent variable. For instance, if we find the same relationship between leadership style and job performance among male leaders as we find among female leaders, then we have successfully ruled out gender as an alternative explanation of our effect.

A third way, though it's somewhat complicated, is to use *statistical control* (see Pedhazur & Schmelkin, 1991). With statistical techniques such as the analysis of covariance, we can remove or control the variability in our dependent variable that is due to the extraneous variable. For instance, if we wanted to test the hypothesis that older workers outperform younger workers on some task because of their greater experience, we would need to control for variables that might be related to age. We could use statistical approaches to make sure that the older group and younger group do not differ on intelligence, quality of supervision, training opportunities, and so on. This would allow us to be more certain that any differences in performance between the two groups are due to experience, because we have controlled for the other potential explanations.

## PRACTITIONER FORUM

Douglas Klein

### Douglas Klein

*MA, 1989, I/O Psychology, New York University*
*Former Principal Member and Chief Leadership Advisor at*
*Sirota Survey Intelligence*

As a practitioner helping companies uncover and overcome obstacles to performance, I have been using field-based research (primarily surveys, but also unobtrusive research methods) for over 20 years. Moreover, reliable, valid, data-driven insights have been fueling strategic decision making in organizations for some time now (although there are still unfortunate examples to the contrary). Gone are the days when successful companies made million-dollar decisions based on unreliable information or management hunches. This is as true for deciding whether to build a new plant as it is for implementing a new leadership development program.

My clients routinely focus on the independent, dependent, and control variables impacting business effectiveness. Recently, a major retailer wanted to understand the relationship between how it led and managed and business results. The hypothesis was that certain leadership and management practices (independent variables) had direct and measurable impacts on business outcomes such as customer satisfaction, employee engagement, operational efficiency, and financial performance (the dependent variables). The company's employee survey data (collected through self-administered surveys) were correlated with existing archival data available for each retail location (e.g., customer ratings, performance metrics, financial performance, turnover, etc.) using a quasi-experimental design. However, we knew that locations in rural areas would have lower financial performance and urban areas would have lower customer service ratings (due to increased volumes), so location-type was used as a control variable. The findings helped this retailer understand why certain locations performed better than others (after controlling for confounding variables) and helped it anticipate future returns on investment in people (and helped it prioritize upcoming spending across a number of potential asset classes).

I/O psychologists help companies recognize the importance of and manage their intangible assets (e.g., people, practices, values, etc.). It is the people who convert a company's tangible resources into business results, so how they are led, valued, managed, and so on plays a huge role in the ultimate success of any organization. Most executives would agree that a weak culture will undermine a sound business strategy every time.

In order to become a successful I/O psychologist providing consultative services, you must understand research theory/methods and statistics and be able to translate learned insights into actions to be taken. A good first step on that path is mastery of the concepts expressed in this chapter on research.

#### Applying Your Knowledge

1. The first paragraph states that reliable, valid, data-driven insights fuel strategic decision making in large organizations. How do the goals of science align with this business practice?

2. Explain how field-based research, such as surveys and unobtrusive methods, could be helpful in gathering information for business decisions.

3. Toward the end of this feature, the difference between the tangible versus intangible assets of an organization is discussed. How would I/O psychologists be particularly suited to understanding and synthesizing both assets to increase productivity?

## Internal and External Validity

With any experiment, the first thing we are interested in is whether our results have **internal validity**, which is the extent to which we can draw causal inferences about our variables. In other words, can we be confident that the result of our experiment is due to

**internal validity**
The extent to which we can draw causal inferences about our variables.

the independent variable that we manipulated, not to some confounding or extraneous variable? Returning to our participation–job satisfaction study, we would have high internal validity if we were confident that participation was the variable that was affecting employees' satisfaction levels. If, however, it was actually the rewards associated with better performance that led to high satisfaction (as I suggested, these rewards might be an extraneous variable), then we couldn't rule out rewards as an alternative explanation for differences in satisfaction; we would thus have internal validity problems.

**external validity**
The extent to which the results obtained in an experiment generalize to other people, settings, and times.

The other major type of validity that is important when designing experiments is external validity, the extent to which the results obtained in our experiment generalize to other people, settings, and times. Suppose we conduct a study in which we find that those employees who are given specific, difficult goals to work toward perform better than those who are simply told to do their best. We want to be able to say that this effect will generalize to other employees in other companies at other times. Obviously, external validity is extremely important to the development of science; to the extent that we devise studies that are low in external validity, we are not moving science forward. For instance, some criticize I/O research done with student participants as not being generalizable to "real-world" employees. If the work that is done with students does not generalize to employees, it is not very useful for increasing our understanding of the phenomenon under study. (For a very thoughtful discussion on this topic, see Landers and Behrend, 2015.)

However, external validity is always an empirical question—that is, a question that can be answered only through experimentation, experience, or observation. We can't simply conduct a study and argue that it is or is not externally valid. Rather, the external validity of this one study is demonstrated by replicating it with different participants, in different settings, at different times. We can also try to use representative samples of the population to which we want to generalize and argue that our results probably generalize to others. However, to be sure, we have to collect additional data.

There is an important trade-off between internal and external validity that often demands the researcher's attention (Cook & Campbell, 1979). As we rule out various alternative explanations by controlling more and more elements of the study to successfully increase our internal validity, what happens to the generalizability of our results? It may decline because, now, a one-of-a-kind situation has been created that is *so artificial* it is not likely to be externally valid. Put more simply, the findings may not generalize to other situations because no other situation is likely to be very similar to the one we've created. So, as we gain control for internal validity purposes, we may lose the potential for external validity.

Of course, if we don't control and rule out alternative explanations, we will not be confident about our causal explanation (internal validity), even if the results have the potential to generalize to other settings and participants. And in any case, if we aren't sure what the results mean, what good is external validity? My point here is that we have to start with internal validity because, without it, our research really can't make much of a contribution to the knowledge in the field. But we also need to balance the two types of validity, as too much control can reduce the extent to which the results are likely to generalize.

## A Model of the Research Process

There are various ways to go about conducting a research project, but in this section we will discuss a general approach that should act as a guide for you in developing and conducting your own research. It should also help you understand how research in psychology progresses through various stages. The model is presented in **Figure 2.2.**

Usually, the first step in any research project is to formulate testable hypotheses. A hypothesis is a tentative statement about the relationship between two or more variables. Hypotheses are most often generated as a result of a thorough review of the literature. Sometimes, however, they arise from the experimenter's own experiences or from a question that has not yet been answered in the published literature. Regardless of how one gets there, hypothesis generation is the first formal step in this process.

**hypothesis**
A tentative statement about the relationship between two or more variables.

The second step involves the actual designing of the study, which we've talked about previously with respect to control, internal validity, and external validity. The two basic choices that need to be made at this stage are who the participants in your study are going to be and what is going to be measured. Although research participants in general can include children, older adults, animals, and people suffering from various disorders, participants in most I/O psychology experiments are either college undergraduates or organizational employees. As for measures, we typically have one or more independent variables and dependent variables.

After the study is designed, it's time to actually go about collecting the data. This can be done in many different ways. Some studies require data collection over more than one time period, whereas others may require the use of more than one group of participants. Some data are collected through face-to-face interactions, other data are collected by mail, and still other data are collected via e-mail or the Internet. We'll talk briefly about some of the more common approaches to data collection in the following sections.

Once the data are collected, the researcher needs to make sense out of them. This is usually done through some sort of statistical analysis, an area in which I/O psychologists are well schooled because the field of I/O is one of the more quantitative fields in psychology. I/O psychologists make great use of the various analytic methods that are available. At this stage of the process, the researcher goes back to the original hypotheses and research questions and uses statistical techniques to test those hypotheses and answer those research questions.

The last step in the research process is writing up the results. This is the point at which the I/O researcher goes back to the original ideas that were used to generate the hypotheses and describes those ideas and the research on which they were based. The researcher will then present the hypotheses and describe in detail the procedures that

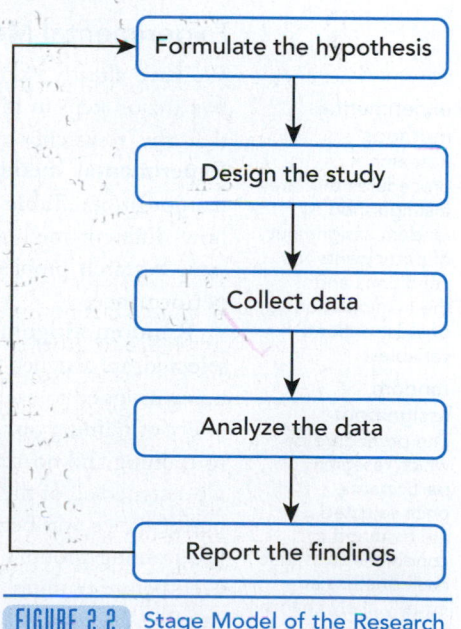

**FIGURE 2.2** Stage Model of the Research Process

were used to carry out the research. The last two sections of the write-up include a presentation of the results and a discussion of what they mean, how they fit into the existing literature, how they help to solve a problem, and what implications they have for organizational functioning.

Ideally, this paper can be published in a journal that is an outlet for research of this type and that allows researchers to communicate their findings to other scholars and practitioners. Papers like this one provide important information that benefits employers, employees, and organizations as they all work to be more productive and effective. Sometimes these research reports are presented at national conferences, serve as work toward a student's master's or doctoral degree, or meet the requirements of a psychology course or an honors curriculum. Whether one is writing up the results of an honors project, a small study done for an experimental psychology class, or a major project to be published in one of the top I/O journals, the process is the same in terms of the steps involved in the research, as well as in the actual written presentation of the research project. For guidelines, see the *Publication Manual of the American Psychological Association* (American Psychological Association, 2009).

## TYPES OF RESEARCH DESIGNS

There are various ways in which studies are designed to answer a particular research question. In this section, we will consider the most frequently employed methods and look at some examples to further your understanding.

### Experimental Methods

We have already examined the inductive–deductive cycle of research, as well as the five major steps in the research process. Now we turn to the experimental methods that the researcher can employ in order to answer particular research questions. **Experimental methods** are characterized by two factors: random assignment and manipulation. **Table 2.2** presents a learning aid to help you better understand how different methodologies and data collection techniques can be applied to the same research problem—in this case, the effect of training on individual employee performance.

**Random assignment** refers to the procedure by which research participants, once selected, are assigned to conditions such that each one has an equally likely chance of being assigned to each condition. For instance, if we were interested in measuring the effect of training on job performance, we would want to randomly assign participants to training and no-training conditions so as to provide a fair test of our hypothesis. If we assigned all of the good performers to the training condition and found that their performance was better than that of the no-training group, the reason could be that the training group was composed of better performers than the no-training group even before training. In other words, pretraining performance could be an extraneous variable. To control for this and other potential extraneous variables, we use random assignment to conditions. Of course, it is possible that even with random assignment

**experimental methods**
Research procedures that are distinguished by random assignment of participants to conditions and the manipulation of independent variables.

**random assignment**
The procedure by which research participants, once selected, are assigned to conditions such that each one has an equally likely chance of being assigned to each condition.

## TABLE 2.2 Research Designs and Methodologies

The effect of training on individual employee performance can be investigated in many different ways, such as the following:

| Research Design | Methodology | Example |
| --- | --- | --- |
| Experimental | Laboratory experiment | Student participants are randomly assigned to the training condition (experimental) or the no-training condition (control); then performance is measured. |
| | Field experiment | Employees in a manufacturing organization are randomly assigned to the training condition (experimental) or the no-training condition (control); then performance is measured. |
| | Quasi-experiment | All the employees in one department of a manufacturing organization are assigned to the training condition (experimental), and all the employees in another department of the same organization are assigned to the no-training condition (control); then performance is measured. |
| Observational | Naturalistic observation | The researcher watches individuals as they receive or do not receive training and records what they experience as well as the individuals' performance behaviors. |
| | Archival research | The researcher identifies an existing data set that includes whether or not individuals experienced training and also individuals' performance levels. |
| | Survey | Employees are given a questionnaire that asks them how much training they have received at their organization and what their most recent performance appraisal ratings were. |

we could end up with all of the good performers in one condition and the poor performers in the other condition, but random assignment makes this very unlikely. To make sure our random assignment "worked" we might measure performance at the beginning of the research to confirm that there are no significant differences on performance across groups.

The second necessary factor associated with experimental methods is the **manipulation** of one or more independent variables. With experimental designs, we don't just measure our independent variables; we systematically control, vary, or apply them to different groups of participants. In our training–job performance example, we systematically provide training to one group of participants and no training to another. Random assignment and manipulation of independent variables are the keys to controlling extraneous variables, ruling out alternative explanations, and being able to draw causal inferences. In other words, these two techniques increase the internal validity of our experiment. They are the reason that experimental designs almost always have higher internal validity than observational designs.

**manipulation**
The systematic control, variation, or application of independent variables to different groups of participants.

**Laboratory Experiments** One type of experimental methodology is the laboratory experiment. Random assignment and manipulation of independent variables are used in a laboratory experiment to increase control, rule out alternative explanations, and increase internal validity. Most laboratory experiments take place in a somewhat contrived setting rather than a real-world work setting. For instance, two of my former students and I conducted a study in which undergraduates were randomly assigned to one of four conditions (Medvedeff, Gregory, & Levy, 2008). The four conditions varied in the type of feedback given (positive or negative) and the nature of the feedback (process based or outcome based). We were interested in whether these differences influenced how likely participants were to request more feedback. We found that the feedback manipulations (positive vs. negative and process vs. outcome) mattered, and participants did seek more feedback in some conditions than in others.

The findings revealed that participants paid more attention to the additional peer information than to the additional self-rating information. Because of our random assignment of participants to experimental conditions and our careful manipulation of the additional information (i.e., the self-ratings and peer ratings), we were able to rule out other plausible alternatives and argue that the difference in final judgments was due to different degrees of trust in the sources of the additional information.

Recall the internal validity–external validity trade-off that we discussed earlier. Laboratory experiments give rise to that very problem. Although they are typically very high in internal validity because of the extent to which researchers have control of the laboratory context, their external validity, or generalizability, is often questioned because of the contrived nature of the laboratory setting. In an attempt to counter this criticism in the study described above, my colleague and I invited as participants only those students who were also employed at least part time. In addition, the majority of our participants had real-life experience in conducting performance appraisals. This factor improved the external validity of our study because our participants were much like the population to whom we wanted to generalize. That they had actual real-world performance appraisal experience made the task we asked them to do (i.e., make performance judgments) appear more reasonable, thus increasing external validity. Imposing enough control to maintain high levels of *internal validity*, having realistic scenarios, and using participants who are representative of the working world for *external validity* are important issues in experimental designs.

**Field Experiments and Quasi-Experiments** To overcome the problems associated with the artificiality of laboratory settings, I/O researchers sometimes take advantage of the realism of field settings and do field experiments. Here, we still use random assignment and manipulations of independent variables to control for extraneous variables, but we do so within a naturally occurring real-world setting. Admittedly, these experiments are not used a great deal in I/O research because it is difficult to find real-world settings in which random assignment and manipulations are reasonable. Organizations are typically not willing to allow a researcher to come in and randomly assign employees to a training or no-training group because such arrangements could disrupt productivity and organizational efficiency.

**field experiment**
An approach to research that employs the random assignment and manipulation of an experiment, but does so outside the laboratory.

A more viable alternative is a **quasi-experiment**, which resembles a field experiment but does not include random assignment (Cook & Campbell, 1979). Quasi-experiments usually involve some manipulation of an independent variable, but instead of random assignment of participants to conditions, they often use *intact* groups. In our training–job performance study, for example, it would be difficult to find an organization that would allow random assignment of individuals to conditions, but it might be possible to assign departments, work groups, or plants to conditions. In this case, perhaps four work groups could be assigned to the training condition and four others to the no-training condition. And to control for potential extraneous variables, we could measure and control for any preexisting differences between the two experimental conditions in terms of experience, gender, performance, attitudes, and so on. Quasi-experiments are very common in I/O psychology because they are more feasible to conduct than field experiments but still allow for reasonable levels of internal validity.

**quasi-experiment**
A research design that resembles an experimental design but does not include random assignment.

## Observational Methods

Studies that employ **observational methods** are sometimes called *correlational designs* because their results are usually analyzed by correlational statistics, which we will talk about a bit later in this chapter. This kind of research is also often described as *descriptive* because we focus exclusively on the relationships among variables and thus can only describe the situation. Descriptive studies are not true experiments because they don't involve random assignment or the manipulation of independent variables. In these designs, we make use of what is available to us, and we are very limited in drawing causal inferences. All we can conclude from such studies is that our results either do or do not indicate a relationship between the variables of interest. Although we can use this approach in either the laboratory or the field, it is much more common in the field because it is here that we are usually limited in terms of what we can control.

**observational methods**
Research procedures that make use of data gathered from observation of behaviors and processes in order to describe a relationship or pattern of relationships.

In consulting with one company, we were interested in the relationship between job satisfaction and performance of the company's employees. To examine this issue, we administered a job satisfaction survey to 200 employees at a company and then measured their performance using their supervisor's rating. Through statistical analysis, we concluded that job satisfaction was related to performance, but we could not conclude that satisfaction causes performance because we had not manipulated satisfaction or randomly assigned employees to satisfaction conditions. Indeed, it might be that performance causes job satisfaction, as the better performers are rewarded for their performance and, therefore, are more satisfied (Lawler & Porter, 1967). The only way we could have actually examined causality in this situation would have been to manipulate job

John Rensten/Digital Vision/Getty Images

**A CLOSER LOOK**
Why can't we infer causality using observational methods?

satisfaction—an option that seems both nonsensical and potentially unethical. Can you think of a company that would allow you to come in and make some employees satisfied with their jobs and others dissatisfied so that you could examine the effects of these conditions on performance? Certainly, the company that hired me would not have allowed me to do that. In such situations, we typically use observational methods and draw conclusions about relationships rather than about causality.

Descriptive research can be very important in a couple of ways. First, although we can't infer causality from such research, we can often gather data that describe a relationship or pattern of relationships. These data can then be used to generate more causal hypotheses, which in turn can be examined with experimental designs. Second, in some cases, there is a great deal to be gained by description alone. Recall that description is one of the basic goals of science. Indeed, some important scientific findings are entirely descriptive, such as the Periodic Table of Elements in chemistry. Descriptive research in I/O psychology can be very important as well, such as when we use surveys to measure the work-related attitudes of organizational employees. This information is certainly useful for employers who may be trying to decide if it is worth implementing a new reward program for their employees. In addition, it can be integral to us as researchers who are trying to enhance our understanding of work processes.

Prediction, you may remember, is another goal of science—and such studies can be very useful in predicting behavior in certain situations. So, although observational research is not as strong as experimental research with respect to inferring causality, it is important for other reasons.

# DATA COLLECTION TECHNIQUES

There are various ways in which data can be collected for a research study. In this section, we will focus on some methods of data collection in I/O psychology, proceeding from the least to the most common approaches.

## Naturalistic Observation

Perhaps the most obvious way to gather data to answer a research question about a behavior is to watch individuals exhibiting that behavior. We use observation in both laboratory and field settings in which we are interested in some behavior that can be observed, counted, or measured. *Naturalistic observation* refers to the observation of someone or something in its natural environment. One type of naturalistic observation that is commonly used in sociology and anthropology, though not so much in I/O psychology, is called *participant observation;* here, the observer tries to "blend in" with those who are to be observed. The observational technique more often used by I/O psychologists is called **unobtrusive naturalistic observation**, in which the researcher tries not to draw attention to himself or herself and objectively observes individuals.

For example, a consultant interested in the effect of leadership style on the functioning of staff meetings might measure leadership style through a questionnaire and

**unobtrusive naturalistic observation**
An observational technique whereby the researcher unobtrusively and objectively observes individuals but does not try to blend in with them.

then observe the behaviors and interactions that take place during a series of staff meetings conducted by various leaders. Note that, although unobtrusive naturalistic observation can be a very fruitful approach for gathering data, the researcher needs to be aware of the possibility that she is affecting behaviors and interactions through her observation. No matter how unobtrusive she tries to be, some people may react differently when an observer is present.

## Case Studies

Somewhat similar to naturalistic observation, **case studies** are best defined as examinations of a single individual, group, company, or society (Babbie, 1998). A case study might involve interviews, historical analysis, or research into the writings or policies of an individual or organization. The main purpose of case studies (as with other observational methods) is description, although explanation is a reasonable goal of case studies, too. Sigmund Freud is well known for his use of case studies in the evaluation of his clients, but an I/O psychologist might use a case study to analyze the organizational structure of a modern company or to describe the professional life of a Fortune 500 CEO. I/O consulting firms often use case studies for PR purposes to showcase the good work that they do and to increase business for the firm. Case studies are not typically used to test hypotheses, but they can be very beneficial in terms of describing and providing details about a typical or exceptional firm or individual. Of course, a major concern with this approach is that the description is based on a single individual or organization, thus limiting the external validity of the description.

**case studies**
Examinations of a single individual, group, company, or society.

## Archival Research

Sometimes social scientists can answer important research questions through the use of existing, or "secondary," data sets. **Archival research** relies on such data sets, which have been collected for either general or specific purposes identified by an individual or organization (Zaitzow & Fields, 1996). One implication is immediately clear: The quality of research using an archival data set is strongly affected by the quality of that original study. In other words, garbage in–garbage out. Researchers cannot use a weak data set for their study and expect to fix any problems inherent in it. Indeed, lack of control over the quality of the data is the chief concern with archival research.

**archival research**
Research relying on secondary data sets that were collected either for general or specific purposes identified by an individual or organization.

This issue aside, archival data sets can be very helpful and, in fact, are used a great deal by I/O psychologists. Available to them are data sets that have been collected by market researchers, news organizations, behavioral scientists, and government researchers. One of the largest and most extensively used in the employment area is the data set containing scores on the General Aptitude Test Battery (GATB), which was developed by the U.S. Employment Service in 1947. It includes information on personal characteristics, ability, occupation, and work performance for over 36,000 individuals. The GATB has received a good deal of attention for many years, and these data were employed in many research studies as well (Doverspike, Cober, & Arthur, 2004).

Certainly, the use of secondary data sets can be very beneficial to researchers in that they do not have to spend huge amounts of time developing measures and collecting data. Going back to Figure 2.2, we find that steps 2 and 3 are already completed for the researcher who embarks on an archival study. In addition, many of the archival data sets available for use were collected by organizations with a great deal more resources than any one researcher would tend to have. Such data may also be richer in that many more variables may be involved than a single researcher would be able to include. A final strength of archival data sets is that they often include both *cross-sectional data,* which are collected at one point in time from a single group of respondents, and *longitudinal data,* which are collected over multiple time periods so that changes in attitudes and behaviors can be examined. Again, given the limited resources of most researchers, these types of data would typically be difficult to obtain.

## Surveys

It certainly seems obvious that if you want information from people, one way to gather it is to ask them. This is the very basis of survey methodology. Surveys involve selecting a sample of respondents (or participants) and administering some type of questionnaire. They are terrific tools for gathering data on employees' attitudes and beliefs about their organizations, their supervisors, their coworkers, and many other aspects of the world of work. It follows that surveys are probably the most frequently used method of data collection in I/O psychology. I'm certain that you have had at least some experience with surveys. You might have filled one out at a restaurant to rate the quality of the food or service, completed one on the warranty card that came with your new iPad, or answered questions on the telephone about what you watch on TV or what candidate you are likely to vote for and why. Surveys are, quite frankly, everywhere. Chances are that, if you have conducted any experimental research at all (such as an undergraduate research project, an honors project, or an experiment for another psychology class), you used a survey to some extent.

**surveys**
A data collection technique that involves selecting a sample of respondents and administering some type of questionnaire.

**Self-Administered Questionnaires** *Self-administered questionnaires* are surveys that are completed by respondents in the absence of an investigator. The primary example is the mail survey, which is mailed or e-mailed to respondents, who complete it and return it to the experimenter. Sometimes, however, we use the term *self-administered questionnaire* to refer to situations in which the respondent fills out the survey in the presence of the researcher (as in research you may have participated in for extra credit in an introductory psychology course). In these situations, the respondent is provided with a written survey that asks a series of questions requiring responses along some scale of agreement or frequency. This is a very common approach to collecting survey data.

Self-administered questionnaires are also common in field settings, where employees are often asked about their attitudes and beliefs about their jobs and organizations. For instance, job satisfaction is typically measured with a self-administered survey. Aside from the research goals linked to surveys, organizations routinely survey their employees to gather useful information for future organizational planning and

Rae Grant Design

**A CLOSER LOOK**
Why are self-administered surveys useful?

decision making, as well as to give employees a voice in company policies. Self-administered surveys are particularly useful for three reasons. First, they are relatively easy to administer. Second, they can be administered to large groups of people at the same time. Finally, they can provide respondents with anonymity, which makes them feel more comfortable and increases the likelihood that their responses will be honest.

On the negative side, with mail surveys in particular, the researcher is dependent on the respondents returning the surveys. These response rates can be quite low. When only a small percentage of the sample completes and returns the survey, conclusions drawn from the data may be very inaccurate. Also, unless the researcher is available during the administration of the survey, respondents cannot easily get clarification on questionnaire items they do not understand. Despite these limitations, however, self-administered surveys are both popular and useful in the field of I/O psychology.

**Interviews** An alternative to the self-administered questionnaire is the investigator-administered survey, or *interview*, in which the investigator asks a series of questions orally rather than in writing. Interviews are conducted usually face-to-face but sometimes over the telephone. Either way, the process is much the same. Interviews tend to be more time-consuming than self-administered questionnaires because they are usually done one-on-one. Still, there are some clear benefits to this approach. First, response rates tend to be higher, as people are less likely to turn down a face-to-face interview than to throw away a mail survey (Babbie, 1998). Second, ambiguities about what a question means that may arise with mail surveys can easily be resolved in interviews because the interviewer is available to provide answers. In the I/O domain, interviews are commonly used to gather data about employees' attitudes, concerns over the need for more management attention, applicants' skills and abilities, whether or not applicants fit a particular job very well, and employees' promotability.

## Technological Advances in Survey Methodology

Technology seems to play an increasingly larger role in our lives, so it should be no surprise that it also has a widespread effect on the research enterprise and, in particular, data collection. One innovation in this area is the use of web-based surveys or mobile surveys to replace or supplement paper-and-pencil ones. The web has much to offer as a data collection tool because participants can answer survey questions quickly, easily, and on their own time schedule and they can often do so on their smartphones or other mobile devices. Researchers are then provided with the survey data electronically in a ready-to-analyze format. Some researchers (Cole, Bedeian, & Feild, 2006) have been examining whether web-based versions of surveys are equivalent to paper-and-pencil versions—that is, are the measurement properties sufficiently similar that a web-based survey can be used instead of a paper-and-pencil one and vice versa? For instance, do people respond more on the favorable end of the scale when the survey is conducted on the web than when it is conducted via paper and pencil? Although additional research is needed, it appears that well-developed surveys for web administration can be created to be parallel to paper-and-pencil versions and that the two can demonstrate measurement equivalence. That is, the measurement structure, reliabilities, means, and so on are about the same regardless of the form of the administration. These studies suggest that web-based survey administration is proving to be a valuable alternative to paper-and-pencil administration (Leung & Kember, 2005).

Kohei Hara/Digital Vision/Getty Images

**A CLOSER LOOK**
How might the experience of taking an electronic survey differ from a face-to-face survey? In what ways are they the same?

This is not to say that no differences between paper-based and electronic surveys exist. Researchers analyzing over 3.5 million job applicants in a selection context (see Chapters 6 and 7 for more on selection) have identified differences in cognitive ability scores between the paper surveys and electronic surveys (web-based, mobile, etc.), however, they found little or no differences on demographics, personality, and measurement invariance (Arthur, Doverspike, Muños, Taylor, & Carr, 2014). Overall, researchers have found that the differences between these survey formats tend not to be large or frequent (Casler, Bickel, & Hackett, 2013), and thus electronic surveys have the potential to meaningfully change survey research (see Paolacci & Chandler, 2014, for a discussion of data quality and sampling issues).

As a result of these positive findings, electronic surveys have become a commonly used tool for researchers. New web-based applications for delivering these surveys are being created and introduced to the market with great speed. Here is one example of the recent innovation in this area: Hofmann and Patel (2015) propose a cost-effective, user-friendly approach that uses a web-based app called SurveySignal. Short messages are sent to participants through smartphones or other mobile devices at fixed or random intervals. These messages link the participants to mobile surveys created with common online survey software (e.g., Qualtrics). Participants answer a series of questions through Qualtrics, and data collection is completed. Of course, an advantage of this approach is that researchers can easily measure constructs and behavioral reports over time and follow up with participants as needed for additional data collection.

SurveySignal uses a data collection technique called **experience sampling methodology (ESM)**, which can be used to capture momentary attitudes and psychological states. Participants are contacted at some predetermined time by the researcher who then signals the participants to answer a series of questions. This method predates mobile technology, but smartphones are being used effectively in ESM research. For example, participants may receive a text or similar alert, after which a series of questions asking the participant about his or her feelings, attitudes, emotions, and behaviors appears on the phone. ESM provides an effective way to measure moment-to-moment attitudes and emotions and has become particularly popular among researchers working in the area of emotions (Bono, Foldes, Vinson, & Muros, 2007; Dimotakis, Scott, & Koopman, 2011).

For instance, ESM has been used to demonstrate stronger relationships between real-time measures of general affect and affective measures of job satisfaction than between real-time measures of general affect and more traditional cognitive measures of job satisfaction (Fisher, 2000). Another study used ESM with a sample of cheerleader instructors to measure their emotional states and perceptions of their behaviors on a momentary basis while interacting with cheerleader students (Beal, Trougakos, Weiss, & Green, 2006). The use of this technique allowed the researchers to gain a better view of emotions and behaviors as well as of how individuals regulate those emotions on a moment-by-moment basis (see Chapter 10 for a discussion of emotional regulation). A more recent study used e-mail notifications to signal employees to respond to survey items on their smartphones. They studied how work-related events predicted fluctuations around employees' trait levels of personality, and they identified personality types that appear to be more sensitive to certain workplace events (Judge, Simon, Hurst, and Kelley, 2015).

Among the newest trends is the use of an online panel, a form of crowdsourcing that serves as an online marketplace where employers can hire workers for single tasks

**experience sampling methodology (ESM)**
A technique that allows researchers to obtain repeated real-time reports of phenomena such as moods and emotions through the use of technology such as smartphones and other mobile devices.

or short-term assignments. Researchers have begun to see these panels as a source for recruiting research participants for some small compensation. Amazon's Mechanical Turk (MTurk) is the most commonly used and well-known online panel. Compared to paper-and-pencil surveys, the flexibility and reach of MTurk and similar sites make it easier for researchers to expand their pool of participants beyond college students. I/O practitioners anticipate great potential for sites like MTurk to aid in research and data gathering. Studies proposing both advantages and criticisms of these sites appear in the literature seemingly every day. One especially important paper analyzed 10 individual experiments of the type that would traditionally be conducted in the lab, but were conducted using MTurk (Crump, McDonnel, & Gureckis, 2013). Rather than simply comparing a paper-and-pencil survey to a mobile survey, these researchers conducted experiments with all the complexity that you would find in a lab setting, but using only the MTurk procedures. They concluded that MTurk provides a valid methodology with results that mirror traditional experiments and has the potential to be a revolutionary tool. This is definitely an area to continue to monitor for future developments.

## MEASUREMENT

We have talked about science, theories, and research design in this chapter, but, although these are all very important to the research enterprise, they are worthless without careful measurement. **Measurement** is defined as the assignment of numbers to objects or events using rules in such a way as to represent specified attributes of the objects (Stevens, 1968). For I/O psychology, this often means that we are quantifying individuals along some attribute. An **attribute** is a dimension along which individuals can be measured and along which they vary. Thus, for instance, we could devise a test of cognitive ability in which job applicants respond to a series of questions or problems, allowing us to *measure* their intelligence; or we could have undergraduates complete a survey of their satisfaction with school, allowing us to *measure* their school-related attitudes. In either case, we are attempting to assign numbers to individuals that indicate how much or how little of an attribute they possess. Ultimately, our goal is to use these measurements or data in our statistical analyses to answer our research questions.

One very important point here is that psychology is very different from other areas, such as the physical sciences. For instance, few measurement problems are likely to occur in the measurement of the weight of an object, provided that one has an accurate scale (an inaccurate scale would be a huge problem). However, when we are measuring an employee's attitude about her supervisor, there are many things that can make that measurement inaccurate—many sources of *measurement error*. By this I mean that if the employee had a particularly bad interaction with the supervisor that day, or wasn't feeling well, or was worried about a sick child, the measurement of her attitude might not be accurate or might differ from the measurement of her attitude next week when a whole host of new variables are involved.

**measurement**
The assignment of numbers to objects or events using rules in such a way as to represent specified attributes of the objects.

**attribute**
A dimension along which individuals can be measured and along which they vary.

Measurement in the behavioral sciences is especially difficult because there isn't an infallible scale, gauge, thermometer, ruler, or calculator that can be used to measure attitudes, beliefs, desires, and behaviors. Thus, when we measure a person's creativity, commitment to the organization, job satisfaction, or motivation, there is greater potential for measurement error than when we measure a person's weight or height. For this reason, we need to be particularly careful in developing our measures. The process of measuring a quality or construct and using it to predict job performance is indeed common in the field, which is why accuracy is very important to this process.

## Reliability

The consistency or stability of a measure is its reliability. Three points are relevant in this context. First, keep in mind that if we are going to use a test score as a predictor of on-the-job performance (much like SAT scores are used as predictors of success in college), it is imperative that the predictor be measured reliably. Second, recall that I mentioned measurement error as getting in the way of accurate measurement. Now you should be able to see that measurement error is what renders measurement inaccurate or unreliable. An individual's score on a mechanical comprehension test will not be a perfect representation of the individual's mechanical comprehension; perhaps he missed some questions because he didn't read them correctly, or mistakenly filled in the wrong ovals, or, for that matter, got some questions correct simply by guessing.

There is always some measurement error that causes the person's score to be a less-than-perfect indicator of his mechanical comprehension. The farther that score gets from his actual level of mechanical comprehension, the more inaccurate or unreliable the test is. Third, reliability is extremely important because we cannot accurately predict attitudes, performance, or behavior with a variable that is not measured very well. In other words, reliability provides a ceiling on our prediction accuracy—what we will call *validity* in subsequent sections. First, however, there are a few types of reliability that may be particularly important for different situations. We'll turn to these reliability types now.

**Test–retest reliability** reflects the stability of a test over time and is, therefore, often called a *coefficient of stability*. To demonstrate test–retest reliability, we might give our mechanical comprehension test to a group of participants and then administer the same test to the same group six weeks later. Assuming that the participants did not somehow improve their mechanical comprehension in the interim (e.g., by taking a training course or gaining additional job experience), their scores at the first test administration should be about the same as their scores at the second administration. Scores that varied, however, would reflect measurement error, indicating that our measure was not perfectly reliable. Virtually no measure we would use in I/O psychology is perfectly reliable. We can only hope to minimize the error as much as possible so that most of the high (and low) scorers at the first administration are also the high (and low) scorers at the second administration. This outcome would demonstrate acceptable levels of test–retest reliability.

**reliability**
The consistency or stability of a measure.

**test–retest reliability**
The stability of a test over time; often called a *coefficient of stability*.

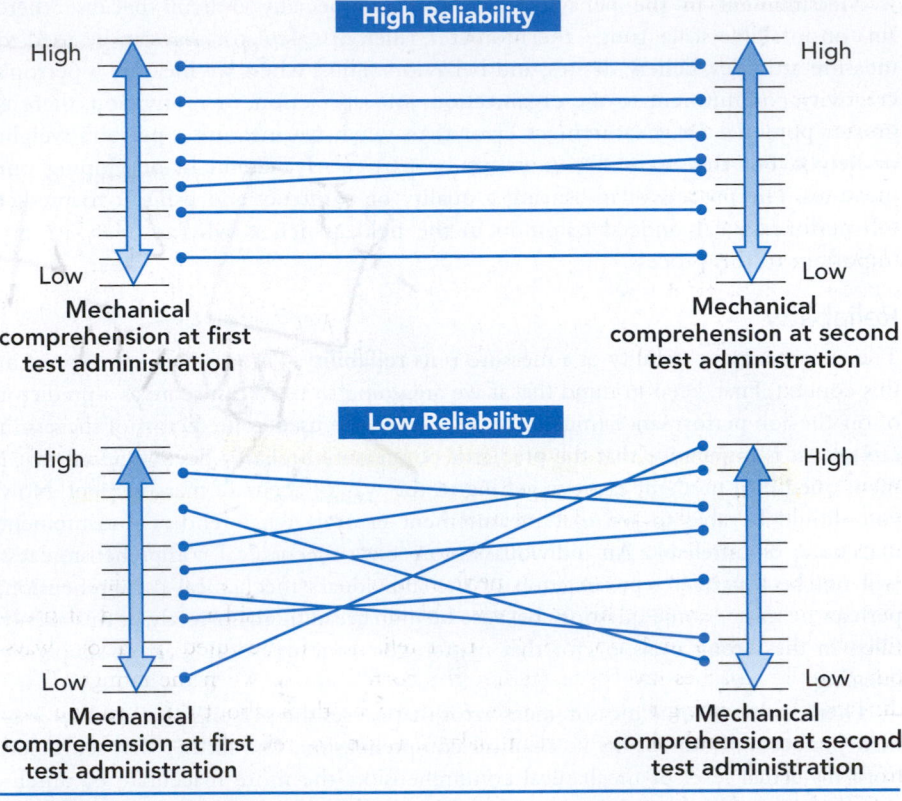

**FIGURE 2.3** Test–Retest Reliability

**Figure 2.3** shows what seven individuals' pairs of scores on mechanical comprehension might look like when the measure has high versus low reliability. Each line represents one person, and the dots on either end represent that person's score at two different time periods. Notice that when the test has high reliability, the high scorers are the same people across both test administrations but that this is not the case when the test has low reliability.

**parallel forms reliability**
The extent to which two independent forms of a test are equivalent measures of the same construct; sometimes called *equivalent forms reliability* or a *coefficient of equivalence.*

**Parallel forms reliability** (sometimes called *equivalent forms reliability)* is often referred to as a *coefficient of equivalence* because it reflects the extent to which two independent forms of a test are equivalent measures of the same construct. In other words, we might want to have two versions of the same test—an approach often used in large, multiple sections of a course to prevent cheating. The important thing is to ensure that the two tests are measuring the same thing. The issue of parallel tests has become very significant in recent years given society's increasing concern that the disabled be treated fairly. We will consider this issue in the context of selection in Chapters 6 and 7, but, for now, note that there are situations in which different tests ought to be developed for applicants or employees who are disabled. Again, we would want to demonstrate that the test for disabled persons is equivalent to the test for nondisabled persons. Similarly, as noted earlier, the use of computerized testing has become popular (Stanton & Rogelberg, 2001). It is important to be able to demonstrate that when measuring, say, cognitive ability, a computerized test is equivalent to a paper-and-pencil test (see the previous section, Technological Advances in Survey Methodology).

An approach to estimating reliability that is similar conceptually to test–retest is what is commonly called **interrater reliability**, which is the consistency with which multiple raters view and thus rate the same behavior or person. This is often relevant in the performance appraisal arena, where we might want to consider how two or three judges rate someone's performance so that we aren't relying on just one judge who may have his or her own biases—we'll consider this kind of situation in more detail in Chapter 5. Interrater reliability is measured in various ways, but many approaches involve examining the correlation between the ratings of two different judges rating the same person. One way to think about this is to conceive of the judges as multiple tests, which makes this kind of reliability somewhat similar to *parallel forms*.

The final form of reliability that we'll discuss is **internal consistency**, which gives an indication of the interrelatedness of the test items. We wouldn't want an item on an IQ test that doesn't seem to fit with the rest of the items because that would suggest that the item is not measuring the same thing as the other items. Internal consistency tells us how well our test items are hanging together. We can estimate internal consistency in two different ways. First, we can split the test in half by odd or even question numbers and see if the even half of the test is equivalent to the odd half—a measure of *split-half reliability*. If all of these items load together and are measuring the same construct, then the scores on one half of the test should be strongly related to scores on the other half of the test. Second, we can determine whether there is consistency among a set of items by looking at the correlations among all the items—a measure of *inter-item reliability*, referred to as *Cronbach's coefficient alpha* in some situations and *Kuder-Richardson 20* in others (for a more in-depth discussion, see Gatewood, Feild, & Barrick, 2007). By looking at the correlations among all pairs of items, researchers can identify any items that are unrelated to the others and would therefore be a source of unreliability of the scale.

As I've suggested, reliability is very important, and one of our goals should always be to have high reliability. A rule of thumb used by many researchers is that all measures should have reliability levels of at least .70. But because measurement

© Rainer Holz/Corbis

**A CLOSER LOOK**
Here, we see multiple judges rating the same behavior very differently. What kind of reliability problem does this represent?

**interrater reliability**
The extent to which multiple raters or judges agree on ratings made about a particular person, thing, or behavior.

**internal consistency**
An indication of the extent to which individual test items seem to be measuring the same thing.

consistency, though important, is not usually our ultimate goal in I/O psychology, we also need to spend some time talking about validity—the extent to which our test measures what we believe it measures and how well it predicts other things. Just as a reminder, you can think of this as a two-step process. First, you have to develop a sound, *reliable* measure. Second, because you will probably want to use that measure to predict attitudes, performance, or behavior, your focus will turn to *validity*. It is important to distinguish the two types of validity associated with research studies that we talked about earlier in this chapter (internal and external) from the validity of a test, which is our focus now.

## Validity of Tests, Measures, and Scales

**construct validity**
The extent to which a test measures the underlying construct that it was intended to measure.

The validity of a measure is most precisely considered in terms of construct validity, the extent to which a test measures the underlying construct it was intended to measure. A construct is an abstract quality, such as intelligence or motivation, that is not observable and is difficult to measure. In a general sense, our test of mechanical comprehension is valid if it really measures mechanical comprehension.

**construct**
An abstract quality, such as intelligence or motivation, that is not observable and is difficult to measure.

There are two types of evidence that we use to demonstrate construct validity. First, content validity is the degree to which a test or predictor covers a representative sample of the quality being assessed. In other words, if you were being tested on Chapters 1, 2, and 3 of this book, a content-valid test would be one that covers the entire domain of material presented in those three chapters. Have you ever taken a test that seemed to cover the minor stuff and didn't ask anything about large sections of chapters? You were probably upset about that test and, although you didn't know it at the time, you were upset because the test was *not* content-valid—it didn't fairly and accurately reflect the domain of material in such a way as to be representative of that domain. In an employment setting, performance appraisal measures should be content-valid such that an employee's performance appraisal reflects all the important elements of his or her job, not just one or two.

**content validity**
The degree to which a test or predictor covers a representative sample of the quality being assessed.

The second type of evidence that we use to demonstrate construct validity is called *criterion-related validity*. The focus here is on whether the test is a good predictor of attitudes, behavior, or performance. We will discuss this type of validity at greater length in Chapter 7. For now, however, let us simply define the two approaches to criterion-related validity. First, predictive validity refers to the extent to which test scores obtained at one point in time predict criteria obtained at some later time. For instance, does our test of mechanical comprehension, when given to applicants, successfully predict their on-the-job behavior once they are hired? In traditional selection situations of this kind, I/O psychologists attempt to develop tests or predictors that companies can use to make employment decisions. The same approach is used for admitting students to college and graduate school: SAT scores and GREs have been shown to be predictive of success in college and graduate school, respectively—as have GPAs in both cases (Camara & Kimmel, 2005; Kuncel, Hezlett, & Ones, 2001; Powers, 2004).

**predictive validity**
The extent to which test scores obtained at one point in time predict criteria obtained in the future.

**concurrent validity**
The extent to which a test predicts a criterion that is measured at the same time that the test is conducted.

Second, concurrent validity refers to how well a test predicts a criterion that is measured at the same time that the test is administered. For instance, we might measure a group of employees' current job attitudes and, at the same time, measure their performance. These two measures would give us evidence of the concurrent validity of job attitudes to predict performance. We still want to make the argument that our test predicts a future criterion, but sometimes predictive validity studies are extremely time-consuming and difficult (if not impossible) to conduct, leaving concurrent validity studies as the more viable option. We will discuss the differences between these two approaches in Chapter 7, but I want to emphasize here that both approaches are used to demonstrate that a test is related to a criterion such as job performance. **Figure 2.4** depicts a situation in which one cognitive ability test predicts job performance well (high validity) and another does not (low validity). In the case of the high-validity test, those who score well also perform well on the job; those who don't score well also don't perform well on the job. In the case of the low-validity test, however, one's score does not seem all that related to one's job performance.

In the preceding paragraphs, we discussed how criterion-related validity (both predictive and concurrent) is used to demonstrate the construct validity of a measure by showing that it is related to or predicts measures of other, similar constructs. This situation describes convergent validity. However, in order to demonstrate that a particular measure is construct-valid, we must also demonstrate that the measure is not related to measures of dissimilar constructs—that it shows divergent validity. For

**convergent validity** The degree to which a measure of the construct in which we are interested is related to measures of other, similar constructs.

**divergent validity** The degree to which a measure of the construct in which we are interested is unrelated to measures of other, dissimilar constructs.

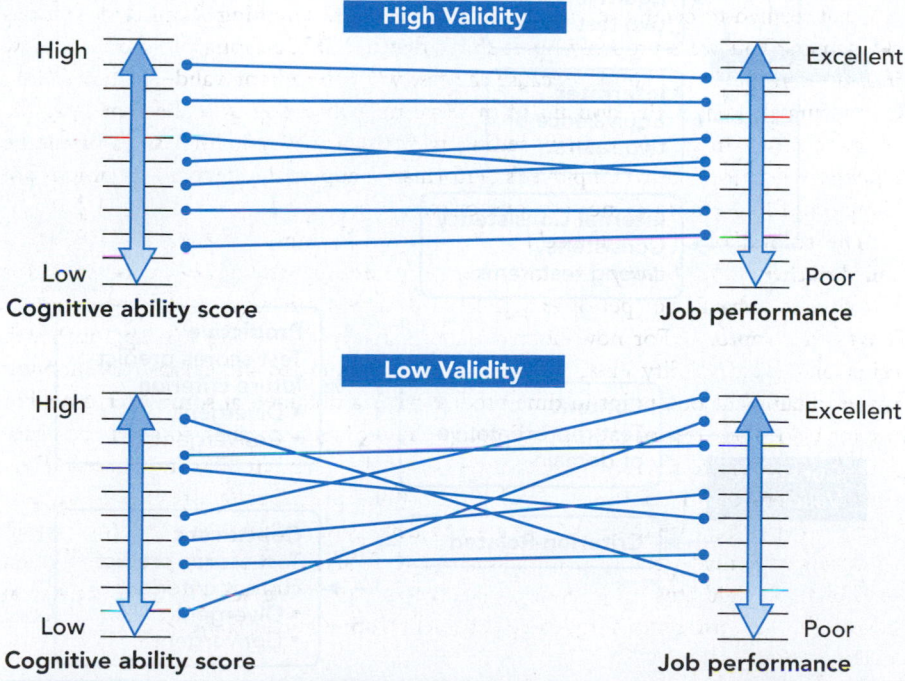

**FIGURE 2.4** Criterion-Related Validity

instance, if we were developing a new measure of job satisfaction, we would need to demonstrate convergent validity by showing that our new measure is strongly related to other, existing measures of job satisfaction. Divergent validity would be demonstrated by showing that our new measure is not strongly related to measures of organizational commitment, job involvement, and satisfaction. The point here is that we can be confident that our new measure is measuring the construct that we intended (e.g., job satisfaction) and not another construct (e.g., organizational commitment) only if it relates to measures of other constructs in the way that it should, based on the definitions of those constructs.

Convergent and divergent validity can be demonstrated through both predictive and concurrent validation designs, which are discussed in more detail in Chapter 7. In the meantime, **Figure 2.5** provides a helpful summary of the major types of reliability and the approaches used to demonstrate construct validity that we've discussed.

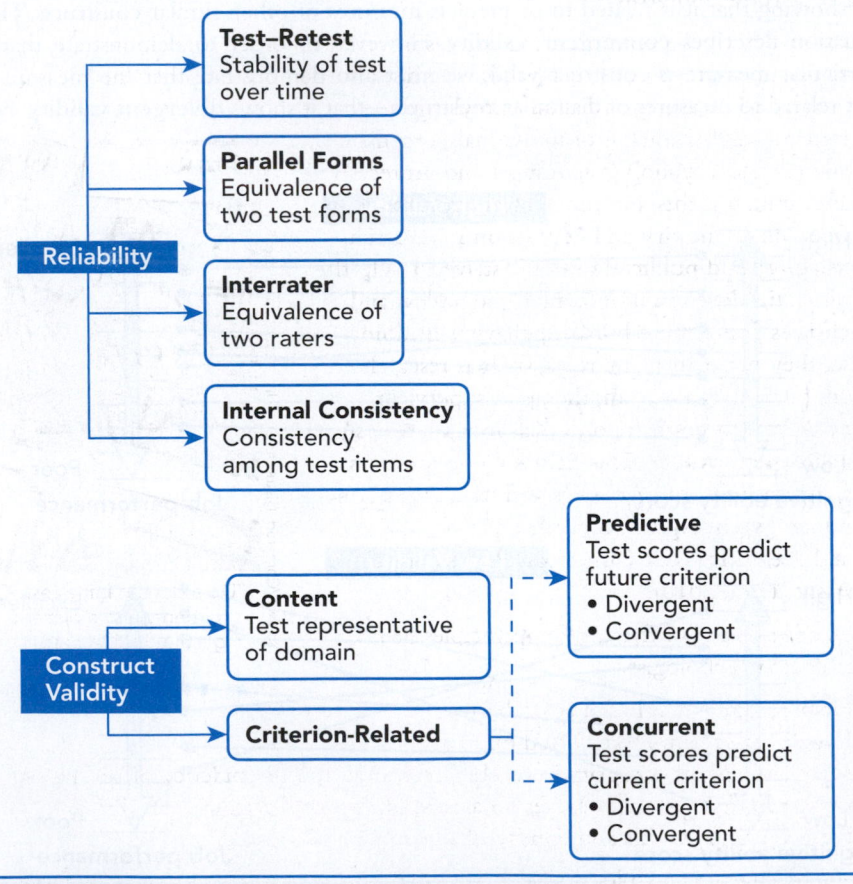

**FIGURE 2.5**  Summary of Reliability Types and Approaches to Construct Validity

# ETHICS

We have been talking about the research enterprise with a focus on reliability and validity. Careful and accurate measurement is important, but so are ethical considerations. I/O psychologists and other researchers are expected to maintain a sense of ethics while doing their work. We will discuss ethics throughout the book, as it is a very important aspect of both research and business. We will consider things like ethical reasoning, moral judgment, and ethical behavior. In this section, however, we will introduce the ethical code and focus on the ethics involved in conducting research.

There are various sets of ethical and professional rules and regulations governing the work of psychologists. The chief ethical code for psychologists is the *Ethical Principles of Psychologists and Code of Conduct* of the American Psychological Association (APA). It covers the work of psychologists in research, teaching, clinical practice, and organizational consulting, among other areas. The preamble gives a nice flavor of the code's purpose and goals:

> Psychologists are committed to increasing scientific and professional knowledge of behavior and people's understanding of themselves and others and to the use of such knowledge to improve the condition of individuals, organizations, and society. Psychologists respect and protect civil and human rights and the central importance of freedom of inquiry and expression in research, teaching, and publication. They strive to help the public in developing informed judgments and choices concerning human behavior. In doing so, they perform many roles, such as researcher, educator, diagnostician, therapist, supervisor, consultant, administrator, social interventionist, and expert witness. This Ethics Code provides a common set of principles and standards upon which psychologists build their professional and scientific work (American Psychological Association, 2010).

"Do a double-blind test. Give the new drug to rich patients and a placebo to the poor. No sense getting their hopes up. They couldn't afford it even if it works."

Mike Baldwin/Cornered. Distributed by Universal Press Syndicate

The code consists of five general principles that serve as goals for psychologists:

1. Helping others while doing no harm
2. Establishing relationships based on trust
3. Maintaining high integrity in teaching, research, and the practice of psychology
4. Being fair and just in all professional relationships and actions
5. Respecting the rights and dignity of all people

These general principles should guide the behavior of psychologists in all facets of their professional work.

**A CLOSER LOOK**
Why is this scientist's suggestion ethically wrong according to the five principles outlined on this page?

With respect to research, the ethical code provides some additional stipulations. First, research studies must be approved by the supporting institution, such as a university or hospital. There is typically a mechanism for this approval that involves what is called an Institutional Review Board (IRB), charged with reviewing each research project and considering ethical and safety regulations. Second, research participants are to be treated fairly and their decision to participate in research is to be an informed one. Informed consent requires providing participants with information about the purpose of the study, their right to decline participation, potential risks and benefits to participants, and where to direct questions about the research. Third, psychologists are required to maintain confidentiality of participants' data and sometimes to protect participants' anonymity. Fourth, researchers are ethically bound to avoid the use of deception in research whenever possible. If deception is necessary, researchers are required to debrief participants about the true nature of the deception. Finally, there are ethical requirements for the care and use of animals in research.

**informed consent**
Participants signifying (usually in writing) their willingness and desire to participate in a particular research study after being provided with important and relevant information about the risks, procedures, and benefits of such participation.

## STATISTICS

After we collect our data, we need to present them in a way that allows us to draw conclusions about what the data mean with respect to our hypothesis and the research literature. This usually involves a summary of the data, often referred to as *descriptive statistics*. A statistic is an efficient device for summarizing in a single number the values, characteristics, or scores describing a series of cases. The first group of statistics we'll discuss are measures of central tendency.

**statistic**
An efficient device for summarizing in a single number the values, characteristics, or scores describing a series of cases.

### Measures of Central Tendency

*Measures of central tendency* characterize a *typical* member of the group in that they represent the "best guess" as to the nature of any case chosen at random from the group. They present a way of characterizing the group with just a few relevant numbers. These measures can be very useful in comparing the various conditions or groups in one's study.

**Mode** The most frequent single score in a distribution is called the mode. The following data set reflects the job satisfaction levels of nine employees on a job satisfaction survey that ranges from a low of 1 to a high of 50. What is the mode in this data set?

**mode**
The most frequent single score in a distribution.

$$1 \quad 1 \quad 1 \quad 10 \quad 12 \quad 26 \quad 33 \quad 45 \quad 50$$

Clearly, the mode is 1, as it is the most frequent score in the data set. But this example demonstrates why the mode is not usually the best measure of central tendency for describing psychological data: 1 is not the single number we would choose to describe the data set overall. (The mode tends to be useful only in situations involving categorical data, as when we say that the modal religion among Americans is Protestantism.)

**Median**  The score in the middle of the distribution is termed the **median**. In other words, it is the score above which half the distribution falls and below which the other half of the distribution falls—it's the score that cuts the distribution in half. In the data set above, the median is 12. In this example, the median is probably not the best measure of central tendency either, though it seems more descriptive than the mode. One interesting and important feature of the median is that it is not particularly sensitive to extreme scores, meaning that an extreme score in a distribution does not affect the median much, if at all.

**median**
The score in the middle of the distribution.

**Mean**  The most useful measure of central tendency is usually the **mean**, which is the arithmetic average of a group of scores. Almost all inferential statistics that we use are based on it. In our example above, the mean is 19.89—and you can see that this value gives a more accurate picture of the data set than does the mode or median. If you were to pick a single value to describe the data in this simple example, 19.89 would be the best one to choose, as it is more representative than either 1 or 12. One problem with means, however, is that they are sensitive to extreme scores; a single extreme score can have a drastic effect on them. Let's consider another data set. Rather than job satisfaction, let's say that it now reflects the number of days absent in a three-year period among the same nine employees:

**mean**
The arithmetic average of a group of scores, typically the most useful measure of central tendency.

$$1 \quad 1 \quad 1 \quad 10 \quad 12 \quad 26 \quad 33 \quad 45 \quad 400$$

Note that only one number has been changed—50 has become 400—but that value is by far the most extreme one, such that the mean is now 58.8 rather than 19.89. Clearly, this one value has a huge effect on the mean. What is the median in our new data set? The median doesn't change; it's still 12 because medians are not sensitive to extreme scores. This suggests that in situations involving extreme scores, a median has some advantages over a mean.

## Measures of Dispersion

*Measures of dispersion* inform us about how closely scores are grouped around the measure of central tendency, usually the mean. These are sometimes referred to as *measures of variability* because they provide information about how much the scores vary from one another. In a sense, we can say that measures of dispersion give us an idea of the "spread-outedness" of the data.

The simplest measure of dispersion is called the **range**, which is the spread of scores from the lowest to the highest. In our original data set, the range is 49, which is the difference between the largest observed score (50) and the smallest observed score (1). This measure appears in published reports of research, but it is not reported as often as the **variance**, which is recognized as the most useful measure of dispersion. To calculate the variance, the researcher subtracts each score from the mean, resulting in differences that are then squared. The next step is to add these squared differences and divide the sum by the total number of scores, which is usually denoted as *N*. In our first data set, the variance is 372.11.

**range**
The simplest measure of dispersion, reflecting the spread of scores from the lowest to the highest.

**variance**
A useful measure of dispersion reflecting the sum of the squared differences between each score and the mean of the group divided by the number of total scores.

**standard deviation**
A measure of dispersion that is calculated as the square root of the variance.

The third measure of dispersion is called the **standard deviation**, which is the square root of the variance. Returning again to the first data set, we find that its standard deviation is $\sqrt{372.11} = 19.29$. We often use this measure because it retains the original metric of the scores. In other words, 19.29 reflects the extent to which employees' job satisfaction levels are spread out on a satisfaction scale that ranges from 1 unit to 50 units of job satisfaction. The variance (372.11), on the other hand, is much more difficult to conceptualize because it is in squared units. The standard deviation is very important for our next topic—distributions of data.

## Shapes of Distributions

**normal distribution**
A mathematically based distribution depicted as a bell-shaped curve, in which most of the observations cluster around the mean and there are few extreme observations.

The **normal distribution** is a theoretical mathematical model based on a population of measures that is infinite in size. This distribution is depicted by what appears to be a *bell-shaped curve,* in which most of the observations are clustered around the mean with increasingly fewer observations as we move out along the continuum in either direction. The normal distribution is important in psychology because many psychological variables are distributed in this way. For instance, intelligence, motivation, performance, personal characteristics, and job attitudes are all believed to be normally distributed in the population. Therefore, the properties of the normal distribution take on added significance.

This bell-shaped curve is presented in **Figure 2.6,** which indicates standard deviation units along the bottom and the percentage of observations that fall within those standard deviation units at the top. In other words, in a normal distribution, 68% (34% + 34%) of the observations in our data fall within 1 standard deviation below the mean and 1 standard deviation above the mean, and about 99% of the observations

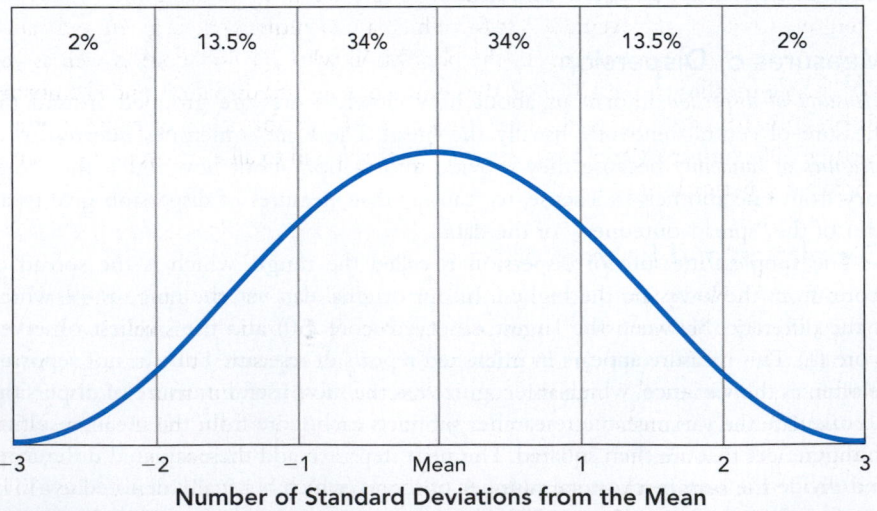

**FIGURE 2.6** The Normal Distribution

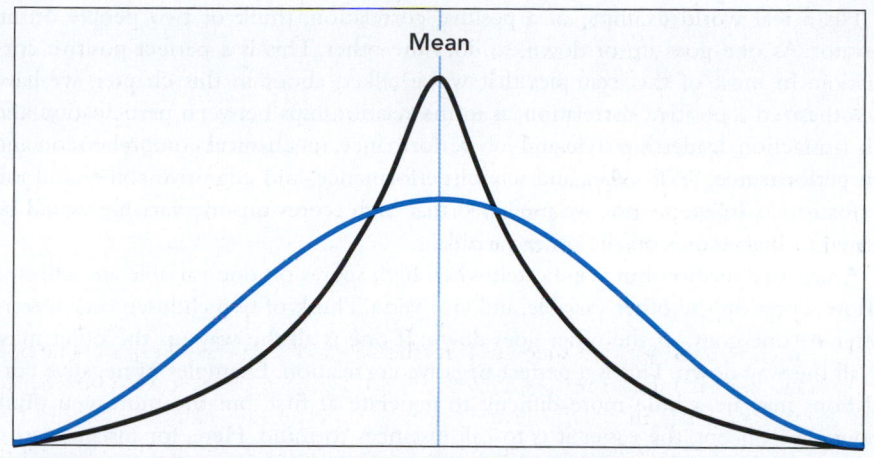

Mean

**FIGURE 2.7** Normal Distributions with Different Standard Deviations

fall within 3 standard deviations of the mean in either direction. Remember that the standard deviation is an index of how far individuals' scores are from the mean. The mean and median have the same value in the normal distribution, indicating that half the observations fall above the mean and half fall below the mean.

**Figure 2.7** shows two normal curves with different standard deviations. The taller curve has a smaller standard deviation than the shorter curve, but both are normal distributions and the same properties of the normal distribution hold for both.

From the properties of the normal curve and an individual's score, we can determine the individual's *percentile* score relative to the rest of the population. You have all taken some type of achievement test for which a percentile score is given, indicating the percentage of other students in the population who did not score as well as you did. This percentile score is based on the mean, the standard deviation, and the normal distribution. We could apply the same process to the performance of employees at a Fortune 500 company to determine how well, in relation to all employees, a particular employee is performing.

## Correlation and Regression

As you undoubtedly are aware by now, I/O psychologists are often interested in the relationship between two (or more) variables. To examine this relationship, we typically use the **correlation coefficient ($r$)**, which measures the strength of the relationship between two variables. A correlation provides information about the *direction* of the relationship, or its sign, and the *magnitude* of the relationship, or its strength. A correlation can indicate a positive or negative relationship, ranging from $-1.0$ to $+1.0$, between two variables. A positive relationship is indicated when high scores on one variable reflect high scores on the other variable and when low scores on one variable reflect low scores on the other variable.

**correlation coefficient ($r$)**
A statistic that measures the strength and direction of the relationship between two variables.

For a real-world example of a positive correlation, think of two people on an elevator: As one goes up or down, so does the other. This is a perfect positive correlation. In most of the examples that we've talked about in this chapter, we have hypothesized a positive correlation, as in the relationships between participation and job satisfaction, leadership style and job performance, mechanical comprehension and job performance, SAT scores and school performance, and cognitive ability and job performance. In every case, we predicted that high scores on one variable would be related to high scores on the other variable.

A negative relationship is indicated when high scores on one variable are reflected in low scores on the other variable, and vice versa. Think of two children on a teeter-totter. As one goes up, the other goes down. If one is all the way up, the other must be all the way down. This is a perfect negative correlation. Examples of negative correlations may be a little more difficult to generate at first, but the more you think about the concept, the easier it is to call instances to mind. Here, for instance, are a few negative correlations that we might predict: job satisfaction and the amount of time absent from work, supervisor–subordinate relationships and subordinate resignations, employee sanctions and promotions, and job performance and the number of grievances filed against the employee. In all these instances, we expect high scores on one variable to be related to low scores on the other. We expect satisfied employees to seldom be absent, employees who get along well with their supervisors to be unlikely to resign, employees who are sanctioned by their company to be passed over for promotions, and good performers to have few grievances filed against them.

© Bill Grant/Alamy

© moodboard/Alamy

**A CLOSER LOOK**
How does an elevator represent a positive correlation and how does a teeter-totter represent a negative correlation?

The magnitude or strength of a correlation ranges from 0 to 1, with larger numbers indicating a stronger relationship. It's important to realize that although a correlation can range from −1.0 to +1.0, correlations of −.50 and +.50 have the same magnitude—the only difference being the sign. A scatterplot in which all the data points fall along a straight 45-degree line represents a perfect 1.0 correlation, which is so rare as to be nonexistent in psychology. In the behavioral sciences, correlations among variables are almost never larger than .70. Consider the three scatterplots shown in **Figure 2.8.** The first, in the shape of a circle, reflects a correlation of 0. This indicates that a high score on the mechanical comprehension test is just as likely to lead to low job performance as to lead to adequate job performance as to lead to superior job performance; in short, there is no relationship between the two variables. The other two scatterplots indicate rather strong relationships—one in the positive direction and the other in the negative direction.

Correlations are relevant for much of I/O psychology because they are intimately involved in prediction. One step beyond computing a correlation among variables is the statistical procedure called *regression,* which allows us to predict one variable from another. Here we calculate how much variance in our criterion variable is accounted for by our predictor variable—a calculation that is based on the correlation between these variables. The percentage of variance accounted for is called the **coefficient of determination**, and it can be computed from the regression as well as from the correlation. In fact, this percentage is actually the correlation squared, commonly expressed as $r^2$. Returning one last time to our example involving mechanical comprehension as a predictor for job performance, let's measure our employees using a mechanical comprehension test and also measure their on-the-job performance using their supervisors' ratings of their performance. Now imagine that we find a .60 correlation between these two variables, indicating that mechanical comprehension accounts for about 36% ($.60^2$) of the variance in job performance. This correlation tells us that the two variables are related, but it does not tell us anything about whether there is a causal relationship between the two variables. There are many situations

**coefficient of determination**
The percentage of variance in a criterion that is accounted for by a predictor.

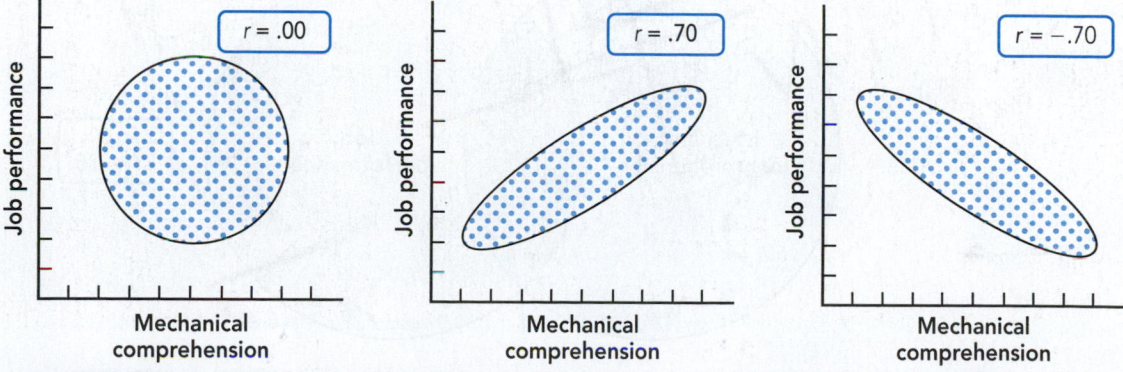

**FIGURE 2.8**  Correlation Examples

where we might find a strong correlation, but this correlation in no way indicates that one variable causes the other—the difficult question of causation largely comes down to our experimental design and the extent to which it uses random assignment and manipulates independent variables.

This statistic sounds confusing, and we will spend a little more time on it in Chapter 6; but, basically, it means that some (i.e., 36%) of the differences among employees on the performance variable could be predicted by the mechanical comprehension test (not everyone is going to perform at the same level). In other words, knowing an individual's score on the mechanical comprehension test is helpful in predicting that individual's level of job performance. **Figure 2.9** describes the relationship between these two variables, using a Venn diagram. As you can see, there is some overlap between mechanical comprehension and job performance. This overlap represents the coefficient of determination. I/O psychology uses correlations and regressions extensively, and we will revisit these throughout the rest of the book.

## Meta-Analysis

**meta-analysis**
A methodology that is used to conduct quantitative literature reviews.

A statistical and methodological technique that is widely used in the social sciences has also gained a very strong following in the I/O area. I'm referring here to **meta-analysis**, a methodology that is used to conduct quantitative literature reviews (Hunter & Schmidt, 1990; Rosenthal, 1991). Prior to the development of this approach in the late 1970s, a researcher conducting a literature review on the relationship between, say, job satisfaction and job performance would conduct a *narrative review* consisting of summaries of all the different findings in the literature; however, there was no mechanism for combining these different findings and providing a best estimate of the true relationship between job satisfaction and job performance. With the development of meta-analysis came a way to combine these many findings and thereby *quantify* the relationship between the two variables.

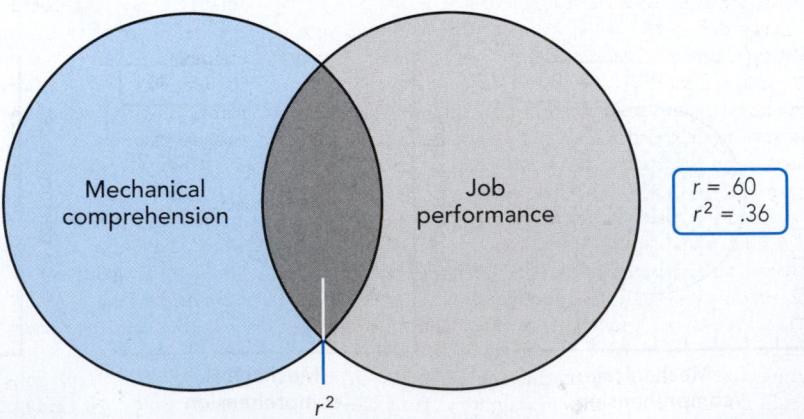

$r^2$

**FIGURE 2.9** Coefficient of Determination

Researchers can use meta-analysis to combine the results from 25, 100, even 1,000 or more studies to arrive at the best estimate of the true relationship. The point here is that statistically combining findings from previous studies is a more accurate way to estimate the true relationship than is focusing on one or two studies that measure this relationship. Of course, as is true with any research, the value of meta-analysis is contingent on how well the meta-analysis is conducted. If a researcher doesn't do a thorough literature review and gather all of the relevant data, then the meta-analysis she conducts will be limited and will not accurately represent the literature. Any coefficient to emerge from this analysis would not be based on a solid sample of the existing data and would thus be flawed.

Despite the potential pitfalls, the benefits of meta-analysis are important and allow us to have a solid estimate of the relationship between various constructs. In the remainder of the book, I present many meta-analytic results as a way of summarizing various findings in the field of industrial/organizational psychology.

## I/O TODAY

### Big Data

One of the most important developments in I/O psychology in the past decade has been the emergence of something known as "Big Data," which refers to massive data sets (potentially millions or even billions of data points) that are rapidly accumulated and contain information on a wide assortment of variables. In the Society for Industrial and Organizational Psychology's review of top trends for 2014, Big Data was ranked #1. Big data is all around us: Social media giants like Facebook and Twitter collect data on users habits, interests, and activities; search engines like Google track the search histories of individual users to allow marketers to provide customized advertisements.

Large data sets have been around for a long time, and have been used by mathematicians, statisticians, and economists. The difference now is that the accessibility of technology and strategies for processing these massive data sets has allowed researchers to focus on what data trends mean for human behaviors and decisions. That is where I/O psychologists come in. As technology makes data collection faster, easier, and cheaper, researchers can collect more data on I/O relevant variables such as job performance or work satisfaction. With this increased data, practitioners can make better decisions about how to hire, promote, and train employees. For example, a large financial firm gathered data about sales rep resumes and their job performance. To their surprise, several characteristics they thought were related to performance (such as where applicants went to school

and what their grades were) did not, in fact, relate. By looking at sales productivity and employee turnover, analysts identified other variables—having a grammatically correct resume and an ability to work with vague instructions—that seemed to be more predictive of sales performance. Implementing new screening processes increased revenue by $4 million within six months (Bersin, 2013).

Large software development and consulting firms have begun using Big Data to make decisions. The software developer SAP helped Macy's department stores develop algorithms to adjust pricing in real time based on inventory. The Big Data–based movement has also opened up the possibility of unique careers for I/O psychologists; for example, consumer research organizations and even dating websites, such as Match.com, can benefit from having someone with psychology training help them sift through massive data sets.

While a solid understanding of research and statistics is essential for working with Big Data, there are a number of other skills that are important for this type of work. Unfortunately, because this field is so new, most graduate programs have not had time to adapt their training to help students learn how to work with Big Data. Because these data sets are so large, conventional statistical packages such as SPSS, SAS, or Excel are unable to handle the calculations. Students need to focus more heavily on programming languages such as Python and Javascript, and must think more strategically about how to present data in a way that makes sense to a lay audience. Fortunately, resources such as coursera.org and codeacademy.com allow I/O psychologists to bulk up their skills for free in their spare time (Maurath, 2014). In any case, it appears that Big Data is not going away anytime soon, and I/O psychologists would be wise to prepare themselves for this new frontier of data analysis, as well as the legal and ethical issues that will accompany it.

### Discussion Questions

1. Imagine you are working for a company that, as its initial screening process, asks applicants to upload their resume and take a brief personality test online. What pieces of data might you collect, and why might these be relevant to someone's performance?
2. One of the downsides of Big Data is that sometimes applicants or consumers feel that the constant data collection is an invasion of their privacy (see I/O Today in Chapter 5 for more on this issue). Do you believe they are right to be concerned? What ethical obligations must I/O psychologists follow to ensure this data is used appropriately?

### References

Bersin, J. (2013, February 17). Big data in human resources: Talent analytics (people analytics) comes of age. *Forbes.* Retrieved from http://www.forbes.com/sites/joshbersin/2013/02/17/bigdata-in-human-resources-talent-analytics-comes-of-age/

Maurath, D. (2014). A critical incident for big data. *The Industrial Organizational Psychologist, 51,* 16–27. Retrieved from http://www.siop.org/tip/jan14/513feat.pdf

### Additional Readings

Lohr, S. (2013, April 20). Big data, trying to build better workers. *The New York Times.* Retrieved from http://www.nytimes.com/2013/04/21/technology/big-data-trying-to-build-better-workers.html

## Summary

Research methods are important to I/O psychology—and all scientific endeavors, for that matter—because research conducted without care is unreliable and worthless. But when we are careful to base our theories on data and to use these data to test and revise the theories, the science of I/O psychology can make a meaningful contribution to the world of work. This science is more than just a matter of commonsense predictions and beliefs. Among its goals are to describe, explain, predict, and control human behavior at work. It is also important to realize that theories are the domain not just of basic science but also of applied scientific disciplines such as I/O psychology. In fact, it is only through careful theoretical development, testing, and revision that we can use our knowledge to describe, explain, predict, and control organizational behaviors and environments.

A major goal of most research in I/O psychology is to be able to draw causal inferences about the relationship between two or more variables. Thus, we must design our studies with an emphasis on internal validity, attempting to control for extraneous variables that could provide alternative explanations for our results. In addition to internal validity, we must concern ourselves with external validity, or the generalizability of our findings.

There are many ways in which I/O psychologists go about collecting data, but the survey is perhaps the one most frequently used. Surveys are very useful in gathering information about attitudes and beliefs. Technological advancements in the use of smartphones and other mobile devices have provided new alternative approaches to survey administration. We may also use observational approaches to measure and record frequency or incidents of particular behaviors or interactions. Archival research is a popular approach as well, given our access to the numerous large-scale data sets that have been collected by the government and private organizations. I/O psychologists often combine these and other data collection techniques in any given study to better examine their research questions.

Without reliable and valid measurement, the research conducted by I/O psychologists would have very little to offer. Researchers must work very hard to eliminate sources of measurement error and to ensure that their measures are tapping the constructs that they were intended to tap. There are a few different approaches to estimating reliability, and each is important for demonstrating the soundness of any particular measure. Validity is important as well, but to talk of validity in general is not very helpful, as the term can mean several different things. In I/O psychology, when we speak of the validity of a test or predictor, we are usually referring to the extent to which the test predicts job performance or some other criterion.

After we have collected our data, the next step is to describe and summarize those data using descriptive statistics such as measures of central tendency and dispersion. Because I/O psychologists are usually interested in the relationships among variables and the prediction of one set of variables from another set, correlation and regression are statistical techniques that are very useful to us. Ultimately, we complete our five-step research process with a written report that summarizes the research project.

In the remainder of this text, we will discuss various content areas of I/O psychology and the research that is conducted in those areas, along with their implications for organizational functioning.

## Key Terms

archival research (p. 45)
attribute (p. 50)
case studies (p. 45)
causal inference (p. 34)
coefficient of determination (p. 63)
concurrent validity (p. 54)
construct (p. 54)
construct validity (p. 54)
content validity (p. 54)
convergent validity (p. 55)
correlation coefficient ($r$) (p. 61)
deduction (p. 32)
dependent variable (p. 35)
divergent validity (p. 55)
experience sampling methodology
   (ESM) (p. 49)
experimental methods (p. 40)
external validity (p. 38)
extraneous variable (p. 35)
field experiments (p. 42)

hypothesis (p. 39)
independent variable (p. 34)
induction (p. 32)
informed consent (p. 58)
internal consistency (p. 53)
internal validity (p. 37)
interrater reliability (p. 53)
manipulation (p. 41)
mean (p. 59)
measurement (p. 50)
median (p. 59)
meta-analysis (p. 64)
mode (p. 58)
normal distribution (p. 60)
observational methods (p. 43)
parallel forms reliability (p. 52)
predictive validity (p. 54)
quasi-experiment (p. 43)
random assignment (p. 40)
range (p. 59)

reliability (p. 51)  
science (p. 29)  
standard deviation (p. 60)  
statistic (p. 58)  
surveys (p. 46)

test–retest reliability (p. 51)  
theory (p. 30)  
unobtrusive naturalistic observation (p. 44)  
variance (p. 59)

## TAKING IT TO THE FIELD

Because I/O psychology tends to rely strongly on empirical data, I/O psychologists must be experts in research design and statistics. One area that I/O psychologists are particularly concerned about is the reliability and validity of measures. In fact, I/O psychologists in consulting firms are often asked for their expertise in understanding how measures work and what measures are best for a certain purpose. Below is an e-mail from Kendall Phillips, the HR manager of the law firm MacLaughlin & MacDougal. She has designed a new selection measure for her firm and needs some feedback from someone who knows more about reliability and validity. Read her e-mail, and provide detailed responses to her questions.

Hello—

Thank you for agreeing to help me with this measure—with all of the financial challenges facing my company, your assistance is appreciated!

First, some background: Our firm currently needs to hire a number of administrative assistants. The demands our lawyers place on our administrative assistants are very high; they often yell at them or ask them to do very difficult things in a short amount of time. We have found that one of the best predictors of these assistants staying more than a couple of months is for them to have very low levels of neuroticism. We used to buy a test (called the WIN) that would measure this, but it has gotten too expensive, and so I've started to develop my own measure (I call my test the Neuroticism Assessment Form, or the NAF). To design my measure, I spoke to a few experts in the personality field, looked at some of the items on other tests of neuroticism, and wrote questions that made sense. I asked a number of current administrative assistants to fill out the WIN and the NAF. I also have job performance ratings for these administrative assistants. Here's what I've found so far:

- The correlation between their scores on the NAF in July and their scores on the NAF in August is .89.

- The correlation between their scores on the WIN and the NAF is .75.

- The correlation between their scores on the NAF and a test of extraversion is .34.

- The correlation between their scores on the NAF and their performance ratings is .30.

So here are my questions for you:

1. Is my test a reliable measure of neuroticism? If not, what else do I need?

2. Is my test a valid measure of neuroticism? What additional information should I collect, if any?

Thanks again!  
KP

Draft a response that clearly answers Kendall's questions. You should indicate what types of reliability/validity she has collected (and whether you think they are adequate) and what types of reliability/validity she has overlooked (and how she can obtain them). Make sure to address *all* forms of reliability/validity you have learned about.

## Critical Thinking Questions

1. Imagine that you are trying to measure attitudes about training at a manufacturing plant. One manager thinks it is better to use a paper survey, while another thinks it would be better to create an online survey that can be taken using a smartphone. What are advantages and disadvantages of each approach? Which do you think would be more effective in this case, and why?

2. Imagine that we want to learn more about how interacting with a boss affects someone's mood. Why might experience sampling method (ESM) be a helpful approach in a study like this? What advantages does that methodology have over asking employees to fill out a "one time only" survey?

3. What are some potential instances of *unethical* behavior in I/O psychology? What makes these instances unethical?

## Application Questions

1. Imagine that a fellow student says to you, "I don't need a study to tell me that lecturing is a bad way to teach students. I know from my own experience that it never works!" How would you convince this student of the value of research? What might be an example of a study you could conduct to see if this student's belief is accurate?

2. Think about a specific behavior you have observed among fellow students. What do you think causes that behavior, and what might be a theory you can develop to explain why that behavior occurs?

3. A researcher has been asked to find a way to help construction workers put on their helmets. Describe a survey study she could conduct. What information would she get from that study? Describe an experimental study she could conduct. What information would she get from that study?

4. Reliability and validity are two separate characteristics of a measurement, but they are related. The chapter notes that you must have reliability (consistency) before you can have validity (accuracy). Provide an example of a measure that is consistent but inaccurate.

5. Correlation coefficients can help us understand how two variables are related. What are two variables that might have a strong positive correlation? A strong negative correlation? A correlation of 0?

## Suggested Readings

**American Psychological Association.** (2010). *Ethical principles of psychologists and code of conduct: Including 2010 amendments.* Washington, DC, http://www.apa.org/ethics/code/. This publication provides the ethical rules and guidelines governing the behavior of psychologists.

**Babbie, E.** (2015). *The practice of social research.* Boston: MA: Cengage Learning. An excellent presentation of research methods that is helpful for both undergraduates and graduate students.

**Dillman, D. A., Smyth, J. D., & Christian, L. M.** (2014). *Internet, phone, mail, and mixed-mode surveys: the tailored design method.* Hoboken, NJ: John Wiley & Sons. The best treatment of survey methodology available. This book provides lots of hints for improving the quality of survey data.

**Leong, F. T. L., & Austin, J. T. (Eds.).** (2005). *The psychology research handbook: A guide for graduate students and research assistants* (2nd ed.). Thousand Oaks, CA: SAGE. A complete treatment of the research process targeted at new psychology researchers. The best book of its kind, it was written to be useful for both advanced undergraduate and graduate students.

**Rogelberg, S. G., Church, A. H., Waclawski, J., & Stanton, J. M.** (2005). Organizational survey research. In S. G. Rogelberg (Ed.), *Handbook of research methods in industrial and organizational psychology* (pp. 141–160). Hoboken, NJ: John Wiley & Sons. A nice compilation of chapters focusing on research methodology linked specifically to I/O psychology. This is a useful reference.

CHAPTER **3**

# Job Analysis

Photo: Rawpixel/Shutterstock

## LEARNING OBJECTIVES

This chapter should help you understand:

- How important job analysis is to HR functioning
- The common terminology used in the area of job analysis
- How to differentiate between task-oriented and worker-oriented job analysis techniques
- How to conduct a job analysis using the Task Inventory Approach, Functional Job Analysis, Job Element Method, Position Analysis Questionnaire, and Common-Metric Questionnaire
- What's included in the *Dictionary of Occupational Titles* (DOT) and how it has been improved through the development of the Occupational Information Network (O*NET)
- What a job description is and how it is used in human resource practices
- What job specifications are and how they are used in human resource practices
- The variety of human resource functions for which job analysis is of great importance
- The newly developing role of technology in the analysis of jobs
- The role of job evaluation in setting compensation levels
- The doctrine of comparable worth and the wage gap

The second part of this book centers on *industrial psychology*, or what has been traditionally called *personnel psychology*. Before discussing the major applications of industrial psychology, you must first have an understanding of the foundation for virtually all of this work—job analysis, the focus of this chapter. Employees get evaluated at work all the time. Think about the person who serves you in your favorite restaurant; she gets evaluated by her boss in various ways, but that evaluation can't be effectively done without the boss and the server knowing the job. That's where the job analysis comes in. Imagine trying to evaluate someone's performance without knowing what the job or what the outcomes of the work are intended to be. Now think about your first job, even as a babysitter or fast-food employee—picture someone appraising your performance without knowing the details of the job for which you were hired.

Unfortunately, job analysis is often taken for granted by I/O researchers and practitioners, but in this chapter I argue that it is the most important building block for industrial psychology. In order to develop predictors to select and place employees in appropriate jobs, to identify criteria used to evaluate employees' effectiveness, and to identify remedial training needs of particular employees, we must first understand the job. We gain this thorough and comprehensive understanding of jobs through job analysis.

Doing performance appraisals without such knowledge would be like cooking a dish without knowing the ingredients, how to prepare them, or how the dish is

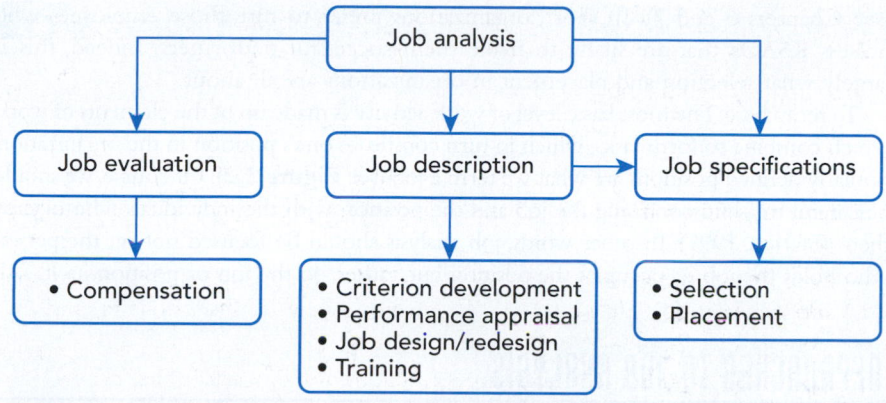

**FIGURE 3.1** Framework for Industrial Psychology

supposed to taste. The job analysis provides the recipe—information that is integral to everything else that follows in industrial psychology. **Figure 3.1** illustrates how job analysis relates to the major *human resource (HR)* functions that will be covered in this section of the text. Throughout this chapter we will talk about the three major products of the job analysis: the job evaluation that is used in setting pay levels in organizations, the job description that relates to what is actually done on the job, and the job specifications that identify the skills that folks need to be able to do the job effectively.

## SOME TERMINOLOGY

**Job analysis** is the process of defining a job in terms of its component tasks or duties and the knowledge or skills required to perform them. Job analysis is the basis for the solution to any human resource problem (Brannick, Levine, & Morgeson, 2007). Before discussing approaches to job analysis, we must familiarize ourselves with some terms that have very specific meanings within this domain. First in the list are elements. An **element** is the smallest unit of work activity, such as pressing a button to start a machine or entering a line of code for a computer program. Multiple elements join together to form a **task**, commonly defined as the activity of work that is performed to achieve a specific objective. For instance, among the necessary elements involved in a cab driver taking his passenger to her destination are turning the key, shifting the transmission into "drive," and pressing the accelerator. Collectively, these elements form a task that is the operation of the vehicle. The tasks performed by an individual in an organization define that person's **position**. A **job** is a collection of positions similar enough to one another to share a common job title. **KSAOs** are the knowledge, skills, abilities, and other characteristics that are required for successful job performance (Primoff & Eyde, 1988). They are very important in I/O psychology because they are the basis for much of the work done in employee selection

**job analysis**
The process of defining a job in terms of its component tasks or duties and the knowledge or skills required to perform them.

**element**
In job analysis, the smallest unit of work activity.

**task**
A work activity that is performed to achieve a specific objective.

**position**
An individual's place in the organization defined by the tasks performed.

**job**
A collection of positions similar enough to one another to share a common job title.

**KSAOs**
The knowledge, skills, abilities, and other characteristics that are required for successful job performance.

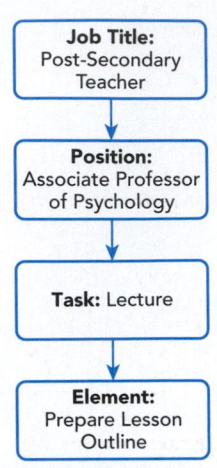

**task-oriented**
Referring to approaches to job analysis that focus on describing the various tasks that are performed on the job.

**worker-oriented**
Referring to approaches to job analysis that examine broad human behaviors involved in work activities.

(see Chapters 6 and 7). In short, organizations prefer to hire those employees who possess KSAOs that are likely to make them successful performers. Indeed, this is largely what selection and placement in organizations are all about.

To recap here: The most basic level of work activity is made up of the elements of work, which combine to form tasks, which in turn constitute one's position in the organization; similarly defined positions are what we term a job (see **Figure 3.2**). Of course, we should be careful to avoid confusing the job and the position with the individuals who occupy them (Harvey, 1991). In other words, job analysis should be focused not on the person who holds the job or occupies the position but, rather, on the job or position itself.

## APPROACHES TO JOB ANALYSIS

Most procedures in I/O psychology can be conducted in various ways. Job analysis is no exception. Whatever the approach, however, the job analyst needs to consider the purpose of the job analysis when deciding on a strategy. One approach may be more beneficial for a given purpose than a different approach. In this section and the one to follow, we will examine a couple of general perspectives taken in the area of job analysis as well as some specific ways in which job analysis data can be collected.

The traditional classification espoused by most job analysis experts over the years categorizes job analysis methods as either task-oriented or worker-oriented (McCormick, 1976). **Task-oriented** techniques focus on describing the various tasks that are performed on the job. **Worker-oriented** techniques examine broad human behaviors involved in work activities (Gatewood & Feild, 2001). Unlike task-oriented approaches, which focus on very specific levels of tasks, worker-oriented job analyses focus broadly on general aspects of the job, such as the physical, interpersonal, and mental factors necessary for completion of the job and the related worker attributes. In fact, a review and analysis in this area also suggests a third category—hybrid methods. These approaches attempt to gather information about the work and the worker at the same time (Brannick et al., 2007). The distinction between the two traditional categories is not always clear; some job-analytic techniques cross over into the other category (Sackett & Laczo, 2003). Furthermore, one approach is not necessarily better than the other; as a job analyst, you can choose a hybrid approach or any combination of pieces from different job-analytic techniques (Brannick et al., 2007) for whatever purpose is being served by your job analysis.

## JOB-ANALYTIC METHODS

For simplicity's sake, this chapter largely employs the traditional task-oriented and worker-oriented distinction, but it also presents the important results of a hybrid approach employed in the development of the Occupational Information Network (O★NET). There are many job analytic techniques, but we will only cover a sampling of the most used approaches. Certain techniques might fit better with particular jobs.

## Task-Oriented Techniques

Task-oriented techniques for conducting job analyses tend to be focused on tasks. (Recall our previous definition of a task as the activity of work that is performed to achieve a specific objective.) One task-oriented approach is called the **Task Inventory Approach**, in which task statements are generated by experts who are familiar with the jobs—**subject matter experts (SMEs)**. These experts may be **incumbents**—that is, people who are currently occupying the job of interest. Or they may be individuals who have expertise or knowledge about the job for some other reason, such as being a supervisor of individuals in that job or an I/O psychologist who has gathered expertise through his or her work. Once a list of task statements has been generated, this list, which can include hundreds of task statements, is usually administered to incumbents, who put a check next to those statements that describe a task that they do on their job. A sample task inventory for the job of college professor is provided in **Figure 3.3**. The task statements that are checked as being done on the job are also often rated as to the importance or criticality of the task to the job and the relative

**Task Inventory Approach**
Task-oriented approach which uses task statements generated by experts familiar with the job in question.

**subject matter experts (SMEs)**
Individuals who participate in job analyses as a result of their expertise.

**incumbents**
Employees who are currently occupying the job of interest.

| Task Statements | Is task done on this job? Yes or No | Importance of task to job | | | | | Relative to other tasks performed on the job, how much time is spent on each of the following tasks? | | | | |
|---|---|---|---|---|---|---|---|---|---|---|---|
| | | 1 Not important at all | 2 | 3 Somewhat important | 4 | 5 Extremely important | 1 Much less time | 2 Somewhat less time | 3 About the same amount of time | 4 Somewhat more time | 5 Much more time |
| 1. Develops written assignments | | | | | | | | | | | |
| 2. Grades exams | | | | | | | | | | | |
| 3. Meets with students individually to help them understand things | | | | | | | | | | | |
| 4. Lectures to groups of students | | | | | | | | | | | |
| 5. Designs research studies | | | | | | | | | | | |
| 6. Collects data | | | | | | | | | | | |
| 7. Mentors and advises students regarding career issues | | | | | | | | | | | |

**FIGURE 3.3** Task Inventory for College Professor

© Corbis

John Howard/Photodisc/Getty Images

**A CLOSER LOOK**
From a Functional Job Analysis perspective, how would a computer technician score on data, people, and things? What would the scores look like for sales jobs?

**Functional Job Analysis (FJA)**
A highly structured task-oriented approach developed by Sidney Fine in which data are obtained about what tasks a worker does and how those tasks are performed.

**Dictionary of Occupational Titles (DOT)**
A tool developed by the Department of Labor in the 1930s that has been used to classify occupations and jobs, consisting of narrative descriptions of tasks, duties, and working conditions of about 12,000 jobs.

time spent on the job doing each task. Together, these pieces of information can provide a thorough analysis, or *picture,* of the job.

In *Functional Job Analysis (FJA),* a highly structured task–oriented approach developed by Sidney Fine many years ago, data are obtained about *what* tasks a worker does and *how* those tasks are performed. (For a summary of this technique, see Cronshaw, 2012.) Specifically, a series of task statements are developed that are believed to be relevant for the job in question. Incumbents or SMEs rate each of these statements (which are similar to those shown in Figure 3.3) on a series of dimensions. These dimensions are what set this approach apart from the standard Task Inventory Approach.

A picture of the job is generated when these task statements have been rated with regard to *data, people,* and *things*—three factors with which employees in all jobs are assumed to interact. One way to understand a job is to know the extent to which these interactions take place and the complexity of those interactions. This is the focus of FJA. A task focusing largely on *data* requires the employee to use cognitive resources in handling information, ideas, and facts. Tasks that are coded along this dimension range from simple comparisons to more complex synthesizing. The *people* dimension refers to the extent to which the job requires employees to use interpersonal resources such as understanding, courtesy, and mentoring. Tasks coded along this dimension range from simply taking instructions to more sophisticated behaviors such as mentoring. Finally, a task that is linked to the *things* scale requires the use of physical resources and includes the use of strength, speed, and coordination. Tasks coded along this dimension range from the simple handling of things to more intricate and precise operations.

In the 1930s, the Department of Labor used FJA to develop the *Dictionary of Occupational Titles (DOT),* a tool that matches people with jobs. Consisting of narrative descriptions of tasks, duties, and working conditions of about 12,000 jobs, the DOT codes each of these jobs according to the data, people, and things dimensions developed by Fine. The information presented in the DOT is based on years and years

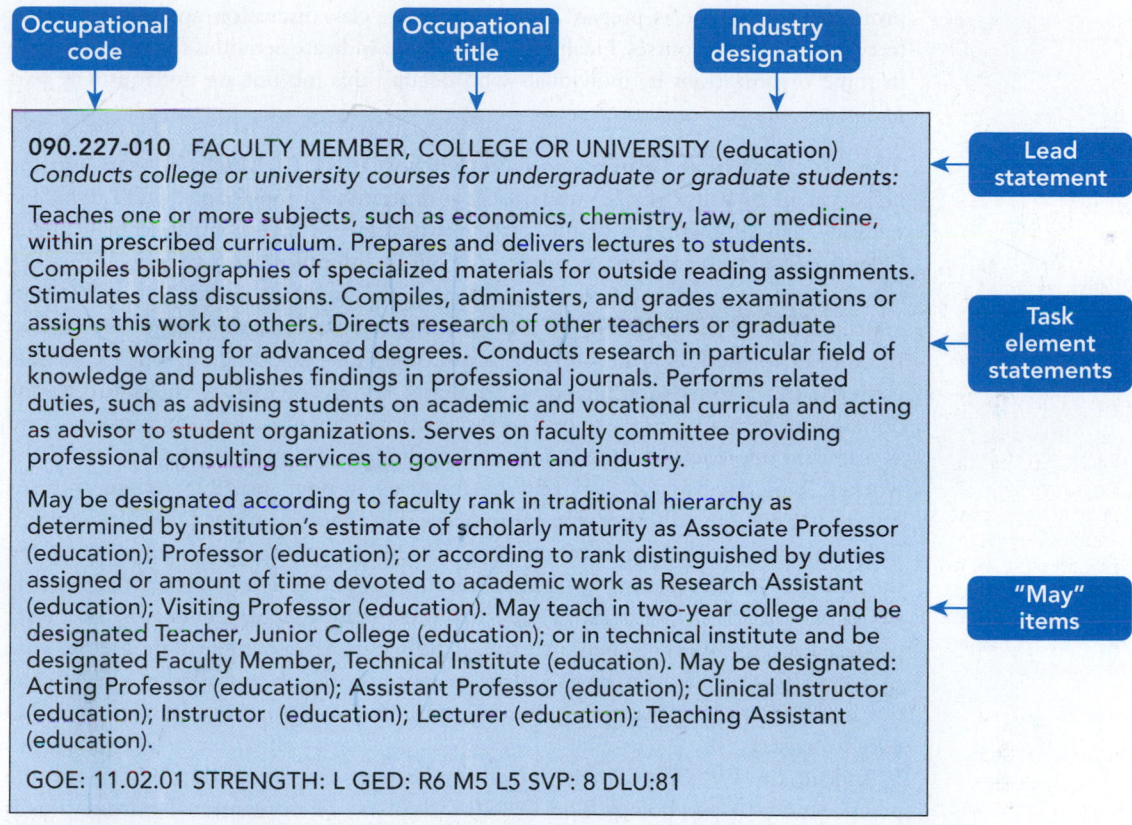

**FIGURE 3.4** DOT Description for Faculty Member

of data collected through job analyses. The DOT presents a hierarchical organization of jobs, with nine major occupational clusters at the uppermost level of the hierarchy. **Figure 3.4** shows the DOT entry for a faculty member, including labels for the particular parts of the entry. The nine-digit *occupational code* is important in that it uniquely identifies this particular job. The first three digits classify the job with respect to its occupational category. The next three digits identify where the job is classified with respect to data, people, and things; in this example, the digits 227 indicate that the job is high on both data (*analyze*) and people (*instruct*) but low on things (*handle*). This probably fits your preconceived notion of what faculty members do, which is to spend a great deal of time working with data and people but less time manipulating tools, equipment, and so on. The *industry designation* in this case is "education."

The *lead statement* is always the first sentence of the description itself, followed by a colon. This statement provides the best simple description of the job. The *task element statements,* which come next, describe with more precision what is done on the job to meet the objectives presented in the lead statement. In other words, college professors teach subjects, prepare lectures, stimulate class discussion, and so on, in order to conduct college courses. Finally, the *"may" items* indicate activities that may be done in some organizations by individuals who occupy this job but are not routinely part of this job in most organizations.

**The Occupational Information Network (O★NET)** About 20 years ago the Department of Labor (DOL) undertook an initiative to replace the DOT, which it viewed as incompatible with the current workplace. This initiative, known as the Occupational Information Network (O★NET), identifies and describes the key components of modern occupations (Occupational Information Network, 2009, January 13) and has replaced the DOT, which has become obsolete as a resource. In contrast to the DOT, the O★NET is not based on FJA; rather, it is based on data gathered in various ways, including an initial review of existing literature in the domains of human performance and occupational analysis. Thus, it is categorized as a hybrid approach because it focuses simultaneously on both the work and the worker. This database of over 950 occupations is now available online (http://onetcenter.org), making it much more accessible than the older DOT. In addition to having data on thousands of jobs, it allows individuals to search for occupations through key words relating to skill requirements, and it is connected to *America's Job Bank* and *school-to-work* initiatives in which schools train students to be better prepared for the workplace and to successfully find employment. The greater ease of access (through the Internet) and its focus on both job and worker characteristics make the O★NET a very useful and attractive tool for organizations and I/O psychologists.

Indeed, the O★NET has widespread implications for the world of work and the practice of I/O psychology. The O★NET database of occupational information is based on the O★NET Content Model, which identifies the structure of information stored in the database. The structure, which is presented in **Figure 3.5**, involves six classes of information: (1) worker characteristics, such as abilities and interests; (2) worker requirements, such as general knowledge and skills; (3) experience requirements, such as past employment history, training, or licensure; (4) occupational requirements, such as generalized work activities; (5) occupation-specific information, such as technical information particular to a certain job family; and (6) occupational characteristics, such as labor market and social information. The database is quite useful for career management; for organizational functions like selection, training, and development; and for researchers trying to better understand organizational performance. Counselors, students, human resource professionals, and researchers are among those who benefit from this DOL initiative.

Research on the O★NET has started to emerge over the past 10 years. For instance, researchers at the University of Nebraska, Omaha, have developed and tested a web-based job-analytic technique using the O★NET (Reiter-Palmon, Brown, Sandall, Buboltz, & Nimps, 2006). More recent work has been focused on matching Occupational Interest Profiles (OIPs) from the O★NET with interest-based assessments often used in career

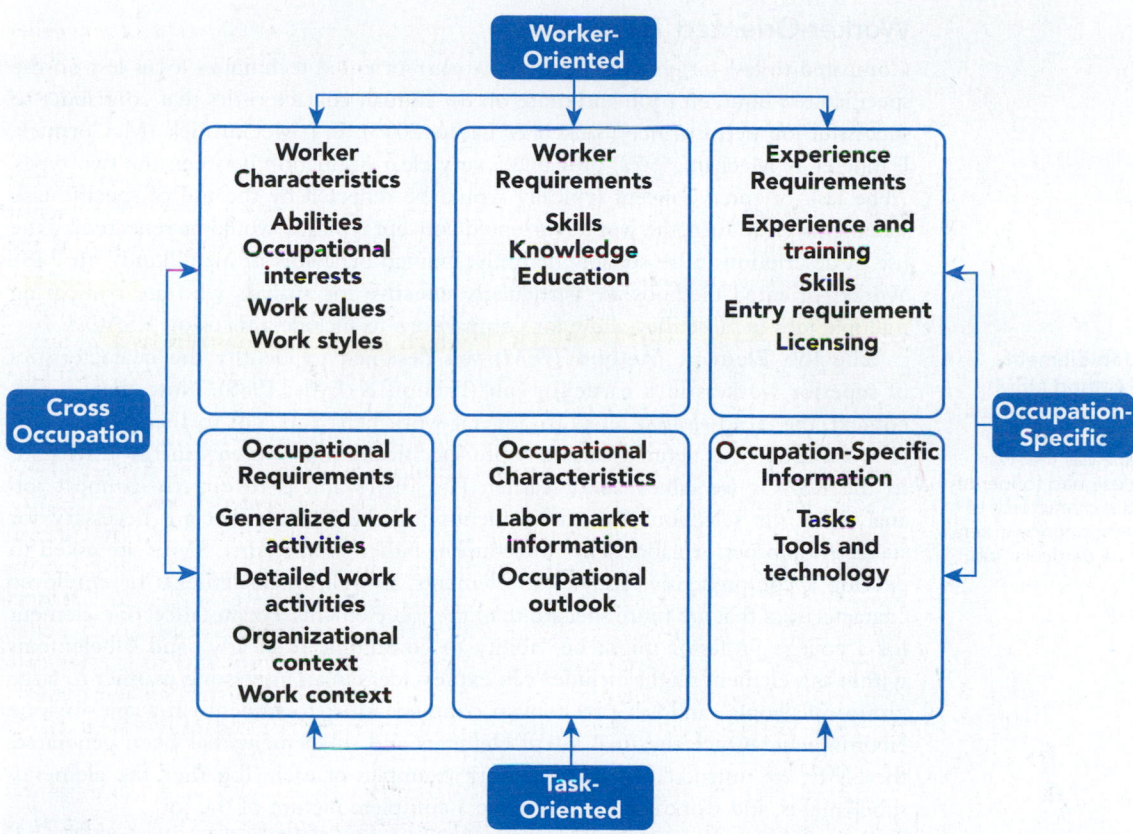

**FIGURE 3.5** O*NET Content Model (Information from http://onetcenter.org)

counseling (Rounds, Armstrong, Liao, Lewis, & Rivkin, 2008). An interesting new study has used information from the O*NET to identify the likelihood of experiencing carpal tunnel syndrome based on various hand exposures such as repetitive movements, movement of objects, reliance on hand/finger speed, and so forth (Evanoff, Zeringue, Franzblau, & Dale, 2014).

Task-oriented approaches to job analysis have been criticized as being potentially too narrowly focused on the tasks for a particular job (Harvey, 1991). Critics say it follows that by focusing microscopically on the tasks of a particular job, we rule out the possibility of making a real comparison across jobs because no job is likely to emerge as similar at such a fine-grained level. In other words, we may miss similarities in jobs because of the high level of technological and behavioral specificity of the tasks and thereby fail to detect more abstract similarities across jobs. Worker-oriented approaches to job analysis address this very problem.

## Worker-Oriented Techniques

Compared to task-oriented techniques, worker-oriented techniques focus less on the specific tasks done on a job and more on the human characteristics that contribute to successful job performance (Sackett & Laczo, 2003). E. J. McCormick (McCormick, Jeanneret, & Mecham, 1972) provided a very clear distinction between the two types: "The task-oriented concept typically would be reflected by the use of specific task statements.... In turn, the worker-oriented concept typically would be reflected by the use of descriptions of reasonably definitive human behaviors of many kinds" (p. 348). Worker-oriented methods are particularly effective for analysts who are comparing multiple jobs because they allow for comparisons to include a focus on KSAOs.

The **Job Element Method (JEM)** was designed to identify the characteristics of superior workers in a particular job (Primoff & Eyde, 1988). Note that, in this context, the word *element* refers to general work behaviors, not to the smallest unit of work activity as defined earlier. More specifically, job elements in the JEM refer to the KSAOs we talked about earlier. The JEM's aim is to directly connect job analysis to the selection context by identifying the KSAOs that are necessary for successful job performance. The procedure is rather simple. First, SMEs are asked to develop a comprehensive list of job elements, as well as subelements or employee characteristics that are more specific than the job elements. For instance, one element for a college professor might be "ability to communicate clearly," and subelements within this element might include "can express ideas in an interesting manner to large groups of people" and "able to explain complex issues to students in a one-on-one environment." Once the final list of elements and subelements has been generated, the SMEs are instructed to provide work examples of each. Together, the elements, subelements, and work examples provide a complete picture of the job.

A common criticism of this approach is that the JEM ignores the specific job tasks, making it difficult to demonstrate that a particular element is related to the job (Gatewood & Feild, 2001)—in other words, a JEM approach may identify "ability to communicate clearly" as an important element, but this isn't a specific job task and may leave us wondering what particular task is important and how the element is related to it. This criticism is consistent with other researchers' (e.g., Harvey, 1991) concerns that job analysis needs to remain focused on observables instead of inferring hypothetical worker traits or abilities. However, much of what we do in psychology involves inferences of some sort, so excluding them seems unreasonable. We can resolve this paradox by realizing that an important focus of job analysis is to ensure that when inferences are drawn, they are based on observable work-related data. The job analyst can choose to focus only on work activities or only on worker attributes or on both, which is consistent with the hybrid approach discussed earlier.

Perhaps the best-known job analysis method is the **Position Analysis Questionnaire (PAQ)**, a standardized instrument that focuses on general work behaviors (McCormick et al., 1972). The PAQ consists of 195 items or elements, 187 of which describe general work behaviors, work conditions, and job characteristics. The incumbent employee or SME decides whether each item pertains to the job in question; each one that does

**Job Element Method (JEM)**
A worker-oriented approach to job analysis that was designed to identify the characteristics of superior workers in a particular job.

**Position Analysis Questionnaire (PAQ)**
A widely used job analysis instrument that focuses on general work behaviors.

## PRACTITIONER FORUM

John Binning

### John F. Binning

*PhD, 1985, I/O Psychology, The University of Akron*
*Director, Research and Development*
*The DeGarmo Group, Inc.*

The DeGarmo Group specializes in designing and administering preemployment selection tests. One of our assessment tools is the DeGarmo Personality Inventory (DPI). The DPI is delivered over the Internet, and job applicant responses are scored and available to client human resource (HR) representatives. What happens between the time an applicant presses the "Finish" button and the HR representative reviews the results is where the real psychological action is!

You will read in later chapters about the Big Five personality factors and how different jobs require different profiles of personality traits. A challenge for HR and talent acquisition professionals is how to determine which personality traits are critical for a particular job. We decided to leverage the vast information available in O★NET to guide the process of determining personality requirements for different jobs.

Our approach unfolds something like this: When an organization wants to hire for a particular job, we find that job in O★NET, and among other information, there are importance ratings for a variety of *work styles*. The work style ratings were determined by having job-knowledgeable people complete job analysis questionnaires about how important the different styles are for different jobs.

The work styles can be interpreted in terms of the Big Five personality factors. For example, one of the O★NET work styles is attention to detail, and this is relevant to the Big Five factor of conscientiousness. We believe that each work style can be meaningfully

mapped onto Big Five factors, and we have automated this process. For any of the thousands of jobs described in O★NET, we can automatically translate the work style ratings into importance scores on the Big Five factors (or facet subfactors) measured by the DPI. Once we know which DPI scores are important for a job, we have our IT staff write the computational code to score job applicants' responses to determine how well their personalities "fit" the demands of that particular job.

To summarize, when a job applicant presses the "Finish" button, his or her responses are mathematically "crunched" into various personality scores and then given different mathematical weights based on the O★NET information, and a final score and interpretive report are generated indicating how well the applicant's personality matches the specific demands of the job. Client HR representatives then use this information to aid in making hiring decisions. This way we apply the science of job analysis and personality to the needs of various organizations.

### Applying Your Knowledge

1. How might the O★NET system be more helpful in job analysis to the DeGarmo Group than the DOT?

2. Given the changing nature of work, why is job analysis so important? How is the DeGarmo Group demonstrating this fact?

3. The DeGarmo Group specializes in trying to match the best applicants to its clients' needs. But what other job-analytic steps are critical for each client organization to take in order to maximize productivity in the hiring process?

---

is evaluated in terms of various dimensions, such as the extent to which it is used on the job, its importance to the job, and the amount of time on the job that is spent on this behavior. These 187 job elements are organized along six dimensions: information input, mental processes, work output, relationships with other persons, job context, and other job characteristics. **Table 3.1** lists these six dimensions, along with two examples of each. A profile of the job emerges as a result of this rather large data collection effort.

| TABLE 3.1 | PAQ Dimensions and Elements | |
|---|---|---|
| **Dimension** | **Description** | **Examples** |
| Information input | Where and how does the worker get the information he uses in performing his job? | Use of written materials<br>Near-visual differentiation |
| Mental processes | What reasoning, decision-making, planning, and information-processing activities are involved in performing the job? | Level of reasoning in problem solving<br>Coding/decoding |
| Work output | What physical activities does the worker perform, and what tools does she use? | Use of keyboard devices<br>Assembling/disassembling |
| Relationships with other persons | What relationships with other people are required in performing the job? | Instructing<br>Contacts with public, customers |
| Job context | In what physical or social contexts is the work performed? | High temperature<br>Interpersonal conflict situations |
| Other job characteristics | What activities, conditions, or characteristics other than those described above are relevant to the job? | Specified work pace<br>Amount of job structure |

Source: McCormick (1979)

Despite its historically widespread use, the PAQ has been the target of at least three major criticisms. First, some data indicate that the reading level of the PAQ is at least college level, if not graduate level (Ash & Edgell, 1975). This is a problem because it limits who can competently do the job analysis and rules out the less educated incumbents in many jobs. Second, the PAQ does not seem well suited for managerial jobs; and, third, the items themselves are too abstract (Harvey, 1993). These criticisms have led other job analysis researchers and practitioners to develop alternative worker-oriented instruments.

**Common-Metric Questionnaire (CMQ)**
A worker-oriented job analysis instrument that attempts to improve the generalizability of worker-oriented approaches through the use of items focused on slightly less general work behaviors.

The **Common–Metric Questionnaire (CMQ)**, developed by Harvey (1993), is one such instrument. Two basic beliefs about worker-oriented approaches to job analysis are reflected in the CMQ: (1) The instrument must comprehensively describe work activities using a common set of items written at a more behaviorally abstract level than the typical task statements, and (2) the rating scale must have the same meaning across all jobs. The focus here is on describing jobs at a level that allows the descriptions to be compared across jobs, as opposed to describing them so abstractly that differences across jobs are lost.

Think back to such task–oriented approaches as the Task Inventory Approach and Functional Job Analysis. In these cases, the focus is on extremely specific tasks conducted on the job, making it very difficult to uncover any similarities across jobs. But the worker-oriented approaches, best exemplified by the PAQ, may be so abstract as to result in the emergence of dissimilar jobs with very similar profiles. For instance, what jobs do you think might emerge with a profile similar to that of police officer? You probably listed things like firefighter, prison guard, and private detective. However, research indicates that one answer is the job of *homemaker* (Arvey & Begalla, 1975). This is probably not one of the jobs you had on your list, but the profiles tend to be similar because both police officers and homemakers are often involved in handling emergencies and troubleshooting. However, I would argue that if the PAQ elements were a little less abstract, these jobs would not emerge as so similar.

The CMQ is computer-based, consisting of 2,077 items that are organized along 80 dimensions. Obviously, one issue with respect to this instrument is its length, but the author reports that over 90% of those who have used the CMQ completed it in less than three hours (Harvey, 1993). A sample question asks whether a particular job involves a skill that requires instruction at a college or university, along with the response scale for that item; the response

scale displays the criticality of this particular skill. The items for all 80 dimensions are set up in a similar way. Its items are more behaviorally specific than those included on the PAQ, its reading level is much lower, and it is relevant for both managerial and nonmanagerial jobs.

**A CLOSER LOOK**
Why are the job profiles of police officer and homemaker so similar according to the PAQ? How would the CMQ address this?

## Advances and Issues in Job Analysis Practice and Research

Technology has played a role in the development of job analyses. For instance, researchers have demonstrated how to use the Internet to generate job-analytic information via the O★NET (Reiter-Palmon et al., 2006). In their work, they emphasized the use of the web to gather and organize job-analytic information with minimal intervention and guidance from a consultant. Other researchers have worked to develop metrics, or quantitative rules of thumb, to help with analyzing and using the mass of job analysis data resulting from technological innovations like the O★NET (McEntire, Dailey, Osburn, & Mumford, 2006). They have developed metrics that would allow organizations to make better use of the existing O★NET data. These metrics, or mathematical formulae, can be used with the O★NET database to answer specific questions in the areas of selection, training, and development, for example, who is the best employee for a particular promotion. Given the ever-increasing use of the O★NET database in organizational analysis, the development and use of related metrics hold even greater potential for organizations.

There has also been considerable advancement regarding issues of SME ratings. For instance, two studies have examined the role of personality and motivation in SME job analysis ratings. One investigation examined the potential role of the self-serving bias in affecting job analysis ratings (Cucina, Vasilopoulos, & Sehgal, 2005).

The authors argued that SMEs may engage in self-serving behavior when asked to identify which traits are important for the jobs. This would suggest that an SME might weight intelligence, flexibility, and creative thinking as important characteristics for successful employees in their job even though others might more objectively not view these characteristics as terribly important.

In a more sophisticated study testing self-presentation in SME ratings, it was found that SME incumbents tended to endorse ability statements as important for job effectiveness even when those abilities were really nonessential (Morgeson, Delaney-Klinger, Mayfield, Ferrara, & Campion, 2004). Individuals were presenting themselves in a positive light to suggest that, in order to do the job that they currently did, one needed to have a plethora of abilities. Individuals may do this unconsciously and without any real plan to alter the objective job analysis, but the result is job analysis data that are inaccurate—and the implications and potential detrimental effects to the organization are very real. For instance, requiring an ability for a particular job because the job analysis identified it as important makes good sense; however, if the ability really isn't essential for the job, it may lead to many competent individuals not being hired for lack of this ability. Other researchers found that one's attitude toward one's job may bias one's job analysis ratings; this was especially the case for tasks that were objectively coded as discretionary (Conte, Dean, Ringenbach, Moran, & Landy, 2005). By "discretionary," the authors mean tasks like "join and participate in community and social organizations," which may not be required as often as other tasks. It appears that SMEs (in this case, incumbents) allow their attitudes about their own jobs as well as the extent to which the task is required to impact job analysis ratings. Further, a recent examination of O★NET data that focused on the source of the job analysis ratings concludes that using both job analytic experts and incumbents to provide job data is the best approach because each may bring meaningful and useful information to the situation (Wamslet, Natali, & Campbell, 2012).

Another recent study argues that the appearance of unreliable competency ratings made by incumbents is due to "job crafting" (Lievens, Sanchez, Bartram, & Brown 2010). For instance, in complex jobs that allow incumbents to make choices that allow them more creativity and flexibility, there are more opportunities for these incumbents to exercise discretion and "craft" their jobs in particular ways. Because employees can tweak their jobs, resulting in something that looks quite different from the way the jobs were originally defined, incumbent ratings of competencies may not agree with the competencies from the original job analysis. Results found that 25% of the differences in the two sets of competency ratings appear to be meaningful differences that emerged because of the job crafting (Lievens et al., 2010). That is, incumbents don't see their jobs as the same—even though the jobs were originally defined as the same—because they have crafted their job to be different based on their skills and weaknesses. Variance in incumbent ratings may not be error at all, but rather a reflection of how incumbents view and craft their own jobs. Therefore, organizations might be wise to encourage employees to craft jobs in ways that are consistent with the strategic plan of the organization.

A newer perspective on job analysis is taken by some recent researchers who argue that we need new types of job analyses. Traditional job analyses assume stable jobs, but jobs have a tendency to change and morph into different-looking jobs, leading some to argue for a novel approach to job analysis (Singh, 2008). With the changing of environments in North American organizations, we need more strategic job-analytic approaches in which experts consider not just the current status of jobs but also how jobs are likely to change and evolve in the future. **Strategic job analysis** is an intentional, systematic process of collecting current and future work-related aspects of a job within the organization's strategic context (Singh, 2008). Although not much has been written about this approach yet, it still represents a potential trend in the discipline. For more information on the concept of strategic job analysis, see J. S. Shippmann's 2013 book *Strategic Job Modeling: Working at the Core of Integrated Human Resources* (Psychology Press).

*In Chapter 2 we talked about variance as a measure of dispersion, or the "spread-outedness" of the scores. Here we are talking about job crafting being responsible for those differences, or variance, in job ratings.*

**strategic job analysis**
An approach to job analysis that considers the status of jobs as they currently exist but also factors in how jobs are likely to change in the future as a result of anticipated organizational or industry changes.

## DEFINING THE JOB: DESCRIPTIONS AND SPECIFICATIONS

The basic goal of job analysis is to define the job in terms of its component parts. As noted earlier, job analysis yields three major outcomes: job description, job specifications, and job evaluation. The first of these will be discussed in a separate section. The second outcome, **job description**, is a written statement of what the jobholders do, how they do it, and why they do it (Cascio & Aguinis, 2010). It presents the *task requirements* of the job. The job description typically includes the job title and descriptions of the tasks and machinery involved, and it sometimes includes information about the working conditions and physical environment, social environment, and conditions of employment. Think about the job of college professor and ask yourself what college professors do, how they do it, and why they do it. Upon answering those questions, you might arrive at the following job description, which looks very similar to the DOT entry for faculty member, presented earlier in Figure 3.4:

**job description**
As an outcome of job analysis, a written statement of what jobholders actually do, how they do it, and why they do it.

> College Professor: Teaches college or university courses within a particular curriculum (e.g., psychology, mathematics, history) to classes of undergraduate and graduate students. Prepares and delivers lectures that conform to a predetermined course outline. Stimulates class discussions in smaller informal groups. Evaluates students' knowledge and achievement through reading, writing, and other assignments as well as through examinations that are graded so as to provide feedback. Conducts research in his or her area of expertise and disseminates the findings of that research in appropriate outlets (e.g., scientific journals, books) to further the knowledge in the field. Provides mentoring and advising to students who are seeking academic degrees. Serves on university committees that serve the interests of students, the university, the government, and the community.

**job specifications**
An outcome of job analysis delineating the KSAOs deemed necessary to perform a job; often called job specs.

The third outcome derived from the job analysis is a description of the *people requirements* that are reflected in the job specifications (often called *job specs*). The job specifications delineate the KSAOs deemed necessary to perform the job. Let's return to our college professor example. We've generated a job description, but what would comprise the job specifications or KSAOs necessary to be a successful college professor? Here is one such list:

- Reading and writing at the post-college level
- Advanced knowledge verified by an advanced degree (master's or doctorate)
- Willingness or desire to work with others
- Ability to communicate clearly
- Ability to communicate in an interesting manner
- Methodological and statistical skills
- Mentoring and advising skills
- A deep knowledge/understanding of one's own discipline

One way to view the relationships among job analysis, job description, and job specifications is to view the job description as stemming directly from the job analysis and the job specifications as being inferred indirectly from the job analysis through the job description. (Look back at Figure 3.1 for this organizational scheme.) For instance, we might use the JEM to develop a picture of the job and to write a job description (like the preceding one) that includes mentoring and advising students who are seeking academic degrees. From the job analysis and this job description, we might infer that successful college professors must have mentoring and advising skills. In short, the job analysis, job description, and job specifications are necessarily intertwined. As you may recall, many experts argue that job analysis should be focused only on observables; inferences about KSAOs from the job analysis should be avoided (Harvey, 1991).

Of course, one of the major purposes of job analysis is to identify KSAOs that can be used in the selection of employees. This process is covered in Chapter 6, but it's worth noting here that even if one limits job analysis to observables that result in a job description, the job analysis and job description must be used to infer job specifications that are of paramount importance for selection and placement. The bottom line is that, as I/O psychologists, we are not simply focused on describing the job; indeed, our longer-term goal is the use of this job analysis information for selection, placement, performance appraisal, and other HR functions.

## Competency Modeling

In Chapter 1, I defined *competencies* as the skills, behaviors, and capabilities that allow employees to perform specific functions. Obviously, this definition is very similar to the one I have specified for KSAOs in this chapter. In fact, many experts consider competencies and KSAOs to be the same thing (e.g., Schippmann et al., 2000). Another way to think about this relationship, though, is to view competencies as sets or groupings of specific KSAOs that allow employees to perform specific organizational functions (Reilly & McGourty, 1998). For example, interpersonal communication may be considered a competency. That competency, in turn, may consist of several KSAOs such as (1) the knowledge of different communication styles, (2) the skill to communicate positive and negative feedback to individuals, and (3) the ability to understand what individuals need to hear from their supervisor to increase their motivation.

*Competency modeling* may parallel job analysis in that both involve describing jobs in a careful and methodical way so that HR practices such as selection and placement can be based on this information (Schippmann et al., 2000). Differences have been observed as well. For example, competency modeling is believed to be more worker-oriented and job analysis more task-oriented (Schippmann et al., 2000).

## I/O TODAY

### The Future of Job Analysis

Although job analysis has historically been a key step in developing solid I/O practices, many researchers and practitioners have suggested that this approach is outdated given the ways that jobs have changed over the past few decades. Technological innovations lead to products that need rapid updates, globalization has increased the pace of competition, and organizations need to be flexible to meet customer needs. As a result, workers are less likely to be hired to do a specific job for the rest of their career; instead, a valuable worker will be able to grow and change with the needs of the company. This, in turn, means that a job analysis can quickly become obsolete.

One potential solution to this problem is competency modeling. In practical terms, competency modeling focuses more on identifying people who have a broad set of capabilities that will help them to adapt as the job changes. In other words, for the role of a retail manager, a job analysis might indicate that the individual must know general management principles and have good communication skills. Competency modeling, meanwhile, might indicate that the manager has a competency in "engaging leadership"—a general competency that might include specific skills such as communication, critical thinking, and charisma. Often, organizations will use competencies such as "mentoring and teaching" or "strategic thinking" at all levels of the organization. A sales representative's version of "mentoring and teaching" might look different from that of a manager's—she might help train new employees or provide in-the-moment feedback to her peers—but arguably, a sales representative who can demonstrate these skills has the potential to one day be an effective manager.

This example helps to illustrate both the benefits and difficulties of competency models. Having broad competencies such as "mentoring and teaching" can provide an organization with a consistent language that can be used with all employees to discuss expectations and performance. Competencies also make it easier to adapt these expectations as the organization changes. However, because competencies tend to be umbrella terms that encompass many different KSAOs, they are not as specific and detailed as a traditional job analysis would be. So while a competency might be more flexible and parsimonious, it also lacks specificity.

Despite these shortcomings, competency modeling is becoming more common among organizations. Researchers have also found that consumers such as HR managers and CEOs are much more interested in adopting competency models rather than conducting numerous job analyses. The challenge for I/O psychologists will be to ensure that these competency models are developed with just as much care and rigor as a job analysis would be.

#### Discussion Questions

1. What situations might lead you to recommend that an organization adopt a competency model approach over a more traditional job analysis approach?
2. How could you use principles for job analysis to help ensure you have created a high-quality competency model?
3. In his 2012 article in *Human Resource Development Review*, Gregory Stevens suggests that using solid research methodology and avoiding "buzzwords" are two possible best practices that practitioners can follow. What other "best practices" might be important to keep in mind if an organization chooses to use competency modeling?

Competency modeling is usually much broader in focus because it tries to build a full framework for HR functioning by defining the responsibilities, skills, knowledge, abilities, personal attributes, and business challenges that are relevant for a particular organization (see Sanchez & Levine, 2009 and Stevens, 2012 for a thorough comparison of the two approaches). Although distinctions exist between the job-analytic approach to identifying KSAOs and the competency modeling approach to building competencies, the two terms are similar enough for our purposes that I will use them interchangeably throughout the text. Please understand, however, that job analysis tends to be a bit more methodologically rigorous, and competency modeling tends to consider organizational strategy a bit more and takes a broader look at the organization.

## THE MANY PURPOSES OF JOB ANALYSIS

As I suggested earlier, job analysis is the foundation for much of industrial psychology. There are two reasons for this. First, a job analysis is necessary to the success of human resource functions. In other words, without a job analysis, many of the HR functions in organizations would be carried out ineffectively. Second, an increased emphasis on laws associated with the workplace has made it more desirable for companies to use job analyses as their first line of defense when accused of an unfair practice. **Table 3.2** presents two cases that demonstrate the need for adequate job analysis to prevent unfair or discriminatory hiring and promotion practices. We will discuss legal issues in more depth in the next few chapters; for now, let's consider job classification, an important purpose served by job analysis.

**TABLE 3.2** Legal Importance of Job Analysis

| Case Description | Legal Ruling |
|---|---|
| *Griggs v. Duke Power* (1971): Among other tests/assessments, Duke Power was using measures of cognitive ability (Bennett and Wonderlic) to make hiring decisions into low-level laborer positions. This resulted in adverse impact against blacks who were hired at a much lower rate than whites. Though the defendant had no job analysis data linking cognitive ability to job performance, they argued that they used a professionally developed test and didn't mean to discriminate against blacks. | The court found the lack of intent to discriminate irrelevant and ruled that tests, even if professionally developed, must be job-related. The burden of proof of demonstrating the job relatedness (business necessity) of the tests/assessments falls on the defendant and the court strongly supported the use of job analysis in this regard. |
| *Albermarle Paper Company v. Moody* (1975): The company was using the same two cognitive ability measures as Griggs, but had not done a validation study until just prior to trial and then did it poorly without a job analysis. | The court ruled that a test validated in one job may be used in another, but only if it is clearly demonstrated to be job-related for the current job. Further, they ruled for the plaintiff because Albermarle had done no analysis of the attributes of the jobs or the skills needed to perform the job. |

## Job Classification

Jobs are often categorized in terms of job families, each of which can then be used as a level of analysis for various personnel decisions. For instance, Word Processing Specialist I, Word Processing Specialist II, and Data Technician I may all be declared parts of a job family called "computer support staff" if the job analyses conducted on each job demonstrated enough overlap to warrant such a designation. If they did, all jobs within this job family would operate under the same benefits package, including number of allowable sick days, number of vacation days, and amount of health benefits. In addition, if a company's 2,000 jobs can be grouped into 100 job families, many of the company's personnel practices will be simplified.

> **TECHNICAL TIP**
>
> Remember that we talked about the importance of test validity in Chapter 2. In particular, criterion-related validity focuses on whether the test is a good predictor of performance. With the legal cases described here, you can see the practical importance of test validity.

## Criterion Development and Performance Appraisal

Performance appraisal is certainly one of the most frequent uses of job analysis data. As we will discuss in Chapters 4 and 5, performance appraisal is one of the most important functions performed by human resource departments. Of course, to conduct a useful and fair performance appraisal, organizations must have clearly stipulated goals, objectives, and criteria on which employees can be evaluated. These criteria should come directly from the job analysis. For instance, if college professors are going to be evaluated annually with respect to their success in teaching, the college must be able to demonstrate that teaching is an important part of a professor's job. (This should be an easy thing to do, but it still needs to be verified by the job analysis.) Suppose that I am evaluated based on the reactions of my students to my classes (and, in fact, I am evaluated in this way every semester), but the job analysis done by my school does not demonstrate that teaching is an integral part of my job. This would be neither fair nor appropriate. Here, of course, I would argue that the problem is not with the criteria but with the job analysis, which did not identify an important element of the job. This example, too, demonstrates the importance of doing a thorough and accurate job analysis because the job analysis is used in important ways.

## Selection and Placement

There is perhaps no area of industrial psychology for which job analysis is more important than selection and placement (see Chapters 6 and 7). Indeed, a major purpose of job analysis is to help industrial psychologists identify the KSAOs that are necessary for successful performance on the job.

Let's turn to the world of construction for an example. In doing a job analysis for the job of an architect, we conclude that spatial skills and knowledge of some basic engineering principles are required. Therefore, when screening applicants, we look for individuals who seem to be knowledgeable and skilled in these areas and hire them. This scenario makes sense, but it may also be too simplistic. For instance, we might ignore the part of our job analysis indicating that architects also need to have some drafting (or drawing) skills because they need to be able to develop plans for new buildings. Given this flaw in our process, we may hire knowledgeable and spatially skilled individuals who do not have the drafting skills to put their ideas on paper. In short, because we weren't careful in conducting and interpreting our job analysis, we may have made costly personnel decisions. Does this cost our company money? It sure does, and it also may cost individuals their jobs.

## Job Design and Redesign

Job analysis may sometimes uncover problems with a particular job that the organization may want to address. For instance, interviews with incumbents may reveal that some of the current equipment used on the job needs to be updated because it cannot keep pace with other, newer equipment during the production process. A company may use this information to purchase newer equipment or to redesign the job so that the current equipment will work more efficiently within the process. Alternatively, PAQ or CMQ data may indicate that employees spend far too much time on a particular facet of the job, information that the company may use to initiate a job redesign intervention to make the work process more efficient. We can see that in this area of I/O psychology, job analyses are often used to make alterations in the work process with the intent of making the company run more efficiently.

Morgeson and Humphrey (2006) developed the Work Design Questionnaire (WDQ) as a comprehensive measure of job design to replace the incomplete and narrow existing measures. The WDQ consists of 77 items along 21 dimensions of work characteristics. The 21 work characteristics can be organized into: (1) task characteristics such as autonomy and task variety; (2) knowledge characteristics that reflect traditional KSAOs; (3) social characteristics that include social support and feedback from others; and (4) contextual characteristics, composed of physical demands and work conditions. Results suggest that the WDQ is a solid measure of work design that relates appropriately to various elements of the O*NET database—it has become a very popular measure for those doing research on job design.

## Training

In many instances, employees are hired into an organization without all the KSAOs necessary to do every facet of their jobs. Sometimes even highly skilled new employees require training to learn the procedures used in a particular organization (see Chapter 8). Job analysis can be used to identify areas in which training programs need to be developed. Ideally, job analysis should identify what work behaviors occur on the job so that the human resource department can develop training programs around these general and specific work behaviors. In addition, given that jobs are *dynamic*—in that they change considerably with changes in technology, in the workforce, and in economic demands—job analysis can be used to identify the extent to which job behaviors have changed to match the times. This information can then be used to develop and target training programs for existing employees.

# JOB EVALUATION

Although we like to think that our job is as important to our particular organization as anyone else's, the reality is that some jobs are more important than others. Job evaluation is a technique based on job analysis that attempts to determine the value or worth of particular jobs to organizations so that salaries can be set accordingly. Most of us would agree that the clerk who works in the hospital restaurant makes a less important contribution to the organization than the chief surgeon. Job evaluation is about trying to quantify differences of this sort so that salaries can be set in a fair manner based on the value or contribution of jobs. Because compensation is often the largest budget item in many companies, it has an important effect on profits and, therefore, attracts a good deal of attention from organizational administrators and HR practitioners.

**job evaluation**
As an outcome of job analysis, a technique that attempts to determine the value or worth of particular jobs to organizations so that salaries can be set accordingly.

## Point System

There are various approaches to job evaluation, but I will focus on the one most frequently used: the point system. This approach involves estimating the value of jobs based on points assigned to various predetermined dimensions (Milkovich & Newman, 1984). Among the most common of these dimensions—referred to as compensable factors to indicate that employees are compensated based on them— are effort, skill, responsibility, and working conditions. The idea here is that jobs requiring more effort and skill, involving more responsibility, and taking place in less desirable working conditions (e.g., outdoors in subzero temperatures versus climate-controlled office buildings) should be more highly compensated than jobs that don't have these characteristics.

**point system**
The most common approach to job evaluation, which involves estimating the value of jobs based on points assigned to various predetermined dimensions.

The steps involved in conducting a point-system job evaluation are rather simple. First, managers or some other group of SMEs use a job analysis to identify the compensable factors. Second, each job is assigned points by a compensation committee with respect to the degree that each has these compensable factors. Third, the points assigned to each job are summed across the factors to arrive at a total score. Fourth, these points are then used to assign wages, with the goal being to maintain equity so that jobs of greater value are better compensated than those of lesser value. Finally, the scores can be plotted against the current wage for existing jobs, providing a clear picture of whether a job is currently undercompensated, overcompensated, or adequately compensated.

**compensable factors**
Dimensions or factors that are used to rate jobs, indicating that employees are compensated based on these factors. Examples include effort, skill, responsibility, and working conditions.

**Figure 3.6** shows an example of this kind of plot to determine how jobs within the organization stack up against each other in terms of the factors and compensation. The line marked "perfect wage equity" represents the ideal situation whereby the number of job evaluation points is exactly proportional to the level of compensation. The line marked "imperfect wage equity," on the other hand, is more realistic but much less desirable. As you can see, jobs evaluated at 125 points are overcompensated at $8.75 per hour rather than the expected $6.25 per hour; jobs evaluated at 350 points are undercompensated at $13.75 per hour rather than the expected $17.50 per hour.

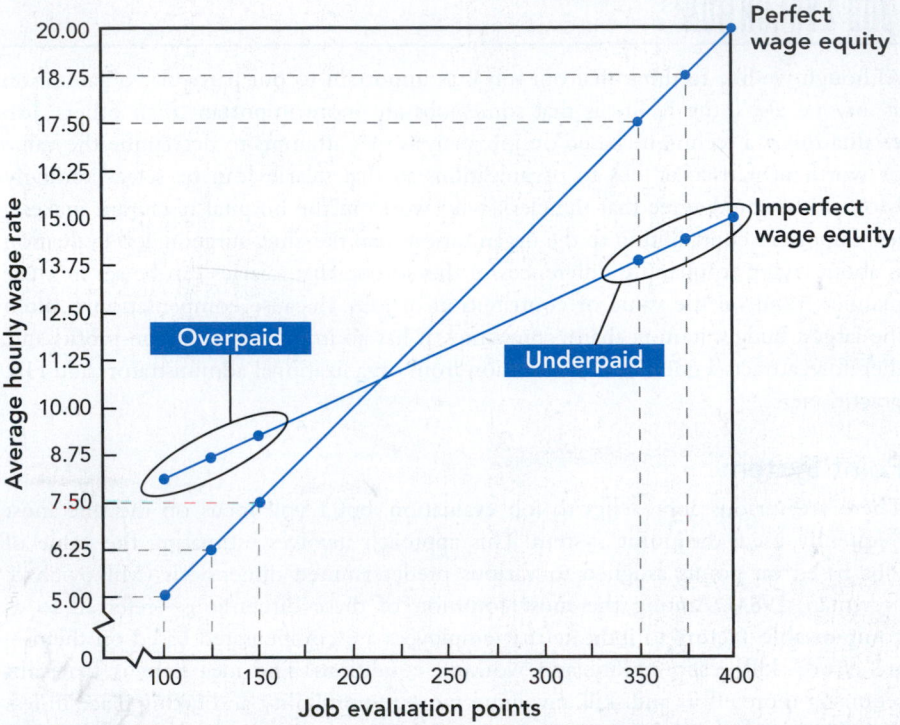

**FIGURE 3.6** Wage Equity and Job Evaluation

Clearly, there are compensation issues to be resolved in this particular organization: Some positions are compensated at a higher rate and others at a lower rate than the job evaluation indicates they should be. Yet once organizations have accumulated and examined such data, they can begin to develop ways to bring wages back in line. For instance, jobs that are undercompensated can be targeted for wage increases, whereas those that are overcompensated can be targeted for wage freezes.

So far, this sounds very scientific, and in some ways it is. But as is often the case with I/O psychology, when we move into the applied arena, things are not quite so simple. In the actual labor market, for instance, individuals in jobs with job evaluation scores between 100 and 200 points sometimes have to be "overpaid"; in other words, there are so few people who will take these lower-level jobs that, to be competitive with other companies, we have to pay higher wages for these jobs than our job evaluation tells us they are worth. At the same time, there may be so many managers interested in upper-level jobs that we can save money by "underpaying" them. Retention of good workers is yet another important issue: We will probably pay what we think is necessary to keep them on the job. In a practical sense, then, companies are likely to use not only job analysis and job evaluation information but also labor market information when setting compensation levels for jobs.

**A CLOSER LOOK**
What role has gender played historically in the compensation levels of jobs? Does gender still play a role?

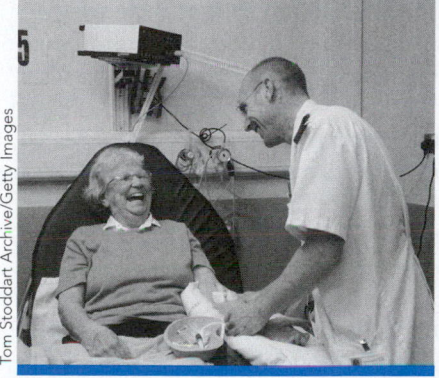

## Comparable Worth

It is a long-established finding that women are paid considerably less than men for similar work. In fact, when a field has become dominated by women, as happened with the administrative assistant profession in the 20th century (for a review, see Lowe, 1987), the rate of pay has decreased. As of 2014, there was a difference of 21.7% between men's and women's wages (Hegewisch & Hartman, 2014; Institute for Women's Policy Research, 2014). This means that, on average, women earn about 78% of what men earn, and this figure has been fairly stable since the mid-1990s, raising concerns about whether women's compensation will ever catch up to men's. There are some projections that suggest the gap may be completely reduced in 2058, but many question whether that is likely (IWPR, 2014). The wage gap is smaller, but still sizable (18%), when we consider salaries one year after graduation (Corbett, & Hill, 2012). A survey of almost 800 Harvard graduates of the class of 2014 reveals some interesting data (Robbins, 2014). First, about 50% of the women graduates received starting salaries under $50,000, while only 28% of men started below $50,000. Second, while only a little under 4% of women accepted positions with starting salaries of over $90,000, about 20% of men did! Even among our most elite institutions we find substantial pay differences. Further, the wage gap does shrink in some industries and when we control for things like hours worked, job choice, etc., but it doesn't disappear; for instance, female administrative assistants earn only 83% of what male administrative assistants earn (Fitzpatrick, 2010).

This issue is a troublesome one, as employees who are doing the same job should be paid similarly regardless of their gender. In fact, the Equal Pay Act of 1963 stipulates that men and women who do work that is *equal* must be compensated similarly. The word *equal* has been interpreted to mean jobs that are the same. But this act does not address the broader issue of gender differences in compensation across dissimilar jobs. For instance, should computer technicians (who are predominantly male) be paid more than executive secretaries (who are predominantly female)? Granted, these jobs aren't the same—but are they equal in terms of their value to the organization? And if they are equal in this sense, shouldn't they be compensated similarly? The Equal Pay Act and the recent Ledbetter Fair Pay Act are discussed in more detail in Chapter 7.

A study (Ostroff & Atwater, 2003) demonstrated that compensation is also affected by the gender composition of one's coworkers. In particular, managers (regardless of gender) who work largely with women are paid considerably less than are managers who work largely with men. Apparently, gender issues in compensation extend beyond just the gender of the employees to the gender composition of the work group as well.

**comparable worth**
A doctrine maintaining that jobs of equal (or comparable) worth to the organization should be compensated equally.

These kinds of questions have given rise to the doctrine of **comparable worth**, which maintains that jobs of equal (or comparable) worth to the organization should be compensated equally. This issue has been linked quite closely to gender differences in compensation. Proponents of comparable worth insist that job evaluation should play a larger role, and the market a smaller role, in setting compensation. They argue that the market is biased and that it artificially sets the compensation for female-dominated jobs lower than for male-dominated jobs. They argue that by focusing on job behaviors rather than on job performers, job evaluation decreases the likelihood of gender bias in compensation (Feder & Levine, 2010).

Opponents of comparable worth argue that there is no bias against female-typed jobs and that women can choose whatever jobs they prefer. They further argue that women are paid less because they choose low-paying jobs that provide greater flexibility or they leave the workforce to raise their families. However, the data do not support these conclusions because female-dominated jobs do not offer more flexibility and most women do not exit the workforce to raise their young children (National Committee on Pay Equity, n.d.). The issue of comparable worth is unlikely to be solved quickly or easily, complicated as it is by market factors and historical trends, potential biases in job evaluation, and both real and imagined gender differences. Of course, we have made progress in this area in recent decades, and with careful and fair practices we can continue to improve the financial situation for women who enter the workforce.

## Summary

Although job analysis tends to receive little empirical attention, it is among the most important areas of I/O psychology, providing the foundation on which all other HR processes are built. This chapter was largely structured around Figure 3.1, which shows the interrelationships among job analysis, job descriptions, job specifications, job evaluation, and the HR functions that are built on these processes. It should be clear by now that without a carefully designed and executed job analysis, HR practitioners and I/O psychologists would have very little to go on in making HR decisions.

Both task-oriented and worker-oriented approaches to job analysis were presented in this chapter, along with a discussion of different methods within each category. Also discussed were the advantages and disadvantages of each approach, the choice of which should depend on the job analyst's purpose. Some developments in the area of job analysis were considered as well. First, although the DOT has been of great importance to the I/O field for many years, the Department of Labor's current undertaking, the O★NET, should provide more updated, useful, and accessible data on occupations and jobs. Second, the CMQ was presented as one of the newer job analysis instruments with great potential to serve the purposes of worker-oriented job analysis methods while avoiding criticisms regarding reading level and work behaviors that are too general.

Job descriptions and job specifications are derived either directly or indirectly from the job analysis and are directly or indirectly connected to a myriad of HR functions. This chapter provided a brief discussion of the links between job analysis and these HR functions; the remainder of the second part of the text will cover these HR functions at length. Finally, we considered the role of job analysis in job evaluation. The Equal Pay Act of 1963 mandates that individuals who do equal work should receive equal pay, but it does not speak to wage gaps between "male-typed" and "female-typed" jobs. The emergence of the doctrine of comparable worth suggests that organizations and society need to do a better job in setting compensation for jobs while taking gender-based job classes into account.

## Key Terms

Common-Metric Questionnaire (CMQ) (p. 82)
comparable worth (p. 94)
compensable factors (p. 91)
*Dictionary of Occupational Titles* (DOT) (p. 76)
element (p. 73)
Functional Job Analysis (FJA) (p. 76)
incumbents (p. 75)
job (p. 73)
job analysis (p. 73)
job description (p. 85)
Job Element Method (JEM) (p. 80)

job evaluation (p. 91)
job specifications (p. 86)
KSAOs (p. 73)
point system (p. 91)
position (p. 73)
Position Analysis Questionnaire (PAQ) (p. 80)
strategic job analysis (p. 85)
subject matter experts (SMEs) (p. 75)
task (p. 73)
Task Inventory Approach (p. 75)
task-oriented (p. 74)
worker-oriented (p. 74)

## TAKING IT TO THE FIELD

Job analysis is one of the most important activities that I/O psychologists can do. Without a thorough job analysis, it becomes difficult to train, assess, and reward employees. There are many ways to do a job analysis, but one of the more commonly used methods is to interview a job incumbent. Using the guide below, interview someone who works at your college/university and then, using the data you gather, write a worker-oriented job description for that position. You may also refer to the O★NET for ideas about this job, but make sure not to copy any phrases from the O★NET.

Here are some tips for writing effective worker-oriented job descriptions:

- A worker-oriented job description is not about what someone does but rather what KSAOs are necessary to be effective in this position. So focus on characteristics rather than tasks.

- It is best to use bullet points for this assignment because you want your document to be as simple as possible for your reader.

- Each bullet point should begin with a present-tense verb, such as *demonstrates* or *knows.*

- Your description should be no longer than two pages; if you find yourself writing more than that, consider how some categories might be consolidated (e.g., "knows laws about food safety" and "follows food safety laws" could be combined into "knows and complies with food safety laws").

- It is important to avoid vague language. Look at what you are writing and consider whether it provides enough information for a job applicant to accurately determine whether he or she would be qualified for the position.

Here are some possible interview questions:

1. What does an effective _____ look like?

2. What does an ineffective _____ look like?

3. What knowledge does someone need to do this job well?

4. What skills does someone need to do this job well?

5. What abilities must someone have to do this job well?

6. What would make someone a "good fit" for this job?

7. Describe a specific example of someone who did something really outstanding in this role—what did they do, and why was it so effective?

8. Describe a specific example of someone who was very unsuccessful in this role—what did they do, and why was it ineffective?

## Critical Thinking Questions

1. One use of job analysis is creating job descriptions. Why is it important to have a detailed and accurate job description? What are some possible outcomes of having a job description that is *not* based on a job analysis and does *not* accurately represent the job?

**2.** Job analysis was an important factor in three court cases presented in this chapter. How is job analysis used in a legal setting? What aspects of a job analysis will make it more likely to hold up in court?

**3.** As noted in the chapter, some proponents of comparable worth argue that compensation for female-dominated jobs is set lower than for jobs dominated by men. These proponents suggest that more rigorous job evaluations could help close the gap. What are some ways in which job evaluation could be used to more effectively determine fair compensation for male- and female-dominated jobs?

## Application Questions

**1.** Find an online job posting. According to this posting, what are some KSAOs required for that position? Are there any KSAOs you believe might be expected but are omitted from this ad? What might be the consequences of this omission?

**2.** Consider a position you currently hold or that you have held in the past. What pieces of information about your job did you know well that you could share with a job analyst? What pieces of information did you not know? Who in the organization would have been better equipped to provide this information to a job analyst?

**3.** Imagine that your college or university is considering using a competency model to ensure that students who graduate have competencies that are necessary in the workplace. What might be some competencies that all students should master by the time they graduate?

**4.** Imagine you have a client who is hesitant to commit to a job analysis. She states that the investment of time and money into developing a job analysis for every position isn't worth it, especially because she thinks that many jobs in the organization will change a lot within the next five years. What might you say to this client?

## Suggested Readings

**Brannick, M. T., Levine, E. L., & Morgeson, F. P.** (2007). *Job and work analysis: Methods, research, and applications for human resource management* (2nd ed.). Thousand Oaks, CA: SAGE. This outstanding treatment of job analysis is useful for both researchers and practitioners.

**Gatewood, R. D., Feild, H. S., & Barrick, M.** (2010). *Human resource selection* (7th ed.). Mason, OH: South-Western College Pub. This is an excellent reference for everything that constitutes industrial psychology, though it is perhaps strongest in its coverage of job analysis and other technical areas.

**O★NET Online.** (2010). *Build your future with O★NET OnLine!* U.S. Department of Labor. Retrieved from http://onetcenter.org/. The U.S. Department of Labor's online database of occupational information provides central characteristics and aspects of both workers and occupations.

**Peterson, N. G., Mumford, M. D., Borman, W. C., Jeanneret, P. R., Fleishman, E. A., Levin, K. Y., et al.** (2001). Understanding work using the Occupational Information Network (O★NET). *Personnel Psychology, 54,* 451–492. This is a detailed discussion of why the O★NET was needed and how it was developed.

**Shippmann, J. S.** (2013) *Strategic job modeling: Working at the core of integrated human resources.* New York: Psychology Press. This book presents some ideas on the future of job analysis and strategic job modeling.

**Wilson, M. A., Bennett, W., Gibson, S. G., & Alliger G. M.** (2012). *The handbook of work analysis: Methods, systems, applications, and science of work measurement in organizations.* New York: Routledge. A very nice overview of job analytic techniques and theory. This provides a current look at the measurement and analysis of jobs and will serve as a great resource for those interested in job analytic issues.

CHAPTER 4

# Criterion Measurement

Photo: Ingram Publishing/Newscom

## LEARNING OBJECTIVES

This chapter should help you understand:

- What the criterion problem is
- How criteria are defined in I/O psychology
- What the criteria for the criteria are
- The difference between the ultimate criterion and the actual criterion
- How to differentiate between criterion contamination and criterion deficiency
- The important issues that revolve around multiple criteria
- Different ways to weight criteria to arrive at a composite criterion
- What dynamic criteria are and how they can affect HR functioning
- The differences between objective and subjective criteria
- The potential role of contextual performance (including counterproductive behavior) in criterion development
- The complex relationships between task behavior, contextual behavior, and counterproductive work behavior

As noted in the last chapter, job analysis provides the foundation on which everything in the field of industrial psychology is built. In this chapter, I will talk about the first aspect of this "everything": criteria. Criteria are quite important to industrial psychology because they reflect organizational or individual performance—and, in a competitive market, companies are driven by performance and profits. Thus, I/O psychologists are often hired to help organizations develop criteria, as well as to implement HR processes that are directly linked to those criteria. Criteria are typically dependent variables that provide an indication of success or performance. For instance, when your instructor grades your paper, he uses criteria. When your boss evaluates your performance and decides on whether or not to give you a raise, she uses criteria. This chapter will present the nuts and bolts of criteria—what they are, how they are developed, how they are evaluated, and what they are used for—along with a discussion of the different types.

## DEFINING CRITERIA AND THEIR PROPERTIES

Every time you evaluate something or someone, you are using criteria—though you're probably not aware of doing so. We even use criteria to evaluate teams such as a work team or a baseball team (for a more complete discussion of team criteria, see LePine, Piccolo, Jackson, Mathieu, & Saul, 2008). When, for the first time, you walked into your dorm room as a freshman or your office cubicle as a new employee, you very likely wondered whether you and the students in that dorm room or the coworkers in the nearby cubicle would get along. In other words, you wondered whether you would like those people. When you did finally decide that Kristen was a pretty cool roommate, you may have made that decision based on her personality (funny, serious, kind, trustworthy), intelligence (smart about academic things, smart about everyday things), hobbies (enjoys sports, music, movies), hang-ups (dislikes people who are stuck on themselves and people who don't clean up after themselves), and so on. You made your decision based on all of these criteria. Consciously or unconsciously, you defined various criteria that led you to the overall evaluation that Kristen was a cool roommate.

"Just measuring your job performance..."

Dave Carpenter/www.cartoonstock.com

Of course, we don't always make the same decisions. For instance, you may have another roommate, Sarah, who doesn't think Kristen is cool at all. Often, when we disagree in this way, it is because we have different criteria. Different judgments may be involved in determining whether Sarah thinks someone is cool versus whether you think someone is cool. For example, Sarah may think it's important to be involved in community service, which Kristen isn't. In other words, you and Sarah come to different conclusions about Kristen because you are using different criteria. At other times, however, we disagree about things not because our criteria differ but because we evaluate people and things differently on the basis of those criteria. When movie critics disagree about a movie, the disagreement is often based not on different criteria but on how the same criteria are evaluated. For instance, one may think the movie is good because the characters are believable, and the other may think the movie is bad because the characters aren't at all believable. Character believability is an important criterion for both reviewers, but their perceptions about the extent to which the movie scores high on this criterion differ, resulting in different evaluations of the film.

In I/O psychology, criteria are defined as evaluative standards that can be used as yardsticks for measuring employees' success or failure. We rely on them not only for appraising employees' performance but also for evaluating our training program, validating our selection battery, and making layoff and promotion decisions. Therefore, if we have faulty criteria, these HR functions would be flawed as well because they depend directly on the adequacy of the criteria. For instance, it seems reasonable to fire an employee because she is not performing at an acceptable level on the performance criterion. However, if that performance criterion is not a good measure of job performance, there is the potential for making a huge mistake by firing someone who may actually be a good worker. In such cases, we leave ourselves vulnerable to lawsuits

**criteria**
Evaluative standards that can be used as yardsticks for measuring an employee's success or failure.

TECHNICAL TIP

*In Chapter 2, we talked a bit about interrater reliability, which is the consistency with which multiple judges evaluate the same thing. This is an example of low interrater reliability because the judges—two movie critics, in this case—don't see the movie similarly.*

**performance**
Actual on-the-job behaviors that are relevant to the organization's goals.

**ultimate criterion**
A theoretical construct encompassing all performance aspects that define success on the job.

(we'll talk about legal issues in the workplace in Chapters 5 and 7). Because key organizational decisions will be made directly on the basis of criteria, organizations need to be sure that these yardsticks are measuring the right thing and measuring it well.

In general, the criterion in which I/O psychologists are most interested is **performance**, which can be defined as actual on-the-job behaviors that are relevant to the organization's goals. Performance is the reason that organizations are interested in hiring competent employees.

Throughout this chapter, I will use the terms *criterion*, *performance*, and *performance criterion* interchangeably.

## Ultimate Criterion

The **ultimate criterion** encompasses all aspects of performance that define success on the job. R. L. Thorndike (1949) discussed this very notion in his classic text *Personnel Selection*, arguing that the ultimate criterion is very complex and not even accessible to us. What he meant is that the ultimate criterion is something we can shoot for, but in actuality we can never completely define and measure every aspect of performance. Doing so would require time and details that simply are not available. As an example, let's say we're interested in defining the ultimate criterion for an administrative assistant's job. Toward that end, we might generate the following list:

- Typing speed
- Typing quality
- Filing efficiency
- Interactions with clients
- Interactions with coworkers
- Creativity
- Written communication
- Oral communication
- Procedural adherence
- Computer skills
- Interactions with supervisors
- Punctuality
- Initiative

This appears to be a fairly complete list, but when I asked two administrative assistants in our psychology department office if they had any to add, they came up with quite a few more that I hadn't thought of, including organizational skills. My guess is that if I gave this list to additional people, they would come up with still other dimensions or subcriteria. The point here is that merely listing all the criteria that define success on the job is difficult enough; *measuring* all of them would be virtually impossible. Thus, the ultimate criterion is a theoretical construct that we develop as a guide or a goal to shoot for in measuring job success.

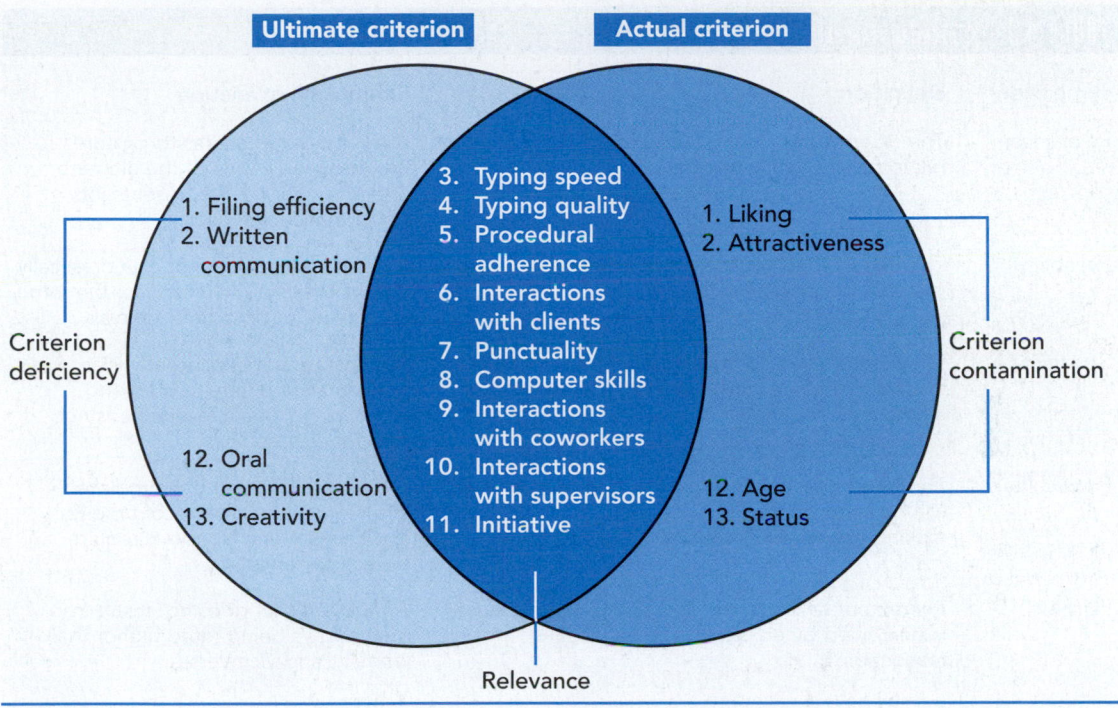

**FIGURE 4.1**  Criterion Properties

## Actual Criterion

The **actual criterion** is our best real-world representation of the ultimate criterion, and we develop it to reflect or overlap with the ultimate criterion as much as possible. **Figure 4.1** illustrates this concept with respect to the administrative assistant job that we discussed earlier. Because we cannot possibly measure every facet of performance that we think is involved in the administrative assistant job and probably could not list everything that would indicate someone's success on the job, we consider only those elements that seem most important and that are most easily measured. Again, as applied psychologists, we need to keep practical issues in mind; we do this by thinking about the time, effort, and cost associated with measuring the different elements of the criteria involved because these are of great importance to the company with which we are working. In a perfect world, everything that is listed as being a part of the ultimate criterion would be included in the actual criterion, but typically this isn't possible. Thus, our actual criterion includes only those elements of the ultimate criterion that we intend to measure.

**actual criterion**
Our best real-world representative of the ultimate criterion, which we develop to reflect or overlap with the ultimate criterion as much as possible.

## Criteria for the Criteria

In this section, we focus on what makes a good criterion. There are many lists of dimensions along which criteria can be evaluated. One of the earliest of these lists

| TABLE 4.1 | Criteria for the Criteria | |
|---|---|---|
| **Dimension** | **Definition** | **Example/Explanation** |
| Relevance | The extent to which the actual criterion measure is related to the ultimate criterion | A measure that seems to capture the major elements of the ultimate criterion; that is, it represents job performance very well |
| Reliability | The extent to which the actual criterion measure is stable or consistent | A measure that does not give drastically different results when used for the same employees at close time intervals |
| Sensitivity | The extent to which the actual criterion measure can discriminate among effective and ineffective employees | A measure that consistently identifies performance differences among employees; that is, everyone is not rated the same |
| Practicality | The degree to which the actual criterion can and will be used by those whose job it is to use it for making important decisions | A measure that can be completed in a reasonable amount of time by a supervisor and does not require excess paperwork |
| Fairness | The extent to which the actual criterion measure is perceived by employees to be just and reasonable | A measure that does not result in men always being rated higher than women, and vice versa |

features 15 dimensions (Blum & Naylor, 1968). In a classic book, John Bernardin and Dick Beatty (1984) delineate more than 25 characteristics that have been examined as yardsticks for measuring the effectiveness of criteria. For our purposes here, I will highlight what I think are the five most fundamental of these criteria for the criteria (see **Table 4.1** for a summary).

**Relevance** The crucial requirement for any criterion is *relevance*, or the degree to which the actual criterion is related to the ultimate criterion. Relevance reflects the degree of correlation or overlap between the actual and ultimate criteria. In a more technical, statistical sense, relevance is the percentage of variance in the ultimate criterion that can be accounted for by the actual criterion. In other words, variance in this context is an index of how much people differ in their ultimate criterion scores. We would like to see as much overlap between the ultimate criterion and the actual criterion as is practical to achieve. Look at Figure 4.1 and note the nine dimensions in the intersection of the ultimate criterion and the actual criterion. These constitute relevance. The overlap itself thus represents the portion of the ultimate criterion that is tapped by our actual criterion. We want this portion of the Venn diagram to be as large as possible, indicating that our actual criterion mirrors the ultimate criterion fairly well. Relevance in this sense is analogous to validity.

**TECHNICAL TIP**

*Recall that in Chapter 2, construct validity was defined as the extent to which a test measures the underlying construct that it is intended to measure.*

Two conditions can limit the relevance of a criterion. The first is **criterion deficiency**, which refers to dimensions in the ultimate measure that are not part of the actual measure. A criterion is deficient if a major source of variance in the ultimate criterion is not included in the actual criterion. We want this part of the Venn diagram to be very small. Figure 4.1 shows the criterion deficiency as a list of dimensions that are in the ultimate criterion but are not part of our actual measure—namely, filing efficiency, written communication, oral communication, and creativity. Our criterion is deficient to the extent that these dimensions are not tapped by our criterion measure but are important to the criterion construct. If these particular dimensions are not terribly important to the criterion construct, then our criterion is not very deficient; but, if they are important, then we may have a problem with criterion deficiency.

The second condition that can limit the relevance of a criterion is **criterion contamination**, which refers to those things measured by the actual criterion that are not part of the ultimate criterion. This is the part of the actual criterion variance that is not part of the ultimate criterion variance. Criterion contamination occurs in two ways. First, it can be caused simply by random measurement *error.* No matter how carefully we develop a precise and accurate measurement, there is always some error in that measurement—unreliability. This measurement error is random in the sense that it tends to even itself out over time, but any single performance measurement may not reflect true performance. For instance, we might measure performance every six months for two years and find that there are some differences in our four performance measurements, even though true performance (i.e., the ultimate criterion) may not have changed.

The second cause of criterion contamination, *bias*, is more troubling given its systematic rather than random nature. Bias is most prevalent when the criteria of interest are judgments made by individuals. It is not unusual for raters to allow their biases to color their performance ratings. For instance, bias would result in criterion contamination if an evaluator, when rating administrative assistants on the dimension of organizational skills, gave a higher rating to those she liked or to those who were more attractive, regardless of actual performance levels. (Two additional examples, age and status, are listed in Figure 4.1.) Sometimes this is done on purpose, while at other times it is unconscious; we will discuss both instances of bias in more detail in the next chapter.

Criterion contamination occurs when the measure of the actual criterion reflects things other than what it should measure according to the ultimate criterion. When we are talking about criteria, a criterion is contaminated if it measures something other than what it is intended to measure, such as likability or attractiveness. Contamination is often a problem in the context of performance ratings, which we will discuss at length in the next chapter.

**Reliability** Although unreliability was mentioned as a potential cause of criterion contamination, its opposite—reliability—is important enough to be listed as a criterion itself. As discussed in Chapter 2, reliability refers to the stability or consistency of a measure. Indeed, an unreliable criterion is not very

**criterion deficiency**
A condition in which dimensions in the ultimate measure are not part of or are not captured by the actual measure.

**criterion contamination**
A condition in which things measured by the actual criterion are not part of the ultimate criterion.

**TECHNICAL TIP**

*In Chapter 2, we defined reliability as consistency or stability in measurement, but unreliability is always present to some degree because we can't measure these kinds of things perfectly.*

Image Source/Getty Images

**A CLOSER LOOK**
Your company has only one opening available for a new technical support staff member. On paper, all the candidates in this photo meet the criteria for the job. Can you think of other characteristics individuals might use in choosing which candidate to hire?

useful. For instance, suppose that we measured an administrative assistant's typing speed on six successive occasions and found that he typed at 50, 110, 40, 100, 60, and 45 words per minute. Such variability in the criterion measure would lead me to conclude that this particular measure is unreliable. When a measure is unreliable, we can't confidently use it in making important decisions. Another way to conceptualize the situation is to ask if this administrative assistant is a fast typist, as the 110 and 100 words per minute might indicate, or a below-average typist, as the 40 and 45 words per minute might indicate. Because the criterion is unreliable, we simply don't know—and the criterion is thus not useful.

**Sensitivity** A criterion must be *sensitive* enough to discriminate among effective and ineffective employees. If everyone is evaluated similarly according to the criterion, then it is not very useful. Suppose Goodyear wants to make a series of promotion decisions based on a performance criterion consisting of the number of tire valves produced by each employee in an eight-hour shift. At first glance, this seems a reasonable criterion; but on closer examination, we find that all 100 employees produce between 22 and 24 tire valves per eight-hour shift. In short, there doesn't appear to be much variability in the performance of these 100 employees on this criterion. The criterion isn't sensitive enough to discriminate between effective and ineffective performers, so Goodyear could not reasonably make promotion decisions based on it. (After all, would it make sense to promote those employees who produce 24 tire valves over those who produce 23?)

Yet there are probably other criteria in this situation that *could* distinguish among the employees. Can you think of any? The first one that comes to my mind is quality. Although all 100 employees produce about the same number of tire valves, there may be some serious differences in the quality of these valves. A second criterion, and one that may be even more sensitive, is the amount of waste each employee leaves behind after producing tire valves. Quite a few other alternative measures would work as well. Every situation is different, of course—but the bottom line is that I/O psychologists work hard to develop sensitive criteria so that confidence can be placed in the criteria on which decisions are based.

**Practicality** I have alluded to the importance of practical issues throughout the book thus far, but here the concept of practicality is tied more directly to organizational functioning. *Practicality* refers to the extent to which a criterion can and will be used by individuals making important decisions. Consider the following example. Let's say I spend an extraordinary amount of time conducting a thorough job analysis using the Common-Metric Questionnaire. Then I develop a set of relevant and reliable criteria that have hardly any criterion deficiency or contamination. But there is one problem: The organization's employees choose not to use the criteria on the grounds that they are too difficult to measure and too abstract to be useful. My error here was that I neglected to consider the usefulness or practicality of the measures and failed to work with the organization's management and other employees in the development process. Indeed, criteria must always be relatively available, easy to obtain, and acceptable to those who want to use them for personnel decisions.

**Fairness** The last element in my list of criteria for the criteria is *fairness*—in other words, the extent to which the employees perceive the criteria to be just and reasonable. Whereas relevance (along with the interplay of deficiency and contamination), reliability, and sensitivity are rather technical concepts, fairness and practicality have more to do with the human element involved in the use of criteria. Here, the issue is whether the employees who are being evaluated along certain criterion dimensions think that they are getting a fair shake. A criterion that is viewed by the employees as unfair, inappropriate, or unreasonable will not be well received by these employees. This point, of course, has widespread implications for organizational functioning and interpersonal dynamics. For instance, it has been found that employees' perceptions of justice are linked to important organizational criteria such as turnover intentions and customer satisfaction ratings (Simons & Roberson, 2003).

## THE CRITERION PROBLEM

You might remember from your introductory psychology class that human behavior is determined by multiple causes, such that it is impossible to point to a particular behavior and demonstrate beyond a shadow of a doubt that the behavior was determined by any one particular cause. Similarly, it is impossible to point to any one performance criterion and argue that it is the perfect measure of performance; performance is simply more complicated than that. In other words, performance (the criterion in which organizations, employees, managers, and I/O psychologists are most often interested) usually includes more than one dimension; some performance criteria are suitable for one type of organizational decision, while other criteria are suitable for a different type of organizational decision. Thus, no one performance criterion fits the bill for all organizational purposes. Given these difficulties, the measurement of performance criteria can be quite complicated. We do not have performance criteria entirely figured out any more than we have human behavior entirely figured out, but, just as we can often predict, understand, and explain human behavior, we can develop, use, and understand criteria in the world of work. However, I will use this opportunity related to our discussion of criteria to present two of the most important elements of the criterion problem.

### Multiple Versus Composite Criteria

Most I/O psychologists believe that performance is multifaceted—in other words, that it is made up of more than one dimension. Look back at the list of criteria I presented for the job of administrative assistant; it should be clear that there are many related, as well as potentially unrelated, dimensions of performance for this job. Belief in a multiple-factor model (Campbell, Gasser, & Oswald, 1996)—the view that job performance is composed of multiple criteria—has been common among I/O psychologists for years. However, many experts in the area have noted that studies of criteria-related issues and, especially, examinations of multiple-factor models have been minimal at best (Austin & Villanova, 1992; Campbell, 1990; Campbell, McCloy, Oppler, & Sager, 1993).

Campbell, one of the leaders in this area, has developed an eight-factor model that he suggests should account for performance variance in every job listed in the *Dictionary of Occupational Titles*, or DOT (Campbell, 1990), and now the O★NET. He asserts that although not every dimension will be relevant for every job, every job can be described adequately in terms of a subset of these eight dimensions. (These are listed in **Table 4.2**, along with definitions and examples.) In addition, he

### TABLE 4.2   Campbell's Taxonomy of Performance

| Performance Factor | Definition | Example |
|---|---|---|
| Job-specific task proficiency | Degree to which individual can perform core tasks central to a particular job | An administrative assistant who does word processing |
| Non–job-specific task proficiency | Degree to which individual can perform tasks that are not specific to a particular job | A plumber who handles phone inquiries and sets up appointments to provide estimates for work |
| Written and oral communication tasks | Proficiency with which one can write and speak | A military officer who gives a formal talk to recruits |
| Demonstrating effort | Consistency and persistence in an individual's work effort | A college professor who goes into the office to continue working on her book even though the university is closed due to a winter storm |
| Maintaining personal discipline | Avoidance of negative behaviors such as alcohol abuse, substance abuse, and rule infractions | An off-duty nurse who avoids excessive alcohol in the event that he is needed in an emergency |
| Facilitating peer and team performance | Helping and supporting peers with job problems | A journalist who helps a coworker writing a story meet the deadline |
| Supervision | All the behaviors associated with managing or supervising other employees | A retail store manager who models appropriate behavior, provides fair and timely feedback, and is available to handle the questions of her subordinates |
| Management/ administration | All the behaviors associated with management that are independent of supervision | A plant manager who gets additional resources, sets department goals and objectives, and controls expenditures |

Source: Information from Campbell, 1990.

maintains that three of these dimensions—job-specific task proficiency, demonstrating effort, and maintaining personal discipline—are necessary components of every job. There appears to be some empirical support for the dimensions he suggests (Rojon, McDowall, & Saunders, 2015).

Returning to our administrative assistant example, let's assume that the job has five criteria that are reflective of performance and that each is important and relatively unrelated to the others. Now, when it comes time to hire, promote, fire, lay off, or increase salaries, which criteria will be used to make these decisions? You see, things would be much easier if performance were one-dimensional, because then we could make all these decisions based on the one criterion without any confusion. For instance, if punctuality were the only dimension of performance that mattered, we could easily make hiring and firing decisions based on that one performance dimension. However, because performance is multidimensional, we have to make some tough decisions about which criteria to use or how to combine them for the purposes of HR decisions. This is a part of the criterion problem: Performance is best represented by multiple criteria, but organizations need to make decisions based on one score, number, or combination of these multiple criteria.

There are at least two alternatives for dealing with this criterion issue. Both focus on creating a **composite criterion**, which is a weighted combination of the multiple criteria, resulting in one index of performance. First, if the five criteria are scored on the same scale, they can be combined using equal weighting. Here, they are simply added up to compute one number that represents the performance of each individual. For instance, if each employee is rated on each dimension along a 1–5 point scale, we could simply add these up and promote the person based on the highest computed score. But on what grounds do we base this decision? Does it seem appropriate to take these five dimensions, which are largely unrelated, and just add them up and call it performance? Doing so would seem to take us back to the problem that Campbell pointed out—we often mistakenly assume that performance is a single construct (Campbell et al., 1993) when, in fact, it is not.

A second alternative composite criterion can also be created through unequal weighting, whereby some procedure is employed to weight the criteria differentially. For instance, it might make sense to employ only those criterion dimensions that seem especially relevant for the particular HR decision that needs to be made and to weight them according to their importance so that the overall weights sum to 1 (see **Table 4.3**). Note that the way in which the information is weighted is a value judgment made by the organization and that this decision should be based on the organization's goals and on research conducted by the organization (Campbell, McHenry, & Wise, 1990). Furthermore, the weighting scheme may vary across HR decisions, such that different weights may be employed for making a promotion decision than for making a termination decision about employees.

An example is provided in Table 4.3, which demonstrates how different dimensions might be used depending on the HR decision in question. In this example, the decision to terminate a particular employee would be based largely on such dimensions

**composite criterion**
A weighted combination of multiple criteria that results in a single index of performance.

| | | |
|---|---|---|
| **TABLE 4.3** | **Combining Criterion Dimensions for the Job of Administrative Assistant** | |
| **Criterion Weights for Promotion to Supervisor** | **Criterion Dimension** | **Criterion Weights for Termination Decision** |
| .00 | Punctuality | .30 |
| .20 | Performance quality | .40 |
| .20 | Interpersonal behaviors | .00 |
| .30 | Leadership behaviors | .00 |
| .15 | Computer performance | .20 |
| .15 | Organizational performance | .10 |

as punctuality and performance quality, somewhat on computer performance and organizational performance, and not at all on interpersonal behaviors and leadership behaviors. On the other hand, leadership behaviors and interpersonal behaviors would be much more important for deciding to promote this person into a supervisory position, whereas punctuality would be much less important.

Still, unequal weighting does not remove the concern that we have now created an index that is somewhat illogical. Let's say that we combine one's score on organizational performance with one's score on productivity. What is this index? What should we call it? What is the construct that it really measures? Finally, haven't we lost the very thing that we wanted to capture with our measures, the multidimensionality of performance? You can see that combining multiple criterion dimensions is a tricky business.

Given these complexities and concerns, you might think it best to keep the criteria separate; but, of course, this causes problems for making HR decisions because you need to make that one hire/don't hire, retain/fire, promote/don't promote decision based on some number or score. A classic article suggests that the issue becomes one of *purpose* (Schmidt & Kaplan, 1971). Its authors argue that if psychological understanding is the primary goal, then multiple criteria should be examined in light of predictor variables without combining them into a composite. On the other hand, if the primary goal is decision making with an economic focus, the I/O psychologist should combine the criteria into one measure and use that as an index of economic success. However, the authors also point out that most applied psychologists should use their weighted composite to make hire/don't hire decisions while at the same time using the multiple dimensions to examine how they relate to various predictors, thereby enhancing the psychological understanding of the performance process and adhering to the scientist/practitioner's ideal—whereby both psychological understanding and applied decision making are important.

## PRACTITIONER FORUM

Jamie Thomas

### Deirdre J. Knapp

*PhD, 1984, Bowling Green State University*
*Vice President, Research and Consulting Operations*
*Human Resources Research Organization (HumRRO)*

Early in my career, I was very lucky to play an important role in seminal research on the criterion domain. This work involved dozens of industrial/organizational psychologists across four organizations and included many of the most renowned academics and practitioners in this field (see discussion of Campbell's work earlier in this chapter).

The project was exciting because a wide array of carefully developed criterion measures were administered across the globe to thousands of soldiers in a variety of army occupations (I was in charge of that part of the project!). The measures included written job knowledge tests; hands-on tests of critical job tasks; peer and supervisor ratings of team, technical, and leadership skills; and ratings of behaviors related to indiscipline and getting along with others. Performance indicators were also retrieved from soldiers' military records. This was a historic opportunity to learn about what it means to "perform."

Considerable effort was made to use the data collected in this project to "model" performance. That is, considering all the scores from all the criterion measures, what performance factors surfaced? The answer has since been corroborated in research on civilian occupations. Six performance factors are relevant to most entry-level jobs:

- Job-specific task proficiency
- Non–job-specific task proficiency
- Written and oral communication
- Demonstrating effort
- Maintaining personal discipline
- Facilitating peer and team performance

Supervisory/leadership and management/administration factors emerge at higher-level jobs.

Most organizations are not able to include all the measures used by the army in this project, nor is it always necessary to examine all possible performance outcomes. Organizations conducting validation studies should first think about what performance factors they want to predict, pick selection tests that would be expected to predict those performance factors, and develop one or more criterion measures that assess the performance factors of interest.

I worked on this project first as an employee of the U.S. Army Research Institute for the Behavioral and Social Sciences and then as an employee at HumRRO (it was a 10-year project). I have continued to use the lessons I learned in much of my work. For example, I've worked with quite a few clients who certify or license professionals in various occupations (e.g., veterinary surgeons, law office managers, physical therapists) and who need valid and fair assessments of job skills. I've also continued to work with the U.S. Army to develop, validate, and implement improved selection procedures.

### Applying Your Knowledge

1. How does the army research project outlined here relate to the criterion problem discussed earlier in this chapter?

2. What is the benefit to researchers and practitioners of having this taxonomy of performance?

3. What attempts were made to ensure that the six criteria that emerged from this study were both valid and reliable?

## Dynamic Criteria

The issue of **dynamic criteria**, measures reflecting performance levels that change over time, has been the focus of much debate in I/O psychology (Austin & Villanova, 1992; Steele-Johnson, Osburn, & Pieper, 2000). This notion may seem unimportant, but let's

**dynamic criteria**
Measures reflecting performance levels that change over time.

consider a situation in which an employee performs well for the first 9 months on the job but by the end of 18 months is performing at unacceptable levels. The problem becomes clearer if we consider a selection context in which measures are developed to predict an individual's performance on the job. The measure—say, a measure of intelligence— might predict performance early on in the employee's career (in fact, we believe that it will, which is why we hired the employee based on an intelligence test to begin with), but not over the long haul. In other words, the validity with which our measure predicts job performance deteriorates over time. This, of course, is a big problem for those trying to staff an organization with people who are most likely to be successful on the job. We will address the selection process in greater detail in Chapters 6 and 7, but, for now, just note that the concept of dynamic criteria raises some important issues.

Some I/O psychologists argued that criteria were not really dynamic at all (Barrett, Caldwell, & Alexander, 1985), but this argument was largely refuted by some more recent empirical work (Deadrick, Bennett, & Russell, 1997; Deadrick & Madigan, 1990; Hofmann, Jacobs, & Baratta, 1993) demonstrating that the relative performance of individuals changes over time. In short, the best worker for the first 6 months on the job is sometimes not among the best workers for the next 6 months on the job.

One study demonstrated that National Hockey League players who had become captains of their team (and thus had a new leadership position) also demonstrated significantly better productivity as operationalized by an index of points based on goals and assists (Day, Sin, & Chen, 2004). In other words, performance levels of players (relative levels) changed and appeared to change as a function of new leadership responsibilities. This study was among the first to try to explain dynamic criteria from a motivational/leadership perspective. A more recent study of an entire cohort of European medical students found an interesting relationship between personality variables and GPA scores (Lievens, Ones, & Dilchert, 2009). The results suggested that personality predicts success later in the curriculum much better than it predicts success in classes taken earlier in the curriculum (which tend to be on a more basic level).

The studies cited above certainly suggest that part of "the criterion problem" is reflected in performance changes over time. Predicting performance is all the more difficult when the performance criterion changes. Keep this point in mind when we discuss the various predictors used in the selection of employees in Chapter 6.

## DISTINCTIONS AMONG PERFORMANCE CRITERIA

Among the many different criteria relevant for various jobs are two traditional types of criteria, which I discuss next. After that, I discuss a third criterion type that has received a great deal of attention from I/O psychologists and organizations in the last 20 years—namely, contextual performance.

**objective criteria** Performance measures that are based on counting rather than on subjective judgments or evaluations; sometimes called *hard* or *non-judgmental criteria.*

## Objective Criteria

Objective criteria are taken from organizational records; often based on counting, they are not supposed to involve any subjective judgments or evaluations. They have

| TABLE 4.4 | Examples of Objective Criteria and Measurement |
|---|---|
| **Criteria** | **Measurement Examples** |
| Absence | Number of days absent per year; number of incidents of absence per year |
| Lateness | Number of minutes late per month; number of incidents of lateness per month |
| Turnover | Percentage of employees who leave the organization over a 12-month period |
| Accidents | Number of accidents per year; number of workers' compensation claims per year |
| Grievances | Number of grievances filed per year; number of grievance cases lost per year |
| Productivity | Number of products produced per day; sales volume in dollars per month |
| Counterproductive behaviors | Dollars lost in theft per year; number of unlikely events (e.g., arson) per year without a reasonable explanation |

traditionally been viewed as the "cleanest" criterion measures because they tend not to necessitate making a judgment call about an employee's performance. Objective criteria are also sometimes called *hard* or *nonjudgmental criteria*, reflecting the belief that they are somehow more solid and believable than other types. **Table 4.4** presents some examples of often-used objective criteria.

Some types of objective criteria are relevant for many different jobs. (These will be discussed in more detail in Chapter 11 when we examine common outcomes of job-related attitudes.) For instance, *absenteeism rate* is often deemed an important criterion by organizations. Related criteria include *turnover rates* and *lateness rates*, which are also used by organizations to evaluate employees and organizational efficiency. Turnover is interesting because, although it generally costs organizations a great deal of money, it can be beneficial to the extent that it involves the replacement of low performers with potentially better performers. Probably the most typical objective criterion is *productivity*, which is usually measured in terms of the number of acceptable products produced in a given time period. This criterion is commonly used in manufacturing plants and assembly lines, where individuals or groups of employees can be evaluated according to how many cars are produced, how many computers are assembled, and so on.

Nonmanagerial jobs lend themselves to objective criteria, but managerial and other higher-level jobs do not. One reason is that most managerial jobs are not based solely on a 40-hour workweek during which the manager punches a time clock; another is that these jobs are not directly linked to a particular item that was produced. Nor are objective criteria appropriate for evaluating college professors, physicians, real estate agents, attorneys, and restaurant managers—with perhaps two exceptions: grievances and counterproductive behavior. The number of *grievances* is a measure of the number of times others have filed complaints about a particular manager. *Counterproductive behavior* is a term that refers to actions, such as theft and sabotage, that reflect the intent to harm the organization in some way.

You may have noted that when I defined objective criteria, I said that these criteria are "not supposed" to require any judgment by others. Indeed, we describe these criteria as objective, and for the most part they are, but they're not completely objective. For instance, a manager can record an employee's absence as being excused, he can record it as being unexcused, or he can fail to record it at all.

On average, objective criteria tend to involve less judgment than do subjective criteria (which we will turn to next). But we need to realize that subjectivity can come into play in virtually all measures of performance. Furthermore, objective criteria can be limited by unexpected factors or situational constraints. For instance, a production employee may not produce at her usual level because her machine has been malfunctioning frequently, thus slowing down her production. The objective criterion would not likely take this into account, but a supervisor could consider it in rating her performance. Performance ratings are typically considered subjective measures of performance, but the subjectivity in this instance is probably a good thing.

## Subjective Criteria

**subjective criteria**
Performance measures that are based on the judgments or evaluations of others rather than on objective measures such as counting; sometimes called *soft* or *judgmental criteria*.

**Subjective criteria** are performance measures that are based on the judgments or evaluations of others rather than on counting. Most published studies on criteria deal with subjective criteria, also called *soft* or *judgmental criteria*. Typical subjective criteria include ratings or rankings of employees by other employees, such as supervisors, coworkers, and subordinates. Of course, these kinds of measures are much more likely to be affected by the biases, attitudes, and beliefs of the raters than are the more objective criteria. On the other hand, they can be an excellent alternative to objective criteria for jobs in which objective criteria don't exist or are insufficient (as in the evaluations of managers). A recent meta-analysis examined the role played by the type of criterion used (subjective versus objective) in assessing the relationship between information sharing among team members and team performance (Mesmer-Magnus & DeChurch, 2009). The researchers found a stronger relationship between information sharing and performance when performance was defined by a behavioral (subjective) measure, such as how much effort was put forth; they argued that this is because the behaviors were more under the control of the team members than were results-oriented (objective) measures, such as sales or profit. As this study suggested, research results can vary as a function of the type of criterion used. As you will see in the

### TECHNICAL TIP

When we talked about correlations in Chapter 2, we said the correlation coefficient was an index of magnitude or strength of relationship. In this example, you can see that magnitude differences can be driven by various factors, such as elements of measurement.

next chapter, we tend to rely largely on subjective criteria, although we may work very hard to make them as objective as possible.

## Contextual Performance

Important work in the area of contextual performance has attempted to expand the criterion domain to include more than just the traditional task performance criteria (Borman, 2004). **Task performance** encompasses the work-related activities performed by employees that contribute to the technical core (what is the actual product, what gets done on the job) of the organization (Borman & Motowidlo, 1997), while **contextual performance** encompasses the activities performed by employees that help to maintain the broader organizational, social, and psychological environment in which the technical core operates (Motowidlo, Borman, & Schmit, 1997). Slightly different renditions of the concept known as contextual performance are *organizational citizenship behaviors (OCBs)* and *prosocial organizational behaviors (POBs)* (Borman & Motowidlo, 1997).

Up to this point, we've focused largely on task performance. An administrative assistant is rated high on task performance if he types quickly and answers phones efficiently, but he is rated high on contextual performance (OCBs or POBs) if he demonstrates enthusiasm, helps his coworker with a problem that she may be having, and works hard to support his organization. Perhaps we can view the basic distinction as one between what is required in the way of on-the-job behaviors (task performance) and other behaviors that are specifically of value to one's workplace and coworkers (contextual performance). I think of contextual behaviors as reflective of employees who go that extra mile rather than putting forth only what is required or expected of them.

There are many different categorical schemes for the dimensions of contextual performance. One such scheme divides these multiple dimensions into five categories (Borman & Motowidlo, 1997). The first pertains to individuals who work with extra enthusiasm and effort to get their jobs done; the second, to those who volunteer to do things that aren't formally part of their jobs, sometimes taking on extra responsibility in the process; the third, to those who help others with their jobs (reflecting what some researchers call sportsmanship or organizational courtesy); the fourth, to those who meet deadlines and comply with all the organization's rules and regulations (reflecting civic virtue or conscientiousness); and the fifth, to those who support or defend the organization for which they work (as when they stay with the organization through hard times or "sell" the organization to others).

Researchers have done extensive work on contextual performance, differentiating it from task performance and arguing for its inclusion in the domain of performance criteria (Hoffman, Blair, Meriac, & Woehr, 2007). They suggest three major distinctions between task performance and contextual performance. First, task activities vary a great deal across jobs (think of the job descriptions for a plumber and for a musician), but contextual behaviors tend to be similar across jobs (a plumber can help a colleague just as much as a musician can). Second, compared with contextual

**task performance**
The work-related activities performed by employees that contribute to the technical core of the organization.

**contextual performance**
Activities performed by employees that help to maintain the broader organizational, social, and psychological environment in which the technical core operates.

activities, task activities are more likely to be formally instituted by the organization as items on a job description or performance appraisal form. Third, task activities have different antecedents. One important study, for example, demonstrated that cognitive ability was more strongly related to sales performance (task activities) than to OCBs such as volunteerism and, similarly, that conscientiousness was more strongly related to OCBs than to sales performance (Hattrup, O'Connell, & Wingate, 1998).

Researchers argue for the inclusion of contextual performance as part of the criterion space, suggesting that these criterion elements can be differentiated from task performance (Podsakoff, Whiting, Podsakoff, & Blume, 2009). Some scholars have begun to propose selection instruments that predict the likelihood of employees exhibiting OCBs (Allen, Facteau, & Facteau, 2004). Recent research has found that individuals make use of their beliefs that applicants are likely to exhibit OCBs in making hiring decisions (Podsakoff, Whiting, Podsakoff, & Mishra, 2011). Participants were shown video clips of applicants answering questions about their tendency and interest in exhibiting OCBs and the results indicated that applicants profiled as high on exhibiting OCBs were rated as better applicants, were rated as more competent, and received higher recommended salaries. Other work has focused on individual difference constructs as predictors of OCBs and for making selection decisions (Chiaburu, Oh, Berry, Li, & Gardner, 2011). This meta-analysis shows consistent and moderate relationships between the Big Five Factors of personality and OCBs. The authors argued that citizenship is especially important for organizational success in contexts that are plagued by limited resources, intense competition, and the need for teamwork. Therefore, using information that predicts citizenship provides an advantage for selection professionals.

Clearly, recent research suggests that the likelihood of contributing to the social and psychological environment of the organization has the potential to play a significant role in selection decisions. Although this work is still in the early stages, it suggests the potential for making hiring decisions based in part on a prediction that certain individuals are more likely to exhibit OCBs than are others.

One framework proposes that OCBs result in favorable relationships among coworkers, which serve as "social capital," and that this capital then affects the organization's performance and effectiveness (Bolino, Turnley, & Bloodgood, 2002). Some scholars have begun to view OCBs as a group-level phenomenon. A recent study of work groups found that relationship conflict and task conflict among group members had negative effects on traditional group task performance; however, task conflict such as disagreements about how best to approach the task increased group-level OCBs and relationship conflict decreased group-level OCBs (Choi & Sy, 2010). However, a recent meta-analysis of 38 studies conducted in the last 15 years that focused on group-level OCBs and performance found a positive relationship between OCBs at the group level, such as group members' ratings of OCBs, and group performance, such as group sales performance or profit margin (Nielsen, Hrivnak, & Shaw, 2009). Furthermore, they reported that group-level OCBs improved social processes (e.g., coordination and communication) within teams. A more recent study took a slightly different approach to examining the relationship between OCBs and organizational effectiveness (Nielsen, Bachrach, Sundstrom, & Halfhill, 2012). In a study of work groups from six different organizations, researchers found OCBs exhibited by organizational work groups were significantly correlated with customers' ratings of the group's performance. The positive correlation indicates that groups that exhibit OCBs are seen by their customers as more effective. This interesting and important effect only held for those groups that were high on task interdependence, which means that the group members relied on each other to complete their work.

You may recall from the historical review of I/O psychology in Chapter 1 that industrial psychology was developed within a measurement framework, resulting in a rather narrow conceptualization of performance as productivity—a measurable outcome. Many now argue, however, that an expansion of the criterion space is more consistent with the modern organization. This more expansive view of performance criteria is illustrated in **Figure 4.2**.

It has become clear with recent research that OCBs are relevant and important across various cultures and international business contexts. For instance, researchers have developed a model of performance criteria for expatriates—employees who are temporarily working and residing in a foreign country. This model includes contextual performance dimensions such as initiative, teamwork, and interpersonal relations (Mol, Born, & van der Molen, 2005). In a Belgian sample, researchers demonstrated that traditional structures or forms of OCBs that have been identified in U.S. samples hold reliably well in this international context (Lievens & Anseel, 2004). However, a recent study of 269 Portuguese men and women working in

**expatriates**
Employees who are temporarily working and residing in a foreign country.

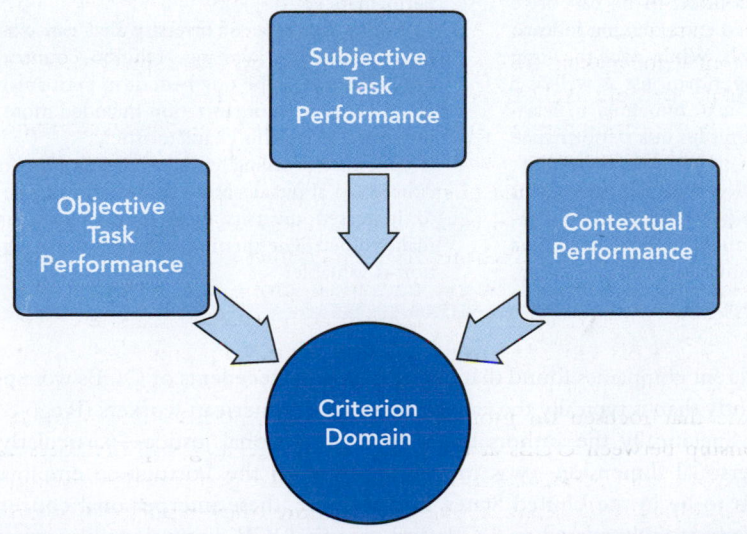

**FIGURE 4.2** Expansion of the Criterion Domain

## I/O TODAY

### Performance and Disability

One of the trickier problems in I/O psychology is known as the *diversity-validity dilemma*—that is, there is sometimes a trade-off between having diversity in an organization, and maximizing performance. There are a variety of reasons why this occurs, but hiring an employee with a disability may provide a good illustration of this dilemma and show why the criterion problem is relevant to this issue.

As you will learn in Chapter 7, employment law indicates that as long as someone can perform the essential components of a job, they are qualified for the job. We also cannot use certain characteristics to discriminate against a qualified worker; disability is one example of these characteristics. Therefore, an individual with a vision impairment could likely be a massage therapist, or someone in a wheelchair could work as a tour guide.

However, along with disabilities come some additional accommodations the organization needs to make, as well as some extra tasks the disabled employee must complete. Take, for example, a tour guide who needs to use a wheelchair. Even though he is qualified for the job, the organization may need to make accommodations for him—perhaps they can only have him lead certain tours that don't involve having to climb stairs. Similarly, this individual may need to receive more training—if the bus he drives uses hand controls so he can drive without foot pedals, he may need extra training to learn how to use these hand controls. While over the long term, this person could likely perform just as well as a nondisabled individual, it may take him time to learn these new tasks, which could limit his task performance in the short term. In addition, if his coworkers don't know how to work with a person with a disability, this can also affect his performance (see Chapter 8 for a review of how diversity training might help his coworkers learn about how to work with him).

As you can see, if we evaluate this employee only on task performance, he may seem like he is underperforming. However, he still might be engaging in valuable performance—he may be a great team member, and he might have some great ideas for the organization, such as how to provide accommodations so that customers with impairments could still enjoy a tour. This example illustrates why it is important for I/O psychologists to help decision-makers understand the other values that come with a diverse workforce, such as better team performance, fewer CWBs, more OCBs, and more robust ideas. I/O psychologists must be thoughtful about defining performance—focusing on only one aspect may lead us to make decisions that reduce the diversity and flexibility in the organization. We must also think carefully and creatively about how to include and support individuals in the workplace, while still ensuring they can do the job well by using training, accommodations, and other tools.

### Discussion Questions

1. Imagine you are in the scenario presented above, and you do notice that your tour guide in the wheelchair has lower task performance than his colleagues. How might you change your criterion for the job? What might be your first steps for addressing his lower task performance?

2. Consider one type of diversity that can exist in an organization (e.g., age, race, religion, country of origin). What might be one benefit in performance that could occur if an organization included more diverse membership on this characteristic?

3. If you were working with an organization that was concerned about decrements in performance related to increased diversity, what arguments might you make to persuade them that diversity in an organization is valuable?

37 different companies found that justice-related antecedents of OCBs were perceived differently than is typically the case among North American workers (Rego & Cunha, 2010). Specifically, the authors found that interactional justice—particularly on the interpersonal dimension—was more important to the Portuguese employees than it tends to be in the United States. Furthermore, these interpersonal concerns were also more strongly related to OCBs and specific OCB dimensions like interpersonal harmony, personal initiative, and conscientiousness than were informational and

distributive justice concerns. The authors argued that these results reflect the fact that Portugal's culture is less assertive, higher on power distance (i.e., it is accepted that power is not shared equally), and more collectivistic (i.e., a focus on the group and loyalty to the group) than that of the United States. As the work of I/O psychologists continues to become more global as a function of the increasing globalization of business and industry, we will likely see additional research with an international focus being conducted.

We have been talking about OCBs as purely positive behaviors; however, some researchers argue that OCBs can actually have negative effects on organizational functioning and the employees exhibiting those behaviors (Bolino & Turnley, 2005; Bolino, Turnley, & Niehoff, 2004). So, the question is whether there are boundary conditions on the positive effects of OCBs. Can focusing too much on OCBs get in the way? The answer appears to be "yes," according to some recent research. In a large study of data from over 3,500 employees, researchers found that time spent on task performance was a better predictor of career outcomes (promotions, salary increases, performance evaluations) than was time spent on OCBs (Bergeron, Shipp, Rosen, & Furst, 2013). Further, they found that, when controlling for time spent on task behavior, there was a zero or negative relationship between time spent on OCBs and outcomes. In other words, it appears that spending too much time on OCBs can get in the way of task performance, but future research is necessary to begin considering what "too much time on OCBs" looks like.

Another study found a curvilinear relationship between OCBs and task performance (Rapp, Bacharach, & Rapp, 2013). This means that task performance is positively affected by exhibiting OCBs up to a point and then OCBs seem to get in the way—this is more evidence for there being some limits or boundaries to the positive effect of OCBs. Finally, a third paper supports the curvilinear relationship (Rubin, Dierdorff, & Bachrach, 2013), but in a study of 352 employees across various occupations the researchers found that the form of the curvilinear relationship between OCBs and task performance varied as a function of other variables, such as the target of the citizenship behaviors (individual vs. organization), autonomy, and accountability. The bottom line is that there are certainly limits to the positive effects of OCBs and the relationships are more complex than we first realized.

**Counterproductive work behaviors (CWBs)** are considered to fall within contextual performance and include those behaviors that somehow harm or detract from the organization, such as theft, sabotage, abuse of others, and withdrawal behaviors (Spector et al., 2006). That OCBs and CWBs are only moderately negatively correlated and seemingly related to different antecedents suggests that these two constructs are quite different from each other, not just the opposite ends of the same construct (Spector, Bauer, & Fox, 2010; Spector & Fox, 2010). In fact, a couple of studies have suggested that CWBs are more strongly related to organizational and individual performance than are OCBs (Dunlop & Lee, 2004; Rotundo & Sackett, 2002). Not only have researchers reported that not all CWBs stem from the same precursors (Spector et al., 2006), but they have also found that sometimes the same people may exhibit both OCBs and CWBs (Spector et al., 2010).

**counterproductive work behaviors (CWBs)** Any behaviors that bring, or are intended to bring, harm to an organization, its employees, or its stakeholders.

© Paul Barton/Corbis

Further, a study of university employees concluded that it was possible to help employees reduce their CWBs through feedback (Ilies, Peng, Savani, & Demotakis, 2013). The researchers found that when individuals who were exhibiting high levels of CWBs were told that their behaviors were undesirable and had negative implications for the organization, these employees reported feeling guilty and rebounded by exhibiting high levels of OCBs. In some way, it appears, they were trying to make up for their bad behavior.

There has been a good deal of recent research aimed at identifying what leads to CWBs, and some of these studies suggest a strong relationship to stress. For instance, one study surveyed over 650 employees at multiple points in time and found that stressors at one time affected the frequency of CWBs at later times. In addition, the exhibition of CWBs then resulted in more stressors at a later point in time (Meier & Spector, 2013) and, thus, there appears to be a vicious cycle operating here, which could result in seriously negative effects for the individual employee and the organization. This relationship makes studies like the one by Ilies et al. even more important as we continue to uncover ways to reduce CWBs to help both individuals and organizations. Other recent research in this area consistently found that when folks run short of self-regulatory resources (sleep, positive affect, energy, self-efficacy, etc.) they experience hostility, anger, and impulsivity, which often leads to workplace deviance or CWBs (Christian & Ellis, 2011; Gino, Schweitzer, Mead, & Ariely, 2011; Thau & Mitchell, 2010). Some really intriguing research has started to tease apart the effect that workplace deviance has on other members of the workgroup or other coworkers. Finally, there is some evidence that when others are indirectly aware of the workplace deviance of their coworkers or have direct observations of the deviance of their coworkers, they, too, are more likely to exhibit deviance (Ferguson & Barry, 2011). We certainly need more research in this area, but this does suggest that deviant employees can help to create a culture in which their deviance spills over to others who then become more likely to exhibit CWBs.

In expanding the criterion to include contextual performance, we should examine how various predictors are related to the various criterion dimensions. Borman and his colleagues' performance model includes two different performance dimensions (task performance and contextual performance) along with two categories of determinants or predictors of these two performance dimensions (cognitive ability variables and personality variables). They report some empirical support for their notion that personality variables are better predictors of contextual performance and that cognitive ability variables are better predictors of task performance (Motowidlo et al., 1997). Indeed, without looking at *both* dimensions of performance, we would likely have a serious criterion deficiency problem and fail to understand how various predictors map onto the different criteria.

# Summary

Traditionally, I/O psychologists have emphasized predictors at the expense of criteria. But this is less the case now that more and more scientists and practitioners have recognized the great importance of developing valid criteria and understanding their role in organizations. Consistent with this observation is the fact that all the HR functions to be discussed in the remainder of the text depend completely on adequate criteria.

In this chapter, the criterion problem was discussed at length and identified as a potential stumbling block to advancing research in I/O psychology. The measurement of performance criteria is as complex as it is important, which is why we speak of the criterion problem. Nevertheless, we are making progress in the process of presenting generally accepted definitions of criteria, examples of criteria, and evaluative standards for criteria, such as relevance, reliability, sensitivity, practicality, and fairness. The ultimate criterion and the actual criterion were defined and discussed, and the traditional view of criteria was explained in detail; also discussed were more recent concerns about the impression that this view can give about the nature of criteria. An actual criterion that does not cover a representative sample of the ultimate criterion was described as deficient, and one that measures things other than what is in the ultimate criterion was described as contaminated.

In discussing the criterion problem, I highlighted two major issues that contribute to that problem. First, I considered the debate regarding multiple criteria versus a composite criterion and suggested that even though, from an applied perspective, a decision needs to be made based on some score or number, the variety of information that comes from using multiple criteria must not be ignored. Performance is surely multidimensional, and multiple criteria are needed to measure it well. Campbell's work in the area of performance modeling and approaches to criteria was highlighted as providing a model for how to proceed in this arena (Campbell, 1990; Campbell et al., 1993). Second, I presented the common belief that criteria are dynamic. This belief is reflected in the relative changes in an individual's performance over time; issues of measurement and prediction were also considered in this context.

Finally, I examined the differences between objective and subjective criteria while considering various examples of each (e.g., measures of productivity, absenteeism, and lateness), as well as supervisor ratings of employees' performance. (The latter are discussed in the next chapter.) In addition, I presented a newer component of performance criteria called contextual performance and considered a great deal of recent research in this area identifying the various antecedents of contextual performance and considering this new line of work within an international context. Lastly, counterproductive work behaviors were also discussed as behaviors that have a negative impact on the organization and other employees. This discussion identified both antecedents of CWBs and their relationships with other organizational behaviors and potential spillover to other coworkers.

## Key Terms

actual criterion (p. 103)

composite criterion (p. 109)

contextual performance (p. 115)

counterproductive work behaviors
   (CWBs) (p. 119)

criteria (p. 101)

criterion contamination (p. 105)

criterion deficiency (p. 105)

dynamic criteria (p. 111)

expatriates (p. 117)

objective criteria (p. 112)

performance (p. 102)

subjective criteria (p. 114)

task performance (p. 115)

ultimate criterion (p. 102)

## TAKING IT TO THE FIELD

Measuring performance is a particularly challenging issue in I/O psychology. It can be especially challenging for jobs where it is difficult to determine exactly what should be measured and whether a measured criterion truly assesses performance. Even seasoned I/O psychologists wrestle with this issue from time to time.

Below is an e-mail from a client presenting you with some challenges related to defining and measuring criteria. Stacia Mattson, who works in the HR department at Collini's Gardening Service, is having some problems. Read the e-mail, and provide critiques and suggestions for Stacia.

Greetings—

Thank you for agreeing to advise me on some tricky issues we've been having at Collini's Gardening Service. We have about 30 gardeners working throughout several regions in Georgia. Currently, we are trying to devise a way to evaluate our gardeners so that we can give our top performers year-end bonuses. Right now, we are considering using the following measures of performance:

- Number of plants that die under the gardener's care for the year

- Number of houses the gardener visits per week

- Satisfaction ratings from the gardener's customers

Could you please critique these measures? In addition, do you have three more suggestions for how we might assess gardener performance that I can bring to my committee as potential options?

Regards,
Stacia

## Critical Thinking Questions

1. Overall criteria are standards used to assess performance. In addition to grades, what are some criteria that could be used to assess the performance of college students? What does *performance* mean for a college student?

2. We know from the text that the ultimate criterion is theoretical, whereas the actual criterion is our best attempt at capturing the ultimate criterion. What are some implications of having *little* overlap (relevance) between an ultimate criterion and

an actual criterion? What would this mean for an organization that is trying to assess the performance of its employees?

3. In this chapter, the author argues that many aspects of performance are dynamic. How could this notion of dynamic criteria be applied to assessing the performance of college students? Have you seen any examples of this at your institution?

4. The evaluation of subjective—as opposed to objective—criteria includes some degree of human judgment. As a result, the evaluation of subjective criteria can be prone to the evaluator's own attitudes and biases. What are some examples of subjective criteria? How might an evaluator's attitudes influence his or her assessment of an employee's performance?

5. Research suggests that coworkers appreciate those colleagues who engage in OCBs. However, research also suggests that engaging in *too many* OCBs can damage task performance. What are some examples of where performing OCBs prevents task performance? What can employers do to encourage their employees to find an appropriate balance between task performance and OCBs?

## Application Questions

1. Consider some of the ways your performance as a student is evaluated (e.g., exams, papers, projects). What might be some examples of criterion deficiency (i.e., what are some aspects of student performance that are not well assessed using these types of measures)? What might be some examples of criterion contamination (i.e., what are some aspects students might be judged on that are not relevant to student performance)?

2. In the United States, there is a great deal of debate about how to distinguish good teachers from poor teachers in public schools. Some people advocate using student scores on standardized tests to determine which teachers are doing well. Other people advocate using student ratings of teachers. What are some pros and cons of each approach?

3. What are some examples of contextual performance that you might have engaged in at your job or in your classes? When were you most likely to perform those behaviors? Did they ever get in the way of your task performance?

4. Imagine that you have a subordinate who has shared something negative about one of his clients using social media (e.g., on Twitter or Facebook). Do you believe this behavior is a part of performance that should be considered during his performance review? Why or why not?

## Suggested Readings

Austin, J. T., & Villanova, P. D. (1992). The criterion problem: 1917–1992. *Journal of Applied Psychology, 77,* 836–874. This is the most thorough published review on the historical use of criteria in organizations. The article contains a great deal of valuable information, but it isn't an easy read.

**Campbell, J. P.** (1990). Modeling the performance prediction problem in industrial and organizational psychology. In M. D. Dunnette & L. M. Hough (Eds.), *Handbook of industrial and organizational psychology* (2nd ed., Vol. 1, pp. 687–732). Palo Alto, CA: Consulting Psychologists Press. This presentation of Campbell's work on modeling performance provides a good overview of his theoretical ideas, along with some empirical findings.

**Lievens, F., Buyse, T., & Sackett, P. R.** (2005). The operational validity of a video-based situational judgment test for medical college admissions: Illustrating the importance of matching predictor and criterion construct domains. *Journal of Applied Psychology, 90*(3), 442–452. As part of a trend to incorporate other criteria into the admissions process for medical schools, this study examines the use of noncognitive criteria, such as interpersonal skills.

**Penney, L. M. & Spector, P. E.** (2008). Emotions and counterproductive work behavior. In N. M. Ashkanasy & C. L. Cooper (Eds.), *Research companion to emotions in organizations* (pp. 183–196). Northhampton, MA: Edward Elgar Publishing. This chapter provides an outstanding overview of counterproductive work behavior and especially focuses on the antecedents leading to counterproductive behaviors. There are many engaging chapters in this book on other topics as well.

**Podsakoff, N. P, Whiting, S. W., Podsakoff, P. M., & Blume, B. D.** (2009). Individual- and organizational-level consequences of organizational citizenship behaviors: A meta-analysis. *Journal of Applied Psychology*, 94(1), 122–141. This recent quantitative summary of the research related to organizational citizenship behaviors is written by some of the leaders in the field.

**Rubin, R. S., Dierdorff, E. C., & Bachrach, D. G.** (2013). Boundaries of citizenship behavior: Curvilinearity and context in the citizenship and task performance relationship. *Personnel Psychology, 66*, 377–406. A clear and interesting look at where OCBs can become part of the problem rather than the solution. More and more research is moving in this direction, and this empirical paper does a very nice job outlining the issues and presenting some important and striking results.

**Schmidt, F. L., & Kaplan, L. B.** (1971). Composite v. multiple criteria: A review and resolution of the controversy. *Personnel Psychology, 24*, 419–434. This article provides a detailed and critical examination of the debate about using composite versus multiple criteria for measuring success.

# Performance Appraisal

Photo: Ragnar Schmuck/Getty Images

This chapter should help you understand:

- The purposes of performance appraisal
- The various formats used in the evaluation of performance
- The effect of rating errors on the appraisal process
- How the broader context in which performance appraisal takes place has various and diverse implications for performance appraisal and organizational functioning
- The role of employee development in the performance management process
- The important role played by legal issues in the performance appraisal process
- The complexities involved in giving and receiving performance feedback

The process of evaluating employees' performance—performance appraisal—is the focus of this chapter. Having our performance appraised is something we've all experienced at one time or another. Of course, we may not have fond memories of our fathers telling us that we didn't weed the vegetable garden well enough or of our Psychology 100 professor telling us that our test scores so far gave us only a C in the course. The types of performance appraisal just described are examples of negative appraisals. But sometimes we did a nice job mowing the lawn or writing a term paper—instances in which we probably received positive appraisals.

There are many domains in which we are held accountable for our performance, but in this chapter we will talk specifically about the role of performance appraisal in organizational life—in which it plays a very important role indeed. In this domain, **performance appraisal** is defined as the systematic review and evaluation of job performance, as well as the provision of performance feedback. However, as you'll soon see, performance appraisal is a lot more interesting than that definition makes it sound.

**performance appraisal**
Systematic review and evaluation of job performance.

## USES OF PERFORMANCE APPRAISAL

Performance appraisal is one of the most important processes conducted in organizations. It has many purposes, of which the three most significant are discussed here. First, performance appraisals are used to make important *personnel decisions,* such as who gets promoted, fired, demoted, or laid off; who gets a large raise, a small raise, or no raise at all; and so on. In efficient organizations, these decisions are not made haphazardly; they are made on the basis of performance appraisal data.

Second, performance appraisals are used for *developmental purposes.* Employees are informed of their performance strengths and weaknesses so that they can be proud of what they are doing well and can focus their efforts on the areas that need some work. On the whole, organizations benefit when employees perform better, and performance appraisal data are used to help employees become better performers. In addition, organizations are interested in seeing their employees advance within the company to other important jobs—an outcome that performance appraisal can facilitate. For example, an employee may be told that she needs to improve her interpersonal skills so that she will be eligible when the next promotion becomes available.

A third purpose of performance appraisal is what I'll call *documentation* of organizational decisions—a purpose that has recently evolved out of personnel decisions and the growing area of personnel law. Now that companies are very aware of the possibility of being sued over personnel business decisions, managers are increasingly using performance appraisals to document employees' performance patterns over time. In cases in which employees are fired for inadequate performance, the organization—if it has kept careful track—can point to detailed accounts of the employees' inferior performance, making it difficult for them to claim that they were fired without just cause. (We will discuss legal issues in performance appraisal later in this chapter.)

On the other hand, performance appraisals that are not carefully developed and implemented can have negative repercussions for both the organization and its employees. For instance, a poorly conceived appraisal system could get the wrong person promoted, transferred, or fired. It could cause feelings of inequity on the part of good employees who erroneously receive smaller raises than bad employees. It could lead to lawsuits in which the company has a very weak defense for why a particular individual was not promoted. Also, it could result in disgruntled employees who decrease their effort, ignore the feedback, or look for other jobs. Even customers are poorly served when an ineffective appraisal system causes employees to operate at less than their peak level of efficiency. Indeed, an ineffective performance appraisal system has widespread implications for everyone involved with the organization, which is why performance appraisal has received so much research attention (for reviews, see Levy & Williams, 2004; Murphy & Cleveland, 1995). A good performance appraisal system is well received by ratees, is based on carefully documented behaviors, is focused on important performance criteria, is inclusive of many perspectives, and is forward looking with a focus on improvement.

"It's one of the advantages of having your own business."

Thomas Bros./Cartoonstock.com

**A CLOSER LOOK**
Performance can be measured in many different ways. How has your performance been measured or recognized in any jobs that you've had, and what made that process useful for you?

# THE ROLE OF I/O PSYCHOLOGY IN PERFORMANCE APPRAISAL

**performance management**
A system of individual performance improvement that typically includes (1) objective goal setting, (2) continuous coaching and feedback, (3) performance appraisal, and (4) development planning.

**coaching**
One-on-one collaborative relationship in which an individual provides performance-related guidance to an employee.

I/O psychologists play a significant role in the area of performance appraisal. They are often hired to help develop and implement performance appraisal systems. I/O psychologists have measurement expertise, as well as a background in both human resources and organizational psychology—areas of knowledge that are integral to successful performance appraisals. Many companies have I/O psychologists in their HR departments who are responsible for what is known as **performance management**, a motivational system of individual performance improvement (DeNisi & Pritchard, 2006). This system typically includes (1) objective goal setting, (2) continuous **coaching** and feedback, (3) performance appraisal, and (4) developmental planning. The key points here are twofold: These four components are linked to the company's goals and objectives, and the system is implemented on a continuous cycle rather than just once per year. Some research has proposed that when an organization is profitable, it is typically more willing to reinvest in human resource practices like performance management, which then impacts employees, supervisors, and the organization itself (den Hartog, Boselie, & Paauwe, 2004). Remember (see Figure 3.1) that performance appraisal stems directly from the job analysis. Performance criteria are identified by the job analysis and used as the central element of the performance appraisal system. Without a careful job analysis, we would likely end up with unimportant or job-irrelevant criteria and appraising performance on the wrong criterion dimensions.

Researchers who specialize in performance appraisal pursue research questions like the following: (1) What is the best format or rating scale for performance appraisals? (2) To what extent do rater errors and biases affect the appraisal process? (3) How should raters be trained so that they can avoid these errors and biases? (4) What major contextual variables affect the appraisal process? (5) How important is the organizational context or culture in the appraisal process? (6) What factors affect how ratees and raters react to performance appraisal? In addition to addressing such questions, I/O psychology, as an empirically based applied discipline, attempts to use basic psychological principles to help organizations develop and implement motivating, fair, accurate, and user-friendly appraisal systems.

## Sources of Performance Ratings

**360-degree feedback**
A method of performance appraisal in which multiple raters at various levels of the organization evaluate a target employee and the employee is provided with feedback from these multiple sources.

Performance feedback can be generated and delivered by various sources. Traditionally, supervisors were charged with conducting the performance appraisal and delivering the performance feedback. This top-down approach continues to be very popular, and it is quite common for an organization to include this type of appraisal as part of the performance management process. However, there are other, more contemporary approaches for the use of feedback sources, with multisource feedback being the most prevalent.

**Multisource Feedback** This method, sometimes called **360-degree feedback** (Fletcher & Baldry, 2015), involves multiple raters at various levels of the organization who evaluate and provide feedback to a target employee. As presented in **Figure 5.1,**

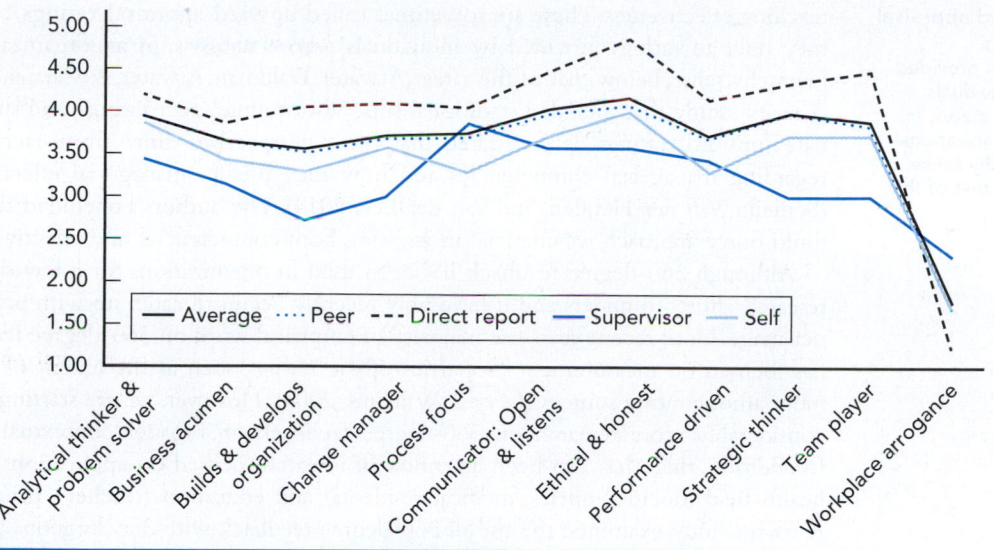

360-Degree Development Report

This sample figure from a 360-degree report shows the scores provided by four raters (and one aggregate score) across eleven "leadership" dimensions on a 5-point scale.
Source: Human Resource Decisions, Inc.

these multiple sources typically include subordinates (or direct reports), peers, supervisors, customers, and clients and even self-ratings. Note the variation that exists between the different raters for each dimension.

These systems are becoming increasingly important to the modern organization in terms of performance assessment and management (Hoffman, Lance, Bynum, & Gentry, 2010). Many companies—such as Home Depot, Procter & Gamble, General Electric, Intel, and Boeing, among others—are using them for a variety of purposes that are consistent with both greater employee expectations and the more sophisticated organizations of the 21st century.

Three basic assumptions are held by advocates of 360-degree feedback systems. First, when multiple raters are used, the participants are happier because they are involved in the process—and this calls to mind the importance of participation alluded to earlier. Second, and perhaps more important, when multiple raters from different levels of the organization rate the same target employee, the idiosyncrasies (and biases) of any single rater are overcome. For instance, if my supervisor doesn't like me and rates me severely for that reason, additional ratings from other individuals that aren't severe should overcome my supervisor's rating and highlight the possibility that there may be a problem with that rating. Third, multiple raters bring with them multiple perspectives on the target employee, allowing for a broader and more accurate view of performance. For instance, universities often require that students rate faculty teaching because it is believed that they have a valuable perspective to share about

**upward appraisal ratings**
Ratings provided by individuals whose status, in an organizational-hierarchy sense, is below that of the ratees.

teaching effectiveness. These are sometimes called **upward appraisal ratings** because they refer to ratings provided by individuals whose status is, in an organizational-hierarchy sense, below that of the ratee (Atwater, Daldman, Atwater, & Cartier, 2000). A recent study that included traditional supervisor ratings, peer ratings, and subordinate (upward) ratings demonstrated that these perspectives differ from each other regarding managerial competencies and how they predict managerial effectiveness (Semeijn, Van der Heijden, and Van der Lee, 2014). The authors concluded that the multisource approach is beneficial in assessing both competencies and effectiveness.

Although 360-degree feedback has been used in organizations for a few decades, research efforts to understand it have only recently begun to catch up with practitioner usage. Until recent years the majority of empirical work on 360-degree feedback has focused on measurement properties of the ratings, such as the extent of agreement among rating sources (Levy & Williams, 2004). However, we are starting to see considerably more research on 360-degree feedback on broader contextual issues. In addition, there has also been an influx of research focused on applications to the health field (doctors, nurses, medical residents) and education (teachers, principals). A recent study examined the use of 360-degree feedback with 385 surgeons (Nurudeen et al., 2015). Results included very high percentages of surgeons reporting that the feedback they received was accurate and reporting that they made changes to their practice as a result of the feedback. Similarly, a large percentage of department heads reported that they believed the feedback provided to their surgeons was accurate. Almost 75% of the participants (raters and ratees) found the process valuable, and over 80% were willing to participate in future 360-degree evaluations. There is even a new app (called Healthcare Supervision Logbook) that allows doctors who are training medical students to provide feedback to the students following a clinical session. The trainees can use the app to provide feedback about the curriculum and training to the doctor trainers (Gray, Hood, & Farrell, 2015). It can also be used to gather patient and peer feedback.

In another recent investigation, this time in the education arena, principals were evaluated with a 360-degree instrument and researchers studied how they reacted to conflicting feedback among sources (Goldring, Mavrogordato, & Haynes, 2015). They found that principals experienced cognitive dissonance (that is, discomfort and tension) when the teacher ratings of their performance were lower than their own ratings of their performance. The authors assert that principals are motivated to reduce the dissonance and that they can do that by either working harder and improving how they do their jobs or by discounting the teacher ratings. The researchers suggest that principals need to be trained in how to receive, evaluate, and use the feedback they are given.

One firm, Human Resource Decision, Inc., employs a 360-degree feedback system that consists of four main tools: (1) a 360-degree development questionnaire, which is administered to multiple rating sources and measures 13 skill dimensions, such as leadership and business acumen; (2) a 360-degree feedback report, which provides the results of the ratings from the various sources, as well as some summary information about ratees' strengths and weaknesses; (3) a development workbook, which helps employees work with and understand the feedback report; and (4) a development guide, which provides suggested readings and activities to improve skills in the targeted areas. This 360-degree system has been used by many companies across a variety of industries.

What does the future hold for 360-degree feedback? Consistent with this chapter's theme of focusing on the social context of appraisal is a list of recommendations to follow for implementing 360-degree feedback: This list includes (1) being honest about how the ratings will be used, (2) helping employees interpret and deal with the ratings, and (3) avoiding the presentation of too much information (DeNisi & Kluger, 2000). The frequency with which it's used in organizations suggests that it will continue to play an important role. Recent research suggests that the following important issues will continue to attract attention: construct validity of ratings, determinants of multisource ratings (such as rating purpose, liking, and personality), and the effect of multisource ratings on employee attitudes and development.

**New Challenges in Telework** Another recent trend in organizations is the increased frequency of telework (see Chapter 11 for information on telework and worker well-being), employees working from home or some other remote location, a practice that is growing rapidly (Golden, Barnes-Farrell, & Mascharka, 2009). This telecommuting results in altered forms of communication. Many employee–employee and employee–supervisor interactions don't take place face-to-face but via e-mails, phone calls, faxes, text messages, conference calls, and so on. This arrangement suggests that supervisors doing performance appraisal must rely on indirect sources of performance information, like gathering information from those who work directly with the employee and reviewing written documentation of work, instead of direct interactions and on-the-job observations. Recent research has demonstrated that when provided with both direct and indirect performance information, supervisors rely more on direct performance information (Golden et al., 2009). Supervisors' tendencies to downplay the indirect information that is frequent in telework suggest potential room for performance appraisal errors and ineffectiveness.

Of course, one important aspect of telecommuting is its relationship with performance. Although there hasn't been a lot of empirical evidence in this area, there is some very recent research. For instance, a survey of 273 supervisor–subordinate dyads found that telecommuting did have a positive effect on performance. The strength of this effect was moderated by various factors, but it's important to note that the effect was never negative (Golden & Gajendran, 2014). That is to say, telecommuting may have a weak or strong positive effect on performance depending on various situational characteristics, but it never has a negative effect. As more evidence of the positive effect of telecommuting on performance, Gajendran, Harrison, and Delaney-Klinger (2015) studied 323 supervisor–subordinate dyads and found that telecommuting was positively associated with both task performance and contextual performance. Further, the effect of telecommuting on performance was strengthened when there was a positive relationship between the subordinate and supervisor. When an employee who experiences a favorable subordinate–supervisor relationship is given the freedom to telecommute, that employee will assume more autonomy, which will be reflected in

**telework**
Working arrangements in which employees enjoy flexibility in work hours and/or location.

Jetta Productions/Blend Images/Getty Images

higher levels of task and contextual performance. For a complete and broad review of telecommuting, I encourage you to read Allen, Golden, and Shockley (2015), who discuss this arrangement from a historical perspective and in terms of a broad array of organizational outcomes.

## Rating Formats

When it comes time for an evaluator to appraise someone's performance, he or she typically uses some type of rating form. There are quite a few options here; in this section, we will discuss the ones most frequently employed.

**Graphic Rating Scales** Graphic rating scales are among the oldest formats used in the evaluation of performance. These scales consist of a number of traits or behaviors (e.g., dependability), and the rater is asked to judge how much of each particular trait the ratee possesses or where on this dimension the ratee falls with respect to organizational expectations. Today, graphic rating scales usually include numerical/verbal anchors at various points along the scale, such as "1/below expectations," "4/meets expectations," and "7/exceeds expectations," and the score is whatever number is circled. Graphic rating scales are commonly used in organizations due, in part, to the ease with which they can be developed and used. **Figure 5.2** provides an example of a graphic rating scale—in this case, one that appraises the extent to which employees are "following procedures."

**Behaviorally Anchored Rating Scales** Behaviorally anchored rating scales, or **BARS** (Smith & Kendall, 1963), are similar to graphic rating scales except that they provide actual behavioral descriptions as anchors along the scale. An example of a 9-point BARS for a nuclear power plant operator's tendency to "follow procedures" is shown in **Figure 5.3**.

BARS are perhaps best known for the painstaking process involved in their development (see Smith & Kendall, 1963). This process can be summarized as taking place in five steps (Bernardin & Beatty, 1984). First, a group of participants—such as employees, supervisors, or subject matter experts (SMEs)—identifies and carefully defines several dimensions as important for the job ("follows procedures," "works in a

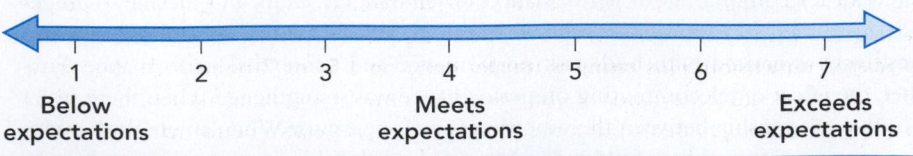

|  |  |  |  |  |  |  |
|---|---|---|---|---|---|---|
| 1 | 2 | 3 | 4 | 5 | 6 | 7 |
| **Below expectations** |  |  | **Meets expectations** |  |  | **Exceeds expectations** |

**FIGURE 5.2** Graphing Rating Scale for "Following Procedures"

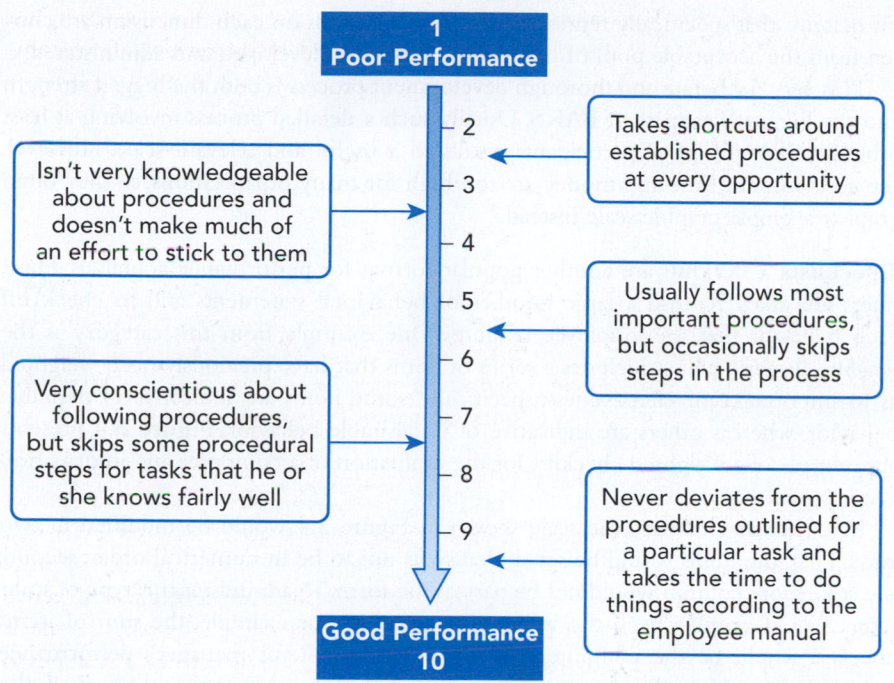

**1**
**Poor Performance**

2

Isn't very knowledgeable about procedures and doesn't make much of an effort to stick to them

3

Takes shortcuts around established procedures at every opportunity

4

5

Usually follows most important procedures, but occasionally skips steps in the process

6

Very conscientious about following procedures, but skips some procedural steps for tasks that he or she knows fairly well

7

8

9

Never deviates from the procedures outlined for a particular task and takes the time to do things according to the employee manual

**Good Performance**
**10**

**FIGURE 5.3**   Behaviorally Anchored Rating Scale for "Following Procedures"

timely manner," etc.). Second, another group of participants generates a series of behavioral examples of job performance (similar to the items in Figure 5.3) for each dimension. These behavioral examples are called **critical incidents**. Participants are encouraged to write critical incidents at high-, medium-, and low-effectiveness levels for each dimension. In Figure 5.3, for example, "Never deviates from the procedures outlined for a particular task and takes the time to do things according to the employee manual" represents high effectiveness, whereas "Takes shortcuts around established procedures at every opportunity" represents low effectiveness.

Third, yet another group of participants is asked to sort these critical incidents into the appropriate dimensions. During this *retranslation* stage, the goal is to make sure that the examples generated for each dimension are unambiguously associated with that dimension. Usually a criterion, such as 80%, is used to weed out items that are not clearly related to a particular dimension: If fewer than 80% of the participants place the critical incident in the correct dimension, the item is dropped. A fourth group of participants then rates each remaining behavioral example on its effectiveness for the associated dimension. This rating is usually done on a 5- or 7-point scale. Any item with a large standard deviation is eliminated because a large standard deviation indicates that some respondents think the item represents effective performance, whereas others think it represents ineffective performance—obviously, a problematic situation.

**critical incidents**
Examples of job performance used in behaviorally anchored rating scales or job-analytic approaches.

Fifth, items that specifically represent performance levels on each dimension are chosen from the acceptable pool of items, and BARS are developed and administered.

This very deliberate and thorough development process is both the biggest strength and the biggest weakness of BARS. Usually such a detailed process involving at least four different groups of participants results in a useful and relevant scale. However, the costs in both time and money are too high for many organizations, so they often employ a simple graphic scale instead.

**Checklists** Checklists are another popular format for performance appraisals. Here, raters are asked to read a large number of behavioral statements and to check off each behavior that the employee exhibits. One example from this category is the *weighted checklist*, which includes a series of items that have previously been weighted as to importance or effectiveness; specifically, some items are indicative of desirable behavior, whereas others are indicative of undesirable behavior. **Figure 5.4** presents an example of a weighted checklist for the evaluation of a computer and information systems manager.

In a real-life situation, the scale shown in Figure 5.4 would be modified in two ways. First, the items would be scrambled so as not to be in numerical order; second, the scale score column would not be part of the form. To administer this type of scale, raters would simply check the items that apply; in our example, the sum of items checked would be the computer and information systems manager's performance appraisal score. Note that as more and more of the negative items are checked, the employee's summed rating gets lower and lower.

| | **Computer and Information Systems Manager** | |
|---|---|---|
| **Check Box (if applicable)** | **Behavioral Descriptor** | **Scale Score** |
| ☐ | Effectively manages backup and computer help systems | +8.5 |
| ☐ | Consults with users, vendors, and technicians on a regular basis | +6.7 |
| ☐ | Stays abreast of technology advancements | +4.4 |
| ☐ | Maintains 40 hours per week in the office | +1.5 |
| ☐ | Doesn't anticipate likely problems | −1.2 |
| ☐ | Pays little attention to financial details | −2.4 |
| ☐ | Rarely provides leadership to his/her work group | −4.6 |
| ☐ | Isn't able to implement necessary changes | −6.7 |
| | **TOTAL SCORE:** | |

**FIGURE 5.4** A Weighted Checklist

*Forced-choice checklists* are also used by organizations, though not as frequently as weighted checklists. Here, raters are asked to choose two items from a group of four that best describe the target employee. All four appear on the surface to be favorable, but the items have been developed and validated such that only *two* are actually good discriminators between effective and ineffective performers. The purpose of this approach is to reduce purposeful bias or distortion on the part of raters. In other words, because all the items appear favorable and the raters don't know which two truly indicative of good performance, they cannot intentionally give someone high or low ratings.

One drawback to this approach is that some raters don't like it because they feel as though they've lost control over the rating process. How would you feel if you had to choose two statements that describe your poorly performing subordinate, but all four statements seem positive? Researchers have recently developed an appraisal format that appears to reduce the bias sometimes associated with other approaches, but without the negative reactions on the part of the raters. Borman and his colleagues developed the computerized adaptive rating scale (CARS), which, although still relatively new to the performance appraisal field, seems to be more sound from a measurement perspective than are other approaches; it also provides more discriminability—that is, the scale does a better job of differentiating between effective and ineffective performers (Borman et al., 2001; Schneider, Goff, Anderson, & Borman, 2003). CARS is an ideal point response method (Drasgow, Chernyshenko, & Stark, 2010) in which raters are given two statements about performance with one slightly above average and one slightly below average. The rater is asked to choose the one that best reflects the ratee's performance. This is followed by two more statements—one more favorable and one less favorable than the point just chosen—and the rater chooses the best option. This continues until all the relevant items have been presented and the best performance estimate/rating has been determined (Borman, 2010).

**Employee Comparison Procedures**  The final category of rating formats, *employee comparison procedures,* involves evaluation of ratees with respect to how they measure up to or compare with other employees. One example of this type of format is *rank-ordering,* whereby several employees are ranked from best to worst. Rank-ordering can be particularly useful for making promotion decisions and discriminating the very best employee from the rest. A second example, *paired comparisons,* involves the comparison of each employee with every other employee. If a manager has only three employees to evaluate, this isn't too difficult a task. (Think about doing this for each of your instructors this semester—comparing each to every one of the others.) However, as the number of ratees increases, so does the complexity of the task. Although this method is one way to arrive at a "clear winner" among employees, it obviously becomes very cumbersome as the number of employees grows.

A third example is called *forced distribution*. Here, raters are instructed to "force" a designated proportion of ratees into each of five to seven categories.

> **TECHNICAL TIP**
>
> The formula N(N – 1)/2 can be used to calculate the total number of comparisons. For example, whereas 3 employees would involve 3 comparisons, 10 employees would involve 45!

A similar procedure is grading on the normal curve, whereby teachers assign grades based on meeting the normal curve percentages (i.e., 68% of the grades assigned are Cs, 13.5% are Bs, 13.5% are Ds, 2.5% are As, and 2.5% are Fs). Sometimes organizations require supervisors to use the same sort of procedure, resulting in the categorization of one-third of the subordinates as average, one-third as below average, and one-third as above average (see the *Time* article "Rank and Fire" by Greenwald, 2001). This is often done because performance ratings are tied to raises and, with a limited pool of money for raises, the company wants to make sure that not too many employees are rated as eligible for a raise and to potentially remove inferior employees from the organization.

To appreciate how employees might feel about this approach, think about how you would feel if your psychology instructor told you that you were to be graded on a normal curve. In other words, if you had an average of 95 in the course but 3% of your classmates had an average of 96 or better, you would *not* receive an A because only 3% can get As. Needless to say, forced distribution is not a popular approach among ratees, whether students or employees, but it was very popular among Fortune 500 companies in the 1990s and early- to mid-2000s. It's estimated that 20% of these organizations employed this practice in the mid-2000s (Grote, 2005), with companies such as General Electric, 3M, Texas Instruments, Microsoft, Ford, Goodyear, and Hewlett Packard among the most ardent supporters. However, some very public lawsuits over the use of these systems have created a controversy regarding the extent to which underrepresented groups tend to be disproportionately ranked in the low category, resulting in adverse impact against these groups (Giumetti, Schroeder, & Switzer, 2015). *Adverse impact* is an important concept in personnel law and may indicate illegal discrimination against a particular group (see Chapter 7 for a more detailed discussion of this issue). Many thoughtful papers and analyses have pointed out other weaknesses in the forced distribution approach, which include the negative reactions of both raters and ratees, the fallacy of forcing some employees into the bottom rung regardless of their true performance, and problems with continuity, where, for example, an employee that was rated average or above average will eventually fall to the bottom rung as the work force is strengthened and perceptions of effective performance change. For these and other reasons, we have recently seen many more companies back away from this approach. You can continue to follow these issues in the popular press, such as in a 2014 piece on the *Wall Street Journal* website called "It's Official: Forced Ranking is Dead" (Deloitte, 2014).

**Contemporary Trends in Rating Formats** Although there has been less research and less written about rating formats in recent years, there are a couple of interesting contemporary trends. First, while there are many rating formats and most are quantitative in nature (i.e., performance is rated in terms of numbers), most of these formats include narrative comments (e.g., your performance on this dimension is above average, but you need to enhance your administrative skills) in some way. It is only recently that researchers have begun examining these narrative comments. Some work has found that supervisors' and subordinates' comments are considerably clearer than the comments from peers (Gillespie, Rose, & Robinson, 2006). A recent conceptual paper proposes a framework for the use of narrative comments in the performance appraisal process (Brutus, 2010) and identifies important characteristics, such as the specificity or breadth of the comments as well as the processes that raters and ratees employ in the use of these narrative comments. This paper provides a framework that can be used to help structure a research program focused on gaining insight into the significance of these and other important characteristics of narrative comments.

Finally, additional outside-the-box thinking has resulted in the use of feedforward interviews (FFIs) for performance appraisal (Kluger & Nir, 2010). This idea is borrowed from appreciative inquiry (see Chapter 14), a part of the positive psychology movement. The FFI is proposed to replace the traditional performance appraisal interview and to facilitate positive change by focusing on employees' strengths, rather than weaknesses, and also to enhance the relationship between the rater and ratee. While promising, there is very little empirical research on the effectiveness of the FFI. However, one new study trained customer service managers in an FFI approach that focused on employees' attention on positive work experiences in which goals were met and success was attained. Researchers found that the performance of subordinates whose managers employed FFI improved more over a four-month period than did those whose managers used more traditional performance appraisal techniques with their employees (Budworth, Latham, & Manroop, 2015). Obviously, more research is needed, but there is some potential for organizations to consider feedforward as an alternative or in combination with feedback.

**An Evaluation of the Various Alternative Methods** Since the 1950s, perhaps no area in performance appraisal has received more research attention than rating type or format. Even in recent years, research has looked at how personality and format may impact performance ratings (Yun, Donahue, Dudley, & McFarland, 2005) as well as how providing ratings via e-mail versus face-to-face meetings impacts the process (Kurtzberg, Naquin, & Belkin, 2005). Researchers have argued that no single format is clearly superior to the others across all evaluative dimensions (Landy & Farr, 1980; Murphy & Cleveland, 1995), though a recent paper that reviewed research on BARS makes a case for the superiority of that approach on some dimensions (Debnath, Lee, & Tandon, 2015). I will make no attempt to argue for one approach over another. **Table 5.1** provides a summary of the advantages and disadvantages of the four major types discussed here. You can use this to decide for yourself which format you would use to evaluate your employees; in some cases, your choice would depend on the situation. Note, however, that companies currently often use a graphic rating scale with various behavioral anchors—basically a hybrid of a graphic rating scale and a BARS.

It's also important to note that there has been a good bit in popular press outlets like NPR and the *Huffington Post* about abolishing performance appraisal all together. This suggestion, however, seems to ignore the important uses of performance appraisal in personnel decisions, employee development, and legal documentation, as outlined at the outset of this chapter. Effective procedures in all three of these areas are necessary for successful organizations. Most organizations value performance appraisal as an important part of the performance management system, but I/O practitioners

**TABLE 5.1** Summary of Appraisal Formats

|  | Advantages | Disadvantages |
|---|---|---|
| Graphic rating scales | 1. Easy to develop<br>2. Easy to use | 1. Lack of precision in dimensions<br>2. Lack of precision in anchors |
| BARS | 1. Precise and well-defined scales—good for coaching<br>2. Well received by raters and ratees | 1. Time and money intensive<br>2. No evidence that it is more accurate than other formats |
| Checklists | 1. Easy to develop<br>2. Easy to use | 1. Rater errors such as halo, leniency, and severity are quite frequent |
| Employee comparison methods | 1. Precise rankings are possible<br>2. Useful for making administrative rewards on a limited basis | 1. Time intensive<br>2. Not well received by raters (paired comparison) or ratees (forced distribution) |

and researchers alike all agree that there is great room for improvement in appraisal systems and the implementation of those systems. I would conclude that this is an example of where we shouldn't throw out the baby with the bathwater.

## Rating Errors

Evaluating another individual's performance accurately and fairly is not an easy thing to do; moreover, errors often result from this process. An understanding of these errors is important to appreciating the complexities of performance appraisal. Research in cognitive psychology has shed considerable light on how the human brain processes information while making decisions. This research has provided I/O psychologists with valuable information that has been applied to the performance appraisal process.

**Cognitive Processes** In a typical company situation, once or twice a year supervisors have to recall specific performance incidents relating to each employee, somehow integrate those performance incidents into a comprehensible whole, arrive at an overall evaluation, and, finally, endorse a number or category that represents the employee's performance over that period. Furthermore, this has to be done for each of 6 to 12 different employees, and perhaps more! With the trend toward flatter organizations, the number of subordinates for each supervisor is increasing steadily, making the task that much more difficult.

Although more complex *cognitive-processing* models of performance appraisal have been developed (see Hodgkinson & Healey, 2008; Landy & Farr, 1980), all such models are consistent with the scheme depicted in **Figure 5.5.** This figure includes two examples of potential error or bias that may come into play at each of the steps shown (see the left and right columns). The first step in this model is the *observation* of employees' behaviors. In many situations, this is done well; the rater may observe a large portion of the ratee's behavior, as when a grocery store manager observes his

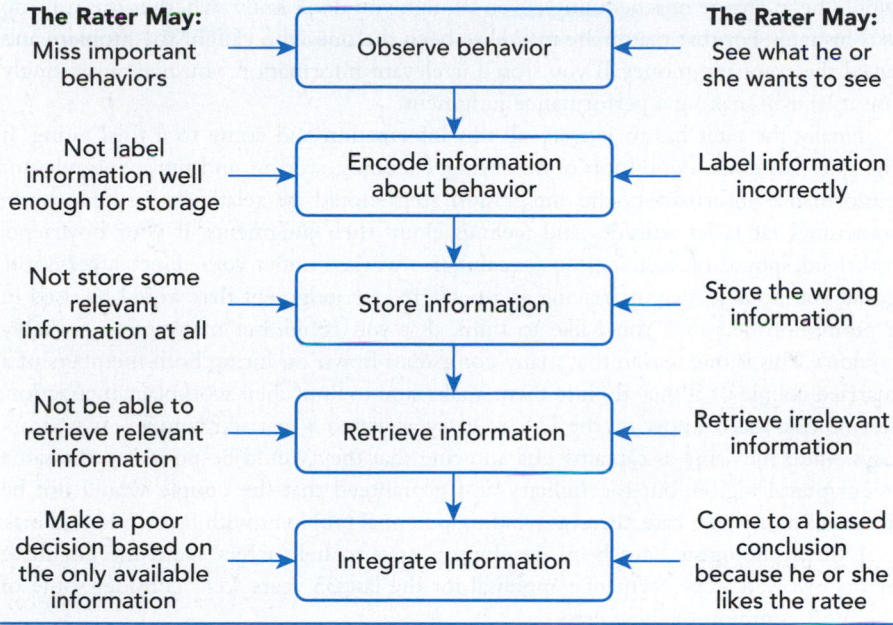

**The Rater May:**
Miss important behaviors

**The Rater May:**
See what he or she wants to see

Observe behavior

Not label information well enough for storage

Encode information about behavior

Label information incorrectly

Not store some relevant information at all

Store information

Store the wrong information

Not be able to retrieve relevant information

Retrieve information

Retrieve irrelevant information

Make a poor decision based on the only available information

Integrate Information

Come to a biased conclusion because he or she likes the ratee

**FIGURE 5.5**    Cognitive-Processing Model of Performance Appraisal

subordinates' performance every day. In other situations, however, raters are unable to observe ratees' performance directly. For instance, professors are often evaluated by their department heads, even though the department heads have little opportunity to view the professors engaging in job-related tasks like teaching.

Second, the observed behavior must be *encoded,* which means that the behavior must be cognitively packaged in such a way that the rater is able to store it. If an observed behavior is encoded incorrectly (e.g., an adequate behavior is somehow encoded as inadequate), the appraisal rating will be affected at a later time.

Third, after encoding, the behavior must be *stored* in long-term memory. Because it is unreasonable to expect that anyone could perfectly store all the relevant performance incidents, some important incidents may not get stored at all.

Fourth, when the appraisal review is being conducted, the stored information must be *retrieved* from memory. In many situations, the rater cannot retrieve some of the important information, leading to an appraisal rating that is based on an inadequate sample of behavior. Also, since performance reviews are difficult and time-consuming, it's not unusual for raters to retrieve irrelevant information and use it as the basis for the performance rating. Think about doing a review of your subordinate's administrative assistant—someone with whom you have very little interaction. In doing this review, you would certainly get input from your subordinate; but later, when doing the final evaluation, you might recall a memo from your subordinate that explained an expensive mix-up in his office in terms of scheduling conflicts. You may consider this when doing the administrative assistant's evaluation (after all, it makes sense that he would be in charge of scheduling), even though you don't know whether this mix-up was his fault. For that matter, he may have been the one who caught the problem and saved the company money. If you stored irrelevant information, you may unwittingly use it later in making a performance judgment.

Finally, the rater has to *integrate* all this information and come to a final rating. If the rater has done a good job of observing, encoding, storing, and retrieving relevant performance information, the integration step should be relatively easy. However, sometimes raters let attitudes and feelings cloud their judgments. If your boyfriend, girlfriend, spouse, or even a close acquaintance worked under your direct supervision, could you be objective in arriving at a performance judgment that would be used in a promotion decision? You'd like to think that you could, but many of us probably couldn't. This is one reason that many companies frown on hiring both members of a married couple or, if they do hire them, make sure to limit their workplace interaction. In one case that I know of, the U.S. military accepted a married couple—two attorneys—into the army as captains, guaranteeing that they would be posted to the same geographical region; but the military also guaranteed that the couple would not be assigned to the same base, thereby avoiding potential problems with favoritism and bias.

I/O psychologists have been developing ways to help raters avoid the cognitive errors involved in performance appraisal for the last 35 years. Let's consider some of the most common of these errors.

**halo**
The rating error that results from either (1) a rater's tendency to use his or her global evaluation of a ratee in making dimension-specific ratings for that ratee or (2) a rater's unwillingness to discriminate between independent dimensions of a ratee's performance.

**Halo** One error that has received a great deal of attention is called **halo**. Halo results from either (1) a rater's tendency to use his or her global evaluation of a ratee in making dimension-specific ratings for that ratee or (2) a rater's unwillingness to discriminate between independent dimensions of a ratee's performance (Saal, Downey, & Lahey, 1980). Halo effects can be positive or negative. A retail manager may evaluate a salesclerk as being very good at connecting with potential customers because she knows that the clerk is very good at keeping the shelves neat and stocked even though competence on this dimension doesn't really indicate that he is competent in dealing with customers. The manager has generalized her evaluation of this clerk from one dimension to another. Similarly, I may assume a student is not going to do well in my class because he hasn't done well in his physics classes.

Sam Diephuis/Blend Images/Getty Images

**A CLOSER LOOK**
What is the difference between halo and true halo?

The early research in this area assumed that all halo was error. However, some people are competent across *all* dimensions—leadership, communication skills, motivating employees, completing paperwork, and so on. Traditionally, I/O psychologists noted high correlations across ratings on these dimensions and concluded that there was a great deal of halo error. However, from a hiring standpoint (see Chapters 6 and 7), organizations tend to target those applicants they believe will be "good at everything." And, indeed, there are employees in all organizations who do seem to be good performers on all performance dimensions. The point here is that some halo results from accurate intercorrelations among performance dimensions (see Goffin, Jelley, & Wagner, 2003; Murphy & Jako, 1989; Murphy & Reynolds, 1988)—what we call **true halo**.

It is also possible that extremely low intercorrelations among performance dimensions (what some have called negative halo because performance on the dimensions seems to be unrelated) may reflect inaccuracy in ratings just as much as strong intercorrelations (positive halo). In a study that reanalyzed some existing data, a curvilinear relationship between halo and accuracy emerged such that both positive and negative halo were found to reduce accuracy (Thomas, Palmer, & Feldman, 2009). In other words, both very strong and very weak associations between performance dimensions may indicate low accuracy. So, we know that halo exists and we understand it better now than we did 30 years ago, but it is complex. Sometimes halo is reflective of true performance and sometimes either positive or negative halo may reflect inaccuracy in ratings.

Rating errors such as leniency, central tendency, and severity (discussed below) are categorized as **distributional errors** because they result from a mismatch between actual rating distributions and expected rating distributions. In other words, the grouping of ratings is much farther toward one end of the distribution or much closer to the middle than what we assume the true distribution to be. Performance is one of those qualities that we expect to be distributed "normally."

**Leniency** Raters commit the error of **leniency** when (1) the mean of their ratings across ratees is higher than the mean of all ratees across all raters or (2) the mean of their ratings is higher than the midpoint of the scale. In other words, if your boss rates her employees higher than all the other bosses rate their employees, or if she gives ratings with a mean of 4 on a 5-point scale, she would be described as a lenient rater. Raters may be lenient because they like their employees or want to be liked. They may think that giving everyone favorable ratings will keep peace in the workplace or that doing so will make them look good as supervisors who have high-performing subordinates. In fact, in a laboratory study examining leniency effects, researchers found that when raters were held accountable to their supervisors (as well as ratees), they were less lenient in their ratings than when they were held accountable only to the ratees (Curtis, Darvey, & Ravden, 2005). This surely has implications for how organizations might want to structure performance appraisal processes.

As with halo, we need to be careful in assuming that distributional errors are really errors. Indeed, it is possible, perhaps likely, that some supervisors really do have better employees or work groups than others, resulting in more favorable ratings that are accurate rather than lenient. For example, the airline chosen as the best

**true halo**
Halo that results from accurate intercorrelations among performance dimensions rather than from rating error.

**distributional errors**
Rating errors, such as severity, central tendency, and leniency, that result from a mismatch between actual rating distributions and expected rating distributions.

**leniency**
The rating error that results when (1) the mean of one's ratings across ratees is higher than the mean of all ratees across all raters or (2) the mean of one's ratings is higher than the midpoint of the scale.

in the nation with respect to service should show higher performance ratings for its service employees than other airlines. So what might appear to be the result of leniency among the evaluators of this airline would in fact be the result of accurate evaluation. Research also suggests that personality can have an impact on one's tendency to be lenient. Specifically, individuals categorized as "agreeable" have been shown to be more lenient than those categorized as "conscientious" (Bernardin, Cooke, & Villanova, 2000; Bernardin, Tyler & Villanova, 2009).

**Central Tendency** Raters who use only the midpoint of the scale in rating their employees commit the error of **central tendency**. An example is the professor who gives almost everyone a C for the course. In some cases, the raters are lazy and find it easier to give everyone an average rating than spending the extra time necessary to review employees' performance so as to differentiate between good and poor workers. In other cases, the raters don't know how well each of their subordinates has performed (perhaps because they are new to the work group or just don't see their employees' on-the-job behavior very often) and take the easy way out by opting for average ratings for everyone. Some research suggests that central tendency error is sometimes a result of the rating scale itself and that simpler semantic differential scales (e.g., ranging from "effective employee" to "ineffective employee") result in a considerable amount of this bias (Yu, Albaum, & Swenson, 2003).

Of course, a given work group or department may be populated largely by average employees. In fact, the normal distribution suggests that most employees really are average, so it is reasonable to have a large percentage of employees rated as such. At times, then, central tendency is a rating error; at other times, though, it simply reflects the actual distribution of performance, which is largely centered around "average."

**Severity** Less frequent than leniency and central tendency is the rating error of **severity**, which is committed by raters who tend to use only the low end of the scale or to give consistently lower ratings to their employees than other raters do. Some supervisors intentionally give low ratings to employees because they believe that doing so motivates them (you will see when we get to Chapter 9, on motivation, that this strategy is not likely to work), or keeps them from getting too cocky, or provides a baseline from which new employees can improve. For some, severity represents an attempt to maintain the impression of being tough and in charge—but what tends to happen is that such raters lose, rather than gain, the respect of their subordinates.

Some work groups include a larger number of low performers than other work groups, so low ratings from the supervisor of such work groups may be accurate rather than "severe." Thus, although we don't see these terms in the literature, we could speak of true leniency, true central tendency, and true severity in much the same way as we speak of true halo. For any given situation, though, it is difficult to determine whether the ratings are affected by rating errors or are an accurate reflection of performance.

The chief problem stemming from distributional errors is that the ratings do not adequately *discriminate* between effective and ineffective performers. In such cases, the majority of ratees are lumped together in the bottom, middle, or top of the distribution. This general problem is often referred to as *range restriction* because only a small

**central tendency**
The tendency to use only the midpoint of the scale in rating one's employees.

**severity**
The tendency to use only the low end of the scale or to give consistently lower ratings to one's employees than other raters do.

part of the scale range is used in the ratings. The difficulty for the organization is that it intends to use performance rating information for personnel decisions such as promotions, raises, transfers, layoffs, and other terminations; but if all the employees are rated similarly (whether as a result of central tendency, leniency, or severity), the ratings do not help in making these personnel decisions. For instance, if everyone is rated in the middle of the scale, who gets promoted? If everyone is rated very favorably, who gets the big raise? If everyone is rated as ineffective, who gets fired?

Employee morale is also affected by nondiscriminating ratings, in that employees who believe they are good employees will feel slighted because their reviews are no better than those of employees whom they view as much less effective. Think about this: Have you ever been passed over for a promotion, only to discover that the person who was promoted, though less deserving than you, was rated similarly to you? You likely experienced feelings of *injustice,* which may have affected not only your subsequent on-the-job performance but also your attitude. These additional implications of nondiscriminating ratings will be discussed in more detail in Chapters 10 and 11.

**Other Errors** Many other rating errors are discussed in the literature, but I will touch on just three more. One is *recency error,* whereby raters heavily weight their most recent interactions with or observations of the ratee. A supervisor who, in rating his subordinate, largely ignores nine months of superior performance and bases his evaluation on only the past three months of less-than-adequate performance is making a recency error. This is similar to the somewhat misguided belief in organizations that all that matters is the question "What have you done for me lately?"

Another error of note, called *first impression error* or *primacy effect,* is the opposite of recency error. Here, raters pay an inordinate amount of attention to their initial experiences with the ratee. A construction foreman may think back to that first day when the new electrician helped out on the site at a crucial time and use this as the basis for his evaluation of the electrician while largely ignoring some major performance problems over the past few months. First impressions tend to be heavily weighted in our everyday lives, as when we form friendships with people with whom we just seem to "hit it off" from the very beginning; they are also used, sometimes ineffectively, in performance appraisal.

Finally, there is the *similar-to-me* error, which occurs when raters tend to give more favorable ratings to ratees who are very much like themselves. We know from social psychology that people tend to make friends with and like being around people who are much like themselves. An old English proverb states: "Birds of a feather flock together." A similar effect occurs in performance appraisal situations, resulting in more favorable ratings of employees similar to the rater than of those dissimilar.

## Rater Considerations

We've talked at length about characteristics of the rating—that is, formats and errors. In this section, we consider important performance appraisal elements that revolve around the rater—namely, rater training, rater goals, and rater accountability.

**Rater Training** We have just discussed some of the common errors that raters make in evaluating the performance of others. An important question asked by I/O researchers and practitioners alike is whether rater training can reduce such errors and improve the rating process (Hauenstein, 1998; Schleicher, Day, Mayes, & Riggio, 2002). There are two main types of rater training in the performance appraisal area. One, known as Rater Error Training (RET), was originally developed to reduce the incidence of rater errors (Spool, 1978). The focus was on describing errors like halo to raters and showing them how to avoid making such errors. The assumption was that by reducing the errors, RET could increase accuracy, the degree to which performance ratings match one's true performance level.

As suggested early on in the development of this approach, however, RET can indeed reduce errors, but accuracy is not necessarily improved (Bernardin & Pence, 1980). In fact, studies have shown that accuracy sometimes *decreases* as a function of reducing error (e.g., Bernardin & Pence, 1980). How can this be? Well, recall our discussion of halo. When raters are instructed not to allow for halo, they are in effect being taught that there is no relationship among performance dimensions and that their ratings across dimensions should not be correlated. But, in many cases, there is true halo, and the ratings *should* be correlated. Thus, rater training may have reduced the correlation across dimensions that we used to assume was error, resulting in artificially uncorrelated ratings that are now inaccurate.

A second type of rater training, called Frame of Reference (FOR) Training, was designed by John Bernardin and his colleagues to enhance raters' observational and categorization skills (Bernardin & Beatty, 1984; Bernardin & Buckley, 1981). Bernardin's belief was that to improve the accuracy of performance ratings, raters have to be provided with a frame of reference for defining performance levels that is consistent across raters and consistent with how the organization defines the various levels of performance. In other words, for a fast-food employee, on the dimension of cleanliness, all raters must know that, on a 5-point scale, a 5 would be indicated by the following behaviors:

> Table top is wiped down in between runs of burgers. Ketchup and mustard guns are always placed back into their cylinders and never left sitting on the table. Buns are kept wrapped in plastic in between runs of burgers. Floor around production area is swept at least once per hour and mopped once in the morning and afternoon. All items in the walk-in refrigerators are placed on the appropriate shelves and the walk-ins are organized, swept, and mopped periodically.

FOR training attempts to make that description part of all raters' performance schema for the level of "5/exceptional" performance. The hope is that by etching this performance exemplar in the raters' minds, the training will render each rater better able to use it consistently when observing, encoding, storing, retrieving, and integrating behaviors in arriving at a final rating. The goal is to "calibrate" raters so that a score of 5 from one rater means the same as a score of 5 from any other rater. Popular procedures for FOR training have since been developed (Pulakos, 1984, 1986). In these, raters are provided with descriptions of the dimensions and rating

**Rater Error Training (RET)**
A type of training originally developed to reduce rater errors by focusing on describing errors like halo to raters and showing them how to avoid making such errors.

**Frame of Reference (FOR) Training**
A type of training designed to enhance raters' observational and categorization skills so that all raters share a common view and understanding of performance levels to improve rater accuracy.

scales while also having them read aloud by the trainer. The trainer then describes ratee behaviors that are representative of different performance levels on each scale. Raters are typically shown a series of videotaped practice vignettes in which individuals (stimulus persons, or ratees) are performing job tasks. Raters evaluate the stimulus persons on the scales; then the trainer discusses the raters' ratings and provides feedback about what ratings should have been made for each stimulus person. A detailed discussion ensues about the reasons for the various ratings.

Research has consistently shown that FOR training not only improves appraisal accuracy (Sulsky & Day, 1994) but also is generally recognized as the most effective approach for improving rater accuracy (Meriac, Gorman, & Macan, 2015). A couple of recent studies have suggested that combining FOR training with *behavioral observation training (BOT),* which focuses on teaching raters how to watch for certain behaviors and avoid behavioral observation errors, may improve the recognition or recall of performance behaviors (Noonan & Sulsky, 2001; Roch & O'Sullivan, 2003). One current concern, however, is that very little field data are available on the FOR technique. Most of the research showing that FOR training improves accuracy has been conducted with students in laboratory settings (see Uggerslev & Sulsky, 2008). For instance, in a recent meta-analysis that found strong moderate effects of FOR training on various accuracy measures, only 2 of the 39 manuscripts identified since 1994 described research studies that did not use students (Roch, Woehr, Mishra, & Kieszczynska, 2011). There were more studies in this literature review that did use FOR training in field settings, but these studies were not direct tests of the effectiveness of FOR and could not be included in the meta-analysis. The next step is to find a way to bring FOR training research into more organizational settings, but doing so requires some modification to the rather expensive and time-consuming process.

**Rater Goals and Accountability** The effect of rater goals/motivation, along with accountability related to the appraisal process, is also quite important and has been the focus of considerable recent research. Raters may have different goals for various reasons. For instance, a particular rater may want all of her subordinates to be rated above a certain level or to have developed in particular areas. These kinds of goals or objectives may affect the ratings provided or the rating process in general. Sometimes this is reflected in raters "bending the rules" or making performance-based judgment calls to enhance individual or organizational performance (Veiga, Golden, & Dechant, 2004); at other times, these goals are reflected in how the rating process is implemented.

Mero and his colleagues have demonstrated that raters who were held accountable to various goals or objectives, such as rating accurately or rating leniently, actually provided ratings consistent with those goals (Mero & Motowidlo, 1995). One step further, it was shown that certain types of raters are more affected by accountability pressures than are others (Mero, Guidice, & Anna, 2006). For instance, raters who are high on conscientiousness tend to be strongly affected by accountability pressures, which is reflected in a felt need to justify one's ratings, some anxiety about the task, and higher-quality performance ratings.

These researchers have also found that the accountability effect was altered as a function of the status of the audience and the manner of being held accountable (Mero, Guidice, & Brownlee, 2007). For example, raters who expected to be held accountable for their ratings in a face-to-face meeting with a high-status session administrator provided more accurate ratings than those who anticipated justifying ratings only in writing. Finally, Wong and Kwong (2007) demonstrated a clear relationship between rater goals and rating patterns. When raters were asked to maintain harmony within the work group, they increased their mean ratings and tended not to discriminate between ratees.

## Contemporary Performance Appraisal Research

For many years, practitioners and researchers believed that rating-scale formats were integral to the success of performance appraisal systems and that *accuracy* should be the chief goal of any performance appraisal system. Because of these two common beliefs, much of the early research in this area focused on the context of performance appraisal as it related to rating formats and rater errors. Format and error research has taught us a great deal about the processes and errors involved in arriving at a performance judgment. However, performance appraisal is not a stand-alone process that can be examined in isolation but, rather, a complex process that takes place in a very rich and sophisticated social–psychological climate, or **context**. Hence, the remaining sections of this chapter will focus on contemporary issues that better emphasize that context (see Levy, Cavanaugh, Frantz, Borden, & Roberts, in press; Levy & Williams, 2004).

**context**
The social-psychological climate in which performance appraisal takes place.

**The Importance of the Social–Psychological Context** Many experts have suggested a more direct research focus on the context in which the appraisal takes place, arguing that this context colors the entire appraisal process. The context in which performance appraisal takes place includes not only the social and legal climates in which the organization exists but also the political and emotional climates and cultures within the organization itself (Ferris, Munyon, Basik, & Buckley, 2008).

These context-related topics include an examination of (1) the use of employees' reactions to the appraisal rather than *accuracy* as a criterion for evaluating performance appraisal systems, (2) how the relationship between the supervisor and subordinate affects performance appraisal, (3) the role of organizational politics in the appraisal process, (4) the importance of trust in the appraisal process, (5) the use of multiple feedback sources rather than just the supervisor's feedback in the appraisal process, and (6) the value of providing employees with knowledge about the appraisal system and the opportunity to participate in the appraisal process. This list represents just a small sampling of the context issues at the core of current performance appraisal research (see Levy & Williams, 2004, for a complete review). With our movement away from an emphasis on formats and errors, we are beginning to increase our understanding of the process itself and to apply that understanding to the use of appraisals in organizations. The next few sections will consider some of this new context-based research.

**Reaction Criteria** Traditionally, performance appraisals were evaluated with respect to how "accurate" they were, in the sense of being free from errors. But as you now know, there are problems with accuracy and error measures. As early as 1984, researchers suggested that future appraisal research should begin to move beyond psychometric criteria due to the measurement problems inherent in that approach and instead focus on *qualitative criteria* (Bernardin & Beatty, 1984) and *reaction criteria* (Cawley, Keeping, & Levy, 1998). Both phrases refer to the role played by raters' and ratees' reactions in the appraisal process (Hedge & Teachout, 2000; Keeping & Levy, 2000).

One research focus has been the potential importance of raters' and ratees' favorable responses to the appraisal system or process (e.g., Findley, Giles, & Mossholder, 2000). In fact, until this past decade, the relative lack of research attention directed toward reaction criteria instead of psychometric and accuracy criteria led researchers to refer to reaction criteria as one class of "neglected criteria" that might be critical in evaluating the success of an appraisal system (Murphy & Cleveland, 1995). It seems reasonable to expect that subordinates' reactions to appraisal systems would have just as much impact on the success and effectiveness of an appraisal system as the more technical aspects of the system. Indeed, researchers have suggested that reactions are usually better indicators of the overall viability of an appraisal system than are narrower psychometric indices such as leniency or halo (Bernardin & Beatty, 1984). After all, one may develop the most technically sophisticated appraisal system, but if that system is not accepted and supported by employees, its effectiveness will ultimately be limited. Indeed, due to the changing nature of performance appraisals and organizations, worker reactions toward performance appraisal may play an increasingly important role in appraisal processes as the procedures and systems continue to develop (Hedge & Borman, 1995).

Despite the relative neglect of reaction criteria, several studies have attempted to investigate various appraisal characteristics that elicit or at least contribute to positive employee reactions. For instance, it has been demonstrated that for a sample of bank tellers, appraisal satisfaction was affected by both appraisal characteristics (e.g., frequency of appraisals) and organizational variables (e.g., employees' understanding of their jobs). Furthermore, bank tellers who reported a positive relationship with their supervisors and a low amount of ambiguity about their roles in the organization were more satisfied with the appraisal system (Dobbins, Cardy, & Platz-Vieno, 1990).

One study demonstrated that subordinates reported less anger and higher perceptions of justice when supervisors provided justification for their ratings (Tata, 2002). Furthermore, we have seen that performance appraisals viewed as unfair by subordinates have tended to be related to ratees' emotional exhaustion (Brown & Benson, 2003). (We will talk more about organizational justice in a later section of this chapter and in Chapters 9 and 10.) This research has great implications for appraisal in organizations because it suggests that organizations and supervisors can do certain things to increase the likelihood that employees will respond favorably to the performance appraisal process—namely, provide frequent performance feedback and relevant job-related information to employees.

A recent study modeled the goals-feedback-reactions-subsequent goals path and determined that emotional reactions to feedback play a significant role in determining future goals (Ilies, Judge, & Wagner, 2013). The authors argue that emotion and cognition are instrumental in determining ensuing goals and that this process has important organizational implications for performance as evidenced through the established literature on goal-setting (see Chapter 9 for further discussion of goal-setting theory).

Justin Kruger and David Dunning have done some very interesting research arguing that there are people who are so unskilled that they aren't skilled enough to know how unskilled they are (Kruger & Dunning, 1999). The Dunning-Kruger effect is a cognitive bias that basically suggests that unskilled individuals overestimate their abilities and do not have the meta-cognitive skills to even realize that they are doing this. As you can imagine, this lack of judgment can cause a variety of problems for individuals and organizations when it comes to properly setting and evaluating goals. Some of Dunning's more recent work has extended this to the feedback arena, where he shows that individuals who are unskilled and unaware are also uninterested in learning and getting better (Sheldon, Dunning, & Ames, 2014). These researchers found that those individuals who were low on emotional intelligence (EI)—an individual's ability to deal effectively with his or her emotions and the emotions of others (see Chapter 6)—also tended to overestimate their emotional intelligence (Dunning-Kruger effect). Interestingly, when given feedback and the opportunity to use that feedback to improve, these individuals were unlikely to do so. More specifically, they tended not to drop their self-ratings of EI much even after feedback; they tended to evaluate the test as poor and inaccurate; and they showed less interest in self-improvement, which was measured by, among other things, their interest in purchasing a book called *The Emotionally Intelligent Manager*. Those low on EI were much less interested in purchasing the book and when they did express an interest in purchasing the book, they were willing to spend far less than those who were high on EI. They were, as Sheldon and colleagues noted, unskilled, unaware, and uninterested in learning! The results from this line of research are consistent with those that practitioners often tend to see in organizations: The people who need feedback the most either don't get it or are not receptive to it, but rather react to it in a negative, disparaging way. This tendency complicates the feedback process, which relies on managers who will work hard to create an atmosphere where employees hear, receive, accept, and use feedback to improve.

**The Supervisor–Subordinate Relationship** Researchers and practitioners have discussed the relationship between supervisors and subordinates in terms of *leader–member exchange (LMX) theory,* which emphasizes the idea that supervisors have different types of relationships with different subordinates (Engle & Lord, 1997; see Chapter 13 for a more detailed discussion). Performance appraisal research has virtually ignored the role of leader–member exchange in subordinate reactions to the appraisal process (Wexley & Klimoski, 1984), but LMX is important in this connection. For instance, a study found that employees of a telephone company who experienced a high level of LMX with their supervisors (meaning the subordinates had a positive working relationship with their supervisors) were rated high in terms of performance regardless of objective performance indicators, whereas those who experienced a low level of LMX received performance ratings that matched their objective level of performance (Duarte, Goodson, & Klich, 1993). In short, the relationship that an employee has with his or her supervisor plays a role in the performance appraisal process. A recent meta-analysis supports this conclusion, uncovering a .34 correlation between LMX and performance (Martin, Guillaume, Thomas, Lee, & Epitropaki, 2015). Further, the meta-analysis also found that this relationship was mediated by other factors, with trust and empowerment being the strongest. That is, individuals who reported that they had a positive relationship with their bosses also reported high trust and empowerment. These same individuals were also rated favorably by their supervisors with respect to performance.

Digital Vision/Photodisc/Getty Images

**A CLOSER LOOK**
The relationship between supervisor and subordinates, sometimes called LMX, is very important for organizational functioning. How do theory and research related to LMX help us understand the performance appraisal process?

An interesting study demonstrated that the frequency of communication between a subordinate and supervisor interacts with LMX to affect performance ratings. A positive LMX relationship led to favorable ratings when there was also frequent communication, but ratings were less favorable even with a positive LMX when there was little communication (Kacmar, Witt, Zivnuska, & Gully, 2003). This is an excellent example of the connection between the context in which the appraisal takes place and the outcome of the appraisal process. The implication in this case is that understanding the appraisal process within a work group requires an understanding of the relationships among those involved because these relationships affect the appraisal process.

In a recent study of about 220 supervisor–subordinate dyads in Dubai, the authors looked at three of the constructs we have been talking about in this section: LMX, justice, and performance reactions (Pichler, Varma, Michel, & Levy, 2015). They found that the quality of the LMX relationship affected performance appraisal satisfaction through its effect on procedural justice. In other words, if subordinates had a positive relationship with their supervisor, they tended to perceive that they were being treated more fairly and this was reflected in a more favorable evaluation of the appraisal process.

**Organizational Politics** Organizational politics—"deliberate attempts by individuals to enhance or protect their self-interests when conflicting courses of action are possible"—helps delineate the context in which performance appraisal takes place (Longenecker, Sims, & Gioia, 1987, p. 184). Because organizations are political entities, politics plays a role in all important organizational decisions and processes, including performance appraisal (Longenecker et al., 1987). It's important to note that both supervisors and subordinates are affected by the politics of performance appraisal. In particular, Clint Longenecker and his colleagues (1987) have demonstrated through interviews that executives intentionally manipulate appraisals for political reasons (e.g., to send a message to subordinates or to make their own department look good). Research has also indicated that subordinates use *impression management* strategies in an effort to bring about favorable appraisals; in other words, they control their behavior to make a good impression on their superiors (Wayne & Liden, 1995).

A study of more than 800 employees demonstrated that among those who perceived a high level of organizational politics in their company, the ones who were also high on conscientiousness performed better than did those who were not high on conscientiousness (Hochwarter, Witt, & Kacmar, 2000). It appears that the high-conscientiousness employees were able to overcome the politics and perform well. Thus, to gain a better understanding of the appraisal process in an organization, and to affect that process, one needs to have information about the politics of the organization and the work group. Recent research has begun to examine how perceptions of politics relate to constructs like stress, anxiety, and job morale within a performance context. For instance, one study uncovered relationships among perceptions of politics, attitudes, stress, and performance (Rosen & Levy, 2013). In particular, the researchers found that when employees perceive politics at work they also tend to experience stress and anxiety, which impact their work attitudes and result in performance decrement.

In another study, researchers looked at the effect of politics perceptions and rumination on performance (Rosen & Hochwarter, 2014). *Ruminators* are individuals who persist in negative thinking and feeling related to stressors that they experience. In studies of architects, clerical employees, and accountants, researchers found that perceptions of politics operated differently depending on an individual's tendency to ruminate. In particular, they found that politics had a strong negative effect on performance (as well as job satisfaction, tension, and mood) for ruminators, but a much weaker effect for those who tended not to dwell on stress-related forces.

Finally, in a simple but interesting study, researchers observed college interns and found a revealing pattern of results (Liu, Ferris, Xu, Weitz, & Perrewe, 2014). They focused on ingratiation, which is an influence tactic that uses behaviors to curry favor or make oneself look good to others—some of these behaviors are very similar to "kissing up." Liu and colleagues found that interns who use ingratiation tactics are rated as better performers by their supervisors if they are also politically skilled. In other words, if an individual is skilled at ingratiation, it works—his or her supervisor will like them and this will be reflected in positive ratings. However, for those interns who used ingratiation tactics and were not good at it, this tactic resulted in low performance ratings. So, the world of politics, ingratiation, and performance is complicated, but I'm guessing you already knew that. Now you have science to support it!

**Trust and Justice** *Trust* in the appraisal process is the extent to which raters believe that fair and accurate appraisals have been or will be made in their organization. Alternatively, if a rater feels that other raters in the organization are inflating their ratings, that rater may do the same. Bernardin and his colleagues developed a scale called *Trust in the Appraisal Process Survey,* or TAPS, to measure raters' perceptions of the rating behavior of the other raters in their department (Bernardin, 1978; Bernardin, Orban, & Carlyle, 1981). They found that raters who scored low on the TAPS were more lenient raters than those who scored high. This finding indicates the importance of trust on appraisal ratings. In addition, performance appraisal systems that are well received by employees appear to affect employees' trust of top management, suggesting that the performance management system may be an effective tool for enhancing organizational trust (Mayer & Davis, 1999).

In another line of work related to trust issues, researchers have looked at how comfortable raters are with the performance appraisal process (Villanova, Bernardin, Dahmus, & Sims, 1993). In particular, Peter Villanova and his colleagues have shown that scores on a scale they call the *Performance Appraisal Discomfort Scale (PADS)* are related to leniency in such a way that those raters who express great discomfort in evaluating others and providing them with feedback also tend to be among the most lenient raters. In other words, not all raters are equally comfortable doing performance appraisals, and the extent to which raters experience discomfort in this setting is likely to affect the quality of the ratings and other elements of the appraisal process (e.g., interpersonal interactions). In their more recent work, Bernardin and Villanova (2005) have taken an important additional step by showing that raters can be trained to be more comfortable doing performance appraisal, resulting in less leniency. Called self-efficacy training for raters, this new approach seems to have great potential for improving the rating process.

In a recent survey of over 100 individuals with graduate school experience it was found that rater's self-efficacy was strongly correlated with the extent to which the raters were of an independent self-construal. The self is a very important part of psychology and self-construal indicates how one views or thinks about the self in relation to others. Typically, people are either individualistic, which means that they see separation between themselves and others, or collectivistic, which suggests that they see themselves as intricately related to others (Brutus, Fletcher & Baldry, 2009). The more independent as opposed to collectivistic a rater is, the more likely that rater is to be high on self-efficacy. Given earlier research that shows raters who are highly self-efficacious are less likely to be lenient and uncomfortable in the rater role (Bernardin & Villanova, 2005), these findings suggest that self-construal—the extent to which an individual sees him- or herself as connected and dependent on others—is potentially very important for the performance appraisal process.

We will talk about organizational justice in Chapter 9, but the notion of the fairness or justice of a performance appraisal system is an important one to mention here. A carefully designed, psychometrically sound performance appraisal system has the potential to be effective, but that potential can be limited by the justice perceptions of those organizational members who are involved in the appraisal process. If raters or ratees see the appraisal system as unfair or biased, its psychometric quality will be irrelevant—it won't matter how "good" the system is if people perceive it to be unfair. Recent conceptual work argues that performance appraisal research must be broad in its focus and include diverse aspects of the appraisal system, such as justice-related constructs (Thurston & McNall, 2010).

A good deal of performance appraisal research in recent years has focused on justice-related constructs and processes as they relate to performance appraisal. An interesting recent line of work has looked at how a supervisor's implicit person theory (IPT)—the extent to which an individual believes that people can change—impacts performance appraisal. One such research investigation (Heslin & VandeWalle, 2011) demonstrated that supervisors who tend to believe that people can change and develop are perceived by their subordinates as more just in their performance appraisals than are those supervisors who do not believe that people can change. The justice perceptions led to more frequent OCBs and greater commitment to the organization (see Chapter 10 for more on OCBs and organizational commitment). Another interesting application of justice to performance appraisal is found in a study linking negative feedback (feedback indicating subpar performance) to organizational justice (Chory & Westerman, 2009). In their study of 250 working adults, the authors found that the quality of the negative feedback—for instance, the extent to which it was destructive versus constructive or inconsistent versus reliant on clear standards—was strongly related to perceptions of justice. They concluded that managers should focus on providing consistent and constructive feedback to elicit perceptions of justice from employees, hopefully resulting in the feedback being deemed as useful and therefore more likely to be put into practice to improve employees' performance. There is a sizable literature on this (for a more thorough discussion, see Elicker, Levy, & Hall, 2006; Thurston & McNall, 2010), but I want to emphasize the important role played by organizational members' perceptions of performance appraisal fairness.

**Participation** One contextual process variable that has received a great deal of attention in the performance appraisal literature is employee participation. Overall, this research suggests an association between allowing employees to participate in the appraisal process and positive employee reactions toward the appraisal system (Cawley et al., 1998). Specifically, as demonstrated by a meta-analysis, there is a strong positive relationship between participation and a host of reactions to performance appraisal, including (1) satisfaction with the appraisal system and session, (2) motivation to improve as a result of the appraisal, (3) belief in the fairness of the appraisal, and (4) belief in the usefulness of the appraisal (Cawley et al., 1998). In short, when employees are allowed to participate in the appraisal process—by completing a self-assessment or expressing their ideas during the appraisal session or interview—they react more positively to the appraisal than when they are not given the opportunity to participate.

Here, too, the important implication is that organizations and supervisors have interventions available to them that can improve the quality of the appraisal process—in this case, by giving employees a voice in the process.

**Table 5.2** presents the steps to be followed during a performance appraisal interview. Compiled

**TECHNICAL TIP**

*Remember from Chapter 2 that meta-analyses are quantitative reviews of research findings. We use them to draw useful summaries of relationships among variables from many published and unpublished studies.*

## TABLE 5.2  How to Conduct a Performance Appraisal Interview

| Prior to the Interview | During the Interview | After the Interview |
|---|---|---|
| 1. Supervisor should give employee adequate notice about meeting date. | 1. Supervisor should explain the purpose of interview. | 1. Supervisor and employee should independently review major responsibilities and objectives. |
| 2. Employee should do a self-appraisal. | 2. Employee should summarize accomplishments and needs with respect to major responsibilities. | 2. Supervisor and employee should schedule additional meetings to set objectives for the next review period. |
| 3. Supervisor should receive copy of self-appraisal. | 3. Supervisor should do same summary as above, but from his or her viewpoint. | 3. Supervisor and employee should agree on the organizational link between achieving objectives and receiving organizational rewards (compensation, promotions, etc.). |
| 4. Supervisor should review documentation of performance. | 4. Supervisor and employee should discuss whether a developmental need exists with respect to each major responsibility. | 4. Communication channels between supervisor and employee should remain open throughout the review period. |
| | 5. Supervisor and employee should diagnose the causes of any discrepancy, or "gap," between objectives and actual performance. | |
| | 6. Supervisor and employee should develop action plans to enhance performance on each major responsibility. | |
| | 7. Supervisor and employee should summarize performance on each major responsibility and review agreed-upon action plans. | |
| | 8. Supervisor should compliment employee on accomplishments. | |
| | 9. Supervisor should set time and date for future meetings to discuss responsibilities and performance. | |

from various sources (primarily Silverman, 1991), these steps make it very clear that the performance appraisal interview should be a participative process that includes substantial input from the employee. This observation is consistent with findings regarding the importance of participation in the performance appraisal process (Cawley et al., 1998), as well as with the change in management style and structure from autocratic to humanistic that has become pervasive in organizations (Meyer, 1991).

**Providing Performance Feedback** The performance management cycle is a multistage, longitudinal process that is central to the development of employees and the success of organizations (London & Smither, 2002). The key element to this cycle is the extent to which employees receive and use feedback. This focus on employee development has received a great deal of attention. For instance, London and Smither (2002) have presented a comprehensive model of the performance management process in which the chief outcomes are behavior changes, better performance, increased self-awareness, and increased self-confidence. They propose that these outcomes are affected by constructs such as the employee's own feedback orientation (see Linderbaum & Levy, 2007) or receptivity to feedback, as well as the feedback environment as defined by the organization or work group (see Whitaker, Dahling, & Levy, 2007). In other words, employees' development is largely a function of their receptivity to feedback and the organization's approach to or emphasis on feedback.

Continuous employee development has been defined as a "cyclical process in which employees are motivated to plan for and engage in actions or behaviors that benefit their future employability on a repetitive or ongoing basis" (Garofano & Salas, 2005, p. 282). In a recent study, it was demonstrated that how participants responded to employee development goals was affected by their personalities (core self-evaluations, which are related to self-efficacy and self-esteem as well as other traits) and other situational and interpersonal variables (Bono & Colbert, 2005).

As noted earlier, feedback accountability plays an important role in both performance management and, in particular, employee development. Research has found that social support is a key determinant of attitudes toward employee development and that organizational social support for development is likely to lead to a feeling of accountability on the part of the employees (Maurer, Mitchell, & Barbeite, 2002). Supervisors who have experienced the support of their subordinates have reported more feedback accountability and greater self-development initiative, suggesting that the social context is an important element of employee self-development (Rutkowski & Steelman, 2005). Let's talk some more about the feedback process.

**The Feedback Process** Feedback serves an important role in organizations, meeting the needs of employees and employers. London and Smither (2002) highlight the key steps of the performance management cycle. First, employees *attend to the feedback,* which includes anticipating, receiving, and reacting to the feedback. After this initial interaction with the feedback comes the second stage, *processing the feedback,* which

## PRACTITIONER FORUM

Elaine Pulakos

### Elaine Pulakos

*PhD, 1984, Industrial and Organizational Psychology,*
*Michigan State University*
*Executive Director, CEB, and President, PDRI, a CEB Company*

Despite more than 50 years of research devoted to designing effective performance management (PM) systems, we have yet to uncover the key to delivering PM processes that managers and employees agree work well and add value.

Over the past few years, our organization has devoted considerable energy to unraveling where our research and best practices are missing the boat. We've concluded that the answer lies in too much focus on the formal PM system—rating scales, rating criteria, process steps, and so on—and too little focus on informal but key behaviors that actually drive effective performance.

Research has shown that engagement and performance are associated with several key behaviors, for example, articulating clear expectations, providing regular feedback, taking an interest in employees' well-being, and developing the employees.[1,2] These positive, day-to-day behaviors comprise the essence of PM and do, in fact, lead to the promised PM outcomes. However, this is not what we get from our formal PM systems. The disconnect results from the fact that our formal systems tend to drive very intermittent, calendar-based events (e.g., setting goals at the beginning of the year, conducting mid- and end-year feedback reviews) rather than effective, ongoing PM behavior that needs to occur daily.

The behaviors that matter most are deceptively simple yet powerful drivers of performance:

- *Vision.* Alignment between employee activities and the organization's mission is critical. While there are formal processes to achieve this (e.g., cascade goals at the beginning of each year), more is actually gained through regular conversations between managers and employees about alignment between the work and the mission.

- *Action.* While setting expectations is core to PM, it is not the annual goal-setting process that drives outcomes. Rather, it is ongoing expectations that

are set regularly as work changes and evolves. Ongoing, real-time feedback tied to expectations is also essential for high performance. In most formal systems, feedback is programmed into one or two annual review meetings, which are too infrequent to impact performance. In contrast, feedback that facilitates engagement and performance happens informally in day-to-day conversations as work is performed.

- *Growth.* Formal PM systems usually include an annual development review. However, because 80% or more of learning occurs on the job, it is actually development through ongoing job experience and regular coaching that enhances performance and engagement.

The bottom line is that more emphasis needs to be placed on fostering and sustaining the key PM behaviors as we implement PM systems in organizations—to the point that they become intricately woven into the fabric of the organization's DNA.

[1] From Corporate Leadership Council, *Driving Employee Performance and Retention Through Engagement: A Quantitative Analysis of the Effectiveness of Employee Engagement Strategies* (Catalog No. CLC12PV0PD), Washington, DC: Corporate Executive Board, 2004.

[2] From A. Bryant, "Google's Quest to Build a Better Boss," *The New York Times,* March 12, 2011, p. BU1.

### Applying Your Knowledge

1. Given the increase in global competition for the best personnel, what role can performance management play in giving companies a competitive edge?

2. How do the issues covered in this section on contemporary performance appraisal research inform PDRI's focus on vision, action, and growth?

3. In what ways has technology allowed for easier assessment of informal behaviors on a more frequent basis? In what ways does technology perhaps present challenges to such assessments?

includes interpreting, understanding, dealing with, and believing or discounting the feedback. Finally, the last step is *using the feedback,* which involves using the feedback to set goals and to track progress. These three steps are integral to making effective use of feedback; of course, if any of the three steps are ignored or handled ineffectively, this will likely result in feedback-related problems such as misperceptions, anxiety, a lack of understanding, and unwise behavioral choices.

In addition to the important steps of the performance management cycle, we also need to consider qualities or characteristics of the feedback itself if we are to truly understand the process. For instance, what makes for good feedback? What kind of feedback is most effective? A very important study by Kluger and DeNisi (1996) created a stir by arguing that feedback is not as effective and beneficial as we had long thought. They did a meta-analysis of research on feedback interventions and, while showing a positive moderate effect of feedback on performance ($r = .41$), the analysis also revealed that over one-third of the studies showed negative effects and many found no effect at all. The authors fit these results into the historical literature on feedback and argued that we had been misled by this historical literature. They consequently proposed the feedback intervention theory (FIT), which states that feedback is most effective when it is targeted at the task rather than at the self. They have argued that feedback directed anywhere other than to the task (e.g., "You are such a conscientious employee") distracts the individual and pulls resources and attention from the task at hand, which leads to no change in performance or a decrease in performance. This is a popular theory and Kluger and DeNisi have provided some empirical support.

**Feedback Environment and Feedback Orientation** The culture of an organization serves to constrain or enhance the effectiveness of feedback. The term **feedback environment (FE)** has been proposed to embody that culture while also specifically representing an organization's climate and attitude toward feedback. Research has shown that FE includes such dimensions as source credibility, feedback quality, and feedback delivery, among others. A favorable FE has been linked to satisfaction with and motivation to use the feedback (Steelman, Levy, & Snell, 2004) as well as an interest in seeking feedback. In addition, a positive FE has been tied to high levels of commitment to the organization and OCBs (Norris-Watts & Levy, 2004). Another study found that FE affected performance levels through its effects on feedback seeking and role clarity (Whitaker, Dahling, & Levy, 2007).

Whereas FE is the situational side of the feedback processes, the **feedback orientation (FO)** is the individual-difference side. FO is an individual's overall attitude toward feedback or receptivity to feedback. It includes things like perceptions of the utility of feedback, accountability to use feedback, social awareness through feedback, and self-efficacy in dealing with feedback (Linderbaum & Levy, 2010). The argument is that just as organizations or departments can set or create different feedback environments, individuals can differ in their receptivity to or ideas about feedback. Together, FE and FO seem important in understanding and affecting the

**feedback environment (FE)**
The contextual aspects of the day-to-day supervisor–subordinate and coworker–coworker feedback process.

**feedback orientation (FO)**
An individual's overall receptivity to feedback.

feedback process. FO is related to other individual differences such as *learning goal orientation,* which is the extent to which individuals believe learning and development are possible. In addition, employees high on FO also tend to seek feedback more often (Linderbaum & Levy, 2010) and perform better than those low on FO (Dahling, Chau, & O'Malley, 2012). In a recent study of 623 Chinese employees, researchers examined how age might relate to various dimensions of FO and impact feedback reactions (Wang, Burlacu, Truxillo, James, & Yao, 2015). They found that older workers had higher levels of the social awareness dimension and lower levels of the utility dimension of FO than did younger workers. Further, dimensions of the feedback environment related to feedback reactions in ways that were driven by age and FO dimensions. In sum, FO differences across age resulted in different patterns of the relationships between feedback characteristics and feedback reactions (Wang et al., 2015).

Perhaps in the most interesting study of all those that link FE with FO, researchers found that the experience of a favorable or encouraging FE is not a positive thing for all people. In a study of correctional facility employees, they found that for those individuals who were low on FO, a positive feedback environment was not a motivating factor, and in some instances it actually resulted in a negative effect on motivation (Gabriel, Frantz, Levy, & Hilliard, 2014). In other words, if you are someone who does not value feedback and is not very receptive to it, then working in an environment that values feedback and encourages feedback seeking may be a toxic combination for you and is likely to result in a lack of motivation and a good deal of dissatisfaction. This is the only study to examine and find this interesting effect. More research is certainly needed.

With recent research on FE and FO, we are gathering more and more advanced knowledge about the feedback process. This promises to improve both the employee development and performance appraisal processes in organizations.

## Legal Issues in Performance Appraisal

It is illegal in the United States to discriminate in performance appraisals on the basis of non–performance-related factors such as age, gender, race, ethnicity, religion, and disability. In short, no employee can be promoted, demoted, fired, transferred, or laid off on the basis of any of these factors.

In their article on legal requirements and technical guidelines related to performance appraisal, James Austin, Peter Villanova, and Hugh Hindman (1995) make the following recommendations for performance appraisal:

1. Start with a job analysis. Austin and his colleagues especially recommend developing criteria from a documented job analysis.
2. Communicate performance standards to employees in writing.
3. Instead of relying on just an overall rating of performance, recognize that there are separate dimensions of performance that should be evaluated on an individual basis.

4. Use both objective criteria and subjective judgments where possible, and ensure that the subjective judgments evaluate job-related behaviors rather than global personality traits.
5. Give employees access to an appeal mechanism.
6. Use multiple raters rather than one rater with absolute authority.
7. Document everything pertinent to personnel decisions. This recommendation can't be emphasized enough, as one never knows who is likely to bring suit and on what basis. The courts have been clear in such cases: If there is no documentation to support the personnel decision in question, the defendant (i.e., the organization that is being sued for discrimination) is likely to lose the case.
8. Where possible, train the raters; if training is not possible, provide them with written instructions for conducting the performance appraisal.

In an extensive review of court decisions between 1980 and 1995, Jon Werner and Mark Bolino (1997) uncovered more than 300 court of appeals decisions related to performance appraisal. Of these, 109 were related to age discrimination, 102 to race discrimination, and 50 to sex discrimination. The authors attempted to determine which factors were most closely associated with judgments made for or against the plaintiffs (i.e., the employees bringing suit against the company). What they concluded was that, in general, the practical recommendations provided in the literature (e.g., Austin et al., 1995; Barrett & Kernan, 1988; Malos, 1998) seemed consistent with the ways in which the courts make these judgments. For instance, judgment was more likely to be made for the defendant when (1) a job analysis was used, (2) written instructions regarding the appraisal process were provided, (3) employees were provided with an opportunity to review their appraisals, (4) multiple raters agreed on performance ratings, and (5) rater training was used. In addition, these researchers found that rating format (e.g., BARS versus graphic rating scales) didn't seem to matter, as this topic never came up in the judges' written decisions.

On the other hand, the court's view of the fairness of the appraisal process was extremely important. Folger, Konovsky, and Cropanzano (1992) refer to this as the *test metaphor* view of performance appraisal. What they recommend, however, is the *due process metaphor* view of performance appraisal, in which the emphasis is on (1) adequate notice, (2) a fair hearing, and (3) judgments based on evidence. Each of these three components of due process—a familiar term in the legal arena—is built around perceptions of justice. In short, courts value the presence of justice in appraisal systems—an observation that supports continued research on contextual variables of this type.

An interesting trend that promises to get the attention of legal experts working both in and out of organizations is the use of wearable technology, or what has become simply known as "wearables." As I write this chapter, I can look down at my arm and see a Fitbit on my wrist that records my steps, my intense activity, my sleep, my workouts, etc. My iPhone is next to me on my desk and I can use it to pull up the data recorded by my Fitbit—for instance, it tells me that I slept 5 hours and 36 minutes last night, that it took me 15 minutes to fall asleep, that I woke up once and was restless for about 21 minutes (clearly, I was worried about finishing this chapter by today's deadline!). This technology has

**A CLOSER LOOK**
Reductions in force or layoffs are serious business. What are the potential implications of a careless or thoughtless approach to making and implementing these decisions?

been available for years and has certainly caught on in the healthcare market as a way for individuals to monitor their behaviors. It also provides a way for employers to offer incentives for specific healthy behaviors (for example, my wife gets a rebate on her health insurance if she hits certain annual goals for healthy behaviors). In recent years companies have become interested in using wearables for workplace purposes, such as increasing productivity, enhancing employee well-being, and reducing work-related injuries (Rackspace, 2014). In a recent study conducted by the University of London and online hosting company Rackspace, the findings clearly show that wearables (e.g., brain activity sensors, motion monitors, and posture coaches) can benefit both productivity and well-being at work. Theatro, one of the leading designers of wearables, reports a 5% to 10% increase in productivity for companies that have used their wearable device (Dishman, 2014).

Wearables have become a $20 billion industry (Harrop, Hayward, Das, & Holland, 2015)! Although the most common use is currently in the health arena, other workplaces are finding ways to use wearable technology. For instance, in manufacturing industries, wearables can be used for hands-free access to information such as instructions, maintenance guides, real-time interactions with off-site supervisors or trainers, and so on (Openshaw & Greenspun, 2014). H. James Wilson, a leading researcher on human–technology interaction, has coined the term "physiolytics" to describe the link between wearables and data analysis to provide feedback and improve performance (Wilson, 2013). He suggests three kinds of analysis that come from wearables: (1) quantification of movements within physical work environments, such as monitoring and recording goods or products at a distribution center, (2) working with information more efficiently by analyzing the time and motion spent on a task, and (3) analyzing our personal "big data," such as blood pressure, brain waves, and cognitive patterns.

There is a great deal of agreement that the technology of physiolytics has potential for individuals and organizations, but as you can imagine, there are questions of privacy and worries that "Big Brother" will be watching our every move. Privacy concerns are likely to lead to legal issues and lawsuits filed by employees claiming that their rights have been violated (McLellan, 2015; Tremaine, 2015). The use of wearables for organizational purposes is very new, and the jury is out on how well this technology will be received by employees, but I think there is very little doubt that cases will begin making their way through our court systems. It will be very interesting to watch what emerges from this legal activity.

## I/O TODAY

### Technology, Performance Measurement, and Privacy

The advent of digital tools like wearables, online surveys, smartphones, and access badges have undoubtedly improved the rudimentary and cumbersome HR processes of the past. A few decades ago, evaluating employee performance required that managers remember to note their subordinate's activity and manually record it with appropriate documentation. Now, a manager can quickly pull up an evaluation form on a tablet, enter in ratings and comments, and have this feedback saved or delivered to the employee instantly. These digital systems have made previously time-consuming processes like 360-degree feedback vastly more efficient. Employees can download a survey and quickly enter in their ratings, which are saved to a shared database that is used by the other evaluators. Analysts can easily break down these ratings for different teams and individuals. In these examples, technology enhances the performance evaluation process, making it more efficient for the manager and more accessible and easier to manipulate for the analyst.

Innovation in this area is occurring at a rapid pace, and often concerns about privacy get lost in the shuffle. Imagine that a company is able to track an individual's movements by monitoring his or her access badge. This monitoring might give managers valid information about their subordinate's performance—whether employees arrive and leave on time, whether they attend scheduled meetings, and so on. However, this system might also gather a lot of information that is not related to performance and that could be used inappropriately. Perhaps an individual makes many trips to the restroom (due to a medical condition) or a female employee steps out of the office twice a day (maybe she just had a baby and is using her breaks to visit the attached daycare to nurse). If a manager chose to discipline or fire these individuals based on this data alone, these individuals could likely bring discrimination lawsuits.

In general, laws allow companies to monitor their employees closely (Privacy Rights Clearinghouse, 2015). Court cases have upheld video recordings of employees in public spaces, monitoring of e-mails and voice mails, monitoring of company-issued phones, and monitoring of social media activity. There are a few exceptions; in many cases, employees must consent to audio recordings, and several states have enacted laws barring companies from requesting passwords to social media accounts.

Regardless of the law, many employees feel uncomfortable with their employers monitoring them closely. Recently, a woman was fired for deleting an app that tracked her movements even when off the job (Matyszczyk, 2015). While it appears that this is legal because the phone was company-issued, her boss allegedly bragged that he knew where she was going and what she was doing off-hours. This case and others like it beg the question of whether tracking employees is ethical, particularly when data is vulnerable to misuse by supervisors or could be breached by hackers. The boundary between what is and is not legal and appropriate for employers to track will likely be a growing issue for I/O psychologists.

### Discussion Questions

1. Imagine that you are working with cashiers at a retail store. What types of information might you collect to judge their performance? What might be some ways you could use technology to make this process easier?
2. Is it reasonable for employees to be concerned about their privacy at work? What can organizations do to respect employee privacy, while still tracking behaviors that are relevant for performance appraisal?

### References

Matyszczyk, C. (2015, May 12). Woman allegedly fired for deleting iPhone app that monitored her 24/7. *CNET.* Retrieved October 26, 2015, from http://www.cnet.com/news/woman-allegedly-fired-for-deleting-iphone-app-that-monitored-her-24-hrs-a-day/

Privacy Rights Clearinghouse. (2015). Fact sheet 7: Workplace privacy and employee monitoring. Retrieved October 26, 2015, from https://www.privacyrights.org/workplace-privacy-and-employee-monitoring

### Additional Readings

Miller, C., & Wells, S. F. (2007). Balancing security and privacy in the digital workplace. *Journal of Change Management, 7,* 315–328.

# Summary

Performance appraisals are used to make personnel decisions, to provide employees with important job-related feedback, and to document employee performance as a way of protecting the organization from potential legal suits. Industrial/organizational psychologists often play an active and important role in the performance management systems of organizations.

Performance appraisals are available in many formats, including graphic rating scales, BARS, CARS, checklists, and employee comparison procedures. Each format has advantages and disadvantages (see Table 5.1); none have clearly been identified as the single best approach. The process of appraising an individual's performance is very complex and can result in rating errors such as halo, leniency, central tendency, and severity. Two types of rater training, Rater Error Training (RET) and Frame of Reference (FOR) Training, have been established as potentially useful in reducing these errors and/or improving accuracy.

Contemporary performance appraisal research continues to focus on the social-psychological context in which the appraisal takes place. This research indicates that ratee and rater reactions toward the appraisal process are important in measuring the success of an appraisal system. Also relevant to the appraisal process are the relationship between the supervisor and subordinate, the political climate within the organization, the rater's motivation and accountability, and the degree of trust among raters.

Participation is another integral element in the appraisal process. One interesting development in this area is the 360-degree feedback system, in which employees receive performance feedback from peers, subordinates, supervisors, and clients/customers. Self-ratings are commonly included in this system, especially when the only other participant is the supervisor. Although 360-degree feedback is relatively new, research indicates not only that many employees like it but also that it has a great deal of potential for improving the feedback process in general. Employee development continues to grow in importance as both employees and organizations recognize the benefits of employee growth and learning. Employee development not only benefits individual workers but also functions as a source of competitive advantage for organizations that encourage and provide opportunities for development.

Adherence to legal guidelines is also critical to the performance appraisal process. Recent work has identified fairness as important not only to ratees but also to the courts, which appear to weight it quite heavily in making judgments for or against plaintiffs. And while emerging technology, such as wearables, will lead to many interesting and innovative approaches to performance management, it may also raise legal concerns over privacy violations.

As we have seen, performance appraisal has widespread implications for organizations because appraisal information is used for such important personnel decisions as promotions, demotions, layoffs, dismissals, and raises. Obviously, invalid performance appraisal information is likely to result in poor organizational decisions. Our understanding of the appraisal process is thus enhanced by our appreciation of the context in which it takes place.

## Key Terms

BARS (p. 132)
central tendency (p. 142)
coaching (p. 128)
context (p. 146)
critical incidents (p. 133)
distributional errors (p. 141)
feedback environment (FE) (p. 156)
feedback orientation (FO) (p. 156)
Frame of Reference (FOR)
    Training (p. 144)

halo (p. 140)
leniency (p. 141)
performance appraisal (p. 126)
performance management (p. 128)
Rater Error Training (RET) (p. 144)
severity (p. 142)
360-degree feedback (p. 128)
telework (p. 131)
true halo (p. 141)
upward appraisal ratings (p. 130)

## TAKING IT TO THE FIELD

Although this chapter primarily discusses rating formats, errors, and training, performance appraisal also depends heavily on appropriately defining the criteria/criterion, as discussed in Chapter 4. Pai Ng, who is the director of institutional research at Blackwood College, is asking for your advice for a new teaching evaluation that she wants students to complete for their professors each semester. Please read her e-mail below and then respond to her questions, carefully considering both the content and the format of her measure.

Hello again—
    Below you will find the draft of the measure I am planning on trying out this semester. I would like your advice on the current items and any suggestions for additional items. Which items do you feel will be most helpful, least helpful, and why? And do you feel that I'm leaving any items out that would assist in conducting better evaluations? I also have heard about a different rating system known as BARS: What is it, and would this be a good thing to include on our evaluations?
        Pai

### Blackwood College Teaching Evaluation

Please rate the following:

| | Satisfactory | | Good | | Excellent |
|---|---|---|---|---|---|
| Instructor's knowledge about the topic | 1 | 2 | 3 | 4 | 5 |
| Instructor's responses to e-mails | 1 | 2 | 3 | 4 | 5 |
| Instructor's friendliness | 1 | 2 | 3 | 4 | 5 |
| Instructor's use of technology | 1 | 2 | 3 | 4 | 5 |
| Quality of room | 1 | 2 | 3 | 4 | 5 |
| Quality of book | 1 | 2 | 3 | 4 | 5 |
| Quality of assignments | 1 | 2 | 3 | 4 | 5 |

| | Strongly Disagree | | Neutral | | Strongly Agree |
|---|---|---|---|---|---|
| I enjoyed this class. | 1 | 2 | 3 | 4 | 5 |
| This class was interesting. | 1 | 2 | 3 | 4 | 5 |
| I would take another class with this instructor. | 1 | 2 | 3 | 4 | 5 |
| I came to this class most days. | 1 | 2 | 3 | 4 | 5 |
| The instructor's grades were fair. | 1 | 2 | 3 | 4 | 5 |
| This instructor should continue to teach at Blackwood College. | 1 | 2 | 3 | 4 | 5 |

## Critical Thinking Questions

1. Based on what you have read, design a rater training program that will help supervisors assess the performance of their subordinates as accurately as possible. What techniques will you include? What important variables can impact rater effectiveness?

2. The chapter discusses both performance appraisal and the broader performance management system. How do these two concepts differ? How are they related?

3. Several different rating formats are presented in the chapter. If you were designing a performance appraisal process for an organization, what types of scales or formats might you use (e.g. BARS, graphic scales)? Would you use paper-and-pencil formats, or would you use a technology-based approach? What rationale do you have for your choices?

4. Multisource feedback is a tool used to obtain feedback from individuals at various levels of the organization. Frequently, the target employee (the one receiving the feedback) selects the individuals who will provide feedback. What are some potential drawbacks of allowing the target employee to select his or her raters? Should the target employee's supervisor be responsible for selecting raters? How else could raters be determined? How might we incorporate technology into this process?

5. Consider a job you have had in the past, or a job you would like to have. How might you use wearables to measure your performance in this role? How would you feel about that company monitoring your behaviors using this technology?

## Application Questions

1. Imagine that when using a 360-degree performance appraisal system, an employee receives a rating of 3.5/5 from his supervisor, 4.2/5 from his peers, and 2.25/5 from his subordinates. What might be some reasons for these discrepancies? What would you recommend that this individual's supervisor do to gain a better understanding of what these ratings indicate about the employee's performance?

2. Imagine that, in order to assign grades on a group project, your professor requires all group members to provide ratings for one another, which he will consider in grading the project. One group member has been particularly troublesome—she has been argumentative, refuses to accommodate other group members' schedules, and completes the bare minimum amount of work. Would you feel comfortable giving her a poor performance appraisal? Why or why not?

3. Once again, imagine that your professor has asked for your feedback on your fellow group members' performance on a project. This time, you have a group member who is very proactive in volunteering and takes an active role; however, even though she tries very hard, she has a lot of trouble understanding concepts introduced in the class; as a result, often the work she does is not usable for the project. Would you feel comfortable giving her a poor performance appraisal? Why or why not?

4. In many work environments, employees can engage in organizational citizenship behaviors (acts that help coworkers or the organization, even though they are not part of their job), such as staying late to work on a project they are not normally a part of or speaking positively about the organization to other people. Should these behaviors be considered in a performance appraisal? Why or why not?

5. Think of a time when you worked with someone who did not perform as well as you believed he or she should. What sorts of things did this person do/not do that led to a poor performance? If you were asked to deliver feedback to this person, what would you say?

## Suggested Readings

**Allen, T. D., Golden, T. D., & Shockley, K. M.** (2015). How effective is telecommuting? Assessing the status of our scientific findings. *Psychological Science in the Public Interest*, *16*(2), 40–68. A nice review of the telecommuting trend and one that comes at it from a scientific perspective.

**DeNisi, A. S., & Pritchard, R. D.** (2006). Performance appraisal, performance management, and improving individual performance: A motivational framework. *Management and Organizational Review, 2*, 253–277. This is a good resource for understanding the ongoing performance management process and moving away from stand-alone performance appraisals.

**Farr, J. L., & Levy, P. E.** (2007). Performance appraisal. In L. L. Koppes (Ed.), *Historical perspectives in industrial and organizational psychology* (pp. 311–327). Mahwah, NJ: Erlbaum.

This chapter provides a review of the historical development of performance appraisal methods and approaches since the beginning of the 20th century.

**Ferris, G. R., Munyon, T. P., Basik, K., & Buckley, M. R.** (2008). The performance evaluation context: Social, emotional, cognitive, political, and relationship components. *Human Resource Management Review, 18,* 146–163. This excellent follow-up to Levy and Williams (2004) continues the argument for the importance of context in performance appraisal and fleshes out a theoretical framework for additional research and thinking.

**Levy, P. E., & Williams, J. R.** (2004). The social context of performance appraisal: A review and framework for the future. *Journal of Management, 30*(6), 881–905. This comprehensive review of the performance appraisal research since 1995 places a particular emphasis on the social context of performance appraisal.

**Fletcher, C., and Baldry, C.** (2015). Multi-source feedback systems: A research perspective. In I. T. Robertson and Cary L. Cooper (Eds.), *Personnel psychology and human resources management: A reader for students and practitioners.* John Wiley & Sons.

**Smither, J. W., London, M., Flautt, R., Vargas, Y., & Kucine, I.** (2003). Can working with an executive coach improve multisource feedback ratings over time? A quasi-experimental field study. *Personnel Psychology, 56,* 23–44. This study demonstrates the value of working through multisource feedback with a coach and using the feedback to set goals and create action plans for improvement.

# Predictors

Photo: Hill Street Studios/Blend Images/Getty Images

## LEARNING OBJECTIVES

This chapter should help you understand:

- The definition of a test and how to find existing tests used for personnel selection
- The differences between various testing formats, such as speed versus power tests, individual versus group tests, and paper-and-pencil versus performance tests
- The importance of validity coefficients to employee selection
- Definitions, estimates of validity, and examples of the following types of predictors: cognitive ability (both general and specific) tests, psychomotor tests, personality tests, integrity tests, work samples, assessment centers, biographical information, and interviews

Criteria are central to organizations and I/O psychology, but in a selection context we typically don't have access to criteria and instead must use predictors as proxies or substitutes for criteria.

Think about a large law firm that is in the market to hire a new associate right out of law school. Ideally, the firm would like to have some criterion data on the potential applicants before making a decision about which one to hire. However, criterion data (e.g., number of lawsuits won, number of cases argued in district court, billable hours logged per month, etc.) aren't available on the applicants because they haven't been employed as lawyers yet. You can see the catch-22 in which the firm is entangled: It wants to hire the right person, the one who will do the best job; but without bringing the applicant on board and seeing how he or she will do, the firm has no criterion data with which to make a decision.

This is where *predictors* come into the picture. Predictors are used in place of criteria; in fact, they are used to forecast criteria. In this situation, the law firm might rely on such predictors as performance in law school, performance in mock trials, letters of recommendation from law professors, and tests of cognitive ability. Selection is all about prediction, or forecasting. Available data are used to predict who is likely to be successful on the job so that the individual in question can be hired. Predictors are of great importance because we place so much trust in their ability to model criteria. Just as faulty criteria can result in bad organizational decisions such as firing or promoting the wrong employee, faulty predictors can result in hiring the wrong person or not hiring the right person. First, we will consider the different formats of tests that are used in organizations for selection and then we will consider the specific predictors that are used to forecast who is likely to be an effective performer.

# TESTING FORMATS

A test is a systematic procedure for observing behavior and describing it with the aid of numerical scales or fixed categories. Tests are systematic in that they are administered in the same way across groups of people, following some sort of script or listing of procedures. In the broad area of employee selection, tests are used as predictors to forecast performance on the job or some other work-related criterion. Thus, I will use the terms *predictor* and *test* interchangeably in our discussion. This discussion should be of interest to all readers, even those who aren't budding I/O psychologists, because at some point you will need to apply (or already have applied) for a job, a scholarship, or admission to a school. In all these situations, you probably will provide the prospective employer, organization, or school with predictor information. Chances are that these predictors will be used to forecast your potential criterion performance.

To select or develop predictors, we start—once again—with a *job analysis*. Remember that we use the job analysis not only to define the job through identifying what gets done on the job and what it takes to do the job, but also to pinpoint relevant criteria that are important for job success. This information, in turn, helps us to locate, develop, create, or modify predictors that we hope are valid indicators of the criteria. Sometimes we might develop our own tests to tap the KSAOs (knowledge, skills, abilities, and other characteristics) in which we are interested, whereas at other times we might find an established test and modify it or use it in its entirety to tap a particular KSAO. **Figure 6.1** shows a graphical representation of how specific tests may be chosen to measure particular KSAs regarding the job of college professor. These tests are linked directly to the job specifications stemming from the job analysis. The boxes in this figure give examples of specific data that could be used to quantify the KSAs identified from the job analysis. In addition, one or two examples of the type of predictors that might be useful for each of these specific KSAs are provided in the figure. For instance, let's look at a specific ability. The job analysis identifies job specifications; in particular, it specifies "communication ability" as an important KSA. Communication ability can be tapped in a couple of ways. For instance, we can interview candidates and evaluate the communication skills we observe in the interview. In addition to the interview, we could provide candidates with a work sample test in which they are asked to give a lecture on a given topic to a class of undergraduates.

There are some established sources that describe thousands of existing tests, perhaps the best example of which is the *Mental Measurements Yearbook* (Spies, Carlson, & Geisinger, 2010), which has been published for over 50 years and continues to be published biennially by the Buros Institute. This resource provides evaluations of tests in a variety of areas. These evaluations include the psychometric properties, cost, and administration time of the tests, as well as information on how to obtain them.

**test**
A systematic procedure for observing behavior and describing it with the aid of numerical scales or fixed categories.

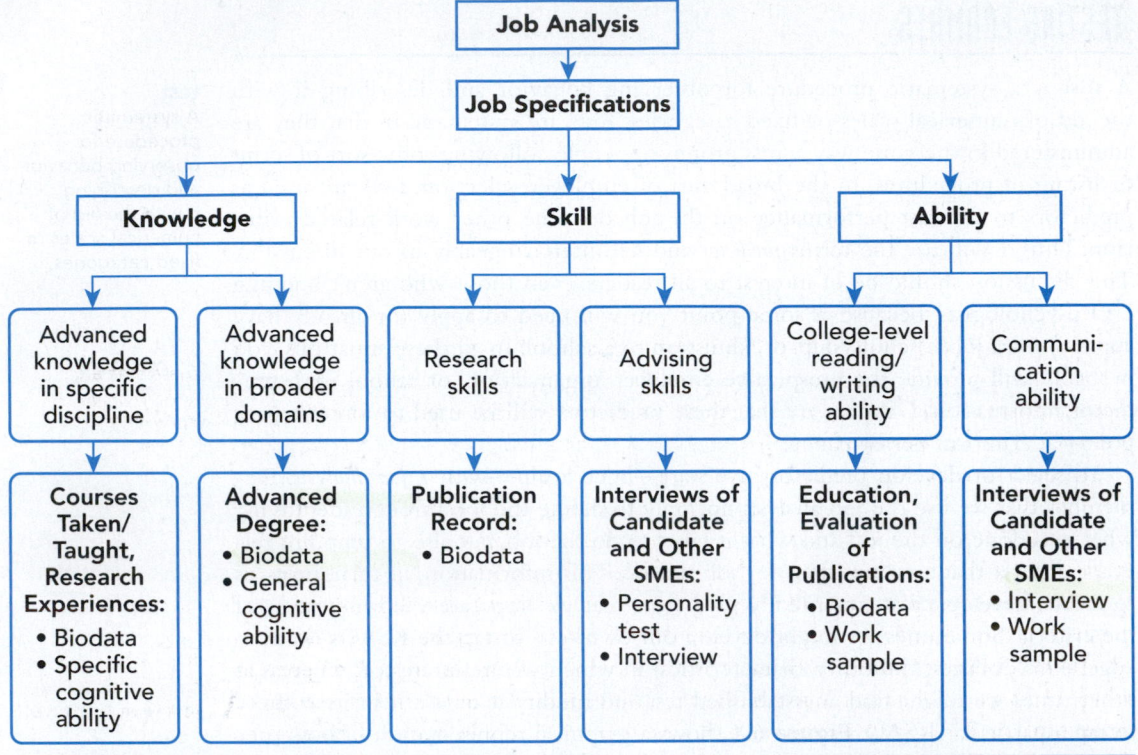

**FIGURE 6.1** Linking Job Analysis to Specific Measures of KSAs

## Computer Adaptive Testing

**computer adaptive testing**
The process through which computer technology is used to identify easier and harder questions for applicants that eventually estimate their true ability level.

A recent trend in testing is the delivery of tests via the computer and sometimes testing that takes place on the Internet. Some computerized tests (e.g., the GRE) are adaptive. **Computer adaptive testing** means that how you score on earlier questions affects the difficulty of subsequent questions. This approach allows for quick and accurate scoring (Educational Testing Service, 2007). If an individual answers an easy question correctly, the next item that is chosen for delivery by the computer is more difficult. If that is answered correctly, another more difficult item follows, but if that is answered incorrectly, then the next question is less difficult than the one the test taker just got wrong. This process is believed to provide more precise measurement and to quickly identify the test taker's ability level through this back-and-forth process that eventually ends at the best estimate of the individual's ability level (for a more detailed discussion, see Farr & Tippins, 2013).

Tests fall into different categories based on their various dimensions. Several of these categories are described in the following sections.

## Speed Versus Power Tests

**speed test**
A test containing relatively easy items with a short time limit in which individuals must complete as many items as they can.

A speed test is composed of relatively easy items with a short time limit in which individuals must complete as many items as they can. One example would be a typing test for a word-processing job. Applicants are instructed to type as much of a writing sample as they can in five minutes, and they are scored on the basis of how much they finished and the number of errors they made. A **power test**, by contrast, has no fixed time limit and tends to be more difficult. Test takers are expected to be able to complete all the items on a power test, but not on a speed test. Most college exams are power tests; although the items are somewhat difficult, students are given what is believed to be enough time to complete them all. In our typing example, however, test takers are not expected to have time to type the entire written sample in the five minutes allotted.

**power test**
A test with no fixed time limits and relatively difficult items.

## Individual Versus Group Tests

**Individual tests** are administered to one person at a time and, thus, are very costly in terms of time and money. Though often used for upper-level managerial positions, these tests tend to be avoided at lower levels because of the costs involved. Intelligence tests such as those developed by Wechsler (WAIS-IV and WISC-IV are good examples of individually administered tests in which an examiner assesses one individual at a time. (For more information on these tests, see Flanagan & Kaufman, 2009; Kaufman, 1994; Lichtenberger & Kaufman, 2012.) Individual tests may take as long as two or three hours to complete and often have to be administered and scored by someone trained specifically on the test in question. More frequently used in organizations are **group tests**, in which many applicants can be tested at one time. For instance, it is typical for a police officer or firefighter promotion test to be given in a group context where all those who meet the requirements are given the test at the same time in the same location. These tests are more conducive to employee selection and, thus, more cost effective—especially in situations in which a company may have 50 or more applicants who need to be assessed for only a few job openings.

**individual tests**
Tests that are administered to one person at a time.

**group tests**
Tests in which many applicants can be tested at one time.

## Paper-and-Pencil Versus Performance Tests

**Paper-and-pencil tests** are the ones we've all most commonly experienced. In such tests, we respond to questions in a test booklet or by marking computer sheets to be scanned. These questions can take several different forms, including essay, multiple choice, true–false, and short answer. Most cognitive ability tests are of this type. Both the ACT and the SAT are paper-and-pencil tests; so are most of your course examinations. However, computer technology has led to "paper-and-pencil" tests being available in computerized versions. A body of literature has emerged that focuses on the comparability of assessing personality or intelligence via Internet-based versus paper-and-pencil tests (Kantrowitz & Dainis, 2014; Karim, Kaminsky, & Behrend, 2014).

**paper-and-pencil tests**
Frequently used tests in which individuals respond to questions in a test booklet or mark answers on computer sheets to be scanned.

One study of 157 German high school students looked at reasoning-ability measures delivered on handheld computers, notebook computers, and paper-and-pencil delivery schemes (Schroeders & Wilhelm, 2010) and concluded that the assessment medium played no meaningful role in individual responses. The issue of proctored versus unproctored tests (i.e., the extent to which the testing environment is monitored by someone) has become an important issue in recent years. The Internet provides a great venue for unproctored employment tests that applicants or candidates can take

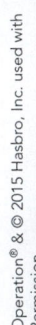

Operation® & © 2015 Hasbro, Inc. used with Permission.

Constantine Pankin/Shutterstock

**A CLOSER LOOK**
What do you think is being tested in each of these photos?

**performance tests**
Tests that require the manipulation of an object or a piece of equipment.

at their convenience. This, however, raises a series of issues about unproctored testing, those related to software and hardware, test security, identity of candidates, and cheating (Tippins et al., 2006). Interestingly, despite these potential concerns, recent research has supported the use of unproctored tests by demonstrating equivalent predictive validities (Beaty et al., 2011) and not showing elevated scores on personality tests (Arthur, Glaze, Villado, & Taylor, 2010). The hottest trend in this domain is mobile testing—the administration of assessments or selection tests on handheld devices such as smart phones. In a recent study of 3.5 million people who took an unproctored test on a mobile or nonmobile device, it was found that it took longer to complete the assessment on the mobile device and the cognitive ability scores were lower (Arthur, Doverspike, Munoz, Taylor, & Carr, 2014). The authors argue that this may be a result of the information-processing difficulty associated with the use of small screen devices or the work distractions present when working on a mobile device vs. a nonmobile device. Despite these differences, a big picture examination of the data indicated that the intercorrelations among all the study variables were incredibly similar across mobile and nonmobile testing, suggesting that the measurements are equivalent. This is a very active research area that will continue to draw attention as the potential benefits from technology continue to surface.

**Performance tests** require the manipulation of an object or a piece of equipment. These include tests of manual dexterity or psychomotor skills, which we will talk about later in this chapter. Most of us would insist that our surgeons have a certain degree of manual dexterity with the instruments necessary for their surgical specialty. This skill could not be evaluated with a paper-and-pencil test but, instead, would require some sort of performance test. (Does the children's game "Operation" ring a bell?) Similarly, manufacturing jobs and trades such as plumbing and electrical work often require manipulation of objects or pieces of equipment.

## PREDICTORS

Many predictors are used for selection purposes, and we will discuss several of these in the following sections; but first, let's revisit a couple of concepts. Recall our lengthy discussion of reliability and validity in Chapter 2 and our application of these concepts to *criteria* in Chapter 4. Reliability and validity are just as important for the predictors that we will discuss here. An unreliable predictor will not be successful in predicting job performance.

Imagine a situation in which you are trying to select automobile mechanics by giving them printouts from a diagnostic machine and asking them to use this information to diagnose a car's problem. This makes sense: Diagnostic skills are important (i.e., they are KSAOs) for mechanics and, thus, ought to be used to predict on-the-job performance. However, suppose we don't realize that in about half of the trials, the diagnostic machine is not working properly. An applicant may appear to make the wrong diagnosis about half the time, thus scoring low on this predictor. In other words, her misdiagnoses may be a result of the diagnostic machine's errors rather than her own errors. In this situation, our predictor score would be unreliable and thus not very useful for predicting performance.

When we talk about the validity of a predictor, we are usually thinking in terms of *criterion-related validity*, discussed in Chapter 2. Keep in mind that the sole purpose of predictors in I/O psychology is to predict some performance criterion. Because we don't have access to performance criteria prior to hiring employees, we use predictors as proxies for the criteria—and it is here that criterion-related validity takes on great importance. If a predictor is not related to a criterion, then the predictor serves little purpose. To avoid this problem, I/O psychologists spend a great deal of effort finding, developing, and validating predictors. In this way, organizations can be confident that selecting applicants based on predictor scores will result in the selection of those with the greatest potential to be successful on-the-job performers.

The correlation is important to selection because it can be used for prediction, which is often the major goal of any selection or testing initiative. In fact, in the context of selection, it has a special name—**validity coefficient (r)**. As an index of the relationship between a predictor and a criterion, it is used by selection researchers and practitioners as evidence that a particular test is a good predictor of job performance. The coefficient of determination can be thought of as the percentage of variance in the criterion variable that is accounted for by the predictor variable. It reflects how well one variable predicts the other. For example, we could use a measure of general cognitive ability to predict job performance, calculate the validity coefficient (i.e., correlation), and square that coefficient (i.e., coefficient of determination) to estimate the amount of variance in a group of applicants' criterion scores that can be accounted for by this group's cognitive ability scores. In other words, we could determine how well measures of general cognitive ability predict individuals' performance on the job, as summarized by the validity coefficient.

Let's take a closer look at predictors in the context of cognitive ability.

> **TECHNICAL TIP**
>
> *Remember from Chapter 2 (page **61**) our discussion about the correlation coefficient as the index of the strength of a relationship. Also, we saw how squaring the correlation coefficient told us how much variance in one variable was accounted for by another variable—the coefficient of determination.*

**validity coefficient (r)**
A correlation that serves as an index of the relationship between a predictor and a criterion, used by selection researchers and practitioners as evidence that a particular test is a valid predictor of a performance criterion.

## Cognitive Ability

Tests of *cognitive ability* are among the most frequently used predictors in selection contexts (e.g., employee selection, college admissions) because of the common belief that mental functioning or intelligence is important for most jobs, as well as for success in school. There are two classes of cognitive ability tests, or what are sometimes called *intelligence tests.* The first are general cognitive ability tests, and the second are specific cognitive ability tests.

**General Cognitive Ability Tests** The Wonderlic Personnel Test (Wonderlic, 1984) has been one of the most frequently used measures of cognitive ability for many years. It's even used (with some controversy) to assess the cognitive ability of professional athletes (e.g., NFL and NBA players) and to attempt to predict how these athletes will perform on and off the field (McCann, 2006). **Figure 6.2** presents a few examples of items similar to those found on the Wonderlic test (as well as other tests of general cognitive ability). A debate over the importance of general cognitive ability in employee selection contexts continues to rage (Beier & Oswald, 2012; Farr & Tippins, 2013; Gardner & Diedrick, 2009; Goldstein, Zedeck, & Goldstein, 2002; Kuncel, Hezlett, & Ones, 2004).

There's a fair amount of evidence suggesting that general cognitive ability accounts for a large proportion of variance in criterion performance (Ree, Earles, & Teachout, 1994; Salgado & Anderson, 2003). For instance, a meta-analysis of various studies in this area indicates that the validity coefficient for measures of general cognitive ability is .53 (Hunter & Hunter, 1984). This means that over 25% of the performance variance in people (i.e., the differences in performance across people) is accounted for or can be predicted by measures of general cognitive ability (the simple calculation is $.53^2$ or $.53 \times .53$, which equals .25 or 25%). It is important, too, to note that general cognitive ability predicts performance similarly across countries such as the United Kingdom (Bertua, Anderson, & Salgado, 2005) and, in general, the European

---

1. **Focused is the opposite of:**
    *a. scattered*  b. concerned  c. helpful  d. gracious

2. **Automobile is to road as boat is to:**
    a. air  b. tracks  *c. water*  d. gasoline

3. **Which of the following months has 31 days?**
    a. September  b. April  c. June  *d. December*

4. **Which number completes the series: 2, 4, 8, 4, 8, 16, 8,**
    *a. 16*  b. 12  c. 8  d. 20

5. **If Bill runs 3 miles in 30 minutes, how many miles will he run in 1½ hours?**
    *a. 12*  b. 6  c. 9  d. 8

**FIGURE 6.2**  **Items Similar to Those Found on the Wonderlic Personnel Test** (Information from Goldstein, H. W., Zedeck, S., & Goldstein, I. L. (2002). g: Is this your final answer? *Human Performance, 15*(1–2), 123–142)

community, where the validity has been estimated at .62 (Salgado et al., 2003). Notice, however, that if 25% (.53²) or 36% (.62²) of the criterion variance is accounted for by this measure, 75% or 64% is left unaccounted for. Is it reasonable to ask if we can do better? This question has been discussed for years, and researchers are continually working to determine what other predictors might help account for a greater percentage of the criterion variance, or what is called *incremental validity*. A recent meta-analysis used more sophisticated statistical techniques to support our knowledge that general cognitive ability accounts for up to 25% of the variance in performance (Lang, Kersting, Hülsheger, & Lang, 2010). In addition, this study found that general cognitive ability wasn't always the most important predictor and that specific cognitive ability sometimes plays a more important role in predicting performance.

**Specific Cognitive Ability Tests** Whereas general cognitive ability tests attempt to predict the likelihood that an individual will perform well in a particular job by measuring the individual's *general* capacity to learn, tests of specific cognitive abilities attempt to predict the likelihood that an individual will do well in a particular job given his or her *specific* abilities. For instance, tests of **mechanical ability** tap comprehension of mechanical relations, recognition of tools used for various purposes, and sometimes actual mechanical skills. The Bennett Mechanical Comprehension Test (Psychological Corporation, 1980) is probably the best known of this type. Sample items from the SRA (Science Research Associates) Test of Mechanical Concepts, another popular test, are presented in **Figure 6.3**.

> **mechanical ability**
> A specific cognitive ability involving a focus on mechanical relations, recognition of tools used for various purposes, and sometimes actual mechanical skills.

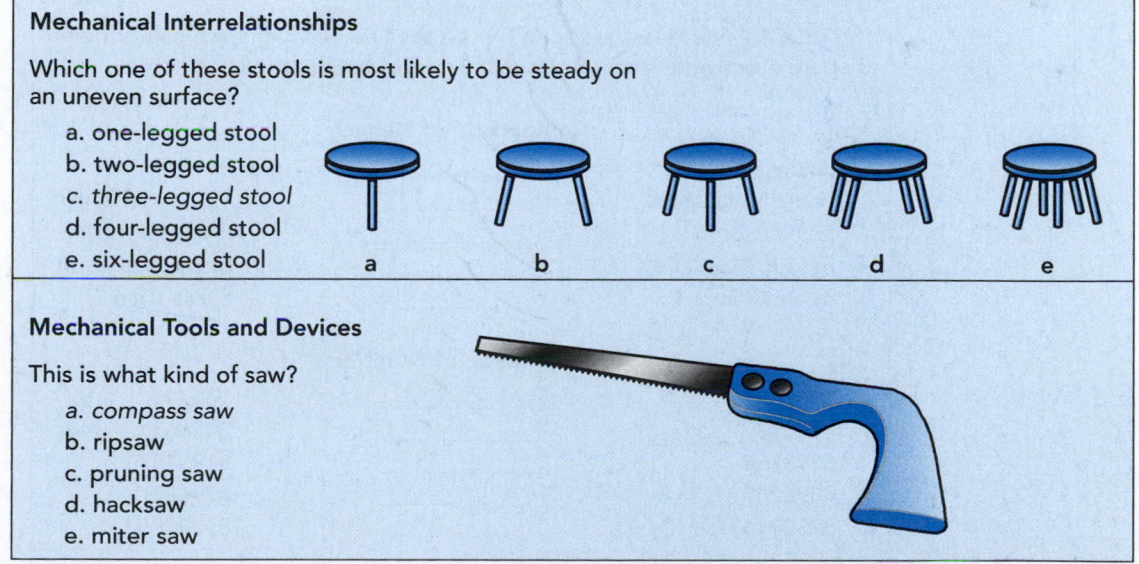

**Mechanical Interrelationships**

Which one of these stools is most likely to be steady on an uneven surface?

   a. one-legged stool
   b. two-legged stool
   c. three-legged stool
   d. four-legged stool
   e. six-legged stool

   a    b    c    d    e

**Mechanical Tools and Devices**

This is what kind of saw?

   a. compass saw
   b. ripsaw
   c. pruning saw
   d. hacksaw
   e. miter saw

**FIGURE 6.3** Sample Items from the SRA Test of Mechanical Concepts (Information from Goldstein, H. W., Zedeck, S., & Goldstein, I. L. (2002). g: Is this your final answer? *Human Performance, 15*(1–2), 123–142)

A test of mechanical ability would be relevant for such jobs as machine operator, factory worker, and engineer, in which mechanical principles are important. Glance back at the framework of industrial psychology presented in Figure 3.1, and you'll see that two of the three major outcomes of job analysis—job description and job specifications—should tell us whether or not mechanical ability is important for the particular job of interest.

Closely related to mechanical ability is spatial ability, a second specific cognitive ability that plays an important role in many jobs. Measures of spatial ability often deal with geometric relations, such as visualizing objects and rotating them spatially to form a particular pattern. Jobs for which these types of tests might be relevant include mechanic and architect.

A third specific cognitive ability, clerical ability, is relevant for numerous important positions, such as secretary, administrative assistant, bookkeeper, and clerk. Most measures of clerical ability focus on both perceptual speed and accuracy in processing verbal and numerical data (Gatewood, Feild, & Barrick, 2007). The most frequently used test is probably the Minnesota Clerical Test, which was developed in 1933 (Psychological Corporation, 1979). This test comprises 200 items, each of which consists of a pair of numbers or names; the respondent is asked to place a check next to the pairs that are identical. Items similar to those found on the Minnesota Clerical Test are presented in **Figure 6.4**. An individual's score is the number right minus the number wrong. This is a speed test in which respondents are not expected to get through the entire list of pairs in the time allotted. Performance on the names subtest has been shown to be related to speed of reading and spelling, whereas scores on the numbers subtest are related to arithmetic skills and computations (Gatewood et al., 2007).

**spatial ability**
A specific cognitive ability involving a focus on geometric relations, such as visualizing objects and rotating them spatially to form a particular pattern.

**clerical ability**
A specific cognitive ability, relevant for jobs such as secretary, administrative assistant, and bookkeeper, involving a focus on both perceptual speed and accuracy in processing verbal and numerical data.

---

*INSTRUCTIONS:* Please place an "X" on the line between each pair of items that are exactly the same. Do as many as you can in the allotted time.

### Comparison of Names

| | | |
|---|---|---|
| Bekky Huber | _____ | Becky Huber |
| Verna MacDonald | _____ | Verna McDonald |
| Frank Giorno | _____ | Frank Giorno |
| Bel Air, Maryland | _____ | Belair, Maryland |
| Sylvia Chinn | _____ | Sylvia Chin |

### Comparison of Numbers

| | | |
|---|---|---|
| 13574 | _____ | 13574 |
| 245693 | _____ | 245663 |
| 5193754 | _____ | 5193457 |
| 4396207 | _____ | 4396207 |
| 8730916375 | _____ | 8739016375 |

**FIGURE 6.4** Items Similar to Those Found on the Minnesota Clerical Test

The validity of measures of specific cognitive abilities tends to hover around .40 to .50, with some consistency across cultures (for a review of the relevant research, see Gatewood, Feild, & Barrick, 2011). For instance, Salgado and colleagues (2003) found validity estimates for the European community to range from .35 to .56. One of the most extensive and thorough studies in the selection area in the past 25 years, the Project A study, was conducted in the military and involved over 4,000 enlisted army personnel (McHenry, Hough, Toquam, Hanson, & Ashworth, 1990). Here, the validity coefficients for general cognitive ability and spatial ability predicting core job performance were .63 and .56, respectively. It is clear that both general and specific cognitive abilities are important predictors of job performance across a wide variety of jobs. However, the same large military study also revealed that these two cognitive predictors did not predict a different criterion, incumbents' personal discipline, very well.

As emphasized in the last chapter, the match between the predictor and the criterion is important. No abilities or skills are predictive of all aspects of performance—I/O psychologists have to rely on the job analysis to identify the important KSAOs for predicting particular on-the-job behaviors. A test of spatial ability would not be predictive of my success as a teacher (and it's a good thing or I'd still be looking for work!) but would likely be very helpful in hiring engineers, architects, or cartographers.

A newer and intriguing intelligence construct is **emotional intelligence (EI)**. EI is the ability of individuals to generate, recognize, express, understand, and evaluate their own (and others') emotions, leading to effectiveness in the workplace and their own personal life (Van Rooy & Viswesvaran, 2004). This construct has become very popular in recent years in part because of the success of Daniel Goleman's 1995 book, *Emotional Intelligence* (Semadar, Robins, & Ferris, 2006). See **Table 6.1** for an example of what EI test items might look like.

Some empirical research has indicated that EI may be an important predictor of performance at work. For instance, one study (Carmeli & Josman, 2006) found significant correlations between EI and task performance ($r = .47$), altruistic citizenship behavior ($r = .26$), and compliance citizenship behavior ($r = .21$). An interesting study using undergraduate business students (Rode et al., 2007) found that EI interacted with a conscientious personality to effectively predict college GPA, group performance, and public-speaking effectiveness. The authors concluded that it's not enough

**emotional intelligence (EI)** Ability of a person to deal effectively with his or her emotions and the emotions of others.

| **TABLE 6.1**   Items from an Emotional Intelligence Test |
|---|
| I adjust my behavior depending on who I am interacting with (e.g., calm and friendly with a child, serious and professional with my boss, etc.). |
| I find myself feeling nervous about situations or events, and I don't even know why. |
| I like learning new things. |
| I know which situations I can handle and which ones will take me outside of my emotional comfort zone. |

Source: *Psychology Today*, Emotional Intelligence Test; accessed June 11, 2015.

to be high on EI; you have to be motivated as well. This particular combination of ability and personality seems to predict performance well and, thus, suggests implications for organizations trying to select those applicants who are likely to be effective employees. Further, even more recent work has concluded that EI is a better predictor of social interactions with peers than general cognitive ability but that general cognitive ability predicts academic performance best (Song et al., 2010).

## Psychomotor Tests

**psychomotor tests**
Tests that measure both the speed and the accuracy of motor and sensory coordination.

Jobs such as packer, machine operator, computer assembler, and electrician require great hand, arm, and finger dexterity. Other positions, such as air traffic controller, nuclear plant operator, and fighter pilot, require excellent sensory abilities such as superior vision and hearing. Measures of motor and sensory abilities known as **psychomotor tests** are often used in the selection of applicants for such positions. Psychomotor tests evaluate both the speed and the accuracy of motor and sensory coordination. One of the best-known tests of psychomotor ability is the Purdue Pegboard (Mathiowetz, Rogers, Dowe-Keval, Donahoe, & Rennels, 1986), which measures an individual's ability to make controlled movements with the hands, arms, and fingertips. Test takers are placed in front of a pegboard on a table and asked to manipulate pegs, washers, and collars in and around the pegboard.

Traditional vision and hearing tests are also used for selection in jobs where a certain proficiency of these senses is required. The Project A study mentioned previously (McHenry et al., 1990) reported a validity of .53 for a psychomotor test battery predicting core job performance across nine jobs. In addition, John Hunter and Ronda Hunter (1984) reported validities of psychomotor tests averaging about .40 across several jobs—a figure that varied according to the type of job. Combining these data, we find that psychomotor tests predict between 16% and 28% of the variance in job performance. Keep in mind that these percentages are not precise, given the diversity of the psychomotor measures, performance criteria, and jobs investigated.

For a more recent example of psychomotor testing, we turn to a study that examined the incremental validity of a perceptual speed test over general cognitive ability in a sample of warehouse workers (Mount, Oh, & Burns, 2008) whose main job was the unloading of trucks and organizing of shipments. The perceptual speed test required individuals to identify names that exactly matched names they had seen earlier, much as they would when unpacking their shipments and organizing them by food item and restaurant name. Results showed that perceptual speed predicted warehouse performance above and beyond what was accounted for by general cognitive ability. In fact, prediction was improved by 15%!

Because a psychomotor test used for the wrong job would likely result in a validity of zero, a careful job analysis is recommended here also. For instance, a perceptual speed test or the Purdue Pegboard would not likely predict the success of a waitress or an insurance sales agent. But when used for appropriate jobs, they can be very useful tools. In fact, a more recent use of psychomotor tests is to examine employees as they work to make sure that they are able to work effectively and are not suffering from excessive fatigue. There is a long history of "fitness for duty" tests used to assess for alcohol or drug impairment in people operating machinery and other dangerous equipment. According to a paper by the Caterpillar mining company, psychomotor vigilance tests that tap reaction times and hand-eye coordination in working employees are being used to ensure that the employees are not suffering from a level of fatigue that would render them unable to function safely (Caterpillar Global Mining, 2011). Remote monitoring and management of driver fatigue are becoming more popular in trucking and other road transport industries. These techniques allow for the monitoring of drowsiness and the provision of drowsiness feedback to the operator to improve alertness and awareness (Aidman, Chadunow, Johnson, & Reece, 2015). This is an intriguing new wrinkle in a very old assessment technique: psychomotor testing.

## Personality Tests

About 40% of Fortune 100 companies use personality assessment to screen job applicants—a $500 million industry in the United States, growing by about 10% per year (http://www.psychometric-success.com/personality-tests/personality-tests-understanding-industry.htm). Compared to many of the other predictors discussed in this chapter, personality tests have received a great deal of attention from the research community (Barrick, Mount, & Judge, 2001; Hurtz & Donovan, 2000).

The word *personality* refers to an individual's traits—or predispositions to behave in a particular way across situations. Personality measurement involves procedures that systematically assign numbers to such characteristics. The most typical measures are self-report questionnaires such as the NEO Personality Inventory (for a review, see Piedmont, 1998), the Hogan Personality Inventory (Hogan & Hogan, 1995), and the Sixteen Personality Factor Questionnaire (for a review, see Schuerger, 1995). Other measures, such as the Minnesota Multiphasic Personality Inventory (MMPI), have been used in employee selection even though scholars have criticized the use of measures for employee selection that were normed, like this one, on a clinical sample and developed for clinical purposes.

Although there are many different personality measures, personality researchers tend to agree that many of them measure the five broad dimensions that make up the Big Five model: openness to experience, conscientiousness, extraversion, agreeableness, and neuroticism. (A helpful mnemonic is to note that the first letters of each dimension spell O-C-E-A-N or C-A-N-O-E.) Of all the personality classification schemes, this is the one used most often by practitioners and researchers alike. To give you a feel for Big Five personality measurement, **Table 6.2** shows a few items from the International Personality Item Pool (http://ipip.ori.org/ipip/).

A good deal of empirical research suggests that personality measures are valid predictors of job performance (e.g., Barrick et al., 2001; Ones, Dilchert, Viswesvaran, & Judge, 2007) and organizational citizenship behaviors (OCBs) (Chiaburu, Oh, Berry, Li, & Gardner, 2011). In fact, this recent meta-analysis demonstrated stronger relationships between openness and agreeableness and OCB than between openness and agreeableness and task performance.

Although it is generally difficult to estimate the size of the validity coefficient between personality and on-the-job performance, meta-analyses estimate that relationship

**personality tests** Tests in which numbers are systematically assigned to individuals' characteristics.

**TABLE 6.2** International Personality Item Pool

| | |
|---|---|
| Extraversion | Am the life of the party<br>Start conversations<br>Keep in the background (R)*<br>Am quiet around strangers |
| Agreeableness | Am interested in people<br>Take time out for others<br>Am not interested in other people's problems (R)<br>Insult people (R) |
| Conscientiousness | Am always prepared<br>Pay attention to details<br>Make a mess of things (R)<br>Shirk my duties (R) |
| Neurotocism (Emotional Stability) | Get stressed out easily<br>Worry about things<br>Seldom feel blue (R)<br>Am relaxed most of the time (R) |
| Openness (Intellect) | Am quick to understand things<br>Spend time reflecting on things<br>Am not interested in abstract ideas (R)<br>Do not have a good imagination (R) |

*(R) indicates that the item's score is reversed before it is used to compute one's total score.
Source: http://ipip.ori.org/ipip/

(.23) to be significant (Barrick et al., 2001). Furthermore, conscientiousness (being dependable and hardworking) and emotional stability have been reported to be the best predictors of performance (Barrick et al., 2001). Accordingly, these two dimensions have received the most research attention. Another benefit of the Big Five model is that the factor structure and other relevant structural information as measured by the NEO Personality Inventory (Revised) hold up consistently across cultures (McCrae & Terracciano, 2005).

Some personality researchers argue that estimates such as the .23 noted above are *under*estimates given that, in most studies, specific personality dimensions are not linked to specific criteria. In particular, some have argued (e.g., Hough, 1998) that the five-factor model comprises dimensions that are too broad, adding that prediction will be improved to the extent that specific personality dimensions are used to predict targeted performance criteria such as effort and leadership, personal discipline, and counterproductive behavior. For instance, a recent investigation demonstrated that those high on conscientiousness and low on agreeableness express greater intentions to be an entrepreneur and exhibit more success as an entrepreneur as predicted by theories outlined by the authors (Zhao, Seibert, & Lumpkin, 2010). Again, I strongly emphasize that no predictor works for all criteria and that job analysis has to allow

for the appropriate match between predictor constructs and criterion constructs
(Borman, Hanson, & Hedge, 1997).

One problem with personality tests is
that individuals can potentially guess the
responses that are likely to result in high
scores—we call this *faking*. For instance,
most applicants would know how to answer
the following question in such a way as to
"look good" to the organization: "I often
think of ways in which I can outsmart my
supervisor—strongly agree or strongly disagree?" It has been argued that the motivation to fake is influenced by demographic
characteristics (e.g., age and gender), indi-

Monkey Business Images/Shutterstock

**A CLOSER LOOK**

What are some
of the potential
advantages and
pitfalls of using
personality testing
for selection
decisions?

vidual differences (e.g., integrity and manipulativeness), and perceptual variables (e.g.,
perceptions of others' behavior and perceptions of organizational justice) (Snell, Sydell,
& Lueke, 1999). Recent work suggests that about one-third to one-half of all applicants
fake (Donovan, Dwight, & Schneider, 2014; Griffith & Converse, 2011) and that these
fakers engage in more counterproductive behavior than nonfakers (Peterson, Griffith,
Isaacson, O'Connell, & Mangos, 2011), have lower integrity and self-efficacy (Gammon,
Griffith, & Kung, 2011), and lower job performance (Donovan et al., 2014). Some argue
that faking reduces the validity of personality measures for selection by 25% (Komar,
Brown, Komar, & Robie, 2008) and that selection decisions are seriously affected because faking substantially affects the rank order of candidates, which can lead to the
wrong people being hired (Peterson, Griffith, & Converse, 2009).

On the other hand, another study (Hogan, Barrett, & Hogan, 2007) showed that
rejected applicants' scores on a personality measure did not improve when they came
back six months later to reapply for the job. The researchers reasoned that not being
hired the first time would result in motivation to score higher on the personality test
the second time around. However, this didn't happen, and these authors argue from
their data that faking is not a serious problem in real-world selection contexts. This
conclusion may be too strong given other research and data, but it certainly makes
clear that we are still unsure of the role that faking truly plays in the selection context.

Some intriguing cutting-edge work is being conducted using eye-tracking machines that are typically used in neuroscience research to link eye movements to
brain activity in the presence of various stimuli. In the I/O application of this work,
researchers have looked at eye movements in studies where they have told participants
to answer the personality items in a way that would make them most desirable for the
job—we call this the fake good condition. A recent study found that those participants
told to "fake" good responses showed more eye fixations on the extreme anchors of
the scales—that is, they were focusing on the extreme responses that would make
them look better (Van Hooft & Born, 2012). They also responded faster to the items
than did those in the nonfaking condition, due presumably to the cognitive processing

time involved in answering honestly vs. faking. One implication of this work is that eye tracking could be used to identify fakers on personality measures. It also has the potential to help us better understand the phenomenon of faking.

As is often the case, there are varying opinions about the benefits of personality assessment for employee selection. Some researchers argue that personality is often inaccurately measured, does not make a large enough contribution to the prediction of job performance, and can be easily faked by applicants (Morgeson et al., 2007). In fact, these same researchers go so far as to suggest that, relative to other predictors, personality tests have low validity for predicting overall job performance and recommend not using published self-report personality tests. They conclude that personality constructs are important in understanding work behavior but encourage researchers to identify and develop alternatives to self-report measures.

## Integrity Tests

**integrity tests**
Tests used in an attempt to predict whether an employee will engage in counterproductive or dishonest work-related behaviors such as cheating, stealing, or sabotage; also called honesty tests.

Among the newest tests used in employee selection are **integrity tests** (also called *honesty tests*), which attempt to predict whether an employee will engage in counterproductive or dishonest work-related behaviors such as cheating, stealing, or sabotage. Since 1988, when the passage of the Employee Polygraph Protection Act prohibited the use of polygraphs for most private-sector jobs, integrity tests have taken on a much more important role in selection (Cascio & Aguinis, 2010).

There are two types of integrity tests. The *overt integrity test* attempts to measure both attitudes toward theft and, through admissions on self-reports, actual theft behaviors. Overt integrity tests might ask respondents to report how often they have stolen from previous employers, whether they believe that lying is okay if one doesn't get caught, and the extent to which they perceive theft to be easy. The *personality-type integrity test* measures personality characteristics believed to predict counterproductive behaviors (e.g., risk taking, emotional instability, dishonesty, and irresponsibility). The purpose of these tests is more hidden from respondents than is that of overt tests. One investigation found that test takers perceived overt integrity tests to have greater face validity (i.e., they appear more believable and useful) and predictive validity than do personality-type integrity tests (Whitney, Diaz, Mineghino, & Powers, 1999). Some recent work has aimed at reducing the concerns that some have about the self-report nature of overt integrity tests by developing conditional reasoning tests designed to implicitly measure the extent to which one rationalizes or justifies counterproductive behaviors or other low-integrity behaviors (Fine & Gottlieb-Litvin, 2013). This research has potential but is still in the very early stages.

Researchers have found clear empirical support for the use of integrity tests. For instance, when a personality-based integrity test was administered to more than 300 prisoners who had been convicted of white-collar crimes (stealing, bribery, extortion, etc.) and to more than 300 white-collar workers in positions of authority in the working world, they found that these groups scored very differently on the integrity test (Collins & Schmidt, 1993). The authors conceptualized the differences as being reflective of "social conscientiousness"—or a lack of it—such that the prisoners exhibited greater tendencies toward irresponsibility and disregard for rules and social norms than did the working managers. Meta-analyses have reported validity coefficients for job performance between .15 and .34 and for counterproductive behavior between .32 and .47 (Berry, Sackett, & Wiemann, 2007; Van Iddekinge, Roth, Raymark, and Odle-Dusseau, 2012). Recently, researchers have found smaller coefficients: .15 for performance and .32 for counterproductive work behavior (Van Iddekinge et al., 2012). There are a few factors that may have contributed to these differences. First, this meta-analysis was more selective in evaluating the quality of the research studies before including them in the analysis. Second, when comparing the studies, it was clear that there were stronger effects for studies that were conducted by integrity test publishers than for those conducted by independent researchers. This difference could reflect the fact that the publishers have a vested interest in the validity of the tests and this interest somehow affects the validity coefficients, although the authors report no reason to suspect this. On the other hand, it could be that the studies conducted by the test publishers provide a more accurate picture and the more pessimistic outlook from the independent researchers is actually inaccurate. More research is needed here, but the authors are careful to point out that we don't know the reason for these differences and can only conclude that the validity differs from test publishers to independent researchers, which should make us cautious before drawing inferences from the literature.

Note that the previous discussion of faking on personality tests is relevant here as well, inasmuch as faking also appears to be possible on some integrity tests (Alliger & Dwight, 2000). Researchers have developed a cognitive lie detection procedure that may help organizations screen out (1) employees likely to engage in misconduct and (2) those likely to provide deceptive answers to screening questions, both of which could improve validity (Walczyk, Mahoney, Doverspike, & Griffith-Ross, 2009).

There isn't much research yet on integrity testing in other cultures. We do know, however, that countries high in power distance (i.e., where members of society accept and expect that power will be unequally distributed) are more likely to use integrity tests (Berry et al., 2007). This is probably because these countries are more comfortable with hierarchically centralized power and less concerned about subordinate employees'/applicants' reactions to this approach to screening.

## Work Samples

Although a cognitive ability test, a vision test, and a personality test may be useful predictors for the position of police officer, none of these tests actually measure on-the-job behaviors; rather, they are used as proxies or replacements for criteria because we don't have access to criteria at this stage in the selection process. With work sample tests, we take a very different approach: Instead of measuring constructs that we hope will predict our performance criterion, we try to duplicate the performance criterion measures and use them as predictors. Work samples are thus miniature replicas of the job. To develop them, we create smaller standardized tests that measure the actual job performance criteria identified by the job analysis.

**work sample tests** Tests that attempt to duplicate performance criteria measures and use them as predictors, thus forming miniature replicas of the job.

In addition to using measures of personality, general cognitive ability, and specific clerical ability, we may find it useful to develop a work sample test for hiring administrative assistants. In fact, this type of test is typically included in a selection battery for the administrative assistant position. As an example in an entirely different occupation, in most academic departments, potential new faculty members are required to present to faculty and students a research study that they have conducted. This approach serves two purposes. First, it provides an opportunity for the department to evaluate the applicant's research after hearing him or her present it for an hour or so. Second, it provides a work sample in the sense that the applicant, if hired, will have to stand up before a group of students and lecture about topics that are in his or her area of expertise. This small sample of behavior is our first clue as to how effective the applicant might be as a teacher in the department.

When work samples are carefully developed, they can demonstrate validities as high as the .50s (Hunter & Hunter, 1984). This means that an individual's performance on a work sample test is a very strong indicator of whether or not this person is likely to be promoted within the company. One meta-analysis reported a validity coefficient of .39 across a series of performance criteria (Roth, Bobko, & McFarland, 2005). The results of these reviews make it clear that work sample tests are among the most valid predictors of criterion performance.

A specific type of work sample test has regained the attention of I/O psychologists in recent years—namely, **situational judgment tests (SJTs)**. These include paper-and-pencil tests or video scenarios that measure applicants' judgment in work settings (Lievens, Buyse, & Sackett, 2005). For instance, applicants might be asked how they would handle a situation in which an employee seemed unable to understand how to solve a particular problem, and they would have to choose from the following response options: (1) continue explaining the problem to the employee, (2) ask someone else to get involved and explain the problem to the employee, (3) discipline the employee for his or her deficiency, or (4) place the employee in a remedial training program. Typically, one of these response options would be scored as the correct answer based on subject matter expert (SME) judgments regarding the best response. In one study, scores on an SJT predicted both the task performance and contextual performance of 160 employees (Chan & Schmitt, 2002). Furthermore, SJTs demonstrated incremental validity over measures of personality, job experience, and cognitive ability.

In a study of over 1,700 medical school candidates in Belgium, researchers found an SJT to demonstrate incremental validity for predicting overall GPA beyond cognitive predictors (Lievens et al., 2005). The most recent meta-analysis published to date found that SJTs measuring teamwork skills and leadership had strong validities for predicting job performance (Christian, Edwards, & Bradley, 2010). The researchers also found stronger validities for video-based SJTs than paper-and-pencil ones. Furthermore, in an earlier meta-analysis, researchers found situational judgment tests that were developed on the basis of a job analysis to be more valid ($r = .38$) than were those not based on a job analysis ($r = .29$; McDaniel, Morgeson, Finnegan, Campion, & Braverman, 2001).

## Assessment Centers

The term **assessment center (AC)** refers not to a particular place or center, but to an approach or method in which multiple raters (called *assessors*) evaluate applicants or incumbents (called *assessees*) on a standardized set of predictors (called *exercises*). Many large companies employ assessment centers. ACs differ in many ways, but a typical one might have the following characteristics: Twelve to fifteen assessees are involved

---

**situational judgment tests (SJTs)**
Paper-and-pencil test or video vignette that provides hypothetical scenarios for candidates to respond to by choosing the best alternative.

**assessment center (AC)**
An approach or method in which multiple raters (*assessors*) evaluate applicants or incumbents (*assessees*) on a standardized set of predictors (*exercises*).

in the center at any given time. The assessment is done by a team of four to six assessors who do not know the assessees and are likely to be two levels above them in the organizational hierarchy. Almost without exception, multiple methods of assessment are used, such as a measure of general cognitive ability, an interview, and various work sample–type exercises. The overall assessment usually lasts two to three days. The assessors receive at least a half-day of training and often stay a half-day after the assessment is complete to finalize scores and write up reports.

© Randy Faris/Corbis

As with much of the testing movement in I/O psychology, assessment centers were developed in the military. They were first created in Germany in the 1930s and later refined during World War II by the British and U.S. military (Gatewood et al., 2007). One important study that employed ACs focused on the career development of young employees as they moved up through the ranks of AT&T (Bray, Campbell, & Grant, 1974). Data were collected on these young men from 1956 through 1965, and more than 300 of them who were tested in the early years of the AC remained with the company through 1965. The AT&T management progress study is the most extensive study of managerial development ever conducted; it created a rich data set that still provides a wealth of information about the relationships between employees' scores on the various exercises and their career progression. The results of the study are very impressive: Of the 72 men who were not promoted by 1965, the assessors had correctly identified 68 (i.e., 94%) as unlikely to be promoted based on their AC performance.

The United Nations uses ACs to select managers for its worldwide operations (Jackson & Schuler, 2000), and they are also implemented throughout Europe. In the United Kingdom, for instance, major banks use them to identify management potential and development needs among upper-level clerical staff. In addition to their widespread use in the private sector, ACs have been extensively employed by metropolitan fire and police departments.

Obviously, an AC is only as effective as the exercises that make it up are valid. In general, considerable evidence suggests that well-established centers are valid predictors for many different performance criteria. The most-cited review of AC validity reports a validity coefficient of .37 for overall AC validity (Gaugler, Rosenthal, Thornton, & Bentson, 1987). More recent reviews found a similar overall relationship and also demonstrated that combining multiple AC dimensions into a composite resulted in a validity coefficient of .45 (Arthur, Day, McNelly, & Edens, 2003; Meriac, Hoffman, Woehr, & Fleisher, 2008). Although the AC dimensions are related to cognitive ability and personality, they improve prediction of job performance above and beyond those predictors (Melchers & Annen, 2010; Meriac et al., 2008). Of course, ACs can also be very expensive in terms of both the time and money involved in assessing employees in a fair and valid way.

Let's now take a closer look at two of the most often used AC exercises: the in-basket and the leaderless group discussion.

**in-basket**

An individual exercise in which assessees are asked to act as a manager in a particular company with certain issues or ideas that need to be considered and responded to.

**In-Basket** An in-basket is an individual exercise in which an assessee is presented with a scenario, such as being newly hired to replace a manager who has had to leave the company abruptly due to a serious illness. The assessee is also provided with information such as an organizational chart and a description of the company mission, along with the kinds of things that would typically appear in a manager's in-basket, such as memos, letters, requests for information, files on grievances, and employee applications. At that point, the assessee is asked to take the one or two hours that are available prior to hopping on a flight to New York for a board of directors' meeting to review all of the in-basket materials and to respond accordingly with memos, letters, decisions, delegations, interview scheduling, and so on. When the time is up, the assessee is asked to describe (using a checklist or a narrative) all of his or her actions and to present a rationale for each.

The idea here, of course, is to place the assessee in a set of circumstances similar to those a manager would experience and to evaluate how well he or she responds. Some refer to in-baskets as simulations or even work samples because they mimic actual on-the-job settings. **Figure 6.5** presents the background information and instructions

> While working on this exercise, you are to be Pat Chandler, who has just assumed the duties of General Manager for the Bradford Consolidated Fund (BCF) in Bradford, New Jersey. The BCF is a nonprofit organization devoted to charitable enterprises. The Fund is now in the middle of their annual fund-raising drive. You were recently hired to replace Georgia McKinley, the former General Manager, who was in an automobile accident and had to resign from her position with the BCF.
>
> Today is Sunday, March 15, the first opportunity you have had to come to Bradford. Your administrative assistant, Harry Stein, has left on your desk a memo along with a number of other items for you to look at and work on during the afternoon. Mr. Stein has also left a list of members of the staff connected with this year's fund-raising drive. You will find this on your desk along with some stationery, pencils, paper clips, and so on for your use.
>
> **The Current Situation:** Your task on this Sunday afternoon is to go through the items, taking appropriate actions as necessary. Keep in mind that you may not finish everything in front of you in the allotted time and it is up to you to decide the order in which to work on the items. You are now actually on the job. Everything you decide to do must be in writing and also recorded on the *Reasons for Actions* form enclosed. Use the stationery provided for memos, letters, lists, and the like. Outline plans or set agendas for meetings you may want to call. Sign papers, if necessary. Wherever possible, clip letters, memos, or notes to the items that they concern.
>
> *Behave as though you are actually on the job. Remember, it is Sunday afternoon, March 15, and you have 30 minutes in the office to get as much work done as you can.*

**FIGURE 6.5** An In-Basket Test: The Bradford Consolidated Fund

## PRACTITIONER FORUM

Matthew O'Connell

### Matthew O'Connell
*PhD, 1994, I/O Psychology, University of Akron*
*Executive Vice President & Co-founder*
*Select International, Inc.*

Predicting future behavior is one of the foundations on which I/O psychology was built. Properly designed selection systems allow us to predict a broad range of future behaviors—or, more specifically, the likelihood of those behaviors occurring—with a surprising level of accuracy.

Whenever you talk about prediction, the first thing you need to determine is what you actually want to predict. That may seem like a very simple question, but in my experience it isn't. Job performance is multifaceted. Consider a sales position. A salesperson may be good at selling—that is, meeting or exceeding quotas—but might overcommit the organization's resources, be poor at organizing his or her own time, and fail to follow up with clients. Would that person be a "good hire"? For some organizations the answer would be "yes," but for many others it would be "no."

That's the reason Select takes a multimethod and multidimensional approach to selection systems, much like a financial advisor looks at an investment portfolio. You wouldn't put all of your money into one stock or even one type of stock. You could strike it rich once in a while, but over the long run your hit rate would be low and you'd have too much volatility. Most of Select's online assessments are multiscale batteries that include a variety of different assessment methods, including personality, situational judgment, applied problem solving, biodata, and interactive simulations. They are combined to create a profile that encompasses

multiple competencies. Once we have a sound battery established, we can focus on how best to weight the competencies, establish cutoffs, and so on. That's where determining the criteria that you're interested in predicting becomes critical. It's relatively easy to set up a profile identifying people who learn quickly and are hardworking. But how likely are they to leave within three months? How well do they handle ambiguity and stress? How well do they get along with others and take feedback? How likely are they to do something unsafe? Ultimately, you have to make trade-offs.

Prediction is not only about selecting the most accurate predictors. Prediction also involves putting them together in a cohesive way to ensure consistency and fairness over time. It involves weighting them to maximize the prediction of important outcomes and establishing cutoffs that allow organizations to meet their hiring needs.

### Applying Your Knowledge

1. In what ways do assessment centers align with the preferred methods for performance prediction used at Select?

2. In what ways do work samples align with the preferred methods for performance prediction used at Select?

3. Given the difficulty and complexity of making accurate, targeted hiring predictions, do you think that assessment measures would be better at limiting poor hires or better at increasing good hires? Why?

---

presented to participants for an in-basket task that I have used for research purposes. Notice that the instructions have the clear purpose of asking the assessee to take actions and make decisions about how to proceed. This is typical of in-basket exercises.

**Leaderless Group Discussion** Whereas an in-basket is an individual exercise, a leaderless group discussion (LGD) is a group exercise designed to tap managerial attributes that requires the interaction of a small number of individuals (Gatewood et al., 2007). Typically, a group of five or six assessees are seated at a conference table,

**leaderless group discussion (LGD)**
A group exercise designed to tap managerial attributes that requires the interaction of a small group of individuals.

## I/O TODAY

### Using Remote Assessment for Selection

Many organizations are turning to remote assessments, unproctored Internet testing, video conference interviews, and similar selection methods in an effort to reduce the cost and time associated with assessing job applicants. With these changes come some concerns about ethics and validity that organizations and I/O psychologists must consider carefully.

Take, for example, the use of a remote assessment center. Instead of performing an in-basket and role play in person, applicants can participate in these activities remotely. They can log onto a website that has a fake e-mail account set up and respond to e-mails in real time. Likewise, the role play could be conducted via video conferencing software.

But I/O psychologists have listed a number of reasons to be concerned about the validity of these new practices—applicants might cheat, encounter issues with technology, or face other issues that are not present in traditional, in-person assessment settings. Initial research on cheating in remote assessment situations is mixed; some research has suggested that cheating is relatively rare and leads to only a small difference in scores, while other research suggests that unproctored cognitive tests show a large inflation of scores compared to tests administered in-person. In other cases, individuals' scores drop in unproctored settings—often because they take tests in distracting environments, or because they are uncomfortable with the technology.

These issues raise questions about the ethics of remote assessment. Some practitioners have voiced concerns about whether it is ethical to use measures that have not been validated in a remote format. Many test developers are also concerned about the integrity of their tests—if items and/or answers are leaked on the Internet, tests that have taken great time and expense to develop might be rendered invalid. Furthermore, avoiding cheating is difficult. Candidates can look up answers, or even have someone else take the test for

them. If candidates are successful at cheating, are we giving an unfair advantage to dishonest applicants?

Although unproctored Internet testing entails a number of risks, companies are embracing it for its convenience. Thus, researchers are focusing their attention on how to prevent and detect cheating. Practitioners have begun using a variety of techniques to help ensure security, such as creating enormous test question banks, using timed tests, monitoring social media for leaks, and asking selected individuals to retake the test in a proctored setting. Another interesting new area of work is something called "data forensics." Data forensics involves identifying what testing behaviors indicate that a candidate may be cheating. For example, if an applicant suddenly starts responding more quickly to items or getting more difficult questions correct when they failed at simpler questions, the program can flag that person's response as suspicious. As the use of smartphones and other technology increases, I/O practitioners will need to continue to consider the benefits and problems with incorporating these tools into the selection process.

### Discussion Questions:

1. As a job candidate, would you prefer a remote assessment or a traditional face-to-face assessment? Why?
2. Imagine that a job candidate you are assessing loses her Internet connection in the middle of a role play. How would you determine how to compare her with other candidates who did not have technical issues?
3. What are some ways you may be able to prevent or detect cheating on an unproctored test?

### Additional Reading:

Arthur, W., Jr., Doverspike, D., Muños, G. J., Taylor, J. E., & Carr, A. E. (2014). The use of mobile devices in high-stakes remotely delivered assessments and testing. *International Journal of Selection and Assessment, 22,* 113–123.

surrounded by assessors at the perimeter of the room who observe the interactions. The group is then presented with an issue to resolve. Sometimes each assessee is given a particular role to play, such as the director of one of the departments involved in the issue; at other times, roles are not assigned. But in all cases, no one is assigned the role of leader (hence the term leaderless). After the group has been provided with background information about the issue in question and given a fixed amount of time to resolve it, the assessors simply sit and observe the interactions; they do not participate at all. The assessees are typically rated on such dimensions as aggressiveness, persuasiveness, interpersonal skills, communication skills, flexible thinking, and listening skills. Scores on these dimensions are used to predict performance-related criteria.

## Biographical Information

The major premise behind the use of biographical information for selection is that past behavior is the best predictor of future behavior. Biographical information can be thought of as any information that is descriptive of an individual's personal history. The idea is that if I want to predict how you will respond in a certain situation, one of the best ways for me to do so is to find out how you have responded in similar situations in the past. Those who work with biographical information often go one step further in considering *any* information about a person's history as potentially useful—even information about hobbies or other activities that are not directly related to the job (Mael, 1991). In the selection context, biographical information is typically collected in one of two ways: through an application blank or a biodata questionnaire.

**biographical information** In the context of selection, any information that is descriptive of an individual's personal history.

**Application Blank** Without a doubt, the application blank is one of the most frequently and widely used selection devices. Whether you are applying for a restaurant job or a faculty position or an executive position at a Fortune 500 company, the chances are good that you will be asked to fill out some sort of application blank. Typically, this form will request historical (as well as current) information such as your educational background, work experience, experience relevant to the job in question, and the names and addresses of previous employers. Most of us have filled out such forms at one time or another. Unfortunately, many companies spend little time developing their application blanks. Some even hand out generic ones, which are available at office supply stores. (Keep in mind that, if these are being used for selection purposes, all the same ethical and legal rules that apply elsewhere to personnel issues apply to the application blank as well.)

The use of generic application blanks suggests that the information the company is asking for has not been developed from a job analysis. But, as we now know, a job analysis is critical. If educational background and work experience are going to be defended as valid predictors of future on-the-job performance, these items have to be backed up by a job analysis. As you can imagine, many companies get themselves into legal skirmishes by using off-the-shelf application blanks rather than developing their own or at least validating the off-the-shelf predictors. For instance, some application blanks routinely include a blank for date of birth, but this information could be used to discriminate in hiring based on age; we will address discrimination as defined by the Age Discrimination in Employment Act in Chapter 7.

**biodata** Personal history information obtained through a biographical information blank (BIB) that asks respondents about their attitudes, hobbies, experiences, and so on.

**Biodata** Although it may be appropriate to think of application blank information as biographical data, the term biodata is usually reserved for the personal history information that is obtained through biographical information blanks (BIBs). BIBs are different from application blanks in that (1) they usually have a multiple choice, yes–no, or Likert-scale format (the last contains answers ranging from "strongly agree" to "strongly disagree"); (2) they ask questions in much broader areas, such as health, hobbies, family history, interests, and social experience; and (3) they contain many more questions (up to about 150) than do application blanks (typically 10–15).

**Table 6.3** presents some items for the job of customer service representative, a person who responds to service complaints or requests from customers over the phone. In the left column of the table are seven predictor dimensions; in the right column are biodata items related to each of those dimensions. In a real-life situation, of course, both the predictor dimensions and criterion dimensions would be developed on the basis of a job analysis. The premise here is that past behavior is a good predictor of future behavior. Thus, for instance, someone with a history of exhibiting patience in socially frustrating situations is likely to respond patiently to customers who are

| TABLE 6.3 | Biodata Items for the Position of Customer Service Representative |
|---|---|
| **Dimension** | **Items** |
| Helping others | How often have you helped someone you didn't know by carrying something for them (e.g., boxes, luggage, groceries)?<br>How often have you stopped to give aid or called someone to assist a stranded motorist? |
| Negotiation skills | When you feel strongly about something, how easily can you persuade others to see your point of view?<br>As a child, when your parents/guardians originally refused to let you do something, how easily could you convince them to change their minds? |
| Interpersonal intelligence | In the past, how easily have you been able to judge the moods of your friends, coworkers, or family members?<br>In the past, when meeting people for the first time, to what extent were you aware of the kind of impression you made? |
| Patience | When you have been in a frustrating interpersonal situation, how often have you been able to be patient with the person or persons causing the frustration?<br>When asked for travel directions by a stranger, how likely are you to voluntarily repeat them if you suspect the person is confused? |
| Empathy | To what extent would your friends describe you as sympathetic?<br>In the past, how easily have you been able to reach out to or express compassion for someone who was upset?<br>In the past, when you've seen a friend or family member upset, to what extent have you actually "felt their pain"? |
| Extraversion | When socializing with a group of people, how often do you feel the group is relying on you to keep the conversation flowing?<br>In the past, how comfortable have you felt in social situations? |
| Oral communication | While in school, if given a choice, how often would you choose to do an oral presentation rather than a written report?<br>In the past, to what extent have you been comfortable in sharing job-related information by having discussions in person? |

yelling about the lack of quality service they've received from the company. Similarly, someone with a history of helping strangers is not only more likely to be satisfied with a customer service job but also more likely to perform better than someone who has never considered it important or rewarding to help others. In short, biodata items should predict on-the-job performance.

For biodata, the validity evidence is quite consistent: It predicts performance quite well (Allworth & Hesketh, 2000). A review of performance predictors for salespeople reported that biodata was the strongest predictor ($r = .52$) of managerial ratings of sales performance (Vinchur, Schippmann, Switzer, & Roth, 1998). And in more extensive reviews, validity coefficients of .37 (Hunter & Hunter, 1984) and .32 (Schmitt, Gooding, Noe, & Kirsch, 1984) have been reported across a series of criteria, including performance ratings. A great resource for further information is the *Biodata Handbook*, one chapter of which provides a summary of meta-analytic reviews of biodata (Stokes & Cooper, 1994). This chapter makes it clear that biodata consistently demonstrate validities between .20 and .46—these tend to be highest for criteria like supervisory ratings of performance and measures of productivity.

## Interviews

As you may have guessed, interviews are among the most popular selection devices and are typically used across all job levels. An interview can be defined as a procedure designed to predict future performance based on an applicant's oral responses to a series of oral questions. The rationale is that the person conducting the interview can gather information through such questions that will allow the organization to make accurate predictions of successful job performance. I was a high school student when I experienced my first job interview at a fast-food restaurant, and every job I've had since then was preceded by an interview. I'm sure that most of you have had interviews of some sort, too.

Two major categories of interviews merit special attention. First, the more traditional *unstructured interview* is constructed haphazardly, with no consistency of questioning across applicants. One candidate may be asked what his particular strengths are and why he is interested in the job, while a second candidate may be asked what her particular weaknesses are and whether she's had any experiences that are especially relevant for the job. The unstructured interview process sometimes results in the organization comparing apples and oranges. For this reason, it is generally considered a less useful technique than the structured interview approach.

The *structured interview* consists of a series of standardized job analysis–based questions that are asked of all job candidates. For instance, when interviewing someone for the job of camp counselor, an interviewer might use questions like "What is it about working with adolescents that attracts you?" "What kinds of nature experiences have you had that prepare you for this particular job?" "Which of your strengths match well with the social and physical requirements of this job?" Each candidate would be asked these questions in the same order, the responses would be noted by the interviewer, and the candidates would receive a score on the interview based on these responses. It is this score that would be used in the selection process. The key to a structured interview is that everyone

**interviews** Procedures designed to predict future performance based on an applicant's oral responses to a series of oral questions.

is asked the same set of questions. This technique not only increases the reliability of the interview process but also allows for a fair comparison among the applicants.

There are two particular structured interview formats that require discussion. First, the **situational interview** focuses on future behavior. Here, the job applicant is presented with dilemmas or situations that are embedded in a work context and asked how he or she would handle the situation (Seijts & Kyei-Poku, 2010). Second, the **behavior description interview** focuses on past behavior—applicants are asked to describe specific ways in which they have addressed various situations in the past. Both situational and behavior description interviews are based on a job analysis, ask consistent questions of each candidate, and use a scoring guide to evaluate the applicant's performance on the interview (Seijts & Kyei-Poku, 2010). Certainly, these features are positively related to the increased validity of the structured interview process.

According to the many reviews of job interview validity conducted between 1960 and 1990, interviews had rather low validity. One well-cited study reported a validity coefficient of only .14 for interviews in predicting supervisor ratings of performance (Hunter & Hunter, 1984). Nevertheless, organizations have continued to use interviews in selection. Among the many possible explanations for this persistence, the most convincing is that the interview is more than a selection device. Indeed, it is a communication process in which the organization gains useful information about the applicant and the applicant gathers useful information about the organization (Cascio & Aguinis, 2010). The interview format may even provide the applicant with a **realistic job preview (RJP)**, which is simply an accurate glimpse of what the job would actually be like. In this way, the applicant can begin to get a feel for the organization's climate, the attitudes among employees, and the interpersonal relationships between subordinates and supervisors.

An early meta-analysis found that interviews overall were predictive of job performance ($r = .37$) and, as expected, that structured interviews were more predictive ($r = .44$) than unstructured interviews ($r = .33$; McDaniel, Whetzel, Schmidt, & Maurer, 1994). Since 1990, interview techniques have been refined (e.g., situational and behavior description interviewing) and more sophisticated meta-analytic techniques have been developed. Reviews using these techniques have reported much better validity for the structured employment interview ($r = .71$) and less validity for the unstructured interview ($r = .20$) (Huffcutt, Culbertson, & Weyhrauch, 2014). Another study demonstrated that structured interviews predict performance over and above general cognitive ability and conscientiousness, thus indicating the incremental validity of the interview (Cortina, Goldstein, Payne, Davison, & Gilliland, 2000). These results suggest that interviews can be very useful in employee selection contexts and that practitioners should attempt to use structured rather than unstructured interviews when possible because they are better predictors of job performance criteria.

Of course, some of the biases discussed in the context of performance appraisal (Chapter 5)—including halo error, contrast effects, and similarity effects—may come into play during interviews as well. For instance, one study demonstrated that interview ratings are affected by nonverbal factors such as physical attractiveness (Burnett & Motowidlo, 1998). However, despite the subjective nature of interview ratings, they tend to be good predictors of on-the-job performance.

---

**situational interview**
An interviewing technique that relies on candidates sharing responses or intentions about job-related dilemmas or situations proposed to them with respect to the new job.

**behavior description interview**
An interviewing technique that relies on candidates sharing examples of past behaviors related to tasks required for the new job.

**realistic job preview (RJP)**
During an employment interview, the presentation of an accurate glimpse of what the job would be like.

One additional point should be made before we leave this topic: Although the employment interview can include many different questions, there are important legal issues involved in deciding what questions *shouldn't* be asked. **Table 6.4** contains a list of legally suspect questions that could be challenged in court and used by plaintiffs to allege discrimination; in the next chapter, we will discuss various employment laws that define what organizations can and cannot ask of applicants.

**Table 6.5** presents validity coefficients for all of the predictors reviewed in this chapter. Notice that general cognitive ability has traditionally been viewed as the best predictor of job performance and it is still among the best, but that structured job interviews have now been shown to be even more valid than cognitive ability. However, the recent meta-analyses on structured interviews raise issues that may lead some to still recognize cognitive ability as the strongest predictor. Psychomotor ability, ACs, and biodata are also among the strongest predictors. Of course, even these consistent predictors seldom account for more than 25% of the variance in a criterion. In one study, for example, researchers examined the extent to which adding predictors to general cognitive ability would help in predicting job performance (Schmidt & Hunter, 1998). What they found was that work sample tests, integrity tests, personality tests, and structured interviews demonstrated incremental validity by accounting for an additional 14% or more of the variance in job performance and that the best two-predictor combination was general cognitive ability and integrity tests (multiple $r = .65$), which together accounted for about 42% of the variance in job performance. One study found that conscientiousness and openness accounted for a significant increment in variance in academic performance beyond that accounted for by intelligence (Chamorro-Premuzic & Furnham, 2008). A new conceptual analysis of existing data across thousands of studies concludes that cognitive ability and personality traits are very important predictors of school, work, and life outcomes (Kuncel, Ones, & Sackett, 2010). The lesson here is that companies and schools should be careful and diligent in choosing which predictors to use in their selection batteries, realizing that using multiple predictors is likely to account for more variance in the criterion and that some predictors tend to be more useful than others in predicting certain criteria.

11-9   e-mail:CLOSETOHOME@COMPUSERVE.COM

© 1998 John McPherson/Dist. by Universal Press Syndicate

**Though it was only his second day on the job, employees were already getting bad vibes about the new division chief.**

**A CLOSER LOOK**
How might a personality test or employment interview have prevented this bad selection decision?

## TABLE 6.4   Interview Questions That Shouldn't Be Asked

| Legally Suspect Questions | Explanation and Alternatives* |
|---|---|
| How old are you? When were you born? | The Age Discrimination in Employment Act (ADEA) does not specifically prohibit an employer from asking an applicant's age or date of birth. However, because such inquiries may deter older workers from applying for employment or may otherwise indicate possible intent to discriminate based on age, requests for age information will be closely scrutinized by the Equal Employment Opportunity Commission (EEOC). |
| Have you ever been arrested? | Being arrested does not imply guilt of any crime; instead, one could ask if the applicant has been convicted of a felony within the past five years. |
| Do you plan on having children? Are you pregnant? | An employer cannot refuse to hire a woman because of her pregnancy as long as she is able to perform the major functions of her job. An employer cannot refuse to hire her because of its prejudices against pregnant workers or the prejudices of coworkers, clients, or customers. |
| Are you a U.S. citizen? | This may lead to discrimination based on national origin. An employer is allowed to ask if an applicant is eligible to work in the United States either as a U.S. citizen or under a government immigration qualification. |
| Do you have a disability? | Employers may not ask job applicants about the existence, nature, or severity of a disability. Applicants may be asked about their ability to perform specific job functions. A job offer may be conditioned on the results of a medical examination *but only* if the examination is required for all entering employees in similar jobs. Medical examinations of employees must be job related and consistent with the employer's business needs. |
| Do you have children? What day-care arrangements will be made if you are hired for this job? | It is unlawful to inquire if an applicant has children (an issue that is certainly not job related). An employer may ask if a candidate has any commitments or responsibilities that might result in considerable absenteeism, but this should be asked of all candidates regardless of gender. |
| Are you actively involved in the National Association for the Advancement of Colored People (NAACP)? | Requesting preemployment information that discloses or tends to disclose an applicant's race suggests that race will be unlawfully used as a basis for hiring. Solicitation of such preemployment information is presumed to be used as a basis for making selection decisions. Therefore, if members of minority groups are not hired, the request for such preemployment information would likely constitute evidence of discrimination. |
| Have you ever been treated by a psychologist or psychiatrist? | All of these questions are probably illegal under the Americans with Disabilities Act (ADA). It is illegal to ask any preemployment questions about illness. |
| Have you ever been hospitalized? If so, for what? | |
| Please list any conditions or diseases for which you have been treated in the past three years. | |
| How many days were you absent from work due to illness in the past year? | |
| Are you taking any prescribed drugs? | |

*Some of this information was adapted from the Equal Employment Opportunity Commission (EEOC) website (http://www.eeoc.gov/).

## TABLE 6.5   Estimates of Validity Coefficients for Common Predictors*

| Predictor | Validity Coefficient Estimate | Source of Estimate | Description |
|---|---|---|---|
| General cognitive ability | .53<br>.48 | Hunter & Hunter, 1984<br>Bertua et al., 2005 | Meta-analysis<br>Meta-analysis |
| Specific cognitive ability | .40–.50<br>.35–.50 | Gatewood et al., 2007<br>Bertua et al., 2005 | Narrative review<br>Meta-analysis |
| Emotional Intelligence | .28–.29 | Joseph et al., 2015; O'Boyle, Forsyth, & O'Boyle, 2011 | Meta-analysis |
| Psychomotor ability | .53<br>.40 | McHenry et al., 2007<br>Hunter & Hunter, 1984 | Meta-analysis<br>Project A data |
| Personality tests | .20–.30<br>.21–.37 | Barrick et al., 2001<br>Oh, et al., 2011 | Meta-analysis<br>Meta-analysis |
| Integrity tests (work performance) | .12–.15 | Van Iddekinge et al., 2012 | Meta-analysis |
| Integrity tests (CWB) | .26–.32 | Van Iddekinge et al., 2012 | Meta-analysis |
| Work samples | .44<br>.39 | Hunter & Hunter, 1984<br>Roth et al., 2005 | Meta-analysis<br>Meta-analysis |
| Situational judgment tests | .24–.38 | Christian et al., 2010 | Meta-analysis |
| Assessment centers | .38–.45<br>.28<br><br>.40 | Arthur, Day, et al., 2003<br>Hermelin, Lievens, & Robertson, 2007<br>Meriac et al., 2008 | Meta-analysis<br>Meta-analysis<br><br>Meta-analysis |
| Biodata | .52<br>.37<br>.20–.46 | Vinchur et al., 1998<br>Hunter & Hunter, 1984<br>Stokes & Cooper, 1994 | Meta-analysis<br>Meta-analysis<br>Narrative review |
| Structured interviews | .71 | Huffcutt et al., 2014 | Meta-analysis |
| Unstructured interviews | .20 | Huffcutt et al., 2014 | Meta-analysis |

*Note: Variability of the coefficients given in this table may be due to the diversity of the studies included in the meta-analyses (e.g., Hunter & Hunter, 1984, versus Bertua et al., 2005) as well as to differences among the predictors and criteria.

## Summary

In this chapter, tests were classified in terms of form as well as the predictor type they represent. The most frequently used selection instruments—cognitive ability tests, psychomotor tests, personality tests, integrity tests, work sample tests, ACs, biographical information, and interviews—were discussed in the context of their role in employee selection. The validity coefficients of these selection instruments are listed in Table 6.5. Note that the variability of these coefficients may be due to the diversity of the studies included in the meta-analyses (e.g., Hunter & Hunter, 1984, versus Schmitt et al., 1984) as well as to differences among the predictors and criteria.

We can draw a few general conclusions. First, it is clear that ability measures (e.g., general cognitive, specific cognitive, and psychomotor) are among the most valid predictors of performance criteria in an employment setting. Second, the validity coefficients for personality tests are not as high as those for most of the other predictors included in our review. Third, nontraditional predictors, such as integrity tests, biodata, work samples, and ACs, are consistently valid predictors of on-the-job performance. Finally, structured interviews tend to be better predictors of job performance than unstructured interviews. In Chapter 7, we will discuss the actual selection process, focusing also on the legalities involved in how organizations use these predictors to hire employees.

## Key Terms

assessment center (AC) (p. 184)

behavior description interview (p. 192)

biodata (p. 189)

biographical information (p. 189)

clerical ability (p. 176)

computer adaptive testing (p. 170)

emotional intelligence (EI) (p. 177)

group tests (p. 171)

in-basket (p. 186)

individual tests (p. 171)

integrity tests (p. 182)

interviews (p. 191)

leaderless group discussion (LGD) (p. 187)

mechanical ability (p. 175)

paper-and-pencil tests (p. 171)

performance tests (p. 172)

personality tests (p. 179)

power test (p. 171)

psychomotor tests (p. 178)

realistic job preview (RJP) (p. 192)

situational interview (p. 192)

situational judgment tests (SJTs) (p. 184)

spatial ability (p. 176)

speed test (p. 170)

test (p. 169)

validity coefficient ($r$) (p. 173)

work sample tests (p. 183)

## TAKING IT TO THE FIELD

One activity that many I/O consultants must address is providing advice to organizations about how to select people for the organization. Because there are many different tools available, consultants must consider what will be reasonable given each client's situation. Pierce Janssen, the CEO of JMF Fireworks Inc., has contacted your boss asking for help redesigning the selection system they use for selecting their pyrotechnicians. Read his e-mail below and provide suggestions for how he might improve his selection battery.

Hello—

Thank you for your help with our selection system—I am looking forward to hearing what you suggest. First, let me tell you a little about the open position. We are looking to hire new pyrotechnicians—that is, the people who are responsible for putting on fireworks shows for a number of clients across the United States. This job entails transporting fireworks to shows, setting them up, programming the choreography, and taking down the setup once the show is completed. In order to do the job competently, pyrotechnicians need the following abilities/characteristics:

- They must be able to lift 80 pounds to shoulder height at least five times per show (the fireworks are quite heavy, and will need to be moved from the truck to the shoot site).

- They need to have good customer service skills (customers will sometimes want to do things that are against regulations; our pyrotechnicians must be effective at being polite but firm so that we follow rules but don't lose customers).

- They must have good attention to detail (small errors can lead to very serious accidents, so our pyrotechnicians need to be careful to not cut corners and to do things by the book).

- They must be cool under pressure (if something goes wrong, they must be able to think quickly and not panic).

- They must also be emotionally stable and not take foolish risks during a shoot.

The last bullet point is fairly well covered by background checks we are required to do by the government. However, we have not always been successful in hiring people who fulfill the other four requirements. Right now, here is our selection process:

- Applicants fill out an application blank I picked up at an office supply store that asks about their age, race, and experience.

- Applicants who look good on the application blank are brought in for an interview. We don't really have an HR department, so the managers typically conduct these interviews. I'm not sure what they ask applicants—they pretty much just ask whatever they want to know and go with their gut on whether they think someone will work out well.

- After applicants pass the interview, we send them to a room where we have a bag of sand that weighs about 80 pounds. We have them lift it from the ground and press it over their head five times.

Any suggestions you have about how we can better select pyrotechnicians would be greatly appreciated. If you can think of anything that we should avoid, that would be very helpful as well.

Pierce

## Critical Thinking Questions

1. What predictors would you use to select a restaurant manager? What is your rationale for including each predictor in your selection battery?

2. Do you think that emotional intelligence is a measurable ability? If so, what is the best way to measure it?

3. What are the advantages and disadvantages of using interviews as a selection measure?

4. Imagine you have been asked to design a role play to help a company select a new CEO. What are important KSAs for a CEO? What might be some ways to capture these KSAs in an assessment center? What might be some examples of issues or problems you would incorporate into this role play?

## Application Questions

1. Many managers look for indications about how someone behaves outside of an interview and testing context. For example, if a candidate shows up late, is dressed in a sloppy way, or fails to send a thank-you note, the manager may no longer consider that person for the position. Do you think this is a valid predictor of performance? Should managers use information like this in making a hiring decision?

2. There has been some recent debate about looking at job applicants' social media information (e.g., Facebook pages, Twitter accounts). Do you believe it is appropriate for managers to look at this type of information about a candidate? Why or why not? Do you think there might be any legal issues with looking at social media?

3. Imagine you are applying for a job and you know the company is looking for a candidate who is very conscientious and extraverted. Do you think the average person would be able to fake these traits on a personality test? How easy would it be for you, given that you have a little background in psychology? What might be some ways you could prevent or limit faking on these types of tests?

4. Have you ever had a job that was described differently from what it actually turned out to be, or that had an aspect that surprised you when you started the job? What happened? What could the organization have done to better prepare you for the actual job?

5. Some workplaces conduct drug testing to ensure that their employees are not using recreational drugs. Do you agree with this practice? When might this practice be justified?

## Suggested Readings

**Farr, J. L., & Tippins, N. T.** (2013). *Handbook of employee selection*. Routledge. This is a terrific resource for selection in general, but it is especially good at addressing the various predictors that are critical to employee selection.

**Furnham, A.** (2008). *Personality and intelligence at work*. London: Psychology Press. This book takes a close look at the role of individual differences at work. It probes the question of whether psychological tests are truly accurate predictors of workplace behavior.

**Gatewood, R. D., Feild, H. S., & Barrick, M.** (2011). *Human resource selection* (7th ed.). Mason, OH: South-Western, Cengage Learning. This is a solid human resource management text emphasizing job analysis and employee selection.

**Guion, R. M., & Highhouse, S.** (2014). Essentials of personnel assessment and selection. New York: Psychology Press. This book, written by two distinguished industrial psychologists, focuses largely on criterion measurement and selection, providing a very thorough treatment of the issues involved.

**Thomas, J. C.** (2004). *The comprehensive handbook of psychological assessment: Vol. 4. Industrial/organizational assessment*. Hoboken, NJ: Wiley. This is part of a four-volume set that wonderfully reviews psychological assessment with sophistication and simplicity. The I/O volume is a great reference, providing a source of tests and data on the tests most often used for assessment at work.

Photo: Susan Walsh/AP Photo

CHAPTER **7**

# Selection Decisions and Personnel Law

## LEARNING OBJECTIVES

This chapter should help you understand:

- The steps involved in validating a selection battery
- Some of the best recruitment strategies used by organizations to recruit individuals to apply for jobs
- The differences between predictive validation and concurrent validation and the steps involved in each
- The importance of cross-validation
- What validity generalization is and how important it has become to I/O psychology
- The three main approaches to selection (multiple cutoff, multiple hurdle, and multiple regression) and the differences among them
- The importance of the utility concept for I/O selection
- The factors that affect the utility of a selection battery (namely, validity, base rate, selection ratio, and cost)
- Important related concepts such as employment at-will, adverse impact, and affirmative action
- What has been rendered illegal by certain U.S. employment laws
- The different forms of sexual harassment
- How the courts seem to be interpreting reasonable accommodation, essential functions of the job, and undue hardship under the Americans with Disabilities Act

In the last few chapters, we have discussed in detail the importance of predictors and criteria in I/O psychology. Recall that Chapter 6 presented a detailed discussion of the common predictors, or tests, that are used in employee selection (see Table 6.5 for a list of those predictors and their validity estimates). In this chapter, we will discuss how an organization might go about using those predictors to select employees.

Let's return briefly to our example from the last chapter, involving the hiring of a new associate by a large law firm. Because the applicants are fresh out of law school, there are no criterion data available, so we will need to use other information to predict performance on the job. How do we go about using these predictors to make hiring decisions? How do we know that our predictors are valid ones? What legal issues come into play in this context of employee selection? For answers to these questions, we need to put together the predictors and the criteria in ways that enable us to do accurate and legal employee selection.

# A BRIEF REVIEW

We will talk about selection decisions in this chapter, but first I want to clarify that much of what is discussed here can also be applied to other personnel decisions, such as promotion decisions and decisions about whom to lay off when staff reductions in force become necessary. For instance, we may give employees a promotion test to determine whom to promote into a management job. The same procedures that apply to validating a selection test can be applied to the validation of a promotion test. Accordingly, in this chapter, I present a general process that can be used to make personnel decisions; I use the selection decision as an example because it is very important to organizations and because research and litigation have focused on this type of personnel decision in particular.

Let's say that we all work for a consulting firm called PE Levy & Associates, which has been hired by CS&J Products, a large manufacturing company, to devise, implement, and evaluate a selection battery that is to be used for the selection of *middle-level managers.* A **selection battery** is a set of predictors, or tests, that are used to make employee hiring decisions. In Chapter 6, we discussed the various types of predictors one by one, but note that, in actuality, it is rare for any of these predictors to be used alone. It is much more likely that organizations will employ a *set* of predictors or a battery of tests as a way of predicting criterion performance. Of course, by this time, you know what the first step is. It's the job analysis—the foundation for everything we do in industrial psychology. Thus, we choose a job-oriented, worker-oriented, or hybrid job-analytic technique, as discussed in Chapter 3. From the job analysis, we generate a *job description* and *job specifications,* and from these we develop performance criteria. We should also be sure to consider the "criteria for the criteria" in developing our measures (see Chapter 3).

Using the job analysis—chiefly, the job specifications information—we develop predictors or select predictors from those that already exist. To decide what type of predictors to use, we'll choose among work samples, assessment centers, biographical information blanks, ability tests, interviews, and so on. In this case, because the job is a managerial one, we should seriously consider the use of work samples and assessment centers, as these seem particularly relevant for the job in question. Also, we should opt for multiple tests, as multiple tests would likely increase the proportion of criterion variance that we could account for.

**Figure 7.1** demonstrates why a selection battery yields better prediction than a single test. In the figure, the squared correlations between each predictor and the performance criterion vary from .10 to .36. Together, they account for about 55% of the variance in criterion performance ($r^2$). The validity coefficient for the battery of predictors is about .74 (i.e., the square root of .55). When the predictors are combined in this way, the validity coefficient is a multiple $R$—the correlation between the combination of all the predictors and the criterion. It's clear, based on the validity coefficient (multiple $R$ = .74) and the amount of variance accounted

**selection battery**
A set of predictors, or tests, that are used to make employee hiring decisions.

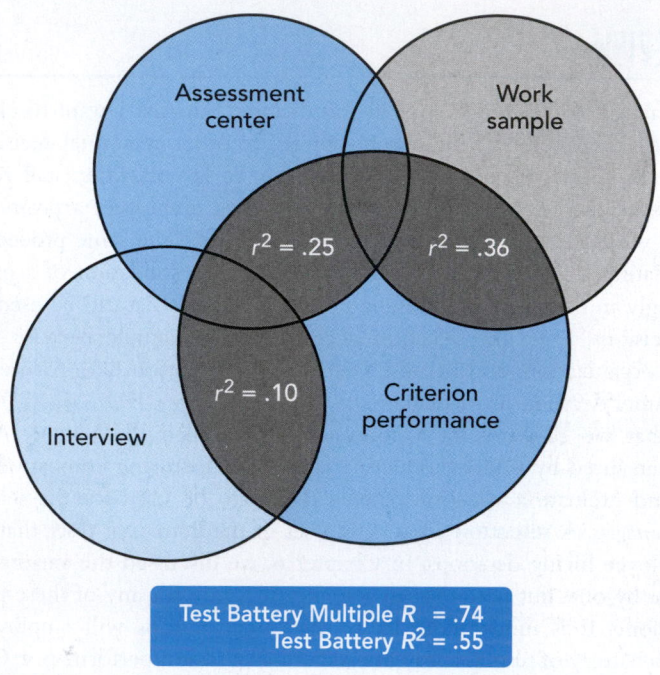

Test Battery Multiple $R$ = .74
Test Battery $R^2$ = .55

**FIGURE 7.1** Selection Battery Example

for ($R^2$ = .55), that using a test battery results in better prediction than using any single test in isolation. Notice also that there is some overlap among the predictors, which means that they are slightly correlated. This explains why, if we add up the individual $r^2$s, we would get .71 rather than .55. The difference between these two numbers reflects the overlap in the predictors. In other words, part of the variance that is accounted for by the work sample test is also accounted for by the assessment center.

Ideally, we want as little correlation among the predictors as possible so that we aren't predicting the same piece of the pie with more than one predictor. In this example, the assessment center is somewhat redundant with the other two predictors. It adds to the prediction, but it makes a smaller unique contribution when you consider its overlap with both the work sample and the interview. If costs were an issue and CS&J Products wanted to use only one predictor, as Figure 7.1 makes clear, using the work sample would be the best choice because it accounts for more variance in the criterion than any other single predictor would. If costs were not an issue, the three predictors as a package would seem to do the best job.

**TECHNICAL TIP**

*Remember that a correlation (r) is used as an index of the relationship between a predictor and a criterion, whereas the coefficient of determination, or the squared correlation (r²), provides information about how much variance in the criterion is accounted for by the predictor.*

# RECRUITMENT

Before we can select employees for CS&J, we must get the applicants interested enough in the jobs to apply. Recruitment, the process of encouraging potentially qualified applicants to seek employment with a particular company, has often been an ignored element of I/O psychology, but it has widespread implications. We could have a large enough budget to make job offers to five lawyers just coming out of law school, but if the applicant pool is weak and the new lawyers are not qualified, selection doesn't really matter very much.

Many organizations report that they have more challenges related to recruiting than to selection (Ployhart, 2006). There are many ways to entice individuals to apply for jobs. Traditionally, jobs have been advertised through college placement offices, newspaper advertisements, employee referrals, job fairs, and, more recently, Internet ads (Breaugh, Greising, Taggart, & Chen, 2003). Newer work in the recruiting area has begun to enhance our understanding of this process a great deal. For instance, research has shown that recruits use the organization's reputation as an indicator of what they expect their job to be like; this reputation also affects recruits' expectations about the pride they will experience working for a particular company (Cable & Turban, 2003; Collins & Stevens, 2002).

Other studies have demonstrated that organizational values affect recruits' attraction to the organization (Highhouse, Hoffman, Greve, & Collins, 2002). Researchers have also shown that individuals aren't attracted to organizations just because of the job attributes (compensation, work environment, etc.); they also strongly consider their subjective evaluation of the organization (e.g., is it an innovative, cool, prestigious place to work?) (Lievens & Highhouse, 2003). In fact, these subjective evaluations appear to be even more important. Research demonstrates the importance of perceived person–environment (PE) fit in recruiting (Ployhart, 2006). Individuals seem increasingly interested in jobs and organizations that seem well suited to them (Yu, 2014). (I introduced the idea of realistic job previews [RJPs] in Chapter 6. You can see how important these RJPs can be for employees and organizations to determine if there is the potential for a good fit.)

The Internet has added a new dimension to recruiting because it reaches an incredibly large audience—one that knows no geographic boundaries (Cober, Brown, Blumental, Doverspike, & Levy, 2000). There have been two elements to this: (1) the general job boards such as Monster.com, LinkedIn.com, and USAjobs.gov, which have broad appeal, and (2) organizations' own employment websites, which focus on attracting recruits for their particular job openings. Some researchers have proposed a model suggesting that applicant attraction is a function of such variables as the aesthetics and usability of the organization's employment website, affective reactions to the website, perceptions of organizational image, and individual applicant differences (Cober, Brown, Keeping, & Levy, 2004). Pieces of this model have been tested, and some of the results suggest that, as predicted, a website's informational content, aesthetic quality, and usability all affect organizational attraction (Cober,

**recruitment**
The process of encouraging potentially qualified applicants to seek employment with a particular company.

**person–environment (PE) fit**
The agreement or match between an individual's KSAOs and values and the demands of a job and characteristics of an organization.

Brown, Levy, Cober, & Keeping, 2003; Selden & Orenstein, 2011; Williamson, Lepak, & King, 2003). Sophisticated technology has been applied to this research area and has extended the work of Cober and colleagues. In a recent study, researchers used eye-tracking devices, which track the movement of a participant's eyes as they read or look at various stimuli, to identify what pieces or elements of the employment website were being looked at the most (Allen, Biggane, Pitts, Otondo, & Van Scotter, 2013). Eye tracking provides an objective indicator of attention—where do participants focus their attention when looking at and navigating a website? Allen and his colleagues found that students fixated on text, particularly text with hyperlinks, more than they fixated on graphics or navigation instructions. The researchers concluded that blocks of text are important when job searchers first begin exploring an employment site and that organizations may not be best served by adding more graphics. Also, it seems that the most important information—the information that the organization really wants the job searchers to see—should be placed in hyperlinked text, because these links attract the visual attention of readers (Allen et al., 2013).

**cybervetting**
The use of social media as part of background investigations used to make employee selection decisions.

Nowhere is the recruiting and selection landscape changing faster than in the area of cybervetting—an assessment of an individual's suitability for a particular job based on information from the Internet (Rose et al., 2010). The popularity of social media has provided an opportunity for organizations to collect information about potential applicants (Preston, 2011). Although there are legal and ethical debates about the use of social media data in the selection process, it appears that most employers are using the Internet to gather information that job candidates do not provide voluntarily or give their permission for potential employers to obtain (Peebles, 2012). In interviews of 45 HR recruiters or hiring managers across many different industries, over 90% of respondents reported that they definitely seek out pictures of job candidates to use in their evaluations (Berkelaar & Buzzanell, 2015). In particular, they reported that they use photographic evidence to disqualify candidates based on lewd behavior, drunk behavior, nudity, etc. The interviews also uncovered a common consensus that social media data are indicators of decision making. Some of the interviewees made it clear that if a candidate left something damaging on their Facebook page that the recruiter could access, it showed a lack of judgment and poor decision-making skills. Clearly, the use of social media has become an important and often used source of data to evaluate potential job candidates. As more and more companies make use of social media in the selection process, legal and ethical issues will continue to swirl around this new approach, leading to some surprising conclusions. One hypothetical situation being discussed is whether a company that *does not* do an Internet search may be found liable for damages if doing that search would have likely uncovered evidence of dangerous tendencies in a candidate who goes on to hurt someone at work (Peebles, 2012). Needless to say, we are just scratching the surface of the legal issues around the use of social media as a screening tool.

Many organizations have quickly learned that the use of social media in recruiting allows them to broaden their potential pool. Job seekers are encouraged to follow companies they find attractive on Facebook, Twitter, LinkedIn, and so on. Talent managers argue that the more people are engaged in the recruiting process, the better.

According to Wikipedia, there are over 200 active social media networking sites, and talent managers are constantly using these sites to contact and engage potential recruits (Lauby, 2010). As the research discussed above makes clear, recruiters are viewing Facebook accounts, personal blogs, and YouTube accounts to get a feel for a candidate's personality and personal behavior.

Informal communication also results in many contacts and, hence, potential job applicants. Often, a company's employees will pass along job information to friends and colleagues, who, in turn, will spread it to other friends and colleagues, greatly increasing the potential applicant pool. This process can be helpful, given that employers tend to be somewhat discriminating about whom they encourage to apply. In this way, informal contacts can help in the screening process. One reason that companies do not want to rely solely on informal contacts is that they could result in discrimination (e.g., if the organization is largely made up of White males, employees' friends and acquaintances are likely to be White males as well); thus, more formal channels are typically used, too. In fact, the more channels that are used to advertise a position, the less likely it is that illegal discrimination will occur, given that increased numbers of culturally and racially diverse people will be aware that the position has become available. (We will spend a great deal of time on legal issues later in this chapter.)

Researchers studying recruiting and racioethnicity (i.e., racial or ethnic differences across people) have proposed a model that describes how culturally distinct group members make decisions about employment at later stages of recruiting, such as during the site visit (McKay & Avery, 2006). One variable that they identify as very important for these racially diverse applicants is the diversity of the community and other available opportunities. They also suggest that some individual difference variables, such as racioethnic identity (i.e., the extent to which an individual's self-concept is defined by membership in a particular racioethnic group), play very important roles. In a companion piece (Avery & McKay, 2006), these scholars provide a framework to help organizations attract female and minority job applicants. This framework is built around organizations demonstrating to applicants that they value and encourage diversity. A recent study found support for this idea by showing that deep-level differences in attitudes and values between the job seeker and the company strongly predicted the seeker's pursuit intentions (Casper, Wayne, & Manegold, 2013). In other words, a company will be more likely to attract job seekers who value diversity, for example, if that company can demonstrate that it has similar values around diversity. Other studies have found that both Black and White participants more carefully process information on an employment website when diversity cues (e.g., the race of people profiled on the

© CJG-Technology/Alamy

**A CLOSER LOOK**

Many organizations now engage in cybervetting. Do you feel it's an efficient and constructive way to get a fuller picture of applicants' job qualifications? Do you feel it's ethical?

website) are included than when those cues are not presented (Walker, Feild, Bernerth, & Bechton, 2014). Careful information processing may allow prospective employees to withdraw their application after uncovering information about a company that they may have missed if they had not carefully processed the data available to them.

For a thorough review of the recruitment literature and a framework for future research, I recommend that you read Rynes and Cable (2003) or a more recent meta-analysis by Uggerslev, Fassina, and Kraichy (2012). For our purposes, however, let's go back to our consulting project and assume that, through varied and appropriate recruitment techniques, CS&J has identified several applicants for its managerial position.

# THE SELECTION DECISION

The rest of the chapter will focus on using a selection battery to decide whom to hire and whom not to hire. Because the work of PE Levy & Associates is based on strong scientific practice and is driven by a strong sense of ethics, prior to recommending any particular selection battery, we set out to demonstrate its validity. There are two general approaches to demonstrating the validity of a selection battery: conducting a *validation study* and *validity generalization*. Let's consider each in turn.

## The Process of Test Validation

In this section, we will look more closely at concepts I have introduced earlier—the validity coefficient, predictors, and criteria. We use a validation study to determine the extent to which a predictor or battery of predictors is related to the criterion of interest, such as on-the-job performance. In other words, it is from a validation study that the validity coefficients we've been talking about are derived. There are two approaches to demonstrating criterion-related validity, but both approaches start with the same up-front work—and for our consulting gig, we've already done that work. In other words, we've started with a job analysis, which allows us to develop or select both predictors and criteria. We examine the links between these two sets of variables through the process of validation.

**Predictive Validation** Predictive validity studies investigate how effective our predictors are at forecasting the on-the-job performance of applicants. Predictors are measured prior to hiring, and criteria are measured after a few months on the job.

In our current example, if we were to pursue criterion-related validity through a predictive validation design, we would be asking if scores on the work sample, assessment center, and interview predict performance at CS&J Products.

To demonstrate predictive validity, we would follow these steps:

1. *Gather predictor data on all of the applicants.* In our example, this means running each applicant through a work sample test, an assessment center, and an interview. Each applicant would be scored on these tests, and a composite score would be arrived at by adding the scores or performing some other computation.

2. *Hire some of the applicants to fill the open positions.* Note, however, that these applicants would be hired on the basis of predictors that are *not* part of our newly developed selection battery. Instead, individuals would be hired according to the company's current selection system, which is probably quite different from the one we are proposing. By following this rather unorthodox strategy, we are more likely to get individuals hired into CS&J who range from low to high on our new predictors. This outcome is very important for the validation process because if we hired only high scorers on the new predictors, we would not be able to determine whether low scorers were unsuccessful on the job because no low scorers would be in our sample.

3. *After several months, gather performance data that can serve as the criteria for our validation study.* Remember that these criteria are developed from the job analysis and that they are intended to differentiate successful from unsuccessful performers.

4. *Compute a validity coefficient between the predictor score and the criterion score that indicates the strength of the relationship between our predictor and our criterion.* We can compute a validity coefficient for the battery as a whole or for each predictor separately. Likewise, we can compute validity coefficients for each particular performance criterion or for our composite criterion.

When this process is complete we have determined how well our selection battery predicts on-the-job performance. This would allow us to begin using this new test if, in fact, the validity evidence indicates that our battery predicts on-the-job performance well. If the validation study shows that the test battery is not a good predictor of job performance, then we have to go back and determine where the problems exist (the job analysis, the measurement of the predictors, the measurement of the criteria, etc.). Future sections of this chapter will address how these tests are used for selection.

Predictive validity studies are difficult to conduct because they require selecting employees based on predictors other than those we are intending to validate—and doing so requires two sets of predictor measures. Obviously, this can be expensive in terms of both the dollars involved in the development and administration of the tests and the time spent by applicants and test administrators.

**Concurrent Validation** Sometimes predictive validity studies are so difficult (if not impossible) to conduct that a concurrent validity study is the more viable option.

To establish criterion-related validity through a concurrent validation study, we would perform the following steps:

1. *Collect data on both predictors and criteria from incumbent employees at the same time.* In our example, this means that incumbents would be run through the work sample test, the assessment center, and the interview and that their performance on these predictors would

**TECHNICAL TIP**

In Chapter 2, we introduced the idea of criterion-related validity, which is the extent to which a test is a good predictor of criteria like job performance. Furthermore, we noted the two types of criterion-related validity—concurrent and predictive. Predictive refers to test scores predicting performance in the future, whereas concurrent shows how well a test predicts performance at the same time.

be scored. In addition, performance data would be collected from current employees. For instance, we might gather performance appraisal data already in the incumbents' files or ask supervisors and peers to provide performance ratings of these incumbents.

2. *Compute a validity coefficient between the predictor score and the criterion score.* Again, this indicates the strength of the relationship between our predictor and our criterion. We can compute a validity coefficient for the battery as a whole or for each predictor separately. Likewise, we can compute validity coefficients for each particular performance criterion or for our composite criterion.

**Table 7.1** presents an overview of each validation strategy. Concurrent validation differs from predictive validation in two major ways: In situations involving concurrent validation, (1) incumbents, rather than applicants, are used as participants, and (2) predictors and criteria are measured at the same time. Although empirical research has not demonstrated many differences between concurrent and predictive validation efforts (Schmitt, Gooding, Noe, & Kirsch, 1984), some I/O psychologists are concerned about the use of concurrent validation because, in their view, incumbents and applicants differ in important ways, such as amount of job experience and potential motivation (Cascio & Aguinis, 2010). Because concurrent designs use incumbents, the results tend to overestimate the validity coefficients (Van Iddekinge & Ployhart, 2008) compared to predictive designs, which use applicants. Some scholars argue that we should be conducting more predictive validation studies to temper this overestimation tendency and to further evaluate the extent of this potential problem (Morgeson et al., 2007; Ployhart & MacKenzie, 2011).

**Cross-Validation** In cases in which predictive or concurrent strategies are used to validate a selection battery, it is a statistical truth that the validity of that selection battery will always be the highest for the sample on which it was validated. In other

| TABLE 7.1  Validation Designs | | |
|---|---|---|
| Element | Concurrent Design | Predictive Design |
| Participants | Incumbents | Applicants |
| Predictor measurement | Time 1 | Time 1 |
| Criterion measurement | Time 1 | Time 2 |
| Selection decision | Made prior to Time 1 and was based on other predictors | To be made between Time 1 and Time 2 and to be based on other predictors |
| Validity coefficient | Correlation between predictor and criterion | Correlation between predictor and criterion |

words, a given selection battery will likely demonstrate lower validity when employed with a different sample—a phenomenon known as validity shrinkage. The statistical explanation for this phenomenon is beyond the scope of this book, but you can find a thorough discussion in Cascio and Aguinis (2010). Here, we consider the general factors involved in our particular situation.

Let's say we find that our selection battery has a validity coefficient (in this case, a multiple *R*) of .74, as depicted in Figure 7.1. If we use this selection battery with another sample of applicants at the same company, the validity coefficient is likely to be smaller. The key question for the generalizability of our results is "How much smaller?" To cross-validate the selection battery *empirically,* we apply the same predictors and criteria to a different sample at CS&J to see how close the validity coefficient is to the original. Specifically, we generate a regression equation using the original predictor and criterion data. We then plug the predictor scores from the new individuals in the cross-validation sample into this original regression equation to obtain a *predicted criterion score.* Correlating this predicted criterion score with the actual criterion score provides the validity coefficient for the new sample, which can be compared with the validity coefficient of the original sample. Of course, we are hoping for only a small amount of validity shrinkage—maybe .05 to .10. If the validity doesn't shrink very much, we can feel comfortable that the selection battery is still valid and ready for use by CS&J to select employees.

To cross-validate the selection battery *statistically,* we correct or adjust the original validity coefficient for measurement error. But the approach we choose, whether empirical or statistical, is less important than our commitment to estimating the cross-validated coefficient. The best estimate of the validity of a particular selection battery is the cross-validated coefficient; yet, because it takes a little extra time and effort, this step is frequently skipped in validation projects.

## Validity Generalization

Obviously, it takes a great deal of effort, time, and money to demonstrate criterion-related validity using concurrent or predictive approaches. An alternative to this approach that has been gaining in popularity over the past 30 years is called validity generalization (VG). One long-standing belief in the selection area was that test validities varied across situations. If this were the case, the selection battery that PE Levy & Associates developed for CS&J would not likely be valid for another company. Indeed, the work sample we developed would work only for this particular company and this particular situation.

The belief that test validities are limited to particular situations is termed situational specificity. John Hunter and Frank Schmidt (1990), however, took issue with this belief and developed methods to examine whether validities are truly situationally specific. Their VG technique was both statistically and conceptually tied to the technique of meta-analysis, which they developed in conjunction with this work. Basically, they argued that by using meta-analytic techniques to weight and combine validity coefficients across situations, we can examine whether validities are situationally specific or generalizable across situations. Their conclusion—for which

**validity shrinkage**
A statistical phenomenon reflecting the likelihood that a given selection battery will demonstrate lower validity when employed with a different sample.

**validity generalization (VG)**
A statistical approach used to demonstrate that test validities do not vary across situations.

**situational specificity**
The belief that test validities are specific to particular situations.

there is a great deal of research support— is that validities do tend to generalize across situations (Murphy, 2003).

Many criticisms and concerns have been raised about the statistical methodology used in VG (Cascio & Aguinis, 2010; Murphy, 2003), and VG is still limited to jobs that are similar to those on which the test was originally validated. For instance, to say that the validity of an in-basket test generalizes is not to say that because it is valid for managerial selection it is also valid for the selection of custodians and ministers, but no test or measure of any construct, regardless of the measure's soundness, is a good predictor for every job (see also *EEOC v. Atlas Paper Box,* 1989).

Another issue regarding VG is that the legal community is often involved in disputes as to whether a particular selection test is legal—an issue we will consider shortly. For now, though, note that, although the courts have traditionally required a validation study to show that a selection battery was valid, in recent years they have viewed VG more favorably, given the caveat that a complete and thorough job analysis is necessary. This job analysis must demonstrate that the job on which the tests were validated is the same as the job for which those tests are being used for selection. In our current example, the implication is that if someone else has validated an in-basket for managerial selection, PE Levy & Associates must be able to show that the CS&J managerial jobs for which we want to use this in-basket are very, very similar to the managerial jobs on which the in-basket was originally validated.

Validation of selection batteries is extremely important not only to organizational performance but also, as we will soon see, to the laws that police our work. There are three main approaches to validation: predictive validation studies, concurrent validation studies, and validity generalization. Each has its strengths and weaknesses, so one's choice should be determined on a case-by-case basis. Whereas there is some agreement among scholars that VG can serve a positive purpose for organizations trying to conduct high-quality selection, although with some limits (see Biddle, 2010, for a more critical view), there is disagreement about the statistical analysis that supports VG. We won't get into the specifics of the statistical debates, but if you are interested, you should read a series of articles published in *Industrial and Organizational Psychology* in 2014 (Volume 7, Issue 4). The lead article raises questions about the use of VG (LeBreton, Scherer, & James, 2014) and the many commentaries that follow provide a diverse set of opinions on the issue.

**synthetic validity**
Validity that is inferred based on the links between job components and KSAOs.

A related approach to validity generalization, called synthetic validity, has existed for over 50 years but has not sufficiently captured the support of researchers or practitioners to make it as popular as these other approaches. Synthetic validity is based on the notion that job components common across jobs are related to the same KSAOs or human attributes (Johnson et al., 2010). Proponents argue for creating large, shared databases of these job components that can be linked to the appropriate KSAOs, allowing for selection to occur based on those KSAOs and without a local validation study. Some argue that this approach is superior to existing approaches (Johnson et al., 2010), while others find it inferior (Harvey, 2010; Schmidt & Oh, 2010) for various reasons, such as a lack of discriminant validity.

## Practical Approaches to Selection

Now that we've demonstrated the validity of our selection battery (including cross-validation), we can provide this information to CS&J Products, assuring its executives that our selection battery predicts job performance quite well. CS&J, being a profit-driven company, is interested in achieving two main goals. First, it wants us to provide the names of people who are likely to be successful performers. This is, after all, why it hired us. Second, it wants us to demonstrate that our selection battery is cost effective. We will consider both of these goals in the next few pages, starting with two major approaches to employee selection: multiple cutoffs and multiple regression.

**Multiple Cutoffs** The multiple cutoff approach is a noncompensatory method of employee selection in which "passing scores," or cutoffs, are set on each predictor. It is considered noncompensatory because applicants, to be eligible for selection, must score higher than these cutoffs on each predictor. In other words, they have to pass each test; scoring well on one test does not "make up," or compensate, for scoring low on another test. Back to our example: In order to be rated as acceptable for the middle-level-manager job at CS&J, applicants have to exceed some minimum level of performance on the work sample test, the assessment center, and the interview. An applicant who excels on the work sample and assessment center but bombs on the interview won't be hired—regardless of the importance of the KSAOs that the interview was designed to tap.

> **multiple cutoff approach**
> A noncompensatory model of employee selection in which "passing scores," or cutoffs, are set on each predictor.

Let's say we had two open positions in the cardiac surgery department. If we simply added up the applicants' scores and selected the two highest scorers as our surgeons, we would pick Dr. Seuss and Dr. Carter. However, both of them failed to reach a critical cutoff score. Although they have the highest total scores, they seem weak in very important areas. How about you? Would you hire the two "top" candidates, or would you invoke a multiple cutoff strategy?

Perhaps the strengths of a multiple cutoff approach are best seen when we consider certain types of jobs. For instance, to select cardiac surgeons, we might use a measure of medical knowledge, grades in medical school, an interview, and a psychomotor test involving fine-grained handwork such as cutting and sewing. I won't speak for you, but a multiple cutoff is the way I want my surgeon selected: An incredibly smart and verbally skilled surgeon who shakes uncontrollably with a scalpel in her hand is of no use to me! It is of paramount importance that candidates pass all the cutoffs for the position of cardiac surgeon. **Table 7.2** presents the names of five applicants for this position, along with their predictor scores. Look this over and decide whom you would select. A second advantage to the multiple cutoff approach is that it is easier for organizational members to understand than more complicated regression-based approaches. However, the noncompensatory nature of the multiple cutoff approach may be a disadvantage in situations where none of the predictors are so important that a low score would result in the applicant not being acceptable. There are situations where organizations would want a strength in one area to be allowed to overcome a weakness in another—this would suggest the use of a compensatory model, which we will get to when we talk about the multiple regression approach.

## TABLE 7.2 Multiple Cutoff Approach: Cardiac Surgeon

| Applicant | Medical Knowledge Test | Medical School GPA | Interview Score | Psychomotor Test | Total Score |
|---|---|---|---|---|---|
| Dr. Pratt | 10 | 8 | 6 | 8 | 32 |
| Dr. Carter | 10 | 10 | 10 | 5 | 35 |
| Dr. Quinn | 9 | 8 | 8 | 7 | 32 |
| Dr. Welby | 9 | 8 | 7 | 10 | 34 |
| Dr. Seuss | 6 | 10 | 10 | 10 | 36 |
| Predictor cutoff | 9 | 7 | 6 | 7 | |

Note: All test scores are on a 1–10 scale, with higher numbers indicating better performance.

**multiple hurdle approach**
A rendition of the multiple cutoff approach in which the predictors are administered in a predetermined order and applicants are measured on the next predictor only if they scored above the cutoff on the previous predictor.

One special rendition of the multiple cutoff approach to selection is the **multiple hurdle approach**. As before, passing scores are set on each predictor, and superb performance on one predictor cannot compensate for below-cutoff performance on another predictor. With the multiple hurdle approach, however, predictors are administered in a predetermined order and applicants are measured on a subsequent predictor only if they scored above the cutoff on the previous predictor.

**Table 7.3** presents scores for seven applicants on four predictors, as well as the cutoff scores for each predictor. Suppose that we have been hired by CS&J to help it select production line supervisors, and we've identified the relevant predictors as

## TABLE 7.3 Multiple Hurdle Approach: Production Line Supervisor

| Applicant | Cognitive Ability Test (Cutoff = 110) | Personality Test (Cutoff = 55) | Work Sample (Cutoff = 80) | Interview (Cutoff = 18) |
|---|---|---|---|---|
| Ripken | 120 | 61 | 88 | 23 |
| Banks | 118 | 59 | 76 | |
| Jeter | 107 | | | |
| Tejada | 108 | | | |
| Yount | 106 | | | |
| Belanger | 104 | | | |
| Aparacio | 121 | 40 | | |
| | Least Expensive | | | Most Expensive |

## PRACTITIONER FORUM

Transportation Security Administration

### Elizabeth Kolmstetter

*PhD, 1991, I/O Psychology, Virginia Tech*
*Assistant to the Administrator and Chief Human Capital Officer,*
*U.S. Agency for International Development (USAID)*

In the aftermath of 9/11, Congress passed legislation mandating a new federal agency, the Transportation Security Administration (TSA), to hire and train a federal workforce of more than 50,000 airport security screeners at more than 429 airports nationwide in less than a year. The TSA implemented high standards during all aspects of creating this new workforce, including the recruiting, selection, training, and certification process. A fair, valid, and defensible selection system was the cornerstone of the success of the workforce federalization. Every screener hired went through the same hiring and training process, regardless of airport size or location.

The assessment process was developed and validated following the principles discussed in this chapter regarding a multiple hurdle approach to selection:

1. Application (online or via telephone)

2. Three-and-a-half-hour multiple-choice test: (a) Aviation Security Screener Employment Test (AS-SET; personality-based), (b) Screener English Test (SET), and (c) Screener Object Recognition Test (SORT; x-ray image test)

3. Structured interview (in-person)

4. Physical abilities test (i.e., baggage lift, baggage search)

5. Medical evaluation (including tests for drugs, vision, hearing, color vision, orthopedic, cardiovascular, etc.)

6. Background investigation (i.e., credit and criminal checks)

7. 45-hour basic screener training (including classroom training with labs, job knowledge test, x-ray image detection test)

8. 60-hour on-the-job training and initial certification (including formal practical skills evaluation, x-ray image detection mastery test)

9. Annual recertification (job knowledge test, x-ray image detection proficiency test, practical skills demonstration)

In its first year, the TSA processed more than 1.7 million applications, tested more than 340,000 applicants, and hired approximately 50,000 screeners. By implementing a job-related selection process, the TSA ensured that less than 2% of the screeners hired failed the training.

The TSA has been very thorough in the development and validation of this complex selection system, but carrying out this process is done with even greater caution. Test security, training of test administrators and applicant assessors, and quality of test scoring are all issues that involve the expenditure of considerable time by the I/O psychologists and other TSA employees and contractors. Although it takes an incredible amount of work, national security is "high-stakes" employment and a priority for this country. The TSA screener selection program has been very successful in selecting qualified screeners while serving society's needs.

### Applying Your Knowledge

1. What are the benefits of the multiple hurdle approach to selection?

2. What other issues are important in the implementation of selection systems?

3. Why should organizations integrate their selection and training programs?

being a cognitive ability test, a personality test, a work sample test, and an interview. The predictors are arranged from least to most expensive because this is typically the way multiple hurdle strategies are conducted. The cognitive ability test can be purchased from a test publisher and administered to applicants in a group, so it is inexpensive in terms of both time and money. But the interview questions probably need to be developed in-house rather than bought off the shelf, and they are typically done one-on-one—so they may require a great deal of time both to develop and to conduct. Applicants proceed to the next predictor only if they successfully jump the previous hurdle (i.e., by scoring above the cutoff on the previous predictor).

As you can see in Table 7.3, only Ripken, Banks, and Aparacio pass the cognitive ability test. Thus, they go on to the next hurdle. But here only Ripken and Banks pass the personality test. They both go on to the work sample test, on which only Ripken survives to the next hurdle. Ripken also passes the interview and would thus be offered the job. (One thing is sure: You won't have an absence problem if you hire Ripken! Absence will be discussed in Chapter 11.) The advantages of this approach mirror those of the multiple cutoff, but also include the potential cost-savings feature. By ordering the hurdles by cost, this approach allows the organization to minimize costs by saving the most expensive assessments for last, when fewer applicants are still in the process. See the Practitioner Forum for an important example of this approach to selection.

**Multiple Regression** We briefly discussed regression analysis in Chapter 2, but we need to spend more time on it here because it is an important technique for determining how we use predictor information to make selection decisions. First, this is a compensatory approach, which means that an exceptional performance on one predictor can make up for a poor performance on another predictor—this is one obvious difference between the multiple regression approach and the multiple cutoff/ hurdle approaches, which are noncompensatory. As with the earlier approaches, the compensatory nature can be an advantage or a disadvantage depending on the job situation and the concerns inherent in making poor selection decisions. Recall that the validity coefficient is an index of the strength of the relationship between a predictor and a criterion. For our present purposes, however, we are interested in more than just this relationship because the focus of selection is on prediction. Accordingly, we use **multiple regression**, a statistical technique that allows us to estimate how well a series of predictors forecasts a performance criterion. This process can get rather complicated, but I will try to present the basics using the middle-level-manager selection scenario that we've been working with.

First, we use our validation data (let's assume a predictive validity design) to generate a regression equation. We do this by regressing the criterion performance of those applicants who were selected on their predictor scores (work sample, assessment center, and interview). The general form of a multiple regression equation is

> **multiple regression** A statistical technique that, when used in the selection context, allows us to estimate how well a series of predictors forecasts a performance criterion.

$$Y = b_0 + b_1X_1 + b_2X_2 + b_3X_3$$

where each X is the individual's score on a specific predictor, each b is the weight for that particular score, Y is the criterion, and $b_0$ is the intercept (i.e., the point at which the regression line crosses the y-axis). Computing the regression equation with our validation data yields the following result:

$$Y_{predicted} = 1.043 + 1.548 \text{ (work sample score)} + .752 \text{ (assessment center score)}$$
$$+ .320 \text{ (interview score)}$$

This equation indicates the best prediction scheme, based on our validation data, for forecasting any individual's criterion performance. In other words, we use the predictor and criterion data from our validation study to determine the best weights for each predictor in arriving at a predicted criterion score.

Second, we apply that prediction scheme (i.e., the regression equation) to our applicant data to arrive at selection decisions. An example is presented in **Table 7.4**, which shows the predictor scores for four new applicants, along with their predicted criterion scores derived from the regression equation. These applicants were not part of the validation sample; rather, we are now using the results of the validation to select from our new applicant pool. Specifically, the predicted criterion scores are derived by plugging each individual's predictor score into the regression equation (as presented in the bottom portion of the table). The table clearly shows that Tomlin is predicted to be the best performer.

The final step is to rank-order all the applicants according to predicted criterion scores and then to select from the top until all the open positions are filled. It's important to note that the regression equation creates the best combination of the tests for maximizing the prediction of the criterion. Based on these data, if CS&J had two open positions, we would make offers to Tomlin and Stokes because, based on our validation study, these two applicants are predicted to be the best performers on the job.

There are a few loose ends here. First, the executives at CS&J may have a very good idea of what is acceptable performance for their company. Thus, they may want to set a cutoff score on the predicted criterion. For instance, based on their standards of what is acceptable employee performance, they may decide that the predicted criterion cutoff is 11.00, which means that no matter how many position

| TABLE 7.4 Multiple Regression Approach | | | | |
|---|---|---|---|---|
| Applicant | Work Sample | Assessment Center | Interview Criterion | Predicted |
| Stokes | 3 | 5 | 7 | 11.69 |
| Dulany | 4 | 2 | 6 | 10.66 |
| Tomlin | 5 | 5 | 8 | 15.10 |
| Blake | 2 | 3 | 5 | 8.00 |

Stokes: $Y_{predicted} = 1.043 + 1.548 (3) + .752 (5) + .320 (7) = 11.69$

Dulany: $Y_{predicted} = 1.043 + 1.548 (4) + .752 (2) + .320 (6) = 10.66$

Tomlin: $Y_{predicted} = 1.043 + 1.548 (5) + .752 (5) + .320 (8) = 15.10$

Blake: $Y_{predicted} = 1.043 + 1.548 (2) + .752 (3) + .320 (5) = 8.00$

**TECHNICAL TIP**

*Of course, as we suggested earlier in this chapter, we would cross-validate the regression equation to make sure that this approach works in more than one context or setting.*

openings are available, they will not hire anyone whose predicted criterion score is under 11.00. In terms of our example in Table 7.4 and based on this cutoff, only Tomlin and Stokes would be considered "qualified" to be hired into CS&J Products. Second, it is possible that the executives at CS&J or PE Levy & Associates feel that it is best to set minimum cutoffs on each predictor. This would involve an approach that combines the multiple cutoff technique with the multiple regression technique—for instance, we might set a cutoff of 4.00 on the work sample test. When using the multiple regression, we could still rank-order applicants based on their predicted criterion scores, but, prior to selection, we would check to make sure that the applicants who fall below 4.00 on the work sample test are withdrawn from the applicant pool regardless of their predicted criterion score. In this case, Stokes and Blake would be removed from the qualified applicant pool.

Think back to our cardiac surgeon example. Given the importance of psychomotor skills and medical knowledge, the use of cutoffs on these predictors, as well as a multiple regression approach, would be a very reasonable strategy for the selection of surgeons.

## Usefulness of Selection Processes

At this point, we can tell the executives at CS&J that we have developed, validated, and cross-validated a selection battery that will result in successful employee selection. We can present them with a few different ways to use the predictor data in making these employment decisions, such as the multiple cutoff approach, the multiple hurdle approach, the multiple regression approach, or some combination of these. Certainly, they will be pleased with what we have to offer. However, they will probably have one remaining question for us to answer: Is it worth it? The executives at CS&J aren't satisfied with knowing that we have developed a valid selection system for them; they also want to know how much better it is than their current system and how expensive (in time and dollars) it will be to switch to and use this new system. These questions all deal with the **utility** of the selection battery—that is, with how useful and cost efficient it is. We will now spend some time discussing the various elements of the selection process that allow us to answer these questions for the organization.

**utility**
The degree to which a selection battery is useful and cost efficient.

**Decision Accuracy** The first element we need to focus on is the accuracy of the selection decision—or, more specifically, the gain in accuracy that is provided by our new selection battery. After all, the whole purpose of our involvement in this project is to improve the quality of the current CS&J workforce by making better employee selection decisions.

**Figure 7.2** depicts all possible theoretical outcomes of our selection situation, as represented by Quadrants 1 through 4. In other words, every selection decision can be characterized by whether the person is hired or rejected and whether the person is successful or unsuccessful on the job. (Of course, we won't know about job performance until after the person has been on the job for a while.)

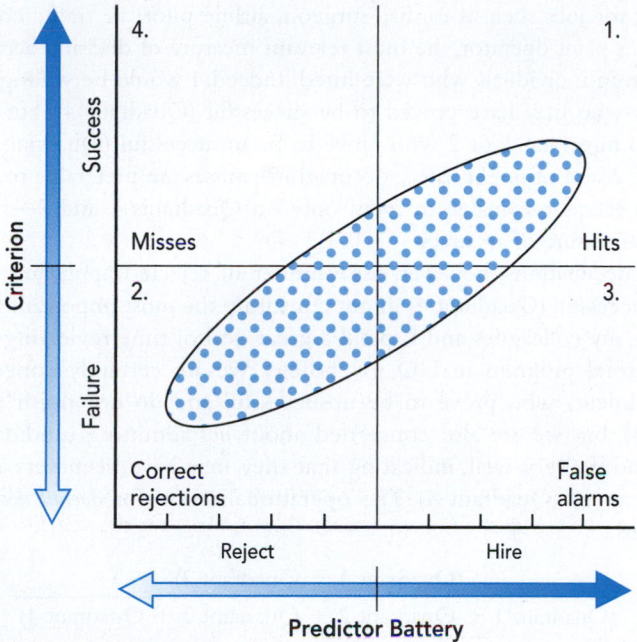

**FIGURE 7.2** Decision Accuracy

The first two quadrants refer to the accurate selection decisions. Quadrant 1, labeled *hits* (sometimes called *true positives*), represents the number of applicants hired on the basis of our selection system who went on to be successful performers. Quadrant 2, labeled *correct rejections* (sometimes called *true negatives*), represents the number of applicants who were not hired and would have been unsuccessful on the job. (Although this number cannot be accessed from our applicant sample because these individuals are never hired, we are able to gather information about such individuals from the validation sample.) The last two quadrants refer to the inaccurate selection decisions. Quadrant 3, labeled *false alarms* (sometimes called *false positives*), represents the applicants who were hired but proved to be ineffective performers. Quadrant 4, labeled *misses* (sometimes called *false negatives*), represents the applicants we didn't hire but should have hired, as they would have been successful performers. (These individuals, too, can be examined only within the validation sample.)

Companies are often interested in knowing only the outcome of the hiring decisions—that is, whether the hired applicants succeed or fail. This information is provided by the following formula for *decision accuracy for hires,* which reflects the percentage of hiring decisions that are correct:

$$\frac{\text{Quadrant 1}}{(\text{Quadrant 1} + \text{Quadrant 3})}$$

Certainly, for jobs such as cardiac surgeon, airline pilot, air traffic controller, and nuclear power plant operator, the most relevant measure of decision accuracy would be derived from individuals who were hired. Indeed, I would be willing to reject 10 airline pilots who may have proved to be successful (Quadrant 4), but I would *not* be willing to hire even 1 or 2 who prove to be unsuccessful (Quadrant 3). In other words, in the realm of public safety occupations, misses are preferable to false alarms! Therefore, it seems reasonable to focus only on Quadrants 1 and 3—hits and false alarms—as a measure of accuracy.

In other occupations, however, the number of rejected applicants who would have been successful (Quadrant 4) might constitute the most important information. For instance, my colleagues and I spend a great deal of time reviewing applications for our doctoral program in I/O psychology. We are certainly concerned about admitting students who prove to be unsuccessful and do not finish the program (Quadrant 3), but we are also concerned about *not* admitting candidates who go elsewhere and do very well, indicating that they may have been very successful in our own program (Quadrant 4). The operationalization for *overall decision accuracy* looks like this:

$$\frac{(\text{Quadrant } 1 + \text{Quadrant } 2)}{(\text{Quadrant } 1 + \text{Quadrant } 2 + \text{Quadrant } 3 + \text{Quadrant } 4)}$$

Regardless of how we define decision accuracy, however, the goal of the selection battery is to maximize the number of hits and correct rejections and to minimize the number of misses and false alarms. All else being equal, the utility of the selection battery is demonstrated by the extent to which it does both.

**Validity** Maximizing hits and correct rejections while minimizing misses and false alarms will occur to the extent that the selection battery is valid. Thus, the first factor that affects the utility of the selection battery is its validity. Figure 7.2 depicts the outcomes of a selection battery with a validity coefficient of about .70. (Compare this figure with the middle panel of Figure 2.8.) Given this degree of validity, the small number of false alarms and misses is not surprising; the selection battery depicted here certainly maximizes the hits and correct rejections. By contrast, **Figure 7.3** depicts the outcomes of a selection battery with zero validity, as represented by a circle. (Compare this figure with the left panel of Figure 2.8.) What makes the lack of validity obvious is the same number of hits, correct rejections, misses, and false alarms. In this case, individuals who score high on the battery of predictors are just as likely to be unsuccessful on the job as they are to be successful; those who score low on the battery of predictors are just as likely to be successful on the job as they are to be unsuccessful. Thus, making a selection decision with a battery that demonstrates zero validity is akin to random hiring and clearly provides no utility to the company. Of course, it is important for organizations to periodically update their job analysis and all of the relevant steps to the selection process (e.g., validation, cutoffs, etc.) to take into consideration any changes that may be taking place in the organization itself, the labor market, the applicants, and current employees.

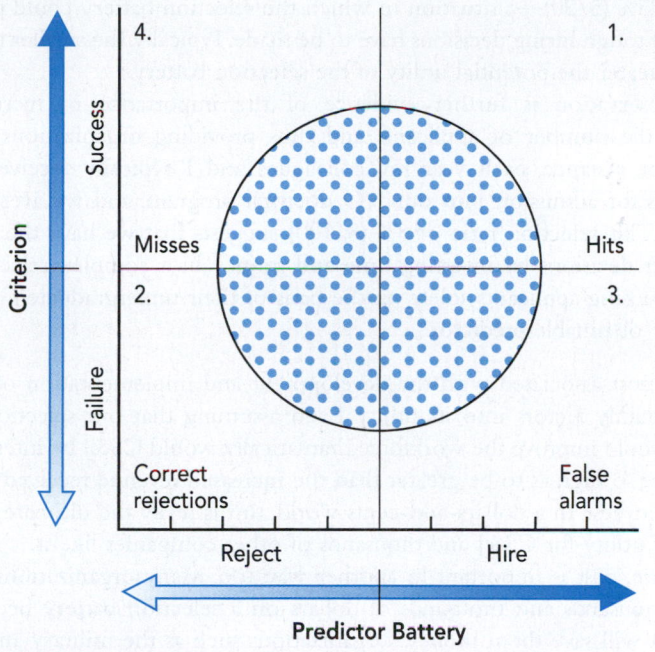

**FIGURE 7.3** The Case of No Validity

**Base Rate** The base rate reflects the percentage of current employees who are successful on the job. In part, this percentage reflects the quality of the previous selection battery (and, perhaps, is affected by other HR processes such as performance management and training) and provides a baseline against which the new selection battery can be compared. Of course, the organization needs to set a cutoff on the criterion so that the base rate can be calculated. In most colleges, for instance, a 2.0 GPA is thought of as the criterion cutoff, and the percentage of current students who meet that cutoff is considered the base rate. Suppose that 30% of the current employees at CS&J perform at a level that CS&J has decided is acceptable. The baseline would thus be 30%, and a new selection battery that resulted in an increase in this base rate would be an improvement over the old selection battery. Of course, if CS&J had a base rate of 90%, it is unlikely that we could develop a selection battery to improve on the current one, and the utility of our newly developed selection battery would be low.

**base rate**
The percentage of current employees who are successful on the job.

**Selection Ratio** The selection ratio is defined as the number of job openings divided by the number of applicants. If CS&J has 20 open positions and 20 applicants, the selection ratio would be 1.00, suggesting that the cost and effort involved in developing and implementing a selection battery are unnecessary because the company would have to hire all available applicants in order to fully staff its organization. On the other hand, if CS&J has 5 open positions and 20 applicants, the selection ratio

**selection ratio**
The number of job openings divided by the number of applicants.

would be 25% (5/20)—a situation in which the selection battery could prove useful, especially if tough hiring decisions have to be made. Typically, the smaller the selection ratio, the greater the potential utility of the selection battery.

This observation is further evidence of the importance of recruitment for increasing the number of applicants and thus providing organizations with more options. For instance, each year my colleagues and I typically receive about 100 applications for admission into our I/O doctoral program, and we average about 8 open slots. This selection ratio of 8% (8/100) suggests that we have the potential to make better decisions by investing time and money in a complex selection battery than by choosing applicants solely on the basis of their undergraduate GPA or some other easily obtainable predictor.

**Cost** The cost associated with the development and implementation of a selection battery certainly factors into its utility. Even assuming that our selection battery is valid and would improve the workforce dramatically, would CS&J be interested in it if the costs are so high as to be greater than the increased revenue received from hiring better employees? In a dollars-and-cents world, this is really the ultimate comparison in terms of utility for CS&J and thousands of other companies like it.

Of course, cost is important in another way, too. Many organizations are willing to spend thousands and thousands of dollars on a selection battery because, in the long run, it will save them money. Organizations such as the military and the upper reaches of the federal government, where a great deal of money is invested in the training and development of new employees, are especially willing to invest in selection. For example, because it is costly to train an astronaut, the false-alarm rate is very significant. Think of it this way: For every new recruit who is selected to be an astronaut, millions of dollars are invested; thus, a great deal of money would be wasted in the training of someone who fails. This is the reason NASA prefers to invest considerable money up front in the selection system. (We'll talk more about training in the next chapter.)

**Putting It All Together** Now that we have discussed all the information that comes into play when evaluating the utility of a selection battery, we can look at how this information is combined to estimate this utility.

With a valid selection battery and knowledge of the organization's base rate and selection ratio, it is possible to estimate the improvement that is likely to follow from the implementation of our newly developed selection battery. Keep in mind that we can only estimate this improvement and that we are still making many assumptions about the performance of the newly hired individuals based on their potential. These high-scoring applicants may not perform well on the job for a whole host of reasons. For now, however, we will have faith that our assumptions and calculations are correct.

Tables have been developed that allow us to estimate the improvement in the workforce that will result from the new selection battery. One version of these is known as the *Taylor-Russell Tables* (Taylor & Russell, 1939). **Table 7.5** presents a portion of these tables corresponding to base rates of 30% and 70% for various levels of validity and various selection ratios. Suppose that the base rate at CS&J Products

## TABLE 7.5  A Portion of the Taylor-Russell Tables

| Base Rate | Validity Coefficient | Selection Ratio | | | | | | | | | | |
|---|---|---|---|---|---|---|---|---|---|---|---|---|
| | | .05 | .10 | .20 | .30 | .40 | .50 | .60 | .70 | .80 | .90 | .95 |
| 30% | .00 | .30 | .30 | .30 | .30 | .30 | .30 | .30 | .30 | .30 | .30 | .30 |
| | .10 | .38 | .36 | .35 | .34 | .33 | .33 | .32 | .32 | .31 | .31 | .30 |
| | .20 | .46 | .43 | .40 | .38 | .37 | .36 | .34 | .33 | .32 | .31 | .31 |
| | .30 | .54 | .50 | .46 | .43 | .40 | .38 | .37 | .35 | .33 | .32 | .31 |
| | .40 | .63 | .58 | .51 | .47 | .44 | .41 | .39 | .37 | .34 | .32 | .31 |
| | .50 | .72 | .65 | .58 | .52 | .48 | .44 | .41 | .38 | .35 | .33 | .31 |
| | .60 | .81 | .74 | .64 | .58 | .52 | .47 | .43 | .40 | .36 | .33 | .31 |
| | .70 | .89 | .62 | .72 | .63 | .57 | .51 | .46 | .41 | .37 | .33 | .32 |
| | .80 | .96 | .90 | .80 | .70 | .62 | .54 | .48 | .42 | .37 | .33 | .32 |
| | .90 | 1.00 | .98 | .90 | .79 | .68 | .58 | .49 | .43 | .37 | .33 | .32 |
| 70% | .00 | .70 | .70 | .70 | .70 | .70 | .70 | .70 | .70 | .70 | .70 | .70 |
| | .10 | .77 | .76 | .75 | .74 | .73 | .73 | .72 | .72 | .71 | .71 | .70 |
| | .20 | .83 | .81 | .79 | .78 | .77 | .76 | .75 | .74 | .73 | .71 | .71 |
| | .30 | .88 | .86 | .84 | .82 | .80 | .78 | .77 | .75 | .74 | .72 | .71 |
| | .40 | .93 | .91 | .88 | .85 | .83 | .81 | .79 | .77 | .75 | .73 | .72 |
| | .50 | .96 | .94 | .91 | .89 | .87 | .84 | .82 | .80 | .77 | .74 | .72 |
| | .60 | .98 | .97 | .95 | .92 | .90 | .87 | .85 | .82 | .79 | .75 | .73 |
| | .70 | 1.00 | .99 | .97 | .96 | .93 | .91 | .88 | .84 | .80 | .76 | .73 |
| | .80 | 1.00 | 1.00 | .99 | .98 | .97 | .94 | .91 | .87 | .82 | .77 | .73 |
| | .90 | 1.00 | 1.00 | 1.00 | 1.00 | .99 | .98 | .95 | .91 | .85 | .78 | .74 |

Source: Taylor & Russell (1939)

is .30 (i.e., 30% of the current employees are performing at, or better than, a level the company views as adequate), the validity coefficient for our new selection battery is .60, and the selection ratio is .40 (i.e., we have 40 openings and 100 applicants). The tables indicate that the predictive efficiency of our new selection battery is .52, which means that with the new selection battery, 52% of the workforce is likely to be successful. Comparing this figure to the current base rate (30%), we see a 22-point improvement

*"Mr. Herman, you made me laugh and you made me cry, but you didn't make me money."*

**A CLOSER LOOK**
What role should economics play in making personnel decisions like firings or layoffs?

in the percentage of successful employees. By contrast, a base rate of .70, a validity coefficient for our new selection battery of .20, and a selection ratio of .30 would yield a predictive efficiency of .78. Comparing this to the current base rate (.70), we see only an 8-point improvement in the percentage of successful employees.

In both of these situations, as a last step, the organization would consider the costs involved in the development and implementation of our new system and ask whether the expenditure is more than offset by the improvement of 22 or 8 percentage points. In addition, even a 5-point improvement for a job like cardiac surgeon would be well worth a hospital's expenditure because it would have such a positive effect on the organization (e.g., improved reputation and fewer malpractice suits), as well as on society at large (e.g., more lives saved). More complex approaches to utility involve estimates of the dollar value of different performance levels, but these are very difficult to calculate. (For a discussion of such approaches and a more sophisticated review and critical analysis, see Boudreau & Ramstad, 2003; Roth, Bobko, & Mabon, 2002.)

In our discussion so far, you have been introduced to not only the various predictors in selection but also various techniques used to make selection decisions and ways to evaluate the effectiveness of these techniques. You should thus have a fairly clear idea about how you could use predictor information to arrive at a selection decision and how cost effective this process might be. But the final component in the selection process—legal issues—is equally important. I present these issues specifically within the context of selection because it is here that they have become most relevant; but please note that legal issues apply to *all* personnel decisions, such as performance appraisal ratings used for promotion, layoffs, firings, salary increments, and training (which we will discuss in the next chapter).

## LEGAL ISSUES IN INDUSTRIAL PSYCHOLOGY

It's hard to believe, but, prior to the early 1960s, discrimination in the hiring of employees was *not* illegal in the United States. For instance, it was accepted practice for companies to have "White jobs" for which African Americans were not even considered. As a reaction to this history of discrimination, the Civil Rights Act of 1964 was designed to provide equality of opportunity and equal treatment of all people regardless of "race, color, religion, sex, or national origin." In 1978, the Equal

Employment Opportunity Commission (EEOC) published the "Uniform Guidelines on Employee Selection Procedures" (hereafter referred to as the Guidelines), which have been adopted as the legal guidelines for employee selection. In 1987, the Society for Industrial and Organizational Psychology (SIOP) published its *Principles for the Validation and Use of Personnel Selection Procedures* (revised in 2003) to serve as a technical guide for those who work in the field of employee selection, with the caveat that the principles were not intended to be perceived as legal guidelines. These two documents have emerged as a how-to guide for personnel decisions. Both are used extensively by professionals in the field and referred to in court decisions. Much of the content discussed in the remainder of this chapter is based on these documents.

## Employment At-Will

According to the common law doctrine of **employment at-will**, employers and employees have the right to initiate and terminate the employment relationship at any time, for any reason or for no reason at all. This approach to employment began in England and was incorporated into the U.S. legal system during colonial times. However, the interpretation of this idea has changed such that companies are sued each year by employees who claim "wrongful discharge" by their employers.

Although employment at-will is still the default employment condition, there are exceptions, such as the existence or implication of an employment contract that prevents either employer or employee from ending the employment relationship prematurely or "just cause" discharge policies, which provide employees with acceptable reasons for discharge (Dunford & Devine, 1998). Such exceptions continue to grow, leaving the law concerning employment at-will in a state of uncertainty (Roehling & Wright, 2004). The most extensive limitation to employment at-will is federal legislation that renders illegal any employment decisions, such as firings and layoffs, that are based on certain conditions such as race and gender. We will discuss these federal laws shortly, but first we need to look at a few other major concepts.

**employment at-will**
A common law doctrine stating that employers and employees have the right to initiate and terminate the employment relationship at any time, for any reason or for no reason at all.

## Adverse Impact

To appreciate the intricacies of employment law as it applies to I/O psychology, you need to understand **adverse impact**. This concept, defined in the Guidelines as the "80% rule of thumb," is the common practical operationalization of discrimination according to the courts. A selection procedure is said to exhibit adverse impact (i.e., to discriminate) against a group if the selection rate (i.e., the percentage of applicants hired) for that group is less than 80% of the selection rate for the group with the highest selection rate. Usually, but not always, it is a minority group that has been hired at a rate lower than that for Caucasians. For instance, if we hired 60 out of 100 Caucasian applicants (a selection rate of 60%), we would avoid adverse impact if we also hired at least 48 out of 100 African American applicants (i.e., 80% of the 60% rate for Caucasians, or 48%). There are also statistical significance tests that may aid in the more accurate identification of adverse impact beyond the more traditional 80% rule (Roth, Bobko, & Switzer, 2006). In fact, some suggest that adverse impact be operationalized by a statistical test along with a practical test (e.g., 80% rule).

**adverse impact**
The most accepted operationalization of discrimination, defined in the EEOC Guidelines as the "80% rule of thumb." A selection battery exhibits adverse impact (i.e., discriminates) against a group if the selection rate for that group is less than 80% of the selection rate for the group with the highest selection rate.

## TABLE 7.6  The Absence and Presence of Adverse Impact

| Case | Majority Selection Rate | Minority Selection Rate | 80% Rule Cutoff | Legal Status |
|------|------------------------|-------------------------|-----------------|--------------|
| #1 | 60 out of 100 Caucasians hired (60%) | 50 out of 100 African Americans hired (50%) | 80% of 60% = 48% | 50% > 48%, thus no adverse impact |
| #2 | 40 out of 50 men hired (80%) | 20 out of 80 women hired (25%) | 80% of 80% = 64% | 25% < 64%, thus adverse impact |

The rationale is that the more ways in which adverse impact is examined the better for coming to an accurate conclusion that will be accepted by the courts (Cohen, Aamodt, & Dunleavy, 2010).

**Table 7.6** illustrates two such cases—one in which adverse impact is absent and one in which it is present. Notice that the actual minority cutoff is determined by multiplying the majority rate by 80%. If the minority rate is less than this cutoff, there is adverse impact; if it is at least equal to this cutoff, there is no adverse impact. Although adverse impact is important, its presence alone does not indicate illegal discrimination.

To understand this better, let's take a general look at how a discrimination case might proceed (see **Table 7.7** for a step-by-step guide).

First, the plaintiff (i.e., the employee who feels discriminated against) must demonstrate a *prima facie* case. In other words, the plaintiff must show, through the 80% rule or some other statistical test, that "on the face of it" the numbers indicate adverse impact. For instance, a Hispanic plaintiff might argue that her not having been hired by a particular company is indicative of a pattern exhibited by this company—a

## TABLE 7.7  Steps in an Employment Discrimination Case

1. Plaintiff files a complaint/lawsuit with the courts.

2. Plaintiff demonstrates a *prima facie* case of adverse impact during the discovery phase of the case.

3. Motions are filed by both sides, such as the plaintiff's request for organizational data or details about procedures.

4. Defendant rebuts the adverse impact analysis by showing the statistics to be inaccurate.

5. Plaintiff refutes defendant's statistical reanalysis of the adverse impact data.

OR

4. Defendant accepts the adverse impact analysis but argues that the selection tests are job related and, therefore, nondiscriminatory.

5. Plaintiff argues that the selection tests are just a pretext for discrimination and that discrimination is the true motivation for the personnel decision.

pattern that shows adverse impact against minorities, including Hispanics. The plaintiff would demonstrate this pattern by providing the company's own data showing that the 80% rule has been violated and that minorities are being hired at a rate less than 80% of the rate for the majority group.

Second, the defendant (i.e., the company) may argue against these statistics by showing that the plaintiff is looking at only some of the data, interpreting the data incorrectly, or considering the wrong data. In this case, however, let's say that the company does not dispute the data but instead admits that adverse impact exists. At this point, the company has a few options to combat the charge of illegal discrimination.

The traditional approach is to demonstrate that, despite the presence of adverse impact, the selection battery is *job related* for all minority groups as well as for the majority group. The job relevance of the selection battery is usually established through a validation study, which makes the case that predictors are tapping the KSAOs shown to be important for success on this job. This is one reason validation studies are so important. If the company can show that the selection battery is valid—such that, regardless of ethnicity, race, and gender, those employees who score high on the selection battery are successful on the job and those who score low are unsuccessful—the courts are likely to recognize this case as an example of adverse impact that is *not* illegal.

Rulings and legislation have made it clear that the defendant must show that each test used in the selection battery was job related—it's not enough to show that the bottom-line result was to hire an appropriate percentage of minorities from the pool deemed acceptable (Posthuma, 2002). This is typically referred to as the *business necessity* defense, where the company argues that business cannot be adequately conducted without people of a certain IQ level, personality type, or educational background and that the people in their candidate pool who fit that criteria frequently happen to be more of a particular gender, race, and so on. Finally, the burden of proof shifts back to the plaintiff to refute the defendant's data or argument by somehow showing the defendant's behavior to be a pretext or an excuse for discrimination.

## Affirmative Action

Before examining some of the major employment laws, we need to consider a far-reaching concept that is very important in this area: affirmative action (AA). It is employed by many organizations to increase the number of minorities or protected class members (i.e., African Americans, Asian Americans, Hispanic Americans, Native Americans, and women) in targeted jobs. Affirmative Action Plans (AAPs) are not a quota system, although the popular press tends to characterize them in that way. This is not to say that quotas never emerge from or develop in parallel to affirmative action programs. But the important point here is that such programs aim to address the discrimination that has existed in many companies and industries throughout history.

affirmative action (AA)
A practice employed in many organizations to increase the number of minorities or protected class members in targeted jobs.

AAPs vary from relatively uncontroversial (as when a company networks with minorities to increase their awareness of job opportunities) to very controversial (as when minorities are hired preferentially). When implemented appropriately, such programs do not result in the hiring of *unqualified* minorities; they may, however, result in the hiring of minority applicants whose qualifications are equal to or perhaps even inferior to those of majority applicants. AAPs have been popular for many years, as evidenced by the inclusion of the following phrase at the bottom of many job advertisements: "This organization is an EEO/AA employer, and qualified minority candidates are encouraged to apply." (EEO/AA stands for equal employment opportunity/affirmative action.)

Much has been written in recent years, in both the popular press and the academic literature, about affirmative action (for reviews, see Harrison, Kravitz, Mayer, Leslie, & Lev-Arey, 2006; Pyburn, Ployhart, & Kravitz, 2008). For instance, some recent studies have examined the stigmatization of AAPs, finding that individuals who benefit from AAPs are sometimes viewed as incompetent (Evans, 2003) and that some people view AAPs as having greater potential benefits to individuals when a justification based on organizational fairness is provided than when it is not (Aberson, 2003).

Perceptions of justice also played a role in a study examining the attitudes of Black applicants toward AAPs. Black applicants viewed an AAP operationalized to show preference for a Black candidate with the same qualifications as a White candidate as *less fair* than similar plans that emphasized special recruitment of Black candidates or that fostered equity between Black and White applicants (Slaughter, Sinar, & Bachiochi, 2002). More recent research found that Black students perceived race-conscious AAPs, such as preferential hiring, as less just than race-blind AAPs, such as active recruitment of minority applicants (Cropanzano, Slaughter, & Bachiochi, 2005). Researchers also found that various forms of organizational justice affected perceptions of organizational attraction and intention to apply. Other research found that the structure or type of AAP, along with perceiver characteristics and how the AAP was described, interacted to affect attitudes toward AAPs (Harrison et al., 2006). A very interesting and sophisticated meta-analysis of studies investigated the effects of stereotyping on the performance and evaluation of AAP targets (Leslie, Mayer, & Kravitz, 2014). The results indicate that the stereotype which depicts AAP targets as lacking competence leads those targets to doubt their own abilities, which negatively impacts their performance. Furthermore, others' perception of low competence and a lack of personal warmth among AAP targets is reflected in performance evaluations. Whereas multiple mechanisms contribute to the problem, the data are clear that stereotype theory explains how targets of AAPs are negatively viewed and the impact that this has on performance ratings and objective performance.

Two court cases have begun to play a central role in how AAPs are viewed and implemented by organizations. However, both of these cases are about college admissions decisions; thus, it is still unclear to what extent these rulings will affect traditional organizational AAPs. The University of Michigan was sued by two Caucasian applicants who argued that they were denied admission to the College of Literature, Science, and the Arts because, even though they were both qualified,

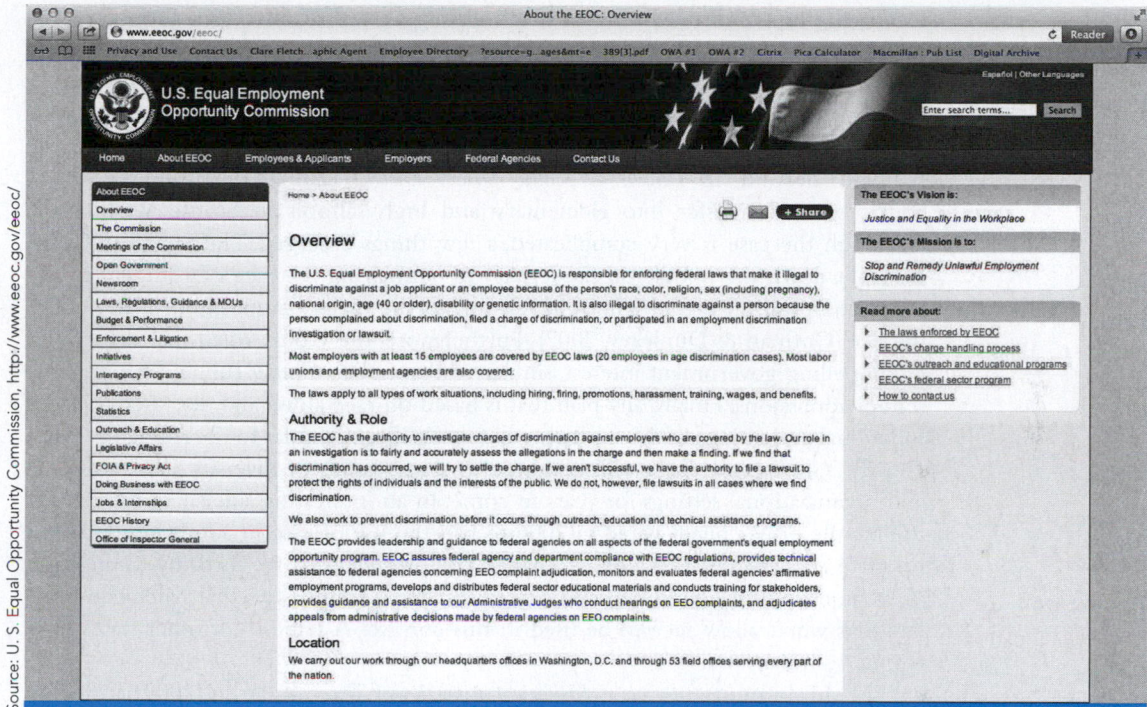

preference was shown to candidates who were classified as "underrepresented minorities" (*Gratz v. Bollinger,* 2003). The Supreme Court ruled for the plaintiffs, citing an admission policy that automatically distributed 20 points (one-fifth of the points needed to guarantee admission) to every underrepresented minority as too global in form. Ignoring individual differences and qualifications among these minority applicants seemed to go against the purpose inherent in diversity initiatives, which is to consider all that individuals bring to the situation and to choose those who are likely to diversify the educational environment.

The University of Michigan Law School was sued by a Caucasian female who also argued that she was denied admission due to racial preferences (*Grutter v. Bollinger,* 2003). The Supreme Court saw this case very differently and ruled for the university. First, the opinion noted that diversity is a compelling interest for the law school. In other words, the Court said that diversity in graduate education, such as law school, can provide educational benefits to the entire student body and is important; it did not make the same statement regarding the undergraduate admission process (see *Gratz v. Bollinger,* 2003). Second, the Court noted that the law school system, which considered race as a "plus" in the admission process (and did not allocate a fixed number of points based on one's race) and which considered various elements of diversity on an individualized basis, did not make race the defining feature of its decision. A terrific summary of these cases can be found in Gutman (2003).

**A CLOSER LOOK**

Why do many organizations publicly emphasize that equal employment opportunity is an important principle underlying how they do business?

Three post-*Grutter* lawsuits are worth noting here. First, in *Petit v. City of Chicago* (2003) the Seventh Circuit Court ruled that there is an even more compelling need for diversity in a large metropolitan police force charged with protecting a racially diverse and divided population than there is in a university. Furthermore, it concluded that the city demonstrated this compelling need and met the *Grutter* standard. Second, in *Parents v. Seattle School District* (2007), the issue was about admission and transfer into elementary and high schools in Seattle, Washington. Although the case is very complicated, a few things emerged. The Supreme Court was split down the middle on the legality of comparing the race of a student to the racial composition of the school in relation to the racial composition of the entire district (Gutman & Dunleavy, 2007). Furthermore, the Court ruled that diversity is a compelling government interest, similar to the earlier *Grutter* ruling regarding law school admissions. Finally, any plan that is based on race alone and does not consider individual evaluations of the students will remain illegal, similar to the ruling in *Gratz*. Clearly, *Grutter* and *Gratz* will continue to shape issues of diversity in educational and organizational settings for years to come. In an interesting sidebar to these cases, the people of Michigan voted in 2006 to ban the use of race in admission decisions for state universities. This doesn't change the precedent as set forth by *Grutter* and *Gratz* and used in continuing and new cases, but it simply says that Michigan has a law that won't allow race to be used in this context. A handful of other states have adopted similar laws.

The third important case is *Fisher v. University of Texas at Austin* (2009), in which Abigail Fisher sued the university, claiming that she was rejected for admission due to an unconstitutional affirmative action policy. The court again supported narrowly tailored AAPs and argued that there is a compelling government interest in achieving diversity in the undergraduate programs at the University of Texas. Although Fisher appealed to the Supreme Court in 2013, it ruled that the lower courts needed to revisit the case because they didn't follow procedures as they should have. The appeals court then ruled that the affirmative action policy was a holistic, narrowly tailored plan, and therefore, rejected Fisher's arguments. Fisher appealed once more to the Supreme Court and that court heard the case once again in December 2015. At the time of publication, the court had not yet decided this case, however there should be a "final" ruling by the time you read this chapter. Although it appears as though the courts are recognizing diversity as a compelling government interest and are somewhat open to AAPs that seem focused on meeting the goals of this compelling interest, the *Fisher v. Texas* decision may have a great deal to say about the use of affirmative action in universities going forward.

**Table 7.8** presents a list of the major U.S. employment legislation prohibiting job discrimination. These are described in the following sections, along with legal cases where appropriate. Presentation of some recent data prior to a full discussion of the legislation may provide some context. You might find a thorough review of employment discrimination sprinkled with some interesting data very helpful (Goldman, Gutek, Stein, & Lewis, 2006). For instance, the four major statutes

| TABLE 7.8 | Major U.S. Employment Legislation | |
|---|---|---|
| **Legislation** | **Year** | **Description** |
| Equal Pay Act (EPA) | 1963 | Prohibits discrimination in pay and benefits on the basis of sex for jobs in the same establishment that require equal skill, effort, and responsibility and that are performed under similar working conditions. |
| Civil Rights Act (Title VII) | 1964 | Makes it unlawful for an employer with 15 or more employees to discriminate against individuals with respect to hiring, compensation, terms, conditions, and privileges of employment on the basis of race, color, religion, national origin, or sex. |
| Executive Order 11246 | 1965 | Prohibits job discrimination by employers holding federal contracts or subcontracts on the basis of race, color, sex, national origin, or religion and requires affirmative action to ensure equality of opportunity in all aspects of employment. |
| Age Discrimination in Employment Act (ADEA) | 1967 | Makes it unlawful for an employer with 20 or more employees to discriminate against individuals who are 40 years or older with respect to hiring, compensation, terms, conditions, and privileges of employment on the basis of age. |
| Americans with Disabilities Act (ADA) | 1990 | Makes it unlawful for an employer with 15 or more employees to discriminate against qualified individuals with disabilities with respect to hiring, compensation, terms, conditions, and privileges of employment. |
| Civil Rights Act | 1991 | Amends the 1964 act and the ADA to allow compensatory and punitive damages but places caps on the amounts that can be awarded. Also provides for jury trials in suits brought under these laws. |
| Family and Medical Leave Act | 1993 | Allows eligible employees to take job-protected, unpaid leave for up to a total of 12 weeks in any 12 months because of (1) the birth of a child and the need to care for a newborn, (2) the placement of a child with the employee for adoption, (3) the need to care for a family member with a serious health condition, or (4) the employee's own serious health condition. |

(Title VII, ADA, EPA, and ADEA—see Table 7.8) resulted in 88,481 charges filed in 2005. Title VII was responsible for the overwhelming majority of these (55,992), and the Equal Pay Act was responsible for the fewest (978).

## Equal Pay Act

As we discussed in the section on comparable worth in Chapter 3, the Equal Pay Act (1963) makes it illegal to provide unequal pay and benefits to men and women who are holding jobs that are equal. The disputes that arise regarding this law usually involve the definition of *equal work*. What is and is not equal is decided on a case-by-case basis. For instance, the court ruled in *Brennan v. Prince William Hospital Corp.* (1974) that male hospital orderlies who were assigned the extra duty of turning patients over in bed did not merit additional pay relative to female nurse's aides who

## I/O TODAY

### Religion in the Workplace

In the past decade, several stories have highlighted the challenges for organizations trying to balance respect for employees' religion with assurances that an individual can meet the essential functions of the job. In 2007, for example, Target accommodated Muslim employees so they would not have to handle pork products. There are numerous other cases where individuals have requested certain shifts to accommodate their prayer schedules.

But sometimes the situation does not offer an easy solution. For example, pharmacists might refuse to fill specific prescriptions because of conflicts with their religious beliefs. These cases often involve emergency contraception and birth control, however, there is a broad range of drugs that a pharmacist might object to prescribing based on his or her religion. This is what happened in the case of Amanda Renz, who visited a K-Mart pharmacy to get her birth control prescription refilled. The only pharmacist on duty was a Roman Catholic, and he refused to fill Renz' prescription due to his religious beliefs. The pharmacist also refused to transfer her prescription to another pharmacy. Despite a call to the store's assistant manager, Renz was not able to get her prescription filled until the following week when another pharmacist was on duty.

This case illustrates some of the complex problems that emerge when religion and the workplace collide. As noted in this chapter, religion is protected under Title VII. However, the chapter also highlights that a protected individual must be able to perform the essential functions of the job. Clearly, dispensing medications is an essential function of a pharmacist's job, but what about a specific subset of medications?

In addition, I/O practitioners might be concerned about how this event might affect customers. It is easy to imagine that if a company fires a pharmacist for refusing to fill a prescription, some customers might boycott; however, the same result might happen if the organization supports the employee's refusal of an important service to the customer.

Other recent developments have also complicated this issue. Several states have issued laws that clarify pharmacists' rights in this situation. Some of these laws prohibit pharmacists from refusing people medication, some allow pharmacists to refuse medication as long as they do not obstruct the patient from getting the medication through other means, and some allow pharmacists to refuse to both dispense the medication and transfer the prescription. Managers, employees, and I/O practitioners need to be familiar with federal regulations like Title VII, but they need to be aware of specific state laws as well.

This issue underscores the need for I/O psychologists to stay up-to-date on laws, politics, and regulations. A recent Supreme Court decision upheld the right of privately held organizations to refuse to pay for employees' birth control (*Burwell v. Hobby Lobby Stores, Inc.*, 2014), while another has required retail stores to hire women who wear headscarves, even though it violates their current dress code (*EEOC v. Abercrombie & Fitch*, 2015). Establishing appropriate accommodations is an ongoing process, and I/O psychologists must understand the implications of new developments on employment law.

### Discussion Questions

1. Imagine you have a pharmacist who says he cannot dispense birth control because of his religious beliefs. What might be some reasonable accommodations you can make for him? What might constitute accommodations that would not be reasonable for your organization?
2. What other issues might large corporations anticipate as the workforce becomes more diverse? How do processes like job analysis and validation help ensure that a selection process is legally defensible?
3. There are a number of changes occurring within the legal system, including naturalizing immigrants, legalization of gay marriage, and legalization of marijuana. How might these changes affect the selection process?

### References

Burwell v. Hobby Lobby Stores, Inc., 573 U.S. 1 (2014).
EEOC v. Abercrombie & Fitch, 575 U.S. 1 (2015).

were not assigned this one extra duty. The courts have made it clear over the years that there must be sizable and reasonable differences in the work to support different pay for men and women (Gutman, 2000).

There have been important developments in recent years regarding equal pay issues. The Supreme Court ruled against Lilly Ledbetter in *Ledbetter v. Goodyear* (2007), stating that even though Ledbetter had been unaware of the way in which her salary was calculated until years later, the statute of limitations (defined as beyond 300 days) began running at the initial payment many years earlier. This was a controversial decision leaving women no recourse unless they find out about the potential wage discrimination early on in the process (Brody & Grodan, 2010). This

Scott J. Ferrell/Congressional Quarterly/Getty Images

led to the 2009 passage by Congress of the Lilly Ledbetter Fair Pay Act, which stipulates that the unfair discriminatory practice occurs every time one is affected by the decision (i.e., each paycheck) and, therefore, that the statute of limitations does not run out. The Ledbetter Act has far-reaching implications beyond the interpretation of the Equal Pay Act and has already played a role in other important cases. For instance, Mary Lou Mikula began working in the Allegheny County Police Department as a grants coordinator in 2001 and was paid considerably less ($7,000) than a male colleague in a similar position. Every time she brought this discrepancy to her superiors they ignored her. After more than five years of her trying to get this issue addressed, she filed a discrimination charge in 2007. The court, citing *Ledbetter v. Goodyear Tire and Rubber Co.,* ruled that she did not file her claim in time and granted judgment for the County. She appealed in 2009 on the basis of the new Ledbetter Act and the court ruled in her favor (National Women's Law Center, 2014).

**A CLOSER LOOK**
In 2009, President Obama signed the Lilly Ledbetter Fair Pay Act into law, providing employees more flexibility to file cases asserting that they have been discriminated against with respect to pay. What kind of steps can organizations take to ensure that they don't fall into the trap of paying people differentially based on qualities like age or gender?

## Civil Rights Act

From its inception on July 2, 1965, the EEOC has been charged with enforcing the principal federal statutes prohibiting discrimination, and Title VII of the Civil Rights Act of 1964 is the most far-reaching one. The Civil Rights Act of 1991, which modified the 1964 act, deals with issues of monetary damages and jury trials, in addition to clarifying each party's obligation in adverse impact cases. Unless noted otherwise, when I refer to the Civil Rights Act (CRA), I am referring to both laws. In general, the CRA prohibits employment discrimination based on race, color, religion, sex, or national origin, thereby making it illegal to base employment decisions on these factors because such decisions would result in discrimination and "unequal opportunity."

One of the most important cases in this area is *Griggs v. Duke Power* (1971), in which the court ruled that even when a company argues convincingly that it had no intention to discriminate, if adverse impact exists, it is incumbent on the company to demonstrate that the selection battery was job related. In *Griggs v. Duke Power,* the plaintiff, Griggs, was an African American male who had not been hired as a laborer; he presented data documenting adverse impact against African Americans. The defendant, Duke Power, responded by saying that the adverse impact was unintentional, but it lost the case largely because it could not demonstrate the job relatedness of its selection battery, as a validation study had never been done. Think about this case for a minute because it is very, very important. What the court was saying, and this still applies today, is that it is illegal to hire only Caucasians, even when they score better on the selection battery, *if the selection battery has not been demonstrated to predict job performance.* Another conclusion from this decision is that even professionally developed tests can be illegal if the company cannot show that the KSAOs measured by those tests are job related (for more information on KSAOs and the *Griggs* case, see Chapter 3).

In *Ricci v. DeStefano* (2009), a more recent case with an interesting twist, the city of New Haven, Connecticut, administered a civil service examination for fire fighters, but upon realizing that there was adverse impact against minority candidates the city chose to throw the results out (the formal term is that they chose not to *certify* the exam). High-scoring White and Latino promotion candidates sued, arguing that this was racial discrimination and the test should have been certified so that they retained their chance for promotion. The lower court found for the defendants and recognized that if the city had used the test it would have been accused of using a test with adverse impact. On appeal, the Supreme Court overturned this ruling, reasoning that just because there was adverse impact doesn't mean the city would have been held liable under Title VII—the city would have had the opportunity to show that the test was job-related. It's not acceptable to simply throw out a test because there is adverse impact, any more than simply demonstrating adverse impact makes a test illegal under Title VII. The issue of job relatedness plays a major role.

Cases of this kind are sometimes called **disparate impact cases** because they involve employment procedures that apparently unintentionally discriminate against or unfairly affect a minority group, that is, the procedures adversely impact that group. In **disparate treatment cases**, by contrast, the discrimination is intentional and a result of differential treatment. Most cases in personnel law are of the disparate impact variety, in which discrimination emerges as a by-product of employment procedures.

In disparate treatment cases, defendants often must show that a particular sex, religion, or national origin is really required or necessary for the job—a **bona fide occupational qualification (BFOQ)**. But this stipulation is interpreted very narrowly by the courts. Imagine the difficulty of convincing a judge that in order to operate your business, you need to hire only females. In fact, this very issue was addressed in an interesting and classic case, *Diaz v. Pan Am* (1971). Diaz was a man

**disparate impact cases** Cases involving employment procedures that apparently unintentionally discriminate against or unfairly affect a minority group.

**disparate treatment cases** Cases involving discrimination that results from intentional differential treatment or behavior.

**bona fide occupational qualification (BFOQ)** A characteristic, such as one's gender, religion, or national origin, that is required or necessary to effectively do the job.

who wanted to be a flight attendant, but because of Pan Am's policy, which favored women to the exclusion of men, he was not selected. Pan Am claimed that gender was a BFOQ and that it was acceptable to hire only women for this job because women provided the intangibles regarding passenger comfort. Think about your most recent flight, and you can probably figure out how this case was decided! The court ruled that the primary function of an airline is to transport passengers safely, and, thus, maintaining safety was the chief job of a flight attendant. A "pleasant environment" is tangential to this primary function; therefore, gender could not be a BFOQ. Even if the "pleasant environment" had been upheld as a primary function, Pan Am would have been in the very difficult position of having to demonstrate that *only* women could provide such an environment—and that would have been difficult to do.

© Jim West/Alamy

**A CLOSER LOOK**
*Diaz v. Pan Am* made it easier for males to be hired as flight attendants. Why is this court ruling important today?

You might be wondering in what circumstances a BFOQ may be supported as a hiring practice. Case law supports the use of a BFOQ in the job of wet nurse, for example. A wet nurse is a woman who can breastfeed and care for a child. The courts have found that the ability to breastfeed is a BFOQ because it is a job that only a woman can perform. Similarly, a BFOQ has been supported by the courts for religious-affiliated schools in hiring only individuals who adhere to the school's beliefs. A classic example of this is that Catholic Jesuit schools have been supported by the courts in only hiring Jesuit teachers because of the specific history and requirements of the Jesuit order (Snider, 2013). The restaurant Hooters presents an interesting case study of how BFOQs may be used. The company has been sued by men multiple times for hiring only "Hooters Girls" as servers. Hooters argues that they are an entertainment establishment and that sex appeal is part of the entertainment and, therefore, hiring women who are scantily-clothed as servers is part of the business and qualifies as a BFOQ. Since all of these cases have been settled prior to going to trial, we don't know how the courts would respond to this BFOQ argument.

In addition to prohibiting discrimination in employment decisions based on race (an issue that certainly receives the most attention in the courts and the popular press), the CRA prohibits discrimination based on *national origin,* such that no one can be denied equal employment opportunity because of ancestry, culture, birthplace, or linguistic characteristics common to a specific ethnic group (EEOC, 2009b). For instance, a company cannot refuse to hire someone because he has an accent unless the company can show that the accent impairs job performance. Since 9/11, the number of claims of discrimination based on national origin has swelled significantly (EEOC, 2009c). The EEOC (2002b) attributes most of that increase to a post-9/11 backlash against Muslims and people of Middle Eastern descent. The EEOC has a website for both employers and employees who have questions about the law regarding discrimination based on national origin as well as a new compliance manual (EEOC, 2002a).

Employment decisions based on *religion* are illegal as well. Furthermore, companies can be required to make reasonable accommodations for individuals' religious practices (EEOC, 2009e). For instance, they may have to provide flexibility in schedules for Jewish employees whose religious practices prevent them from working on the Sabbath if this can be done without undue hardship to the employer.

Protection is also provided to *pregnant women* under the CRA (note the Pregnancy Discrimination Act of 1979 amended the CRA of 1964), which stipulates that discrimination on the basis of pregnancy, childbirth, or related medical conditions constitutes unlawful sex discrimination. The bottom line is that pregnant women cannot be treated differently from other applicants or employees with similar abilities (EEOC, 2009d).

**sexual harassment**
Behaviors such as unwelcome sexual advances, requests for sexual favors, and other conduct of a sexual nature, submission to or rejection of which affects one's job or creates an offensive work environment.

Also prohibited by the CRA is **sexual harassment**, which includes such behaviors as unwelcome sexual advances, requests for sexual favors, and other conduct of a sexual nature, submission to or rejection of which affects one's job or creates an offensive work environment (EEOC, 2007). There are two forms of sexual harassment. The first is *quid pro quo harassment,* which refers to situations in which advancement or continuation in a company is contingent on sexual favors. (*Quid pro quo* means "this for that.") This is the blatant kind of sexual harassment that we tend to hear about most often.

The second form is *hostile work environment harassment,* defined by the courts in *Meritor Savings Bank v. Vinson* (1986) as verbal or physical behavior that creates an intimidating, hostile, or offensive work environment or an environment that interferes with one's job performance. Vinson was abused verbally and sexually by her boss at Meritor Savings Bank, and the court ruled in favor of Vinson, arguing that this behavior was both abusive and "unwelcome." Thus, hostile work environment was established as a type of sexual harassment (Cascio & Aguinis, 2010). During Clarence Thomas's Supreme Court confirmation hearing in 1991, Anita Hill, a lawyer employed at the EEOC, where Thomas was her supervisor, raised issues about his sex-related talk, which she alleged created a hostile work environment. Though not a legal proceeding as such, this was certainly the most famous "case" focusing attention on the issue of sexual harassment. Justice Thomas was confirmed by the Senate after a rather long and difficult hearing and still serves on the Supreme Court of the United States.

Federal legislation (i.e., Title VII) does not recognize sexual orientation as a protected class, leaving lesbian, gay, bisexual, and transgender (LGBT) employees without federal protection against workplace discrimination. Many states have elected, however, to provide protection against discrimination for LGBT individuals in the workplace (Berkley & Watt, 2006). As of publication, 22 states and the District of Columbia ban discrimination in the workplace based on sexual orientation and/or gender identity, and over 100 municipalities in the 28 states without nondiscrimination laws do so as well (ACLU, 2015). Some of this may change as a result of Peter TerVeer who worked for the Library of Congress until he was fired in 2012. TerVeer, a gay man, argues that he was fired because of his sexual orientation, but the Library of Congress counters that his termination was performance-based. TerVeer also claims that he suffered harassment and that his boss created a hostile work environment, which affected his performance. Given that federal legislation does not protect individuals based on sexual orientation, this could be a landmark case because the district court judge ruled that the case could move forward under a Title VII claim. The case is still pending, but it could prove to be a very important one that may change the laws or the way in which sexual discrimination is defined.

## Executive Order 11246

Executive Order 11246, enacted in 1965, prohibits job discrimination by employers holding federal contracts or subcontracts on the basis of race, color, sex, national origin, or religion. This piece of legislation is very similar to the CRA but is specifically relevant for federal agencies and those organizations that do work for federal agencies. For instance, universities fall within this legislation if they are a public school or a private school that has contracts with other federal agencies.

Michael Krasowitz/Photographer's Choice/Getty Images

**A CLOSER LOOK**
In most jobs, individuals cannot be forced to retire at a certain age. What role can BFOQs play with regard to age and employment?

## Age Discrimination in Employment Act

Individuals who are 40 years of age or over are protected from discrimination by the Age Discrimination in Employment Act (ADEA), signed into law by President Lyndon Johnson on December 15, 1967. According to the ADEA, it is unlawful to discriminate against a person who is 40 or older because of his or her age with respect to any employment-related decision (EEOC, 2009a). In addition, it is illegal to indicate any age preferences or limitations in job ads or notices. Exceptions are possible, but only when the company can demonstrate that age is a BFOQ necessary to the conduct of its business.

   *EEOC v. Univ. of Texas Health Science Center at San Antonio* (1983) is one example of a case in which the court allowed age as a BFOQ exception—specifically, by upholding a maximum age of 45 for campus police officers. In its ruling, the court noted that because the job was dangerous and required individuals to be on the beat alone, an age limit of 45 was a reasonable and safe requirement. Another example is that no commercial airline may employ a pilot or copilot who is 65 years old or older. This used to be the Age 60 rule, but was increased in 2006. However, there are still some stipulations that kick in at 60 years of age, such as requiring pilots who are 60+ to go through training to ensure that their skills and judgment are still acceptable (Federal Aviation Administration, 2012). The rationale for these rulings was that age-related decrements in vision and information processing in older individuals hired could lead to safety issues with catastrophic outcomes.

*Cleverly v. Western Electric* (1979) is a classic example of a typical ADEA case. Cleverly, an engineer, was fired six months before his pension benefits were to become fully vested—despite many years of distinguished service. In any ADEA case, plaintiffs must demonstrate that they (1) are members of the protected class (i.e., 40 or over), (2) were doing satisfactory work, (3) were discharged despite satisfactory work, and (4) were replaced by younger persons (Cascio & Aguinis, 2010). Cleverly was able to meet each of these requirements and was awarded back pay. (Western Electric had even made direct statements to him indicating that he was being let go to make way for young engineers!)

## Americans with Disabilities Act

Title I of the Americans with Disabilities Act (ADA), which was signed into law by President George Herbert Walker Bush in 1990 (and took effect on July 26, 1992), prohibits discrimination against qualified individuals with disabilities in employment decisions. To clarify the role played by the ADA in organizations, I will start by defining a few terms. First, according to the EEOC (2005), a person with a *disability* is someone who (1) has a physical or mental impairment that substantially limits one or more major life activities, such as seeing, hearing, speaking, working, learning, and walking; (2) has a record of such an impairment; or (3) is regarded as having such an impairment. However, the law applies not to all disabled employees but only to those who are otherwise qualified for the job in question. By *qualified,* the EEOC means that the person can perform the essential functions of the job—if necessary, with the aid of reasonable accommodations.

**essential functions**
Tasks that are significant and meaningful aspects of the job.

**Essential functions** are tasks that are significant and meaningful aspects of the job. In short, then, it is illegal to deny someone a job because he can't perform tasks that are only tangential to the job. For example, in a company in which heavy lifting is seldom necessary but occasionally useful, the company should be able to make other arrangements when heavy lifting is called for. In those instances, someone with a bad back could still do the essential functions of the job and someone else could do the lifting.

**reasonable accommodations**
Changes or exceptions made by an employer that allow qualified disabled individuals to successfully do a job.

**Reasonable accommodations** are changes or exceptions made by the employer that would allow the qualified disabled individual to successfully do the job. They include redesigning existing facilities so that they are readily usable by individuals with disabilities (e.g., installing an elevator in a building that does not currently have one); restructuring jobs and schedules to allow disabled persons to perform their jobs; and acquiring equipment, devices, training materials, and qualified readers/interpreters to aid disabled persons. An example in this last category would be voice-activated computer software that allows individuals who have lost the use of their hands to create computer documents without having to type them.

**undue hardship**
An accommodation for the disabled that would result in significant difficulty or expense given the employer's size and financial resources.

Employers are required to make reasonable accommodations, but only if such accommodations do not impose undue hardship on themselves. This brings us to our final definition: **undue hardship**, an accommodation that would result in significant difficulty or expense given the employer's size and financial resources.

Since 1990, the components of the ADA have continued to be interpreted on a case-by-case basis. For instance, in *Ethridge v. State of Alabama* (1993), the court ruled that Ethridge, a police applicant, could not perform the essential functions of the job due to his limited use of one hand and that no reasonable accommodation existed. The essential function cited by the court was shooting in a two-handed position. In a more recent case, *Rooney v. Koch Air, LLC* (2005), Rooney alleged that he was fired as a result of his disability. Rooney had injured his back on two occasions and eventually resigned after receiving numerous written reprimands for not doing his job. He sued the company, arguing that he had been discriminated against because of his disability. However, the court ruled that he had never demonstrated a disability because he himself had testified that after back surgery he was able to perform all major life activities such as sleeping, bathing, exercising, and performing basic household chores. The district court's decision was affirmed on appeal.

Huntstock/Brand X Pictures/Getty Images

**A CLOSER LOOK**
Because of the ADA, disabled workers who are qualified for a particular job cannot be rejected for that job because of their disability. How do job analyses and job descriptions affect disabled workers' search for new jobs?

Perhaps the most famous ADA case to date is *Martin v. PGA Tour, Inc.* (1998). Casey Martin was a professional golfer whose right leg was so disabled that when he walked he was placed at significant risk of fracturing his leg. Martin sued the PGA after it refused his request that a reasonable accommodation be made to allow him to use a golf cart on the PGA tour. The PGA asserted that waiving this rule would fundamentally alter the competition and give Martin a competitive advantage. The judge ruled that it was a "gross distortion of reality" to think that providing Martin with a cart would give him a competitive advantage, given his disability and the pain he experiences simply being on his feet. Thus, the judge concluded that the requested accommodation of a cart was eminently reasonable in light of Martin's disability, and this ruling was supported on appeal by the Supreme Court.

On September 25, 2008, President George W. Bush signed into law the ADA Amendments Act, which became effective on January 1, 2009, and was the first legislative change to the ADA of 1990. The new law describes how individuals are evaluated as to the presence of a disability, clarifies what it means to be regarded as having a disability, and expands the list of major life activities to include things such as caring for oneself, concentrating, and working, as well as major bodily functions (e.g., functions of the immune, digestive, respiratory systems, etc.). Although this has clarified some issues around the implementation of the ADA, there remain other issues regarding the definition of essential functions and reasonable accommodation.

The 2008 Addendum to the ADA broadens the definition of a disability, but some already thought the definition of a disability was too broad (Popovich, Scherbaum,

Scherbaum, & Polinko, 2003). A recent analysis and thought-provoking paper focuses on the social model of disability and argues that disability is a sociopolitical construct; this is a huge shift from the medical model that has been the focus for over 100 years (Scotch, 2014). It is this big shift and broadening of the construct that has led to controversy and differing opinions about what a disability is.

## Family and Medical Leave Act

The first piece of federal legislation signed by President Bill Clinton was the Family and Medical Leave Act (FMLA) in August 1993, which allowed eligible employees to take job-protected, unpaid leave for up to 12 weeks owing to family-related issues such as the birth of a child, the serious health condition of a family member, or one's own serious health condition. *Serious health condition* is defined as an illness, injury, impairment, or physical or mental condition that involves inpatient care or continuous treatment by a healthcare provider (Franklin, Gringer, & Cohen, P.C., n.d.). In general, the employee has the right to return to the same position or an equivalent position with equivalent pay and benefits at the conclusion of the leave. The purpose of the FMLA is to provide employees with the opportunity to balance their work and family life and to promote the security and economic stability of the family (U.S. Department of Labor, 2009). On January 16, 2009, revised regulations regarding implementation of the FMLA went into effect. The new recommendations, among other things, provide for extended leave for the families of wounded soldiers, clarify what constitutes serious health conditions, and require enhanced communication between employees and employers regarding these issues. (This balance between work and family life will be considered in more detail in Chapter 11.)

In 2002, California became the first state to pass a paid family and medical leave statute that requires employers to provide six weeks of paid family leave to every eligible employee for each 12-month period. Currently, 17 states have enacted FMLA laws (U.S. Department of Labor, n.d.) that may work in concert with the federal legislation to the benefit of the employee. Employers and employees, though, have raised concerns about the success and effectiveness of the federal legislation (National Coalition to Protect Family Leave [NCPFL], n.d.). It is too complex for our discussion here, but employers have found it difficult to understand and to define what classes of illnesses qualify under the legislation. The confusion and ambiguity have resulted in inconsistency and "intermittent leave," in which employees use the FMLA for, say, three days off from work due to a cold or the flu (NCPFL, n.d.). On the other hand, employees have suffered under the FMLA because many simply can't afford to take 12 weeks off from work without pay. Former Senator Chris Dodd, the author of the 1993 bill, recognized this financial problem and, therefore, introduced the Family Leave Insurance Act of 2007, which would have provided paid leave for 8 of the 12 weeks ("Dodd, Stevens," 2007). The bill has been modified and reintroduced (as the FAMILY Act, by Senator Kirsten Gillibrand and Representative Rosa DeLauro), but has not moved through the legislative process; it was assigned to a congressional committee on March 18, 2015, which will review it and send it on to the House or Senate.

As we have seen, legal issues are tightly linked with employment decisions, especially employee selection. In general, employment laws attempt to ensure *equal employment opportunity* to all individuals. According to the EEOC (2004), it is illegal to discriminate in any aspect of employment such as, but not limited to, the following:

- Hiring and firing
- Compensation, assignment, or classification of employees
- Transfer, promotion, layoff, or recall
- Job advertisements
- Recruitment
- Testing
- Use of company facilities
- Training and apprenticeship programs
- Fringe benefits
- Pay, retirement plans, and disability leave

This is an exciting area that continues to grow and develop. Table 7.8 lists most of the major pieces of employment legislation in existence as of this writing. Because legal work is so driven by court decisions and case interpretations, I suggest that you consult the websites given in the references cited in this chapter for the most recent information on industrial psychology and the law, especially with respect to legal precedent.

## Summary

Whereas Chapter 6 discussed the many types of predictors used in employee selection, this chapter has presented information about how to use those predictors in making selection decisions. Predictive validation, concurrent validation, validity generalization, and synthetic validation were examined in light of how important they are for employee selection. Recruitment was also discussed as an important precursor to employee selection, and the recent role of social media in this process was examined.

Various approaches to the selection process were discussed, including the multiple cutoff, multiple hurdle, and multiple regression techniques. This part of the discussion provided both a how-to guide and an overview of the differences among these approaches. A lengthy discussion of utility followed; here we noted that if a selection battery is not viewed as useful for an organization, the organization is unlikely to be interested in it. We also looked at two ways in which decision accuracy can be operationalized: decision accuracy for hires and overall decision accuracy. Validity, base rate, selection ratio, and cost were identified as important factors affecting the utility of a new selection battery.

The last half of the chapter was spent on legal issues in industrial psychology. The emphasis was on selection, as it is in this area that legal issues tend to emerge most often. First, we discussed the history of the EEOC. Next, we examined employment at-will, adverse impact, and affirmative action, as these are among the most important concepts one must understand in order to appreciate the context and procedures involved in personnel law. Finally, we considered the major employment laws currently in place (see Table 7.8). Distinctions were drawn between disparate treatment and disparate impact, between *quid pro quo* harassment and hostile work environment harassment, between BFOQ defenses and job-relatedness defenses, and between reasonable accommodation and undue hardship.

## Key Terms

adverse impact (p. 223)

affirmative action (AA) (p. 225)

base rate (p. 219)

bona fide occupational qualification (BFOQ) (p. 232)

cybervetting (p. 204)

disparate impact cases (p. 232)

disparate treatment cases (p. 232)

employment at-will (p. 223)

essential functions (p. 236)

multiple cutoff approach (p. 211)

multiple hurdle approach (p. 212)

multiple regression (p. 214)

person–environment (PE) fit (p. 203)

reasonable accommodations (p. 236)

recruitment (p. 203)

selection battery (p. 201)

selection ratio (p. 219)

sexual harassment (p. 234)

situational specificity (p. 209)

synthetic validity (p. 210)

undue hardship (p. 236)

utility (p. 216)

validity generalization (VG) (p. 209)

validity shrinkage (p. 209)

## TAKING IT TO THE FIELD

I/O psychologists, while not lawyers, are sometimes asked to provide information about the legality of a hiring process. While this text is not intended to teach you the details of employment law, it is helpful for you to recognize the key problems to watch out for in a selection system. You have been speaking with Mr. Marshall recently regarding some questions he has about his selection system. You have just received the following e-mail from him.

Hello again—

Per our discussion on the phone, I think I would like to get some input from you about whether I need to make any changes to my selection system. Of course, I will also be consulting with a lawyer, but input from you would be very helpful.

Here's the background of my problem:

I own several pork-processing plants. We have roughly 10,000 employees nationally, primarily based in the Midwest. One of the positions that we need to hire for regularly is in the slaughterhouse. Processing the carcasses is physically demanding work, and many people we hire cannot perform the work effectively for very long. Thus, we end up having to fire quite a large number of employees because of low job performance.

Last year, we had 500 Latino American applicants, 200 Caucasian American applicants, and 400 African American applicants. Out of these applicants, we hired 400 Latino Americans, 300 African Americans, and 120 Caucasian Americans. We did not have any Asian American applicants this year.

To be hired, an applicant must pass three selection tests:

1. The applicant must be low on neuroticism. This is because the gore that occurs on the killing floor can be upsetting; we find that people with moderate to high

levels of neuroticism typically quit within one week. In fact, we completed a validation study, which indicated that neuroticism and job performance were correlated at −.35.

2. The applicant must be able to pass a physical test by being able to squeeze a rod with a certain amount of pressure for two minutes straight. This is because the workers must move sides of pork all day; unless workers have a basic level of strength in their hands, they will not be able to complete the job over an eight-hour shift. We also find that our physical test correlates .25 with job performance. We have found that Caucasian Americans tend to have less hand strength because they are less likely to have worked in jobs requiring manual labor compared to our African American and Latino American applicants.

3. The applicant must have at least one year of experience in either manufacturing or meat packing. It seems that workers who have done this work before are likely to remain in the organization longer. We find that Latino American applicants are much more likely to have experience than any other racial group.

So here are my questions. First, do we have adverse impact? Second, are all three of our selection requirements legally defensible? If any of the processes are not legal, what should I do to make them legal?

Thanks for your help on this!

Regards,

John Marshall

Respond to Mr. Marshall's e-mail. Note that the important part of this assignment is not whether you believe Mr. Marshall's system is illegal; rather, it is your reasons for thinking it is (or is not) legal.

## Critical Thinking Questions

1. How do recruitment and selection fit together?

2. Why is it unheard of for a selection battery to explain 100% of the variance in job performance?

3. Refer back to Figure 7.2 on page 217. What happens to the number of false alarms if you raise the cutoff score? What happens to the number of misses? What might be some reasons for raising a cutoff score?

4. Do you believe the major employment laws offer sufficient protection for all workers in the United States? Why or why not?

5. How do performance appraisal and selection complement each other? How are these two very important processes dependent on each other?

## Application Questions

1. This chapter mentions person–environment fit. When you are looking for a job, what are some cues that indicate an organization is a "good fit" for you? Have you ever been in an organization that wasn't a good fit for you? What happened?

2. In some states, the medicinal use of marijuana is allowed to treat certain conditions, such as glaucoma and anxiety. In these states, do you think it would be legal to require applicants to take a drug test? What might be some problems with implementing this requirement? If an organization wants to use a drug test, what steps might you suggest they follow?

3. How common are BFOQs? Interview five people about their jobs and determine whether someone in a protected class (race, color, religion, national origin, sex, age, disability) would be unable to perform an essential job function.

4. Consider a job you have had. Provide one example of a reasonable accommodation that could be made so an applicant with a disability could do the job. What types of changes do you believe would be unreasonable (i.e., cause undue hardship for the company)?

5. Typically races other than Caucasians are considered to be minorities. Are there any jobs where one might expect a different racial group to be hired more often than Caucasians? In these cases, would you recommend that the organization enact an AAP? Why or why not?

6. In the United States, new mothers are given 12 weeks of unpaid leave. Some countries provide paid maternity leave (e.g., Portugal), paternity leave (e.g., Sweden), or longer periods of unpaid leave (e.g., Japan). What are some advantages and disadvantages of the U.S. policy? What changes (if any) would you make to the U.S. policy?

## Suggested Readings

**Crosby, F. J., Stockdale, M. S., & Ropp, S. A. (Eds.).** (2007). *Sex discrimination in the workplace.* Boston: Blackwell. In this multidisciplinary text, a distinguished group of contributors examine causes of and solutions to sex discrimination. Many firsthand accounts from participants in landmark sex discrimination cases are included.

**Dipboye, R. L., & Colella, A.** (2005). *Discrimination at work: The psychological and organizational bases.* Mahwah, NJ: Erlbaum. Broadly focused, this book explores the various biases that can emerge in the workplace and the implications of these biases.

**International Association of Chiefs of Police website.** (http://www.theiacp.org/). This website provides a wealth of information about social media and its growing importance in the world of work—namely, employee recruitment and selection.

**Leslie, L. M., Mayer, D. M., & Kravitz, D. A.** (2014). The stigma of affirmative action: a stereotyping-based theory and meta-analytic test of the consequences for performance. *Academy of Management Journal, 57*(4), 964–989. An interesting article that helps the reader appreciate the many issues that swirl around affirmative action.

**Outtz, J. L.** (2010). *Adverse impact: Implications for organizational staffing and high stakes selection.* New York: Routledge/Taylor & Francis Group. In this volume, leading selection scholars and practitioners tackle the complex issues surrounding adverse impact.

**Robinson, R. H., Franklin, G. M., & Wayland, R.** (2002). *The regulatory environment of human resource management.* Orlando, FL: Harcourt College. This text presents a nice framework for understanding and interpreting personnel law. A technical presentation is made more user-friendly by many useful examples.

CHAPTER **8**

# Training and Development

Photo: Ciaran Griffin/Stockbyte/Getty Images

## LEARNING OBJECTIVES

This chapter should help you understand:

- How important training is to both organizations and employees
- How to diagnose an organization's training needs through the use of organizational, task, person, and demographic analyses
- The basic principles of learning that affect training success, such as meaningfulness, practice, overlearning, and feedback
- What makes an organization's learning context conducive to successful training
- Each of the various training techniques, as well as their strengths and weaknesses
- The key elements of transfer of training
- The traditional criteria used in training evaluation, along with a newer perspective on these criteria
- How to design a training evaluation study in a number of different ways
- The increasing importance and prevalence of both sexual harassment training and diversity training

In this chapter, we will discuss the extremely important role of training and development in organizations. Surveys consistently report that over 90% of Fortune 500 companies have some type of formal training program. According to the American Society for Training and Development, U.S. organizations spend $126 billion annually on employee learning and development (American Society for Training and Development, 2011). Firms considered to be on the leading edge of training provide their employees between 40 and 45 hours of training per year. The average training budget for the top 125 companies according to *Training* magazine was $30.6 million, which makes up almost 6% of their payroll (Freifeld, 2015).

At a very basic level, we can think of training as being any kind of teaching that is related to one's job—it's about employee development. In previous chapters, we have seen how organizational efficiency is affected by the selection, appraisal, and compensation of employees. This chapter demonstrates how organizational efficiency is also affected by the training of employees.

You might be wondering why training is needed at all if you are careful about your selection system. In other words, if you select high performers, you ought to be able to save a great deal of money on training—because these employees already have the KSAOs (i.e., knowledge, skills, abilities, and other characteristics) necessary to do the job. That logic would be sound if it weren't for a few key issues. First, although a company may hire people who appear to be the most skilled and able of its applicants, they may still need job- or organization-specific training to do the job effectively. For instance, Apple may hire the best and brightest graduates of computer programming

departments worldwide, but if those new hires don't know the Apple infrastructure or computer networking system or aren't familiar with the culture, norms, and procedures that are part of the Apple way of doing business, they will not be effective performers until they are trained in these areas.

A second reason training is so important to organizations is that experienced employees must sometimes be *retrained* because of changes in the job or organization. This issue will continue to grow as continued advancements in technology change the nature of many jobs (Zammuto, Griffith, Majchrzak, Dougherty, & Faraj, 2007), making it necessary for employees to keep up with these technological changes.

Third, training is important for the continued development of employees. Experts believe that training programs can lead to increased organizational commitment and job satisfaction, resulting in increased productivity, decreased absenteeism, and less turnover (Jackson & Schuler, 2000). In other words, training and development efforts result in better employees and a more productive workforce.

Although many definitions of training are available in the literature, the following is one that I believe is particularly good: **Training** comprises the *formal procedures* that a company utilizes to facilitate *learning* so that the resultant *behavior* contributes to the attainment of the company's *goals* and *objectives* (McGehee & Thayer, 1961).

## ASSESSING TRAINING NEEDS

Before even beginning to develop a training program, organizations must identify what, if any, training needs exist. Organizations differ greatly in terms of their training needs (Brown, 2002). For instance, some organizations may need training at the management level, while others need it at the nonmanagement level. Some organizations may require rater training (discussed in Chapter 5), while others would benefit from performance training, and still others may need sexual harassment training. Further, another form of training that is growing in importance and frequency is continuing education, in which employees participate in degree credit courses, nondegree credit courses, personal enrichment courses, and so on. These

**A CLOSER LOOK**
Think of a time when you received some sort of training. Was it effective? Why or why not?

**training**
The formal procedures that a company utilizes to facilitate learning so that the resultant behavior contributes to the attainment of the company's goals and objectives.

courses are often delivered by universities or university extension campuses and are sometimes linked to licensure or certification.

A recent development in this area is what some are calling *competency-based training*. (Recall from Chapter 1 that competencies are skills, behaviors, and capabilities that allow employees to perform specific functions.) Organizations that take this approach to training identify what competencies they want all employees to have and then develop training programs around those competencies (Holton, Coco, Lowe, & Dutsch, 2006). Those companies that are truly innovative and thought leaders in this area consistently tie training to organizational outcomes (Aguinis & Kraiger, 2009). In this section, we will consider how organizations identify their training needs through four types of needs analyses. (For a thorough treatment of needs analysis, see Goldstein & Ford, 2002.)

## Organizational Analysis

Where is training needed in the organization? To answer this question, an organizational analysis is conducted to determine the organization's short- and long-term goals and then to compare those goals to the organization's accomplishments. In this way, the organization can identify which goals aren't being reached, as these areas are likely to be targets for training. I myself have done some training work with a manufacturing company whose organizational analysis indicated that the organization had not been able to achieve one of its important goals—to generate a "team-oriented" relationship among managers and subordinates. The organization believed that a stronger working relationship among supervisors and subordinates would improve productivity. It saw this as a clear need, and I targeted improvement in that area by developing and implementing a training program designed to improve communication among employees, thus creating a shared sense of the organization's purpose and mission.

Organizational analysis should also consider the culture of the organization. Is it an organizational culture that sees training and development as important? If not, this suggests the need to overcome some potential obstacles to training, necessitating careful thought about how best to proceed.

## Task Analysis

What duties, tasks, behaviors, and actions need to be improved? At this level, the analysis is much like the job analyses that we have discussed thus far. The organization or consultant examines the task requirements for the successful conduct of each job, specifying exactly what the new employees are going to do on their jobs. By identifying these tasks, the organization can distinguish between those the new employees are able to do immediately upon beginning employment and those for which they will require some training.

Recall that in Chapter 3 we talked about different types of job analyses. The type most often used to determine training needs is a task-oriented job analysis in which subject matter experts (SMEs), such as incumbents or others who are familiar with the job, respond to a series of items in a checklist format. The responses are collected into a summary that serves as the outcome, or result, of the task analysis—a summary that specifically describes the tasks that are completed on the job. For instance, your local cable company may notice that customers frequently complain that mild windstorms are knocking down their fiber optic cables and disconnecting their service. After comparing the task analysis and the manner in which the cable workers were attaching the cables to the house, the company might conclude that the cable workers did not know how to effectively perform this task. This is a clear instance in which retraining would be very beneficial.

It's important at this point to note that we talked extensively about job analysis as the foundation for selection. We used job analysis to identify the KSAOs necessary to be an effective employee. In a related vein, we use task analysis here to identify the KSAOs that need to be further developed or refined to allow employees to do their job. One way to think about the relationship between selection and training is to view selection as dealing in the raw materials (i.e., the KSAOs that employees bring to the organization) and training as developing or producing the finished product (i.e., the KSAOs that are developed through training and applied to one's job). Both selection and training deal with **human capital**—the skills, abilities, and experiences of organizational members that provide each organization with its competitive advantage or unique aspects.

<aside>
**human capital**
The education, training, and experiences of individual employees that provide value to organizations.
</aside>

## Person Analysis

Who needs the training? A person analysis <mark>gets quite specific, focusing on those employees who actually need training.</mark> Toward this end, it examines how well all employees are carrying out their job responsibilities and duties. For an example, let's return to our cable company scenario. The cable workers are the employees who have been identified as needing some training; in particular, they need training on attaching fiber optic cables to houses so that they aren't easily dislodged. Which of the cable workers are most in need of this training? If the company has 2,500 cable workers but only 500 of them seem unable to grasp this skill, it makes sense to target our training to those 500 employees who appear to need it.

Often, performance appraisal data (see Chapter 5) are used to identify good candidates for training. In addition to traditional performance appraisal ratings, some organizations allow employees to nominate themselves for training in specific areas in which they feel they could further develop as employees. Finally, sometimes organizations will give a test to diagnose employees' strengths and weaknesses and use the test results to indicate who needs additional training. In fact, performance management systems and training programs are often used in concert to develop employees. (We talked about employee development in Chapter 5, and we will talk more about it later in this chapter as well.)

## Demographic Analysis

Traditionally, training needs assessment entailed analyses at the organization, task, and person levels. In the last two decades, however, scholars and practitioners suggest that needs analysis should also take into account the demographic makeup

## PRACTITIONER FORUM

Eric Surface

### Eric A. Surface
*PhD, 2003, I/O Psychology, North Carolina State University*
*Co-founder, President, and Principal I/O Psychologist,*
*ALPS Solutions*

Learning is critical for organizational success. Needs assessment is the primary tool for aligning learning, assessment, compensation, and policy with performance requirements and business objectives. SWA Consulting Inc. works with organizations to help make a difference in learning and performance by helping to create alignment among requirements, learning, assessment, capability, and performance.

Needs assessment is typically initiated when an organization perceives a need or a gap between desired capabilities and current capabilities. Organizations ask us to help identify and specify the gap and to develop strategies to bridge that gap.

A few years ago, Naval Special Warfare Command (NSW) leaders decided SEAL (Sea Air Land) and SWCC (Special Warfare Combatant-Craft Crewman) personnel needed more foreign-language capability. There was limited foreign-language capability in the force and a heavy reliance on interpreters. Mission analysis demonstrated a need for foreign-language capability, especially speaking capability. A gap between the current and desired states existed. How could this gap be closed?

There are typically five strategies to resolve a capability gap: (1) select/hire, (2) train, (3) redesign work, (4) outsource, and (5) adapt strategy, mission and objectives. Which of these strategies make sense depends on the situation. Given the constraints of the context, only training and outsourcing (interpreters) were feasible, but outsourcing had demonstrated problems. The NSW leadership decided that all SEAL and SWCC personnel should receive a minimum amount of training in a mission-relevant language focused on

developing mission-required capability, with some personnel receiving advanced training. NSW needed a thorough training needs assessment in order to develop learning objectives, efficient and effective curricula, and valid assessments focused on its mission-related foreign-language requirements.

My company worked with the advisory group, planned the needs assessment, conducted the language-focused task and KSAO analysis, developed learning objectives, created a curriculum plan, and reviewed existing curricula in conjunction with our partner, the American Council on the Teaching of Foreign Languages, and with learning and subject matter experts at NSW. We developed a comprehensive coding system to relate all learning objectives and activities back to mission requirements, allowing for future curriculum updates.

Although this was a very extensive, domain-focused training needs assessment, need assessments can vary greatly in purpose, focus, scope, and methodology. When approaching a needs assessment, judicious flexibility is required because every situation is different. But transferable lessons can be learned from examples such as the one above.

### Applying Your Knowledge

1. How do you decide which of the five strategies are feasible and appropriate for addressing an identified capability gap?

2. Why would restricting applicants to those with existing high levels of language proficiency *not* work for an occupation that already has very high selection requirements and a very demanding assessment process?

3. Why was a task and KSAO analysis used to determine the foreign-language requirements?

of the organization (Latham, 1988). Basically, this involves determining the specific training needs of various demographic groups, such as those protected by civil rights legislation. For instance, since the Age Discrimination in Employment Act (ADEA) has made it illegal to discriminate in the selection of employees based on age, many companies recognize that older hires may need training that is not necessary for younger employees. One example is technology training. Many older employees may need such training simply because they grew up during an era when technology was less advanced, whereas younger employees have probably picked up these skills throughout their lives.

Another example is training for employees with disabilities. As discussed in Chapter 7, organizations are legally required to make reasonable accommodations for disabled employees. One such accommodation may be the provision of training that helps these employees do their jobs. Another is the redesign of existing training programs to accommodate disabled employees. For instance, a visual-based management skills training program may have to be altered in such a way that vision-impaired employees can participate in and benefit from it. Trainers must avoid discriminating against employees on the basis of gender, race, physical disabilities, age, ethnicity, and religion—in keeping with the laws, policies, and mission of equal employment opportunity.

## LEARNING CONTEXT

Before we discuss the various training methods available, we need to describe the learning context because it is so important to the success of any training program. In short, the context, which includes principles of instructional design, basic principles of learning, and characteristics of the trainee and trainer, largely determines the success of a training intervention. In fact, there has been a great deal of focus on *learning organizations*, companies in which there is an organization-wide concern with and valuing of knowledge acquisition and continuous learning (Garofano & Salas, 2005).

**Continuous learning** is more than just taking lots and lots of courses; it's about learning how to learn. The management guru and scholar Peter Senge (2006) has written extensively about continuous learning, noting that it's about having a personal vision, taking an active role in one's world of work, reflecting on one's experiences, being open to feedback, and making adjustments to how one approaches one's work. It is much easier for employees to embrace this attitude when they are working for an organization that promotes continuous learning.

### Instructional Design

**Instructional design** refers to all activities that are developed and coordinated to support the trainees' learning processes. The first important element of instructional design is determining what is to be learned. Learning can take a variety of forms, but generally it can be categorized as cognitive, psychomotor, or social. Another, more sophisticated scheme presents a series of design features, or learning conditions (e.g., providing feedback, informing trainees of goals), that can be mapped to the various categories of learning (Gagné, Briggs, & Wager, 1992). This approach allows an organization to use existing knowledge to build an effective context or environment for the specific learning targeted by the organization. The last element of instructional design is the planned evaluation (Wang & Wilcox, 2006), which, of course, should be part of every training program (see Training Evaluation, later in this chapter).

**continuous learning**
Directed and long-term effort to learn; stems from an intense desire to acquire knowledge and improve results and from participation in activities that facilitate learning.

**instructional design**
A set of events that facilitate training through their impact on trainees.

## Principles of Learning

**Learning** is defined as a relatively permanent change in behavior that occurs as a result of experience or practice (Wexley & Latham, 2002). Therefore, to understand training, which is all about learning, we need a clearer understanding of the principles that enhance the learning process. In academic circles, the research on learning has been chiefly conducted by cognitive, experimental, and social psychologists. As I/O psychologists, however, we try to apply learning principles to the design and implementation of training programs.

In the following sections, we will focus on some of the more general principles that are important to effective organizational training.

**Active Learning** Learning theory is built on the principle that learning is facilitated if the learner is active during the learning period. By active, we mean that the learner is engaged in activities like practice, problem solving, written communication, verbal interactions, and so on, all with the focus on improving analysis and synthesis of information. This, of course, is why professors always encourage students to take notes or outline reading assignments, talk to others about the material, and write and rewrite key concepts rather than just read the material over and over again. The suggestions from learning theory about **active learning** apply very easily to training in organizations as well. One can read about how to conduct a performance appraisal (PA) interview or be provided with a list of the specifications for the development of a particular product, but a better way to learn these things is to actively practice doing them.

**Size of the Unit to Be Learned** The question here is whether training should be structured in such a way as to present the whole task or only part of the task in a given training session (Goldstein & Ford, 2002)—a distinction sometimes referred to as *whole versus part learning*. According to learning theorists, it is more effective to practice or be trained on the whole task at one time if the task is highly organized, coherent, and interdependent; however, for a complex task that is easily divided into independent components, a more effective strategy is to be trained on each component separately, moving on to the next component after mastering the previous one.

For instance, 25 years ago I had a secretary who was trained on an older generation of computers that used a DOS operating system. When the Windows operating system was introduced, she was already 30 years into her career and not very comfortable with the significant changes in word processing and data manipulation that came with this revolution in operating systems. Obviously, we needed to provide her with some training on the new operating system and the software that was now based on that system. Here, it was much more efficient to teach bits and pieces of the operating system and software programs than to try to teach it all at once. She was uncomfortable with the changes to begin with. To throw it all at her at once would have been overwhelming and she would have likely rejected our efforts.

On the other hand, suppose I've hired a new truck driver to deliver my product to the retail establishments that sell it. Assume also that this driver has no experience driving an 18-wheel tractor-trailer, which is the vehicle I want her to use for deliveries. Does it make sense to teach her how to use the clutch first, then the accelerator, then the side-view mirrors? No, because the overall operation of this vehicle requires that the clutch, accelerator, and side-view mirrors be used in concert. Learning them separately would clearly be ineffective. You can see, then, that the way in which material to be learned is structured can play an important role in the success of a training program.

A related structural question is whether the practice of the task should take place all at once or be spread out over time. Distributed practice refers to training that is divided into segments, usually with rest periods in between; massed practice refers to training that takes place at one time, without breaks. Research has traditionally shown that, overall, distributed practice is better for learning skills and for long-term retention of those skills. In a recent study of sales employees in Germany, it was found that both massed and distributed practice were effective, but distributed practice was superior (Kauffeld & Lehman-Willenbrock, 2009). According to a meta-analysis of 63 studies, distributed practice is especially effective for tasks that are low in complexity, like psychomotor tasks such as the Purdue Pegboard, discussed in Chapter 6 (Donovan & Radosevich, 1999). However, for practical reasons, many organizations don't make the time for distributed practice; instead, they cram in as much as possible during one eight-hour session; an approach that often results in poorly trained employees.

**Meaningfulness of Material** It makes sense that trainees will be more likely to learn new material if they find it meaningful. Accordingly, organizations should incorporate a few elements into their training programs to make the material more meaningful and relevant for the trainees (Wexley & Latham, 2002). First, the trainer should present an overview of the material, which allows the trainees to better understand the objectives of the training program, as well as its procedures. Second, the material should be presented in a way that trainees can easily understand. This involves using terms, examples, and concepts that the trainees can understand and relate to. One obvious application here is the use of job-relevant examples in the training, such as patient-care issues when training nurses and student-related issues when training schoolteachers. Third, sequencing of the material is important. Trainers should present the material in a logical order. For example, in training air conditioner–repair technicians to replace an air conditioner coil, it makes sense to first demonstrate how to disassemble the unit; next, how to take out the old coil; then, how to install the new coil; and, finally, how to reassemble the unit. Any other order of steps would not be logical and could result in less understanding on the part of the trainee.

**Practice and Overlearning** You've heard it said that "practice makes perfect." Although true perfection is rarely achieved, this phrase does suggest that practice is important in almost any learning situation. But *how* one practices—that is, the quality of the practice—also affects what one learns. This last point is an important one to make in a training context, as employees who either don't practice or practice in an inappropriate way do not learn very well. We all fall prey to some bad habits in our home lives as well as our work lives. Often those bad habits develop if we fail to

---

**distributed practice**
Training in which the practice is divided into segments, usually with rest periods in between.

**massed practice**
Training in which all the practice takes place at one time, without breaks.

practice good habits or continue to repeat a pattern of wrong behaviors. Bad habits—such as when children don't wash their hands after using the bathroom or when UPS drivers lift heavy boxes using just their backs, not their legs—can easily develop from faulty practice. Trainers must be aware of the practice sessions of trainees and make sure they are practicing appropriately because, although practice doesn't really make perfect, "perfect practice" is a near-guarantee of quality performance.

**overlearning**
The process of giving trainees continued practice even after they have appeared to master the behavior, resulting in high levels of learning.

**Overlearning** is the process of giving trainees continued practice even after they have appeared to master the behavior, resulting in high levels of learning. You may think this is a waste of time, but, in fact, practicing something so much as to overlearn it increases the likelihood that one will be able to exhibit the behavior quickly, easily, and consistently when called on to do so. Think back to the subject of bad habits. If I stop practicing the use of my turn signal when I drive, eventually I won't be using it at all. However, if I have overlearned this behavior to the point where it becomes second nature to me, I'm likely to use that turn signal forever. The same principle holds true in the workplace. If a secretary is trained to save his document after every page is typed, actually doing so during the training sessions themselves, he is likely to continue this practice because the behavior has been overlearned.

Now let's consider a situation that is truly a matter of life and death. Emergency room (ER) physicians must be trained in such a way that they overlearn certain behaviors because, given the stress and severity of the situations they find themselves in, these behaviors have to be second nature. If a member of my family is rushed to the ER because he can't breathe or his heart isn't pumping, I don't want the ER physician having to think through the steps involved in intubating or defibrillating him—I want these behaviors to be so overlearned that they happen automatically.

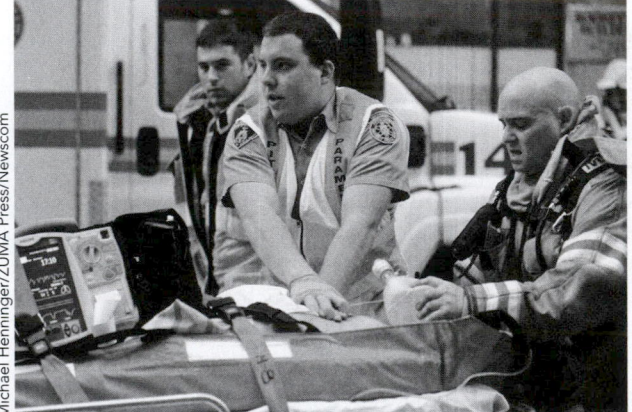

Michael Henninger/ZUMA Press/Newscom

**A CLOSER LOOK**
Sometimes overlearning can increase the likelihood that a task will be performed more quickly, easily, and effectively. What other job-related tasks might it be beneficial to overlearn?

**Feedback** In training situations, it is imperative that participants be given timely and useful feedback about how they are performing. Feedback, also called *knowledge-of-results (KOR)*, serves three purposes in a training context: (1) It provides information that allows trainees to make whatever adjustments may be necessary in their behaviors during training, (2) it makes the learning process more interesting for the trainees and increases their motivation to learn, and (3) it leads to goal setting for improving performance (Wexley & Latham, 2002). Also worth knowing are three important principles regarding how feedback is best delivered to individuals: (1) Feedback works best when it is given immediately following the individual's behavior, (2) immediate and frequent feedback tends to result in the best performance, and (3) both positive and negative feedback have value when delivered in a sensitive yet clear manner. (For an excellent and classic overview of the feedback process, see Ilgen, Fisher, & Taylor, 1979.)

## Individual Differences in Trainees

Although the structural elements of the learning context are important, characteristics of the learner are also important, such as the desire for continuous learning. There are three specific characteristics of the learner that deserve some discussion. First, learning is likely to happen only if the learner is prepared to learn—what is sometimes called trainee **readiness**. Sometimes, individuals are incapable of being taught something because they don't have the necessary knowledge, ability, or experiences to allow them to learn.

Second, individuals' beliefs in their ability to be successful in training and in the job—self-efficacy—can play a very large role (Aguinis & Kraiger, 2009). If trainees aren't convinced of their ability to successfully complete the training program and to apply what they've learned at work, the training process is not likely to be effective. A recent meta-analytic review of 89 empirical studies (Blume, Ford, Baldwin, & Huang, 2010) supports this notion.

Third, the motivation to learn is important as well. We will talk at length about motivation in Chapter 9, but, for now, it's important to understand that if employees are not motivated to be trained, the training is almost certain to fail. I could design the slickest multimedia training program ever, making use of nice color videos and computer simulations—but if you hate your job and aren't motivated to do any better than you're currently doing, you won't work hard during training, and it's unlikely to have much impact on you. Providing useful, immediate feedback to trainees is one strategy a trainer can use to increase motivation. Another strategy is to demonstrate how the training will pay off for the trainee. This answers the "what's in it for me" question, which is a very reasonable one for the employee to ask. If the trainer can show that, by working hard in training, employees will be able to work more easily, perform better, or enjoy their jobs more, motivation is likely to follow.

Some research has focused on these individual differences in trainees. For instance, some training work has taken a different perspective by encouraging trainees to make errors during training. The rationale is that more exploration (trial and error) may help trainees learn at a deeper level and gain a better understanding of the task at hand. Researchers have found that so-called error training was very effective for trainees who were high in cognitive ability and openness. Those individuals who were high on conscientiousness, however, demonstrated reduced self-efficacy as a result of error training (Gully, Payne, Koles, & Whiteman, 2002).

Others who have focused on the role of individual differences (e.g., Big Five factors) in training success found that those high on emotional stability and openness acquired skills in training at a faster rate (Herold, Davis, Fedor, & Parsons, 2002). They concluded from these and other results that individual differences are useful for predicting training success and that early training success has differential effects on later success, depending on the various levels of these individual differences.

## Characteristics of the Trainer

We've seen how the structural properties of the training context, the principles of learning, and individual differences among trainees affect the training process. In some

**readiness**
Possessing the background characteristics and necessary level of interest that make learning possible.

ways, the last piece of the puzzle is a consideration of trainer characteristics. First, Wexley and Latham (2002) suggest that effective trainers establish specific objectives and communicate them clearly to the trainees. Second, trainers should have a solid understanding of how people learn (including the principles of learning discussed earlier) and what role their own approaches or styles can play. Third, communication skills are extremely important. As you might imagine, trainees' attitudes, motivation, and behaviors are likely to be adversely affected by a trainer who communicates in a rigid, closed, negative, and condescending way. Fourth, trainers must realize that different trainees may require a different style or different treatment from the trainer. Although other issues may be important as well, this list provides a good overview of the kinds of trainer characteristics that are likely to be important to training effectiveness.

## Transfer of Training

**transfer of training**
The extent to which the material, skills, or procedures learned in training are taken back to the job and used by the employee in some regular fashion.

Transfer of training is the extent to which the material, skills, or procedures learned in training are taken back to the job and used by the employee in some regular fashion. From the organization's perspective, this principle is integral to the success of the training program. This is the reason that training experts and organizations alike are always concerned about transfer of training (Velada, Caetano, Michel, Lyons, & Kavanaugh, 2007). *Positive transfer* is the organization's goal—the hope is that what is learned in the training program will improve performance back on the job. Sometimes, however, performance declines as a result of training. This outcome is called *negative transfer*.

Irwin Goldstein and Kevin Ford's (2002) classic text on training provides a summary of the literature in this area, as well as some guidelines on how to increase the likelihood of positive transfer. First, trainers should maximize the similarity between the training situation and the job situation. In other words, the training environment should resemble the on-the-job environment as much as possible, an idea that is often called *identical elements theory*. A major cause of negative transfer in many training situations is disparity between these two environments. As an example, let's say we're training employees how to assemble automobile wheels, and we provide all of the materials they need at their workstations, along with an unlimited amount of time to complete the task. However, after these employees successfully complete the training program and get back to their jobs, they find that the materials are not always at their workstations, and, owing to the assembly-line nature of the workplace, they don't have an unlimited amount of time. When the employees try to apply the same procedures they learned in training to the work situation, their performance declines because there isn't enough time to actually use the procedures they learned in training. This is negative transfer.

Second, providing employees with an adequate amount of active practice is essential for positive transfer. This is especially true for new employees learning new tasks. In such situations, practice to the point of overlearning is a good strategy for enhancing transfer because it helps the new employees do these new tasks correctly, despite the additional stress associated with novel situations. Third, trainers should provide different contexts in which employees can practice the desired behaviors. Practice in different contexts with different stimuli (e.g., wheels of different sizes and parts) increases the likelihood that what is learned in training will generalize to a variety of contexts back on the job. Fourth, the trainers, trainees, and manager should work together throughout this entire process. Fifth, expectations for the trainers, trainees, and manager should be made clear up front. And, finally, trainers need to provide on-the-job maintenance programs that are focused on helping employees to continue their learned behaviors. A maintenance program might be a "refresher course" on how to use the hospital's updated medical software. The software may not be new and the medical staff (nurses, physician assistants, medical techs, and so on) should already know how to use it, but occasions like software updates provide the perfect opportunity to remind folks about how the software is supposed to be used, to answer any questions, and to train them on any new features or options.

Baldwin and Ford's (1988) classic paper on transfer of training proposed a model of the transfer process that emphasized, among the other things just discussed, the importance of social support. It has been demonstrated that social service employees reported a lack of transfer from their training experiences due to heavy workloads, excessive time pressures, lack of reinforcement, and lack of feedback (Clarke, 2002). This led to some discussion about the importance of *transfer climate* (Hatala & Fleming, 2007), which consists of peer and supervisory support for transfer. If trainees don't perceive support for transferring what they've learned back to their jobs, the training is likely to be ineffective. Clearly, these findings suggest that the supportiveness of the work context is important in affecting transfer of training.

A recent meta-analysis found that characteristics like cognitive ability, conscientiousness, and voluntary participation were most strongly related to transfer of training. In addition, both transfer climate and social support (peer and supervisor) were consistently related to transfer. Finally, posttraining self-efficacy and posttraining knowledge demonstrated small to moderate correlations with training transfer (Blume et al., 2010). This finding suggests that if trainees have learned a good deal as a result of training and feel more competent than when they started, transfer is more likely to happen. This is very clear evidence for the potential effectiveness of training to improve job performance.

## TRAINING DELIVERY

No book could do justice to all the training techniques that are available to HR practitioners, and we certainly can't cover them all in this one chapter. However, I will talk about a representative sample of the various training techniques. First, I will present some general approaches to training, many of which have been adapted to rely on innovative technology. Then I will conclude with employee-development techniques focused on specific employee competencies, such as leadership skills, and approaches to socializing new employees to the organization.

### General Approaches

Before moving on to a discussion of the types of training, it's helpful to know that research also shows that pretraining interventions aimed at preparing employees for

Rainer Jensen/DPA/Corbis

Yellow Dog Productions/The Image Bank/Getty Images

**A CLOSER LOOK**
What elements of training might make it more successful for transferring back to the job?

the training that ensues are also important ingredients for effective training (Mesmer-Magnus & Viswesvaran, 2010). These interventions typically involve providing information to give trainees a preview of the ensuing training and providing strategies that increase trainees' capability to make the most of the training.

**Lecturing** One of the oldest and most established training methods is the use of simple lecturing to teach trainees important work-related information. This approach is very economical because many employees can be trained at one time. The effectiveness of this technique varies greatly, depending on the training objectives. Specifically, whereas the lecture approach seems useful for teaching trainees facts or helping them acquire knowledge, it may not be very effective for developing problem-solving or interpersonal skills. Additionally, a lecture with a fixed time limit delivered to a moderately sized group of trainees is not likely to include such important learning principles as active practice, overlearning, and feedback. However, in a meta-analysis of training effects, researchers pointed out that even though the lecture method has a bit of a negative reputation based on perceptions that it is a boring technique, their data strongly supported its effectiveness at teaching many different skills (Arthur, Bennett, Edens, & Bell, 2003).

**On-the-Job Training** On-the-job training (OJT) is, and has been for years, the most widely used training technique in organizations. Almost all employees are exposed to some form of it. Bosses often ask incumbents to spend some time working with new employees and showing them the ropes. The assumption underlying OJT is that the new employee can learn by watching an experienced employee doing the job; by talking with that employee about important elements of the job while he or she performs those job elements; and by working with the actual machines, materials, or raw products that are the focus of the job. With this kind of training, too, success is largely dependent on the skills and motivation of the trainer. Reliance on the trainer can be a weakness of OJT unless the trainer is both skilled at training and motivated.

Some companies do OJT without much thought or preparation, or much of a budget for compensating the trainers—and in such cases, it often fails. In fact, some companies use OJT in place of carefully planned training programs. When new employees report to work, incumbents who happen to be working that shift are asked to work with them; this is a prime example of poorly designed OJT because the trainers are chosen based on the happenstance of scheduling and not any particular KSAOs relevant for being a good trainer. In contrast, companies that choose employees to serve as trainers based on their potential to be good teachers, that train the trainers in the proper methods of instruction, that provide incentives for their work as trainers, and that match up trainers with trainees based on their potential to work well together are more apt to have successful training programs (Wexley & Latham, 2002).

**Self-Directed Techniques** Self-instructional techniques allow trainees to work at their own pace and to remedy identified weaknesses. *Programmed instruction (PI)*, the most established of this training type, presents information to the learner while using learning principles to reward and motivate. The first step in programmed instruction is to present material broken down into small elements. Second, these elements are arranged in a logical sequence from simple to complex. Third, following completion of each element, a short test is administered to see if the learners have mastered the material at some criterion level. Finally, the learners are given immediate feedback (KOR). If they answer questions correctly, they are asked to move on to the next stage of the PI. If they answer questions incorrectly, they are given additional information to think about and then asked to revisit those questions until a performance criterion is met.

*Computer-assisted instruction (CAI)* stems largely from the PI approach just discussed, but with one difference: Trainees interact with a computer. Custom-designed software, similar to computer-based testing you may have encountered in an educational setting, presents training information, asks questions to determine what trainees have learned or not learned, and monitors and captures trainee performance. Both information and questions can be presented on the basis of the trainees' responses to previous questions—this is very similar to computer adaptive testing that we discussed in Chapter 6. Thus, fast learners can move through the training program quickly, and slower learners can move at a more deliberate rate with additional practice and tests as needed. Although this individualized approach to training has great potential, careful evaluations of it are lacking.

PI/CAI is clearly based on many of the learning principles reviewed earlier in the chapter, such as KOR, distributed practice, and reinforcement. One obvious advantage of this approach is that trainees can work at their own pace: Those who are quite skilled don't have to waste time waiting for everyone else to catch up, whereas those who are not as skilled can take as much time as they need. Overall, research indicates that PI/CAI techniques result in shorter training times than do other techniques, but PI/CAI training groups often do not show superiority in learning or retention as compared with trainees in control training groups (Goldstein & Ford, 2002).

Some researchers suggest that the learner control inherent in self-directed training programs is counterproductive and makes this method inferior (Bell & Kozlowski, 2002). This control often results in less time spent on-task and the use of poor learning strategies. One study demonstrated that providing self-directed trainees with adaptive guidance during the training process, or simply with information that helps them make more effective learning decisions (i.e., guides them toward what to practice, suggests how best to focus attention, etc.), results in higher levels of knowledge and performance and better transfer (Fulton, Ivanitskaya, Bastian, Erofeev, & Mendez, 2013). This is certainly an area in which we can expect to see more research, such as the study of medical students that found that self-directed learning with respect to CPR was just as effective as more traditional learning with respect to the quality of chest compressions and ventilations (Roppolo et al., 2011).

The training techniques covered thus far have relied on approaches developed before the advent of sophisticated technology. Now we turn to some techniques that have come about as a result of recent technological advances.

**Virtual Reality Training**   For virtual reality training, a simulator is designed to be as realistic as possible so that trainees can easily transfer the skills they gain to the real-life situation. For many jobs, it would be too dangerous, costly, and inefficient to train individuals on the actual equipment to be used in the real-life situation (Wexley & Latham, 2002). Training astronauts is one obvious example (you might want to watch the movie *Apollo 13*, where the importance of the flight simulator to space travel is highlighted); it simply isn't possible to send individuals into space to learn how to be astronauts. They need to learn offsite with carefully developed simulators. Virtual reality training places individuals in a situation that is made as real as possible through high technology. Simulators are also instrumental in the training of airline pilots and military fliers, providing repeated practice and individualized feedback without presenting any actual safety hazards. The simulated hazards are made to seem as real as possible, however. In fact, two important determinants of the effectiveness of the simulators used in virtual reality training are their **physical fidelity**, the extent to which the operation of the equipment mimics that in the real world, and their **psychological fidelity**, the extent to which the behavioral processes needed for success on the job are also necessary for success on the training simulation.

One fascinating example of the great potential of simulation training was presented in a recent study of anesthesiology interns and fellows (Bruppacher et al., 2010). Many studies that evaluate the use of simulations use outcomes in training as the focal variable. This study actually measured how well a two-hour high-fidelity simulation, in which the research lab was turned into a replica of a surgical room with all of the various technology and people available, compared to a more traditional two-hour interactive seminar. The results were very clear: With 60 real cardiac patients, those trainees who had participated in the simulation performed much better than did those who had participated in the seminar. Two expert observers (blind to the experimental conditions) watched the trainees wean 60 cardiopulmonary bypass (CPB) patients off anesthesia and then rated their behaviors on an established

**physical fidelity**
The extent to which the operation of equipment in training mimics that in the real world.

**psychological fidelity**
The extent to which the essential behavioral processes needed for success on the job are also necessary for success in the training simulation.

checklist and an established global skills–rating scale. Although both types of training were effective, the simulation was superior. The authors believe that this type of high–fidelity simulation may be useful for training in other high–stakes clinical settings as well.

An even newer offshoot of virtual reality or simulation training is *gamification*, which uses computer-based simulation games for purposes of training and development. A few important conclusions have emerged from a recent meta-analysis of over 50 research reports and 6,000 trainees participating in simulation games (Sitzmann, 2011). First, training using simulation games results in higher self-efficacy, better learning, and greater retention than trainees taught by other methods. Second, in particular, training via gamification was 17% more effective than lecture approaches and 5% more effective than discussion techniques. Third, the authors conclude that based on their results and other technology-related meta-analyses, technology-delivered instruction can have substantial effects on learning outcomes.

**Multimedia Techniques** Many large consulting firms that specialize in training, such as Development Dimensions International (DDI; www.ddiworld.com), have invested extensively in elaborate multimedia training programs. Though not fancy, videos are still quite popular; in fact, they are often used in organizations for behavioral modeling. Audiovisual techniques are believed to be at least as effective as, and often more effective than, traditional live lectures. The flexibility they allow—in terms of reshowing segments, pausing at various segments, repeating earlier segments, and stopping the presentation prior to showing the correct approach—makes them particularly appealing. In fact, some training procedures, such as those involved in a medical operation, would be impossible during a live lecture but quite feasible using audiovisual means (Wexley & Latham, 2002).

Not surprisingly, trainees often report greater interest in and satisfaction with training conducted through multimedia presentations than with training of the live-lecture variety. Even in universities, you will find that instructors often supplement live lectures with multimedia elements. This method of teaching is supported by the belief that students are more interested in and pay more attention to information presented in a multimedia format.

**Distance Learning** In addition to including video, audio, and computer technologies in workforce training, many organizations make use of technology for distance learning (DL), which is the delivery of educational or training materials,

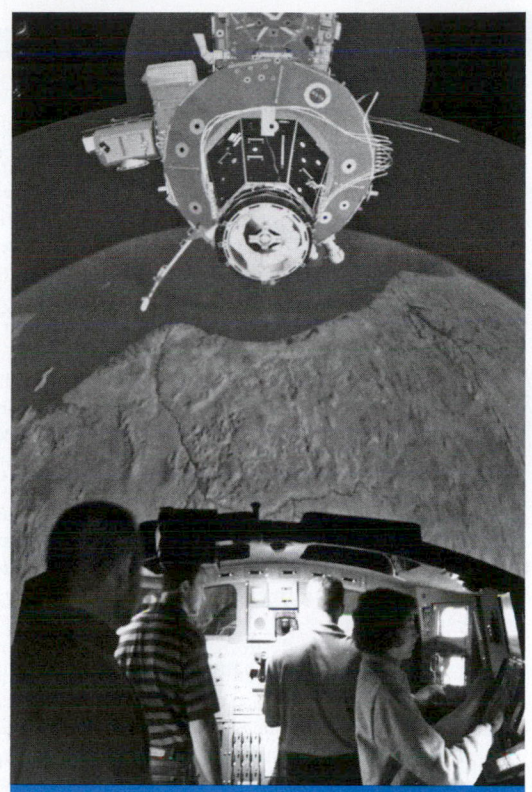

NASA

**A CLOSER LOOK**
What is the rationale behind using simulators to train astronauts?

**distance learning (DL)**
The delivery of material to all participants at the same time even though participants are separated by geographical distance.

## I/O TODAY

### Gamification in Job Training

As you've read in this chapter, gamification refers to the use of gaming mechanics (such as virtual worlds, leaderboards, and unlocking achievements) to train employees, and it represents an exciting new trend within the training realm. Arguably, this technique appeals to computer savvy workers and can help to motivate employees to complete training and hone their skills. Gamification as a concept is not new; for decades, academic and military institutions have often found ways to incorporate game components such as badges, achievements, and points to encourage certain learning behaviors. More recently, websites such as LinkedIn and Fitocracy use gamification to encourage learning and behavior on the part of their members. Even health insurance companies and political candidates have used gaming techniques to encourage certain behaviors in their customers and constituents. But the application of these techniques to training software has grown in popularity over the past few years.

One recent case study from Pep Boys, an aftermarket automotive retailer, illustrates what gamification is and why it can be helpful. Pep Boys discovered that their safety and loss prevention awareness training program was not as effective for preventing thefts and injuries as they'd hoped. Trainers soon realized they had a problem with sustained transfer; associates would learn the content from the training modules but would quickly revert to their old behaviors shortly after the training ended.

Pep Boys partnered with the software company Axonify to create a solution rooted in gamification. Associates would answer brief questions about safety and theft, and receive an opportunity to play a slot machine game to win prizes. When an associate missed questions, he or she would receive a short training module that refreshed their memory. The entire process took approximately 90 seconds to complete and could be done during downtime at work. According to a white paper summarizing the process, over 95% of associates participate in the game regularly, and theft has dropped by 55% (Axonify, n.d.).

It is easy to see how this approach might be used in other contexts. New sales reps might receive awards for learning about new products, or call center representatives might earn achievement levels for increasing their call volume by a certain percentage. A number of other major companies, including Google and Walmart, have also incorporated gamification in their training. So the question for I/O psychologists is, does gamification actually work? As you might expect, the answer is "It depends."

In order for gamification to produce positive results, it must rely on solid training and motivation theories. First, developers must identify exactly what behaviors or skills need to be targeted, and who the intended audience is. Second, they must ensure that the incentives provided by the game are valuable and fun to the participants. Third, they need to take care not to create a counterproductive training module—the program won't be successful, after all, if productivity decreases as employees spend their time playing games! As you can see, this process follows the development and analysis strategies outlined in this chapter. Gamification holds many potential benefits for employers and employees by making learning and practicing fun, but trainers must be thoughtful about when gamification is appropriate and how best to implement it.

### Discussion Questions

1. Consider a behavior (in a job or in a class) that someone needs to master. What might be some ways you could incorporate gamification to help people learn this behavior?
2. In some cases, gamification may not be appropriate, or it might not work well in a certain situation. What might be some circumstances where you would *not* recommend gamification?

### References

**Axonify.** (n.d.). *Pep Boys case study*. Retrieved June 25, 2015, from http://www.axonify.com/wp-content/uploads/2012/08/PepBoys_CaseStudy-Final.pdf

### Further Reading

Yu-kai Chou, founder of gamification consultants The Octalysis Group, provides a number of case studies outlining how gamification has been used to change behaviors on his blog: http://www.yukaichou.com/gamification-examples/gamification-stats-figures/#.VWW-IkZN9dc

usually through electronic means, to people at different locations at the same time. For instance, at the University of Akron, we offer our introductory psychology class via distance learning to about 100 high school students per year. This is typically done by broadcasting the on-campus course to other campuses and using technology to allow offsite students to see and communicate with one another as well as the instructor. Perhaps you have taken a class or two via this approach. This format has become so popular that there is now a "National Distance Learning Week" sponsored by the United States Distance Learning Association (www.usdla.org), which sponsors distance learning research across education and training in organizations. This same agency also holds a national conference to share and disseminate research on distance learning.

Burgess and Russell (2003) summarize the many benefits of DL programs as articulated by various organizations. These include (1) the most efficient use of high-quality instructors and instruction, (2) learners' assumption of more responsibility for personal success, and (3) very clear cost savings. Perhaps the latest buzz in this area is around mobile learning, in which handheld devices (e.g., iPhones) are used by employees for learning. The revenues from the U.S. market for mobile-learning products and services reached $1.6 billion in 2014 and is projected to reach $2.1 billion by 2019; as the devices get more sophisticated and the networks get faster, it is anticipated that more and more training will be delivered through mobile devices (Ambient Insight Research, 2015). A recent analysis reports that 73% of the organizations surveyed are delivering training through mobile devices (Freifeld, 2013). This is certainly an area where I/O psychologists will be focusing more of their research attention in the future.

© DPA Picture Alliance Archive/Alamy

**A CLOSER LOOK**
High-tech presentations, such as this neuroanatomy lecture being delivered to medical students at the University of Leipzig, are quite common in today's technological age. What are some of the advantages of training that is conducted using multimedia?

**E-Learning** Training delivered via the Internet (e-learning or web-based training) is quite popular. I should point out that sometimes terms like e-learning, distance learning, distance education, and online learning are used interchangeably, but scholars believe that this adds to the confusion around what these various approaches are (Moore, Dickson-Dean, & Galyen, 2010). I define e-learning as learning that involves tools that are web-based, web-distributed, or web-capable (Nichols, 2003). Using an Internet browser, employees at remote sites can sort through, read, and work with information made available by the company. A few benefits of web-based training are worthy of mention. First, it's easy to update and change information because it's stored in one location and transmitted across company intranets or the Internet. Second, the training can be done at work or any other location that's convenient for the trainee. Third, the training can be set up so that trainees can share information with one another via discussion groups, chat rooms, webinars, blogs, bulletin boards, or even Twitter accounts (Boller, 2012).

Research suggests that web-based training is slightly more effective than traditional classroom-based training (Welsh, Wanberg, Brown, & Simmering, 2003). In a study of eighth grade chemistry students, researchers found that students experiencing web-based learning showed better conceptual understanding and were able to apply what they learned better than did the students who experienced traditional classroom-based learning (Yen, Tuan, & Liao, 2011). There is also some evidence that trainees react favorably to web-based instruction (Goldstein & Ford, 2002). A study of 47 learners (organizational employees who participated in an e-learning course) found that their computer attitudes were positively related to successful transfer, as were perceptions of the system's usability (Park & Wentling, 2007). A great deal of research seems necessary for organizations to acquire the information they need to make reasoned decisions and choices about the potential for web-based delivery of training and how best to deliver such training.

One of the first studies that attempted to isolate and examine potentially important variables in the e-learning domain specifically investigated learner control, which is the degree of control that trainees are given over instructional elements during training (Orvis, Fisher, & Wasserman, 2009). This laboratory study proposed that learner control (along with personal variables like goal orientation and training motivation) would affect learning through training satisfaction and off-task attention. The researchers argued that if individuals were given control over things such as a play/pause button, text that parallels the video, an interactive outline of themes with additional links, and a pop-up, key points feature that could be turned on or off, they would spend less time off-task, devote more cognitive resources to the training, and be more satisfied with the training. Results indicated that those participants who had more control spent less time off-task taking mental breaks and reported more satisfaction and greater utility of the e-learning process and its content. Further, learner control had a positive impact on learning through these meditational variables. Providing control to learners appears to be an effective way to impact training effectiveness. Additional research will likely explore and identify other important related constructs and techniques.

VM/Getty Images

**A CLOSER LOOK**
Why might a company employ e-learning methods to train its employees?

It seems clear that technology-based training has become the preferred choice for training delivery across large and, to a lesser extent, smaller corporations. In particular, the growth of DL and e-learning is staggering and has become a dominant training delivery method across the United States and other technology-focused countries. Furthermore, there is also a current emphasis on combining e-learning with traditional classroom learning in what is referred to as *blended learning* (Holton et al., 2006). This newer approach provides flexible and user-friendly training programs to a diverse population of employees. Burgess and Russell (2003) suggest that blended learning might be a superior approach to 100% e-learning by facilitating more interaction among trainees. In a survey of over 100 companies by The Oxford Group (2013), it was found that 86% of the companies used blended learning, that the companies surveyed expect mobile learning, virtual classrooms, and webinars to increase in frequency as part of blended learning, and that there are problems and obstacles that still need attention in creating and providing high quality blended learning.

## Employee Development–Based Approaches

The techniques we've discussed thus far are general methods that can be used in a variety of jobs. In this section, however, we will consider some techniques that are specifically associated with employee development and leadership skills training. This type of training, in its many forms, has become a huge part of what HR departments do because the development of employees for continued employment and advancement is key to organizations' success.

**Orientation Training and New Employee Socialization** Though not always treated as a formal training technique, socialization is usually the first element of training that new employees experience. Organizational socialization, sometimes called onboarding, is the process by which an individual acquires the attitudes, behaviors, and knowledge needed to participate as an organizational member (Goldstein & Ford, 2002) and moves from being an organizational outsider to becoming an organizational insider (Bauer & Erdogan, 2011). This is done both formally and informally. Formally, it may include orientation meetings conducted by the HR staff in concert with line managers, social receptions, policy workshops, and tours of the organizational facilities. (When I was hired into my first academic job, my first formal experience was the new faculty orientation and lunch, during which new faculty were introduced to the administration and to one another.) The socialization process for new employees can be very important in that it determines their first impression of the organization, supervisors, and coworkers. This is also the time when new employees learn the formal and informal rules, procedures, and expectations of the organization or work group. In a very interesting recent experiment, researchers were able to actually compare three different approaches to onboarding within the same company (Cable, Gino, & Staats, 2013). Employees of a business process outsourcing company were assigned to either an individual identity condition that focused on individuals' strengths and how they could bring them to their work, an organizational identity condition that focused on the elements of the organization that fostered pride, or a control condition that used

**organizational socialization** The process by which an individual acquires the attitudes, behavior, and knowledge needed to participate as an organizational member.

a traditional onboarding process that highlighted job requirements and information about the organization. The results were clear: When the organization focused on newcomers' personal identities rather than organizational identities or job descriptions, there was lower turnover and greater customer satisfaction.

Some scholars suggest the use of peer mentors. A mentor can serve as a companion throughout the onboarding process, orient the newcomer as he or she works through paperwork, procedures, and so on, and eventually transition to long-term coach and sounding board (Ross, Huang, & Jones, 2014).

**Coaching** Like organizational socialization, coaching is not considered as a training technique in many classic treatments of organizational training. I'm discussing it in this chapter because its focus is on developing employees and helping them to get better at their jobs, which is, in large part, what training is all about. When I talk to I/O practitioners about the really big issues in their organizations, I invariably find that coaching is one of the first things they mention.

Coaching was introduced in Chapter 5 as a one-on-one collaborative relationship in which an individual provides performance-related guidance to an employee. It is the process by which supervisors provide subordinates with advice and information about current performance and discuss ideas for developing them as employees and setting goals for improving their performance (Whetten & Cameron, 2002). In short, it is a training and motivational technique used to improve performance that serves three functions (Heslin, Vandewalle, & Latham, 2006):

1. Guidance: Clearly communicating performance expectations, performance outcomes, and suggestions for improvement
2. Facilitation: Helping employees analyze and explore ways to solve problems and enhance performance
3. Inspiration: Challenging employees to aspire to and realize their potential

Many organizations invest considerable resources in teaching their managers how to conduct effective and useful coaching sessions. In other words, not only are nonmanagerial employees trained *through* coaching, managers themselves are also trained *to do* effective coaching.

Some researchers suggest that the feedback orientation of the employee, such as the extent to which he or she welcomes guidance and coaching, interacts with the feedback culture of the organization to determine the effectiveness of coaching (London & Smither, 2002; Steelman, Levy, & Snell, 2004). At least one empirical study has shown that coaching has an effect on managerial behaviors such as goal setting, the amount of feedback shared with subordinates, and the extent to which managers ask others for input and ideas. All of these, of course, are important managerial behaviors. Managers in this study who were coached were rated more favorably by subordinates than were those who did not experience any coaching (Smither, London, Flautt, Vargas, & Kucine, 2003).

*Executive coaching* is similar to coaching as I've described it, except that the coach is typically a consultant external to the organization who develops a coaching relationship with a mid- to high-level executive in the organization. Executive coaching is used to develop executives and improve their skill sets and capabilities to make them more effective leaders. In addition, a common goal of executive coaching is to prepare these individuals to step into an even higher-level executive position within the organization. This practice has grown considerably in the last 10 to 15 years. It has been estimated by the International Coach Federation that companies invest close to $2 billion in executive coaching and receive a rate of return of 3.44 times the original investment (International Coach Federation, 2015). In other words, companies spend a lot of money on executive coaching, but get a great deal back in revenues, social capital, and other benefits.

As executive coaching has become more and more popular over the years we are starting to see more conceptual and empirical work on this important approach to growing and developing executives. Some research has investigated the style and influence tactics of executive coaches. For instance, a survey of over 100 executive coaches revealed that, when trying to get the coachee to fulfill a request, they tend to use rational persuasion, inspirational appeals, information delivery, and consultation more often than they use exchange, pressure, personal appeals, and reliance on others (Lewis–Duarte & Bligh, 2012). The authors also found that specific tactics were tailored to certain goals. The goal most often reported by executive coaches was getting coachees to demonstrate commitment to the request, which consisted of not just an agreement, but also of enthusiasm and effort to make whatever change was suggested. Another study found that the coach's mood had a significant impact on the style the coach used in interacting with the coachee and that style predicted coachee perceptions about his or her relationship with the coach (Ianiro & Kauffeld, 2014).

Researchers have argued that the quality of the coaching relationship is very important to the effectiveness of the coaching enterprise (Gregory & Levy, 2010). Others have extended this notion to similarity in gender, race, and personality suggesting that the relationship will be of a higher quality if the coach and coachee are matched on constructs like these. However, recent empirical evidence calls this match idea into question. For instance, one study found that neither similarity based on gender or based on perceptions of values, interests, and personality had any effect on coaching outcomes (Bozer, Joo, & Santora, 2015). Further, in a study of 156 coach–coachee pairs, researchers found that the quality of the coaching relationship was the key factor related to coaching outcomes, but that personality match played no role (de Haan, Duckworth, Birch, & Jones, 2013).

**Behavior Modeling** Because working well with others is so important for managers, developing interpersonal skills is of great interest to organizations. Based on Albert Bandura's (1986) work on social imitation, or social learning theory, behavioral modeling is one technique that seems well suited for improving interpersonal skills. You might recall from your introductory psychology or social psychology class that Bandura did the Bobo doll study in which kids watched adults act aggressively against a blow-up doll and later, when given the opportunity, acted aggressively toward the doll themselves. The theory's main argument is that most social behavior is learned through observation.

Social learning theory has been successfully applied to training for the past 35 years. An especially good example of the use of behavior modeling in organizational training is provided by Gary Latham and Lise Saari (1979), who developed nine training modules to train managers to interact effectively with their subordinates. The modules focused on, for example, socializing a new employee, motivating a poor employee, overcoming resistance to change, and dealing with a problem employee. The trainees met for two hours per week for nine weeks. The training format included (1) an introduction to the topic; (2) a film that demonstrated a manager modeling effective behaviors, which were highlighted in earlier and later films as well; (3) a group discussion of the effectiveness of the model; (4) practice in role-playing the desired behaviors in front of other trainees and the trainer; and (5) feedback from the training class regarding the effectiveness of each trainee's role-play.

Latham and Saari assigned half the supervisors to the training condition and half to a control condition that did not involve the behavior modeling training. (The latter group did eventually receive the training, but not until this segment of the study was completed.) The training resulted in positive trainee reactions, better scores than the control group on a learning test given a few months after the training, and better on-the-job performance than the control group when measured one year later.

**Business Simulations** This technique is somewhat similar to the case study approach used in business education. Managers are given a brief introduction that includes some background about a fictitious company, an explanation of a situation, organizational problems, and the organizational goals and then asked to make managerial decisions that subsequently affect the situation and context. These simulations, or management games, differ from case studies in that they are usually set up to be competitive in the sense that managers are organized into teams and the teams develop their own ideas, procedures, and solutions. In addition, as decisions are made on a round-by-round basis, they are presented to the trainers, who provide feedback and make alterations to the environment on the basis of those decisions. The next round begins with new and additional decisions to be made by the various teams.

Although the games are designed to model an entire organization, they can often be categorized on the basis of their functional purpose (Wexley & Latham, 2002). Thus, there are many types of management games, such as marketing, finance, production-management, and quality-management games. These games are often well received by trainees because they are interesting to participate in and are perceived as relevant and realistic. They are also effective in helping employees understand the complexities and interdependence of the different departments within organizations. Although there has been little empirical evaluation of management games and some critics argue that trainees often become so interested in the competition that they lose sight of the general principles that the game was designed to teach (Goldstein & Ford, 2002), one recent study did show that the use of a management game resulted in more positive behavior change and greater learning than was found in the case study condition and also resulted in high levels of enjoyment and engagement (Kenworthy & Wong, 2005). Of course, as with simulators, the effectiveness of management games is clearly linked to their fidelity—that is, how realistic they are and how well they reflect the KSAOs necessary to do the job.

**Corporate Universities** Many companies have begun making long-term investments in their workforce through, in part, the development of institutes, or "universities," focused on continuous training and development. These corporate classrooms have modern facilities with up-to-date technology that allows for effective learning and transfer onsite. General Electric began this trend in the 1950s, but substantial development of the corporate university didn't take place until the 1990s (Gould, 2005). As you might imagine, Disney is among the leaders in the development and use of a corporate university. Walt Disney's mantra was "keep the place clean, keep it friendly, and make it fun." Disney University is designed to live up to that very clear message. Every employee experiences Disney University (located at the corporate headquarters in California) and is taught the importance of the brand: Disney values, Disney history, and Disney traditions (Lipp, 2013). On-the-job training immediately follows orientation at Disney University.

Other famous corporate universities include McDonald's Hamburger University in Virginia and Apple University in Cupertino, California. Apple University was created by Steve Jobs and sometimes hires faculty from other universities to teach the classes onsite. It is all very secretive, with no pictures of any of the classrooms or details about the curriculum available. Rumors have persisted that classes are occasionally taught by some pretty famous instructors; for example, employees who sell Beats™ might find themselves working with the founder, Dr. Dre (Chen, 2014). Some companies have moved much of what was done onsite at the corporate university to an online system. For example, the physical campus of Caterpillar Institute has been replaced by Caterpillar University, an online training facility. Others, of course, like Apple and Disney, seem very committed to their physical versions of the corporate university because they see them as ideal for orienting and training employees in the way, manner, values, history, and goals of their organizations.

As organizations continue to become more focused on continuous learning and the management of knowledge within the company, corporate universities should grow in importance. In fact, one framework suggests that the corporate university be placed at the center of organizational learning because it has implications for knowledge systems, networks and partnerships, learning processes, and people processes (Prince & Stewart, 2002).

The development of the corporate university stems in large part from the societal trend called the Third Wave (Toffler, 1980), in which the world's industrialized economies evolve into knowledge-based societies (Rademakers, 2005). Organizations have begun to recognize the importance of knowledge, learning, unlearning, and relearning at the organizational level and the continuous development of their human capital. Corporate universities have international appeal, too. In China, for instance, they have grown rapidly over the last 10 years, and their focus is often on the use and management of corporate knowledge (Qiao, 2008). Therefore, corporate universities appear to be one way to enhance the potential for continuous learning.

## TRAINING EVALUATION

Any intervention employed in an organization needs to be evaluated. Unfortunately, training evaluation is often not done because many training practitioners don't have the mind-set necessary to conduct an evaluation, others lack confidence in the success of their training program and are afraid to do an evaluation, and still others won't allocate resources to the evaluation (Wang & Wilcox, 2006). However, a careful evaluation is really the only way that an organization and employees can be certain that the intervention has been effective. Accordingly, I have two objectives in this section: (1) to discuss the criteria used to evaluate training programs and (2) to present a few evaluation designs that are used in these evaluations.

### Training Criteria

By this time, you certainly recognize the importance of criteria (see Chapter 4). The criteria for training programs are just as important as the criteria used to evaluate employees or validate selection systems. The "criteria for the criteria" apply here as well. Indeed, the criteria used in the evaluation of training programs, as with all other criteria, have to be relevant, reliable, sensitive, practical, and fair.

**Kirkpatrick's Taxonomy** By far the most frequently used categorizing scheme of training criteria is based on the work of Donald Kirkpatrick in the late 1950s and early 1960s (for a contemporary view on Kirkpatrick's work, see Giangreco, Carugati, & Sebastiano, 2010). Recognizing that training is a multifaceted endeavor, Kirkpatrick identified four types of criteria to use in the evaluation of training programs (Kirkpatrick, 1976). The first type, reaction criteria, has traditionally involved trainees' attitudinal reactions to the training program. These are measured with survey or questionnaire items that tap trainees' feelings about the training. Overall, organizations hope that their training program is liked by the trainees and that the trainees value the experience. However, evaluating a training program at the reaction level is probably not enough to provide solid evidence that the training program has been effective.

The second type, learning criteria, reflects how much of the material is actually learned in the training program, as measured by a knowledge test at the conclusion of the training program. The idea here is that because the training program was designed to teach certain material, a test is needed to measure the extent to which the trainees learned that material. Sometimes this knowledge test is given prior to the training program as well as afterward so that trainees' improvement can serve as an index of how much learning occurred. Such learning can be categorized or measured in terms of (1) *cognitive outcomes*, such as amount of knowledge gained; (2) *skill-based outcomes*,

**reaction criteria**
In Kirkpatrick's taxonomy, trainees' attitudinal reactions to the training program; along with learning criteria, also called internal criteria.

**learning criteria**
In Kirkpatrick's taxonomy, criteria that reflect how much of the material is actually learned in the training program; along with reaction criteria, also called internal criteria.

such as speed of performance as a result of training; and (3) *affective outcomes*, such as the strength or centrality of trainees' attitudes about the content presented during training (Kraiger, Ford, & Salas, 1993).

The third type, behavioral criteria, involves changes that take place back on the job. These are the criteria most closely linked to transfer of training. It should be clear that an evaluation of a training intervention that didn't include measures of behavioral criteria would be seriously flawed because, from the organization's standpoint, learning without transfer is not very useful.

The fourth and final type, results criteria, refers to the ultimate value of the training program to the company. Recall that in Chapter 7 we discussed the *utility* of a selection system. Results criteria are the focus of utility for a training program as summed up by the organization's question: "Was the training worth it?" Even if the evaluation indicates that trainees responded favorably to the training program (reaction criteria), learned the material well (learning criteria), and used what they learned to improve their performance on the job (behavioral criteria), the training program is arguably *unsuccessful* if the costs incurred in developing and conducting the training far outweighed the performance improvements. In other words, although the training may appear to have worked in many ways, it still wasn't "worth it" from the organization's perspective.

Note that, as these four sets of criteria are not always related to one another, an evaluation of a training program on the basis of just one or two would probably be insufficient. Indeed, although many training evaluation programs focus exclusively on reaction and learning criteria (sometimes called *internal criteria* because they exist within the training program), doing so is problematic because organizations are often most interested in behavioral and results criteria (*external criteria*), as these are more relevant for the conduct of the organizations' business.

**Augmented Framework** G. M. Alliger and his colleagues (Alliger & Janak, 1989; Alliger, Tannenbaum, Bennett, Traver, & Shotland, 1997) have worked extensively with Kirkpatrick's taxonomy of criteria. They presented an augmented framework, summarized in **Table 8.1**, alongside Kirkpatrick's traditional framework; the table also includes some example measures generated to fit our earlier example of weaning CPB (cardiopulmonary bypass) patients off anesthesia. Here, I want to highlight just some of the differences. First, the newer framework recategorizes reactions in terms of affective reactions and utility reactions. *Affective reactions* are the attitudes or feelings that Kirkpatrick referred to in his original conceptualization of reactions, whereas *utility reactions* are trainees' beliefs about the transferability or utility of the training program. Imagine a training program that is technologically and visually dynamic, with lots of bells and whistles to engage the user. Trainees may find this program to be fun and exciting, but at the same time they may determine that it is not a good simulation of the job and does a poor job of teaching them lessons that they can transfer back to the job. This example demonstrates the value of utility reactions that go beyond just one's affective reactions. Alliger and colleagues suggest that utility reactions are important elements of training evaluation and different enough

**behavioral criteria**
In Kirkpatrick's taxonomy, criteria that refer to changes that occur due to the training program that take place back on the job; along with results criteria, also called external criteria.

**results criteria**
In Kirkpatrick's taxonomy, the ultimate value of the training program to the company; along with behavioral criteria, also called external criteria.

**TABLE 8.1** Training Criteria Frameworks

| Kirkpatrick's Taxonomy | Augmented Taxonomy of Alliger et al. | Applied to Anesthesia Weaning Study, Bruppacher et al. |
|---|---|---|
| Reactions | Reactions:<br>Affective reactions<br>Utility judgments | To what extent was the simulation engaging? How certain are you that the simulation will be helpful in surgery? |
| Learning | Learning:<br>Immediate knowledge<br>Knowledge retention<br>Behavior/skill demonstration | Ratings of observers regarding knowledge, skills, and behaviors during the simulation |
| Behavioral | Transfer | Checklist of behaviors transferred to real patients, such as:<br>Restores adequate ventilation<br>Checks cardiac rhythm<br>Determines when pump flow can be stopped |
| Results | Results | Measurements of patient health after weanings<br>Long-term recuperation<br>Success of procedure |

Source: Based on Alliger et al. (1997).

from trainees' feelings to be considered separately. Another study also reports empirical support for multiple dimensions of the reactions level, including utility reactions (Morgan & Casper, 2000).

Second, Alliger and colleagues recategorized learning criteria in terms of three distinct types: (1) *immediate posttraining knowledge* measures, which resemble the traditional Kirkpatrick criterion and usually refer to multiple-choice tests of knowledge; (2) *knowledge retention* measures, which are similar to immediate posttraining knowledge measures, except that they are administered at a point later than immediately after training and thus give a better indication of the extent to which the information learned during training is retained for some time after training; and (3) *behavior/skill demonstration* measures, which more precisely evaluate behavior in the training context and differentiate it from behavior exhibited on the job. The final change reflected in the augmented framework involved a change in terminology from *behavioral criteria* to *transfer criteria*. Here, too, the intention was to differentiate behavioral changes that take place in training from behavior transfer that takes place on the job.

The meta-analysis of Alliger and colleagues reveals, at best, only modest correlations among the various criteria. Affective and utility reactions were correlated more strongly with each other ($r = .34$) than with other criteria, as we would expect. But utility reactions correlated more strongly with on-the-job performance (i.e., transfer) than did affective reactions, immediate learning, or retained learning, suggesting that this new category of utility reactions is more useful for the prediction of job performance than are more traditional criteria such as affective reactions and learning criteria.

Another meta-analysis of about 160 studies is among the first thorough quantitative reviews of training effectiveness to be published (Arthur et al., 2003). A couple of interesting results emerged. First, the effect sizes for training effectiveness across Kirkpatrick's four criteria ranged from .60 to .63, indicating a medium to large effect of training. In other words, whether measuring reaction, learning, behavioral, or results criteria, training clearly works. Second, as noted earlier in this chapter, although the lecture method of training delivery has the reputation of being boring, the data indicate that it is a very effective technique. Thus, perhaps this "low-tech" approach still has much to offer. Finally, a recent study took a very interesting approach; they argued that the frequency of training evaluation would positively relate to transfer of training because with evaluation comes more knowledge, feedback, and accountability leading to better transfer (Saks & Burke, 2012). Their focus was on transfer as the outcome variable as a function of the frequency with which specific levels of evaluation criteria were employed. In a survey of 150 training professionals, they found that more frequent evaluation at the behavior and results level resulted in better transfer immediately after training and six months after training. These results are significant because, as we have already discussed, when organizations cut costs and don't do an adequate job of training evaluation, they also tend to not do evaluation at the behavior and results level, which this study shows to be most important for transfer.

## Evaluation Designs

Once we have chosen how to specifically measure training effectiveness (at the reaction, learning, behavioral, or results level), we turn to identifying an effective design or experimental methodology to employ. Quasi-experiments are the most viable alternatives for the evaluation of training programs. (**Table 8.2**

| TABLE 8.2 Training Evaluation Designs | | | | |
|---|---|---|---|---|
| Design | Group | Time 1 | Training Intervention | Time 2 |
| 1. Pre/post design | Experimental | $M_1$ | Training | $M_2$ |
| 2. Pre/post design with a control group | Experimental | $M_1$ | Training | $M_2$ |
| | Control | $M_3$ | | $M_4$ |
| 3. Solomon four-group design | Experimental I | $M_1$ | Training | $M_2$ |
| | Control I | $M_3$ | | $M_4$ |
| | Experimental II | | Training | $M_5$ |
| | Control II | | | $M_6$ |

**TECHNICAL TIP**

*In Chapter 2, we noted that a quasi-experiment is much like a field experiment, except that, unlike a field experiment, participants are not randomly assigned to conditions. In a quasi-experiment, as in this instance, we can take the people already in a particular group and assign the whole group to the training or control condition.*

summarizes three such designs.) First, let's say we have 400 people in our organization undergoing training at the same time and we are interested in finding out whether the training results in *changes* in various criteria. For instance, do the trainees know more about the material on which they were trained after participating in the training program (a question of learning criteria)? Do they perform better on the job after participating in the training program (a question of behavioral or transfer criteria)?

In this situation, we would use all 400 trainees in what is called a *pre/post design*, which allows us to measure these various criteria prior to training ($M_1$) and again after training ($M_2$). The change on these measures (an improvement, we hope) would be indicated by a larger $M_2$ than $M_1$ and would reflect the effectiveness of the training program. One weakness with this design, however, is the lack of a control group, which prevents us from drawing a direct comparison between our training participants and others who did not experience training.

Second, let's say we assign 200 trainees to the training (experimental) condition and 200 others to the no-training (control) condition. This design, often described as a *pre/post design with a control group*, is very similar to the previous design except that it involves a control group. In other words, measures are obtained both prior to and after training, but this time they apply to both the experimental condition and the control condition. In addition, the control group can be provided with some other kind of training, such as an old training program, in an attempt to compare the effectiveness of the old program with the newly designed one. With the addition of a control group, this design is stronger in terms of internal validity than is the previous design because we are able to make not only pre- and postcomparisons ($M_2 - M_1$ versus $M_4 - M_3$ in Table 8.2) but also comparisons between the experimental and control groups ($M_2 - M_4$). If the difference between $M_2$ and $M_1$ is larger than the difference between $M_4$ and $M_3$, and if $M_2$ is greater than $M_4$, we can be fairly certain that the training program was effective in terms of the criteria that we evaluated.

The third design presented in Table 8.2 is called the *Solomon four-group design*. In terms of internal validity, this is a superb design because it includes two training (experimental) groups as well as two nontraining (control) groups, each with 100 trainees assigned to it, allowing us to draw *several* useful comparisons. However, it is also very costly in terms of both dollars and resources—precisely because it involves multiple groups, numerous participants, and multiple measures. Thus, although it is a very strong design from a research perspective, organizations find it impractical and are seldom willing to use it for their training evaluation studies.

**TECHNICAL TIP**

*Remember that a control group includes the research participants who do not receive the experimental treatment. We are typically interested in comparing those who received the treatment with those who did not receive it so that we can determine whether the treatment had its intended effect.*

# TRAINING AND ISSUES RELATED TO DIVERSITY

Diversity issues related to race, ethnicity, age, and gender have become increasingly important to organizations and employees alike. In this section we'll discuss sexual harassment and workplace diversity. These are not training delivery techniques or associated with particular elements of a learning context, but are more about skills and knowledge important for contemporary organizations. As the makeup of organizations changes with respect to race, ethnicity, sexual preference, age, and other important personal variables, it becomes paramount for organizations to be aware of these changes and to train and prepare employees for these changes. Training around these skills and knowledge elements is our next topic.

## Sexual Harassment Training

As discussed in Chapter 7, sexual harassment is prohibited by the Civil Rights Act and includes behaviors of a sexual nature, submission to or rejection of which affects one's job or creates an offensive work environment (Equal Employment Opportunity Commission, 2007). Sexual harassment has received a great deal of attention over the years because of some very high-profile cases, such as Supreme Court Justice Clarence Thomas' confirmation hearings and the Monica Lewinsky scandal that led to the impeachment trial of President Bill Clinton. Herman Cain's presidential bid in 2012 was derailed by accusations from multiple women about inappropriate sexual language and behavior. Two of the women worked with Cain at the National Restaurant Association, which settled those cases out of court.

Eric Thayer/Getty Images

In an interesting review (Gutek & Koss, 1993), the consequences of sexual harassment are categorized in terms of three dimensions. First, harassment has widespread implications on *work outcomes*, such as interpersonal relationships at work, an alteration in the direction of one's career, satisfaction with the job, and commitment to the organization. Second, *psychological and somatic outcomes* result from sexual harassment. For instance, it appears that women who are sexually harassed experience reductions in self-esteem, life satisfaction, home satisfaction, and self-confidence, sometimes also becoming angry, hostile, irritable, and depressed. Physical symptoms that emerge as a result of sexual harassment include gastrointestinal problems, teeth grinding, nausea, weight loss, and insomnia. Finally, sexual harassment has negative effects on the *organization* (Gutek & Koss, 1993). Turnover and absenteeism attributable to harassment incur direct costs; indirect costs also accrue in the form of low motivation, inability to focus on work, and time spent on reacting to the harassment. Finally,

**A CLOSER LOOK**

In 2012, Republican presidential hopeful Herman Cain was forced to end his primary campaign after multiple allegations of past sexual harassment surfaced. How should employees proceed if they feel like they have been or are being sexually harassed?

organizations can be torn apart by sexual harassment investigations, resulting in a divided workforce and increased conflict among employees. One study found that 50% of manufacturing and social service employees studied reported experiencing sexual behaviors at work in the previous two years (Berdahl & Aquino, 2009). These behaviors included sexual jokes or stories, the display of sexual materials, and inappropriate touching. Further, experiencing these behaviors at work predicted negative personal outcomes like withdrawal from work and poor psychological well-being.

Because prevention is the best tool against sexual harassment, the Equal Employment Opportunity Commission (EEOC) and other agencies encourage companies to offer sexual harassment training. In fact, many organizations offer such programs, most of which employ behavior modeling through the use of videos (Meyer, 1992). In one study, participants who saw a sexual harassment training film perceived sexually oriented work behaviors as incidents of sexual harassment to a greater extent than did individuals who did not see the film (Blakely, Blakely, & Moorman, 1998). Thus, the authors concluded that the film sensitized the participants to sexual harassment and what constitutes it. In addition, they found that males who had not viewed the film tended to rate items such as "making sexually suggestive remarks or behaviors around a female subordinate" as less sexually harassing than did males who had seen the film and females in both the film training group and the control group. (For further discussion of how men and women view and respond differently to the work group climate for sexual harassment, see Kath, Swody, Magley, Bunk, & Gallus, 2009.)

A review of the literature supports these findings, and an empirical study accompanying this review demonstrates the same effect in a large sample of govern-ment employees (Antecol & Cobb-Clark, 2003). Overall, these intriguing results suggest that (1) behavior modeling may help some individuals become more sensitive to sexual harassment behaviors and (2) males and females may view behaviors differently with respect to their potential for being sexual harassment. However, what these studies do not show convincingly is the extent to which these changes in attitudes or beliefs transfer back to on-the-job performance, which is really the most important point—to eliminate sexually harassing behaviors from the workplace. A recent review and conceptual paper suggests that rather than focusing solely on improving individuals' skills, organizations should work to address sexual harassment at the organizational level by creating a climate of awareness of and opposition to sexual harassment (Hunt, Davidson, Fielden, & Hoel, 2010). Another paper focused on sexual harrassment training programs used by the military. The findings suggest a very broad model that includes traditional techniques, such as skill-based training, a well-disseminated policy, reporting mechanisms and remediation procedures, as well as regular self-assessments of sexual harassment climate perceptions that can be used for immediate and careful intervention (Buchanan, Settles, Hall, & O'Connor, 2014). Obviously, a great deal more work is necessary in the area of sexual harassment training, but this is one area in which such work promises to pay huge dividends for organizations and their employees.

## Workplace Diversity Management and Training

That demographic changes are affecting the nature of the workforce and are expected to continue to do so is not news to anyone, but data and projections from the Bureau of Labor Statistics present an especially interesting picture in this regard. Individuals 55 years of age and older made up about 12% of the U.S. workforce in the 1990s. In 2012, that age group made up 21% of the workforce, and it is projected to make up 26% of the workforce by 2022 (U.S. Bureau of Labor Statistics, 2014). These projections reflect the aging baby boomers who either choose or need to work longer than did earlier generations. This aging workforce creates exciting changes and challenges for HR functions such as training.

The diversity in the U.S. labor force is increasing at an amazing rate, and the outlook for 2016 paints a very different picture than we have been accustomed to seeing. For instance, there has been an unprecedented growth in the Latino workforce, as it fulfilled earlier projections by surpassing the African American workforce in 2006. In addition, by 2022, it is projected that women will make up almost 47% of the workforce; African Americans, 12%; and Latinos, 19%.

These data trends along with the increasing globalization of organizations result in a very dynamic situation in which organizations must change at a very fast pace to keep up with the changing context in which they exist. This changing nature of the workforce necessitates new HR approaches to managing that workforce. Diversity must become a bottom-line issue if companies are going to be able to compete for—and keep—the best and the brightest. As a result, diversity management (including training) has burst onto the scene as a multibillion dollar industry (Sleek, Michel, & Mikulak, 2014). Most government agencies and almost 70% of private organizations polled by the Society for Human Resource Management provide some type of diversity training (Carrns, 2010). Here are a few examples of the top companies for diversity management according to DiversityInc (DiversityInc, 2015):

1. *PricewaterhouseCoopers* is highly rated for diversity in recruitment, mentoring, and LGBT employees. They are especially effective in terms of diversity with women, with women holding one-third of the top-level leadership positions and almost half of the next level positions. All managers participate in formal mentoring with a focus on helping the majority white, male managers to understand the importance of diversity and inclusion. They are also known for their flexible workplace culture, and they started an advisory board for openly gay and lesbian partners in 2004.

2. *Marriott International* has been among the leaders in this area for many years and is highly rated for LGBT employees and supplier diversity. The company also created a series of diversity councils to help implement corporate-wide initiatives. It created the Diversity Ownership Initiative and now reports over 790 minority- and female-owned hotels, with a goal of 1,000 by 2020. Nine women lead divisions with revenue greater than $100 million. They launched a cutting-edge marketing campaign in 2014 called #lovetravels focusing on reaching LGBT, Black, and Latino customers.

3. *AT&T* continues its reputation as one of America's most forward-thinking organizations regarding issues of diversity. It is highly rated in eight different

categories including supplier diversity, mentoring, and diversity councils. The chairman and CEO (Randall Stephenson) created and continues to chair the Executive Diversity Council. Employee-resource-group participation and management participation in mentoring has doubled in the past two years. AT&T's supplier-diversity leadership is the model for others—18% of its expenditures to direct contractors are to minority-owned business enterprises, making it the highest ranked company in this regard.

As you can see from these examples, the most successful companies in the world are focusing on diversity issues by emphasizing recruitment, selection, retention, and training. The last of these categories, diversity training, has three primary objectives: (1) increasing awareness about diversity issues, (2) reducing biases and stereotypes that interfere with effective management, and (3) changing behaviors so that a diverse workforce can be more effectively managed (Hanover & Cellar, 1998).

In an interesting study, over 700 HR professionals were asked a series of questions about diversity practices (Rynes & Rosen, 1995). The researchers found significant relationships between the perceived success of the diversity training and the following variables: (1) diverse top management teams, (2) high priority given to diversity relative to other business issues, (3) top management support, (4) managerial rewards for supporting diversity, (5) presence of a diversity manager, and (6) mandatory managerial attendance.

Empirical support for the effectiveness of diversity training has increased in the last 10 years. For instance, one review found that as a result of diversity training, employees had a better understanding of the value of diversity and the organization's diversity goals, better diversity management skills, and more effective diversity-related behaviors (Kulik & Roberson, 2008). Another interesting study found that diversity training that focused on similarities among groups rather than group differences resulted in less backlash or pushback from trainees. These trainees also developed better conflict resolution skills (Holladay & Quinones, 2008). Most studies examining the effectiveness of diversity training programs have focused on posttraining learning rather than transfer of learning back to the job. Obviously, the extent to which what is learned in training is applied to work behavior is extremely important. Fortunately, a recent empirical study did evaluate transfer and demonstrated that transfer was predicted by the extent to which skills were learned in training and the favorability of the work environment for use of these new skills (Roberson, Kulik, & Pepper, 2009).

There has been a backlash from some employees about mandatory diversity training programs, the perception being that they advantage nontraditional employees (Kulik, Pepper, Roberson, & Parker, 2007). This has led some companies to make these programs voluntary, but the effectiveness of voluntary programs is still very unclear. An interesting alternative approach to traditional diversity training (and its mixed results) (Chavez & Weisinger, 2008) is the notion of creating a "culture of diversity" within organizations. The scholars who suggest this approach recommend that organizations focus on creating a relational culture in which people feel proud of their uniqueness while still being socially integrated into the larger group. Furthermore, the inclusive culture should be maintained by the organization, but employees must be held responsible or accountable for their learning and development, relying on one another and growing as a result of the uniqueness of others. Finally, they suggest that the organization needs to create an organizational strategy that takes advantage of the multiple perspectives of the various individuals. This notion of a culture of diversity may be helpful in many situations in which diversity training has not worked; it may strengthen the commitment to and understanding of diversity issues in organizations as well.

The effects of organizational diversity on organizational performance have been mixed. Some argue that diverse organizations are not as effective because the heterogeneous groups of employees experience communication, coordination, and conflict problems. Others argue that more diverse organizations are more effective because diversity results in better decision-making strategies and more openness to new ideas. A recent study of government employees addressed these very issues (Choi & Rainey, 2010). In this study of 150,000 federal employees, it was found that racial diversity was negatively related to organizational performance, which is certainly troubling to those of us who believe in the value of diversity. However, there was an important caveat: Diversity management moderated the relationship such that, in agencies where diversity was well managed, diversity had a positive effect on performance. So effective management is a great way to realize the positive effects of diversity in organizations, but diversity that isn't well managed may result in negative effects.

## Summary

This chapter was structured around five major areas. First, we discussed how organizations are diagnosed with respect to training needs. The organizational analysis identifies where training is needed in the organization, the task analysis identifies which behaviors or duties have to be improved through training, and the person analysis identifies those employees who need to be trained. In addition, demographic analysis may indicate the training needs of particular employee populations.

Second, the learning context and its role in training effectiveness were considered. Some learning principles were defined and then applied to specific training issues. As discussed, these principles can play a critical role in the success of a training program. For instance, we noted that trainees may fail to learn effectively if the material to be learned is too extensive and cumbersome; if the material is not meaningful; if practice is rarely used or done poorly; if the desired behaviors are not overlearned; and if immediate, specific feedback is not provided. We also discovered that the transfer of learned behaviors and skills back to the workplace is contingent on many factors that make up the learning context.

Third, we discussed training delivery methods, with an emphasis on the role technology has played in the development of new and varied approaches. Many of the most frequently used specific techniques were discussed, along with examples and empirical evidence.

Fourth, we examined the evaluation of training programs. We discussed Kirkpatrick's four levels of criteria (reaction, learning, behavioral, results), as well as the augmented framework presented by Alliger and his colleagues. In addition, we discussed a few commonly used training evaluation designs.

Finally, we spent some time considering a recent trend in the training literature—diversity. In particular, we discussed issues related to both sexual harassment training and general workplace diversity training, with a consideration of the role these play in today's organizations and an examination of effectiveness where possible.

## Key Terms

active learning (p. 250)

behavioral criteria (p. 269)

continuous learning (p. 249)

distance learning (DL) (p. 259)

distributed practice (p. 251)

human capital (p. 247)

instructional design (p. 249)

learning (p. 250)

learning criteria (p. 268)

massed practice (p. 251)

organizational socialization (p. 263)

overlearning (p. 252)

physical fidelity (p. 258)

psychological fidelity (p. 258)

reaction criteria (p. 268)

readiness (p. 253)

results criteria (p. 269)

training (p. 245)

transfer of training (p. 254)

## TAKING IT TO THE FIELD

I/O psychologists draw from many different areas of psychology (e.g., educational psychology, social psychology) in order to design training programs and assess their effectiveness. While the best training designs typically begin with an in-depth understanding of what is lacking in employees that is necessary for good performance, we can often provide solid recommendations based on some general information about employee performance. Read the e-mail below from Imani Dixon, the owner of the Ocho Rios Bar, and provide some suggestions for how she might solve her problem.

Hello—

Thank you for your help with my troubles. Ocho Rios is a bar in Daytona, Florida. We serve regulars most of the year, but around spring break, we get a large number of vacationers, which requires us to add a number of seasonal employees for a few months. Thus, we have to be able to train a large number of servers quickly and cheaply to prepare for the increase in business. I don't have time to spend a whole day training each new employee, so they have to learn on the job.

Right now, new servers shadow another server for two days to learn the menu and how to work the register. Then we allow them to serve during the afternoon, when we are less busy, until they think they are ready to serve drinks at prime time. If we get too many complaints, we fire the server.

We have a number of problems that occur each year. First, the new servers don't always do their job. I discover them smoking, talking on their phones, or talking with other staff while customers are waiting for fresh drinks. Second, they are not always very friendly to customers. They think their job is just to serve the drinks, but customers who have fun while they are at our bar are more likely to spend money and to come back again. Finally, sometimes I find that a server who has supposedly been trained doesn't know the menu, can't work the register, and messes up orders.

How should I change my training to help these servers learn their jobs? I have a lot of turnover among servers, so it has to be cheap and something that can be done anytime I need to replace someone who has quit. Also, what can I do to eliminate the problems I am having with servers who either forget what they have learned or don't do what they are supposed to do because I am not watching them?

Cheers,
Imani

## Critical Thinking Questions

1. E-learning is a popular tool for delivering training programs. Organizations tend to favor e-learning because it is easy to update, easy to deliver, and convenient for both the organization and trainee. However, like any training program, e-learning has some disadvantages. What are some disadvantages associated with e-learning? If you have experienced e-learning, what did you find to be advantages and disadvantages of the approach?

2. The chapter discusses the notion of *transfer of training*. Why is transfer of training so important? Pretend you are a training coordinator in an auto wheel assembly plant. What steps would you take to enhance transfer of training among your training participants?

3. As discussed earlier in the book, an important part of I/O psychology is the relationship between predictors and criteria. How can you relate training programs and their subsequent outcomes to this idea of predictors and criteria? How would you assess this relationship? What implications does this have for the relationship between selection and training?

4. Imagine your professors decided to use gamification to motivate students to learn. Instead of losing points by getting wrong answers on exams, you would earn points and badges by demonstrating that you are competent on specific topics. Would you find this approach motivating? What might be some problems with this approach?

## Application Questions

1. Imagine you are working in a company that has had some difficulties with employees making racially insensitive comments or jokes. However, employees view going to diversity training as a punishment that only racist people require. How might you convince employees of the benefits of diversity training? What might be some activities the company could do to help employees think more carefully about their comments?

2. According to some media sources, employers report that new graduates lack adequate critical thinking, communication, and time management skills when they begin their first jobs. Is there any truth to this complaint? What might universities do to better help students prepare for the work world? What can students do to prepare themselves? What might make it difficult for new graduates to transfer what they have learned at school to the workplace?

3. Think of a time when you overlearned something. How did it happen? How was that overlearning useful?

4. Imagine an organization has provided training on teamwork skills to their employees, and a subsequent knowledge test indicates the employees have learned what they are supposed to. However, these employees are not using their skills on the job—they speak rudely to teammates and sometimes fail to do their share of the work. What might be the issue? How could you address the problem?

5. I/O practitioners are often confronted with training programs that have been created without much thought for ensuring that the training is accessible to minority groups. What might be one step you, as a consultant, could take to make training more accessible for an individual who is: (a) elderly? (b) vision-impaired? (c) from a different country?

## Suggested Readings

**Aguinas, H., & Kraiger, K.** (2009). Benefits of training and development for individuals and teams, organizations, and society. *Annual Review of Psychology, 60(1),* 451–474. This current review by two outstanding scholars provides a nice overview of recent trends and problems inherent in the training literature.

**Arthur, W., Jr., Bennett, W., Jr., Edens, P. S., & Bell, S. T.** (2003). Effectiveness of training in organizations: A meta-analysis of design and evaluation features. *Journal of Applied Psychology, 88(2),* 234–245. This quantitative review of training effectiveness is the most relied-upon resource for drawing inferences about training success.

**Chavez, C. I., & Weisinger, J. Y.** (2008). Beyond diversity training: A social infusion for cultural inclusion. *Human Resource Management, 47(2),* 331–350. This paper takes a relational approach to diversity and provides some intriguing ideas about how to infuse diversity into organizations.

**Freifeld, L.** (2015, February 10). Training magazine ranks 2015 top 125 organizations. *Training.* Retrieved July 25, 2015, from http://www.trainingmag.com/training-magazine-ranks-2015-top-125-organizations. A great website that provides lots of information about what cutting-edge companies are doing in the diversity area.

**Klein, H. J., & Polin, B.** (2012). Are organizations on board with best practices onboarding? In C. Wanberg (Ed.), *The Oxford handbook of organizational socialization* (pp. 267–287). New York: Oxford University Press. This is a very readable chapter that provides a nice summary of onboarding. Further, the book is a great resource for organizational socialization and all that is entailed in this important organizational initiative.

**Kraiger, K., Passmore, J., dos Santos, N. R., & Malvezzi, S.** (2014). The psychology of training, development, and performance. New York: Wiley-Blackwell. This is a great book for those interested in delving more into training and development. It is quite comprehensive and goes into just the right amount of depth per topic.

**Kulik, C. T., & Roberson, L.** (2008). Diversity initiative effectiveness: What organizations can (and cannot) expect from diversity recruitment, diversity training, and formal mentoring programs. In A. P. Brief (Ed.), *Diversity at work* (pp. 265–317). Cambridge, UK: Cambridge University Press. This chapter provides a thorough literature review and analysis about diversity in organizations. The book is a great source for scholarship and useful applications for diversity at work.

# Motivation

Photo: Hero Images/Getty Images

## LEARNING OBJECTIVES

This chapter should help you understand:

- The importance of work motivation to organizational psychology
- How the three major categories of motivation theories differ from each other
- The similarities and differences among the various need–motive–value theories of motivation
- How cognitive choice theories emphasize the rationality of human behavior
- The similarities and differences between equity theory and expectancy theory
- How important self-regulatory processes are to work behavior
- The major principles and findings with respect to goal-setting theory
- Why discrepancies are so important to goal-directed behavior
- The widespread use and success of organizational behavior management programs for improving motivation and performance
- How successful goal setting (including management by objectives) is as an applied technique for improving motivation and performance
- What job enrichment approaches have to offer organizations and the various ways in which enrichment can be employed
- The current trends with respect to job crafting and how individuals change and create jobs to better fit their needs and to serve the organization

As discussed in Chapter 1, the Hawthorne Studies in the 1920s and 1930s provided a stable foundation for organizational psychology. Prior to this work, I/O psychology was largely about industrial psychology. The Hawthorne Studies opened the way for researchers to realize that systems of rewards and punishments created by organizations, relationships among workers, organizational norms, and individuals' perceptions of where they fit into the organization were all key elements of the workplace. For instance, one analysis points to operant conditioning by explaining the Hawthorne effect in terms of feedback and rewards (Parsons, 1974). Regardless of the particular explanation, the Hawthorne Studies encouraged researchers in the field to study the role of motivation and other organizational elements in work environments.

**organizational psychology**
The systematic study of dispositional and situational variables that influence the behaviors and experiences of individuals and groups at work.

As Edgar Schein (1980) noted in his classic book, organizational psychology "is intimately tied to the recognition that organizations are complex social systems, and that almost all questions one may raise about the determinants of individual human behavior within organizations have to be viewed from the perspective of the entire social system" (p. 6). In other words, as organizational psychologists, we cannot study an individual's work behaviors without considering the entire context in which that individual works and lives. **Organizational psychology**, then, can be formally defined as the systematic study of dispositional and situational variables that influence the behaviors and experiences of individuals and groups at work (Lawson & Shen, 1998).

Accordingly, this final part of the text covers the following organizational psychology topics: motivation, job attitudes, stress and worker well-being, group processes and work teams, leadership, and organizational theory and development. As in the industrial psychology part of the book, much of our discussion will focus on individual performance and organizational effectiveness.

Of all the topics typically considered within the realm of organizational psychology, motivation draws the most interest and attention from scientists and practitioners alike. In fact, it is likely that more journal space over the years has been devoted to work motivation than to any other area of organizational psychology (Steers, Mowday, & Shapiro, 2004). The fact that this topic is especially important to management is evidenced by the following quotes by managers from various companies:

"The workers today aren't willing to put out the extra effort that is required to do a nice job."

"Everybody wants something for nothing—they all want the big pay, nice benefits, and to work in a nice air-conditioned office, but they don't want to work hard for any of those things."

"It's really not that they can't do the work. Most of my workers are pretty competent; they just seem to want to take shortcuts around doing the work—they just aren't motivated."

As an I/O psychologist, I am often asked by organizational managers and executives about what can be done to improve the motivation of their workforce. One theme that I have emphasized throughout this book is the complexity of human behavior at work. This complexity explains why we need to use multiple tests (i.e., a selection battery) for employee selection and why we are fortunate if our battery accounts for 30% of the variance in performance. It also explains why even the most skilled and competent professionals are not always the best performers. Ability is an important predictor of individual performance, but so is motivation. The brightest and most skilled workers in the world will not be successful if they are not motivated to be successful. In this chapter, we take a very detailed look at work motivation.

Among the many definitions of **work motivation**, one that strikes me as particularly useful is to view it as a force that drives people to behave in a way that energizes, directs, and sustains their work behavior (Steers et al., 2004). Work motivation is *energizing* in that it results in the expenditure of effort. It *directs* effort or behavior in a particular way or channels it toward a particular object or place. In other words, having energy is not sufficient to characterize a worker as being motivated; there must also be some direction or purpose to that energy. Finally, work motivation is not fleeting; rather, it *sustains* effort over a period of time.

Motivation is an abstract internal concept that cannot be seen, touched, or measured directly. We infer motivation from employees' behaviors; we operationalize it by measuring behavior choice, intensity, and persistence. It is important to note

**work motivation**
A force that drives people to behave in a way that energizes, directs, and sustains their work behavior.

**TECHNICAL TIP**

*Remember from Chapter 4 that performance is operationalized as actual behaviors on the job relevant to the organization's goals.*

that motivation and performance are different constructs, although many individuals seem to confuse the two. It's not unusual for managers to immediately attribute performance problems to the motivation of the employees involved. As I mentioned earlier, performance is much more complicated than that. Motivation is an important antecedent of performance, but so are ability, the right equipment, organizational support, and freedom from organizational constraints. For now, we will focus on motivation.

## THEORETICAL PERSPECTIVES

The following three subsections are based on a framework presented by Ruth Kanfer (1990) that involves three major categories of motivation theories. But before I continue, I'd like to clarify one point of confusion. A happy worker is not always a productive worker. There has been a belief for many years among lay folks that these two constructs are strongly linked, but the relationship between job satisfaction and performance is only moderate in size (Fisher, 2003). I introduce this notion here to simply suggest that motivation and performance are much more complex than we sometimes realize. This complexity will be clear as we discuss the various theories of motivation that follow.

### Need–Motive–Value Theories

Approaches to motivation from the need–motive–value perspective emphasize the role of personality traits, stable dispositions, needs, and values. In other words, individuals are motivated to perform a particular behavior as a result of these four factors. The most frequently cited theories of work motivation in this category focus on **need**, a force that organizes perceptions, beliefs, cognitions, and actions, giving rise to behaviors that reduce the force and bring about a steady state (Pinder, 1984). Let's look now at four need–motive–value theories of work motivation.

**need**
A force that organizes perceptions, beliefs, cognitions, and actions, giving rise to behaviors that reduce the force and bring about a steady state.

**Maslow's Hierarchy of Needs** Maslow's theory assumes, in part, that we are all aroused by biological and instinctive needs and that people behave as they do in order to satisfy those needs. For example, an individual who is hungry is experiencing a hunger need; the behavioral pattern that follows that experience of hunger (which may include walking to the refrigerator and grabbing a snack) is exhibited to reduce or satisfy that hunger need. Hunger is one of the physiological needs at the bottom of Maslow's hierarchy of needs (see **Figure 9.1**). *Physiological* needs are those for food, shelter, and water—the basic needs for existence. *Safety* needs, one level up, are the needs to be free from threat and danger. Then come *love* needs (sometimes called *social* needs), which have to do with our needs for affiliation, belonging, and friendship. The *esteem* needs, at the next level, are those for respect from others, self-confidence, and belief in oneself.

Finally, at the top of the hierarchy is the need for *self-actualization*—the need to fulfill one's potential. Quite a few years ago, the army ran an advertising campaign that included the motto "Be all that you can be"—this is what I think Maslow meant by self-actualization. A recent analysis (Koltko-Rivera, 2006) of Maslow's later writings concludes that he actually considered a level above self-actualization called *self-transcendence*, which focuses on causes beyond the self, such as social justice, art, and faith.

Maslow argued that humans are motivated first by lower-order needs and that when these needs are met, higher-order needs become more important as motivators of behavior. Thus, if someone is dying of hunger, the need for food will take precedence over all the other needs above it; but once this need is satisfied, the safety needs become more important, and then the love needs, and so forth up the hierarchy.

One organizational implication of this theory is that different employees are likely to be at different places in the hierarchy, such that no one thing can be assumed to motivate *all* employees. For instance, one employee may be motivated to earn money that he

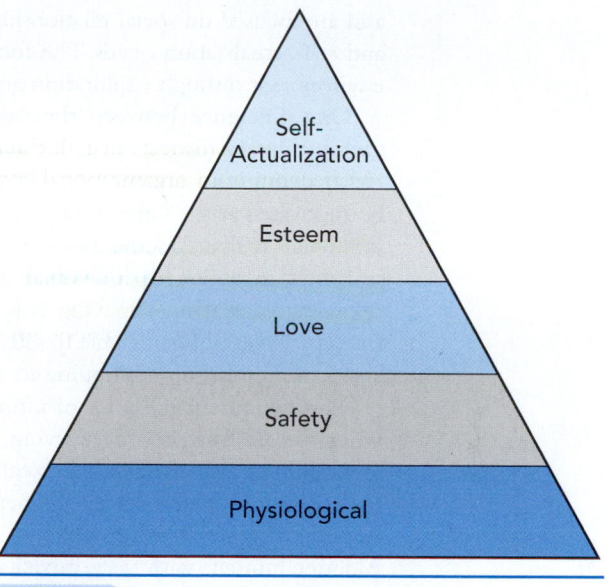

**FIGURE 9.1** Maslow's Hierarchy of Needs

needs right now to pay for his wife's cancer surgery, whereas a second employee may be focused on gaining the respect of her peers because she is at a different stage in her life. The second employee, then, would be motivated to behave in ways that result in her being respected and appreciated by her colleagues—she would be motivated by esteem needs—whereas the first employee would be focused on physiological and safety needs.

This theory of human motivation was popular in organizational psychology during the 1950s and 1960s but has since fallen out of favor because there isn't much empirical support for it. In fact, few empirical tests of this theory have ever been conducted. The reason has to do with the difficulty of testing needs theories— and with the hypothetical nature of needs themselves: We can't see or touch them, or manipulate them, or measure them. This makes it very hard to empirically test whether needs are important causes of human behavior at work. Yet Maslow's theory still remains popular among managers and students of organizational behavior (Payne, 2000; Pinder, 2008).

**Alderfer's ERG Theory** Whereas Maslow's theory was chiefly rooted in his own clinical observations, Alderfer set out to empirically generate a theory of motivation that focused on the subjective states of need satisfaction and desire. He proposed that satisfaction is an internal state resulting from the attainment of one's goals. Desire is similar to such concepts as want or intensity of need strength. Alderfer developed three categories of needs that somewhat parallel Maslow's five levels. First, there are *existence* needs, analogous to Maslow's physiological and safety needs (e.g., pay and fringe benefits). Second are *relatedness* needs, which correspond to Maslow's love needs and are focused on social relationships. Finally, *growth* needs parallel Maslow's esteem and self-actualization needs. The focus here is on interacting successfully with one's environment through exploration and mastery of it.

One difference between the two theories is that ERG (existence–relatedness–growth) theory suggests that all three categories of needs can operate simultaneously rather than in the sequence suggested by Maslow. Thus, for instance, an employee can be motivated at the same time by existence, relatedness, and growth needs. A second difference is that Alderfer posited a *frustration–regression hypothesis*, which allows for situations in which an individual who is frustrated at a higher level of need then refocuses energy on satisfying a lower-level need. For example, someone who is frustrated over not being able to satisfy her growth needs at work may take a step back and focus instead on continuing to satisfy her relatedness needs.

This hypothesis has a lot of intuitive appeal because it makes sense to think that when we are frustrated over trying to do too much or to be too successful, we can focus instead on maintaining excellence in another way until we are reenergized to resume our attack on the higher-order needs. More research has been done on Alderfer's theory than on Maslow's, but, with few exceptions, it was conducted by Alderfer himself, with very mixed results. Some of his predictions were supported; others weren't.

**Herzberg's Two-Factor Theory** In the 1950s, Frederick Herzberg and his colleagues (Herzberg, Mausner, & Snyderman, 1959) proposed that the determinants of job satisfaction were different from those of job dissatisfaction. In other words, providing employees with some things will result in job satisfaction and motivation, whereas providing them with other things will result in satisfaction that looks and feels more like neutral affect. This was a rather controversial statement at the time because it suggested that job satisfaction and job dissatisfaction were not at opposite ends of a continuum but, rather, were different constructs entirely.

Two-factor theory suggests that *motivators*—like recognition, interesting work, responsibility, reinforcement for work well done, and potential advancement—are what lead employees to be satisfied with and motivated by their jobs. Motivators have to do with job content: Their presence results in job satisfaction and motivation, but their absence results only in neutrality. *Hygienes*, on the other hand, are related to job context. Examples include supervision, salary, and working conditions. The presence of hygienes results in only a minimal level of satisfaction or neutrality. True job dissatisfaction results from not having hygienes; true satisfaction only results from having motivators.

**Figure 9.2** shows how Herzberg's two-factor theory of needs maps onto the Maslow and Alderfer theories we've discussed. The implication from two-factor theory should be obvious: To ensure that your workforce will be satisfied and motivated to perform, it is not enough to provide for a reasonable context by altering working conditions and pay. The content of the job, such as interpersonal relationships and recognition for one's contributions to the workplace, must be taken into account as well.

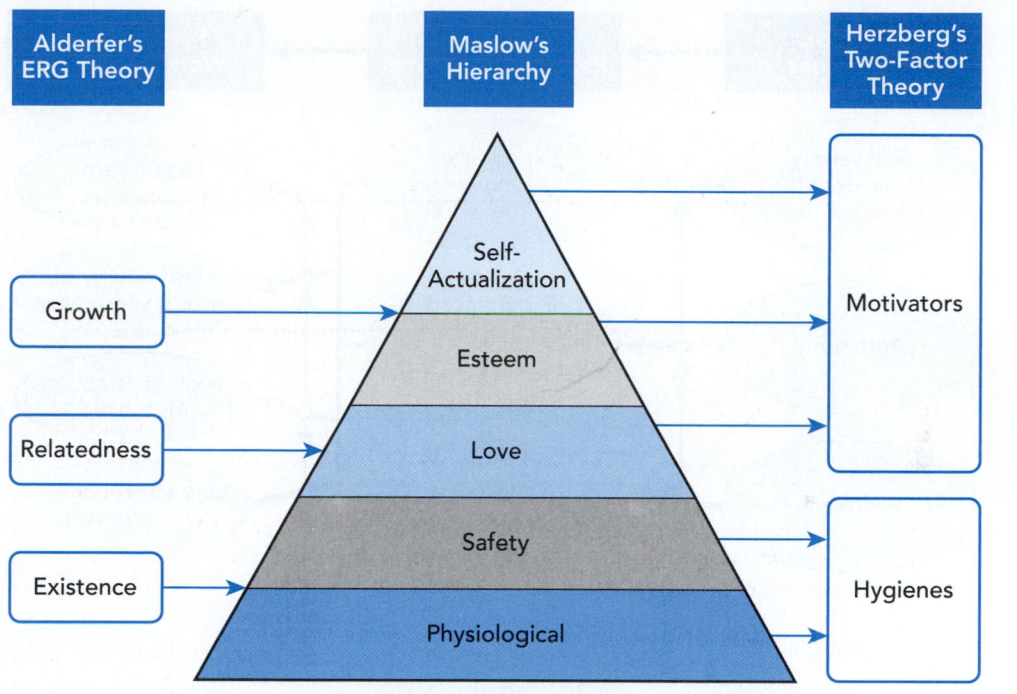

**FIGURE 9.2**    Overview of Need Theories

There has been considerably more empirical investigation of this theory than of the other need theories we've discussed, but the results have been mixed. Nevertheless, although this is purely anecdotal, I have heard many practitioners argue (sometimes convincingly) that they see two-factor theory play out before them every day in their organizations. Some, for instance, have dealt with employees whose decent offices and wages prevent them from being dissatisfied but are not sufficient to make them truly satisfied or to motivate them to do their jobs well. Perhaps there is some truth to these anecdotes. Recent interest in the area of positive psychology seems quite consistent with Herzberg's ideas. **Positive psychology** is the study of positive human attributes such as well-being, optimism, creativity, and spirituality. Researchers working in this area find that happiness is more than just the absence of unhappiness and that factors like wealth are unrelated to long-term life satisfaction (Sachau, 2007). Perhaps Herzberg wasn't so far off after all! We'll look at positive psychology more closely in Chapter 14 when we focus on organizational development.

**Job Characteristics Theory**    In this more contemporary example of need–motive–value theories, the emphasis is on matching individuals to jobs or changing jobs to better fit individuals. In building on Herzberg's earlier work and proposing their *job characteristics theory*, Richard Hackman and Greg Oldham (1980) argued that motivation is determined by the joint effects of individual differences in personality and

**positive psychology**
The study of human strength and well-being rather than weakness and disorders.

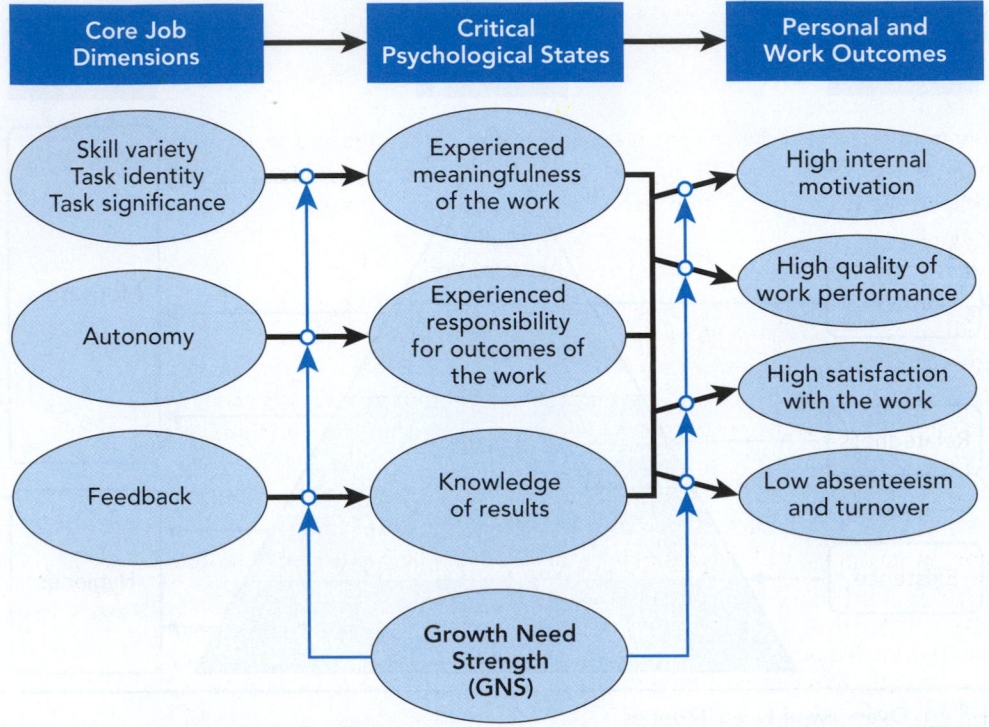

FIGURE 9.3 The Job Characteristics Model (Source: Hackman & Oldham (1976))

characteristics of the job; they also developed a model (see **Figure 9.3**) that explains how jobs influence attitudes and behaviors. Any job, they said, can be described by five *core job dimensions:* skill variety, task identity, task significance, autonomy, and feedback. Jobs vary along these dimensions; some have more of one and less of another. These dimensions influence the three *critical psychological states* that are necessary for motivation.

In particular, jobs that employees perceive as *meaningful* lead them to assume *personal responsibility* for the outcomes they produce; in addition, these jobs are likely to motivate employees to put forth some effort by providing them with *knowledge of the results* of these efforts. Such jobs would be described as having high motivating potential. (Figure 9.3 shows how the five core job dimensions map onto these psychological states.) For instance, employees are more likely to experience meaningfulness if their job requires skill variety (and thus doesn't involve the same old thing every day), provides task identity (such that employees can point to some aspect of their work as being the result of their own efforts), and provides task significance (such that employees' tasks appear to matter to coworkers or others in society at large). The final element of the model concerns the *personal and work outcomes* that follow from the psychological states. These include high internal motivation to work hard and excel, high quality of work performance, high satisfaction with the work, and low absenteeism and turnover.

This model has at least two major implications. The first is that jobs should be designed with the core dimensions in mind. Because positive outcomes are believed to follow from these core dimensions, it seems reasonable to design and redesign jobs to be high on skill variety, task identity, task significance, autonomy, and feedback. (We will talk more about this issue in the section on Applications of Motivational Theories to Organizational Problems.)

Second, some thought should be given to the placement of employees in jobs. Although the core dimensions are arguably positive for most employees, there are likely to be individual differences among them. For instance, autonomy may be much more important to one employee than to another, suggesting that the first employee should be placed in a job involving a great deal of autonomy, while the second employee should be given a job in which he simply follows someone else's direction. According to Hackman and Oldham, **growth need strength**, or the extent to which individuals value or desire fulfilling higher-order needs, moderates the relationships among the variables in the model. For instance, if fulfilling higher-order needs is not an important goal for a particular employee, then meaningfulness of work probably doesn't matter much for that employee.

**growth need strength**
The extent to which individuals value higher-order needs or desire to fulfill them.

A recent meta-analysis found strong support for the job characteristics model, including the mediational role of experienced meaningfulness of work (Humphrey, Nahrgang, & Morgeson, 2007). This comprehensive study also examined the role of social and work context characteristics in addition to the more traditional job characteristics, which the authors combined with a few others and referred to as motivational characteristics. Furthermore, 34% of the variance in work performance and 55% of the variance in job satisfaction were accounted for by the various characteristics they examined. The authors also found that experienced meaningfulness of the work served as the most important mediator of the relationships between motivational characteristics and work outcomes.

Most experts would agree that job characteristics (motivational characteristics) play an important role in the motivation of employees. One investigation in the health insurance industry in the United Kingdom looked at a job redesign intervention. The intervention lasted six months and had positive effects on employee well-being through job characteristics like job control, skill utilization, feedback, and participation (Holman, Axtell, Sprigg, Totterdell, & Wall, 2010). A series of three studies involving fundraisers and lifeguards found that performance increased for those workers who experienced an intervention to increase the significance of their tasks (Grant, 2008). This effect appears to be mediated by increased perceptions of social impact and social worth and is strongest for individuals who are low on conscientiousness and have strong prosocial values. It's clear in this study that workplace interventions can affect important outcome variables through their effect on job characteristics.

Job characteristics theory is considered a theory of intrinsic motivation because of its emphasis on personal mastery and control. Another popular theory of intrinsic motivation is Deci's (1975) cognitive evaluation theory, which assumes that individuals adopt

Image Source/Getty Images

Cultura RM/Ricky John Molloy/Getty Images

**A CLOSER LOOK**
How do you think these two different work environments might affect someone's work-related motivation?

either an intrinsic or extrinsic motivational orientation. Ryan and Deci (2000) describe their newer formulation of this theory, self-determination theory (SDT), as being focused on specifying factors that explain variability in intrinsic motivation. The theory postulates that social–contextual events (e.g., reception of feedback or rewards) that enhance perceptions of competence improve intrinsic motivation. However, in order for intrinsic motivation to develop, a person must feel that those perceptions of competence are self-determined and attributable to one's own ability or effort.

The theory further proposes a self-determination continuum ranging from amotivation (no self-determination) to intrinsic motivation (total self-determination), with levels of extrinsic motivation in between, each varying in the level of self-determination (Gagné & Deci, 2005). According to SDT, social environments impact personality development and self-regulation in either positive or negative ways (Deci & Ryan, 2000). To foster high levels of well-being and motivation, these environments must satisfy basic psychological needs. As the theorists argue, need satisfaction provides "innate psychological nutriments that are essential for ongoing psychological growth, integrity, and well-being" (p. 229). Three needs must be satisfied for optimal psychological health and well-being: first, *competence*, which stems from successes and leads to self-efficacy; second, *relatedness*, which is the need to feel a sense of belonging or connectedness to other individuals or groups; third, *autonomy*, which is experienced when one feels a sense of personal control over his or her own actions. So, the theory proposes that individuals are self-determined when they feel successful and competent, are connected to others, and have control over their own actions.

Some researchers have reported that SDT is especially relevant in describing the motivation of older workers (Claes & Heymans, 2008). The focus groups employed in this study reported that older workers tend to achieve when given more responsibility, more face time with their boss, and greater autonomy. Research in this area continues to examine when and how individuals become intrinsically motivated, as well as when providing external reinforcement reduces intrinsic motivation (see Dickinson, 1989, for a behaviorist viewpoint on this issue). This latter phenomenon is called the *overjustification effect* and is illustrated in the following story.

> Mr. Warren was an elderly man who lived alone on a dead-end street. All the children in the neighborhood gathered to play at the end of the street every day after school, making a lot of noise outside Mr. Warren's house. One day, Mr. Warren came out of his house and explained to the boys that he loved hearing them having fun outside, and so he would pay them all 50 cents to come back and do it again the next day. The kids were excited, and the first thing they did after school the next day was to gather outside Mr. Warren's house and make even more noise. Mr. Warren followed through on his promise and encouraged the boys to come back again the next day for additional money.
>
> However, when they came back the next few days, Mr. Warren explained that he was running out of money and couldn't pay them as much. The boys weren't very happy, but they came back until one day Mr. Warren only had a dime for them. The boys were very disappointed and their leader, a young boy named Jerry, protested, saying that it wasn't worth their time and they wouldn't be back anymore. The boys left and never played in front of Mr. Warren's house again.
>
> Mr. Warren looks more rested these days since he has returned to getting in his late-afternoon nap every day without interruption!

Although this story is cute and certainly makes the point that extrinsic motivation can get in the way of, or reduce the effect of, intrinsic motivation (i.e., self-determination), extrinsic motivation doesn't always have this negative effect. For instance, in a recent study of employees in many different employment sectors and jobs in China, it was found that controlled (more extrinsically determined) motivation did not negatively impact performance or need satisfaction (i.e., competence, relatedness, and autonomy). Further, although autonomous work motivation (intrinsically determined) is most important, controlled motivation still has positive benefits even if these employees are also extrinsically motivated (Moran, Diefendorff, Kim, & Liu, 2012).

## I/O TODAY

### Results-Only Work Environments

Positive psychology and self-determination theory (SDT) are major influences on innovations in employee motivation. More and more, I/O psychologists are moving away from the concept that workers must be forced to do their jobs and toward the idea that workers can be encouraged to find their work genuinely interesting and engaging. One intriguing new approach in this area is the results-only work environment (ROWE).

ROWE was developed by Jody Thompson and Cali Ressler when they were HR employees at Best Buy in the early 2000s. Thompson and Ressler observed that traditional approaches to work focused on time spent at the office rather than whether or not the work was getting done. For example, under the traditional model, if an individual finished a project more quickly than expected, she might be expected to find more work, or show up for her regular workday even if she had nothing to do. ROWE, on the other hand, suggests that if this worker has met her goals, it is acceptable for her to leave for the day.

ROWE gives workers a great deal of freedom in how they accomplish their goals. Given that autonomy is a key component of SDT, the theory might predict

*(Continued)*

that workers in ROWEs are more intrinsically motivated and ultimately demonstrate higher levels of performance compared to traditional work structures. In fact, researchers have seen that groups using ROWE demonstrate gains in productivity and lower rates of turnover compared to groups not using ROWE (Moen, Kelly, & Hill, 2011). ROWE also appears to have a number of other helpful outcomes, such as improving workers' health behaviors and allowing working mothers to have more at-home meals with their children (Hill, Tranby, Kelly, & Moen, 2013).

Because ROWE is so new, only a few studies conducted by sociologists have been published. And although ROWE has been implemented in a number of different organizations, Best Buy dropped the approach in 2013 amid concerns about profitability. Best Buy's spokesperson, Matt Furman, noted, "It makes sense to consider not just what the results are, but how the work gets done. Bottom line, it's 'all hands on deck' at Best Buy, and that means having our employees in the office as much as possible to collaborate and connect on ways to improve our business" (Lee, 2013).

Despite some setbacks, ROWE is likely to continue to be implemented in organizations in the future. Workers from the millennial generation (typically defined as those born between 1985 and 2000) tend to value flexibility in the workplace. Organizations may need to devise creative ways to motivate these workers to keep them engaged. For example, given that these millennial workers strongly value volunteerism, more organizations are allowing employees to take time off to volunteer in the community. These workers also value more work–life balance, and thus organizations are finding new ways for workers to have flexible schedules that allow them to juggle their families, travel, and other outside interests. Positive psychology will likely play an important role in the analysis of worker motivation as well; employees want to feel fulfilled by their jobs, and devising ways that they can have autonomy over their work will help keep people in their jobs for longer periods of time.

### Discussion Questions

1. Imagine that you have to make the decision about whether or not to implement ROWE in a workplace. What might be some benefits of using this approach? What concerns would you have about ROWE?

2. SDT works by helping workers to feel competent, autonomous, and connected to their work. In your own experiences, what factors have helped you feel this way about your work?

### References

Hill, R., Tranby, E., Kelly, E., & Moen, P. (2013). Relieving the time squeeze? Effects of a white collar workplace change on parents. *Journal of Marriage and Family, 75*, 1014–1029.

Lee, T. (2013, December 13). Best Buy ends flexible work program for its corporate employees. *Minneapolis Star Tribune*. Retrieved from http://www.startribune.com/no-13-best-buy-ends-flexible-work-program-for-its-corporate-employees/195156871/?refer=y

Moen, P., Kelly, E., & Hill, R. (2011). Does enhancing work-time control and flexibility reduce turnover? A naturally occurring experiment. *Social Problems, 58*, 69–98.

## Cognitive Choice Theories

Cognitive processes involved in decision making and choice are the focus of this next approach to motivation. The assumption here is that people are neither passively driven by inner needs nor controlled by their environment. Rather, people are active decision makers who strive to be rational in choosing what to do, how much effort to exert, and so on. Two theories based on this assumption are equity theory and expectancy theory.

**Equity Theory** In the early 1960s, J. Stacy Adams proposed a model of motivation called *equity theory* that focused on social justice. According to this model, behavior is initiated, directed, and maintained by individuals trying to preserve some internal psychological balance (Adams, 1965). Equity theory stemmed in part from the earlier work of Leon Festinger, who developed the theory of cognitive dissonance—a theory that explains how and why we change our behaviors or beliefs to be consistent with other behaviors or beliefs. The idea behind equity theory is that people's perceptions and beliefs about the fairness of their treatment at work affect their motivation, attitudes, and behaviors.

We have all experienced situations at work or at school in which we have felt mistreated. Have you ever thought that you worked too hard on a class project to get only a C, whereas someone else in the class didn't work very hard at all yet received a B? How did you respond? Did you talk to the teacher about how unfair the grading was? Did you stop taking classes from that instructor? There are many ways to respond to situations in which we feel we are not being treated fairly. Let's look at the mechanics of equity theory a bit more closely.

Equity theory is based on the notion that we compare the ratio of what we bring to a situation (i.e., inputs) and what we get out of it (i.e., outcomes) with what others bring to and get out of the same situation. Underlying these comparisons are four main postulates:

1. People strive to maintain a state of equity.
2. When inequity is perceived, a state of tension results.
3. When faced with this tension, people are motivated to reduce the tension.
4. The greater the magnitude of the perceived inequity, the greater the motivation to act to reduce the tension.

In an organizational setting, inputs can include abilities, effort, resources such as money or education level, and anything else employees possess that helps prepare them to do their jobs. Outcomes include wages, benefits, feelings of satisfaction, and anything else the employees receive as a result of their inputs. **Table 9.1** presents lists of potential inputs and outcomes. Suppose Bill is a market researcher for NBC and works with three other market researchers who are at approximately the same level in the organization. Bill has a master's degree and five years of experience with NBC; he puts in overtime and believes that he works very hard and is quite competent. He makes $69,000 a year but feels that he doesn't get many benefits, accolades for his hard work, or sufficient appreciation. He notices that no one else in his group has a master's degree and that no one else has more than three years of experience. However, all four market researchers make the same salary.

In this situation, Bill perceives inequity because when he compares his input/outcome ratio to that of his coworkers, the ratios aren't equal. He brings more to the job but gets no more than the others. In fact, this is a classic case of inequity, but not because Bill gets less than he deserves; rather, inequity has resulted because, compared with what others have to offer, what Bill has to offer gets him *relatively* less than they get.

Employees can reduce perceived inequity in several different ways. Let's apply a few of these to Bill's situation. The first thing he can do is *change his inputs*. Bill can stop working so hard and

| TABLE 9.1 Potential Inputs and Outcomes | |
|---|---|
| **Inputs** | **Outcomes** |
| Education | Compensation |
| Effort | Benefits |
| Ability | Recognition |
| Skills | Self-Concept |
| Knowledge | Experience |
| Experience | Learning |
| Diversity | Opportunities |
| Vision | Satisfaction |

avoid working overtime. Of course, with respect to changing inputs, he is limited to altering his effort. He can't suddenly not have a master's degree anymore—this input is relatively fixed. On the other hand, if Bill felt that he was getting more than he deserved, he could reduce the inequity by going back to school and obtaining more training, thereby increasing his inputs.

A second way to reduce perceived inequity is to *change outcomes*. Bill can present his concerns to his boss and ask for a raise, a promotion, additional benefits, more recognition, and so on. Obviously, Bill is dependent on his boss for increasing the outcomes, but he can certainly get the ball rolling by asking for them.

A third way, though perhaps not always a wise one, is to *alter his perceptions*. Bill can attempt to convince himself that his ratio is about the same as his coworkers'. In other words, he can decide that he doesn't really work any harder than they do and that, although he has a master's degree, they have more practical experience from previous jobs than he does. Although this may seem like he's "tricking" himself, this option can be reasonably successful in the short term by reducing the tension that arises from perceived inequity. Whether there are long-term costs associated with this strategy is another matter.

Empirical support for equity theory is generally mixed (Pinder, 1998). According to some studies, when people who are paid on the basis of how much they produce (i.e., a piece-rate system) feel that their rate of pay is not enough, they tend to produce more but at a lower quality (Mowday, 1991). There is some evidence, though not a great deal, that when individuals believe their hourly pay rate is too low, they tend to reduce their inputs—for example, by reducing their effort (Mowday, 1991). The authors of a meta-analysis on pay satisfaction couched their study in terms of equity theory and discrepancies (Williams, McDaniel, & Nguyen, 2006). They reported that people's level of satisfaction with their pay was determined by the difference between what they were paid and what they felt they should be paid. A recent study reported that college students did a cost-benefit analysis akin to what is proposed by equity theory when deciding whether to participate in research and whether to attend class (Miles, Cromer, & Narayan, 2015). Incidentally, the students felt that both participating in research and attending class had positive benefits even after considering costs.

One problem with equity theory, however, is its prediction that if individuals believe they are *paid too much*, they will change their inputs to make the situation more equitable. In other words, if you believe you are getting more and better outcomes from your job than those received by your coworkers, all of whom have the same inputs as you, you will be motivated to make this situation more fair either by working harder to *earn your extra outcomes* or by telling your boss that you are being paid too much for what you do. As you can imagine, there isn't much research to substantiate this prediction. Have you ever worked with people who thought they were overpaid and offered to take a cut in pay? Such situations are rare, but studies have shown that inequity in either direction (i.e., getting too little or too much) can lead to burnout (van Dierendonck, Schaufeli, & Buunk, 2001) and negative organizational outcomes (Scheer, Kumar, & Steenkamp, 2003).

A newer construct called **equity sensitivity** was developed to account for the notion that people differ in terms of their sensitivity to overreward or underreward situations (O'Neill & Mone, 1998). This construct has been quite useful in predicting attitudes and behaviors as a function of various inequitable situations. Depending on how employees score on equity sensitivity measures, they are classified as *benevolents*, who tend to be more tolerant of underreward inequity; as *entitleds*, who always want overreward; or as *equity-sensitives*, who truly desire the state of equity or balance. Some research has shown a relationship between these categories and such factors as job satisfaction, effort, organizational commitment, and turnover (Allen & White, 2002). An interesting study of employees who were completing their MBAs found that more OCBs were exhibited when perceptions of organizational justice were high (Blakely, Andrews, & Moorman, 2005). In addition, benevolents performed more OCBs than entitleds regardless of their justice perceptions—this makes some sense as benevolents tend to be less responsive to inequity. Finally, entitleds exhibited the fewest OCBs when organizational justice was low. This finding is consistent with entitled's focus on overreward: With low justice, there isn't much likelihood of overreward, so these individuals withhold their OCBs.

Equity theory has served as the foundation for one of the hottest topics in 21st-century organizations—**organizational justice**, the term used to refer to the role of fairness in the workplace. The term was coined by Jerald Greenberg in the 1980s to describe individuals' interest in and concern with fairness-related activities that take place at work. Organizational justice is viewed as a class of motivated behaviors or attitudes that are engaged by different individual and contextual characteristics. Justice perceptions result in both affective and cognitive responses that determine ensuing behaviors.

Adams's (1965) work on equity theory focused on fairness with respect to outcomes, which has become known as *distributive justice*. More recently, researchers and practitioners alike have become interested in *procedural justice*, or the extent to which the procedures and processes used at work are perceived to be fair by employees. An interesting pair of studies recently demonstrated that procedural justice affected task performance through intrinsic motivation (Zapata-Phelan, Colquitt, Scott, & Livingston, 2009). Across two studies and varied measures, the researchers found that the use of fair decision-making procedures is one potentially useful way to improve both students' and employees' levels of intrinsic motivation and resulting performance. Finally, a third dimension of organizational justice has received considerable interest in recent years—*interactional justice*, or the way in which decisions and procedures are communicated to employees. This last dimension focuses more on the extent to which individuals are provided information about the rationale and purpose of organizational decisions. In fact, this dimension has been further divided by some scholars and researchers into interpersonal and informational subdimensions. *Interpersonal justice* is the extent to which people are treated with respect and politeness by supervisors or others. *Informational justice* concerns explanations provided to people about decisions or outcomes that provide useful information. We will look at the effect of organizational justice on job satisfaction in Chapter 10.

**equity sensitivity**
An individual difference indicating the extent to which people are affected by overreward or underreward situations.

**organizational justice**
The study of people's perceptions of fairness in organizational contexts.

**Expectancy Theory** One of the most popular theories of work motivation is based on the work of Victor Vroom (1964) and stems from the much earlier work of Edward Tolman (see Tolman, 1932). Vroom's expectancy theory includes a model termed *valence–instrumentality–expectancy (VIE)*. The major premise of this model is that people's behaviors result from conscious choices among alternatives and that these alternatives are evaluated with respect to valence, instrumentality, and expectancy. Its basic assumption, to which its critics have objected, is that individuals are rational and make rational decisions. Although the model is called VIE theory, my students have found it more helpful when I discuss the elements in a different order: E–I–V.

We know that rational decision making doesn't always occur, but it certainly does some of the time. Expectancy is defined as an individual's belief about the likelihood of achieving a desired performance level when exerting a certain amount of effort. **Figure 9.4** presents the VIE model, along with two examples. A student might ask

**expectancy**
An individual's belief about the likelihood of achieving a desired performance level when exerting a certain amount of effort.

| Education example | Getting an A on the test will be valued to the extent that it makes one feel like something has been accomplished. **Or** Getting an A on the test will be valued to the extent that it is perceived to lead to other valued outcomes. |
|---|---|

| Organizational example | Getting a favorable performance review will be valued to the extent that it makes one feel like one has performed well. **Or** Getting a favorable performance review will be valued to the extent that it is perceived to lead to other valued outcomes. |
|---|---|

**Value**

**Effort** → **Expectancy** → **Performance** → **Instrumentality** → **Outcome**

| Education example | Will studying 3 hours result in getting an A on the test? | Will getting an A lead to other valued outcomes (e.g., getting an A in the class)? |
|---|---|---|
| Organizational example | Will working 60 hours per week result in a favorable performance review? | Will getting a favorable performance review lead to other valued outcomes (e.g., getting a raise)? |

**FIGURE 9.4** Expectancy Theory: Concepts and Examples

how likely it is that studying three hours for a test will result in getting an A on the test, whereas a computer programmer might ask how likely it is that working 60 hours a week for the next three months will result in performance that is good enough to receive a favorable performance review. Expectancy is sometimes referred to as the effort–performance link—a link that should be clear from these two examples.

Instrumentality is the perceived relationship between the performance of a particular behavior and the likelihood that a certain outcome will result from that behavior—this is sometimes viewed as the performance–outcome link. In our school example, instrumentality is the extent to which getting an A on the test is likely to lead to other favorable outcomes, such as an A for the course or graduating with honors. In the workplace example, it is the extent to which getting a favorable performance review is likely to result in a pay raise or a promotion. In both examples, instrumentality is reflective of one outcome leading to another outcome.

Valence, which literally means "value," is the expected level of satisfaction to be derived from some outcome. An outcome is positively valued if an individual expects to be satisfied by obtaining it. As Vroom (1964) noted, an outcome is more likely to be valued if other positive outcomes are likely to stem from it. In other words, if one outcome is instrumental for other outcomes, that first outcome is likely to be positively valued.

In our school example, getting an A on the test may be valued in and of itself because it makes a student feel as though she has accomplished something important. In addition, if getting an A on the test is likely to lead to an A for the course (instrumentality), and if getting an A for the course is important to her (value), then getting an A on the test is positively valued as well. Similarly, our computer programmer may value a positive performance review because it makes him feel that he is doing a good job. In addition, he is likely to value a positive performance review if he believes that the review will result in a large pay raise (instrumentality) and if the pay raise is important to him (value).

Monkey Business Images/Shutterstock

Putting all this together, Vroom (1964) suggests that individuals' beliefs about values, instrumentalities, and expectancies interact psychologically to create the motivational force to act in such a way as to bring pleasure and avoid pain. In other words, we tend to do things that make us pleased and proud and not to do things that displease or disappoint us. Motivation is a multiplicative function of these three concepts, which means that if any of the three is 0, there is no motivation. For instance, if getting an A on the test is *valued* and believed to be *instrumental* for obtaining other valued outcomes such as an A in the course, but the student believes that it is completely unrealistic to *expect* that pulling an all-nighter is going to result in getting an A on the test, then she won't pull an all-nighter.

**instrumentality**
The perceived relationship between the performance of a particular behavior and the likelihood that a certain outcome will result from that behavior.

**valence (value)**
The expected level of satisfaction to be derived from some outcome.

**A CLOSER LOOK**
How is study behavior affected by expectancy, instrumentality, and valence?

Although she perceives high levels of value and instrumentality, her 0 expectancy results in the choice not to exhibit the behavior (i.e., pulling an all-nighter).

A major implication of the VIE model is that if the organization can identify the weak link in the chain, then it can work to rectify it. I chose the performance review example because this is an area in which motivation often breaks down. Although some employees may value a favorable performance review in and of itself, most value it only if it leads to something else. (See Chapter 5 for more details about performance appraisal.) The organization needs to recognize that employees are not likely to exert great effort at work if they don't see the performance review leading to something else of value, such as a pay raise, a promotion, additional benefits, a better job situation, or increased responsibility and autonomy. Indeed, the organization can fix this instrumentality problem by clarifying the links between performance and other outcomes. For instance, the performance review can be used as a basis for important organizational rewards, and employees can be made explicitly aware of this link.

A very intriguing study examined new entrepreneurs to see the effect of VIE constructs on important outcome variables (Renko, Kroeck, & Bullough, 2011). In particular, valence, instrumentality, and expectancy were related to participants' intentions to begin a new firm, but even more interesting is the finding that V, I, and E worked through intentions to impact the sales income and health of the new venture up to 2.5 years later. These results are especially interesting because we know from a great deal of data that most new entrepreneurs exit the start-up process before getting the new venture off the ground—it appears that V, I, and E may be very important predictors of future entrepreneurial success.

A meta-analysis exploring the results of almost 80 studies that tested all or part of the VIE model (Van Eerde & Thierry, 1996) uncovered a few important findings. First, the relationship between the individual VIE components (valence, instrumentality, expectancy) and the work-related outcomes is stronger than that between a score that combines the VIE components and the work-related outcomes. In other words, although the multiplicative combination of the components may not predict outcomes very well, the data are clear that outcomes are related to the three components. Second, many of the studies reviewed were flawed because they examined the model in terms of comparisons between people rather than in terms of predicting how an individual person is likely to behave. The model was developed by Vroom to account for how motivated an individual is to exhibit a certain behavior versus a different behavior—it was not developed to compare one person's motivation to perform a particular behavior with another person's motivation to perform that same behavior. Finally, the correlations between the VIE components and attitudes/intentions were stronger than those between the VIE components and behaviors (e.g., performance, effort, and choice). Based on these findings, the authors concluded that the VIE components are clearly related to work criteria. VIE theory has since been applied to a diverse set of work-related criteria, such as occupational choices, job choices, decisions to participate in an employee involvement program, strategic decision making (Ambrose & Kulik, 1999), and test-taking motivation (Sanchez, Truxillo, & Bauer, 2000).

## Self-Regulation Theories

Self-regulation theories revolve around goal-directed behaviors. The idea here is that motivation is directly linked to self-regulation, or the manner in which individuals monitor their own behaviors and make adjustments to those behaviors in the pursuit of goals. Motivation is translated into behavior as a result of self-governing cognitive mechanisms. Unlike needs–motives–values theories and cognitive choice theories, self-regulation theories come into play after a goal has been chosen. They explain how time

**self-regulation**
The manner in which individuals monitor their own behaviors and make adjustments to those behaviors in the pursuit of goals.

gregepperson/iStockphoto/Getty Images

**A CLOSER LOOK**
Do you think your performance tends to increase as the difficulty and specificity of the goals increase?

and effort are allocated across various activities, all of which are directed toward attaining that goal. And whereas the former theories deal with intentions or choices, self-regulation theories deal with *volition*, or will (Kanfer, 1990). That is, given the choice to pursue a particular goal or exhibit a particular behavior, how do we go about pursuing that goal or exhibiting that behavior?

**Goal-Setting Theory** Kurt Lewin's early work on "level of aspiration" (Lewin, Dembo, Festinger, & Sears, 1944) provided the foundation for the most researched and well-established theory of work motivation—goal-setting theory. Largely developed by Edwin Locke, this model suggests that goals affect behavior in four ways (Locke & Latham, 2006). First, goals direct our attention to a particular task or element of a task. Second, goals mobilize on-task effort. In other words, they allow us to focus our effort appropriately to move toward their attainment. Third, goals enable us to be persistent as we strive toward their attainment. Without goals, we would often give up and move on to something else. Finally, goals help us facilitate strategies that can be used at a higher cognitive level to move toward their attainment.

Locke and others have conducted empirical research in this area for over 40 years (for a review, see Locke & Latham, 2002). This wealth of data has provided us with a great deal of useful information, but I will summarize only a few of the major findings. First, people tend to perform better when they are assigned or choose difficult, specific goals than when they are assigned or choose easy goals or no goals. Second, the goal-setting effect—namely, improved performance as a result of difficult, specific goals—occurs only when individuals accept and are committed to those goals. (For this reason, providing your employees with a difficult, specific goal that they don't accept and don't care about achieving will not result in increased motivation or performance.) Third, feedback about a person's performance in relation to the goal positively affects that performance.

These three well-supported propositions combine to produce goal-setting theory's key statement: *Motivation is enhanced when employees accept and are committed to specific, difficult goals and when feedback about progress toward those goals is provided.* This effect has been found in literally hundreds of studies in both the laboratory and the field, in both the United States and elsewhere; in addition, it holds true for over 100 different tasks, as well as for diverse samples along dimensions of race, gender, age, mental ability, and work experience (for a review, see Locke, 1990). More recently, study of the goal-setting effect has been extended into such areas as group goal setting (Wegge & Haslam, 2005) and goal strategies of athletes (Senécal, Loughead, & Bloom, 2008). Goal-setting theory is not only one of the most successful motivation theories in terms of demonstrating consistent support for its propositions, but it is also among the simplest. This simplicity (along with its strong results) has made it a favorite technique for HR practitioners who are interested in altering the behavior or effort of their employees. We will discuss some applications of goal-setting theory a bit later in the book.

**Social Cognitive Theories** Social cognitive theories, which gained prominence in the 1960s, stress the interplay of both behavioral and cognitive elements in motivation. Emerging as a result of dissatisfaction with the way in which behaviorism ignored the role of cognitive processes in motivation, this approach emphasizes the cognitive, behavioral, individual, and environmental factors that work together in determining motivation (Kanfer, 1990).

The most important of these social cognitive theories was developed by Albert Bandura (1986), who views self-regulation as made up of three major components. The first is *self-observation*, which refers to the extent to which we pay attention to specific aspects of our behavior. Because we are limited processors of information, we cannot attend to all dimensions of our behavior; thus, we have to choose which ones will occupy our attention. It is through this process that we are able to monitor our behavior, performance, feedback, and goals to allow for motivational strategies to develop. The second component is *self-evaluation*, which accounts for the attention that individuals devote to feedback processes. Specifically, it is how we evaluate our own performance and effort. Third, *self-reactions* are the internal responses to self-evaluation. Some of these are affective reactions, such as being disgruntled with our performance toward a goal or being overjoyed with the progress that is being made. Others are behavioral reactions, which may involve an increase in effort, a goal shift, or abandonment of the goal altogether.

Another crucial element of Bandura's theory is what he calls **self-efficacy expectations**—that is, individuals' perceptions of their ability to successfully complete a task or attain a goal. Bandura (1986) has argued that strengthening one's self-efficacy enhances motivation to attain a particular goal; other researchers view self-efficacy as

**self-efficacy expectations** Individuals' perceptions of their ability to successfully complete a task or attain a goal.

being intimately related to the *expectancy* component of VIE theory. Indeed, people do tend to be more motivated to take on a particular task when they feel competent to do that task and expect that they can do it well. Although self-efficacy is an individual-level construct, organizations can certainly play a role in developing employees' levels of self-efficacy. For instance, organizations can help an employee develop a healthy level of self-efficacy through training and feedback that is focused not just on weaknesses, but also on strengths, as suggested by a positive psychology approach. (We discussed positive psychology early in the chapter, but will consider it in more detail in Chapter 14.) Bandura's social cognitive theory specifically views motivation as resulting from the joint influence of self-efficacy expectations and self-reactions to discrepancies between current performance and some standard or goal (Kanfer, 1990). Bandura and Locke (2003) argue that a strong belief in one's performance efficacy or ability is essential to mobilize and sustain the effort necessary to succeed. We form intentions, along with plans and strategies for carrying out our intentions. As self-regulators, we adopt personal standards (i.e., goals) and monitor our actions by self-reactive influence. (For a contrasting view in which self-efficacy is sometimes believed to be negatively related to motivation and performance, see Vancouver, More, & Yoder, 2008.)

In keeping with Bandura's emphasis on self-efficacy, some social cognitive researchers have linked motivational principles to other individual-difference variables such as goal orientation (DeShon & Gillespie, 2005). For instance, *learning goal orientation* (i.e., the extent to which individuals approach problems with an emphasis on learning and developing) has been linked to both motivation and affect in the performance of complex tasks; *performance goal orientation* (i.e., the extent to which individuals approach problems with a focus solely on performance) has been linked to motivation and affect in the performance of simple tasks (Steele-Johnson, Beauregard, Hoover, & Schmidt, 2000).

Bell and Kozlowski (2002) have argued that goal orientation, self-efficacy, and ability interact in affecting performance. Specifically, they found that a learning goal orientation was adaptive for high-ability individuals but not for low-ability individuals. Furthermore, high-ability individuals experienced a decrement in performance that was determined by high levels of performance orientation. Finally, Van Yperen and Janssen (2002) found that high job demands felt by those employees who were high on performance orientation and low on learning orientation resulted in low job satisfaction but that the same was not true for those low on performance orientation and high on learning orientation.

Several researchers have proposed and developed *control theory*, which is essentially a social cognitive motivational theory with a negative feedback loop at its core (see Johnson, Chang, & Lord, 2006). The basic premise of control theory is that this negative feedback loop results from the comparison of performance feedback with some goal or standard. If people perceive a discrepancy between the feedback and the standard, they are motivated to reduce that discrepancy in some way. The objective in such cases is to control the situation so that the feedback and the standard match—or, in control theory lingo, to keep the sensed values (feedback) in conformity with the reference value (standard).

koinseb/iStockphoto/Getty Images

Control theory is certainly not limited to the social sciences; in fact, it did not even originate there. Rather, control theory in the social sciences has developed from work done in technical areas such as engineering, which employs the term *control system* to illustrate the process in question. (For criticisms of this approach as too mechanical a description for human behavior, see Bandura & Locke, 2003.) The best example of a control system is a thermostat that operates by sensing the temperature in the room and comparing it with the standard or preset temperature. If the preset temperature is higher than the sensed temperature, the thermostat turns on the furnace to reduce this discrepancy, bringing the sensed temperature (feedback) in line with the preset temperature (standard). Now, what does a thermostat have to do with motivation? A quick look at one of the best-articulated and empirically supported control theories of motivation—developed by Charles Carver and Michael Scheier—will provide an answer. **Figure 9.5** presents a simple graphical representation of a control system.

According to Carver and Scheier (1998), most behaviors entail feedback control. Consider the following scenario:

> If your standard for a day's work is to "be productive," how do you decide at day's end whether you've met your goal? You look at the hard evidence of what you've done, and you look at some concrete comparison point (guidelines provided by a work assignment, or perhaps performance of other people engaged in similar activity). In sum, to compare your behavior against an abstract standard, you often seek out concrete information that facilitates the abstract comparison. (p. 32)

This very simple principle has given rise to a complicated but useful theory of motivation. The basics of Carver and Scheier's theory stem largely from earlier work on control theory, but these authors have developed many important related issues that have helped researchers gain a better understanding of motivation. For instance, they have conducted many studies demonstrating that the more self-focused individuals are, the more often they engage the feedback loop and concentrate on comparisons that reveal information about existing discrepancies (Carver & Scheier, 1998). By *self-focused*, the authors

**FIGURE 9.5** **Control System** (Source: Information from Lord & Levy (1994) in *Applied Psychology: An International Review. Moving from cognition to action: A control theory perspective.*)

mean simply the degree to which individuals focus attention on themselves. Being self-focused, they argue, is more likely than not being self-focused to lead to reactions (both affective and behavioral) that stem from perceiving a discrepancy (when a discrepancy exists) between one's standard and feedback.

The scenario I just borrowed from Carver and Scheier seems quite simple, but their theory points out that the process of gathering, receiving, and interpreting feedback from various sources is quite complex. Think back to Chapter 5, in which we discussed the use of 360-degree feedback in organizations for the purposes of individual development, as well as more formal performance appraisal processes. Obviously, individuals are presented with a wealth of feedback from a 360-degree system, and sorting out and choosing which feedback to use in the feedback loop is a complicated issue. I mention this here only to reiterate that although examples can be simplified to better illustrate control theory and its processes, the theory's operation is, in actuality, much more complex.

For example, control theory has been used to focus on the volitional and strategic elements of motivation (Diefendorff & Lord, 2003). Researchers have demonstrated that individuals who were volitional and formed implemental intentions (i.e., specific goals and a plan for acting on those goals) performed better than those who did not, regardless of their particular strategy. However, strategy quality interacted with implemental intentions to result in the best performance. Thus, both volitional and strategic domains are important parts of the motivational system. In a large-scale review, researchers have recently found that implementation intentions have a sizable effect on goal attainment (Gollwitzer & Sheeran, 2006).

Carver and Scheier (1998) have argued that people are goal-directed and that we use not only goals but also intentions, values, and wishes in our daily lives to move forward. Furthermore, researchers have presented an interesting application of control theory to emotions, explaining the process through which individuals regulate their emotional displays over time (Diefendorff & Gosserand, 2003). However, we don't always reach our goals—and when it appears as though we aren't going to make it, we have an important decision to make: Persevere or throw in the towel? Carver and Scheier suggest that giving up—what they call *disengagement*—is not always a bad thing. Indeed, they argue that it is a natural and necessary part of self-regulation. There are times when a goal is unattainable, and continuing to shoot for it can have serious detrimental effects on one's psychological well-being and ultimate success. But the essential point here is that both continued effort and giving up are necessary parts of adaptive self-regulation. Think about the time you were shooting for an A in a particular class but kept getting Cs on the exams. At some point, revisiting your goal and making an adjustment to it probably helped you move forward (perhaps you passed the course with a B and learned something about yourself in the process). Or imagine a work situation in which you are focused on achieving $10,000 in sales for the quarter, but as the weeks go by, it becomes clear that this goal is unattainable because of a downturn in the economy. Are you better served by continuing to bang your head against the wall or by reevaluating your goal and attempting to move forward toward another reasonable goal?

Hopefully, you see that the answer to this question is to go easy on your head and come up with an alternative goal that is still motivating, resulting in individual and organizational productivity. This holds for supervisors as well in the sense that it can be wise for them to take a step back and help employees readjust their goals downward when that appears to be a reasonable strategy.

# APPLICATIONS OF MOTIVATIONAL THEORIES TO ORGANIZATIONAL PROBLEMS

The first half of the chapter was spent looking at the most popular and empirically supported theories of motivation. Given that I/O psychology is an applied field with applied goals and issues, the rest of this chapter is devoted to applications of these theories to real-world organizational problems, including a discussion of how organizations can and do impact employee motivation. Of course, there are many applied ways that organizations can impact the motivation of their employees; I'll present a few of them here.

## Organizational Behavior Management

Behavior analysis is a science that seeks to understand the behavior of individuals by analyzing environmental influences. It has two main branches: experimental behavior analysis and applied behavior analysis (American Psychological Association, 2015). Applied behavior analysis has emerged from the basic experimental scholarship and has had considerable success in helping psychologists understand behaviors of social or personal importance. The **organizational behavior management (OBM)** approach to improving motivation and performance in organizations is one application area or approach within the broader domain of applied behavior analysis. OBM can be defined as the application of the principles of behavioral psychology to the study and control of individual and group behavior within organizational settings.

OBM has been applied to organizations across the globe and typically focuses on the ABC model: A stands for the *antecedents* of the behavior, B stands for the *behavior* itself, and C stands for the *consequences* of the behavior (Wilder, Austin, & Casella, 2009). It is important that the antecedents for desired behaviors be in place within the organization. For instance, employees must have the equipment and training to be able to do the job well. But the consequences are perhaps the most important part of this approach, as they are the rewards that follow the desired behaviors. These can range from seemingly small rewards such as verbal recognition to large rewards such as a salary bonus or additional vacation days. We are beginning to see more work on what is called *pay for performance* (see Cadsby, Song, & Tapon, 2007; Rynes, Gerhart, & Parks, 2005), which is one direct way to link consequences to behaviors. The better employees perform, the more

**organizational behavior management (OBM)** The application of the principles of behavioral psychology to the study and control of individual and group behavior within organizational settings.

## TECHNICAL TIP

*In Chapter 8 we talked at length about the needs analysis that is so necessary to identify specific training needs in an organization. Targeting the behaviors that need to be changed as a part of this behavior approach is quite similar to a needs analysis.*

they get paid. This behavioral approach to the management of human resources can be summarized in five steps (Stajkovic & Luthans, 1997). First, the behaviors that need to be changed are targeted. This step is much like a needs analysis that is done in the area of training. Second, the targeted behaviors are measured so that the organization has a baseline against which to compare behaviors that occur after the intervention. Third, the links between both current rewards and punishments and behaviors are examined. Fourth, the organization intervenes with a program that sets goals concerning the targeted

ColorBlind Images/Getty Images

**A CLOSER LOOK**
In what ways do awards and rewards motivate people?

behaviors and links various rewards to the attainment of those goals. Finally, there is an evaluation phase in which the success of the intervention is determined by comparing resultant behaviors with baseline behaviors in terms of the program's goals.

OBM has been used extensively in organizations (Wilder et al., 2009). Let's look at one example in the area of safety improvement, where OBM has been very popular (Grindle, Dickinson, & Boettcher, 2000). An injury prevention model was applied in a large industrial plant to reduce lost time due to injuries and to increase safety behaviors (Sulzer-Azaroff, Loafman, Merante, & Hlavacek, 1990). Three departments with the highest injury rates were identified; the number of employees totaled about 250. The researchers identified behavioral targets for each department and observed behaviors such as safe lifting of heavy materials, use of safety glasses and appropriate safety shoes, immediate clean-up of wet floors, and storage of chemicals in designated areas. In addition, they recorded accident data, including medical visits and lost time due to injuries or accidents.

After implementing the intervention program, which included meetings about safety, weekly safety posters, small rewards and reinforcements, and setting of goals, the researchers noted some drastic improvements. First, safety behavior goals were attained at a rate of over 90% across departments. Second, this period was the best in the history of the company in terms of injury rate and person-hours worked. Third, workers' comments about the program and the improvements were overwhelmingly positive. Results like these are typical of OBM programs, demonstrating the usefulness of this approach in improving motivation and performance behaviors. In fact, a meta-analysis (Stajkovic & Luthans, 1997) reported an average effect of .5 standard deviation on performance ($d$ effect size = .51). What this tells us is that the use of OBM, which is based on reinforcement theory, resulted in a sizable performance improvement in the various companies studied.

**TECHNICAL TIP**

Remember that a standard deviation indicates how much spread there is in a set of data. It can also be used to indicate the size or magnitude of an effect. A .5 standard deviation means that the difference in performance between those who use OBM and those who don't is quite sizable.

## Goal Setting and Management by Objectives

Goal-setting theory has received considerable attention from practitioners and has been applied across the world in every type of organization imaginable with very consistent success. Let's look at one recent example of a study conducted by behavior analysts applying the science of applied behavior analysis. Since pizza delivery has become such a huge industry (perhaps nowhere more so than on college campuses!), delivery drivers' safety has become a subject of concern. Pizza deliverers have accident rates that are three times higher than the national average, resulting in fatalities and personal injuries that cost companies millions of dollars (Ludwig & Geller, 1997, 2000). In a 1997 study, pizza deliverers ($N = 324$) from three different pizza stores were observed going out on and returning from deliveries. Observers were stationed in the windows of nearby businesses with a clear view of the streets on which the pizza stores were situated. Three specific behaviors were observed: (1) whether the drivers used their seat belts, (2) whether the drivers used their turn signals when leaving or entering the pizza store's parking lot, and (3) whether the drivers made a complete, slow-rolling, or fast-rolling stop when entering the street from the store's parking lot.

These three behaviors were observed for six weeks to establish a baseline. At this point, deliverers were randomly assigned into a participative-goal, an assigned-goal, or a control condition. Those in the participative-goal group took part in a discussion-based meeting, participative goal setting, and four weeks of group feedback. Those in the assigned-goal group took part in a lecture-based meeting, were assigned a goal (the same goal that was arrived at participatively in the participative-goal group), and underwent four weeks of group feedback. The control group received no intervention at all. The targeted behavior in all three conditions was the percentage of complete stops, and the goal in both goal-setting conditions was 75%.

**Figure 9.6** presents a summary of the observation data for four periods: the six-week baseline phase, the four-week intervention phase, the four-week withdrawal phase (after the feedback posters were removed), and the ten- to eleven-week follow-up phase. The data clearly indicate that both the participative-goal and assigned-goal groups made a larger

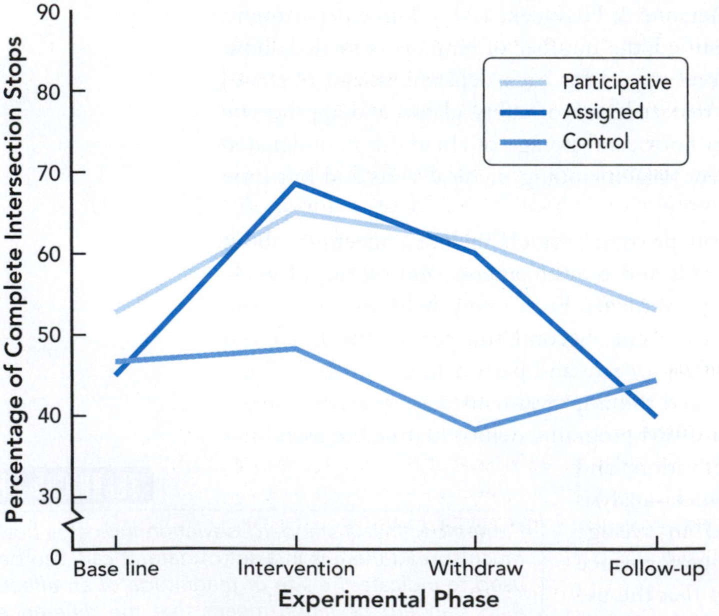

**FIGURE 9.6** Pizza Delivery Results—Intersection Stops (Source: Ludwig & Geller (1997))

number of complete intersection stops and that this improvement in safety behavior continued for some time (though for longer in the participative-goal than in the assigned-goal condition).

Interestingly, the observers also coded other behaviors that were not part of the intervention, including seat belt use. (Although seat belt use was observed, it was never mentioned in the meetings, nor was group feedback ever presented on this behavior.) **Figure 9.7** presents the relevant data for seat belt use. Here, only participative goal setting seemed to improve safety behaviors and to maintain that improvement— an especially interesting outcome given that seat belt use was not part of the intervention. Apparently, participative goal setting that

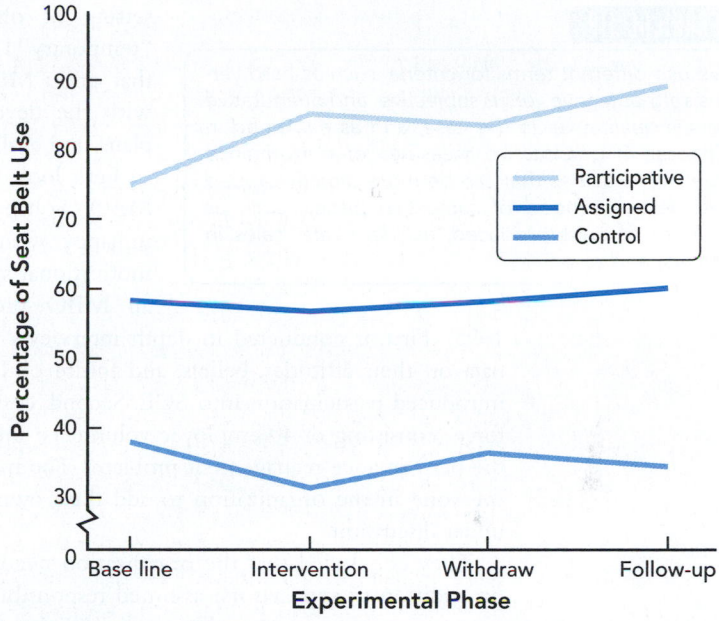

**FIGURE 9.7** Pizza Delivery Results—Seat Belt Use (Source: Ludwig & Geller (1997))

focused on one particular safety behavior improved other safety behaviors as well. (Similar results were found for turn signal use.) The power of goal-setting programs like this one is very clear: People respond very effectively to feedback that is coupled with difficult, specific goals.

Another practical application of goal setting involves what is called *management by objectives (MBO),* a managerial technique widely used in the Western world since the late 1950s (Pinder, 1998). MBO dates back to the work of Peter Drucker at both General Motors and General Electric. Drucker's approach to management centers on the importance of performance objectives and involves two essential factors: (1) a system for establishing work-related goals and (2) a procedure for assessing a person's performance as compared with those goals.

The MBO process consists of four basic stages. First, managers and subordinates participatively set objectives for subordinates over a specified time period. For instance, they may agree on an increase in sales of 15% over the next six-month period. Second, subordinates develop an action plan, or how-to map, describing the ways in which they intend to achieve those goals. In our current example, it would stipulate the manner in which subordinates will increase sales by 15% and might include a marketing strategy, subgoals for the development of new business contacts, and so on. Third, at the end of the period, managers conduct a performance review that examines the progress made since the last formal meeting, when the objectives were set. Finally, the process comes to a temporary conclusion with the participative

*We use different terms for criteria, such as hard ver-sus soft, objective versus subjective, and quantitative versus qualitative. In this case, and as explained in Chapter 4, quantitative measures of performance refer to measures that can be more directly tapped with less likelihood of subjective biases, such as number of units produced, accident rate, sales in dollars, and so on.*

setting of objectives for the next period. By "temporary" I mean that this phase is the only one that ends; MBO continues in a cyclical manner with the development of new objectives, action plans, and evaluations over time.

Let's look at an example of an application of MBO. Southern California Edison (SCE) was unhappy with its performance management and motivational system and thus began implementing an MBO program (Moravec, Juliff, & Hesler, 1995). First, it conducted in-depth interviews with employees to gather important data on their attitudes, beliefs, and future outlooks with regard to SCE. This step introduced participation into SCE. Second, consultants were hired to oversee a task force (consisting of 40 employee volunteers) intended to generate some solutions to the performance management problems. The members of this task force encouraged everyone in the organization to add their own perspective to the important issues under discussion.

They concluded that the organization needed a system in which (1) employees (in addition to supervisors) assumed responsibility; (2) the focus was on values and future growth, not past problems; and (3) the discussion was not a control tool but, rather, supported a partnership between employees and supervisors. The new MBO system emphasized that supervisors and employees should collaboratively define objectives, develop strategies to attain the objectives, determine ways to measure performance relative to the objectives, and then periodically reevaluate the objectives and adjust them where appropriate. Both supervisors and employees reported that this program had been successful, noting that they felt energized by becoming active participants and appreciated the enhanced openness that had become the culture in the company.

According to a meta-analysis of the MBO literature, 97% of the evaluation studies reviewed found increases in productivity; the mean rise in productivity across those studies with quantitative measures of performance was over 40% (Rodgers & Hunter, 1991). This finding suggests that an organization that was producing 100 units of its product per month prior to an MBO intervention is likely to produce 140 units per month after the intervention. The meta-analysis also revealed that MBO programs tend to result in greater performance improvement when they are supported by upper-level management. This observation is consistent with what we know about most organizational interventions: Support from the top is often necessary for their success. We will see other examples of this in the remainder of the book.

© Robert Garvey/Corbis

**A CLOSER LOOK**

Why do more frequent collaborative meetings between management and workers to define goals tend to affect performance and outcomes?

## Job Enrichment

We have already discussed job characteristics theory, Hackman and Oldham's (1980) model of job design that stemmed from Herzberg's earlier work on two-factor theory. One way in which organizations apply this approach to job design is through job enrichment. **Job enrichment** is the process of increasing the motivating potential of jobs—specifically, by strengthening the key motivating characteristics identified by job characteristics theory. Let's briefly look at a couple of organizational interventions along these lines.

Our first example concerns an article about improving the teaching of psychology that argues for the use of job characteristics theory for "course enrichment"—a process similar to job enrichment. The author specifically proposes that the job characteristics model can serve as a theoretical framework for increasing the motivational potential of college courses (Catanzaro, 1997). She suggests that instructors can increase skill variety among students by requiring a wider range of skills through varied written and oral assignments.

For instance, in an I/O course, the instructor could (1) ask students to write about how theories of motivation are used by employers and employees at their place of employment; (2) structure a debate that considers the pros and cons of affirmative action; (3) illustrate task significance through applications of what is learned in class and discussions of their implications for organizations and employees; or (4) give an assignment that requires students to conduct a job analysis of some real job (e.g., interviewing incumbents) or to develop a proposal that outlines a potential selection battery for their current position. Each of the five core job dimensions we discussed earlier (skill variety, task identity, task significance, autonomy, feedback) could be emphasized in the design of such a course in order to enrich its content and increase its motivating potential. A study of over 200 psychology students found that four of these five core dimensions were related to outcome measures such as course motivation, satisfaction, and performance (Bloom, Yorges, & Ruhl, 2000).

**job enrichment**
The process of increasing the motivating potential of jobs, often by strengthening the key motivating characteristics identified by job characteristics theory.

## Job Crafting

In this chapter I've talked about motivation at work and provided both overviews of general theories and details of precise theories. Among the topics we covered were job design and job enrichment. I'd like to close this chapter by providing some information and ideas about some newer approaches and conceptualizations with respect to jobs. A recent special issue of the *Journal of Organizational Behavior* (Vol. 31, Issues 2–3) was titled "Putting Job Design in Context." This fascinating issue argued that jobs (and organizations) have changed so dramatically over the past few decades that new questions have emerged with respect to the nature and design of jobs (Grant, Fried, Parker, & Frese, 2010).

In the final piece published in this special issue, Oldham and Hackman (2010) write about **job crafting**, in which employees have the flexibility to customize or modify their own job. This is an interesting idea, but we don't know much about it. The authors raise some interesting questions. For instance, do the benefits that accrue from job crafting result from the changing of the job or the participation and

**job crafting**
The process through which employees are allowed to customize, modify, and craft their own job with respect to tasks, responsibilities, and processes.

involvement of employees in making the changes? If the benefits do result from the actual job crafting, what leads to these changes? Why are people more productive and more satisfied after job crafting? Who is more likely to want to participate in job crafting? Who is more likely to follow through with it? What are the characteristics of supervisors who allow and encourage job crafting?

Although we don't have well-supported answers to these questions, we are beginning to learn more about this interesting phenomenon. One study argues that the manner in which job crafting plays out is largely affected by one's place in the organization (Berg, Wrzesniewski, & Dutton, 2010). Interviews of 16 higher-ranked employees (e.g., senior managers) and 17 lower-ranked employees (e.g., associates) uncovered interesting differences. Employees in lower-ranked jobs identified others as the barriers to job crafting—limits imposed on them by supervisors and others did not give them the power to craft their jobs. Therefore, they focused on being adaptive and proactively acting on opportunities that arose to gain support for crafting. Employees in higher-ranked jobs, on the other hand, saw themselves as the biggest obstacles to crafting. They often felt limited by their expectations of how they and others *should* do their work. Therefore, they focused on adjusting their own expectations and making changes where they saw possibilities. Ironically, it appeared as if higher-ranked employees actually saw less opportunity for job crafting because of self-imposed constraints, whereas lower-ranked employees saw more opportunities and worked intentionally to alter their environments and adjust others' expectations.

A daily diary study that measured job crafting constructs from employees in the Netherlands for five consecutive days produced some interesting findings. Among the most intriguing was that the relationship between job crafting and work engagement (see the Practitioner Forum in this chapter for more discussion of engagement) demonstrated a motivational role for job crafting (Petrou, Demerouti, Peeters, Schaufeli, & Hetland, 2012). The authors conceptualized job crafting in light of demands and resources, and their results suggest both positive and negative consequences. They found that seeking daily challenges was positively correlated with work engagement and that seeking to reduce demands on a daily basis was negatively correlated with work engagement. In another daily diary study, it was found that when employees felt more self-efficacious on a given day, they were more likely to mobilize resources for job crafting on that day, resulting in greater enjoyment at work, which related positively to their job performance on that day (Tims, Bakker, & Derks, 2012). This study clearly shows the potential positive impact of job crafting through employee enjoyment and performance.

Denise Rousseau has introduced the idea of *idiosyncratic deals* (i-deals) in which employees negotiate with supervisors about their own job conditions and arrangements (Rousseau, 2001). A recent study demonstrated that more successfully negotiated i-deals followed from leader–subordinate relationships characterized as favorable (Hornung, Rousseau, Glaser, Angerer, & Weigl, 2010). Further, the i-deals were related to more favorable job characteristics, greater employee initiative, and more employee engagement. A recent longitudinal study of managers in the United

## PRACTITIONER FORUM

Anne Herman

### Anne Herman

*PhD, 2008, I/O Psychology,*
*University of Nebraska, Omaha*
*Senior Vice President, Analytics and Performance,*
*United Way of the Midlands*

This chapter does a great job of outlining the different motivational theories you'll see operating across different aspects of the workspace. Over the past decade, one of the most common areas where many of these theories have converged, and so where many researchers are now focusing, has been in how to create an engaged workforce.

Much of the energy relating to work motivation in organizations is focused on engaging current employees and, to a lesser extent, finding and attracting talent that has the capacity to be engaged. There is a reason for this: There is substantial evidence that organizations that show higher levels of engagement also show better results with respect to customers, financial performance, and employee retention.

Though different engagement models are used, they all include a commitment to and involvement in the organization. Most believe that the state of being engaged results in higher discretionary effort put forth.

Since 2008, many clients and other organizations have asked me if the challenging economic climate is causing lower engagement levels in the workforce. Both my practice experience and research generally show that it is still possible to maintain strong levels of and/or improve employee engagement. Almost all companies have been confronted with significant challenges not seen in the past 50 years. Many organizations have had to make difficult decisions around divesting lines of business, engaging in other types of restructuring, and even examining and taking action on staff redundancies. But it has been possible to continue to cultivate motivated and engaged employees.

The organizations that have been better at keeping workers engaged, and have in many cases also experienced better business performance, did well on three primary criteria: (1) They took action on what mattered most to their employees' engagement. (2) Their executive leadership did the best they could to keep employees informed about what was happening (strong communication) and to provide a vision of the future that instilled confidence and was motivating. (3) They created environments where the focus was on the customer, and employees had the tools they needed to fulfill organizational goals.

No doubt we will learn much more about how to engage workers as research continues in this complex area.

### Applying Your Knowledge

1. Why do you think engagement is so crucial to an organization's success?

2. How much do you feel people are internally motivated versus incentivized through various leadership and organizational strategies?

3. Of the three criteria outlined above relating to worker engagement and better organizational outcomes, which do think is the most important? Why?

States and China found that managers who receive more i-deals also tend to exhibit more behaviors to strengthen and help the organization. Further, the relationship between i-deals and voice behavior was mediated by things like having a flexible orientation at work, building social networks, and trusting the organization (Ng & Feldman, 2015). Clearly, the receipt of i-deals can have very positive effects on employee behaviors, which impact organizational outcomes.

In another study, these same authors were interested in whether the promise of future i-deals could make up for past breaches of promises. In other words, if a company has violated a psychological contract (i.e., employees' beliefs about mutual obligations and expectations between themselves and their employers) with its employees, is the promise of future i-deals an effective way to rebuild that relationship? The authors found that the effect of past breaches on affective commitment was weaker when future i-deals were promised and the employees perceived many external job opportunities (Ng & Feldman, 2012). The authors conclude that breaches may not strongly affect these employees because of the options they perceive outside the organization and also because they see the promise of future i-deals as an indicator of their competence and, thus, they deem themselves likely to be competitive for those external opportunities. However, when promised future i-deals in a market in which they don't see many external options, employees tend to believe that the future i-deals will be violated just like the past psychological contract was. These results suggest a complex arrangement in which both the promise of future i-deals and the external job opportunities are important. We need a great deal more research on concepts like job crafting and i-deals because there is much more to learn about the nature of jobs in our dynamic work context.

## Summary

Few topics in I/O psychology have been as thoroughly explored as work motivation. In the first part of this chapter, I presented the most commonly cited theories of work motivation; in the second part, I focused on applications of these theories to organizational problems. Three sets of theories were considered: need–motive–value theories, cognitive choice theories, and self-regulation theories. Although need–motive–value theories are no longer as well accepted by researchers and academics as they were 40 years ago, they are still popular in business settings. First, we discussed Maslow's hierarchy of needs; then we examined two approaches that are related to Maslow's work, ERG theory and two-factor theory. Job characteristics theory and cognitive evaluation theory were also considered in this category, as they clarify the different motivational potentials that are inherent in jobs and people.

Cognitive choice theories, which view motivation and behavior as rational processes rather than as a function of inherent needs or values, were discussed in terms of two important theories: equity theory and expectancy theory. The latter—presented in the context of VIE theory—was described as the most rational theory of them all. Each of its three components was discussed in terms of recent meta-analytic research on expectancy theory. The conclusion drawn was that these three components seem related to motivation, though not always in the multiplicative manner predicted by the theory.

Self-regulation theories were discussed last. In this context, goal-setting theory was presented as one of the simplest and most empirically supported models of work motivation. Social cognitive theories were described as extensions of goal-setting theory that provide potential explanations for why goals are so important to individual motivation and performance. All three sets of theories have received a great deal of attention in the literature, some of which was reviewed in the text.

In the second part of the chapter, I presented applications of motivation theories to organizations. OBM was discussed as a very successful technique (particularly in the area of improving organizational safety) that stems from reinforcement theory. A similar approach was followed with respect to goal setting and management by objectives. There appears to be a great deal of support for these goal-based interventions as well. Finally, I discussed job enrichment and its potential for organizational improvement. In addition, some of the more cutting-edge thinking around job crafting and idiosyncratic deals was presented, and a series of questions was generated that could drive future research.

## Key Terms

equity sensitivity (p. 295)
expectancy (p. 296)
growth need strength (p. 289)
instrumentality (p. 297)
job crafting (p. 309)
job enrichment (p. 309)
need (p. 284)
organizational behavior management
    (OBM) (p. 304)

organizational justice (p. 295)
organizational psychology (p. 282)
positive psychology (p. 287)
self-efficacy expectations (p. 300)
self-regulation (p. 299)
valence (value) (p. 297)
work motivation (p. 283)

## TAKING IT TO THE FIELD

Many companies struggle with motivating their employees—a problem that consultants frequently see among their clients. Thus, it is important to know which theories of motivation have empirical support and how each theory can be applied to an actual situation. One of your clients, Ken Cooper, has been struggling with keeping his employees motivated at Blues Bus Tours, Inc., a small tour company in Nashville. Ken has received some advice, but he would like a second opinion. Provide a critique of the advice he has received, and provide an additional, empirically-supported intervention that he might consider trying.

Hello—
Thanks for being willing to talk with me on such short notice. Recently, our tour guides have been unmotivated—they are coming into work late and putting forth the minimal amount of effort. We've been receiving more complaints from clients, and we're starting to get worried that this will impact our bottom line. However, there simply aren't very many people around who are a good fit for leading tours (it requires that they be away from home for long periods of time, so people with families have some difficulty with the job). So I would rather try to motivate the

employees I have than try to replace them. I spoke with a colleague who used to work in an HR department, and she suggested the following solutions:

- Tour guides are unmotivated because the job is too complex. According to the job characteristics model, tour guides should have only a few simple tasks that are clearly outlined in an employee handbook, and these tasks should be done the same way on every tour.

- Both equity theory and two-factor theory suggest that paying employees more will get them to work harder. You should give all the unmotivated tour guides raises to help with this issue.

- So what do you think? Should I follow this advice? What might be one other thing I could do to help motivate my employees, and what theory supports its use?

Thanks!
Ken

## Critical Thinking Questions

1. What on-the-job behaviors would you expect an employee with a high level of motivation to demonstrate?

2. What are some ways that managers or instructors have attempted to motivate you? Did it work? Which theory of work motivation do you believe best relates to your examples?

3. As noted in this chapter, studies on job crafting have found that seeking out daily challenges is positively correlated to work engagement, whereas seeking out reduced demands is negatively correlated. What reasons might account for this relationship?

4. Under what circumstances do you think pay-for-performance systems motivate or fail to motivate employees? Why? Please couch your answer in terms of the motivation theories discussed in this chapter.

5. What is one area (at work or in school) where you feel you have high self-efficacy, and one area where it is low? How has this affected your motivation? Your performance? What are some steps you might take to improve self-efficacy in areas where it is low?

## Application Questions

1. Imagine you have a friend who is currently dissatisfied with her job. She feels that she puts a great deal of effort and time into her job yet is passed over for promotions and awards. What would you suggest she do to feel more motivated about her job?

2. Interview a friend, family member, or associate about his or her work environment. Consider the three needs for optimal health and well-being, as described in Ryan and Deci's self-determination theory: *competence, relatedness,* and *autonomy.* Based

on your interview, what interventions would you recommend to this person's employer to meet these needs?

3. Consider the job of a babysitter. Based on control theory, what are some examples of feedback that babysitters might look for to determine whether they're doing a good job? Where might they look to find a "standard" for babysitters that they can compare to their own behaviors to determine whether they are successful?

4. The manager of a graphic design studio wants to improve the quality of his company's output. He decides he is going to set a goal for his staff: "We will make $100,000 in commissions within the next three months." What are some problems with his goal? What would you suggest as a more effective goal?

5. A company has fired a department manager after repeated complaints from his staff that he failed to meet with them for performance reviews or provide them with adequate feedback on their work. The new manager wants to use the i-deals model to build a better supervisor–subordinate relationship with her team. What are some challenges she might face in instituting this new system? What ways might she be able to overcome these challenges?

6. Job crafting is a relatively new idea in the field. What are some advantages of allowing employees to customize their own jobs? What are some disadvantages? Have you had opportunities to craft your own job?

## Suggested Readings

**Greenberg, J., & Colquitt, J. A. (Eds.).** (2005). *Handbook of organizational justice.* Mahwah, NJ: Erlbaum. This volume, edited by two prominent researchers on the topic, is a great overview of recent thinking about organizational justice.

**Latham, G. P.** (2012). *Work motivation: History, theory, research, and practice.* Thousand Oaks, CA: SAGE. This is a terrific book by a leading motivational scholar who makes this text very user-friendly.

**Latham, G. P., & Budworth, M.** (2008). The study of work motivation in the 20th century. In L. L. Koppes (Ed.), *Historical perspectives in industrial and organizational psychology* (pp. 353–382). Mahwah, NJ: Erlbaum. This is a great resource for any psychology history buff; this particular chapter does a thorough job of tracing developments in work motivation.

**Pinder, C. C.** (2014). *Work motivation in organizational behavior.* Upper Saddle River, NJ: Psychology Press. My personal favorite! I've used Pinder's earlier book in my classes for almost 20 years and highly recommend this newer version as well. It is a very complete treatment of motivation, written at a level that makes it accessible for undergraduates as well as graduate students.

**Steers, R. M., Mowday, R. T., & Shapiro, D. L.** (2004). Introduction to special topic forum: The future of work motivation theory. *Academy of Management Review, 29*(3), 379–387. This is the introduction to a special issue on work motivation in one of the field's most respected journals. This paper gives a nice overview of the historical development of work motivation, and the other papers spend considerable time looking to the future and setting a research agenda for the field.

# Job Attitudes: Antecedents and Consequences

Photo: Odilon Dimier/PhotoAlto/Getty Images

## LEARNING OBJECTIVES

This chapter should help you understand:

- The role played by attitudes in predicting behavior
- Why attitudes are sometimes unrelated to behavior
- What job satisfaction is and how it is measured
- What determines a person's level of job satisfaction
- How job satisfaction affects important organizational outcome variables
- The three major components of organizational commitment
- What determines a person's commitment to his or her organization
- What commitment profiles are
- How organizational commitment affects important organizational outcome variables
- What types of withdrawal behaviors are important to organizations
- What types of counterproductive behaviors are concerns for organizations
- The role played by emotional labor in organizations
- The effect that perceived organizational support has on employee attitudes and behaviors

Have you ever had a job you didn't like? Did the fact that you didn't like the job affect your performance? Why didn't you like the job? Was it your supervisor, coworkers, the work itself, or the pay that led to your dissatisfaction? Do you say good things to people about your current company, school, or institution, or do you give the impression that you'd rather work anywhere but there? Do you identify with your job, occupation, or college major? In other words, is what you do an important part of who you are, or is it just something you do? All of these questions have to do with job-related attitudes, which are the focus of this chapter.

Like most of us, you've probably experienced the anger and frustration that come with working in a job you don't like. There's the feeling that you're wasting your time, and each minute of the day seems like an hour. Even routine tasks, which by themselves should not be so unpleasant, become unbearable. These negative experiences can become so pervasive that their effects trickle into other parts of your life. Before you know it, you're arguing with your spouse or your mom more frequently and running out of patience with your friends or children more quickly. On the other hand, when you really love your job, your thoughts are occupied not with the tasks you have to do at work but, rather, with the opportunities and programs that you get to experience, and you want people to know what you do for a living and why it's the best job in the world.

The difference between a job that we hate and one that we love is very real. In this chapter, we will discuss job satisfaction because this is the attitude that organizations seem most interested in and researchers know the most about. We will also discuss organizational commitment, work centrality, job involvement, perceived organizational support, and emotional labor.

## ATTITUDES, INTENTIONS, AND BEHAVIORS

In I/O psychology, when we talk of attitudes, we are usually interested in the relationship between attitudes and intentions or behaviors. In this context, an intention is one's tendency or proclivity to act. An attitude can be defined as the degree of positive or negative feeling or belief a person has toward a particular person, place, or thing (Fishbein & Ajzen, 1975). As you might imagine, humans have many work-related attitudes. These have to do with supervisors, coworkers, the job environment, the work that is done on the job, and even the amount of respect received on the job.

**attitude**
The degree of positive or negative feeling or belief a person has toward a particular person, place, or thing.

### Why Study Job Attitudes?

Before we delve into job attitudes, it makes sense to understand why such attitudes are important. First, it has long been assumed that job attitudes influence work behavior, which explains why managers and executives are so interested in them. Second, for humanitarian reasons, improving employees' job attitudes is a desirable goal in and of itself. As Edwin Locke (1976) notes, happiness is the goal of life—and making people happy at work should be a goal of organizations. Third, studying job attitudes can help us understand the complexities of our work lives as well as of our nonwork lives. For these reasons and others, researchers and practitioners alike have been, and continue to be, very interested in job attitudes. However, before exploring specific job-related attitudes, we need to examine a popular model of the attitude–behavior relationship.

### A Useful Model

The *theory of planned behavior*, as it is known, was developed from an earlier model called the *theory of reasoned action* by Icek Ajzen and his colleagues (Ajzen & Fishbein, 1980; Ajzen & Madden, 1986; Fishbein & Ajzen, 1975). It is a rational choice model much like expectancy theory and equity theory, discussed in Chapter 9 in the context of cognitive choice theories of motivation. These researchers subscribe to the view that people consider the implications of their actions before deciding whether to engage in a particular behavior (Ajzen & Fishbein, 1980). From this perspective, the determinants of an action are one's intentions to perform the action (Ajzen & Fishbein, 1980). Thus, in a sense, predicting behaviors is not that difficult; if we want to predict whether an employee will work hard on a particular project, the most efficient approach is to ask her whether she intends to work hard. All else being equal, there should be a fairly strong relationship between her intention and her behavior.

Because our goal is to understand human behavior, however, just knowing that someone does what she intends to do is not that illuminating. We need to be able to predict the intention as well. This is where attitudes come into play. The theory

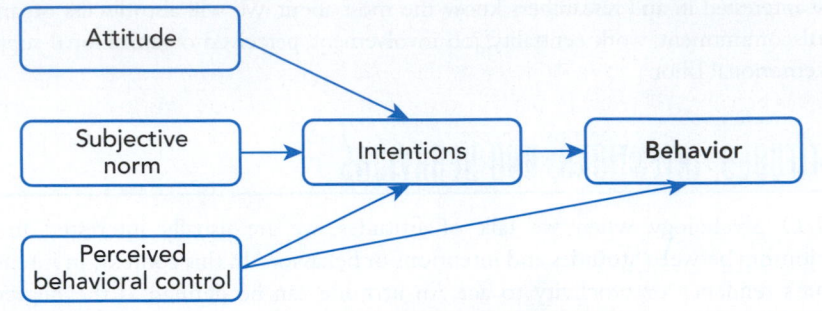

**FIGURE 10.1** **Theory of Planned Behavior** (Information from Ajzen & Madden, 1986)

of planned behavior is useful here because it depicts the relationships among attitudes, intentions, and behaviors (Ajzen & Fishbein, 2005; Ajzen & Madden, 1986). **Figure 10.1** presents a simplified version of the model, which clearly shows that attitudes and subjective norms affect intentions, which in turn affect behaviors. A **subjective norm** is an individual's perception of the social pressures to perform or not perform a particular behavior. The theory of planned behavior maintains that a person's intention to act is a function of both the subjective norm for that act and his attitude toward that act. For example, he will intend to meet his deadline if meeting deadlines is the norm at his office and if he has a positive attitude about meeting deadlines. The theory also maintains that his intention to meet the deadline is the best predictor of whether his actions will result in him actually meeting the deadline.

As shown in Figure 10.1, **perceived behavioral control** is also an important element of the theory. Perceived behavioral control is the individual's belief about how easy or difficult performance of the behavior is likely to be (Ajzen & Madden, 1986). Although an individual may be favorably disposed to a particular act and perceive the social norms as being in favor of the act, she may not perceive that she has any control over performance of the act. For instance, a factory worker may recognize that the norm is to produce 200 units of product per eight-hour shift; she may also want to achieve this level of performance. But if she believes that this action is out of her control because of equipment breakdowns, this perceived behavioral control should be considered when predicting her behavior. In effect, she won't produce 200 units because of a lack of control.

This calls to mind the role played by expectancy in the motivational model known as *VIE theory* (see Chapter 9, page 296). You may recall that no matter how valued or instrumental a certain performance level is, if the individual does not believe that a particular amount of effort can lead to that performance level, there will be no motivation to exhibit that level of effort. The theory of planned behavior goes one step further in suggesting that even if an employee has an intention to exhibit the behavior, if she perceives that she can't do so because of a lack of control, she won't.

**subjective norm**
An individual's perception of the social pressures to perform or not perform a particular behavior.

**perceived behavioral control**
An individual's belief about how easy or difficult performance of a behavior is likely to be.

**TECHNICAL TIP**

*Recall that VIE theory proposes that individuals' behaviors result from conscious choices based on perceptions of value, instrumentality, and expectancy.*

The work of Ajzen and his colleagues is important as we proceed with our discussion of crucial job attitudes. The theory of planned behavior will become even more useful as we try to make sense of the relationships between specific job attitudes and job behaviors. We will revisit this theory from time to time as a way of explaining some of the empirical findings in the I/O literature on attitudes and behaviors. Let's turn to the most important of these attitudes: job satisfaction.

## JOB SATISFACTION

Job satisfaction is one of the most researched areas of I/O psychology, in part because it has long been viewed as relevant for organizational effectiveness; it is an aspect of the attitude–behavior link discussed earlier, but in an applied setting.

Job satisfaction interests all of us. In fact, we all seem to have an opinion on the subject. Some insist that the key to job satisfaction is money; others claim that it's working conditions; still others believe that it's employee input. The list goes on and on—and it makes for lively discussions at work and in the grocery store but does not always help us to understand the construct. So let's get a bit more scientific. According to Locke (1976), job satisfaction can be defined as a pleasurable, positive emotional state resulting from the cognitive appraisal of one's job or job experiences. The same author notes that job satisfaction stems from our perceptions that our jobs are fulfilling. In other words, we tend to be satisfied in our jobs if we believe that we are getting what we want out of them. Note also that job satisfaction has both an affective component (emotional state) and a cognitive component (the appraisal or evaluation). We will return to this shortly.

**job satisfaction**
A pleasurable, positive emotional state resulting from the cognitive appraisal of one's job or job experiences.

### Antecedents

**Figure 10.2** presents a framework for studying and thinking about job satisfaction. On the left side of the figure are the antecedents of job satisfaction—the characteristics or factors that lead to job satisfaction. On the right side are the consequences—the outcomes or results of job satisfaction. Below I discuss a sampling of the research in support of these antecedents and consequences, but see the list of suggested readings at the end of the chapter for great places to learn more.

**Job Characteristics** The first category of antecedents consists of *job characteristics*, which include not only the five core job dimensions postulated by Richard Hackman and Greg Oldham's (1980) job characteristics theory (see Chapter 9) but also workload. The premise here is that one's satisfaction with a job is affected by the structure of the job and what it provides. Look back at Figure 9.3 (page 288) and you will notice that satisfaction is one of the hypothesized outcomes in job characteristics theory. Research has demonstrated a consistent relationship between employees' perceptions of the characteristics of their jobs and their level of job satisfaction (Spector & Jex, 1991). The more employees perceive that their jobs provide autonomy, task identity, task variety, task significance, and job feedback, the more satisfied they report being with their jobs.

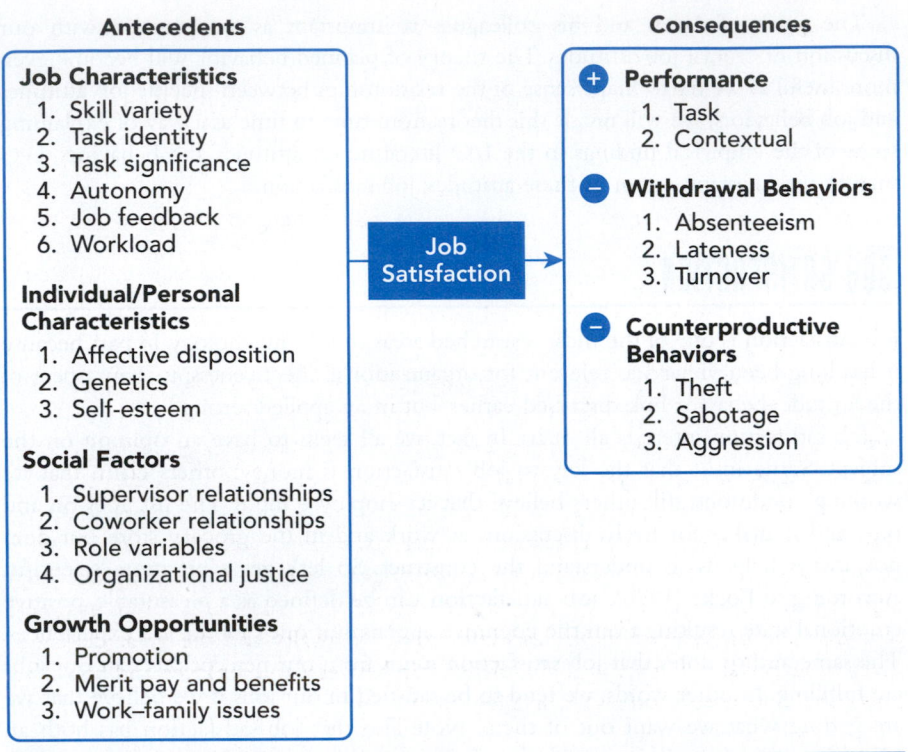

**FIGURE 10.2**  Framework for Job Satisfaction

A meta-analysis that reviewed 28 studies found that correlations between the core job dimensions and job satisfaction ranged from .32 (task identity) to .46 (autonomy; Loher, Noe, Moeler, & Fitzgerald, 1985). Another study reported that the match between worker preferences regarding such variables as work schedule, shift, number of hours, and organizational staffing policies regarding those same variables was positively related to employee attitudes such as job satisfaction (Holtom, Lee, & Tidd, 2002). Other studies indicate that employees who feel overloaded at work—which often leads to stress—tend to be dissatisfied with their jobs. Furthermore, research has indicated that personality traits such as self-esteem affect job satisfaction through their effects on job characteristics (Judge, Bono, & Locke, 2000). Although stress is also important in this context, we will discuss that in more detail in Chapter 11.

In a look back and to the future, Greg Oldham and Richard Hackman (2010) argue that work design is commonplace in organizations with a continued emphasis on job characteristics. However, as a result of the change from a manufacturing to a service economy, the approach has evolved and will continue to evolve. They propose that the social aspects of work have taken center stage because of the prominence of social interactions in contemporary work organizations, where product teams, service teams, and technical teams rule the day. In fact, a very large meta-analysis in this area reports that social characteristics (e.g., interdependence, feedback from others, social support) have been empirically linked to job satisfaction, accounting for as much as 24% of the variance in individuals' job satisfaction scores (Humphrey, Nahrgang, & Morgeson, 2007).

Oldham and Hackman (2010) suggest that research on interactions inside and outside the organization, social support, interdependence, interpersonal feedback, and coordination among employees will become the focus of job characteristics and work design initiatives in the 21st century. Thus, it follows that research should also focus on these social aspects of work. A recent meta-analysis of over 200 studies across 23 countries shows that the relationship between an employee and his or her boss (this relationship, which is called leader–member exchange or LMX, will be discussed in Chapter 13) is positively related to levels of job satisfaction (Rockstuhl, Dulebohn, Ang, & Shore, 2012). The relationship was very strong regardless of culture, but it was stronger in individualistic (Western) cultures ($r = .55$) than in collectivistic (Eastern) cultures ($r = .45$). The authors suggest that the difference may be due to the situation in collectivistic cultures where attitudes like job satisfaction are also influenced by loyalty and the great deference given to leaders, leaving the specific relationship between an employee and his or her boss (LMX) to have a somewhat smaller effect.

**TECHNICAL TIP**

Remember from Chapter 2 (page 61) that correlations range in magnitude from − 1.0 to + 1.0, and the larger the number (in either direction), the stronger the relationship. Positive correlations mean that as one variable goes up, so does the other. Correlations in the .30 to .40 range are considered moderately strong relationships. A correlation above .50 is typically considered an index of a strong relationship.

**Individual/Personal Characteristics** A sizable body of research suggests that people have stable characteristics that predispose them to respond positively or negatively to job contexts (e.g., Staw & Ross, 1985). In other words, some people tend to be satisfied with their jobs over the course of their careers, while others tend to be dissatisfied. Barry Staw and Jerry Ross (1985) found moderate correlations between satisfaction measures over time and even saw evidence of this stability in job satisfaction scores when individuals changed jobs. In other words, there seems to be some consistency in job satisfaction levels for individuals over the course of their careers—some folks tend to be satisfied (or not satisfied) with their jobs over their whole careers even if they change jobs and sometimes even if they change occupations. These data suggest that there is likely some dispositional element to job satisfaction. Yet other research has shown that job enrichment and other organizational interventions designed to "improve" jobs still have the potential to raise individuals' levels of satisfaction

© Hero Images Inc./Alamy

**A CLOSER LOOK**
What job characteristics do you notice here that might affect performance?

(Gerhart, 1987; Steel & Rentsch, 1997). This suggests that it's not all dispositional because for some people changes in job characteristics or the job itself results in changes in job satisfaction levels. When we are talking about human behavior, which is largely what psychology deals with, it's pretty common to recognize the importance of both dispositions and situations—this research provides another important and clear example of this.

**affective disposition**
The tendency to respond to classes of environmental stimuli in predetermined, affect-based ways.

Some researchers in this area have argued that the stability we see in job satisfaction scores over time stems from **affective disposition**, or the tendency to respond to classes of environmental stimuli in predetermined, affect-based ways (Judge & Hulin, 1993). In other words, some individuals respond to the world in a positive way, while others respond in a negative way. Someone with a positive affective disposition might be more upbeat, energized, and happy as opposed to someone with a negative affective disposition, who may be more down, weary, and sad. In a review that revisits the situation versus disposition debate, researchers concluded that one's affective disposition can strongly impact what is experienced in the workplace, how it is evaluated, and how it is remembered (Staw & Cohen-Charash, 2005).

Another group of researchers have taken a slightly different perspective, focusing on genetic differences as an explanation for the stability in job satisfaction. In particular, they argue that genetic factors might influence the way in which individuals respond to their work contexts (Arvey, Bouchard, Segal, & Abraham, 1989). We know that genes affect intelligence, personality, interests, and attitudes—so why not job satisfaction? These researchers used an often-studied group of twins from the Minnesota Study of Twins Reared Apart to examine the extent to which twins who were separated at (or soon after) birth had similar levels of job satisfaction much later in life. They found that the proportion of variance in satisfaction resulting from genetic factors was about 30%, a statistically significant number. Thus, there appears to be some genetic contribution to an individual's level of job satisfaction (Ilies & Judge, 2003).

Some attention has been paid to the idea that individuals with high self-esteem tend to be satisfied with their jobs (Brockner, 1988; Lopez & Greenhaus, 1978). In one study, researchers examined the role played by core self-evaluations in both job satisfaction and life satisfaction (Judge, Locke, Durham, & Kluger, 1998). By *core self-evaluations*, the authors mean the fundamental evaluations we make about ourselves—a concept that includes self-esteem and generalized self-efficacy (Judge, Bono, Erez, & Locke, 2005). Their results strongly support the link between self-esteem (and other core self-evaluations) and both job and life satisfaction. The authors concluded that core evaluations of the self have consistent effects on job satisfaction regardless of the job. In other words, how people view (or evaluate) themselves directly affects how they experience their jobs and their

**TECHNICAL TIP**

*A longitudinal study is one in which the researcher measures participants on the same variables at numerous points in time to see whether respondents have changed over time. In the Steel and Rentsch (1997) study presented here, the researchers showed that job characteristics predicted job satisfaction later in time even after controlling for job satisfaction earlier in time. Of course, job satisfaction rates at Time 1 and Time 2 were positively correlated, but even with that correlation, job characteristics predicted job satisfaction at Time 2. This is a great way to show the effect of one variable on another even after controlling for another variable.*

lives. In some research that combines individual differences with job characteristics, studies of students and employees found that individuals high on core self-evaluations tended to choose more complex tasks and were more satisfied with their jobs as a result (Srivastava, Locke, Judge, & Adams, 2010). This research shows very nicely how the interplay of both individual differences and job characteristics likely impacts job satisfaction and, potentially, other outcome variables.

A related variable is **organization-based self-esteem (OBSE)**, which concerns employees' perceptions of their value as organization members (Pierce, Gardner, Cummings, & Dunham, 1989). In other words, OBSE reflects one's degree of work-related self-esteem. It seems reasonable to expect that individuals who view themselves as valuable to the organization would also report higher levels of job satisfaction than would individuals who don't perceive themselves as valuable. This is exactly what researchers found in a study of healthcare workers (Chen, Goddard, & Casper, 2004). OBSE was strongly correlated with job satisfaction ($r = .58$) and even predicted job satisfaction, organizational commitment, and job involvement.

**organization-based self-esteem (OBSE)** A measure of how valuable employees view themselves as organization members.

**Social Factors** Other antecedents of job satisfaction can be considered social factors; these include interactional and relational variables at work. For instance, employees' relationships with their supervisors and coworkers seem to be important indicators of whether these employees are satisfied with their jobs. Think back to a job that you really liked—one in which you were really motivated to work hard, looked forward to going to work, and never "watched the clock." I've asked many students over the years to do the same; when I then asked them to describe what made the job so great, most started by saying something like, "I had this great boss" or "My manager was a great woman who really knew how to work with people and didn't play head games with us."

Research indicates that job satisfaction is also affected by the demographic similarity between supervisors and subordinates (Wesolowski & Mossholder, 1997), by the way in which supervisors assign tasks (Blau, 1999), and by the extent to which subordinates perceive that supervisors have violated their psychological contract (Rosen, Chang, Johnson, & Levy, 2009). The **psychological contract** consists of employees' beliefs about what they are entitled to receive because of promises made to them by their employer (Robinson, 1996). Clearly, the relationship we have with our bosses has an important effect on how we react to our jobs.

**psychological contract** An employee's idiosyncratic beliefs about the terms and conditions of the reciprocal agreement with his or her employer.

Recent research has also shown how individual differences and social factors come together to affect job satisfaction. In a study of 200 Chinese employees, results demonstrated that a proactive personality—a dispositional tendency toward taking personal initiative—led employees to establish high-quality relationships with their supervisors (leader–member exchange), resulting in high levels of job satisfaction (Li, Liang, & Crant, 2010). Like the study discussed earlier that showed the interplay between individual differences and job characteristics (Srivastava et al., 2010), this research shows how individual differences and social constructs work together. It should be clear that job attitudes like those discussed in this chapter are affected by the meshing of various types of antecedents.

The next thing people with great jobs often tell me is that they like their coworkers. It's nice, they say, to work with a great group of people who pitch in for each other and make work fun. You can look at this from another perspective, too. Think of a job that you really disliked and ask yourself what was so bad about it. Most of us will zero in on the people—coworkers—as a major reason for their job dissatisfaction because it was not a supportive, helpful, trustworthy, or enjoyable bunch to be around.

Research supports the importance of coworker relations as an antecedent to job satisfaction. One study proposed that organizational restructuring that influences the nature of work interactions affects coworker relationships, which, in turn, affect job satisfaction (Howard & Frink, 1996). Indeed, this study found that after the departments in a few city governments were restructured, attitudes about coworkers predicted job, as well as life, satisfaction. A recent survey of 490 managers reported that 73% of them cited good relationships with coworkers as the key to job satisfaction (Rennie, 2007).

Role variables also affect job satisfaction. If you have ever had a job in which you were not completely sure of your role or function in the organization, you can understand the negative effect that such ambiguity has on job satisfaction. Ambiguity is something that most people feel very uncomfortable with, especially with respect to the expectations associated with one's job.

Another important variable is organizational justice, or fairness, now one of the most investigated concepts in I/O psychology (see Chapters 9 and 14 for a detailed discussion of organizational justice). Studies have examined the role of this variable in determining employees' levels of job satisfaction and other work-related attitudes (e.g., Liao & Rupp, 2005). By **organizational justice** I mean simply the role of fairness in the workplace. The question here is whether employees' perceptions of the fairness of policies, procedures, and treatment affect their attitudes, behaviors, and performance. In a study that developed and validated a measure of just interpersonal treatment (Donovan, Drasgow, & Munson, 1998), justice was correlated with various job satisfaction measures even after controlling for affective disposition, indicating that justice is an important predictor of job satisfaction regardless of one's affective disposition. Further research has demonstrated that organizational fairness affects job satisfaction through its effect on perceived organizational support and leader–member relationships (Masterson, Lewis, Goldman, & Taylor, 2000; Rhoades & Eisenberger, 2002).

In sum, employees' levels of job satisfaction are likely to be affected by the quality of the interpersonal relationships they experience at work. These relationships are affected by how well the employees get along with their supervisors and coworkers, as well as by their perceptions of role clarity, organizational fairness, and organizational support.

**Growth Opportunities** The last group of factors that can affect job satisfaction are what I call *growth opportunities*, such as the employee's perception that there is potential to grow, advance, or be promoted within the organization. The obvious antecedents here include whether someone is paid well, is provided excellent benefits, and is offered the opportunity for advancement. Each of these factors is related to job satisfaction. Pay for performance was discussed as a motivational technique in the last chapter; some

**organizational justice**
The role of fairness in the workplace.

research studies show that this motivational approach results in increased job satisfaction (Green & Heywood, 2008). However, a meta-analysis shows that pay level was only weakly correlated with job satisfaction (Judge, Piccolo, Podsakoff, Shaw, & Rich, 2010). The authors argued that when individuals get pay increases, they are more satisfied in the short term, but then they revert back to original levels of satisfaction because the new pay level quickly becomes the normal/expected level.

A recent study looked at both situational and dispositional variables as they relate to job satisfaction among young adults (Keller & Semmer, 2013), but the researchers were most interested in the role that growth rates in these variables played in affecting job satisfaction. They found that both situational and dispositional variables were important, but that the best predictors were the extent to which participants were able to grow on these variables. Even more interesting was the finding that if there was no growth on the dispositional or situational variables, job satisfaction actually decreased! It appears that young adults are strongly affected by opportunities for growth in important variables.

**A CLOSER LOOK**
How would your job attitudes be affected by a boss like the one Colin Farrell played in the movie series *Horrible Bosses*? Why?

In the next chapter, on work-related stress, we will discuss many issues related to work–family conflict. For now, however, note that the conflict or stress one experiences as a function of valuing both one's family and one's job affects both job and life satisfaction (Bruck, Allen, & Spector, 2002). According to a meta-analysis, work–family conflict was negatively correlated with both job satisfaction ($r = -.31$) and life satisfaction ($r = -.36$; Kossek & Ozeki, 1998). Thus, it appears that employees with high levels of conflict tend to be less satisfied with their jobs (and their lives in general) than are employees with low levels of conflict. Other findings suggest that this relationship is slightly stronger for men than for women and considerably stronger for dual-career than for single-career couples. In addition, the conflict appears to be more strongly related to satisfaction if it is the work domain that is "interfering" with the family domain rather than the other way around. We'll revisit these interesting findings in Chapter 11.

## Measurement and Dimensions

We have been discussing job satisfaction without considering the manner in which it can be measured. More important, we have been conceptualizing job satisfaction in a general sense so that the antecedents could be considered separately from the complexities inherent in the measurement process. At this point, however, we need to consider the measurement of job satisfaction from a multidimensional standpoint.

Traditionally, job satisfaction has been assessed at the global level with questionnaire items like "In general, I like my job" or at the facet level with items determining how satisfied employees are with their pay, supervisor, and so on. Both approaches seem reasonable, so the choice may depend on the organization's purpose. But I would also argue that including measures at the facet level provides more fine-grained, or specific, data that can be useful in diagnosing organizational problems and developing organizational interventions.

One of the most frequently used and best-validated measures of job satisfaction is the Job Descriptive Index, or JDI (Kinicki, McKee-Ryan, Schriesheim, & Carson, 2002; Stanton et al., 2002). Developed in the 1960s (Smith, Kendall, & Hulin, 1969), it measures satisfaction along five dimensions (and an overall dimension): satisfaction with the type of work itself, satisfaction with pay, satisfaction with coworkers, satisfaction with promotion opportunities, and satisfaction with supervision. **Figure 10.3** presents sample items from each facet, along with a sample item from the overall dimension (i.e., "Job in General"). This scale is so well established that it is often used today to validate and develop other measures of job satisfaction (e.g., Whitaker, 2007).

---

In the blank beside each word or phrase below, write

____ 1  for "Yes"
____ 2  for "No"
____ 3  for "?"

**Work on Present Job**
How well does each of the following describe your work?
____ Fascinating
____ Routine
____ Satisfying
____ Boring

**Opportunities for Promotion**
How well does each of the following describe your opportunities for promotion?
____ Good opportunities for promotion
____ Opportunities somewhat limited
____ Promotion on ability
____ Dead-end job

**Present Pay**
How well does each of the following describe your present pay?
____ Income adequate for normal expenses
____ Fair
____ Comfortable
____ Bad

**Supervision**
How well does each of the following describe your supervision?
____ Supportive
____ Hard to please
____ Impolite
____ Praises good work

**Coworkers**
How well does each of the following describe the people you work with?
____ Stimulating
____ Boring
____ Slow
____ Helpful

**Job in General**
How well does each of the following describe your job most of the time?
____ Pleasant
____ Bad
____ Great
____ Worthwhile

**FIGURE 10.3** Sample Items from the JDI and the Job in General (JIG) Scale (Source: Bowling Green State University, Department of Psychology, 2009)

## PRACTITIONER FORUM

Brian Welle

### Brian Welle
*PhD, 2004, I/O Psychology, New York University*
*Manager, People and Innovation Lab*
*Google*

I lead the People and Innovation Lab (PiLab) at Google. We are a group of psychologists, organizational behaviorists, and researchers whose projects include, among other things, the measurement of employees' beliefs, attitudes, opinions, and behaviors.

My team collects and analyzes data to help business leaders and human resource professionals make better decisions that affect Googlers (i.e., employees at Google). In an engineering company like Google, all decisions, whether from our sales team, engineers, or human resources, are guided by data. I/O psychologists are like the engineers of HR: We play a pivotal role by collecting, analyzing, and interpreting data for people-related decisions.

We use several methodologies and research tools in the PiLab. One of our most useful tools is surveys, and the best example of these is Googlegeist, our annual employee opinion survey. The Googlegeist survey is sent to all Googlers around the world and provides them the opportunity to tell us about the facets of the workplace that are most important to them: from satisfaction with their jobs, to confidence in their leaders, to perceptions of the company's culture. It also assesses constructs that predict Google-valued outcomes, including the speed and quality of decision making, and innovation. The data we collect through Googlegeist have enabled us to significantly improve our employee

development programs, to help our leaders develop and improve, and even to guide business decisions.

Employee opinion surveys are useful tools. They provide a snapshot of people's beliefs and attitudes; however, they are not as good at determining cause-and-effect relationships. We therefore turn to experimental and quasi-experimental research to dive a bit deeper into key behaviors. We have, for example, conducted studies that reveal the best way to motivate retirement-savings behavior and time-series experiments to help Googlers eat healthier.

These examples, from surveys to experiments, illustrate how important psychological research is at Google. Attitudes, opinions, perceptions, and actual behaviors are the foundation for many things that organizations like Google care about, both from a business and an employee well-being perspective. We devote a lot of time to conducting research to understand the perspectives of our employees and using their data to make Google the kind of place where they are proud to work.

### Applying Your Knowledge

1. Why does Google use different research methods to gauge employee attitudes versus behaviors?

2. What are some ways in which an organization might benefit from taking the time to assess employee attitudes and perspectives?

3. Based on what you've read about the JDS in this chapter, how does the Googlegeist sound similar? How might it differ?

---

A scale along similar lines was developed in connection with the Job Diagnostic Survey, or JDS (Hackman & Oldham, 1980), which measures job characteristics (see Chapter 9). This latter scale measures satisfaction as a function of pay, security, social factors, supervision, and growth (see **Figure 10.4**). There are many other measures of facet satisfaction, but the JDI and the JDS are well known and psychometrically sound.

Overall measures of job satisfaction are plentiful as well. For instance, both the JDI and the JDS include a measure of overall job satisfaction. The JDS measure is presented in **Figure 10.5.** Another large-scale approach to measuring job attitudes is related to

### How satisfied are you with this aspect of your job?

| Extremely dissatisfied | Dissatisfied | Slightly dissatisfied | Neutral | Slightly satisfied | Satisfied | Extremely satisfied |
|:---:|:---:|:---:|:---:|:---:|:---:|:---:|
| 1 | 2 | 3 | 4 | 5 | 6 | 7 |

**Pay**

☐ The amount of pay and fringe benefits I receive.

**Security**

☐ The amount of job security I have.

**Social**

☐ The chance to get to know other people while on the job.

**Supervisory**

☐ The amount of support and guidance I receive from my supervisor.

**Growth**

☐ The amount of personal growth and development I get in doing my job.

**FIGURE 10.4** Sample Items from the JDS (Information from Hackman, J. R., & Oldham, G. R. (1980). *Work Redesign.* Upper Saddle River, NJ: Pearson. © 1980 by Pearson Education, Inc.)

| Disagree strongly | Disagree | Disagree slightly | Neutral | Agree slightly | Agree | Agree strongly |
|:---:|:---:|:---:|:---:|:---:|:---:|:---:|
| 1 | 2 | 3 | 4 | 5 | 6 | 7 |

☐ 1. Generally speaking, I am very satisfied with this job.

☐ 2. I frequently think of quitting this job. (R)

☐ 3. I am generally satisfied with the kind of work I do in this job.

☐ 4. Most people on this job are very satisfied with the job.

☐ 5. People on this job often think of quitting. (R)

Note: An (R) indicates that the item is "reverse-scored" because of the way it is written, so that a high score is actually recorded as a low score.

**FIGURE 10.5** JDS Measure of Overall Job Satisfaction (Information from Hackman, J. R., & Oldham, G. R. (1980). *Work Redesign.* Upper Saddle River, NJ: Pearson. © 1980 by Pearson Education, Inc.)

L. H. Lofquist and R. V. Dawis's (1969) theory of work adjustment, which proposes that employees seek to maintain correspondence with their environment. The idea here is that employees want their jobs to fulfill their needs and desires. The Minnesota Satisfaction Questionnaire, which was developed on the basis of this theory, totals 100 items that measure 20 different facets of satisfaction. However, a short form of the scale (with just 20 items) has also been used very successfully for measuring overall satisfaction.

Three versions of the Faces Scale (Kunin, 1955, 1998), which measures the affective component of job satisfaction rather than the cognitive component, are depicted in **Figure 10.6** and have also been frequently used to measure overall satisfaction. The Faces Scale can be used in many different situations because it is largely nonverbal and thus easier for verbally unskilled employees to complete. It is easily adapted for measuring various facets of satisfaction as well.

Which of the following faces best expresses your feelings about your job (tasks, compensation, supervision, growth opportunities, etc.)?

Put a check under the face that expresses how you feel about your job in general, including the work, the pay, the supervision, the opportunities for promotion, and the people you work with.

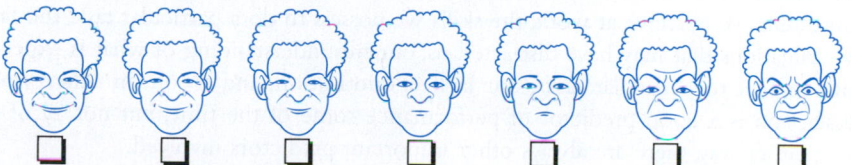

Circle the number below the face that expresses your current level of job satisfaction, including your feelings about the work, the pay, your coworkers, job security, and opportunities for growth.

| 10 | 9 | 8 | 7 | 6 | 5 | 4 | 3 | 2 | 1 |

**FIGURE 10.6** **Three Versions of the Faces Scale** (Information from: (top and middle) Kunin, T. (1955). The construction of a new type of attitude measure. *Personnel Psychology, 8*, 65–77; (bottom) Dunham, R. B., & Herman, J. B. (1975). Development of a female Faces Scale for measuring job satisfaction. *Journal of Applied Psychology, 60*(5), 630. © The American Psychological Association.)

## Consequences

Now that we've described job satisfaction, what factors determine it, and how to measure it, we need to consider its consequences for organizations and employees. We return to the theory of planned behavior in considering the role of work-related attitudes in organizations. As illustrated in Figure 10.1, attitude is only one of four variables that are instrumental in the prediction of an individual's behavior. Although we hope that an employee's attitude will strongly predict her behavior, we have to realize that behavior is very complicated and that other important variables will also play a part in the prediction. Hence the old axiom "A satisfied worker is a productive worker" is not always accurate. What if that satisfied worker is incapable of doing what is required on her job? What if, despite her satisfaction, the norm at work is to do just enough to get by? What if her job satisfaction doesn't lead to an intention to work hard because her supervisor doesn't require much effort to give a favorable performance review? In all these situations, despite a high level of satisfaction, this employee is not likely to perform well; the attitude–behavior relationship is thus small or nonexistent. There are many antecedents to behavior other than attitudes. Expecting a strong relationship between attitudes and behaviors might be unrealistic in many situations.

**Performance** I have just suggested that the satisfied worker may or may not be a productive worker—an outcome that depends on many other variables. Think about this. Have you ever had a job in which you were not very satisfied but still did decent work? For that matter, did you sometimes perform better than others who were much more satisfied than you? Were you ever satisfied at work because you were performing well? Sometimes our performance is not a function of our job satisfaction at all but, instead, satisfaction may stem from performance or may be determined by the constraints we perceive at work, the skills we possess to do a particular task, the family obligations that may have distracted us, our misunderstanding of what is expected with respect to particular tasks, our lack of motivation, and so on. In other words, satisfaction is a good predictor of performance some of the time, but not all of the time; either way, there are always other important predictors involved.

To talk in a general sense about the satisfaction–performance relationship is to ignore all these other potential variables. It's reasonable to do so as long as we keep in mind that these variables exist and that we shouldn't expect an extremely strong relationship between satisfaction and performance. A good general estimate of the relationship (i.e., the correlation) between satisfaction and performance is somewhere around .30 (Judge, Thoresen, Bono, & Patton, 2001). Furthermore, the correlation tends to be stronger for employees in highly complex jobs. A more recent meta-analysis takes a more sophisticated analytic approach and reports a large correlation ($r = .59$) between overall job attitude and work effectiveness (Harrison, Newman, & Roth, 2006). Even the meta-analyses don't always agree due to the particular studies included and the particular focus of the research, but we can reasonably conclude that job satisfaction and performance are moderately correlated.

A new and intriguing study examined the role of culture in the job satisfaction–performance relationship. This meta-analysis of 208 independent studies found that the satisfaction–performance relationship was stronger in those cultures that were high on individualism and low on uncertainty avoidance (Ng, Sorensen, & Yim, 2009). In other words, cultures in which individuals act in accordance with their own desires and preferences (as opposed to those of the collective) and those in which dynamic change is favored (as opposed to having an emphasis on stability) tend to have stronger satisfaction–performance relationships, probably because individuals in these cultures are rewarded for behaving in accordance with their own wishes and believing in their own independence—thus, if satisfied, they perform well.

Another variable to consider is *contextual performance,* also known as *organizational citizenship behavior,* or *OCB* (see Chapter 4). Contextual performance refers to behaviors that are not formally part of one's job description—that is, behaviors that have more to do with social elements at work than with task elements. Research has examined the relationship between job satisfaction and contextual performance as well; in fact, the most studied antecedent of contextual behaviors is job satisfaction. For instance, in a study of machine operators, satisfaction with coworkers, supervision, and pay was significantly correlated with various dimensions of OCB (Lowery, Beadles, & Krilowicz, 2002). Furthermore, in a study of U.S. government employees and various kinds of employees in Saudi Arabia and Egypt, moderate to strong correlations were found between job satisfaction and OCBs (Tang & Ibrahim, 1998). These correlations ranged from .22 to .57, depending on the type of satisfaction and the type of OCBs measured.

**Withdrawal Behaviors** Performance is one outcome variable of interest to organizations, but withdrawal behaviors are important as well. The three most common withdrawal behaviors are absenteeism, tardiness, and turnover.

We have all missed a few days of work here and there because of illnesses or other uncontrollable events such as a funeral, jury duty, a doctor's appointment, or a child's play or pageant. No one would suggest that employees should come to work every day regardless of illness, personal problems, or other important considerations. The Bureau of Labor Statistics reports that, on average, employees are absent about four days per year due to illness or personal concerns. This doesn't sound like much, but absenteeism costs companies a great deal of money. The cost of absenteeism continues to rise, and some estimates have the cost of unplanned absenteeism at $3,600 per year for hourly workers and $2,600 per year for salaried employees (Circadian, 2005). The federal government reports that musculoskeletal injuries like carpal tunnel syndrome account for 62% of all workers' compensation claims, costing $15–20 billion per year, and result in a great deal of absenteeism ("Carpal Tunnel Syndrome," 2005). A recent survey by the Society for Human Resource Management (SHRM) proposes that the total cost of employee absenteeism can reach 22% of a company's payroll (Society for Human Resource Management, 2014).

One survey found that only 33% of unscheduled time off was due to personal illness, which means that there are other explanations for 67% of unscheduled absences; chief among these are family issues and personal needs. A popular model of absenteeism developed by Richard Steers and Susan Rhodes (1978) accounts for some of these alternative explanations. A simplified version of this model is depicted in **Figure 10.7**. First, notice that *job satisfaction* is an integral variable in the model,

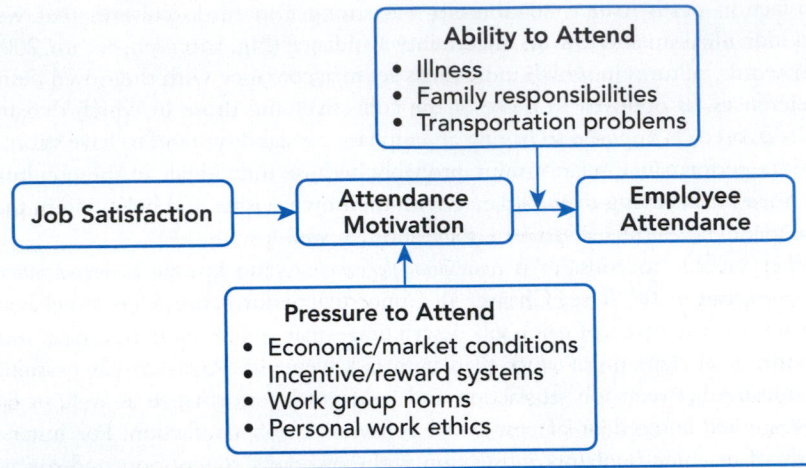

but also notice that it is rather far removed from *employee attendance* and that there are many variables in between. Some studies have found low to moderate correlations ($r = -.15$ to $-.25$) between job satisfaction and absenteeism (Hackett & Guion, 1985; Scott & Taylor, 1985), whereas others have demonstrated a stronger relationship. For instance, in a study based on the personnel records of over 300 city employees in Israel, a moderately negative correlation ($r = -.47$) was found between job satisfaction and voluntary absence, which includes everything but excused absence due to sickness or family obligations (Sagie, 1998). Still other studies have reported relationships close to zero (e.g., Goldberg & Waldman, 2000).

Second, notice that in Figure 10.7 the closest predictor to attendance is *attendance motivation*. This should remind you of the work of Ajzen and his colleagues (Ajzen & Fishbein, 2005), who argued that the best predictor of a behavior is the intention to exhibit that behavior. In Ajzen's models, attitude leads to intention, which affects behavior—much like satisfaction leads to attendance motivation, which then influences attendance. Third, notice that attendance motivation is affected by *pressure to attend*. For example, if an individual has very little money and depends on his job to buy food and shelter, then he is unlikely to behave in ways that might cost him his job, such as being consistently absent from work. This individual would experience pressures to attend that might not be experienced by someone who is independently wealthy. Fourth, notice that *ability to attend* takes into account whether employees actually have control over their attendance behavior. (Think back once more to Ajzen's work and you'll find that this variable is similar to the notion of perceived behavioral control.)

In short, attendance motivation is likely to affect attendance behavior only if the employees involved have control over their ability to attend. Consider the case of an employee who is very motivated to attend but needs to stay home to take care of a son who has chicken pox. This inability to attend would affect the relationship between her attendance motivation and her attendance behavior. She doesn't go to work, but it's not because she's unmotivated to attend work. In fact, research on more than 200 employed, married parents has found positive relationships between the number of children under six years of age and absence, and between child-care difficulties and absence (Erickson, Nichols, & Ritter, 2000).

The Steers and Rhodes model of absenteeism makes it very clear that although job satisfaction can be an important predictor of absenteeism, the absenteeism process is much more complicated than that. As discussed in the section on satisfaction and performance, expecting a strong direct relationship between satisfaction and any outcome variable is unreasonable given the complexities of human behavior. A recent study found support for many of the propositions presented in the Steers and Rhodes model, accounting for 46% of the variance in employee absenteeism (Steel, Rentsch, & Van Scotter, 2007) and demonstrating satisfaction to be important.

Much less research has been conducted on tardiness, or lateness (see some recent work by Foust and her colleagues: Elicker, Foust, O'Malley, & Levy, 2008; Foust, Elicker, & Levy, 2006), but some older work by Gary Blau (1994) has proved especially interesting. Blau suggests that there are different types of lateness and that one common type, which he calls *chronic lateness,* is significantly predicted by job satisfaction. In his study of hospital employees, he found a $-.39$ correlation between job satisfaction and one's tendency to be chronically late. The Steers and Rhodes model of absence has also been applied to lateness; here, the results indicate that job satisfaction has a small direct effect on attendance but that both motivation to be on time and ability to be on time are important determinants of lateness (Bardsley & Rhodes, 1996).

One last withdrawal behavior is a very important one: turnover, which can have huge cost implications for organizations. Think of some of the major topics discussed thus far. Organizations invest a great deal of time, effort, and money in things like recruitment, testing and selection, training, and performance evaluation. If the employee chooses to leave the company, not only is that money no longer working for the company, but the process must begin again. The Society for Human Resource Management has estimated that it costs $3,500 to replace an employee making $8.00 per hour (Blake, 2006)—these are our most recent figures, but it is likely that the true cost has risen since the time of this study. Other estimates have suggested it costs 1.5 to 2.5 times the employee's annual salary to replace him or her (Cascio, 2003).

The average turnover rate in the United States in 2014 was 15.7% (http://www.compensationforce.com/2015/03/2014-turnover-rates-by-industry.html). Of course, the flip side of all this is that turnover can be good for companies if departing employees were ineffective and can be replaced by more effective ones. This is often the case when employees are fired or when ineffective employees select themselves out of the organization. For our present purposes, however, let's think about situations in which organizations lose employees they would have preferred to keep.

A recent investigation was able to show that employees whose satisfaction levels change also report changes in turnover intentions (Chen, Ployhart, Thomas, Anderson, & Bliese, 2011). The results suggest that one's intent to leave a job changes more as

**A CLOSER LOOK**
Can you think of a coworker you were glad to see leave the organization? How did your job attitudes change when this person left?

a function of a decrease in satisfaction than as a function of the level of satisfaction. There are broad implications for the importance of tracking attitudes over time; doing so may provide greater insight into employees' attitudes and perhaps even allow organizations to better predict when turnover intentions are likely to increase and become a serious threat to the organization.

Traditionally, researchers have looked at two main antecedents of turnover: (1) perceived ease of movement, or the extent to which employees can find alternative jobs, and (2) perceived desirability of movement, or the desire to change jobs, which has largely been operationalized with respect to job satisfaction. In general, a modest relationship has been found between job satisfaction and turnover (Griffeth, Hom, & Gaertner, 2000; Lee, Mitchell, Holtom, McDaniel, & Hill, 1999), with correlations between −.20 and −.30. **Figure 10.8** shows a simplified version of Hom and Griffeth's (1991) model. Along one path to turnover, job satisfaction affects the extent to which an individual begins thinking about quitting; a second path leads from job satisfaction to a job search and comparisons of alternatives. Both paths eventually result in a

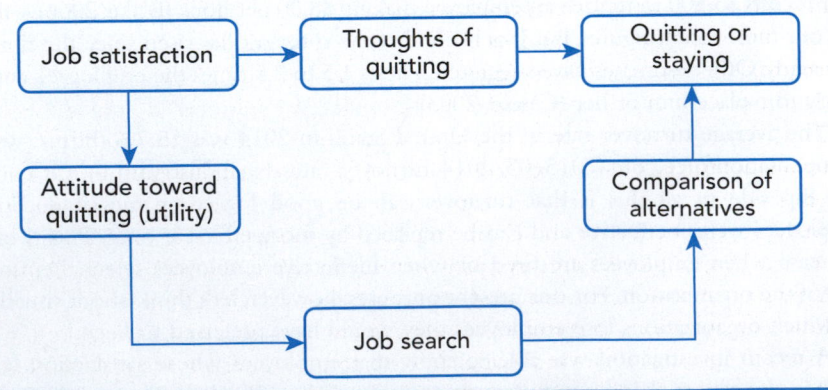

**FIGURE 10.8**  Modified Model of Turnover (Information from Hom & Griffeth, 1991)

decision to stay or go. A more recent study demonstrated that the relationship between job satisfaction and turnover varies as a function of psychological well-being, or PWB (Wright & Bonett, 2007). Namely, the negative relationship tends to be much stronger when people are low on PWB rather than high on PWB.

Indeed, job satisfaction is often integral to the turnover process, but we must also realize that some individuals leave companies because they can't pass up an incredible opportunity elsewhere or because they want to relocate for personal reasons, such as taking care of an ailing parent. In other words, turnover may be less related to the current job than to alternative job opportunities or personal circumstances. For example, consider earlier cutting-edge work on turnover, involving what Thomas Lee and his colleagues call the *unfolding model* (Mitchell, Holtom, Lee, Sablynski, & Erez, 2001; Sablynski, Lee, Mitchell, Burton, & Holtom, 2002), in which four different paths to turnover are hypothesized. Along the first path, turnover results from a *shock to the system* (e.g., an unsolicited job offer, a change in one's marital status, a job transfer, a firm merger), and job satisfaction is completely irrelevant. This model provides other turnover paths and some interesting alternatives to traditional beliefs about the turnover process.

A recent empirical investigation extended the work of Lee and his colleagues by successfully categorizing 86% of a sample of accountants into one of the four proposed paths (Donnelly & Quirin, 2006), lending support to the unfolding model. Additional support comes from a recent study that found half the voluntary turnover from a national study was due largely to family reasons or an unsolicited job offer (Lee, Gerhart, Weller, & Trevor, 2008). This study demonstrates the importance of paths to turnover that don't include or emphasize job satisfaction. Organizational withdrawal happens for many reasons, but thanks to thirty years of cutting edge research we have many supported theories that have helped us to understand the processes involved.

**Counterproductive Work Behaviors** Employees engage in various activities that are detrimental to an organization, including antisocial behaviors, dysfunctional behaviors, and workplace deviance. Here I use the phrase counterproductive work behaviors (CWBs), defined as any behaviors that bring, or are intended to bring, harm to an organization, its employees, or its stakeholders. Counterproductive behaviors include arson, blackmail, bribery, sabotage, theft, fraud, psychological withdrawal, interpersonal violence, and sometimes absence and lateness (Giacalone & Greenberg, 1997). Frustration is the centerpiece in one model of antisocial behavior (Spector, 1997). It argues that when an employee is frustrated and thus dissatisfied (i.e., when something interferes with his goals or objectives), his potential for antisocial behaviors increases. Recent work has shown that abusive behaviors are driven by anger, whereas withdrawal is more related to boredom and depression (Spector et al., 2006). This work argues that there are some different patterns in antecedents for the various CWBs.

A review of the literature found that young dissatisfied employees were most likely to engage in counterproductive work behaviors (Lau, Au, & Ho, 2003); it has also been demonstrated that individuals low on conscientiousness were most likely to exhibit counterproductive behaviors (Salgado, 2002). More generally, the correlations between job satisfaction and counterproductive behaviors range from $-.10$ to $-.25$

**counterproductive work behaviors (CWBs)**
Any behaviors that bring, or are intended to bring, harm to an organization, its employees, or its stakeholders.

(Boye & Jones, 1997). A recent study of 74 employees found that the effect of hostility on workplace deviance was mediated by job satisfaction (Judge, Scott, & Ilies, 2006). In other words, hostility led to a decrease in job satisfaction, which resulted in more workplace deviance. Although relatively little empirical research has been conducted in this area (because measuring counterproductive behaviors requires "catching" people in the act), the notion that employees' work-related attitudes play a role seems reasonable and is becoming the focus of more research.

In sum, job satisfaction is an important organizational variable. However, although we know a great deal about the antecedents and consequences of job satisfaction, we have probably been guilty in the past of expecting too much from it (Fisher, 2003). That is, we have anticipated very strong relationships between job satisfaction and organizational behaviors. In recent years, however, we have begun to realize the important, but limited, role played by job satisfaction in organizational processes. Our understanding of how satisfaction fits into the bigger picture of organizational and individual functioning continues to grow. The questions that we have asked in the past about the small direct effects of job satisfaction on various outcomes have led to research that is now helping to build more accurate models of organizational functioning.

## ORGANIZATIONAL COMMITMENT

Organizational commitment (OC) is the second most frequently studied attitude in the workplace, but it has captured much less attention than job satisfaction. These two attitudes tend to be positively related at a moderate level, with correlations around .30 to .40. However, there has been some controversy over the causal order of these two variables (Kinicki et al., 2002) without a resolution as to which variable causes the other or whether there is a particular causal order at all.

Organizational commitment is broader in scope than job satisfaction given that the target is the "organization" rather than the "job." Furthermore, it is often reported that OC is more stable over time than is job satisfaction, which can fluctuate with daily or even hourly changes at work; OC doesn't fluctuate quite so much. In this section, I will define the various dimensions of organizational commitment and present a brief discussion of some of its antecedents and consequences. In a general sense, workplace commitments can be viewed as bonds or attachments to something related to work (Klein, Molloy, & Cooper, 2009). Organizational commitment can be defined as the psychological attachment to an organization. However, to really understand this attitude, we need to consider three components of commitment that have been defined in the literature.

**organizational commitment (OC)** The psychological attachment that binds an employee to the organization.

### Components

In the last 20 years, John Meyer has studied organizational commitment more thoroughly than anyone else in the field (Allen & Meyer, 1996; Meyer & Allen, 1997; Meyer, Stanley, Herscovitch, & Topolnytsky, 2002; Meyer, Stanley, & Parfyonova, 2012). Meyer and Allen conceptualize commitment as having three components, and they have developed a measure of each one. An example of these measures, which are the most frequently used and accepted in the literature (Meyer & Allen, 1997), is presented in **Figure 10.9**.

| Disagree strongly | | Disagree | | Disagree slightly | | Neutral | | Agree slightly | | Agree | | Agree strongly |
|---|---|---|---|---|---|---|---|---|---|---|---|---|
| 1 | | 2 | | 3 | | 4 | | 5 | | 6 | | 7 |

### Affective Commitment

☐ 1. I would be very happy to spend the rest of my career in this organization.

☐ 2. I really feel as if this organization's problems are my own.

☐ 3. I do not feel like "part of the family" at my organization. (R)

☐ 4. I do not feel "emotionally attached" to this organization. (R)

☐ 5. This organization has a great deal of personal meaning for me.

☐ 6. I do not feel a strong sense of belonging to my organization. (R)

### Continuance Commitment

☐ 1. It would be very hard for me to leave my organization right now, even if I wanted to.

☐ 2. Too much of my life would be disrupted if I decided I wanted to leave my organization right now.

☐ 3. Right now, staying with my organization is a matter of necessity as much as desire.

☐ 4. I believe that I have too few options to consider leaving this organization.

☐ 5. One of the few negative consequences of leaving this organization would be the scarcity of available alternatives.

☐ 6. If I had not already put so much of myself into this organization, I might consider working elsewhere.

### Normative Commitment

☐ 1. I do not feel any obligation to remain with my current employer. (R)

☐ 2. Even if it were to my advantage, I do not feel it would be right to leave my organization now.

☐ 3. I would feel guilty if I left my organization now.

☐ 4. This organization deserves my loyalty.

☐ 5. I would not leave my organization right now because I have a sense of obligation to the people in it.

☐ 6. I owe a great deal to my organization.

Note: An (R) indicates that the item is "reverse-scored" because of the way it is written, so that a high score is actually recorded as a low score.

**FIGURE 10.9** **Affective, Continuance, and Normative Commitment Scales** (Source: Meyer, J. P., & Allen, N. J. (1997). *Commitment in the Workplace: Theory, Research, and Application* (pp. 118–119). Thousand Oaks, CA: SAGE. © 1997 by SAGE Publications.)

**affective commitment**
Emotional attachment to an organization, characterized by a strong belief in and acceptance of the organization's goals and values, a willingness to exert effort on behalf of the organization, and a strong desire to remain a part of the organization.

The first and most studied component of organizational commitment, **affective commitment**, is characterized by (1) a strong belief in and acceptance of the organization's goals and values, (2) a willingness to exert effort on behalf of the organization, and (3) a strong desire to remain a part of the organization (Mowday, Steers, & Porter, 1979). This component can be thought of as the employee's emotional attachment to the organization. Second is **continuance commitment**, which has to do with the costs that are associated with leaving the organization. This component is sometimes referred to as *sunk-costs commitment* because it concerns attachment to an organization as a function of what the employee has invested in it (Shore, Tetrick, Shore, & Barksdale, 2000). An employee might have high continuance commitment because leaving the organization would cost him a great deal in retirement earnings (high sacrifice continuance commitment) or because he has no other better options (low alternatives continuance commitment). Third is **normative commitment**, sometimes called *moral commitment,* which reflects one's obligation to continue employment with the organization. Individuals who are high in normative commitment tend to believe that they ought to stay with the company regardless of what it offers them.

**continuance commitment**
Attachment to an organization as a function of what the employee has invested in it; also called *sunk-costs commitment.*

## Antecedents

**normative commitment**
Attachment to an organization that reflects one's obligation to continue employment with the organization; also called *moral commitment.*

**Figure 10.10** presents a heuristic framework for thinking about and studying organizational commitment. On the left side of the figure, antecedents are grouped

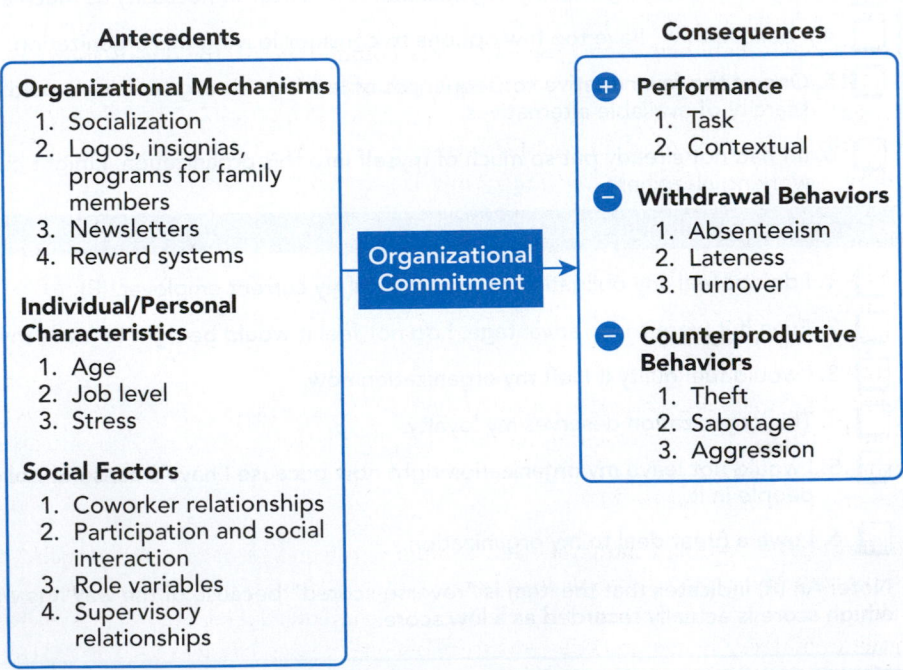

**FIGURE 10.10** Framework for Organizational Commitment

into three categories to enhance the understanding of the commitment construct. We will discuss each of these categories in turn.

**Organizational Mechanisms** Have you ever noticed all the little things that organizations seem to be doing these days to get employees committed to the company? Some organizations have company stores that sell items with the company logo emblazoned all over them (coffee cups, shirts, hats). The use of logos and insignias on merchandise for employees and their children (what "organizational team player" wouldn't want his or her child to have a hat that says Apple or Goodyear?) may serve various purposes, but one is clearly to increase the commitment of employees.

**A CLOSER LOOK**
What do companies hope to achieve by providing their employees with merchandise displaying their company logo?

No empirical studies have examined the success of this approach thus far, but, speaking for myself, I proudly wear a sweatshirt from Virginia Tech (one of my alma maters). The same process occurs with respect to organizations. Newsletters can also increase the strength of employees' identification with or involvement in the organization. Hearing about the charity work the company has done, the new employees who have been hired, the employees who are retiring after 30 years of distinguished service to the company, the company's goals and objectives over the next five years, and how the CEO is a great champion for the company in the local community can all help to increase employees' commitment to the organization.

Of course, there are more formal mechanisms as well, in the form of reward systems, that give employees trips for positive performance, provide gift certificates for employees of the month, pay for furthering employees' education, and so on. Meyer and Allen (1997) view such mechanisms as leading to affective commitment—specifically, by communicating to employees that the organization is supportive of them, by treating them fairly, and by enhancing their sense of personal importance and competence. Other research, too, has demonstrated that affective commitment is influenced by employees' perception that organizational policies, procedures, and programs are fair (Konovsky & Cropanzano, 1991; Sweeney & McFarlin, 1993). One way an organization can demonstrate support for its employees is by offering flexible work alternatives. For instance, a recent study of 393 employees who telecommute found that the more telecommuting these employees were allowed to do, the less exhaustion they experienced from their job and the more committed they were to the organization (Golden, 2006).

**Individual/Personal Characteristics** Examining situational characteristics such as the organizational mechanisms discussed previously would be incomplete without considering individual characteristics as well. Individual employees bring to their jobs many qualities, attitudes, beliefs, and skills—what we often refer to as *individual differences;* these differences are often related to job attitudes such as organizational commitment. In one of the largest meta-analyses done in the area of commitment (Meyer et al., 2002), a few

## I/O TODAY

### The Relationship Between Unions and Job Satisfaction

Given that unions are intended to improve working conditions and benefits, we might expect that workers who are unionized will be more satisfied than nonunion workers; however, research suggests this is not necessarily the case. According to a 2010 study by Benjamin Artz, first-time union workers experience an uptick in satisfaction initially, but then decrease in their work satisfaction the longer they are with the union; their satisfaction only recovers after they leave the union. In another study, it was found that dissatisfaction is even more pronounced for female workers (Artz, 2012).

Why might unionization have this negative effect on satisfaction when it is intended to make workers more satisfied with their jobs? The most obvious suggestion might be that dissatisfied employees are more likely to unionize, and there is some support for this theory. However, research suggests that the relationship between satisfaction and unionization is more complex than this. One study noted that an increase in red tape and bureaucracy was associated with lower levels of job satisfaction; members who were committed to the union perceived less bureaucracy, but those who were not committed perceived more (Davis, 2013). Thus, individuals who are not initially committed to the union may be irritated with the additional red tape that exists within the organization.

Furthermore, unions make it difficult to get accurate assessments of satisfaction. First, satisfaction is usually assessed through surveys, and the individuals who are motivated to complete these surveys tend to be those who are strongly dissatisfied. In addition, unions can fan the flames of discontent in order to advocate for change from management; thus, low ratings of satisfaction may reflect a biased attitude that is intended to elicit a change from management (Powdthavee, 2011). There are a number of other issues affecting data collection, such as the fact that union and nonunion members are not randomly assigned (for example, perhaps people who are more prone to dissatisfaction will be more likely to join a union) (Cotti, Haley, & Miller, 2014). In fact, in their own data where they controlled for a number of selection effects, Cotti and colleagues found a positive relationship between union membership and satisfaction, which was explained by the fact that union members felt they had more voice in what occurs in an organization. These researchers also suggest that if organizations provide workers with more autonomy and influence in the workplace, those actions might alleviate the need for unions altogether. As you can see, there are a number of reasons why we see the overall negative relationship between union membership and satisfaction, and some variables actually may hide what is, in fact, a positive relationship between the two variables.

It is interesting to note that the research cited here was not done by I/O psychologists (in fact, most of the studies cited above were conducted by researchers trained in economics and business, not psychology). Historically, I/O psychologists have not been heavily involved in research on unions. However, I/O psychologists can provide some useful tools that allow unions and management to work together better. For example, I/O psychologists can conduct satisfaction surveys, suggest interventions, and help management and unions negotiate agreements. Concepts such as engagement, perceived organizational support, and justice can help I/O psychologists find ways to keep workers satisfied and productive, whether a union is present or not.

### Discussion Questions:

1. What are some ways that the work of an I/O psychologist can benefit both employers and unions?
2. Imagine that your client, a manufacturing plant, wants their workers to improve productivity by 20%, and the union asserts this is not possible. What are some I/O tools and concepts you could apply to this situation to help management and the union find an acceptable compromise?

### References:

Artz, B. (2010). The impact of union experience on job satisfaction. *Industrial Relations, 49,* 387–405.

Artz, B. (2012). Does this impact of union experience on job satisfaction differ by gender? *Industrial and Labor Relations Review, 65,* 225–243.

Cotti, C. D., Haley, M. R., & Miller, L. A. (2014). Workplace flexibilities, job satisfaction and union membership in the US workforce. *British Journal of Industrial Relations, 52,* 403–425.

Davis, R. S. (2013). Unionization and work attitudes: How union commitment influences public sector jobs. *Public Administration Review, 73,* 74–84.

Powdthavee, N. (2011). Anticipation, free rider problems, and adaptation to trade unions: Re-examining the curious case of dissatisfied union members. *Industrial and Labor Relations Review, 64,* 1000–1019.

### Additional Readings:

Lefkowitz, J. (2005). The values of industrial-organizational psychologists: Who are we? *The Industrial-Organizational Psychologist, 43.2.* Retrieved from http://www.siop.org/tip/backissues/Oct05/03lefkowitz.aspx.

individual-difference variables were identified as important predictors of organizational commitment. Across 53 different samples, researchers found a .15 correlation between age and affective commitment, indicating that the older employees are, the more affectively committed they are. This could be the result of more experience or tenure on the job, or it could be that as we age we are increasingly likely to end up in a job that we like, and thus we become emotionally attached to it.

One of the more interesting new findings involves the potential role of guilt. A recent paper presents results from both the laboratory and the field (Flynn and Schaumberg, 2012) indicating that more guilt-prone individuals—that is, people who are more apt to feel guilty—tend to work harder because they feel more affective commitment to their organization. Individuals who have a tendency to feel guilty seem more motivated to fix the situation and perform better to remove their guilt because they become more committed to their organization as a result of the guilt.

In the previously discussed Meyer et al. meta-analysis, the researchers also found a .16 correlation between organizational tenure and affective commitment, suggesting that individuals with more tenure in the organization are more committed to the organization than are individuals with less tenure. Specifically, they discovered a stronger relationship between organizational tenure and continuance commitment ($r = .21$) than between organizational tenure and affective commitment, thus supporting what we know about these two components of commitment: As employees' tenure with an organization increases, their sunk costs—and hence their continuance commitment— also increase.

**Social Factors** The last category of antecedents revolves around social interactions and relationships. A recent study of 514 attorneys in Hong Kong found that perceptions of justice were related to organizational commitment, but the relationships were mediated through perceived organizational support (Loi, Hang-yue, & Foley, 2006).

Organizational support has been found to be one of the strongest predictors of affective and normative commitment (Meyer et al., 2002). For instance, the extent to which a boss treats employees considerately ($r = .34$) and communicates often and openly with them ($r = .45$) is related to the employees' level of organizational commitment (Mathieu & Zajac, 1990). Role variables are important antecedents of affective commitment, given consistent negative correlations between certain concepts—like role ambiguity (when employees are not sure what is expected of them) and role conflict (when role expectations are inconsistent)—and organizational commitment (Meyer et al., 2002). Organizational justice has been identified as an important predictor of both affective and normative commitment (Meyer et al., 2002), with correlations tending to fall in the .30s.

## Consequences

In Figure 10.10, the potential consequences of organizational commitment are divided into three categories—performance, withdrawal behaviors, and counterproductive behaviors.

**Performance** It is reasonable to assume that any work-related attitude will be more favorably viewed by organizational practitioners if that attitude is directly related to job performance. However, as we noted in an earlier section, expecting strong direct relationships between job satisfaction and performance outcome variables is not reasonable, given the complexity of performance. The same advice holds for organizational commitment: Don't expect a strong direct relationship between commitment and performance. Still, we can try to understand what the empirical data indicate about the relationship that does exist. For instance, in a national sample of almost 300 workers, affective commitment served as an antecedent of innovative performance (Ng, Feldman, & Lam, 2010), suggesting a potentially important role for commitment in organizational innovation. Looking at innovation is a nice new wrinkle in this literature, and so is looking at commitment at the group level. A recent study of service sector employees in the United Kingdom showed that affective commitment measured at the group level (i.e., the average commitment score for a particular geographical site or location) was significantly negatively related to both group-level customer complaints and average customer service times (Conway and Briner, 2012).

Studies report correlations between affective commitment and task performance ranging from .15 to .25. Similarly, contextual performance appears to be consistently related to affective commitment in a positive way, less consistently related to normative commitment, and unrelated or somewhat negatively related to continuance commitment (Meyer et al., 2002). Two reviews found a stronger relationship between OC and performance when performance was extra-role (i.e., OCBs) rather than in-role (i.e., task performance) (Meyer et al., 2002; Riketta, 2002). Finally, a study found that even after controlling for procedural justice and job satisfaction, affective commitment accounted for a significant amount of variance in altruistic OCBs (such as helping other employees), suggesting that it might be more important than satisfaction or justice in predicting OCBs (Schappe, 1998). The author of this study concluded that employees' feelings about their organization may manifest themselves in terms of OCBs that are important to organizational functioning.

**Withdrawal Behaviors** Affective commitment and absence appear to be correlated to a small but significant degree. For instance, one study found a −.18 correlation between affective commitment and the frequency of absence incidents over a 12-month period (Gellatly, 1995). A second study found a −.22 correlation between the affective commitment of bus drivers and the frequency of absence incidents that were under the drivers' control (Hackett, Bycio, & Hausdorf, 1994). Again, think back to the attendance model in Figure 10.7 and recall the many variables other than attitudes that play a part in determining absence behavior; a direct correlation of about −.20 should not be surprising. In fact, the best estimate of the relationship between affective commitment and voluntary absence is −.22 (Meyer et al., 2002). Not as much research has explored continuance or normative commitment. However, one recent study looked at all three components of commitment and their relationships with absence in a sample of U.K. secondary school employees (Woods, Poole, & Zibarras, 2012).

As expected, normative ($-.45$) and affective ($-.53$) commitment had negative relationships with absence frequency, but these were stronger than might be anticipated based on the existing literature. Continuance commitment was not significantly related to absence. However, they did find that both normative and continuance commitment interacted with age in predicting absence. The negative effect of normative commitment and the positive effect of continuance commitment were both stronger for older workers than younger workers. It may be that older workers who feel tied to their organization because of location or retirement benefits (continuance commitment variables) don't see turnover as an option and so choose the other obvious type of withdrawal—absenteeism. On the other hand, older workers with a low sense of obligation to the organization may find absenteeism as an easy way to respond to stress or issues at work that push them away from their workplaces. So, this study seems to identify all three components as important for absenteeism, but the most interesting finding may be that older employees who feel very little obligation to the organization or who have a lack of options or alternatives to their current job are those most likely to be absent from work.

Organizational commitment has a long-standing association with turnover (see Mowday et al., 1979). This association is clear in my earlier presentation of the three characteristics that define a highly committed employee, the last of which is *a strong desire to remain a part of the organization*. By definition, organizational commitment should be negatively related to the turnover process. The meta-analyses vary a bit, but the relationship between affective commitment and actual turnover is approximately $-.15$ to $-.25$.

Much stronger correlations ($-.40$ to $-.50$) are typically found between affective commitment and intentions to leave a job (e.g., Marique & Stinglhamber, 2011), which is consistent with the theory of planned behavior described earlier. For instance, a study of 316 Belgian employees reported a .57 relationship between affective commitment and intent to quit (Vandenberghe, Bentein, & Stinglhamber, 2004). Interestingly, intent to quit predicted actual turnover very well 18 months later ($r = .38$). Both normative commitment and continuance commitment are significantly and negatively related to withdrawal cognitions as well, but the relationships are smaller than with affective commitment ($r = -.33$ and $-.18$, respectively). Another study has found similar and consistently strong effects in a Chinese sample (Cheng & Stockdale, 2003). For normative commitment, Meyer and his colleagues have found a similar pattern but weaker relationships, with correlations ranging from $-.20$ to $-.38$ (Meyer et al., 2002).

Some very recent research has positioned organizational commitment as an important mediator between various other constructs and turnover or turnover intentions. Turnover intentions are often studied in turnover research because of the difficulty in measuring actual turnover and the consistently strong relationship between turnover intentions and actual turnover. I'd like to share a couple of examples of research on commitment as a potential mediator. In a study of 168 part-time MBA students/full-time white-collar employees in Malaysia, researchers proposed and found that affective commitment mediated the relationship between distributive justice and turnover intentions (Poon, 2012). The correlation between affective commitment and turnover intentions was quite large ($r = -.68$), indicating that employees who were not emotionally attached to the organization were more likely to intend to leave the organization than were those who were emotionally attached. Further, they found that affective commitment mediated the relationship between distributive justice and turnover intentions such that employees who felt like they were fairly rewarded for their performance were also committed to the organization and less likely to be actively looking to leave the organization. Not to complicate things here, but I think it's interesting that the researchers also found that this mediational chain was moderated by perceptions of procedural justice such that the degree of emotional attachment to the organization mattered most in affecting turnover when people felt like the procedures used in interacting with them were not fair (i.e., they were low on procedural justice). To summarize, when employees don't get what they perceive to be fair outcomes, they tend not to be committed to the organization or positively emotionally attached and, therefore, are more likely to look for a job and intend to leave the organization. This negative effect of commitment on turnover intentions is strengthened if they also believe that their supervisors are relying on unfair procedures in making workplace decisions.

In another recent investigation of commitment and turnover intentions (Jehanzeb, Rasheed, & Rasheed, 2013), researchers surveyed 251 Saudi Arabian employees and found a strong, negative relationship ($r = -.48$). Further, they found that the availability of organizational training programs positively impacted employees' levels of emotional attachment, which was related to turnover intentions—again, this suggests a mediational relationship even though the authors did not use statistical analyses to test it in this way. Finally, another recent study broadened the notion of commitment and chose to focus on affective occupational (rather than organizational) commitment, which is the emotional attachment one has to his or her occupation rather than to his or her specific organization (Weng & McElroy, 2012). Similar, albeit somewhat weaker, results were found with affective occupational commitment being negatively related to turnover intentions ($r = -.23$). In a regression analysis, the authors found that occupational commitment accounted for 13% of the variance in turnover intentions after controlling for demographic and other variables. In addition, they demonstrated that occupational commitment mediated the relationship between satisfaction with career growth and turnover intentions. The more satisfied employees were with their career progress, the more committed they were to the occupation and the less likely they were to look for a job change.

A few things are clear from these studies. First, the relationship between commitment and turnover is substantial and significant across many studies. Second, the relationship holds up across many different samples in different cultures. Third, commitment serves as a mediator between other constructs and turnover intentions.

**Counterproductive Behaviors** Although there has not been a great deal of research on the role of organizational commitment in counterproductive behavior, there are various reasons to expect a relationship. One model of counterproductive behavior that emphasizes the role of frustration in the process suggests a likely relationship between frustration and a lack of commitment to the organization (Spector, 1997). Other recent work indicates that the values and goals communicated by an organization have a significant effect on the frequency of counterproductive behaviors. Because one important characteristic of an organizationally committed employee is a strong belief in and acceptance of the organization's goals, it follows that commitment ought to be negatively related to the frequency of counterproductive behavior. In fact, a meta-analysis has uncovered that this relationship is $-.36$ (Dalal, 2005).

Indeed, companies that embrace such organizational values as treating employees with fairness, empowering employees, and demonstrating interpersonal cooperation report higher levels of trust than do companies that do not embrace these values (Boye & Jones, 1997). A recent study sought to extend the results of the Dalal (2005) meta-analysis. In a survey of 120 employee–supervisor pairs from two organizations in South Korea, researchers found a similar negative relationship ($r = -.32$) between employees' reports of their affective commitment and supervisor reports of deviant workplace behaviors, a construct similar to CWB (Gill, Meyer, Lee, Shin, & Yoon, 2011). Further, they also found a significant, but smaller, correlation between continuance commitment and deviant workplace behavior ($r = .15$); as expected, employees who felt bound to the organization through sunk costs and through having few alternatives were more likely to exhibit deviant workplace behavior. This relationship is neither as strong nor as consistent in their data, but it does indicate a relationship nonetheless.

Finally, another recent study examined affective commitment as a mediator in the relationship between Big Five personality factors and workplace deviance (Guay et al., 2016). This research surveyed bank teller–supervisor pairs in South Korea and found strong support for the mediational effect of affective commitment in the relationship between personality and workplace deviance. Further, this study demonstrated that affective commitment was significantly related to both organizational deviance (e.g., dragging out work in order to get overtime or taking property from work without permission) ($r = -.25$), and interpersonal deviance (e.g., cursing at someone at work or publicly embarrassing someone at work) ($r = -.24$). Recent research seems to indicate that organizational commitment is an important antecedent of workplace deviance.

## Organizational Commitment Profiles

A recent trend in the commitment literature has focused on commitment profiles. Meyer and Herscovitch (2001) were probably the first to argue convincingly for the importance of the interactions among the three components of organizational commitment, or what are called commitment profiles. Gellatly, Meyer, and Luchak (2006) advanced the field by arguing that any component of organizational commitment should be interpreted in a context that includes the other components of commitment. For instance, understanding how one experiences continuance commitment and what continuance commitment relates to depends in part on the context that is created by the other components of commitment. A good deal of empirical work has followed from this paper and others that have argued for commitment profiles. The notion of a commitment profile moves us from a variable-centered approach to a person-centered approach that classifies groups of individuals into a particular profile based on their relative score on each of the three components of organizational commitment. It is this notion of commitment profiles that continues to garner a great deal of attention. Breaking each component of commitment into two levels (high and low) and crossing the three in all possible ways leaves us with the potential for eight separate commitment profiles, as suggested by Meyer and Herscovitch.

Somers (2010) used cluster analysis in a sample of 572 hospital workers to create commitment profiles. Seven of the eight possible profiles emerged with only a dominant normative commitment (i.e., people who were high on normative commitment, but low on both continuance and affective commitment) not emerging. He found the lowest intent to turnover in the profile that was comprised of high normative and high affective commitment and in the high commitment profile (i.e., high on all three components). The low commitment profile (i.e., low on all three components) and the dominant continuance commitment profile (i.e., high on continuance and low on the other two) reported the greatest intent to turnover. As expected, the highest actual turnover rate was for the low commitment group and the lowest turnover rate was for the high commitment group. Another similar study (Somers, 2009) replicated some of the results just discussed, but found a couple other interesting pieces. First, the affective–normative dominant profile (i.e., high on affective and normative commitment and low on continuance) resulted in the lowest level of job stress and in less stress than the highly committed profile (i.e., high on all three). This difference in stress levels in these two profiles suggests that continuance commitment gets in the way and actually leads to more stress than if one is only highly committed based on affect and moral obligation. Further, the study concludes that, based on analyses of various profiles, the dominant affective–normative profile provides the most benefits to organizations in terms of retention, psychological well-being, and OCBs.

Two other recent studies employed a more sophisticated design and analytic strategy called latent profile analysis to identify the commitment profiles. One study sampled 712 university employees in Belgium and identified five of the same profiles as other studies such as the ones described above (Stanley, Vandenberghe, Vandenberg, & Bentein, 2013). A few interesting results were uncovered. First, all the profiles that included a high level of affective commitment showed the lowest mean level of turnover intention. These results suggest that it doesn't matter much what affective commitment is paired with since it seems to limit turnover intentions. Perhaps the most interesting finding is that the dominant continuance profile folks (those with high continuance commitment and low affective and normative commitment) thought about leaving more often than did the highly committed profile because, according to the researchers, they are continuously evaluating their situation with their current organization and considering the alternatives and risks that are commonly associated with continuance commitment. However, despite the strong intentions to quit the organization, these same high continuance commitment folks displayed turnover numbers as low as the affective dominant profiles. This is likely a result of the few alternatives available to these individuals and the sacrifice or losses they would experience if they did leave their organization. Remember that continuance commitment reflects employees who feel bound to the organization because they don't perceive that they have many other alternatives and they would lose things like retirement benefits or seniority if they left the organization.

Finally, a study of 403 employees in three human services organizations attempted to link commitment profiles to motivation and, in particular, to self-determination theory, which we talked about at length in Chapter 9. In addition to finding similar profiles to the other studies we've discussed, this study uncovered a few very interesting findings (Meyer, Stanley, & Parfyonova, 2012): (1) satisfaction of all three needs (autonomy, competence, and relatedness) integral to self-determination theory was greatest in the two profiles in which both affective and normative commitment were high; (2) individuals in the uncommitted profile group had the lowest need satisfaction scores overall; (3) OCBs were displayed more often by the fully committed group and the dominant affective–normative group; (4) positive affect and work engagement were greatest and negative affect and health complaints were lowest in the fully committed group and the dominant affective–normative group; and (5) well-being indicators were less favorable in the dominant continuance group than any other group except the uncommitted group. Like the results of Somers (2009), the dominant affective–normative commitment profile appears to have the most positive benefits for both employees and the organization. It appears that when normative commitment is paired with high affective commitment, normative commitment is experienced in a positive light as a moral imperative that internally drives an individual's behavior. Clearly, if organizations are interested in keeping their employees satisfied, motivated, psychologically healthy, and more engaged, they should attempt to connect with their employees through agreement on the organization's goals and values and encourage employees to see that remaining with the organization is the right thing to do. The data clearly indicate that the combination of high affective and high normative commitment is a win–win for the organization and the employee.

Robin Beck/Getty Images

**A CLOSER LOOK**
How might the campus-like environments at places like Apple, Google, and Facebook (pictured here) influence an employee's commitment?

# ADDITIONAL JOB ATTITUDES

Although job satisfaction and organizational commitment have received by far the most attention from employee attitude researchers, a few other attitudes deserve mention: job involvement and work centrality; perceived organizational support; and emotions in the workplace.

## Job Involvement and Work Centrality

**job involvement**
The extent to which employees are cognitively engaged in their jobs.

**workaholic**
An individual whose high drive to work and high job involvement become so intense that they result in work–life imbalance issues.

**work centrality**
The degree of importance that work holds in one's life.

Job involvement and work centrality are closely related to each other and to organizational commitment; they also have a long history in I/O psychology. **Job involvement** is the extent to which employees are cognitively engaged in their jobs (Paullay, Alliger, & Stone-Romero, 1994). In extreme cases, employees may become **workaholics**, meaning that they enjoy the act of working (although they tend not to enjoy their particular job) but are obsessed with it and devote great personal time to it at the expense of other important life roles (Ng, Sorensen, & Feldman, 2007). **Work centrality**, on the other hand, is defined as the degree of importance that work, in general, holds in an employee's life (Paullay et al., 1994). This attitude usually develops as a result of socialization, reflecting the nature of our individual role models as we grow and mature. One distinction between job involvement and work centrality is that the former focuses on one's particular job, whereas the latter concerns work in general. Although we know less about these two constructs than about the others discussed in this chapter, research continues to illuminate the role they play in organizations.

According to two studies, for instance, job involvement, work centrality, and organizational commitment are moderately intercorrelated, with relationships between .25 and .45 (Hirschfeld & Feild, 2000; Paullay et al., 1994). Based on the relationships among these three constructs, one study of over 300 employees (Hirschfeld & Feild, 2000) concluded that affectively committed employees tend to identify with their work roles (work centrality) and are engaged in their jobs (job involvement). A meta-analysis examining the potential effects of work centrality on employee work outcomes demonstrated that work centrality is positively related to salary level, number of promotions, and career satisfaction (Ng, Eby, Sorensen, & Feldman, 2005).

Second, an investigation of over 280 public-sector employees found that job involvement moderated the effect of job insecurity on outcomes such as negative job attitudes, health problems, and psychological distress (Probst, 2000). In particular, job insecurity had stronger effects on these outcomes for individuals who were highly involved in their jobs. This makes a great deal of sense: If you are invested in your job and engaged by it, then job security is likely to be very important to you and job insecurity is more likely to lead to negative attitudes and both physical and psychological distress.

More attention has been directed at workaholism in recent years. A longitudinal study of 191 employees of a Dutch university found that rigid personal beliefs, such as the belief that self-esteem is contingent on good performance, predicted compulsive work behavior (one dimension of workaholism) six months later (Van Wijhe, Peeters, & Schaufeli, 2014). They also found that people who reported that they tend to continue working because they want to make sure that they've done enough or they are concerned that they haven't worked hard enough also tended to work both compulsively and excessively six months later. Finally, they found a significant relationship between working compulsively and exhaustion. The researchers argue that there may be opportunities to use these results to build cognitive interventions that may change the way people think about self-esteem and working hard, and thus reduce workaholism.

Another very interesting study found that daily work activities done at night tend to have a more severe negative effect on evening happiness and energy for workaholics than they do for nonworkaholics (Bakker, Demerouti, Oerlemans, & Sonnetag, 2013). In contrast, because nonworkaholics tend to enjoy work more than workaholics, they are more apt to enjoy daily work activities done in the evening than workaholics, who would probably need a different release. The authors also found that physical exercise during leisure time resulted in individuals feeling happier and more rested before bedtime. Interestingly, this effect was stronger for workaholics— a finding that suggests physical exercise in the evening may be a very effective way for workaholics to prevent their workaholism from negatively affecting their happiness. Nonworkaholics do not have the same compulsion to work and may find other ways to detach from work during their leisure time.

Some recent work focusing on workaholism has found that workaholics in general experience more work–life imbalance and less life satisfaction than do nonworkaholics (Aziz & Zickar, 2006). This kind of thinking has led researchers to begin hypothesizing about and examining the boundaries between work and home and the different ways in which people define them (Kreiner, Hollensbe, & Sheep, 2009). We will consider work–family issues in Chapter 11.

## Perceived Organizational Support

**Perceived organizational support (POS)** has been defined by Rhoades and Eisenberger (2002) as employees' global beliefs concerning the extent to which the organization values their contributions and cares about their well-being. A review by these authors of over 70 empirical studies identified the major antecedents and consequences of POS. A more recent and extensive meta-analysis was driven by organizational support theory, which suggests that employees form an overall perception about the extent to which the organization cares about them (Kurtessis et al., 2015). The researchers found overwhelming support for the theory and how POS relates to various antecedents and outcomes. For instance, the results indicate that among the more strongly related antecedents of POS are: perceptions of supervisor treatment, transformational leadership style, psychological contract breach (negatively related), organizational politics (negatively related), developmental opportunities provided by the organization, and role conflict (negatively related). Among the more important consequences of POS are: affective commitment, trust

**perceived organizational support (POS)** Employees' global beliefs concerning the extent to which the organization values and cares about them.

in management/organization, job satisfaction, burnout (negatively related), OCBs, and turnover intentions (negatively related). This review makes clear the importance of POS in organizations and will, I believe, help to frame future research in this important area.

## Emotions in the Workplace

**emotion regulation**
The ways in which individuals monitor their emotions and the expression of those emotions.

**emotional labor**
The effort, planning, and control required by employees to express organizationally desired emotions during interpersonal interactions.

In recent years, the role of emotions in the workplace has attracted a great deal of research attention. One topic of interest is generally referred to as **emotion regulation**, or the ways in which individuals monitor their emotions and the expression of those emotions (Gross, 1998). **Emotional labor** is a slightly more specific term, defined as the effort, planning, and control required by employees to express organizationally desired emotions during interpersonal interactions (Morris & Feldman, 1996).

It is believed that there are two forms of emotion regulation: *amplification,* or faking/exaggerating pleasant emotions, and *suppression,* or hiding displays of felt emotions such as anger or jealousy (Cote & Morgan, 2002). Much of the work on the regulation of emotions or on emotional labor has focused on service jobs that emphasize interactions with customers because it is believed that employees in these jobs must constantly regulate their emotions and the expression of them.

Some research suggests that emotional labor is linked to substance abuse, absenteeism, work-related stress, and psychological distress, whereas other research has found these relationships to be weak and inconsistent (Zapf, 2002). One consistent finding, however, is that employees who experience *emotional dissonance*—whose true feelings are different from the emotions they project on the job—experience higher rates of stress (Grandey & Brauburger, 2002). For example, people who tend to see the world in rather rigid and negative ways may experience emotional dissonance as customer service representatives, who are required by their job to be pleasant, helpful, and encouraging. This disconnect between their true feelings and what's required of them at work is likely to lead to stress, burnout, and, ultimately, poor customer service. (See Chapter 11 for a more detailed discussion of stress.)

Regulation of emotions at work has become an area of great interest for scholars as indicated by the number of interesting and sophisticated studies recently conducted. I will discuss a few of those recent studies to give a flavor for what is going on empirically in this area. Employees who need to manage their emotions at work can do so in various ways. Traditionally, researchers have referred to two different techniques: deep acting and surface acting (Hochschild, 1983). Deep acting involves not just controlling the display of emotions, but also modifying one's inner feelings to match the display of affect or emotions. Surface acting involves "faking" emotions outwardly without changing one's inner emotions or feelings. Similar to deep acting is a more recent idea referred to in the literature as *automatic regulation* in which authentic displays of emotion are presented (i.e., the display matches one's true feelings/emotions), but this happens without conscious acting—it is an automatic display of naturally felt emotions (Diefendorff, Croyle, & Gosserand, 2005).

In a recent series of studies, researchers have linked the use of deep acting and automatic regulation of Dutch restaurant servers, taxi drivers, and other service employees with tips they received (Hülsheger, Lang, Schewe, & Zijlstra, 2015). In one of the studies, the researchers trained German hairdressers to use cognitive change and attentional processes to support the use of deep acting and automatic display of naturally felt emotions. They found that those participants who used the training information received significantly more tips than did those in the control group, suggesting that those who deep act and automatically regulate are financially rewarded for these behaviors. The researchers argue that because customers are usually looking to save money and tipping is voluntary, tipping is a strong indicator of customers' emotions or attitudes about their service experience. These results demonstrate the idea of emotional contagion in which the server's emotions spread to others including customers. It follows that employees' use of emotion regulation likely has effects beyond their own tips and likely results in more business and a better outcome for the company.

In a related study, researchers coded phone calls received by a medical billing office that included an expression of negative emotions from the customer (Little, Kluemper, Nelson, & Ward, 2013). The calls were coded for the expressed emotions of the customer service representative and the customer as well as for the way in which the customer service representative tried to deal with the customer's negative emotions. They found that problem-focused coping, trying to get at the core issue and fix it, reduced the intensity of negative emotions and increased the positive emotions, whereas emotion-focused coping, attempts to reduce the negative emotions through small talk or telling a joke, actually increased the intensity of negative emotions. This study also suggests that training is important and that some customer service representatives may be trying to help manage customer emotions in a way that intensifies the customer's negative emotions.

Other studies have looked at characteristics of individuals who are especially good or bad at emotion regulation. For instance, a recent study looked at how individuals use both surface and deep acting and whether there are subsets of individuals who use these two strategies in similar ways (Gabriel, Daniels, Diefendorff, & Greguras, 2015). These researchers used two studies to identify five different profiles of emotional labor with different antecedents and outcomes. For instance, deep actors (high on deep acting/low on surface acting) differ considerably from surface actors (low on deep acting/high on surface acting), and both differ from regulators (high on deep acting/high on surface acting). There were many interesting differences across the five profiles; here are just a few: (1) being high in positive affectivity increased the likelihood of being a deep actor as compared to a regulator; (2) being high on customer orientation meant that one was very unlikely to be a surface actor; (3) surface actors exhibited higher emotional exhaustion, lower job satisfaction, and higher felt inauthenticity than all other profiles. These results suggest that deep acting or low levels of emotion regulation are most beneficial for employee well-being—perhaps managers can use this information in a selection or training context.

© Radius Images/Corbis

Another intriguing look at individual differences and affect regulation is found in a recent paper with a focus on affect spin, which is the variability in affective experiences (Beal, Trougakos, Weiss, & Dalal, 2013). Someone who is high in affect spin likely experiences lots of different affective dimensions whereas someone who is low on affect spin tends to experience a small subset of affective dimensions reliably. In their study of restaurant servers in the United States and Canada, they found that those who were high in affect spin experienced more strain and fatigue as a result of surface acting. This was expected based on previous studies that have shown those high in affect spin tend to react more strongly to environmental conditions. There are other, more complicated results in this study, but the implications are that understanding affect spin may help managers get a better handle on the strain and fatigue experienced by employees and may also give some clues about anticipating absenteeism, turnover intentions, and other important outcome variables.

One particularly fascinating study focused on coffeehouse baristas and service with a smile (Barger & Grandey, 2006). Trained coders observed 220 employee–customer interactions, recording both employee and customer behaviors. They found that the strength of employees' smiles predicted customer satisfaction and customer ratings of service. The authors warn, however, that fake or forced smiles sometimes backfire, since other research has demonstrated that inauthentic displays of emotion lead to less positive customer impressions (e.g., Grandey, Fisk, Mattila, Jansen, & Sideman, 2005).

The existing work on emotional labor has numerous relevant applications. For instance, emotional dissonance, given its links to stress and burnout, has implications for selection systems that determine how well employees fit into the hiring organization—a factor known as *person–organization fit* (for a comprehensive discussion of this and other "fit" constructs, see Kristof-Brown, Zimmerman, & Johnson, 2005). Not surprisingly, customer service representatives are likely to be more successful at their jobs if their emotional makeup is somewhat consistent with the emotional regulation required in those jobs. A preliminary job analysis conducted by an I/O professional is a vital step in helping to ensure not only person–organization fit but also employee–job fit. Ideally, applicants who believe that people should help themselves and not expect others to help them at all, who don't enjoy interacting with people, and who believe that customers are never right should be screened out by such predictors. Think about it: How many times in the past few weeks have you walked into a store and been "served" by a customer service employee who was clearly unable to do the emotional labor required of that job and really didn't care much about you as a customer? Additional research on emotional labor promises to enhance our understanding of organizations and increase organizational effectiveness.

## Summary

This chapter is divided into four sections. First, I presented some background information on attitudes, behaviors, and the relationship among them. At the outset, I discussed the theory of planned behavior as a model of this relationship and then referred to it throughout while trying to make sense of the links between work-related attitudes and organizational outcomes. The work of Ajzen and Fishbein provided a nice foundation for the more work-specific issues that were discussed later in the chapter.

Second, after considering various reasons why I/O researchers and practitioners are interested in job attitudes, I presented a detailed overview of job satisfaction, using Figure 10.2 as a basis for discussion. I cited research dealing with the four main classes of antecedents to job satisfaction: job characteristics, individual/personal characteristics, social factors, and growth opportunities. All of these antecedents appear to make important contributions to employees' levels of job satisfaction. I also discussed a few scales that measure job satisfaction, included examples of those scales, and considered the multidimensional nature of job satisfaction. To conclude this section on job satisfaction, I discussed at length three classes of organizational outcome variables (consequences) that appear to be substantively linked to job satisfaction: performance, withdrawal behaviors, and counterproductive behaviors.

In the third section, I presented Figure 10.10 as a working heuristic for our discussion of organizational commitment. Throughout, I reviewed Meyer and Allen's three-component model: affective commitment, continuance commitment, and normative commitment. I also classified the antecedents of organizational commitment as organizational, individual, or social in nature. Each of these sets of variables seems to have potential effects on organizational commitment. Indeed, recent research in this area demonstrates that performance, withdrawal behaviors, and counterproductive behaviors are all influenced by organizational commitment. Organizational profiles were examined as a newer focus of commitment research. Finally, in the context of other work attitudes, I discussed the role played by job involvement, work centrality, perceived organizational support, and emotions in the workplace.

## Key Terms

affective commitment (p. 340)

affective disposition (p. 324)

attitude (p. 319)

continuance commitment (p. 340)

counterproductive work behaviors (CWBs) (p. 337)

emotion regulation (p. 352)

emotional labor (p. 352)

job involvement (p. 350)

job satisfaction (p. 321)

normative commitment (p. 340)

organizational commitment (OC) (p. 338)

organizational justice (p. 326)

organization-based self-esteem (OBSE) (p. 325)

perceived behavioral control (p. 320)

perceived organizational support (POS) (p. 351)

psychological contract (p. 325)

subjective norm (p. 320)

work centrality (p. 350)

workaholic (p. 350)

## TAKING IT TO THE FIELD

One particularly difficult part of work is learning how to deliver bad news in a way that preserves an employee's positive feelings and attitudes toward the job. However, because job satisfaction is a well-researched topic, I/O psychologists have many different ways to approach this problem. One of your long-standing clients, Karen Strazinski, manager of River Valley Bank, has experienced some problems surrounding a bank closure. She is looking to you to help her strategize how she can salvage morale among workers who will not be laid off.

Hello—

Thanks again for agreeing to help me with my problem. Here's some background into the problems River Valley Bank is experiencing. Previously, we had two bank locations: Green River and South Bend. Due to economic issues in the area, we have recently closed the Green River location. We were able to offer a few jobs at South Bend to our best Green River employees, but we couldn't take them all. Those who were laid off received a month's salary as their severance package.

The problem is with the employees at South Bend. Despite our assurances that their jobs are safe, the employees are demoralized, unmotivated, and afraid they will lose their jobs. There have been more absences and tardiness, and a handful of our best South Bend employees have left for other jobs. In their exit interviews, many of them have stated that they liked their jobs, but that they would rather "jump ship" now than get laid off down the road.

I know that employees spend a lot of time talking about the Green River closure, and gossiped that it is just a matter of time before layoffs come to South Bend. This is not true, and I've told them this. However, the closing of Green River was not handled well, and many employees were genuinely surprised by the closure. I think the employees who were transferred from Green River are not helping the situation, as many of them are upset about the transfer.

This is obviously a tough situation for everyone. Clearly, telling them that they are safe is not working. But the poor performance that's occurring really will put South Bend in jeopardy, so we need to get this bad trend turned around. What steps would you suggest I take to help improve morale here at South Bend?

Karen

Write an e-mail responding to Karen's problems. Be sure to provide her with specific ways by which she can bolster morale during this difficult time at her company.

## Critical Thinking Questions

1. Is employees' job satisfaction stable over time, or can it vary? How could an organization modify its work environment in order to increase employees' job satisfaction?

2. How might the varying forms of organizational commitment become manifest in employees' on-the-job behavior?

3. Assume you have been hired by an organization to survey the job attitudes of its employees. Your survey cannot exceed a certain number of items due to concerns that it will take the employees too long to complete. If you only have time to

administer valid, reliable measures of *three* job attitudes, which attitudes would you measure and why?

**4.** How has the emphasis on service industries had an effect on the study of emotion regulation and emotional labor?

## Application Questions

**1.** Compare two jobs you have held and your overall satisfaction with those jobs. Was your satisfaction similar in both jobs? If so, why do you think that is? If not, what affected your satisfaction?

**2.** It is common in consulting work to encounter managers who believe that job attitudes do not matter—if someone quits, they will just hire another person to replace that person. What might you say to these types of managers?

**3.** Imagine you have to tell one of your best employees that she will not be getting her expected bonus check this year due to financial problems in the company. What might you tell her to ensure that she will still feel satisfied with her job, even though she will be disappointed about her bonus check?

**4.** The chapter discusses emotional labor (when employees must fake positive emotions or hide negative emotions). Provide an example in which you had to engage in emotional labor and how that experience made you feel about that situation.

**5.** If you were to win enough money in a lottery so that you would never need to work again if you didn't want to, would you still work? Why or why not?

## Suggested Readings

**Burke, R. J.** (2006). *Research companion to working time and work addiction.* Northampton, MA: Edward Elgar. Contributing authors explore the fascinating and relatively new phenomenon of workaholism.

**Elfenbein, H. A.** (2008). Emotion in organizations: A review and theoretical integration in stages. *The Academy of Management Annals, 1,* 315–386. Elfenbein provides an excellent overview of emotion in organizations, with particular attention paid to specific job attitudes such as job satisfaction.

**Meyer, J. P., Stanley, L. J., & Parfyonova, N. M.** (2012). Employee commitment in context: The nature and implication of commitment profiles. *Journal of Vocational Behavior, 80*(1), 1–16. A great overview of commitment profiles and how they impact organizational processes written by the unquestioned leader in research on organizational commitment.

**Holtom, B. C., Mitchell, T. R., Lee, T. W., & Eberly, M. B.** (2008). Turnover and retention research: A glance at the past, a closer review of the present, and a venture into the future. *The Academy of Management Annals, 2,* 231–274. The foremost researchers on turnover and retention explore the past, present, and future state of research into why employees stay with or leave their organizations.

# Stress and Worker Well-Being

Photo: skynesher/Getty Images

## LEARNING OBJECTIVES

This chapter should help you understand:

- The difference between stressors and strains
- How coping skills help individuals handle stress
- Warr's environmental determinants of well-being
- Many of the important issues that are involved in work–family conflict
- The importance of family-friendly employee benefits
- The ways in which companies are helping employees balance their work and family lives with as little stress as possible
- The particular complexities faced by dual-earner couples
- Why job loss and underemployment are among the most severe sources of stress that individuals ever experience
- The factors that trigger workplace violence in the United States today

Has something like this ever happened to you?

After waking with a headache, probably the result of staying up until 3:00 AM studying for two final exams that happen to fall on the same day, you go to the refrigerator to find there's no milk for your cereal. You instead gobble down a Pop-Tart while reviewing your notes for your psychology exam—and suddenly realize that you never got the notes for the day you missed to attend your grandmother's funeral. After unsuccessfully trying to call a couple of friends in the hope of catching a quick glimpse of their notes, you go back to studying and get frustrated because you just can't seem to remember all the definitions that are likely to be on the exam. Finally, you grab your backpack and head for the bus. As you close the door behind you and step outside, your foot sinks into eight inches of snow that you didn't even realize had fallen overnight. It's now 9:00 AM, and you realize it will take a lot longer to get to class. Making it to your 10:00 AM exam will be tight—and your psychology professor makes no exceptions for makeups or tardiness.

Or how about something like this?

You wake up in the morning and just don't feel right. You get out of bed and notice that you have a little headache. After your shower, you sit down to eat breakfast and read the morning news, but you can't seem to finish an article—your mind keeps wandering. Before leaving for work, you pull out your calendar and remember that your day includes a meeting with a supervisor who usually asks to see you only when she has a problem with your work, a meeting with a disgruntled subordinate who thinks he should have been promoted but you think should be fired, about four hours of administrative paperwork, and a sexual harassment training session because your department has been guilty of some serious violations in this area.

These situations involve stress—a word that is often thrown around casually. In this chapter, I will define the major components of the stress process in a more formal way and discuss stress as it relates to work. In addition, I consider some modifications that organizations are implementing to reduce the stress that is so prevalent in today's workplaces. The chapter concludes by focusing on one of the most terrifying outcomes of excessive stress—workplace violence.

## STRESSORS AND STRAINS

There continues to be disagreement and even confusion among psychologists regarding the key terms used to describe stress and strain. I refer to *stress* in a general sense throughout the chapter, but I am more specific when I use two important terms. Stressor refers to any seriously disruptive event, situation, or individual. For instance, we experience a stressor when we feel "stretched too thin." The opening scenarios of this chapter presented many examples of stressful events and elements, or stressors, such as anxiety over a work meeting, the death of a close family member, the prospect of being late for class, and so on. Strains, on the other hand, are undesirable personal outcomes resulting from the experience of stressors. In other words, stressors lead to strains. Employees who are particularly stressed at work may experience sickness, low-quality performance, increased absence, poor communication, and many other strains. An upset stomach, for example, is the strain that stems from the stressor of a tight deadline. The short fuse and general crankiness of a worried employee is the strain resulting from the stressor of impending layoffs. This process of stressors leading to strains is what we generally refer to as stress—when we talk about a stressful process, we really mean that we have experienced stressors that have now caused strains or undesirable outcomes. Let's tease these apart a bit more.

**stressor**
Any disruptive event or force that pushes a psychological or physical function beyond its range of stability, producing a strain within the individual.

**strains**
Undesirable personal outcomes resulting from the combined stressful experiences of various life domains.

### Stressors

There are many models of workplace stress. Each has unique elements, but most share several elements as well. **Figure 11.1** was developed on the basis of two such models (see Bhagat, Allie, & Ford, 1995; Cartwright & Cooper, 1997). Though not perfect, this figure presents a reasonable picture of stressors and strains, along with two of the most important coping strategies. In particular, note that the sources of stress are categorized in ways that we have seen elsewhere in the book (e.g., in the Chapter 10 discussion of job satisfaction). Intrinsic factors such as poor working conditions (e.g., low lighting, excessive noise, and poorly designed office space) tend to lead to perceived stress, as do long hours, excessive travel, and lack of control over one's job.

This last factor—lack of control—has been found to play an especially important role in employees' stress levels. According to Robert Karasek's (1990) demand–control model of stress, for example, stress is a function of the psychological demands of work

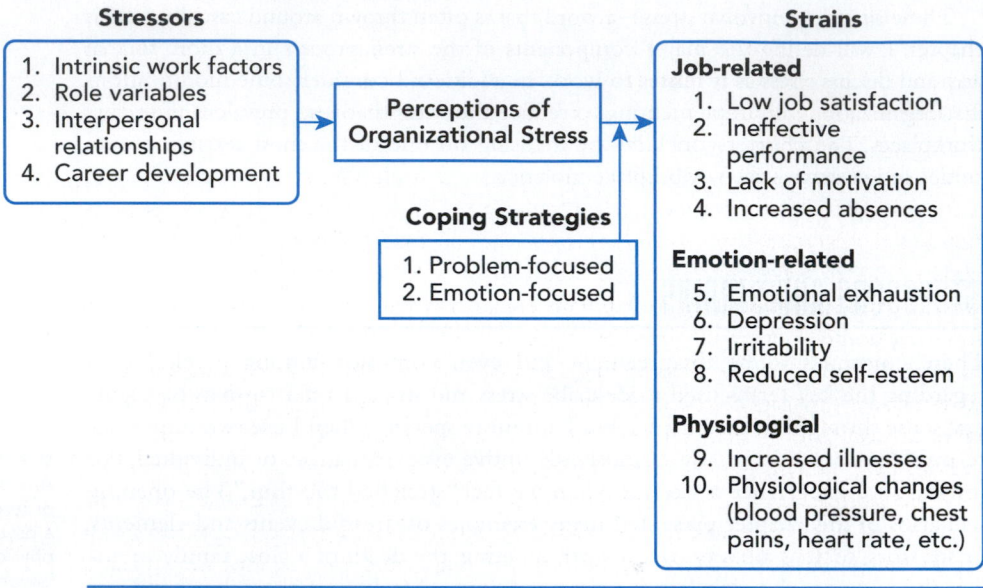

**Stressors**

1. Intrinsic work factors
2. Role variables
3. Interpersonal relationships
4. Career development

**Perceptions of Organizational Stress**

**Coping Strategies**

1. Problem-focused
2. Emotion-focused

**Strains**

**Job-related**

1. Low job satisfaction
2. Ineffective performance
3. Lack of motivation
4. Increased absences

**Emotion-related**

5. Emotional exhaustion
6. Depression
7. Irritability
8. Reduced self-esteem

**Physiological**

9. Increased illnesses
10. Physiological changes (blood pressure, chest pains, heart rate, etc.)

**FIGURE 11.1**   General Stress Model

and the amount of decision latitude (i.e., control) that employees are provided (see also Theorell & Karasek, 1996). Since the inception of this model, many studies have demonstrated links between low levels of workplace control and psychological and physical problems such as heart disease, depression, exhaustion, job dissatisfaction, stomach ailments, and absenteeism (reviewed in Karasek, 1990). More recent work has demonstrated links between excessive workload and time pressure (i.e., stress) as well as major depressive and generalized anxiety disorders (Blackmore et al., 2007; Melchior et al., 2007).

The job demands–resources (JD-R) model of stress is an extension of the demand–control model. Job demands are physical, psychological, social, or organizational elements of the job that require effort from the individual. Resources are the physical, psychological, social, or organizational elements of the job that facilitate the completion of work goals (Bakker & Demerouti, 2007). Basically, an individual perceives stress when the demands of the job are not met by the available resources. For example, if a task demands a high degree of cognitive focus, but I don't have the cognitive resources to focus on the task, then the JD-R model predicts that I will perceive stress, which leads to negative outcomes or strains. In a study of 278 Canadian physicians, researchers found that both demands and resources predicted emotional exhaustion (what we'll call burnout a bit later in this chapter). Heavy job demands (e.g., workload) predicted emotional exhaustion, whereas resources (e.g., autonomy) were positively related to accomplishment and negatively related to physical symptoms (Lee, Brotheridge, & Lovell, 2010).

Another stress model that has received a great deal of support in the literature is the conservation of resources (COR) model, which argues that individuals work to acquire and keep resources that they may need to ward off stress (Hobfoll & Shirom, 2000). When individuals believe that they either don't have or are losing the resources they need, perceptions of stress increase, resulting in strains. A comprehensive review of the application of the COR theory in organizations found that resource loss played a critical role in the stress process and that limiting resource loss was a key to prevention of stress and post-stress intervention (Westman, Hobfoll, Chen, Davidson, & Laski, 2004). An interesting empirical study built on the COR theory found that employees who expend great resources to maintain engagement at work experience increased strains at home as operationalized by work interfering with family life (Halbesleben, Harvey, & Bolino, 2009). This finding suggests that even though organizations tend to want active, engaged employees, the COR theory demonstrates that the effort it takes to maintain the necessary resources at work can sometimes lead to strains felt at home. We will talk about work–family conflict in more detail later in this chapter.

Role variables are another important workplace stressor. A role is a set of behaviors expected of a person who occupies a particular position in a group. Role ambiguity results when role expectations are unclear and employees are thus not sure what is expected of them. Role conflict, on the other hand, occurs when role expectations are inconsistent, as when a supervisor sends employees mixed messages about their roles. For instance, your boss might tell you to be creative and to take initiative—but when you do so, he says that you aren't following company policy. Alternatively, you may get conflicting messages about your role from two different people, such that your subordinate sees your role one way and your boss sees it another way. Needless to say, both role ambiguity and role conflict can lead to workplace stress. A recent study has found that political skill and organizational support can lessen the negative effects of role conflict (Jawahar, Stone, & Kisamore, 2007).

Another source of stress has to do with interpersonal relationships at work. Employees who have bad relationships with their supervisors and coworkers tend to be more stressed than are individuals whose interpersonal relationships are more favorable. If you can recall a stressful job situation that you have experienced, you can also likely recall relationships with your colleagues at that job that were contentious or lacking in trust. It has always been my belief that the people I work with actually have more to do with my stress levels and attitudes toward my job than the job itself does. Indeed, bad interpersonal relationships tend to be stressful regardless of whether they occur in the context of one's job, school, neighborhood, or family.

As noted in Chapter 1, many people define themselves, at least in part, by what they do. Our jobs and careers are important parts of our lives. Thus, it is very stressful to reach a point where opportunities for additional advancement or job security are lacking. In their aptly titled book *Working Scared*, Ken Wexley and Stan Silverman (1993) argue that the stress, nervousness, and uneasiness associated with the changing nature of work have left many of us working scared: scared of being downsized, fired, or considered less competent—and thus more expendable than younger and cheaper employees. More recently, the United States experienced an economic recession

**role**
A set of behaviors expected of a person who occupies a particular position in a group.

**role ambiguity**
A situation that results when role expectations are unclear and employees are thus not sure what is expected of them.

**role conflict**
A situation that results when role expectations are inconsistent, as when a supervisor sends employees mixed messages about their roles.

unlike any seen in decades. We couldn't glance at a newspaper without learning of massive layoffs at one major company or another.

Despite the recession and its potential role in organizational life, very little research has directly examined the role of the recession on employees. One recent study, however, found that recession-related stressors like increased workload and reorganization of work were related to strains and job satisfaction (Jones, Sliter, & Sinclair, 2015). The notion of work ability, or an individual's capacity or capability to continue working, was very important during the recession because of the increased possibility of losing one's job. A recent study operating from a JD-R model found that demands and resources were related to outcomes such as absence through the relationship with perceived work ability (McGonagle, Fisher, Barnes-Farrell, & Grosch, 2015). For instance, the more demands (e.g., time pressure, negative environmental conditions, etc.) that were experienced on the job, the lower the perceived work ability and the more absence from work.

## Strains

Strains are experienced everywhere in the workplace. A partial list is presented in Figure 11.1, which groups them into three categories: job-related, emotional, and physiological. The first category, job-related strains, can occur, for example, when you have a job that creates a great deal of stress or when you probably aren't terribly satisfied with that job or motivated by it. Indeed, a lack of satisfaction and motivation often leads to low effort, high absenteeism, high turnover, and low productivity or ineffective performance (Cartwright & Cooper, 1997). Workplace stress costs companies up to $190 billion annually in U.S. healthcare expenses alone. The biggest stressors are high demands at work, concerns over health insurance, and work–family conflict (Blanding, 2015). Jeffrey Pfeffer and colleagues have conducted a very interesting and comprehensive meta-analysis in which they identify nine stressors that have increased the nation's healthcare costs by 5% to 8%, and determined that job insecurity increased self-report of poor health by 50%, long hours increased mortality by almost 20%, and high-demanding jobs raised the likelihood of a physician-diagnosed illness by 35% (Lynch, 2015). They also argue that more deaths are caused by these workplace stressors than are caused by diabetes or influenza in the United States. Based on these findings, Pfeffer and his colleagues conclude that the environment that workers operate in should receive a great deal more attention from organizations than it currently does (Goh, Pfeffer, & Zenios, 2015).

© Sadie Dayton/Anyone/amanaimages/Corbis

**A CLOSER LOOK**

Burnout can be debilitating for people. Do you think that individuals have much control over burnout, or is it more a function of characteristics of the job?

The second category of strains is emotional strains. Stress certainly takes a toll on us emotionally. One clear indicator that I'm stressed at work is that I have much less patience with my children and become irritable. After a particularly stressful day at work, when my kids acted up (as they all do), I was very quick to lose my temper and seemed unable to understand that they were doing exactly what kids their age do.

Sometimes employees become so stressed that they experience burnout, a condition characterized by (1) *emotional exhaustion,* or being overextended by one's work; (2) *depersonalization,* or a cynical view of others and the work role that often results in detachment; and (3) *reduced personal accomplishment,* or the belief that one is no longer very useful or successful at one's job.

Burnout was originally believed to be limited to the helping professions, such as medicine and psychology (Cordes & Dougherty, 1993). Since then, however, it has been recognized as a more widespread phenomenon (Demerouti, Bakker, Nachreiner, & Schaufeli, 2001) and linked to characteristics of jobs (e.g., workload, control, rewards, social relationships, fairness, and values) rather than to dispositions of people (Maslach, 2003). Work-related stress can be so overwhelming that some individuals lose a sense of self or begin to lack self-esteem. In cases of chronic high stress, they may even become depressed. Furthermore, burnout has effects on job performance, organizational commitment, and turnover (Eatough, Chang, Miloslavic, & Johnson, 2011; Jawahar et al., 2007).

The third category of strains is physiological in nature. There is considerable evidence for the role of stress in physical conditions. One study, for instance, found both life stress and work stress to be significant predictors of the frequency of serious illnesses (Bhagat et al., 1995). Over 600,000 people die of heart disease in the United States every year, which accounts for one in every four deaths (Centers for Disease Control and Prevention, 2015). Stress plays an integral role in heart disease, and workplace stress is a major culprit. The leading causes of disability in the U.S. workforce are heart disease and stroke, and 735,000 Americans have a heart attack every year (Centers for Disease Control and Prevention, 2015).

In addition, there is a widespread belief that managers experience a great deal of stress and, anecdotally, it seems that the level of stress has been increasing in recent years. A study of more than 800 upper-level managers reported some interesting results along these lines (Cavanaugh, Boswell, Roehling, & Boudreau, 2000). According to the researchers, stress is either *challenge-related* or *hindrance-related.* Challenge-related stress—which results from time pressures at work, high levels of responsibility, and job overload—is positively related to job satisfaction and negatively related to searching for a new job. In other words, stress related to being challenged at work has positive outcomes for the manager and for the organization. The researchers also found that hindrance-related stress—which results from constraints that interfere with one's work—is negatively related to job satisfaction and positively related to job searching and voluntary turnover. Hindrance-related stress is often due to red tape, organizational politics, and job insecurity. However, a recent study found support for the idea that some stressors may be appraised as both challenge and hindrance (Webster, Beehr, & Love, 2011). The study also found that hindrance-related stressors were consistently associated with negative outcomes, but that even when things like workload and responsibility are categorized as challenge-related, they had a positive relationship to physical strain. Clearly, these two types of stress have potentially important and sometimes differential effects on outcome variables.

**burnout**
A condition that occurs when employees become so stressed that they experience emotional exhaustion, depersonalization, and a sense of reduced personal accomplishment.

## I/O TODAY

### PTSD and STSD

Although we often think of posttraumatic stress disorder (PTSD) as a strain limited to people in the military, psychologists actually find that PTSD occurs in a number of occupations and for a wide variety of reasons. In some cases, individuals may personally experience dangerous situations. Firefighting and law enforcement are obvious examples where an employee may be exposed to traumatic experiences that lead to symptoms of PTSD. Medical personnel, such as ambulance rescue workers, and journalists, particularly those who have worked in war zones, also demonstrate relatively high levels of PTSD. Even a brief, isolated exposure to a dangerous situation, such as a bank robbery, can trigger PTSD in individuals.

However, PTSD does not only arise when someone is in physical danger; oppressive or abusive work conditions can also lead to symptoms, such as nurses in hospitals who have experienced high levels of bullying from doctors, patients, or even other nurses. Prolonged exposure to these environments can lead to many strains such as burnout and PTSD (Laschinger & Nosko, 2015).

A new area of exploration involves a construct similar to PTSD—secondary traumatic stress disorder (STSD). In STSD cases, an individual may not personally experience a risk to their own life, but they witness the suffering or dying of other people. As you might imagine, there are many jobs where this is a routine experience, such as among emergency room personnel. However, STSD can occur in some unexpected places. One study looked at risk for STSD among train drivers who are involved in accidents where someone is seriously injured or killed by the train (Yum et al., 2006). Recent research has also been exploring exposure to disturbing media, such as video recordings of rapes or deaths. For example, computer forensics investigators who had to view child pornography as part of their investigation reported higher levels of STSD (Perez, Jones, Englert, & Sachau, 2010). In court proceedings, individuals, including judges, juries, bailiffs, and lawyers, may have to view disturbing media. In addition, exposure to disturbing media can occur accidentally, such as an IT worker who accidentally finds violent videos on a customer's computer.

In some jobs, experiencing circumstances that are linked to PTSD or STSD is unavoidable. However, I/O psychologists play an important role in finding ways that organizations can identify and reduce the psychological impact of disturbing experiences. Research has demonstrated that work support, training, and workload all affect the experience of these disorders (Hensel, Ruiz, Finney, & Dewa, 2015). Additional research will help us understand how to structure jobs to limit the negative effects these experiences have on workers.

### Discussion Questions

1. Consider other examples of jobs where someone might personally experience or witness a distressing event. What are some interventions or precautions that the organization can provide for that person to help treat or prevent PTSD/STSD?

2. In jobs where someone is regularly exposed to disturbing events or media, do you believe it is a better approach to have a small group of people dealing with this work over a long period of time, or do you believe it is better to regularly rotate people out of these jobs? What are the benefits and problems with these approaches?

### References

Hensel, J. M., Ruiz, C., Finney, C., & Dewa, C. S. (2015). Meta-analysis of risk factors for secondary traumatic stress in therapeutic work with trauma victims. *Journal of Traumatic Stress, 28*(2), 83–91.

Laschinger, H. K. S., & Nosko, A. (2015). Exposure to workplace bullying and post-traumatic stress disorder symptomology: The role of protective psychological resources. *Journal of Nursing Management, 23*, 252–262.

Perez, L. M., Jones, J., Englert, D. R., & Sachau, D. (2010). Secondary traumatic stress and burnout among law enforcement investigators exposed to disturbing media images. *Journal of Police and Criminal Psychology, 25*, 113–124.

Yum, B. S., Roh, J. H., Ryu, J. C., Won, J. U., Kim, C. N, Lee, J. E., & Kim, K. Y. (2006). Symptoms of PTSD according to individual and work environment characteristics of Korean railroad drivers with experience of person-under-the-train accidents. *Journal of Psychosomatic Research, 61*, 691–697.

### Further Readings

Sliter, M., Kale, A., & Yuan, Z. (2014). Is laughter the best medicine? The buffering effect of coping humor on traumatic stressors in firefighters. *Journal of Organizational Behavior, 35*, 257–272.

## Coping with Stress

Stress is clearly a problem for many employees, but fortunately there are coping mechanisms that can help. Coping is defined as efforts that help people manage or reduce stress. For instance, to handle the stress that comes with reduced supervision because of cutbacks in managerial positions, employees can develop their own responsibilities and objectives and seek high-quality feedback from coworkers, supervisors, and subordinates.

Coping mechanisms take two general forms: problem-focused coping and emotion-focused coping. Problem-focused coping involves behaviors or actions targeted toward solving or handling the stress-inducing problem itself. One example might be compromising with a coworker on a particular conflict. Emotion-focused coping, on the other hand, involves cognitive, or thought-related, strategies that minimize the emotional effects of stress-inducing events. Examples include rationalizing or intellectualizing, looking for the "silver lining," and making the best of a bad situation.

One study suggested that the effectiveness of coping depends on the coping method, the particular stressor, and one's view of oneself (i.e., self-efficacy; Jex, Bliese, Buzzell, & Primeau, 2001). For instance, researchers have shown the coping process to be very complex in situations in which employees have to adjust to an organizational merger over time (Fugate, Kinicki, & Scheck, 2002). An interesting study conducted in Germany and Switzerland found that the extent to which employees used their time away from work to psychologically detach from work was key to protecting their well-being and keeping them engaged at work (Sonnentag, Binnewies, & Mojza, 2010). So the better we use our downtime from work, the less stressed we will be and the fewer strains we'll experience.

A recent study showed that emotional competence (EC) training can improve employee subjective and physical well-being (Kotsou, Nelis, Gregoire, & Mikolajczak, 2011). Emotional competence is the ability to understand, express, and manage feelings (it is similar to emotional intelligence, discussed in Chapter 6). EC has been linked to general well-being as well as work and academic performance. This interesting study of 132 participants found that those randomly assigned to an EC training program—which included group discussions, role-play, and self-observation—showed a significant improvement in EC along with a decrease in perceived and objective stress, a decrease in physical complaints, and improved social relationships (Kotsou et al., 2011). Incredibly, these changes lasted for over a year. Obviously, there is great potential in this kind of intervention as a coping technique.

In addition to coping styles, social support can play a huge role in helping us deal with stress. I'm sure you've experienced this firsthand. It's always easier to handle stress-inducing events or situations if you have others around to provide the kind of support you need. In the workplace, for instance, credible senior-level employees or peers who make an effort to convince you that you can succeed may help you push through stressful situations and rise to the occasion. Quite a few studies have demonstrated the importance of social support in dealing with stress (e.g., Bliese & Britt, 2001;

**coping**
Efforts that help people manage or reduce stress.

**problem-focused coping**
A coping style that involves behaviors or actions targeted toward solving or handling the stress-inducing problem itself.

**emotion-focused coping**
A coping style that involves cognitive, or thought-related, strategies that minimize the emotional effects of stress-inducing events.

Zellars & Perrewé, 2001). For instance, problem-focused coping along with supervisory support of family-related issues results in a decrease in work–family conflict (Lapierre & Allen, 2006); problem-focused coping results in reduced strain (Searle, 2008). Even family support can contribute to lowering stress at work.

## ENVIRONMENTAL DETERMINANTS OF WELL-BEING

As I pointed out in Chapter 1, employment is a central element of our lives. Certainly, some individuals are more apt than others to define and view themselves with respect to their jobs or occupations; but all in all, our work is important to most of us. In his research and writing, Peter Warr takes a very useful approach toward helping I/O psychologists gain an understanding about work processes. He has spent years developing his model of the environmental determinants of well-being (Warr, 1999, 2007a; 2011) and has applied this model to job-related well-being, which is a function of people's feelings about themselves in relation to their jobs (Warr, 1999). Indeed, Warr argues that the workplace is central to mental health. His framework provides a way of further investigating how individuals interact with the workplace.

Warr's 10 environmental determinants of well-being are listed in **Table 11.1**. The more employees experience these determinants on the job, the less likely they are to experience negative well-being, which, according to Warr, is reflected in anxiety, displeasure, and depression rather than enthusiasm, pleasure, and comfort. Let's consider each of the determinants in turn.

### TABLE 11.1 Warr's Environmental Determinants of Well-Being

| Environmental Determinants | Links to I/O Theory |
| --- | --- |
| 1. Opportunity for personal control | Job characteristics theory |
| 2. Opportunity for skill use | Job characteristics theory |
| 3. Variety | Job characteristics theory |
| 4. Environmental clarity | Job characteristics theory |
| 5. Valued social position | Job characteristics theory |
| 6. Externally generated goals | Intrinsic motivation and reinforcement theories |
| 7. Availability of money | Intrinsic motivation and reinforcement theories |
| 8. Physical security | Maslow's hierarchy of needs, ERG |
| 9. Supportive supervision | |
| 10. Opportunity for interpersonal contact | |

*Opportunity for personal control* refers to one's ability to control situations and events at work. We have discussed in various chapters (and earlier in this chapter) the importance of participation, freedom to choose, and job autonomy. *Opportunity for skill use* is the extent to which employees are encouraged to use and develop skills. Not having the opportunity to develop their skills can be stifling for employees, resulting in a negative sense of well-being. Employees who enjoy *variety* at work don't do the same old thing each day but, rather, have an assortment of tasks and responsibilities. *Environmental clarity* has to do with whether employees have a clear understanding of current and future expectations, as reflected in the amount and quality of feedback they receive at work. *Valued social position* is the extent to which employees gain prestige or a sense of accomplishment from their work.

Do these first five determinants remind you of anything? Recall that in Chapter 9 we discussed job characteristics theory and the effect of factors like feedback, autonomy, skill variety, task significance, and task identity on certain psychological states, which lead to outcomes such as job satisfaction, high motivation, and high work quality. In this sense, the work of Warr is consistent with job characteristics theory. Table 11.1 lists this theory and others in relation to each of Warr's environmental determinants.

*Externally generated goals* and the *availability of money* may be familiar from previous discussions about motivation. In this context, goals have to do with task demands; a job that requires very little from employees is not likely to be challenging or stimulating. And although having money doesn't guarantee positive well-being, not having what one considers to be enough money can result in a devastatingly negative sense of well-being. Much the same can be said about *physical security,* which has to do with working conditions and safety.

The last two determinants, *supportive supervision* and *opportunity for interpersonal contact,* deal with the social atmosphere at work. As discussed in previous chapters in the context of interpersonal relationships, having an understanding, supportive, and effective boss is quite important to employees' well-being, as are their opportunities for social interactions with peers, supervisors, subordinates, and customers.

Warr (1999) has reviewed dozens of empirical studies demonstrating the relevance of these factors to well-being in the workplace. For the most part, the more one's job provides these factors, the more positive one's well-being is likely to be. However, where some of these determinants are concerned, there may be a point at which more *isn't* better. For instance, employees tend to be favorably disposed toward jobs that demand a lot from them and provide a good deal of responsibility. However, too many demands and too much responsibility can easily result in overload, stress, and a negative sense of well-being. In fact, jobs that combine very high demands with very low opportunity for control tend to be extremely stressful. Although Warr places considerable emphasis on the environmental (i.e., job-related) determinants of well-being, he also makes it clear that one's job environment and experiences are not wholly independent of other life experiences. We turn now to a discussion of the two most salient elements of individuals' lives, work and family, which appear to be quite closely linked.

## WORK–FAMILY CONFLICT

Never before has the interplay between work and family been the focus of so much talk at work, at home, in the neighborhood, at places of worship, and, especially, in research labs across the United States. In the last 20 to 30 years, the American family has undergone some significant changes that have had widespread impact on organizational life as well. In this section, I consider some of these changes and what they typically mean for today's employees who try so hard to successfully juggle their work and family responsibilities.

### Theoretical Models

Recent models of work–family conflict have begun to examine its bidirectional nature. In other words, family life affects work life, and work life affects family life. The conceptual model presented in **Figure 11.2** clearly shows that both organizational and personal variables have an impact on work–family conflict and work–family enrichment, which have both organizational and personal outcomes. Work–family conflict (WFC) exists when the two domains don't fit well together and results in one role having a negative effect on the other (Hammer, Cullen, Neal, Sinclair, & Shafiro, 2005). Work–family enrichment occurs when attitudes and behaviors are believed to have a positive carryover from one domain to the other (Greenhaus & Powell, 2006). Traditionally, this kind of approach has been termed a *spillover model*. Another form of spillover was identified by a study that found commuters to perceive greater stress than noncommuters. Furthermore, driving experiences during their morning commute (especially for men) affected their aggression and hostility at work for the rest of the day (Hennessy, 2008). Another study, this one conducted in China, found that workers who experienced more work–family conflict tended to drink more alcohol and that

**work–family conflict (WFC)** A model of work–family relations in which work and family demands are incompatible.

**work–family enrichment** A model of work–family relations in which positive attitudes and behaviors are believed to carry over from one domain to the other.

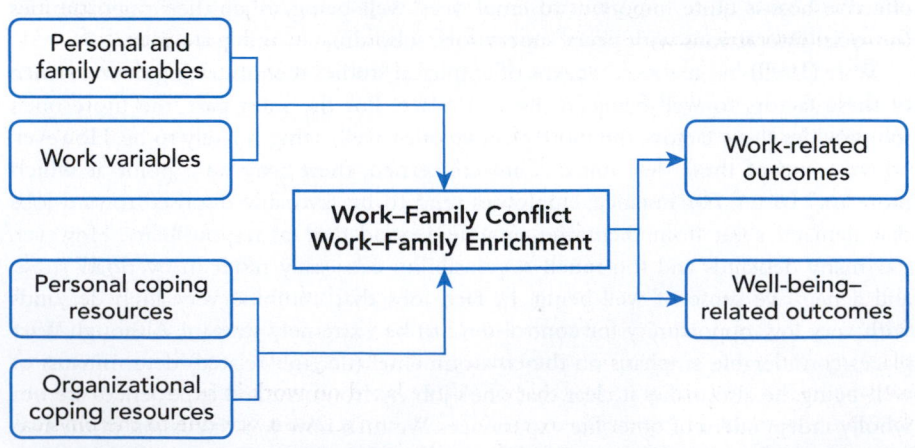

**FIGURE 11.2** Conceptual Model of Work–Family Interface

this relationship was affected by peer drinking norms and social support (Wang, Liu, Zhan, & Shi, 2010).

An interesting study of Israeli workers explored various work-based and family-based coping techniques for dealing with or minimizing *work interfering with family* (WIF) *conflict* and *family interfering with work* (FIW) *conflict*. The authors showed that different coping techniques seem to work better for different people—in other words, the success of coping strategies may be a function of people and situations (Somech & Drach-Zahavy, 2007). For instance, they found that

© Rick Gomez/Corbis

**A CLOSER LOOK**
How do WIF, FIW, spillover, and interventions affect employees' relationships with their families?

nontraditional women and traditional men deal with FIW conflict by exerting extra effort at work and delegating responsibilities at home. This allows them to focus on their jobs, which are very important to these two groups, while also serving the needs of the family. Vastly different patterns emerged for nontraditional men, who chose to emphasize the family and delegate at work so that work didn't interfere with their family role.

Considerable research support exists for the effects of work–family conflict on both personal and organizational outcomes. For instance, employees with high levels of work–family conflict tend to be less satisfied with their jobs ($r = -.31$) and their lives ($r = -.36$) than their low-conflict counterparts (Kossek & Ozeki, 1998). Furthermore, the spillover is stronger for WIF conflict than for FIW conflict. In addition, a recent and thorough meta-analysis demonstrated convincingly that work domain variables such as job involvement and job stress influence WIF conflict, which impacts family satisfaction (Ford, Heinen, & Langkamer, 2007). On the flip side, family domain variables like family conflict and family stress influence FIW conflict, which impacts job satisfaction.

These interesting results suggest the importance of both work and family and even explain how one might spill over to affect the other and vice versa. However, we need to be wary of our Western bias: Because most I/O psychology research has been conducted in predominantly White Western cultures, we cannot conclude that these findings generalize across other cultures. For example, a recent study (Grzywacz et al., 2007) using in-depth interviews of Latinos employed in the North Carolina poultry-processing industry concluded that these employees experienced little WFC as compared with the studies we've discussed to this point. The researchers argued that this was due to the collectivistic nature of the Latino culture, where hard work is valued and seen as securing one's family's well-being. Little conflict is perceived between work and family because of the value placed on work in service to the family. Latina women did experience more WFC, but much of it was due to the physical demands of their jobs. Other studies have also found other cultural differences in WFC, as well as gender differences (e.g., Grzywacz, Almeida, & McDonald, 2002).

The common belief has always been that women give their family roles greater priority than do men, even when comparing men and women with careers outside the home (see Grzywacz et al., 2007). It follows, then, that the career satisfaction of women versus men should be more affected by work–family conflict. Martins, Eddleston, and Veiga (2002) found this to be the case in their survey of more than 1,000 professionals from more than 100 organizations: WFC was not significantly related to career satisfaction for men ($r = -.07$), but it was for women ($r = -.23$). Furthermore, they found that this pattern held up for women at all ages; but for older men, work–family conflict became more important. That is, for men over 40, work–family conflict was significantly related to career satisfaction ($r = -.26$), suggesting that men reprioritize their life domains as they age, making family more central. The authors note that this finding is consistent with early theoretical work suggesting that men are less willing to sacrifice family relationships later in their lives and thus are less tolerant of work–family conflict.

In another interesting study, Baltes and Heydens-Gahir (2003) applied Baltes's *life management theory* to WFC. Basically, they found that individuals who identify and set goals, who develop and refine strategies for achieving those goals, and who are flexible enough to employ alternative approaches when the initial targeted approach isn't working both perceive less job and work stress and report low levels of work–family conflict. It's also important to understand that boundaries help individuals to keep domains separate or allow for some interaction across domains. Some people want very segmented domains with thick boundaries separating them; others want more integrated domains with thin, more permeable boundaries. A model of boundaries involved in WFC has been proposed that emphasizes the match between one's desired boundaries and one's environment (Kreiner, Hollensbe, & Sheep, 2009). Furthermore, this very interesting model proposes four general tactics used to manage our boundaries: behavioral (e.g., using technology), temporal (e.g., blocking off segments of time), physical (e.g., creating a separate work space at home), and communicative (e.g., setting and communicating rules to others). In recent years, this model has been used by others in framing the issues around the management of work-life balance. For instance, Kossek, Ruderman, Braddy, and Hannum (2012) used Kreiner et al.'s work to help them identify individual behaviors in managing interruptions between work-family roles and new work-family dual identities. They found that what matters more than whether an employee integrates across his or her roles or keeps the roles separate is whether one feels in control of these boundaries, and feeling in control is related to positive work-family outcomes (Kossek et al., 2012).

## Organizational Support and Interventions

We have talked about the importance of social support throughout the book and noted the importance of organizational support in Chapter 10. These ideas have been extended into the domain of supervisor support as well and, in particular, supervisor support around the role of the family. Leslie Hammer and her colleagues have been leaders in this area and recently developed a multidimensional measure of *family supportive supervisor behaviors* (FSSB). A family supportive supervisor is one who values and appreciates an employee's desire to find a balance between work and family. Hammer and her colleagues found that their new measure demonstrated incremental validity over more general social support measures in predicting various outcomes related to work-family issues as well as job satisfaction and turnover (Hammer, Kossek, Yragui, Bodner, & Hanson, 2008). Among the important implications of this work is that supervisors may be very supportive of employees at work doing their jobs and not supportive of family. This is an interesting idea with significant consequences for organizations as work-family demands increase and balance continues to be a high priority among employees.

In addition, it's worth noting that work-life balance experts argue for the importance of intervention studies rather than simple correlational studies in this area. Hammer and her colleagues recently conducted an intervention study around FSSB. They were interested in whether a work-family intervention targeted at increasing employee perceptions of family-specific support would lead to positive outcomes like increased job satisfaction, decreased turnover intentions, and improved physical health (Hammer, Kossek, Anger, Bodner, & Zimmerman, 2011). They found that, among other things, the FSSB training had an impact on employees who perceived the family-specific support and reported great job satisfaction and lower turnover intentions. They did not find this mediational effect for physical health, however. Although the results were considerably more complex than this summary might indicate, it's fair to say that the training resulted in behavior changes (i.e., more FSSB) on the part of the supervisors, which were noticed by employees and impacted employee health and work outcomes (Hammer et al., 2011). Further, the supervisors reported that they liked the training, which also bodes well for its use going forward.

A study of 1,100 employers from the 2012 National Study of Employers (Matos & Galinsky, 2012) found that organizational flexibility and a supportive work-family culture was positively related to employee engagement, job satisfaction, intentions to stay with employers, less negative spillover from work to home and from home to work, and better mental health. In addition, two trends emerged from 2005 to 2012: (1) employers are providing more flexible options for employees to manage their time (e.g., flex time, time off for emergencies, flex place) now than they were in 2005; and (2) employers are providing fewer options that allow employees to move from full-time to part-time or to take career breaks for personal reasons than they were in 2005. So, it appears that employers are providing more day-to day flexibility to manage one's own time, but providing less flexibility in career-related changes regarding employment status (e.g., full-time vs. part-time). This trend is especially interesting in light of a very recent survey by RecruitiFi (an expert recruiting service) of over 1,000 U.S. employees in which it was found that people are volunteering and requesting part-time work so as to experience a better work-life balance and the other perks that come with a flexible schedule (PR Newswire, 2015). The respondents recognize that there are negative implications of going part-time, such as a loss of money, prestige, and job insecurity, but they feel the benefits more than make up for the potential negative implications.

A 2012 survey of almost 2,000 workers reported signs of prolonged stress in attitudes about work (Jayson, 2012). The researcher argues that just showing up for work has replaced the focus on performance—work has become drudgery for many and "being present" has become one of the most important priorities for workers who have to overcome burnout, stress, fatigue, and overwork just to show up to their place of employment. Another survey of 5,000 U.S. households found that only one-third of the workers surveyed were pleased with their workload and 63% reported extreme fatigue, high levels of stress, and feeling like they had lost control (Jayson, 2012).

Some research has found that work-family issues are paramount immediately after the birth of a child. A recent study has shown how, for new moms returning to work four months after childbirth, job resources predict work–family enrichment and job demands predict work–family conflict (Carlson et al., 2011). For instance, having control over one's schedule buffered against negative effects of conflict and job security was related to work-family enrichment. In a special issue of the *International Journal of Stress Management*, researchers (O'Driscoll et al., 2003) found that organizational and supervisory support for family life were related to key stressors and strains, suggesting an important role for family-friendly policies in organizations. And, in fact, many companies offer family-friendly programs, or what are often called *work-life supports* (Sahibzada, Hammer, Neal, & Kuang, 2005), to alleviate some of the stress experienced by workers. **Table 11.2** provides a list of some of these programs.

### TABLE 11.2  Work-Life Supports Offered by Organizations

| Traditional Benefits | Nontraditional Benefits |
|---|---|
| Child-care benefits<br>  Onsite child-care centers<br>  Informational assistance<br>  Financial assistance<br>  Sick-child care | Convenience benefits<br>  Onsite physicians, dry cleaning,<br>  postal services, etc.<br>  Take-home meals<br>  Preferred banking |
| Elder-care benefits<br>  Counseling<br>  Informational assistance<br>  Geriatric care management<br>  Financial assistance | Health promotion benefits<br>  Onsite fitness centers<br>  Health screening<br>  Flu shots<br>  Counseling services |
| Flexible work arrangements<br>  Flextime<br>  Part-time options<br>  Job-sharing<br>  Telecommuting | Education assistance benefits<br>  Tutoring<br>  Tuition reimbursement<br>  Scholarships<br>  Student loan assistance |
| Leave/time-off policies<br>  Maternity leaves<br>  Family and medical leaves<br>  Parental leaves<br>  Educational leaves | Housing assistance programs<br>  Relocation programs<br>  Seminars<br>  Home-purchase savings accounts<br>  Preferred mortgage arrangements |
|  | Group purchase programs<br>  Discounts at local merchants<br>  Auto-purchase arrangements<br>  Group auto and home insurance |

Data from 2,810 employees surveyed in the 2002 National Study of the Changing Workforce provide an interesting look at work-life supports (for a summary, see Bond & Galinsky, 2006). Fifteen practices/policies (i.e., supports) were identified to define what is meant by workplace flexibility. Many of these are listed in Table 11.2. A 2012 follow up to that 2002 study has uncovered some very interesting findings (Matos & Galinsky, 2012). For instance, employers have cut back on some of the work-life supports they offer employees, especially those that directly cost the company money, like healthcare and pension plans. However, employers have invested more heavily in providing employees with flexibility around work times, work places, and time off during the work day to attend to personal/family issues. Finally, nonprofit companies and companies with diverse top-level leadership seem to provide more support to their employees.

This analysis by income level suggests that we still have far to go in giving support to those who may be most in need of some workplace flexibility. However, we need to recognize that even things that are generally positive for organizations and employees alike may have a potential downside, too. For instance, a recent study surveyed 454 telecommuters from a high-tech firm. This study found that telecommuting reduced the extent to which work interfered with family (WIF) but *increased* the extent to which family interfered with work (FIW)—and this increase was larger for larger households (Golden, Veiga, & Simsek, 2006). Apparently, for employees who spend considerable time telecommuting from home, there is the potential for the family domain to interfere with work outcomes.

Let's look at a few particularly innovative programs. NRG Insurance is a Seattle company that won a 2006 Alfred P. Sloan Award for Business Excellence in Workplace Flexibility (Families and Work Institute, 2007). This is one of the largest woman-owned brokerage companies in the United States, where all employees are required to work at home one day per week; that way, according to the company owner, they can concentrate better without the phones ringing all around them. All staff members take a three-hour break one Friday afternoon per month and get one month off (a paid sabbatical) every five years.

Another Sloan winner is Intel, which gives all 5,000 employees in a microchip manufacturing plant in Arizona two consecutive months off, fully paid, every seven years. Intel argues that this allows employees to come back rested and recharged, able to throw themselves back into the very demanding world of innovation and creativity. Employees can also tap additional time to further their education—and Intel pays the bill.

*Fortune* magazine publishes an annual list of the 100 best companies to work for based on surveys and an audit of the company's culture ("100 Best Companies," updated annually). Google is at the top of the 2015 list and has been for six straight years! A few Google perks include free/unlimited gourmet food and snacks, free rides to and from campus, pets permitted at work, paid paternity/maternity leave, generous benefits for spouses of "googlers" who pass away (e.g., half of the employee's salary for 10 years, $1,000 per month benefit for each child, etc.), an onsite child-care center, an onsite fitness center, subsidized gym membership, telecommuting,

## PRACTITIONER FORUM

E. Jeffrey Hill

### E. Jeffrey Hill

*PhD, 1995, Family and Human Development, Utah State University*

*Professor, School of Family Life, Brigham Young University*

I worked at IBM for over 30 years. In one five-year stretch, I had five different IBM jobs and lived in Washington, Utah, New York, Georgia, and Arizona. I traveled extensively and worked long hours.

I found myself becoming a casual occupant in our home. I missed birthdays, ball games, plays, concerts, recitals, and parent–teacher conferences. I began to worry that I was living to work instead of working to live.

In 1990, I was offered a promotion to do employee surveys for IBM. But the job was in New York and the commute horrendous. I decided to accept the job with conditions. I reasoned with my future boss that I could better design surveys and analyze results through a modem from my home. To my surprise, she agreed to let me try it.

The difference in my life was immediate. Instantly, I gained an hour and a half a day because I didn't have to drive to and from work. I could roll out of bed early with an exciting idea and immediately type it into the laptop.

I became more focused, energized, and productive at work. Without the constant interruptions of coworkers, I was able to deliver higher-quality surveys and analyses in less time. The arrangement worked so

well that soon four of my colleagues were working from home as well.

In the mid-1990s, IBM began to implement what was called the "virtual office" in a big way. Soon 25,000 IBMers no longer had dedicated IBM offices but were given laptops, cell phones, and pagers. Controlled research findings were similar to my personal experience. On the work side, telecommuting at IBM was associated with increased productivity, higher morale, greater organizational commitment, and better customer relationships. On the family side, telecommuting was found to have a positive influence on family relationships and well-being.

Sure, it's true that telecommuting works better in some jobs than others. But for me and thousands of telecommuters I have studied at IBM and in other companies, the flexibility alluded to in this chapter has been a positive step toward resolving work–family conflict.

### Applying Your Knowledge

1. Discuss Dr. Hill's experience of telecommuting in the context of the benefits described in this chapter.

2. Why is schedule flexibility so important to workers in the 21st century?

3. What are the potential long-term benefits of telecommuting for IBM (or any other company)?

---

an emphasis on green technologies, options to control projects one works on, choice of departments to work in, and a nondiscrimination policy that includes protections related to sexual orientation and domestic partner benefits for same-sex couples.

Whole Foods Market is a natural and organic food market that employs over 76,000 people. It provides between 85% and 100% healthcare coverage, subsidized gym memberships, a compressed workweek, and telecommuting options, along with same-sex partner benefits and a nondiscrimination policy. These and other benefits have kept them on the list for quite a few years. I would encourage you to read through the *Fortune* list, its measurement approach, and the descriptions of what

© Scott Adams/Dist. by United Feature Syndicate, Inc.

**A CLOSER LOOK**
Certainly, most managers have a better handle on the importance of work–family issues than Alice's boss does. In real life, what are the pros and cons of letting employees work from home?

various companies are doing. Think about what factors would be most important to you at this point in your life and perhaps how your values and priorities might change over time.

We now turn to a more detailed discussion of three work-family supports that are being more frequently offered by organizations as well as one work-family trend that continues to grow in importance.

## Family-Leave Policies

As discussed in Chapter 7, the first piece of legislation signed into law by President Bill Clinton was the Family and Medical Leave Act (FMLA), which allows eligible employees to take job-protected, unpaid leave for up to 12 weeks because of family-related issues such as the birth of a child, the serious health condition of a family member, or one's own serious health condition (see also the new regulations discussed in Chapter 7, which went into effect in January 2009). The United States is actually a late arrival in this respect; many other countries have had formal family-leave programs and laws in place for over 30 years. However, the United States continues to trail most other developed countries that offer more extensive programs with leaves built around compensation and flexibility. Nevertheless, many U.S. companies provided some form of family leave to their employees before it was mandated by law; indeed, many states have had family-leave policies for state employees since 1978.

Hungary and Sweden first introduced parental leave in 1967 and 1974, respectively. **Parental leave** was developed to enable employees to combine work and family responsibilities related to child rearing; many countries provide for this type of leave for children up to the age of three and, in some cases, until school age. Belgium has a rather distinctive program: Employees can take a *career break*, with an allowance payable by unemployment insurance, provided that the employer hires an unemployed person to replace the worker on leave.

**parental leave**
A program offered by organizations that enables employees to combine work and family responsibilities related to child rearing.

Although family-leave programs can provide great relief for many employees for whom juggling family and work responsibilities is a major priority and an increasingly complex task, such programs are not without their problems. According to the U.S. Department of Labor, over 30% of those individuals who receive limited or no pay during their leave report cutting their leaves short of what they needed and about 40% report that they would have extended their leaves if they could have afforded to do so (U.S. Department of Labor, 2015). Some experts in this area advocate making family leave affordable for the majority of workers who cannot utilize it in its current form. Many other bills have been introduced in Congress to expand the FMLA, but none have worked their way through the congressional system yet. The most recent is the Family Leave Insurance Act of 2009, which was assigned to a congressional subcommittee in March 2015, and should be sent on to the House or Senate in 2016 (see Chapter 7 for more details). This bill would amend the FMLA to provide paid leave for 8 of the allowable 12 weeks. Of course, many foresee this kind of law as resulting in huge unemployment costs to employers.

## Child-Care Benefits

If you have children and work outside the home, then you know how frustrating it can be to balance your work responsibilities with the care that you want to provide for your kids. Many studies have linked child-care difficulties not only to employee absenteeism, tardiness, productivity, and leaving work early, but also to indirect effects on coworkers' productivity (e.g., Erickson, Nichols, & Ritter, 2000; Tetrick, Miles, Marcil, & Van Dosen, 1994). In fact, a general conclusion is that an employee who fills the dual role of full-time employee and parent (i.e., who has a child under the age of 18 living at home) tends to experience lower psychological well-being, decreased life and marital satisfaction, and increased work–family conflict (Sahibzada et al., 2005). Given the effect of child-care problems on employee morale, productivity, and well-being, many companies have begun to give serious attention to child-care benefits and other child-care programs.

**A CLOSER LOOK**
How might the availability of affordable child-care options affect employees' absenteeism, attitudes, and productivity?

Four of these child-care benefits are listed in Table 11.2. Some organizations provide resources that inform employees of other child-care facilities in the area. They may also provide some financial assistance to employees to help cover the high costs of child care. But perhaps the most interesting benefit is the onsite child-care center. This is a popular feature—25 of the 100 best companies to work for in the most recent *Fortune* magazine list provide this support. In a survey of employees who worked at hospitals with onsite child-care centers, researchers found that active users of the onsite center were more likely to believe that the center was a good recruitment and retention tool for the company than were those employees not actively using the center (Kossek & Nichol, 1992). Also, those using the center

Yellow Dog Productions/Getty Images

held more positive attitudes toward managing their work and family responsibilities than did those who weren't using the center. A report by the National Conference of State Legislatures notes that of all family-related issues, child-care issues are the most commonly cited problem. Further, companies report increased instances of absence and leaving work early as a result of child-care issues. The report notes that employers who sponsor child-care benefits have employees with better morale, less turnover and absenteeism, and higher productivity (Hahn, 2007). Other studies (e.g., *Kids at Work: The Value of Employer-Sponsored On-Site Child Care Centers*, 2004) report that companies save hundreds of thousands of dollars in operations costs (i.e., wages) by having an onsite child-care center that allows employees to remain at work with fewer distractions.

## Elder-Care Assistance

Some might say that child care was the family-friendly emphasis of the 1980s and 1990s (Perry-Jenkins, Repetti, & Crouter, 2000), but for the first few decades of the 21st century, the emphasis will most certainly be on elder care. It is expected that going forward half of the workforce will be caregivers in the very near future (Smith, 2012). In fact, according to the AARP, 43.5 million adults are currently unpaid caregivers (AARP, 2015).

Here is the typical profile of a caregiver: a 49-year-old employed woman who works about 35 hours per week and spends about 24 hours per week caring for her elderly female relative who is 69 years old with a long-term physical condition. She is married or living with a partner, her average household income is $54,700, and she has been providing care for four years (National Alliance for Caregiving, 2015). Most problematic is the fact that 47% of adults in their 40s and 50s have a parent over 64 and are either raising or financially supporting a child who is 18 or under (Parker & Patten, 2013). These individuals with such great familial responsibilities have been labeled the *sandwiched generation* because they provide care to both their children and their parents—and often feel stuck in the middle. Obviously, financing child care and elder care at the same time can be extremely costly, and the enormous stress these caregivers experience often results in health problems of their own. In addition to providing financial support to both their children and their parents, they are relied on by both for emotional support.

The statistics are amazing. The U.S. Census Bureau projects that by 2030, over 20% of U.S. residents will be 65 or over as compared to 13% in 2010—this is about 80 million people by 2030 (Ortman, Velkoff, and Hogan, 2014). Furthermore, the fastest-growing subpopulation of the elderly comprises people over 85, who are most likely to be in need of care ("America in 2050," 2012).

Given these demographics, employers have begun to respond to elder-care needs; according to one estimate, 75% of employers claim to provide time off (paid or unpaid) to employees to provide elder care with no risk to their jobs (Matos, & Galinsky, 2012). As more and more employers begin to recognize the importance of elder-care benefits to employees, this percentage should increase considerably (much as the percentage of child-care programs has done). Some recent data are likely to motivate

Jose Luis Pelaez Inc./Blend Images/Getty Images

**A CLOSER LOOK**
How is the baby boomer generation forcing modern-day companies to evaluate their elder-care benefits?

employers to move quickly in this direction: The MetLife Caregiving Cost Study reports that U.S. companies lose between $17 billion and $34 billion annually on lost productivity due to caregiving responsibilities (MetLife Mature Market Institute, 2006). Caring for elderly parents from afar costs companies 15 million workdays per year. The major expenditures include replacement costs for employees ($6.6 billion), absenteeism costs ($5.1 billion), and costs due to workday interruptions ($6.3 billion). The most prevalent elder-care services offered by organizations are resource and informational assistance, dependent-care accounts, seminars, counseling, and long-term insurance (Work Options Group, 2006). Some employers have begun reimbursing their employees for elder-care expenses, with a limit on the funds provided, and certain large companies have even established onsite intergenerational day-care centers (e.g., Oakwood Healthcare). Perhaps the fastest-growing benefit is geriatric care management, whereby the employer provides certified professionals to go to an elderly person's home and assess his or her well-being and specific needs (Prudential Financial, Inc.). Furthermore, the professional may also provide an onsite review of an elder-care facility for the employee (Gonzalez, 2004). Other organizations provide long-term insurance for parents, grandparents, and so on (e.g., Cornell University) and 80 hours per year of backup care, such as PNC bank (Halzack, 2013).

Experts who work in the areas of family-friendly benefits and elder care argue that caregiving for the elderly directly affects employees' performance, causing them to report late for work, to work fewer hours, and, sometimes, to resign or retire early (Seaward, 1999). Of 22.4 million individuals who indicated in a 2007 AARP survey that they were providing care to an older parent or friend, about half reported that they took time off, came in late, and worked fewer hours because of their caregiving responsibilities (Crute, 2007). Conversely, employees who don't have to worry about caring for an elderly individual are more satisfied with their jobs as well as more productive (Seaward, 1999). According to Ceridian Corporation, the largest dependent-care resource provider, 16% of employee caregivers leave the workforce to provide full-time care (Gonzalez, 2004). Recent surveys show that 69% of caregivers report rearranging their work schedules, decreasing their hours, or taking unpaid leave to meet their caregiving responsibilities (Family Caregiver Alliance, 2012).

**dual-earner couple**
A couple in which both members are employed and maintain a family life.

## Dual-Earner Couples

We turn now to a discussion of dual-earner couples, a trend in the world of work that is clearly and logically linked to work–family conflict. A **dual-earner couple** is one in which both members are employed and maintain a family life. As this topic plays a role in the changing nature of work and the demographic characteristics of the current labor force, let's add a few more statistics to the mix. In 2014, 70% of mothers with children were in the labor force (U.S. Bureau of Labor Statistics, 2015). According to the Census Bureau, only 17% of U.S. households conform to the traditional model of a dad who brings home the wages and a mom who stays home and takes care of the kids.

One motivating factor for women to work in addition to their spouses is that they now make about 82.5% of what men make—up from 63.9% in 1980 (Institute for Women's Policy Research, 2015). We discuss the issues of comparable worth in Chapter 3. In fact, a survey by Catalyst, a research group that focuses on working women, found that 85% of the respondents listed increased income as the biggest advantage of a dual-earner situation and that 56% noted a lack of time as the biggest challenge (Kate, 1998). In a very interesting study of 50,000 adults across 25 countries it was found that daughters of working mothers completed more years of education, were more likely to be employed in leadership roles, and made more money than daughters of nonworking mothers (Miller, 2015). So, clearly, additional income is not the only benefit of working mothers to their children.

mother image/Getty Images

In an interview in *Forbes* magazine, Ralph Gomory, former president of the Sloan Foundation and former director of the research labs at IBM, provided an interesting take on the notion that everyone is working harder and putting in more hours: "It's not that one individual is working longer so much as that two people are now doing three jobs. In the past, one person did the working job and the other one brought up the family, took care of the home, built a social network or anything else you want to describe in that category. It was never recognized as a job. But it was" (quoted in Machan, 1999).

In other words, for the dual-earner couple there are now two jobs outside the home and one inside. Needless to say, this situation takes more effort and is more difficult. As for the job of taking care of the home and the kids, men still do less than their fair share—even when their wives are working full

**A CLOSER LOOK**
How do role-sharing dual-career marriages differ from conventional dual-career marriages?

time. North American women do about two-thirds of routine household tasks such as cooking and cleaning. There is also evidence that this imbalance exists in many other countries throughout the world (Lothaller, Mikula, & Schoebi, 2009). In general, women report doing over 13 hours of household labor per week compared to just under 7 hours for their male spouses (Lachance-Grzela & Bouchard, 2010).

In a national sample of 234 sandwiched-generation dual-earner couples, Hammer and colleagues (2005) uncovered longitudinal crossover effects regarding both work–family conflict and work–family enrichment. Crossover effects refer to the transmission of stress, strain, and depression from one member of a couple to the other. For instance, they found that husbands' work–family enrichment (i.e., positive spillover) was negatively related to wives' depression one year later; a parallel effect was found from wives' family–work enrichment to husbands' depression. This is the first study to highlight the important role of a dyad member's positive spillover from work to family or family to work in the well-being of the other member of the dyad. An even more recent study of dual-earner parents in the Netherlands found support for a model in which one partner's job demands affect his or her WIF conflict. The resources he or she must channel into the job leave little reserves for home activities; this increases demands on his or her partner at home, affecting the partner's level of FIW conflict and leading to the partner's exhaustion (Bakker, Demerouti, & Dollard, 2008).

Another study took a different approach by surveying over 170 career-oriented college women in the United States about their expectations and desires regarding future careers and family life (Hallett & Gilbert, 1997). Based on the responses, the authors classified each student as expecting either a *conventional dual-career marriage*, in which the female maintains primary responsibility for the home and the children while simply adding a career to her responsibilities, or a *role-sharing dual-career marriage*, in which both spouses actively pursue careers and actively involve themselves in the household and parenting. One interesting finding was that women who expected a role-sharing marriage were significantly more likely than their conventional counterparts to be committed to a lifelong, time-consuming career. In addition, having a spouse who would involve himself in managing the household and parenting the children was more important to those women looking for a role-sharing marriage than to those looking for a more conventional dual-career relationship. The authors concluded that many college-educated women today are thinking about their futures in ways quite different from those of earlier generations.

More recent work in this area has continued to explore attitudes toward dual-career marriage. An interesting study tracked college senior women over time (beginning in 1993) and found that while in college they reported wanting to have a career and family and that 16 years later (2009) two-thirds of them were employed full-time, 91% were married, 75% were mothers, and 57% were combining full-time employment and motherhood (Hoffnung & Williams, 2013). The researchers also found that the "have it all" women (parent and full-time career) were more likely than traditional women (parent and part-time career or no career) to be married to less educated spouses and had less concern about separation from their children because of work responsibilities. Most of the women still wanted to have it all and many of the traditional women still wanted to return to the workforce.

No longer must women choose between a career and a family; today's college-educated women believe that both are possible. Fortunately, many are leading the way in demonstrating how to make this work so that everyone involved can benefit.

I conclude this section on work–family conflict with a quote from a commencement speech delivered by Brian Dyson, author and former COO of Coca-Cola (*The Whistle*, 1991):

> Imagine life as a game in which you are juggling some five balls in the air. You name them—work, family, health, friends and spirit—and you're keeping all of these in the air. You will soon understand that work is a rubber ball. If you drop it, it will bounce back. But the other four balls—family, health, friends and spirit—are made of glass. If you drop one of these, they will be irrevocably scuffed, marked, nicked, damaged or even shattered. They will never be the same. You must understand that and strive for balance in your life.

I don't think it's much of a stretch to predict that the companies emerging as future national and world leaders are likely to be the ones that subscribe to the belief that work-family issues are very important to today's worker and helping employees handle the associated stress is beneficial to the organization. In fact, a close look at today's top-drawer companies suggests that this is already happening. In *Fortune* magazine's "100 Best Companies to Work For," the most important criterion is the extent to which these companies are helping employees balance work and life issues. Its list for 2016 includes some companies you will recognize: Google, Quicken Loans, Hyatt Hotels, Wegmen's, Walt Disney, and Prudential; all of which provide many of the work-life supports listed in Table 11.2 ("100 Best Companies," 2016).

## PSYCHOLOGICAL EFFECTS OF JOB LOSS

Recall that in Chapter 1, when highlighting the reasons why I/O psychology is important and relevant to most of us, I focused on the fact that a large part of who we are is, in some way or another, tied to what we do.

I talked about how being a psychology professor is an integral part of who I am. It affects not only the way I live my life but also my perceptions, beliefs, and attitudes. Is the same true for you? Certainly, some of us identify with our occupation or job more than others; but I really believe that, for the overwhelming majority of us, our occupation is central to who we are. That said, it shouldn't be a surprise to learn that losing one's job is a profoundly stressful event. In fact, research has consistently found job loss to be among the 10 most stressful events in a person's life (Maysent & Spera, 1995). Recent research demonstrates that job loss is a major life stressor that substantially predicts health issues (Strully, 2009) and is related to mortality and suicide (Eliason & Storrie, 2009). For some, it can be almost as stressful as the loss of a loved one.

Jobs are important to us for various reasons (Cartwright & Cooper, 1997). First, of course, they provide the financial means for living our lives in the manner that we desire. Second, they provide time structure to our day. They determine what time we get up, when we eat lunch, what we do in the afternoon, and when we are available to be home for dinner. If we were to suddenly lose our jobs, this structure would fall apart and leave us unmotivated and without direction. Third, jobs provide an opportunity to use our existing skills and to develop new ones. Without this opportunity, people can become stagnant and bored. Fourth, for most of us, an important feature of our jobs is social interaction with people outside our family. Human beings are social animals, and we all need some degree of social interaction. Our jobs provide an opportunity to interact not only with people who have interests and skills in common but also with those who differ from us in these respects. In other words, at work we have the opportunity to interact with various kinds of people.

Fifth, our jobs help provide a purpose to our lives—in the form of both short-term day-to-day goals and long-term goals regarding career development and advancement. A sense of purpose is crucial; without it, individuals can get stuck "spinning their wheels." Finally, we tend to get a sense of identity and even prestige from our jobs. Being a professor is important to me in part because it is a job that I value and a job that many others in society value—I am pleased with the prestige that goes with being a professor. I didn't choose this profession for that reason alone, of course; but the sense of identity that I receive from my job is very important for my sense of well-being.

## The Hard Facts

Whether we call it "rightsizing," "downsizing," "layoffs," or "reductions in force," there's no denying that U.S. corporations have been reducing the size of their workforces at alarming rates since the late 1980s. From July 1989 to June 1990 alone, nearly 81,000 positions were eliminated in 1,219 U.S. corporations (Schwartz, 1990). Some of the most stable and reliable companies in the world—including United Airlines, DuPont, General Electric, and General Motors—have laid off workers in record numbers. According to one estimate, over 43 million jobs were lost in the United States from 1979 to 1999 (McKinley, Zhao, & Rust, 2000). About 80,000 people lost their jobs because of layoffs in each month of 2004 (Weber, 2004).

The most extreme period of job loss in the United States since World War II took place from October 2008 through March 2009—712,000 jobs were lost per month during that six-month period, which was the height of recession (U.S. Bureau of Labor Statistics, 2011). In the third quarter of 2008, 1,330 mass layoffs were initiated, with 218,000 employees separated from their jobs (U.S. Bureau of Labor Statistics, 2008). (A mass layoff is a company action in which at least 50 employees are separated from their jobs.) The average size of the layoff during this period was 164 employees, but 48% of the layoffs affected between 50 and 100 employees. Almost 50% of the layoffs were in the manufacturing and construction industries.

Worse still, one study using a very large employment database has reported that U.S. workers are even more concerned about losing their jobs than the data suggest they should be—anxiety about job loss has existed for a very long time (Rudisill & Edwards, 2002). A perceived lack of career opportunities is related to psychological distress and poor health (Melzer et al., 2010). In a very large review of the literature, researchers concluded that job loss is substantially related to depression, suicide, antisocial behavior, and substance abuse (Goldman-Mellor, Saxton, & Catalano, 2010). According to Carol Wilson, a vice president of a firm specializing in employee assistance, when a layoff is announced in a company, 20% of the remaining employees leave the organization either physically or emotionally; another 60% take a "wait and see approach" (Wilson, 2004).

Let's consider some empirical work that looks specifically at layoffs. In a study of employees who had lost their jobs as a result of a company closing, coping resources were examined as predictors of distress and reemployment (Gowan, Riordan, & Gatewood, 1999). The researchers operationalized problem-focused coping as job search activity and emotion-focused coping as distancing oneself from the job loss. Their results indicated that the more social support employees had, the better able they were to distance themselves from the job loss. Social support (along with lack of financial resources) also led to job search activities. But employees' ability to distance themselves from the job loss (measured by items like "I remind myself that other people have been in this situation and that I can probably do as well as they did") appeared to be the key variable, as it was negatively related to distress about the job loss and positively related to reemployment.

Unfortunately, a recent study of laid-off workers has linked layoffs to symptoms of PTSD (posttraumatic stress disorder) like depression, fixation on the job loss, and anxiety. In addition, this study also found that those who had the most negative reactions to the layoffs also tended to be underemployed one year later (McKee-Ryan, Virick, Prussia, Harvey, & Lilly, 2009). In other words, the perceived fairness of the layoff event affected the severity of the PTSD symptoms, which were linked to a tendency to be underemployed in the future. We will discuss underemployment near the end of this section.

Another line of research has focused on the stress and pressure involved in being layoff survivors—that is, employees who have survived a layoff but who are left at the workplace to deal with its aftereffects. A review of the literature in this area showed that layoff survivors tend to be less productive, less trusting of the organization and supervisors, more angry and anxious about their futures, and more likely to suffer from low morale and low job satisfaction (Grunberg, Anderson-Connolly, & Greenberg, 2000). In addition, employees' perceptions of the fairness of the process, organizational commitment levels prior to the layoff, and levels of self-esteem affect how survivors respond to the layoffs (see Brockner, Wiesenfeld, & Martin, 1995; Wiesenfeld, Brockner, & Martin, 1999).

**A CLOSER LOOK**
How can being laid off affect people's mood, interactions with their spouses, and satisfaction with their marriages?

Some research examining *managers* as layoff survivors has given careful consideration to procedural justice, organizational commitment, and ensuing managerial behavior (Wiesenfeld, Brockner, & Thibault, 2000). The results from the two studies reported in this article indicated that managers (as opposed to nonmanagers) who perceive injustice in how layoffs are handled tend to report low self-esteem, which seems to be partly a function of their high levels of organizational commitment. They also exhibit less effective managerial behaviors than are necessary in times of organizational change and direct these less effective behaviors toward subordinates, who report a less supportive work environment. A series of studies has also shown perceptions of justice to be very important in determining how employees respond to various organizational changes such as the violation of one's psychological contract (the expectations and responsibilities shared between employees and their employers) and layoffs (Edwards, Rust, McKinley, & Moon, 2003; Kickul, Lester, & Finkl, 2002).

**underemployment**
When a worker is in a job that, by some standard, is inferior or below his or her capacity or ability.

Another very interesting trend with great implications for organizations is **underemployment**, which has to do with people employed in jobs that are somehow inferior and have them working under their capacity or ability levels. As a result of the recent recession and scaling back of many jobs, a great number of individuals find themselves underemployed. The Bureau of Labor Statistics indicates that almost 9 million workers have had to work part-time because full-time jobs were unavailable to them (U.S. Bureau of Labor Statistics, 2010). Using the broad definition of underemployment above, estimates range from 17% to 33% of the population being underemployed and predict a positive trend going forward (McKee-Ryan & Harvey, 2011). In many instances, underemployment entails a well-educated and skilled individual who is in a job that requires less education and skill than he or she possesses. In addition to not using their education or skill set, these underemployed individuals are often being undercompensated. The research is clear that there is a consistent negative relationship between underemployment and individual outcomes like job satisfaction, job involvement, work alienation, and organizational commitment, as well as withdrawal cognitions/behaviors like job search, intent to turnover, and turnover behaviors (McKee-Ryan & Harvey, 2011).

One recent study of 215 employees found that those who believed they were overqualified for their current jobs exhibited more counterproductive behaviors than did those who believed they were appropriately qualified employees (Luksyte, Spitzmueller, & Maynard, 2011). Further, the behaviors seem to stem from the cynicism dimension of burnout—these employees become burned-out by being in jobs that they feel are below them with little hope for growth and promotion; thus, they become cynical and exhibit counterproductive behaviors. The negative implications for both organizations and other employees are obvious and potentially quite damaging (see Chapter 4 for a discussion of counterproductive work behaviors).

Finally, a new line of research has begun investigating a model of job uncertainty in the downsizing process (Paulsen et al., 2005). This study found that, for a sample of Australian hospital employees whose hospitals were undergoing large-scale restructuring and downsizing, job uncertainty and feelings of personal control were quite low at the anticipation stage of the downsizing, when the environment was most turbulent. The study also found that personal control mediated the negative effects of job uncertainty on both emotional exhaustion and job satisfaction in the anticipation stage and for survivors at the implementation stage. Personal control appeared to be less important in the aftermath of downsizing, when the environment became more stable. A couple of recent studies have pursued these ideas and demonstrated that the threat of unemployment leads to job insecurity, which is related to strains such as lowered job satisfaction and organizational commitment and elevated psychological distress and turnover intentions. The researchers also found that perceptions of control can play a role here as well, as they appear to mediate the relationship between job insecurity and the various strains (De Cuyper, De Witte, Vander Elst, & Handaja, 2010; Elst, De Cuyper, & De Witte, 2011).

## Environmental Determinants—Revisited

I close this section by returning briefly to Warr's environmental determinants of well-being (see Table 11.1). As you may recall, Warr argues that the more employees experience these determinants on the job, the more likely they are to experience positive well-being. Another way to look at the importance of work in our lives is to consider the potential effect that losing one's job has on each of these determinants, along with the more general effect of job loss on overall well-being.

First, work tends to provide people with *opportunity for personal control*; when they lose their jobs, they experience a considerable loss of control, which, in turn, affects their well-being. Second, job loss largely eliminates *opportunity for skill use*, causing some individuals to feel that their skills are being wasted. Third, *variety* is important, and doing the same old thing has a negative effect on job-related well-being. But when one's job is lost, doing the same old thing becomes more the norm than the exception and often involves unappealing activities like standing in unemployment lines and searching the Internet for potential jobs. Fourth, *environmental clarity* helps employees define their roles, but without jobs, they lose all sense of their roles and lack environmental clarity altogether. Fifth, the sense of *valued social position* that employees derive from their jobs is damaged when they lose their jobs, thereby affecting their general sense of self-esteem and self-worth.

Sixth, people without jobs tend to lose focus on their *externally generated goals*; because there are no demands placed on them by their jobs, supervisors, or organizations, they engage in little activity or achievement. Certainly, job security provides both *availability of money* and *physical security*, the seventh and eighth factors in Warr's list; but when people lose their jobs, both are gone, creating anxiety-arousing circumstances that affect every facet of their lives. Ninth, *supportive supervision*—a form of social support—is obviously relinquished when a job is lost. The tenth and last determinant of job-related well-being is *opportunity for interpersonal contact*—one of the main benefits provided by a job. When employees lose their jobs, they are cut off from the outside world, or at least from a circle of people who were an important part of their lives. For some, a large void is left. For others, interpersonal contact is experienced through job search behaviors, but the quality and depth of that contact pale by comparison to what used to occur at work.

I have reviewed these environmental determinants to demonstrate how significant job loss can be. When we look at Warr's model, what becomes quite clear is how much we actually receive or gain from our jobs. When we lose our jobs, we lose a great deal—more than any of us (including myself) can understand until it happens to us.

The last area we need to cover in this chapter stems in part from our discussion of how damaging job stress can be. In very extreme situations, it can even result in workplace violence.

## WORKPLACE VIOLENCE

Violence in the workplace has become a very important topic for organizations, employees, and researchers. The trends are indeed staggering. According to the U.S. Bureau of Labor Statistics, homicide is one of the leading causes of death among American employees (along with falls and transportation accidents). From 2006 to 2010 there were, on average, over 551 homicides at work per year in the United States (U.S. Bureau of Labor Statistics, 2013). Shootings accounted for 78% of the homicides in 2010. Assailants with no known relationship to the victims account for two-thirds of the homicides. Of the homicides in 2010, 27% were in retail, 17% in government, and 15% in leisure/hospitality. There was a decrease in 2014 with only 404 homicides constituting 9% of the total deaths at work (BLS, 2013).

In July 1993, Northwestern National Life Insurance Company conducted the first comprehensive assessment of fear and violence in the workplace. It surveyed 600 full-time American workers and, in generalizing these data to the U.S. workforce as a whole, uncovered some startling facts. It found that more than 2 million American workers self-reported that during the preceding 12 months they had been victims of physical attacks; 6 million, that they had been threatened; and 16 million, that they had been harassed (Northwestern National Life Employee Benefits Division, 1993). This amounts to one out of every four full-time U.S. workers.

In 2009, 572,000 employees were victims of nonfatal violent crimes while they were at work (Centers for Disease Control and Prevention, 2014). The National Institute for Occupational Safety and Health (NIOSH) lists the following risk factors for the likelihood of being assaulted at work (Biles, 1999):

- Having contact with the public
- Being involved in the exchange of money
- Delivering passengers, goods, or services
- Having a mobile workplace (e.g., taxicab or police cruiser)
- Working with unstable persons (e.g., healthcare, social services, criminal justice settings)
- Working alone or in small numbers

One study developed and validated a measure for identifying the risk for workplace violence by focusing on 28 different job characteristics that have been reported in the literature as being related to workplace violence (LeBlanc & Kelloway, 2002). Along with those characteristics listed by NIOSH, this additional measure asks about whether the job involves serving alcohol, caring emotionally or physically for others, disciplining others, handling weapons, or making decisions that influence other people's lives. The study reported significant correlations between 22 of the job characteristics and reports of violence. Furthermore, researchers found that this scale was more strongly related to violence from individuals outside the organization (e.g., customers) than from those inside the organization (e.g., other employees). Other research has shown that most violence at work is initiated by what are called "organizational outsiders" (nonemployees) rather than "organizational insiders" (employees) (LeBlanc & Barling, 2004). Finally, researchers have made it clear that even though insider-initiated violence is not as frequent (nor, usually, as deadly) as outsider-initiated violence, it still frequently occurs and has devastating effects for its victims (LeBlanc & Barling, 2004).

Interest in workplace violence has increased in the past 30 years or so. In fact, prior to the events in Edmond, Oklahoma, in 1986, most Americans weren't even aware of the potential impact of workplace violence. It was at the Edmond Post Office that Patrick Sherrill went on a rampage that resulted in the death of 14 of his coworkers before he took his own life. This event, and others that followed, resulted in the coining of the term *going postal* to refer generically to wild episodes of violence at work. What set Sherrill off isn't completely clear, but we do know that his performance record at work was spotty and that he wanted to get revenge on his shift supervisor, who was his first victim in the onslaught.

This atrocious crime is the first well-known incident of workplace violence in the United States, and it marks the beginning of the escalating trend toward workplace violence that we just discussed. In recent years, I/O psychologists, social psychologists, organizational development experts, and others have begun a systematic examination of this phenomenon. The remainder of this section briefly highlights the results of their research.

**Figure 11.3** presents a profile of the dangerous employee. This profile is consistent with a 1995 study published by the U.S. Department of Justice and the FBI that discovered some interesting trends after reviewing 89 incidents of serious violence in the workplace (Duncan, 1995). First, 97% of the murderers were male, and over 70% were White. Second, the average age of the perpetrators (nearly 40) was a bit higher than that of nonworkplace murderers (under 30). Third, in each of the 89 incidents, a firearm was used to commit the crime. Fourth, almost 90% of the perpetrators were current or former employees. Fifth, many of the perpetrators had a history of psychological or personality disorders and an affinity for weapons. Sixth, they often exhibited warning signs, such as extremely erratic behavior, threats of violence, irrational thought processes, and agitated mood, just prior to the incident. These characteristics and the profile in Figure 11.3 are consistent with a report by the FBI

FBI via Getty Images

**A CLOSER LOOK**
Former Navy electrician's mate, 34-year-old Aaron Alexis, killed 12 people at the Washington Navy Yard in 2013 after being discharged from the service in 2011 after a long list of disciplinary problems. Why do you think organizational insiders sometimes exhibit violence at work?

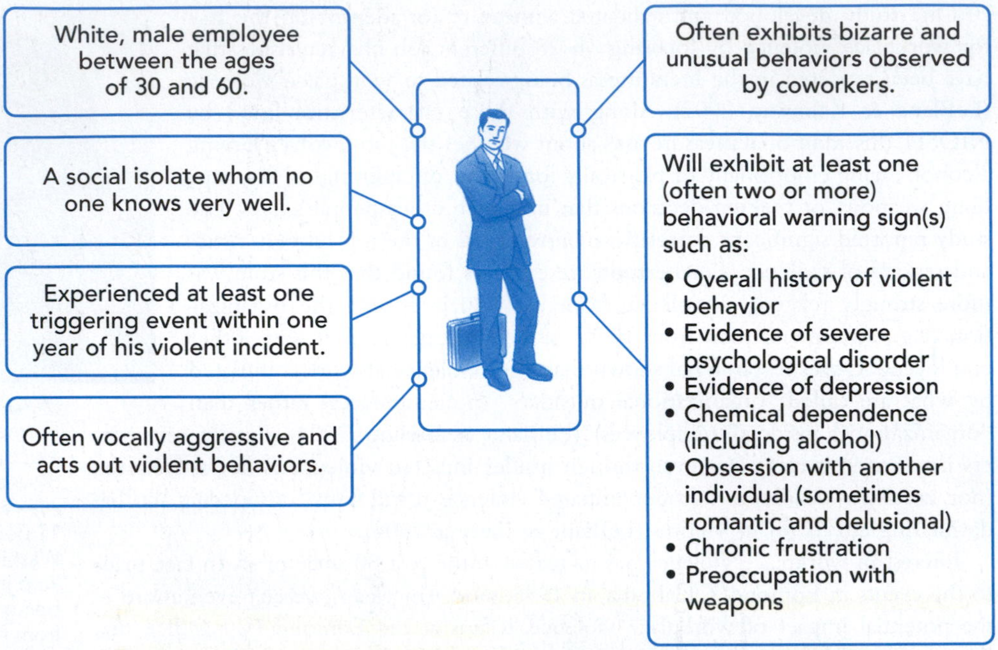

White, male employee between the ages of 30 and 60.

A social isolate whom no one knows very well.

Experienced at least one triggering event within one year of his violent incident.

Often vocally aggressive and acts out violent behaviors.

Often exhibits bizarre and unusual behaviors observed by coworkers.

Will exhibit at least one (often two or more) behavioral warning sign(s) such as:
- Overall history of violent behavior
- Evidence of severe psychological disorder
- Evidence of depression
- Chemical dependence (including alcohol)
- Obsession with another individual (sometimes romantic and delusional)
- Chronic frustration
- Preoccupation with weapons

**FIGURE 11.3**  Profile of the Lethal Employee

(U.S. Department of Justice, FBI, 2002), which lists the following risk factors or problematic behaviors:

**organization-motivated aggression** Attempts by someone inside or outside the organization to cause injury or to be destructive as a result of some organizational factor.

**organization-motivated violence** The negative effects on people or property that result from organization-motivated aggression.

- A mishandled termination/disciplinary action
- Bringing weapons onto work site
- Drug or alcohol use on the job
- Holding a grudge over a real or imagined grievance
- Personal emotional disturbance
- Hypersensitivity to criticism
- Recent acquisition/fascination with weapons
- Obsession with supervisor or coworker or employee grievance
- Preoccupation with violent themes

A useful model of workplace aggression has been developed (O'Leary-Kelly, Griffin, & Glew, 1996). It uses the term **organization-motivated aggression** to refer to attempts by someone inside or outside the organization to cause injury or to be destructive as a result of some organizational factor; the term **organization-motivated violence** refers to the negative effects on people or property that result from the aggression. **Figure 11.4** presents this model of organization-motivated aggression, which demonstrates the importance of both the organizational environment and individual characteristics. Some individuals are clearly more disposed toward violent

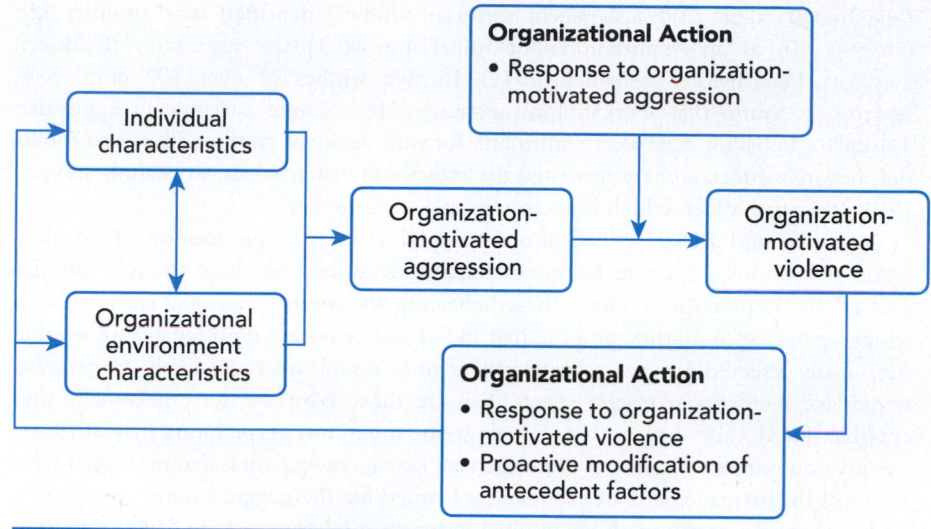

**FIGURE 11.4**  A Model of Organization-Motivated Aggression (Information from O'Leary-Kelly et al. (1996)).

or aggressive behavior than others (again, see Figure 11.3), but organizations that are rigid, punitive, and aggressive themselves may also encourage aggressive behavior on the part of employees (Tobin, 2001). The model further indicates that the way in which the organization responds to the aggressive behavior moderates the extent to which the aggression results in violence and other negative outcomes.

A second model of organizational aggression extended this earlier work (Martinko & Zellars, 1998). Though extremely complex, it builds on Figure 11.4 by focusing on the individual characteristics. The authors' literature review led to four reliable conclusions: (1) High levels of frustrating events in the workplace lead to a greater incidence of aggression and violence; (2) employees who tend to exhibit violent and aggressive behavior also tend to have been rewarded in the past for this pattern of behavior and to have had role models who were violent and aggressive; (3) employees who believe that what happens to them is beyond their control (i.e., those who are high on external locus of control) are more likely than others to respond to negative events in an aggressive or violent way; and (4) males are considerably more likely than females to be aggressive and violent in the workplace. A recent study found results consistent with this model. For instance, employees' perceptions of how controlling their supervisor was played an important role in creating psychological workplace aggression, such as making disparaging remarks about one's supervisor (Dupré & Barling, 2006).

A fifth reliable finding has to do with a series of seemingly minor frustrations at work that may serve as a trigger for aggression (Tobin, 2001). A meta-analysis concludes that interpersonal conflict, trait anger, job dissatisfaction, negative affectivity, and situational constraints all predict interpersonal and organizational aggression

(Hershcovis et al., 2007). A recent series of studies identified workaholism (see Chapter 10) as an important factor impacting workplace aggression (Balducci, Cecchin, Fraccarol, & Schaufeli, 2012). In two studies of over 700 employees, researchers found that workaholism accounted for unique variance in aggressive workplace behavior even after controlling for interpersonal conflict. They also found that negative affect/anxiety mediated the effect—in other words, workaholics experience negative affect, which leads to workplace aggression.

Martinko and Zellers (1998) also developed a series of propositions. First, they argue that some aggressive behaviors happen without conscious thought on the part of the perpetrator; in effect, these behaviors are purely emotional reactions to a trigger event. Second, they propose that individuals who are emotionally susceptible (i.e., easily affected by events happening around them) are more likely to perceive workplace incidents as trigger events than are those who are not emotionally susceptible. Third, they suggest that in ambiguous situations, perpetrators may attribute negative outcomes to a general cause such as "management," such that personnel who are most like management are likely to be blamed for the trigger events.

An extension of this work has resulted in newer models proposing that a triggering event is perceived and processed differentially, resulting at times in aggressive behavior (Douglas et al., 2008; Harvey, Summers, & Martinko, 2010). These models distinguish among different cognitive-processing paths that foster different types of aggressive behavior and report results from the literature supporting the role of attributions or cognitive processing as being central to how individuals react to triggering events. In a recent investigation of 233 employees in China, researchers found that hostile attribution bias (the tendency to aggressively blame others) and negative reciprocity beliefs (the tendency to react to negative treatment with negative treatment) led to a stronger relationship between workplace incivility and workplace aggression. When individuals are treated badly, their hostile attribution bias and negative reciprocity beliefs tend to determine whether they will exhibit deviance or aggression at work. Those who are high on hostile attribution bias and have negative reciprocity beliefs tend to react to the incivility with aggressive behaviors (Wu, Zhang, Chiu, Kwan, & He, 2014). It is becoming clearer through these various models and empirical studies that cognitive processing in the form of attributions or some other mechanism plays an important role in whether an individual will show aggressive behavior at work.

All these models provide useful summaries of what we know about workplace aggression and violence. But even more important, they provide directions for future work in this area. For instance, one practitioner suggests that strategies to reduce bullying and workplace violence should include surveillance, training, coaching, and the development of HR policies, such as selection, performance management, and reward systems (Ferris, 2009). A large-scale review of workplace violence interventions concluded that to reduce violence against healthcare workers (which is quite frequent) organizations need to emphasize training and techniques to deal with combative patients and to better cope with potentially violent patients. For a reduction in violence in the retail industry, where incidents are also quite frequent, the author's review indicates that environmental designs, like enhanced lighting to increase visibility and a limited cash handling policy, are effective (Wassell, 2009). One final point: We must not assume that all (or even most) aggressive behaviors in the workplace involve fatal physical assaults. In actuality, such incidents often entail subtle, covert, or verbal types of aggression, the majority of which are directed at coworkers rather than at supervisors (Neuman & Baron, 1998). But of course it is the heinousness of the murders and rampages, in combination with the media spotlight, that makes them more salient than more typical incidents such as verbal threats, arguments, paybacks, and assaults among coworkers.

## Summary

The purpose of this chapter was to discuss stress as it manifests itself in the workplace. I began the chapter with a look at stressors, strains, and coping. After defining these important terms and briefly considering stress in general, I presented a model that indicates various sources and outcomes of job-related stress. In the second section, I highlighted Warr's model of environmental determinants of well-being as a way of thinking about how employees' jobs can affect their well-being. (Later in the chapter the same model was used to show how job loss and underemployment can result in anguish.)

In the third section, I focused on work–family conflict. Given the importance of this area to both employees and organizations, I devoted a substantial amount of space to discussing it. In particular, I defined work–family conflict and enrichment, presented a conceptual model to demonstrate how work and family interact with each other and related variables, and emphasized the various struggles faced by people who are working and nurturing a family at the same time. I then discussed the benefits that some organizations currently provide employees to help them deal with this conflict— benefits such as family-leave policies, child care, and elder care. Because more and more married people are dual-earner couples, I also considered some of the issues that make this situation stressful and explained how companies can help reduce the stress associated with juggling multiple careers and family responsibilities. Throughout this section, specific companies' work-life supports were highlighted to provide a sense of the many family-friendly benefits and services being offered to help reduce employees' stress.

The last two sections took a darker turn. First, I discussed the psychological effects of job loss and underemployment in light of the increased number of layoffs at major U.S. corporations and the perceived threat of being laid off experienced by so many employees in the 21st century. Then I presented some incredible statistics indicating the rise of workplace violence. In this context, employees at risk of becoming perpetrators were profiled, some recent research was reviewed, and a discussion was presented of two recent theoretical works that attempt to model the process through which workplace aggression and violence occur.

## Key Terms

burnout (p. 365)

coping (p. 367)

dual-earner couple (p. 380)

emotion-focused coping (p. 367)

organization-motivated aggression
(p. 390)

organization-motivated violence
(p. 390)

parental leave (p. 377)

problem-focused coping (p. 367)

role (p. 363)

role ambiguity (p. 363)

role conflict (p. 363)

strains (p. 361)

stressor (p. 361)

underemployment (p. 386)

work–family conflict (p. 370)

work–family enrichment (p. 370)

## TAKING IT TO THE FIELD

Work–family conflict is a growing concern among U.S. organizations. There are many practical issues that must be considered when designing programs to help support workers with families. One of your clients, Dutler Accountancy Firm, has reached out to you for some advice on a current problem they are encountering. Read the e-mail from Michael Yurttas, and draft a response with some recommendations.

Hello—

Thank you for taking the time to help me out with this problem.

Dutler Accountancy Firm has historically had quite a bit of difficulty recruiting and retaining female accountants. Part of this is because the field tends to be male-dominated; however, over the past decade, we have put forth a great deal of effort on recruiting and selecting qualified women for many of our positions. Unfortunately, we seem to be having much difficulty retaining these women.

We recently conducted a focus group with female employees from all levels of the company. From these sessions, it's become evident that our workplace policies are not a good fit for women with families. However, I'm not sure that we can change some of these policies to satisfy our female employees.

Throughout most of the year, we have a typical 9-to-5 workweek. However, during the two months leading up to tax season, our accountants often have to work 60 to 70 hours each week. Of course, we provide them with overtime pay for these long weeks. It became clear during our focus group sessions, though, that women, particularly women with children, do not find this work model effective. Many of our working mothers indicated that the long workdays were wreaking havoc with their child care. Many women also indicated that this timing sometimes conflicted with spring break, which prevented them from joining their families on vacations. Obviously, we can't cut back their hours during this time—the work has to get done, and we have very strict deadlines. It also doesn't make sense to hire more full-time workers—we have enough people at our firm to get the work done when it isn't tax season. In fact, sometimes we don't have enough work during the rest of the year to keep our workers busy.

We would really like to find a way to encourage women to stay with our organization. What suggestions do you have for us?

Sincerely,
Mike Yurttas

## Critical Thinking Questions

1. You learned at the beginning of this chapter that stressors lead to strains, which are the negative outcomes of stressful experiences. Based on what you read, what are some ways that people can keep stressful experiences from leading to strains? What are some advantages and disadvantages of these coping mechanisms?

2. Some unique employee benefit programs and perks were noted in this chapter. What are some new, innovative benefit programs that you think organizations should consider implementing for their employees? If you were exploring the job market right now, what kind of programs would you look for in your next employer?

3. Dual-earner couples are becoming increasingly common. What are some of the challenges faced by individuals in these dual-earner roles? How might organizations help their employees alleviate, or lessen, some of these challenges?

4. Work–family conflict is an important topic in I/O psychology and an important issue for organizations and their employees alike. A related but lesser-known concern is family interference with work. What do we mean by family interference with work? Is it a bigger issue for some people than for others? Why?

## Application Questions

1. Consider a recent stressful event you experienced at work. What types of job-related, emotional, and physiological strains did you experience as a result of this event? What are some problem-focused and emotion-focused coping strategies you might have used? What could the organization have done to help you deal with this stress?

2. Telecommuting is becoming more popular in a number of different companies. Consider your own schoolwork and how productive you are when you are working at home or in your dorm room, compared to when you are in a computer lab or a library. What are some benefits you have found to working at home? What are some difficulties? If you've taken an online course, how does that environment compare to a traditional classroom setting? What changes have you needed to make to your work habits to ensure you finish your online class successfully?

3. If you were to take a new job right now, what types of benefits would be most appealing to you? How might those benefits help you avoid common stressors such as work-family conflict, healthcare concerns, and job demands? Do you think you would find those same benefits helpful five years from now? Why or why not?

4. Underemployment is a common problem in the United States. Think of a time when you were stuck in a job or a class that was too easy and failed to challenge you. What were some frustrations you had with that situation? Do you think these frustrations would become more or less intense the longer you were in that situation? Did you take any steps to try to add challenge to that experience, and if so, what were they?

**5.** Imagine that a friend was recently laid off. He has only been unemployed for a few weeks, but already he is feeling depressed and hopeless about finding another job. What might you do to help him? What advice would you offer him?

## Suggested Readings

**100 best companies to work for.** (2015). *Fortune.* Retrieved February 6, 2016, from fortune.com/best-companies/. This very interesting annual report from *Fortune* magazine is a fun read; it provides cutting-edge examples of the workplace supports provided by some of the more progressive companies, both large and small.

**American Psychological Association.** (2004). *Public policy, work, and families: The report of the APA presidential initiative on work and families.* This report presents cutting-edge knowledge and a thorough summary of the social science research on the challenges faced by working families and their employers. It's a very readable account of what we know and don't know about some very complicated and important issues.

**Cartwright, S., & Cooper, C. L.** (1997). *Managing workplace stress.* Thousand Oaks, CA: SAGE. This book provides a readable treatment of stress at work and offers approaches and techniques for dealing with stress.

**Hammer, L. B., Kossek, E. E., Anger, W. K., Bodner, T., & Zimmerman, K. L.** (2011). Clarifying work–family intervention processes: The roles of work–family conflict and family-supportive supervisor behaviors. *Journal of Applied Psychology, 96*(1), 134. An interesting study showing the importance of training and work-family supports.

**Maertz, C. P., & Boyar, S. L.** (2011). Work-family conflict, enrichment, and balance under "levels" and "episodes" approaches. *Journal of Management, 37*(1), 68–98. This is a comprehensive review of the work-family literature with a framework to help your understanding.

**McGonagle, A. K., Fisher, G. G., Barnes-Farrell, J. L., & Grosch, J. W.** (2015). Individual and work factors related to perceived work ability and labor force outcomes. *Journal of Applied Psychology, 100*(2), 376–398. An interesting study that uses a longitudinal design to show that work ability predicts work outcomes like absence and retirement.

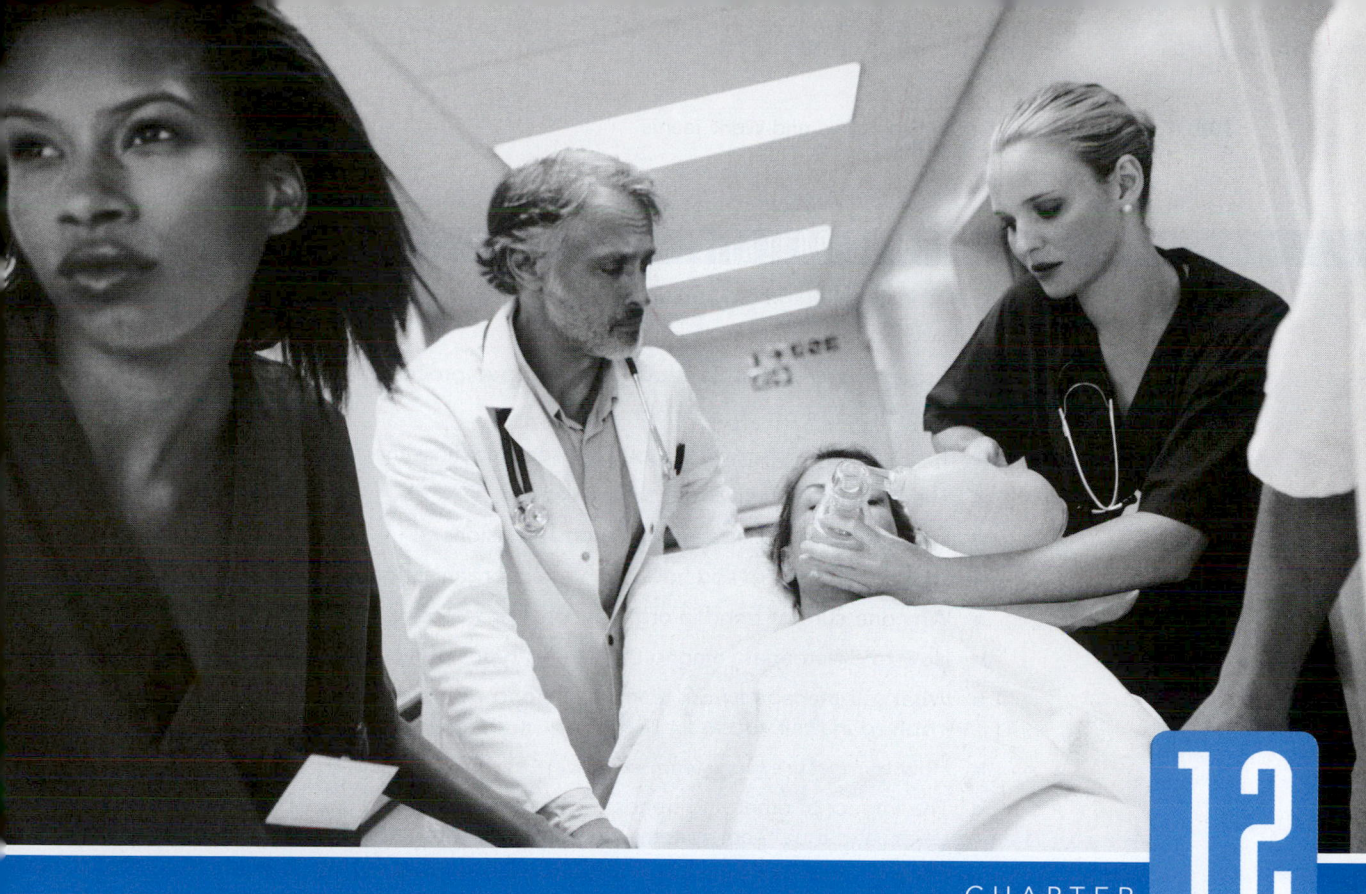

CHAPTER **12**

# Group Processes and Work Teams

Photo: Abel Mitja Varela/Getty Images

| **397**

## LEARNING OBJECTIVES

This chapter should help you understand:

- How social influence affects group behavior
- Group cohesion and its importance in group processes
- The stages of group development
- The implications for work groups of social loafing and free riding
- The stages of effective decision making
- Why groups don't always make good decisions
- What groupthink is and how it can affect organizations
- Why one current trend in organizational processes is the use of work teams
- How to differentiate among the various types of work teams
- What self-managed work teams are, along with some of the processes involved in their success
- How to measure work-team effectiveness and what factors affect it
- The impact of emerging trends such as the expanding use of virtual teams and multiteam systems, and the increased focus of teamwork in selection decisions

At some point during your education, you probably worked with other students on a group project. It may have been a book report in the fifth grade, a science project in the tenth grade, or a term paper in your freshman year of college. Group projects are a common way for students to learn about relevant material, develop interpersonal skills, and achieve goals that may have been more difficult to achieve individually.

Groups are quite prevalent in our day-to-day lives as well. I was a member of a softball team for over 10 years, I participate in various groups at church, and I've done some volunteer work as part of a group. You may have been a member of the Boy Scouts or Girl Scouts, and perhaps you are in a sorority or fraternity. Maybe your parents belonged to the Rotary Club or a neighborhood association. Groups, it seems, have always played a role in people's lives, from playgroups in early childhood to social or service groups in late adulthood. In the years between, people in the workforce encounter various groups in the workplace as well.

Though typically considered a specialty area within social psychology, group processes have been extensively examined by I/O psychologists interested in organizations that use work groups. In this chapter, I deal with the role of such groups in organizations. Specifically, I review some of the basics of group processes, apply them to groups at work, consider what I/O psychologists know about work teams, and discuss the great potential that teams have for transforming organizations.

# GROUPS VERSUS TEAMS

A **work group** is "an interdependent collection of individuals who share responsibility for specific outcomes for their organizations" (Sundstrom, DeMeuse, & Futrell, 1990). Other definitions, too, emphasize that members of work groups have interrelated goals; in short, a collection of people is not a group unless the individuals share common goals that affect one another. For instance, five people sitting in close proximity on a subway do not constitute a group; but when the subway doors get stuck, they become a group that works together to achieve such interrelated goals as getting the door open, contacting emergency personnel, comforting children who may be scared, and so on. *Formal groups* are subunits that the organization has actually established (e.g., committees, small departments, work crews), whereas *informal groups* develop apart from the official structure of the organization and exist relatively independently of it. Informal groups often emerge among employees who work in close proximity and interact frequently. They may consist of employees who get together for a working lunch, go through training together, or study together for a certification exam.

All organizations have both formal and informal groups. Formal groups are discussed at greater length in this chapter, but first we need to recognize how powerful and important informal groups can be. Informal groups serve a variety of functions, including the following:

1. They satisfy social needs such as friendship and companionship.
2. They satisfy security needs in that they make employees feel safe and connected.
3. They facilitate cooperation among employees.
4. They regulate social and task behaviors such that organizational norms and procedures are disseminated.

In the past, researchers drew a distinction between work groups and work teams; they argued that the former consist of individuals who work together but can do their respective jobs without the other members of the group, whereas the latter consist of individuals who are truly interdependent such that they must "work together" to get their jobs done. Many contemporary researchers, however, use these terms interchangeably, arguing that the distinction is unnecessary, sloppy, and not widely recognized (Sundstrom, McIntyre, Halfhill, & Richards, 2000). I myself use both terms to refer to the same idea: *Work groups* were defined at the beginning of the chapter, and *work teams* are discussed later on in the context of organizations, but I do not mean to imply any qualitative difference between the two terms.

**work group**
An interdependent collection of individuals who share responsibility for specific outcomes for their organizations.

Alina Solovyova-Vincent/Getty Images

**A CLOSER LOOK**
Librarians perform a variety of interdependent functions in order to facilitate the operation of their institution. How does this system reflect characteristics of a group versus a team? How might this distinction be unnecessary in a context like the one shown here?

# SOCIAL INFLUENCE IN GROUPS

Social psychologists spend a great deal of time studying the ways in which groups affect individual behaviors. In this section, we will review some major concepts related to group processes that have traditionally been studied by social psychologists but that I/O psychologists now apply to organizations.

## Norms

**norms**
Shared expectations about appropriate ways of responding in a group.

Norms are shared expectations about appropriate ways of responding in a group. As such, they are guidelines that serve an important organizational function, sometimes by stipulating certain behaviors as off-limits or inappropriate. *Descriptive norms* define what most people tend to do, feel, or think in a particular situation; *prescriptive norms* suggest what people *should* do, feel, or think in a particular situation (Forsyth, 1999). As you might imagine, employees who violate descriptive norms are viewed as unusual or different, but those who violate prescriptive norms are viewed as dysfunctional—that is, bad employees.

Sometimes groups sit down and list their norms; more often, norms develop gradually as group members become more comfortable with their place in the organization—and more comfortable with each other. Norms may also be passed down by employees who were members of the group at an earlier time. New employees, rather than changing existing norms, tend to adapt or adjust to them.

I have had experience with an organization in which the norm was for employees not to use their sick days at all. It was very clear to new employees that unless they had to be hospitalized, they were expected to be present at work; that way, their sick days would accumulate for years and years and would allow them to retire early. However, new employees who did not see the value in carrying over their sick days but preferred to stay home when ill essentially violated a prescriptive norm at this organization, leading at times to interpersonal conflict. A recent model of counterproductive work behavior (CWB) proposes that group norms and other team processes interact with individual-level variables to impact the frequency of CWB (O'Boyle, Forsyth, & O'Boyle, 2011).

## Roles

We have discussed roles elsewhere in this text (see especially Chapters 9 and 11), but let's take a more formal approach here. First, consider the context of behavior. An individual's behavior is jointly determined by internal forces (e.g., values, attitudes, and needs) and external forces (e.g., social pressure and job requirements). In other words, behavior is a function of both the person and the situation. Kurt Lewin (1951), widely recognized as the leader of the scientific study of groups, put it a bit differently: Behavior is a function of the person and the environment, or

$$B = f(P, E)$$

Second, the term *role concept* is used to describe how people perceive the various situational forces acting on them. For example, my role as a father is composed of what I think a father is supposed to do and, in particular, what I think *I* am supposed to do as a father. Similarly, my role as a psychology professor consists of how I interpret the expectations and demands of the environment to arrive at what I think I am supposed to do, how I should behave, and what my chief purpose is as a psychology professor.

Third, as defined in Chapter 11, a *role* is a set of behaviors expected of a person who occupies a particular position in a group or organization. The process by which a group or organization establishes distinct roles for various members of the group or organization is called **role differentiation**. This is accomplished through formal job descriptions, rules, and task requirements, as well as by supervisors, subordinates, and coworkers who communicate expectations and beliefs to individual employees. Thus, for example, a computer programmer at Apple knows what her role is not only because it is spelled out in the job description and other formal organizational documents but also because it is defined through discussions and interactions she's had with her supervisor and other computer programmers. A recent study of Major League Baseball teams found that player experience and skills were related to team performance. Further, these characteristics were especially valuable when held by those who occupied the core roles on the team and when the team allocated more resources to the core—here defined as pitchers and catchers (Humphrey, Morgeson, & Mannor, 2009).

Especially when combined with the work stress caused by role conflict and role ambiguity (again, see Chapter 11), role differentiation within work groups can become quite complicated. With this in mind, let's now examine two of the more important dimensions of groups—conflict and cohesion.

**role differentiation**
The process by which a group or organization establishes distinct roles for various members of the group or organization.

## Conflict

As norms and roles are important elements that help determine how groups operate, it should not be surprising that there is sometimes conflict within teams. You have probably experienced conflict in groups that you have been a member of, such as class project groups, bands or musical groups, sports teams, or church groups.

Researchers generally agree that conflict comes in three different forms (O'Neill, Allen, & Hastings, 2013). First, *relationship conflict* is the tension and friction that emerges in interpersonal relationships and can harm team performance. *Task conflict* results when team members have different ideas, beliefs, or viewpoints regarding the work to be done. It is interesting to note that though this task conflict can be harmful to performance, in some instances it can also be beneficial to the effectiveness of the team, which may benefit from the various perspectives brought to bear on a task or issue.

Finally, *process conflict* emerges when group members have incompatible ideas about how the work should be accomplished. This conflict often results in a performance decrement because members cannot find common ground, producing little collaboration. Among the many interesting findings of their meta-analysis of over 6100 hundred teams, O'Neill et al., found that task conflict had a positive effect on decision-making teams, but a negative effect on project and production teams. These findings suggest that the different perspectives and viewpoints of team members are helpful in a decision-making context. In addition, the negative effects of relationship and process conflict were stronger in teams with greater tenure, suggesting that these types of conflict play a more serious role in long-standing teams perhaps because the conflict resurfaces again and again and team members have difficulty moving past the hurt and anxiety.

## Cohesion

**cohesion**
The strength of members' motivation to maintain membership in a group and of the links or bonds that have developed among the members.

At some point in your life, you have probably been part of a group in which the members were very close-knit, expressed a unified commitment to the group, and shared similar beliefs about issues relevant to the group. You may also recall that morale was generally high in that group. All of these elements are related to **cohesion**, defined as the strength of members' motivation to maintain membership in a group and of the links or bonds that have developed among the members. Cohesion is seen as (1) both a binding force that pushes members together and a combative force that tries to pull them apart; (2) group unity, or "we-ness," in which group members feel such a strong sense of belonging that they put the goals of the group above their individual goals; (3) a special type of interpersonal attraction; and (4) an aspect of "teamwork" (Forsyth, 1999). Some groups are cohesive because they consist of close personal friends, others are cohesive because the members feel a strong sense of belonging, and still others are cohesive as a result of great teamwork (Cota, Evans, Dion, Kilik, & Longman, 1995).

Examples of cohesive work groups are widespread; think of the many work groups depicted on television. Any of the many medical dramas on television, for instance, have routinely presented the emergency-room employees as belonging to a very cohesive group whose members get along well; are committed to one another, the patients, and the hospital; share similar beliefs about medicine and patient treatment; and are clearly motivated to maintain affiliation with the group. Interestingly, some of the storylines of these popular TV shows have been about the conflict that results when someone disrupts the cohesiveness of the group by disagreeing with other group members or violating a group norm. In reality, of course, many work groups are not very cohesive. They consist of employees who don't get along very well, who see things very differently, and who remain affiliated with the other group members only because doing so is part of their job.

Cohesion has both positive and negative consequences for groups and organizations. The negative consequences, which are largely related to group decision making, are discussed in a later section. For now, however, I focus on the positive consequences. Most managers, if asked to choose between supervising a cohesive work group and a noncohesive work group, would quickly opt for the former. Faced with a similar choice, you would probably do the same. What, then, are the positive consequences of cohesion?

First, a great deal of research across athletic, industrial, and educational settings demonstrates that members of cohesive groups report being more satisfied than do members of noncohesive groups (Forsyth, 1999). Think about your own experiences in this regard. I would predict that you have more positive things to say about the cohesive groups you've belonged to than about the noncohesive groups. There tends to be less tension and anxiety in cohesive groups because their members get along, like one another, have similar goals and objectives, and work well together.

Second, group cohesion is positively linked to performance (Kerr & Tindale, 2004). One of the truly great groups of the 20th century was the Disney group that worked together in the early days of Walt Disney's success (Bennis & Biederman, 1997). Creative, hardworking, and cohesive, this group made incredible contributions to the world of animation and film.

*Yellow Dog Productions/Iconica/Getty Images*

Indeed, two meta-analyses support a positive relationship between cohesiveness and performance (Evans & Dion, 1991; Mullen & Copper, 1994). Both meta-analyses identified a series of moderators that affect the strength of this relationship, as did a recent study employing sophisticated virtual laboratory methods. This study found support for the argument that the causal relationship between cohesiveness and performance varies as a function of type of task and type of cohesiveness (Fullagar & Egleston, 2008). The results suggested that social cohesiveness (interpersonal attraction) affects performance on tasks requiring social interaction; however, on tasks that don't require much social interaction, performance impacts task cohesion (group commitment to the task). In other words, when there isn't much social interaction, performance of the task is necessary before task cohesiveness can be developed. Research has consistently found task cohesion, as opposed to social cohesion, to be more strongly related to many outcome variables such as team performance (Carless & De Paola, 2000).

Cohesion plays a role in many diverse contexts. For instance, in a study of elite ice hockey players, it was discovered that perceptions of team cohesion predicted the tendency to return to the team in the following year (Spink, Wilson, & Odnokon, 2010). Have you experienced both cohesive and noncohesive groups at work, at school, or in social circles? If so, you know that the differences between the two types of groups are striking. But how do cohesive groups develop?

## Group Development

Traditionally, theories and models of group development agree that groups pass through various stages as they develop. One model that many group researchers have endorsed is the five-stage version proposed by Bruce Tuckman in the 1960s (Tuckman, 1965; see also Tuckman & Jensen, 1977). We'll examine this model in some detail because it provides a solid general view of group development.

Tuckman believed that groups develop while passing through five stages over time (see **Table 12.1**). In the first stage, groups go through an orientation period that Tuckman referred to as *forming;* group members spend time getting to know each other. This is followed by a period of conflict called the *storming* stage, in which group members

| TABLE 12.1 | Tuckman's Five Stages of Group Development |
|---|---|
| **Stage** | **Group Processes** |
| 1. Forming | Members get acquainted. Interactions are polite, tentative, exploratory, and sometimes guarded. |
| 2. Storming | Interactions are characterized by disagreement. Members question one another more pointedly. Some conflict emerges. |
| 3. Norming | Unity is established. Members become more cohesive. Roles, standards, and relationships develop. Trust increases. |
| 4. Performing | Members become focused on productivity and goal achievement. Task orientation is high. |
| 5. Adjourning | Roles are terminated. Relationships weaken, and members become much less dependent on one another or the group. Some degree of stress or tension is likely. |

have moved beyond polite conversation and actually begin disagreeing with one another, questioning one another's ideas and beliefs, and openly revealing who they are.

In the third stage, a structure-building stage that Tuckman referred to as *norming,* group members become more cohesive and establish unity among themselves. During the fourth stage, members are focused on productivity, or *performing.* It typically takes a while before a group is productive, occurring after the members have a better feel for one another.

Of course, some groups never make it to this stage. Having stagnated at the norming stage, they fail to reach their potential in terms of productivity. Examples of unproductive groups can be found in numerous studies of combat groups, civic groups, and personal-growth groups. On the other hand, we have all experienced truly productive groups that reached the performing stage. It is exhilarating to be part of a group that grows and matures into a productive arm of society, whether at work, a house of worship, or school.

The final stage involves the dissolution of the group, or what Tuckman called *adjourning.* This stage can be planned for, as when a work group charged with a particular project dissolves because the project is finished. Sometimes, however, groups dissolve due to lack of performance or group members' dissatisfaction. The organization itself may decide that a particular group is no longer successful or useful. At other times, work groups are dissolved for financial reasons, as when group members are laid off or asked to take on more work that necessitates their being pulled out of the group.

Change is stressful regardless of the context, especially when one has spent considerable time as a member of a group, only to see it disband. The stress that accompanies the dissolution of a team was made very clear to me by my oldest son when he was eight years old. He loved playing baseball and soccer in the local recreation leagues; every time the season ended, he became very sad and told me how much he was going to miss his teammates and the fun that comes from working together to score more than the other teams. I always pointed out that he would see the same guys in school, at church, and around the neighborhood, but he would say that it wasn't the same because they wouldn't be a team anymore. Indeed, when we affiliate with others in close situations and work interdependently to achieve a goal, it's hard to accept the end of that relationship.

We need to be careful about generalizing this process to all groups all the time. Some groups may go through the five stages in a different order and spend more time at one stage than at another. Other groups may stop short of making it through all the stages; still others may skip a stage or two.

Gersick's work on models of *punctuated equilibrium* presents an alternative in which groups fluctuate more quickly among these and other stages of development (Gersick, 1989). This model has become extremely popular in describing how groups form, and it's a stark contrast to Tuckman's more traditional linear stage view. This more complex model argues that all groups don't pass through these stages one step at a time. In many instances, groups will oscillate between stages or perhaps even go through them in a different order. According to this model, groups go through inactive periods where very little is happening and then, as a result of time and an awareness of deadlines, a spike in activity occurs and group activity picks up. Sometimes groups adopt a task-focused approach early on, but not much happens until about half their time allotment is gone, and then they shift into gear.

In a recent study of MBA students using a sophisticated business simulation, results showed that a group's business charter or a plan for how the group would operate interacted with performance strategies to determine group performance (Mathieu & Rapp, 2009). What is most interesting for our purposes is that about halfway through the simulation—as would be suggested by the punctuated equilibrium model—the performance of the groups with a low-quality performance strategy declined drastically, while the performance of the groups with a high-quality performance strategy was maintained or began a steady incline. As suggested by the theory, when groups realize they are about halfway through their task, they tend to become more active and therefore to enact their strategies and approaches.

Another approach has been proposed in which groups may actually develop in a way that combines the traditional stage model and the punctuated equilibrium model. Chang, Bordia, and Duck (2003) compared Gersick's punctuated equilibrium model with a stage approach and found that the two models together explain group formation fairly well. They argued and demonstrated that each model is useful when looking at a particular unit of analysis. For instance, the punctuated equilibrium model describes the discontinuous changes in a group's pacing and task activities over time, but a stage model describes the continuous manner in which a group's structure changes over time. So in the 1990s, the pendulum swung away from linear stage models like Tuckman's and toward Gersick's punctuated equilibrium model; but today some researchers (e.g., Chang et al., 2003) and theoreticians argue that it may have swung too far and that the models complement each other in providing a better understanding of group functioning.

Recent work in the area of group development has produced some interesting results. One study argues that Tuckman's linear model of group development is fundamentally different from the punctuated equilibrium model (Garfield & Dennis, 2012). The authors propose that these two models do not just present two ways of looking at group development, as many have suggested, but that they are distinct models that operate in different contexts. Garfield and Dennis predicted and found that groups with well established routines that are understood by the group members develop within a punctuated equilibrium model because they can quickly get to work. However, those groups that do not operate with understood routines must first figure out how the work is to be done and come to some agreement about that work. These groups tend to follow a stage model, such as Tuckman's, where the groups have to go through the stages of forming, storming, etc. before they can make progress on the task at hand.

Another recent study (Raes, Kynd, Decuyper, Van den bossche, & Dochy, 2014) examined a sample of about 40 professional Belgian teams and observed that actual team learning—learning that involves sharing information, collaborating on proposals and ideas, and honest interaction that may lead to conflict—only happens in the later stages of team development. The authors concluded that teams do not learn in the early stages of team development, but rather tend to operate as separate individuals at those stages. As structures develop and trust grows in the latter stages of development, teams start to learn together. Future research will continue to explore the various ways in which groups evolve and develop.

## Social Loafing and Other Group Phenomena

The idea of social loafing was first analyzed and presented in the early 1900s by Max Ringelmann, who noticed that individual effort in a wide variety of tasks often decreased with increases in the size of the group. What later became known as social loafing refers to the reduction in individual effort that occurs when people work in groups instead of alone. The point here is not that groups, as a whole, work less hard than individuals but, rather, that individuals, in many situations, work less hard in groups than they do when working alone. Ringelmann and others noticed this effect across a variety of tasks such as rope pulling and clapping.

Since Ringelmann's early work, social loafing has been empirically demonstrated by additional researchers on such tasks as making noise, working on mazes, writing, swimming, and problem solving. Although there are various explanations for this effect (Pinder, 1998), most researchers agree that people are less likely to "loaf"

**social loafing**
The reduction in individual effort that occurs when people work in groups instead of alone.

(1) when they believe that their individual efforts can be identified and (2) when others are going to be personally affected by their effort. Some argue that social loafing is especially pervasive in groups and usually occurs because people don't expect their efforts on group tasks to be as directly tied to valued outcomes as their efforts on individual tasks (Karau & Williams, 1993). You may recognize this explanation as being based on the expectancy theory of motivation.

When Stephen Zaccaro (1984) conducted a study in which students were given the opportunity to "loaf" in groups, he found that social loafing occurred only among group members who were working on a task low in attractiveness. The opposite effect, *social enhancement,* occurred among group members who were working on a task that was high in attractiveness. In the latter case, individuals in larger groups performed better than those in smaller groups. Other research has also demonstrated that social loafing is less likely to occur in cohesive groups than in noncohesive groups (Karau & Hart, 1998; Karau & Williams, 1997); thus, variables other than task attractiveness may affect the likelihood of social loafing in any given situation (Goren, Kurzban, & Rapoport, 2003).

Some research has examined the role that cultural variables play in group phenomena like social loafing. For instance, research has generally supported the idea that North Americans socially loaf more than the Chinese. However, a recent study demonstrated a more complicated relationship. Chinese workers actually performed at a level that matched their coworkers'—this was especially the case in public contexts (Hong, Wyer, & Fong, 2008), where the authors argue that Chinese employees prefer not to stand out. So, while it's true that Chinese tend to socially loaf less than North Americans (probably due to their collectivistic nature, as opposed to the more individualistic nature of North Americans), it's actually more complicated than that.

Group dynamics can get even more thorny. Sometimes, for instance, employees do less than their share of the work but still share equally in the rewards. Known as free riding, this situation appears to happen when employees perceive that their efforts are not necessary to group success and rewards. In such cases, other group members become concerned that their coworkers are holding back, at which point they reduce their own efforts to the level they believe is being exhibited by their coworkers. This outcome, called the sucker effect, occurs when group members decide they will no longer be played for a sucker and thus reduce their effort—even if it results in failure on the task. Have you ever experienced this in a group project for class? Kerr and Tindale (2004) discuss other complex group effects such as *social compensation,* which occurs when individuals increase their efforts on collective tasks because they don't anticipate much help from their group members. You can see, then, how complicated social processes can become, with potentially far-reaching effects on organizational functioning.

**free riding**
A situation that occurs when employees do less than their share of the work but still share equally in the rewards.

**sucker effect**
An outcome that occurs when group members become concerned that their coworkers are holding back, at which point they reduce their own efforts to the level they believe is being exhibited by their coworkers.

# GROUP DECISION MAKING

Think about the roles that various groups play throughout the world. We often entrust groups with the greatest responsibilities. Groups run major national and international companies that affect our economy and lives (e.g., boards of directors); groups run universities and colleges that influence our own and our children's education (e.g., boards of trustees); groups decide the fate of our accused criminals and provide the only means of protection for the unjustly accused (e.g., juries); we even entrust our physical health and well-being to groups when faced with serious illness (e.g., surgical teams). Although most of us would agree that as citizens of the United States we live in an individualistic society, we must not lose sight of the importance of groups—especially considering the power and responsibility we hand over to them to make crucial decisions. In this section, we will consider both effective and ineffective group decision making.

## Decision-Making Processes

Although no two groups make decisions in exactly the same way, certain elements can be said to characterize most successful decision making. There are various ways to break down these elements (Schilling, Oeser, & Schaub, 2007); I do so by relying on the five steps outlined in **Table 12.2**.

Before any intensive work can be done to solve a problem by making a particular decision, groups must first *diagnose the problem*. Group members must come to some agreement about the nature of the problem, the goals of the group with respect to this problem, and the obstacles the group should be sensitive to and then prepare to overcome. Although at first glance this step in the process appears rather straightforward, research indicates that many groups don't spend enough (or any!) time on it (Forsyth, 1999). Some common mistakes at this stage include confusing facts with opinions and looking for scapegoats. For instance, the members of a salary-equity task force charged with identifying and resolving apparent differences in pay between men and women may mistake as a fact what is merely their opinion—that the pay differences are based purely on skills and experience—and thus distort their perception of the problem.

The second step of effective decision making is to *generate solutions*. This discussion-oriented stage involves communication among group members in which they process the problem and group goals while trying to identify potential solutions. A useful technique here is **brainstorming**, in which all members of a group generate potential solutions without fear of having their suggestions criticized by other members. The purpose is to create

**brainstorming**
A technique in which all members of a group generate potential solutions without fear of having their suggestions criticized by other members.

Pete Souza/The White House/MCT via Getty Images

**A CLOSER LOOK**
What steps go into effective decision making?

## TABLE 12.2 Five Steps to Effective Group Decision Making

| Step | Description | Common Mistakes |
|---|---|---|
| 1. Diagnose the problem | Group members come to an agreement on the nature of the problem. | Confusing facts with opinions<br>Confusing symptoms with causes |
| 2. Generate solutions | Group interaction is focused on understanding the problem well enough to identify potential solutions. | Suggesting irrelevant solutions<br>Looking at what should have been done rather than looking forward |
| 3. Evaluate solutions | Group members consider each solution in terms of its potential for success and failure. | Failing to consider the potential downside to each solution<br>Attacking the person who proposed a particular solution rather than focusing on the solution itself |
| 4. Choose a solution | Group members come to some agreement on the best solution. | Allowing powerful members of the group to dictate the solution chosen<br>Biasing a particular solution because it's politically correct |
| 5. Develop an action plan and implementation | Group members determine steps to follow in carrying out the decision and monitoring progress. | Preventing some members from being involved even though they were part of the decision process |

Source: Information from *Decision Making: A Psychological Analysis of Conflict, Choice, Commitment* by Irving L. Janis and Leon Mann (1977).

an atmosphere in which each group member feels comfortable generating solutions—and, indeed, the group is arguably best served by having a long list of such solutions.

One mistake sometimes made at this stage, however, is to raise irrelevant solutions, thereby throwing the group off task. Another mistake is to rely on "old" solutions rather than remaining open and willing to think creatively about the problem. In general, research suggests that the effectiveness of brainstorming is reduced when (1) members have to wait their turn or are otherwise delayed in their opportunity to share, thus blocking the free flow of ideas (this is called *production blocking*); (2) members are apprehensive about voicing their ideas to the group; and (3) members are more motivated by concern for how "good" they look in comparison with others than by concern for generating viable solutions (Forsyth, 1999).

Several decades of research have shown many instances in which brainstorming results in worse performance than that of nominal groups (i.e., individuals not working together or groups in name only). This performance decrement has been the major criticism of brainstorming. More recent work, however, has begun to challenge these negative findings and provide some solutions for improving the effectiveness of this technique, such as employing a trained facilitator to minimize production blocking (Kerr & Tindale, 2004).

annebaek/iStock/Getty Images Plus

Perhaps the most intriguing solution is the recent development of "electronic brainstorming," in which software allows individuals to type in their ideas without production blocking, with anonymity, and with other group members' ideas available to them at any time on the screen. Some research has demonstrated the superiority of this approach to the use of nominal groups (for a review, see Nijstad, Stroebe, & Lodewijkx, 2003), which may result in greater interest in electronic brainstorming in the future. Although we have not seen much done with this technique in psychology as of yet, it has become quite popular in more technical spheres. However, one recent psychological application of this approach to the study of social loafing found that teams composed of individuals who were familiar with each other performed better using electronic brainstorming, which is consistent with the extant literature on traditional brainstorming where familiar teams also perform better (Fang & Chang, 2014).

The third step, *evaluating solutions,* follows directly from the previous one. Specifically, the group critically evaluates each of the solutions proposed during the brainstorming procedure, accepting those that seem workable and rejecting those that do not. At this point, it's important for the group to consider the worst-case scenario regarding each alternative when deciding whether to eliminate it from further consideration. For instance, if our salary-equity task force decides to explain pay differences in terms of the importance of jobs held by the respective genders, the result could be a worst-case scenario involving angry female employees whose commitment to the organization is compromised. This could then lead to dissatisfaction with their jobs, a decrement in performance, high turnover rates, potential suits brought against the company, and depleted morale.

*Choosing a solution* from those on the list is the fourth step of the process. After considering the potential benefits and weaknesses of each alternative and eliminating those that are not workable or that would have negative consequences, the group must compare the remaining solutions and pick the best one for implementation. Groups choose solutions in various ways. Forsyth (1999) discusses some common approaches:

- *Delegating:* The group provides information to the chairperson, who makes the decision. (Alternatively, a subcommittee speaks for the whole group.)
- *Averaging individual inputs:* Group members make individual private decisions, which are then averaged to arrive at a group-level decision.
- *Majority rules:* The group votes, and the majority viewpoint becomes the group's choice.
- *Group consensus:* The group members discuss the issue until they reach a unanimous agreement.

Potential mistakes at this stage include allowing those with power to dictate the chosen solution and biasing the benefits and weaknesses to support a "favorite" solution.

Finally, after the decision has been made to enact a particular solution, the group begins to *develop an action plan and implementation* of that solution. Detailed action steps and methods for monitoring and evaluating progress toward the solution are developed. Let's say our salary-equity task force decides to conduct a reevaluation of job classifications and wage scales; toward this end, it must develop a plan that includes timelines, steps in the process, and objectives for each step. After the action plan is ready, implementation begins, with each step monitored and evaluated along the way.

Although success is not guaranteed, consideration of the issues raised in each of the preceding five steps is certainly more likely to result in effective decisions than ignoring such issues. Of course, groups can also undergo these steps with varying degrees of commitment, which explains why some decisions are good ones and others are not so good.

## Ineffective Decision Making

The fact that groups are asked to make many of our important decisions doesn't mean they always do it well. Indeed, in American culture we often poke fun at groups, especially committees, through humor—such as the *Cathy* comic strip in this chapter and the several *Dilbert* cartoons throughout the book. Forsyth (1999), for instance, quotes the all-too-common view that "committees consist of the unfit appointed by the unwilling to do the unnecessary." Now perhaps that's a bit extreme, but we have all had bad experiences as part of a group decision-making effort or been adversely affected by an inadequate group decision-making process.

**Process Loss**    In 1972, Ivan Steiner suggested the following *law of group performance:*

Actual Productivity = Potential Productivity − Losses Due to Faulty Processes

Here, "potential productivity" refers to all the positive things that can come from group work, such as shared responsibilities and the variety of skills brought to bear on a particular problem. At the end of the equation, however, is the category of

**cathy**®                                                                 **by Cathy Guisewite**

© 1990 Universal Press Syndicate

Does the group in this cartoon exhibit any of the five steps to effective group decision making outlined in Table 12.2?

**process loss**
Any nonmotivational element of a group situation that detracts from the group's performance.

"losses due to faulty processes," or process loss, which refers to any nonmotivational element of a group situation that detracts from the group's performance. For example, coordination problems among group members result in process loss, as when one employee works on her part of a group task without coordinating her efforts with other members who are doing related parts of the task. Actual productivity is adversely affected by process loss, a key element groups need to be aware of so that they can take advantage of the benefits of group processes rather than being limited by potential disadvantages.

A program of research by James Larson and his colleagues (Larson, Christensen, Franz, & Abbott, 1998; Larson, Foster-Fishman, & Franz, 1998) has focused on the factor of shared versus unshared information in terms of its effect on decision making. *Unshared information* is that held by only one group member; *shared information* is that held by all group members. According to these researchers, one reason we entrust important decisions to groups is that we assume a larger pool of relevant information is being brought to bear on the problem. As their studies have shown, however, groups are not particularly effective at pooling unshared information; indeed, group decisions tend to be determined more by shared information.

This finding is ironic, given that the notion of pooling unshared information is one of the assumed strengths of group decision making. Larson and his colleagues argue that to improve the quality of group decision making, the pooling of valuable unshared information should be encouraged (see also Brodbeck, Kerschreiter, Mojzisch, Frey, & Schulz-Hardt, 2002). One technique they suggest is for leaders to employ a "participative" style of leadership. Participative leadership simply describes leaders who include others in the making decisions and implementing policy. This method has received some qualified research support (Larson, Foster-Fishman, et al., 1998), but more work needs to be done regarding how to encourage groups to take advantage of one of their potential benefits—the pooling of unshared information. One recent study examined individuals from multiple plants in nine different countries and found that the relationship between organizational structure and learning was positively affected by the extent to which the national culture supported participative leadership (Huang, Rode, & Schroeder, 2011).

The process loss that we see in many group failures often centers on communication problems. Some researchers have argued that process losses often stem directly from not sharing information and arriving at decisions too quickly (Van Ginkel & van Knippenberg, 2009). In addition, problems emerge when group members don't discuss foundational ideas regarding the group task—that is, when they don't discuss how they see the task or their perceptions of what the task requires. Researchers assigned 252 students to groups of three and invited them to work on a cooperative decision-making task dealing with retail stores and a few important marketing and operating decisions (Van Ginkel, Tindale, & van Knippenberg, 2009). They found that group reflection about the nature of the task affected group members' information sharing and elaboration, which in turn affected decision quality. Indeed, communication about task perceptions and reflection on what the task entails are important determinants of effective decision making.

**Groupthink** Without a doubt, the most talked-about group decision-making error is groupthink, defined by Irving Janis (1972) as a mode of thinking that individuals engage in when the desire to agree becomes so dominant in a cohesive group that it tends to override realistic appraisal of alternative courses of action. In such instances, group members become so focused on sticking together and following through as a cohesive group that their decision making is clouded or biased. Indeed, groupthink has been presented (by Janis and others) as an explanation for various poor decisions made throughout the history of the United States.

An especially compelling example has to do with Japan's attack on Pearl Harbor on December 7, 1941. U.S. military commanders in Hawaii had been provided with a great deal of information about Japan's buildup for this attack; as a group, however, they never really took the situation seriously. They didn't strategically place aircraft carriers in the Pacific, where they could have provided some warning of the attack, and they didn't deem the threat real enough to warrant any military buildup on the part of the United States. Thus, there was absolutely no warning at all until the Japanese bombers were directly overhead, attacking our defenseless ships and airfields (Janis & Mann, 1977).

Although some researchers argue that the empirical data about groupthink are mixed at best and perhaps better characterized as weak (e.g., Park, 2000), others suggest that additional research is needed—both to examine the theoretical variables involved and to expand these variables to include other potentially important constructs (Henningsen, Henningsen, Eden, & Cruz, 2006). Many experts agree, however, that the groupthink construct presents a useful framework for analyzing and combating ineffective group decision making (Mulrine, 2008).

Regarding the *antecedents* of groupthink, what do you think are some of the factors likely to lead to this phenomenon? Not surprisingly, Janis has presented a list of these factors in his model of groupthink (see **Figure 12.1**). The primary necessary

**groupthink**
A mode of thinking that individuals engage in when the desire to agree becomes so dominant in a cohesive group that it tends to override the realistic appraisal of alternative courses of action.

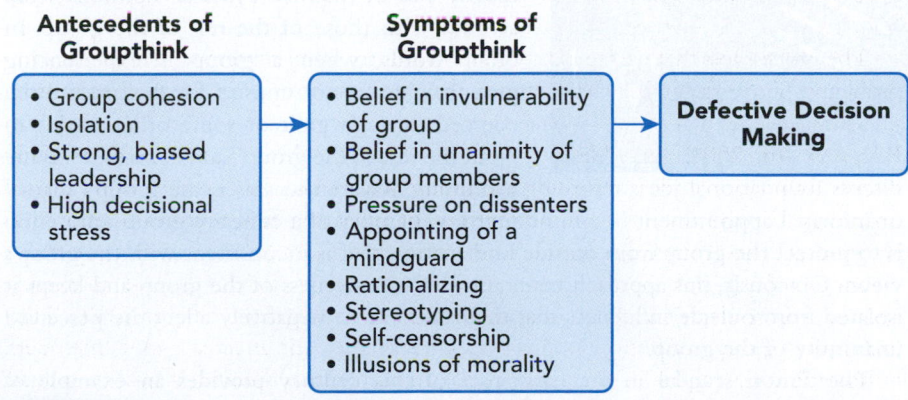

**FIGURE 12.1**  **Janis's Model of Groupthink** (Information from Janis & Mann, 1977, p. 132)

antecedent for groupthink to occur is *cohesion* (Janis, 1982). Members of cohesive groups often feel such a strong sense of belonging that they put group goals above their own individual goals. The implication here is that group members may even avoid expressing a dissenting opinion because they believe group unity to be more important; in this case, group cohesion is problematic.

Groupthink is also more likely in groups that are *isolated* from others. This makes sense, given that isolation from others limits the dissenting opinions that could be shared with the group. *Strong, biased leadership* is another important antecedent of groupthink. Strong leaders have a tendency to "dictate" the direction of the group and even some of its opinions. In your own experience, have you ever tried to get a group to listen to your opinion about something, only to be silenced by the group leader, who had a seemingly solid explanation of why your opinion wasn't relevant? The last antecedent of groupthink is *high decisional stress,* which refers to situations in which a decision needs to be made quickly and the context in which it exists is very important and emotionally charged.

As for the *symptoms* of groupthink, take another look at Figure 12.1, in which eight such symptoms are listed. Limited space prevents me from discussing all of these, but I will mention briefly a few of the more interesting ones. First, in situations involving groupthink, members tend to believe that they are *invulnerable* to harm and *unanimous* in their beliefs. I always think of Watergate as a great example of this; the accounts and interviews of those involved with the Nixon White House—the principal players on the Committee to Reelect the President (CREEP)—make it very clear that these people never considered the possibility that they could be caught, brought down, and damaged, much less that they were doing anything "wrong."

**mindguard**
A member of a cohesive group whose job it is to protect the group from outside information that is inconsistent with the group's views.

Two other symptoms that seem to go hand in hand with the ones just discussed are *pressure on dissenters* and *appointment of a mindguard.* When groupthink occurs, a great deal of pressure is usually put on members whose opinions seem at odds with those of the rest of the group. In other words, when a group is experiencing groupthink, it is not unusual for dissenters to be coerced through guilt or some other means to "join the rest of the group" and contribute to the unanimity. Related to this is the group's formal or informal appointment of a **mindguard**, a member of a cohesive group whose job is to protect the group from outside information that is inconsistent with the group's views. Obviously, this approach maintains the cohesiveness of the group and keeps it isolated from outside influences that might otherwise negatively affect the perceived unanimity of the group.

Kenneth Lambert/AP Photo

**A CLOSER LOOK**
In what ways does the culture and collapse of Enron, which engaged in systematic accounting fraud leading to its bankruptcy, reflect the dangers of groupthink?

The Enron scandal in the early part of this century provides an example of groupthink. Team members were pushed hard to deliver results, and dissent among executives or against adopted company strategies was suppressed. Highly ranked employees felt pressure to go along with deals and decisions in order to maintain their status within the company (Prindle, 2010). The culture was one of unrealistic demands and high pressure, in which employees, led by strong, coercive leaders, were compelled to toe the company line. In the end, a combination of poor financial decisions and accounting fraud led to bankruptcy for the company and criminal charges for several of its executives (Lardner, 2002; Riordan & Riordan, 2013).

Finally, the steps to effective decision making presented earlier (see Table 12.2) should be followed in the hope of eliminating or preventing groupthink altogether. The more carefully the problem is diagnosed, the more tightly focused the group is in identifying potential solutions, the more critically the potential solutions are evaluated, the more carefully a final solution is chosen, the more precisely the action plan and implementation are carried out, and the less likely groupthink is to emerge.

## WORK TEAMS OF THE 21ST CENTURY

Collaboration, which is an important concept for 21st-century organizations, is reflected in two or more people engaged in interaction with each other who are also working toward a common goal (Patel, Pettitt, & Wilson, 2012). A recent conceptual framework suggests seven major factors of collaboration (context, support, task, interaction process, teams, individuals, and overarching factors) (Patel et al., 2012). In the remainder of this chapter, I will focus on one very important factor of collaboration: teams.

Although I made it clear at the outset that I would use the terms *work group* and *work team* interchangeably, I predominantly use the latter in this last section in order to be consistent with the growing I/O literature. In this literature, work teams are essentially defined as work groups in which the actions of individuals are interdependent and coordinated; each member has a specified role, and the team has common goals and objectives. But regardless of the specifics of the definition, a growing organizational trend that cannot be denied is the steady increase in work teams across every segment of the industrial sector.

### Mental Models

Group learning is an important element in the functioning of work teams. Group learning can be viewed as an outcome—a new shared understanding among group members. The process of group learning includes sharing a new understanding, storing it, and being able to retrieve it (Goodman & Dabbish, 2011). This shared understanding is more than just an aggregation of beliefs across people; it is actually a property of the team (Goodman & Dabbish, 2011).

Related to the notion of group learning is a concept called shared mental models. First, a **mental model** is an organized knowledge structure that enhances the interaction of an individual with his or her environment (Mathieu, Heffner, Goodwin, Salas, & Canon-Bowers, 2000). Mental models allow people to make sense of the world around them—to describe, explain, and predict what's happening in

**mental model**
An organized knowledge structure that helps an individual make sense of the world around him or her.

## PRACTITIONER FORUM

Tom Ruddy

### Tom Ruddy
*PhD, 1989, I/O Psychology, Bowling Green State University*
*Vice President of Human Resources WW Businesses*
*Becton Dickinson*

Much of what you've learned in this chapter about work teams rings true in the real world of corporate America. At Xerox and Siemens, I became familiar with these concepts while implementing empowered teams for over 14 years in over 36 countries worldwide. For Xerox's global customer service organization, the empowered team implementation process consisted of several steps: (1) form teams (controlling size and composition), (2) understand and communicate the company vision, (3) develop a team mission, (4) define team goals, (5) establish team norms of behavior, (6) clarify team member roles, and (7) document and follow key work processes (e.g., communication, meeting, and work processes).

We used these team start-up steps during team training as a way to get teams up and functioning. We sometimes found that there was a lack of clarity in one of these key areas, which affected the team's success. The completion and monitoring of these process steps would often ensure effective team functioning.

As my own study and observation of over 3,000 teams has demonstrated, team members' ability to follow agreed-upon processes and norms is more predictive of good team functioning than is the extent to which team members "like" each other. While positive personal relationships do not hurt team functioning, such relationships are not necessary or sufficient to create

high-performance work teams. My work at Siemens with virtual teams that operate across multiple countries and time zones has highlighted the fact that well-defined processes and behavioral expectations are the critical factor in making teams successful.

Our research data, based on over 16 separate studies on Xerox and Siemens teams, has identified the following critical organizational context factors in team performance: (1) team-based support structures (e.g., team-based incentives, performance feedback systems), (2) management leadership and coaching, and (3) technical resources (e.g., pagers, laptops, real-time communication devices). The presence or absence of these factors has an impact on the ability of teams to develop effective team processes (i.e., the seven start-up steps mentioned previously) and drives performance (e.g., customer satisfaction, employee satisfaction, and expense management).

### Applying Your Knowledge

1. Why is team cohesiveness related to tasks more important than general liking among team members?

2. In what ways are Dr. Ruddy's experiences regarding team development consistent with the punctuated equilibrium model?

3. How do virtual teams differ from traditional face-to-face teams with regard to the importance of team processes and organizational context factors?

---

**shared mental models**
Organized structures combining the knowledge, beliefs, and understandings of two or more individuals that help coordinate their efforts.

their environment. Individuals need to be able to describe, explain, and predict the attitudes and behaviors of their team members so that effort can be coordinated; this is where **shared mental models** come into play. They are structures that allow team members to use their own knowledge and understanding in choosing behaviors that are coordinated and consistent with their teammates' behaviors (Mathieu et al., 2000).

As you can imagine, shared mental models become very important for high-functioning teams that don't have extra time to discuss issues and situations, are under considerable pressure, and need to work quickly and carefully. These team members need to be on the same page and to understand one another's thought patterns and tendencies so they can coordinate their efforts. Studies have found that the extent to which mental models are shared among team members determines team performance through effective team processes such as strategy formation, coordination, cooperation, and communication (Mathieu et al., 2000). Furthermore, a recent study found that individuals are better able to retrieve and rely on team expertise throughout the organization when there is strong communication among the team members (Yuan, Fulk, Monge, & Contractor, 2010)—that is, individuals are more apt to call on others' expertise and understand where expertise lies in the organization when there are strong connections among the minds of team members.

## Types of Work Teams

As I/O psychologists began studying work teams more intensively, it became clear that such teams could be grouped into five different categories (Sundstrom et al., 2000). These are summarized in **Table 12.3**. First, *production teams* are groups of employees who produce the output. They tend to be front-line employees in that they are responsible for production at the front end. Second, *management teams* coordinate workers who report to them as the product is being made, developed, or refined. They aren't on the front line but are instead responsible for the planning, staffing, budgeting, and logistics of work projects. Third, *service teams* consist of employees who

| TABLE 12.3  Types of Teams | |
|---|---|
| **Production teams** | Front-line employees producing tangible output<br>Often self-managed, self-led, self-directed<br>*Examples:* Electronics assembly units, coal mining crews, candy production crews |
| **Management teams** | Corporate executive teams; regional steering committees<br>Coordinate other work units under their direction<br>Responsibilities include planning, budgeting, staffing<br>*Examples:* Top management teams, military command teams, healthcare teams |
| **Service teams** | Attend to the needs of customers<br>Serve many customers at one time<br>*Examples:* Flight attendants, hospital emergency units, retail sales groups |
| **Project teams** | Created for the duration of a project<br>Cross-functional<br>Disband at completion of project<br>*Examples:* New-product teams, research units, research and design project groups |
| **Advisory teams** | Solve problems and recommend solutions<br>Very popular in organizations<br>Temporary<br>*Examples:* Quality circles, employee involvement teams, university advisory group to the president |

work together to attend to the needs of customers. One example of a service team is the group of flight attendants who assist you and other passengers on an airplane.

Fourth, *project teams* are formed to carry out specific projects only and are then dissolved upon project completion. These may also be referred to as cross-functional teams, especially when they involve team members from diverse departments of the organization, each with its own function. For instance, a book publisher might assign a particular book to a cross-functional team that will handle all the procedures necessary to get the finished product into stores. Members of this team might include someone from production, marketing, finance, and circulation.

These various team members are responsible for working with one another while at the same time focusing on their individual responsibilities to best serve the company's interest with respect to this one particular book or project. Harley-Davidson, for example, uses cross-functional teams extensively in the production of its motorcycles. Typically, each line of motorcycle is designed, manufactured, and marketed by a specific team consisting of a program manager from the design department and representatives from the departments of manufacturing, purchasing, and marketing (Brunelli, 1999). Another example might be an Apple phone application development team that includes programmers, a graphic designer, a writer, a marketing professional, and a business development expert. In this scenario, cross-functional teams in which each of these team members is necessary for success might be formed to bring a product to market.

Finally, we come to *advisory teams,* sometimes called *parallel teams* because they are developed to work separately from but in parallel to production processes (Sundstrom et al., 2000). A company may have an employee involvement team, for example, or a college may have an advisory group whose chief task is to keep the president informed about morale on campus and other faculty/student issues. Typically, members of advisory teams serve for a limited term, after which they are replaced by new members. A book called *The Third Opinion,* by Saj-Nicole Joni (2004), describes advisory team members as external thinking partners who may help the executive deal with a particular problem or with big-picture issues.

In their review of work-team literature published between 1980 and 1999, Sundstrom and his colleagues (2000) reported that 33% of the research focused on service teams, 17% on production teams, 14% on management teams, and 14% on project (or cross-functional) teams. Interestingly, despite the obvious popularity of advisory teams, very few studies have formally examined this newer approach to management and productivity. Future research is certainly called for, given the prevalence of these teams in organizations today. It would be helpful to know how successful these teams are, how they are received by employees, and how they are viewed by upper-level management. A contrary position was proposed in a recent paper in which the authors suggest that distinguishing among types of teams is not that useful (Hollenbeck, Beersma, & Schouten, 2012). The authors argue that there are multiple team taxonomies and no consensus on how to truly categorize teams. They suggest that it really doesn't matter what we call the particular team (production or project); what matters are the dimensions that serve as the foundation for team types. They propose three underlying constructs that provide the foundation for all teams: (1) skill differentiation, or the degree to which members have specific skills,

**cross-functional teams**
Work teams that are composed of members from diverse departments of the organization, each with its own function; also called *project teams.*

(2) authority differentiation, or the extent to which decision making is entrusted to certain members or subgroups, and (3) temporal stability, or team members' history of working together and expectation of collaborating into the future.

We have just discussed one popular scheme for categorizing work teams (again, see Table 12.3) and wondered aloud if categorizing teams is that important. Another important dimension along which teams differ has also received both popular and scholarly attention—namely, the extent to which work teams are self-managing, self-directing, self-leading, and self-regulating. These terms, which are often used interchangeably, refer to work teams that assume complete responsibility for a final product or an ongoing process (Mohsen & Nguyen, 1999). In short, the self-managed work team (SMWT) is responsible for monitoring and controlling the overall process or product, as well as for doling out specific tasks to team members. These teams often schedule their own work, do routine housekeeping, and maintain their own equipment; some may even participate in discussions of budgets, performance appraisals, or training (Sundstrom et al., 2000).

In the 1980s, only about 5% of American organizations used work teams; by 1992, this figure had grown to about 20% (Mohsen & Nguyen, 1999). It has been reported that 72% of Fortune 1000 companies had at least one SMWT in 1999 (Lawler, 2001)—SMWTs are discussed in more detail later in this section. Xerox, Chrysler, Apple Inc., Texas Instruments, and Frito-Lay are among the leaders at the forefront of the teams movement. This emphasis on teams reflects the growing realization that the complexity of work in the 21st century requires collaboration. Many different skills and so much knowledge are required that individuals can no longer accomplish certain tasks on their own.

Traditionally, organizations have taken a "command-and-control" approach to operations. Generally, organizations have been viewed as machine-like systems that were all about order, predictability, and control (Ashmos & Nathan, 2002). Some theorizing suggests that in the current global environment of rapid and discontinuous change, the emphasis should be on being flexible enough to change as the organization encounters more complex and varied situations (Henningsen et al., 2006). An alternative way to characterize effective teams is as sensemakers. In this way, teams can help the organization get to know itself, its history, and its future. To serve this purpose, teams need to be flexible, independent, and self-empowered rather than a command-and-control arm of the organization.

SMWTs seem to fit this sensemaking framework quite well. Research has demonstrated that autonomy and empowerment, essential features of these types of teams, are positively related to team effectiveness. Some research has found that empowered teams were not only more productive than less empowered teams but also had higher levels of customer service and more favorable attitudes (Kirkman & Rosen, 1999). Similarly, another study found that, in cases in which team members' tasks were

**self-managed work team (SMWT)** A work team that is responsible for monitoring and controlling the overall process or product, as well as for doling out specific tasks to team members.

© John Fedele/Blend Images/age Fotostock

**A CLOSER LOOK**
What are some of the factors that can lead to success of SMWTs? What are some of the pitfalls?

interdependent, autonomy had a positive effect on work-team effectiveness (Langfred, 2000). In other words, when team members were dependent on each other for the completion of their tasks, their autonomy as a team was an important predictor of team success. However, in some instances, SMWTs are not effective in managing themselves. A recent study suggests that conflict among team members can lead to ineffectiveness in SMWTs (Langfred, 2007).

## Work-Team Effectiveness

An important question is how to evaluate the effectiveness of work teams. Among the various ways to do so, one of the best is a framework developed by Susan Cohen (Cohen, 1994; Cohen & Bailey, 1997). According to this framework, there are three major dimensions of work-team effectiveness: (1) *team performance,* which concerns how well the team is performing and includes such variables as productivity, quality of output, and the degree to which costs are controlled in this process; (2) *attitudes* of team members, which reflect such variables as quality of work life, trust in management, organizational commitment, and job satisfaction; and (3) *withdrawal* behaviors, such as turnover, absence, and tardiness.

Another dimension might be *diversity,* which has become a popular topic among scholars. Team diversity is usually conceptualized and measured with respect to the ways in which members differ on one or more attributes (Jackson & Aparna, 2011). These attributes may include relational characteristics, like age, gender, and personality traits, or more task-related characteristics, like credentials, skills, and tenure. Although there are studies linking team diversity to outcomes, researchers agree that there isn't enough evidence yet to allow for firm conclusions about how these various attributes related to team diversity influence work teams (Jackson & Aparna).

Another useful way to think about the effectiveness of teams is to consider two types of behaviors (McIntyre & Salas, 1995): **taskwork**, which involves the task-oriented aspects of work, and **teamwork**, which involves the process-oriented aspects of work. Whereas taskwork entails specific individual behaviors or duties that are required for success, teamwork includes the wide range of activities aimed at maintaining and enhancing team performance. Teamwork revolves around communication and coordination among team members, feedback, team cohesion, and norms (Levy & Steelman, 1997). Most team experts argue that both taskwork and teamwork are integral to successful team performance. In other words, if teams are to be successful, it isn't enough for members to fulfill their individual duties; they must also work together toward common goals.

Whether we use the term *teamwork* to describe a great NBA team, the board of directors of General Electric, or the cross-functional groups at Harley-Davidson, the importance of teamwork is clear. Further insights into this area are likely to emerge from research that has begun to examine the level at which team data should be analyzed—for example, at the level of individual perceptions, perceptions aggregated across team members, and perceptions combined across teams at the organizational level.

A second important question concerns the factors involved in increasing work teams' effectiveness. In an extensive review of the literature on work teams, researchers

**taskwork**
Activities, behaviors, or actions that involve the task-oriented aspects of work.

**teamwork**
Activities, behaviors, or actions that involve the process-oriented aspects of work.

## I/O TODAY

### Age Diversity in Teams

The topic of "diversity" within teams has received a lot of attention in the last few decades. In this context, diversity can refer to any number of characteristics, including race, gender, and nationality. One aspect of diversity that garners a lot of discussion among I/O practitioners is age diversity. The "Boomer" generation (typically defined as people born between 1946 and 1964) has remained in the workforce longer than their predecessors, leading to increased interaction with "Generation X" (born between 1965 and 1984) and "Millennials" (born between 1985 and 2000). Research suggests that different generations hold different values and interests, which can sometimes make team interactions difficult when these cross-generational workforces mix.

While some of the differences among generations can be attributed to age alone, there are also a number of social, cultural, and political influences that are different for each generation. Boomers have typically been taught that the way to achieve the "American Dream" is through hard work and long hours. Success means lots of face time in the workplace and foregoing vacations in favor of professional interests. Boomers also tend to value pay over other perks. Meanwhile, Millennials are accustomed to having information at their fingertips immediately. They tended to be much more closely supervised as children, and tended to have schedules that emphasized achievement. Their parents also often addressed conflict for them, and as a result, these Millennials tended to rely on their parents to keep them organized and advocate for them. In the workplace, they tend to be interested in flexible work arrangements, self-development, and continuous feedback.

Given these trends, it is easy to see where conflicts among teammates might arise. If a team has a meeting, a member who is a Millennial may expect to be able to teleconference in, have his opinions and input granted equal respect and consideration, and be allowed to multitask. A member who is a Boomer may be put off by this behavior—from her perspective, this colleague is failing to be fully present at the meeting and is disregarding her more experienced perspectives. At the same time, both individuals might have a lot to offer if they can understand the different ways they approach the workplace.

How can I/O psychologists address some of these conflicts? First, they can develop training programs that will help employees understand some of these generational differences, and help them to avoid stereotypes. I/O psychologists also might create training programs for managers to help them learn how to manage differing needs and expectations in the workforce, such as addressing interpersonal conflicts, finding different ways to motivate workers, navigating work–family conflict, and appraising performance. I/O psychologists can also look for ways to help workers focus on their similarities and common goals, rather than allowing them to dwell on their differences. I/O psychologists are working to develop strategies that allow them to leverage multiple perspectives, whether they come from differences in age, race, culture, gender, or any number of other factors.

### Discussion Questions

1. What are ways you might learn more about perspectives that are different from your own? What resources might you use to help you better understand diverse team members?

2. If you were to see a team member engaging in behavior that was normal to her, but that was clearly confusing or offensive to other team members, how might you address it?

### Suggested Readings

The *Journal of Managerial Psychology* devoted Volume 28, Number 7/8, to the issue of age diversity. The guest editorial below is an introduction to the issue, and provides a summary of articles in that particular volume.

Hertel, G., Van der Heijden, B. I. J. M., de Lange, A. H., & Deller, J. (2013). Facilitating age diversity in organizations—part II: Managing perceptions and interactions. *Journal of Managerial Psychology, 28,* 857–866.

identified five categories of factors that appear to be important predictors of work-team effectiveness: organizational context, group composition and size, group work design, intragroup processes, and external group processes (Sundstrom et al., 2000). **Table 12.4** presents some examples of each of these categories.

## TABLE 12.4 Predictors of Work-Team Effectiveness

| Organizational context | Rewards |
| --- | --- |
| | Goals and feedback |
| | Training |
| Group composition and size | Cognitive ability of group members |
| | Personality traits of group members |
| | Demographic characteristics of group members |
| Group work design | Member task interdependence |
| | Member goal interdependence |
| Intragroup processes | Group cohesion |
| | Group efficacy or communication processes |
| External group processes | Communication outside the group |
| | External interaction patterns |

Source: Information from Sundstrom et al. (2000).

One category in particular has received considerable attention of late: group composition. A series of studies have built on this notion, paying particular attention to personality traits of team members. For instance, a recent study found that teams with high variability on extraversion and low variability on conscientiousness were the most effective (Humphrey, Hollenbeck, Meyer, & Ilgen, 2011). Apparently, teams will function best if all teammates are conscientious about their work, but in high-functioning teams, this conscientiousness is accompanied by significant differences in people's interpersonal styles and other individual differences. In another interesting study, it was demonstrated that when an individual perceives that his or her team member really needs help with a task—what the literature calls *backup behavior*—the personalities of the helper and the recipient of help play an important role (Porter et al., 2003). For instance, team members higher on conscientiousness delivered more backup to one another, whether it was really needed or not; those high on extraversion secured more backup from others, regardless of their true need for help, than did those low on extraversion.

A recent meta-analysis identified group composition variables as very important to group effectiveness (Stewart, 2006; see also Bell, 2007). In particular, team performance improves when members have high cognitive ability, favorable personality traits, and relevant expertise. The author also found significant relationships between task design variables and team effectiveness as well as between leadership skills of team leaders and effectiveness (see Chapter 13 for more discussion of leadership skills).

Another recent meta-analysis found that demographic diversity among team members was unrelated to team effectiveness (Horwitz & Horwitz, 2007). However, the authors did find that diversity related to the task, such as expertise and education, was positively related to team effectiveness. Finally, an intriguing analysis of movie production over a 30-year period showed that team diversity with respect to newcomers and old-timers had favorable effects on movie-making innovation (Perretti & Negro, 2007). Certainly, these studies have implications for how organizations will consider diversity in constituting work teams in the future.

## CURRENT TRENDS

Sundstrom and his colleagues (2000) suggested that the use of work groups or teams would continue to expand in the areas of service, production, and project completion. They also suggested that work teams would continue to become more fluid; in other words, the teams would be assembled in such a way as to make use of various people, including employees from other units and other companies. Today, some organizations use teams as a way to link or partner with other organizations. The definition, development, and use of teams will continue to evolve as organizations find new and interesting ways to make use of them. Let's look at a couple of those new and interesting uses of teams.

### Virtual Teams

With the increase in telecommuting and electronic work, the use of virtual teams promises to expand (Zaccaro & Bader, 2003). Virtual teams are composed of members who work in different cities or countries and communicate via e-mail, fax, web pages, and videoconferencing. Such team members may be working on the same sales account or for the same client but rarely do so face-to-face. Increases in creativity and innovation are believed to be positive outcomes of virtual teams (Martins & Shalley, 2011).

There is the potential for virtual teams to be very effective. One major advantage is that team members can communicate, collaborate, and create regardless of their location, time zone, weather, and so on. Face-to-face meetings are not necessary to keep projects moving along. Communication is obviously central to this process, and the organization must be certain to establish guidelines and rules regarding communication along with the necessary resources to allow for effective communication and collaboration.

Most larger organizations today employ virtual teams to some extent (Hertel, Geister, & Konradt, 2005), and it is not just a U.S. phenomenon; virtual teams are popular in Europe and other parts of the world. Some recent theoretical works suggests that the degree to which a team functions on a virtual basis stems from contextual features, such as organizational boundaries; temporal dynamics, such as time pressures; and task–media–member compatibility, such as synergy among members' abilities and available technologies (Kirkman & Mathieu, 2005).

Various dimensions have been identified as requirements for categorizing a team as virtual; at a minimum, virtual teams must use computer-mediated communication, and most experts agree that they should also be geographically dispersed (Johnson, Bettenhausen, & Gibbons, 2009). Furthermore, teams can be categorized on a virtuality dimension from almost completely face-to-face communication to almost completely computer-mediated communication. In other words, there are gradations of virtuality, with some teams being somewhat virtual and others being mostly virtual (Berry, 2011).

A recent study of employed MBA students found that compared to all other groups that used less computer-mediated communication, those who used computer-mediated communication at least 90% of the time reported lower levels of positive affect, task effectiveness, and affective commitment (Johnson et al., 2009). The authors conclude that there is a tipping point—when about 90% of communication is computer-mediated—where virtual teams become less effective. Another way to view this finding is that even a small amount of face-to-face time may further enhance the performance of virtual teams.

Research on virtual teams has expanded substantially in recent years and may be the biggest area of growth in the team literature. In a wonderful review of the last ten years of virtual team research, Gilson, Maynard, Jones, Young, Vartiainen, and Hakonen (2015) provide some really interesting findings and suggestions. I will touch on a sampling of both recent research trends and future opportunities. We'll begin with the recent trends. First, virtual team research was originally focused on laboratory studies where teams were artificially created for the research, but now we are seeing more case studies of real virtual teams. These studies measure the extent to which team work is done virtually or what is called *team virtuality*. Second, earlier research was focused largely on relational attributes such as age, gender, and personality. Recent work has emerged that focuses more on task attributes such as group composition, culture, multiteam membership, time devoted to the team, and task interdependence. Third, globalization has become an emergent theme of virtual teams in a number of ways. For instance, research is being conducted by a more diverse group of scholars and teams have become more global with team members located in different cities and countries. Research has also focused on cultural diversity and the role that major cultural dimensions—such as collectivistic versus individualistic cultures—play in virtual teaming. Fourth, a great deal of research has demonstrated how important leadership is to virtual teams and scholars continue to examine how teams adapt to virtuality as a function of leadership (e.g., Andressen, Konradt, & Neck, 2012; Hoch & Kozlowski, 2012).

Gilson et al. (2015) also provide a thoughtful list of virtual team research opportunities to take us into the next decade. First, most of the virtual team research up to this point has examined knowledge-intensive workers, like software engineers and physicians. We need to better understand how virtual teams operate with team members at other skill levels and in other industries. Perhaps there is no greater need than to examine virtual teams in the healthcare sector, where teamwork is the default approach and technology is truly changing the face of medicine. Second, to truly understand team dynamics we need research that takes a longitudinal perspective rather than the more traditional cross-sectional research designs. Longitudinal studies would allow us to model causal effects, such as what factors cause teams to be effective and what outcomes flow directly from effective teaming. Third, perhaps the biggest need going forward is new, sophisticated, comprehensive research on computer-mediated communication (CMC).

CMC refers to any communication that takes place across multiple electronic devices and it represents the technology that helps foster and coordinate teamwork within an organization. CMC products are being developed at a rapid pace and many of these products appear to have great potential to impact the efficiency and effectiveness of work teams. As you might guess, among these CMC techniques are collaboration tools, meeting tools, document editing/creating tools, social media tools, and project management tools (Gilson et al., 2015). I'm quite certain there will be great progress made in this area and future research will have huge impacts on how teams function and operate going forward. This is a truly exciting time for team researchers and organizations that value the contributions made by work teams.

Ariel Skelley Blend Images/Newscom

**A CLOSER LOOK**
What unique benefits and challenges do video-conferencing and virtual teaming present to the healthcare sector? How can research on virtual teams in this field impact the development of tools and strategies in other fields?

## Team Member Selection

Another trend worth discussing has to do with selecting employees to work in a team environment. Think back to Chapters 6 and 7, which discussed the various predictors and procedures used for hiring employees. As you might recall, the selection process always begins with a job analysis to identify what tasks are done on the job (job description) and what knowledge, skills, abilities, and other characteristics (KSAOs) employees need to have in order to do the job successfully (job specification). We also talked about the use of ability tests, personality tests, work sample tests, and so on as techniques for predicting how effective or successful particular individuals are likely to be in a particular job. Given this background and review, what additional kinds of information might we want to know about applicants prior to hiring them into a job that exists within a team-based environment? I certainly wouldn't want to hire onto a production team someone who is highly self-involved and cannot or will not get along with others. In short, it makes sense from a selection standpoint to consider applicants in light of their desire and ability to work in a team environment.

Some earlier work began examining this issue, which has now become an important and growing trend in the team area. For instance, a laboratory experiment in which students worked together on group decision-making tasks found that work-team performance was predicted by students' preferences for and attitudes about working in teams, as well as by their perceptions of group confidence and ability (Jung & Sosik, 1999). The authors of this study argued that group preference appears to be a stable individual disposition and thus can be used to select individuals for group membership, increasing the likelihood that those selected will be suitable for and will perform well in team-based work environments.

Another study examined the mental abilities and Big Five personality traits (see Chapter 6) of more than 600 employees to determine the relationship between these variables and group performance (Barrick, Stewart, Neubert, & Mount, 1998). The authors concluded that selecting team members with higher levels of general mental ability, conscientiousness, agreeableness, and emotional stability appears to improve team performance—and that just one team member who is low on agreeableness, conscientiousness, or extraversion can result in increased stress and decreased performance among team members.

As with any selection situation, it is imperative that predictors be linked to criteria; indeed, the organization must assume responsibility for demonstrating this link when it chooses its predictors. A more recent study showed that conscientiousness, extraversion, and teamwork knowledge significantly predicted the contextual performance of team members (Morgeson, Reider, & Campion, 2005).

Other researchers have developed an instrument specifically geared toward identifying individuals likely to be successful in a team environment. Known as the Teamwork Test, the measure identifies KSAOs that more effectively predict teamwork than taskwork. The following KSAOs are tapped by this measure: conflict resolution, collaborative problem solving, communication, goal setting and performance management, and planning and task coordination (Stevens & Campion, 1999). The Teamwork Test is a situational judgment test in which respondents are provided with hypothetical teamwork situations and asked to select, from multiple solutions, which one they would likely use. Correct answers are determined on the basis of the research literature. The authors found that scores on the Teamwork Test were correlated with ratings of teamwork performance and that these ratings were predicted even after aptitudes and abilities measured by nine other different tests had been controlled for. The implication is that the Teamwork Test can be used for selection purposes in identifying individuals who are most likely to thrive in a team environment (Miller, 2001).

In recent years we have seen the development of the Team Role Test, which is intended to tap into one's knowledge about team roles, including in which situations certain roles are more important (Mumford, Van Iddekinge, Morgeson, & Campion, 2008). The researchers believe that an understanding and recognition of the various roles team members play are related to team effectiveness. The researchers present some data linking knowledge about task, social, and overall team roles to team effectiveness; furthermore, knowledge of team roles improved prediction of team effectiveness above and beyond cognitive ability and Big Five personality constructs (Mumford et al., 2008).

More recently, the Team Role Experience and Orientation (TREO) test has been developed, which, the creators argue, improves upon the Team Role Test by measuring orientations, past behaviors, and behavioral predispositions, rather than just assessing team knowledge of roles (Mathieu, Tannenbaum, Kukenberger, Donsbach, & Alliger, 2015). The authors did a very thorough job in the development and validation of this new scale, including demonstrating that responses to the TREO predicted peer ratings of team behaviors three months later. Because this scale is so new, we will have to wait and see how other researchers use it and how vital it can be in helping us understand, explain, and predict team functioning.

## Multiteam Systems

Finally, one last trend to discuss in the area of teamwork is the notion of **multiteam systems (MTS)**, which can be defined as "two or more teams that interface directly and interdependently in response to environmental contingencies toward accomplishment of collective goals" (Mathieu, Marks, & Zaccaro, 2001). It is becoming more common in various industries—including healthcare, software development, and military—to find MTS operating as a major component of the work. Teams within this system may have individual subgoals that are hierarchically organized with the superordinate goal (the highest goal) requiring interdependent activity among the component teams that make up the MTS (Zaccaro, Marks, & DeChurch, 2012). One element that makes MTS very interesting is that other than where interdependent action or collaboration is required, the component member teams are often free to work, think, and operate in their own unique, diverse ways. However, with respect to the points of necessary interdependence, the component member teams must come together in agreement and uniformity. You can see how complex this can get with diverse teams that operate independently and yet have to function as part of a MTS with a collective goal that requires that they come together in uniform ways and with a shared approach. MTS research is beginning to ramp up, and we are seeing this new construct gaining more interest and attention from both researchers and practitioners.

**multiteam systems**
Tightly coupled teams that work on collective goals.

## Summary

This chapter introduced the concepts of work groups and work teams and discussed the processes involved in the use of such groups in organizations. I began by defining work groups and reviewing group processes. Then I discussed social influence in groups in the context of norms, roles, conflict, cohesion, and social loafing, applying those elements to organizational functioning. I also presented Tuckman's model of group development and the popular punctuated equilibrium model, as well as theories that seek to combine these models.

Group decision making was another area emphasized in this chapter. Because groups are entrusted with important organizational decisions, I spent considerable time discussing a process that, when followed, is likely to result in effective decision making. This five-step process emphasizes the quality of the social interaction among group members—an issue I discussed in connection with some of the common mistakes made at certain points in the process. This topic led logically to ineffective decision making, with a particular emphasis on groupthink. Here I presented historical examples of groupthink and discussed its antecedents and symptoms in light of organizational situations.

In the last section, I focused on work teams, which have become incredibly popular in modern-day organizations. I discussed various types of work teams and gave examples of each, placing particular emphasis on self-managed work teams both because of their prevalence in organizations and because of their inherent complexities. I also provided a few examples of organizations currently using work teams, introduced the idea of shared mental models, and identified the determinants of work-team effectiveness. I concluded the chapter with a discussion of current trends such as the growth of virtual teams and multiteam systems.

## Key Terms

brainstorming (p. 408)

cohesion (p. 402)

cross-functional teams (p. 418)

free riding (p. 407)

groupthink (p. 413)

mental model (p. 415)

mindguard (p. 414)

multiteam systems (MTS) (p. 427)

norms (p. 400)

process loss (p. 412)

role differentiation (p. 401)

self-managed work team (SMWT) (p. 419)

shared mental models (p. 416)

social loafing (p. 406)

sucker effect (p. 407)

taskwork (p. 420)

teamwork (p. 420)

work group (p. 399)

## TAKING IT TO THE FIELD

Building effective teams can often be difficult. In many organizations, work groups tend to forget that they are part of a larger organization and become competitive with one another for resources and attention. One of your clients, Siran Belekdanian, has come to you for advice on how to build better teams at WeldCo. Please read her e-mail, and provide three suggestions for how she can improve the teamwork within her organization.

Hello—

Thank you for being willing to work with me on this project. Here at WeldCo we have two main departments. First, we have salespeople, who sell updated welding equipment to plants. Second, we have service people, who provide training on the equipment and repair the equipment when it breaks down. Over the past year, the relationship between these two departments has been strained.

Our salespeople have recently been promising faster training and repairs than our service department can handle. On the one hand, the sales department has been claiming that it needs to promise these quick turnaround times to close sales. On the other hand, we have also been experiencing an increase in customer complaints because the service side has not been able to do what the salespeople promise. In fact, some of the service people are actively slowing down in order to make the salespeople look bad.

I'm not sure what to do next. I've tried to explain to both groups separately that even though they are in separate departments, we are on the same team. Ultimately, we have the same goal—we want the customers to be happy. I tell them that they need to work together to be successful and get the job done, but they continue to undermine each other. How can I help them understand that the two departments need to come together and act as a team? What are some first steps we could make toward improving the relationships between the two departments?

SB

## Critical Thinking Questions

1. Say you are a high-level manager in an organization. How would you go about assembling a team for a very important work project?

2. What does diversity mean in the context of work teams, and how does it impact team effectiveness?

3. How might work groups prevent groupthink?

4. What makes virtual teams so effective despite the potential complexities?

5. How has the globalization trend impacted work teams?

## Application Questions

1. What is an example of a group you've been a part of that was highly cohesive? What made it that way? How could some of those qualities be instilled in a workplace team?

2. Consider a time when you experienced social loafing in a group (in a class or at work). What were some aspects of the situation that caused social loafing to occur? What could your instructor or boss have done to decrease social loafing?

3. Consider a group that you are currently a part of. In your opinion, do you find that the group follows Tuckman's model as it has continued to develop, or does it follow the more oscillating style of punctuated equilibrium? Give some specific examples to support your opinion.

4. Imagine you are working with a virtual group to put together a presentation on teamwork. How might you use technology to help you communicate, share ideas, and design your presentation slides? What parts of that experience do you think would be most difficult, and how might you overcome them?

5. Consider a job you once had or a group project you worked on in a class. In order to work well with others, you likely had a shared mental model. Give some examples of what might have been part of this mental model you shared with other group members.

## Suggested Readings

**Gilson, L. L., Maynard, M. T., Jones Young, N. C., Vartiainen, M., & Hakonen, M.** (2015). Virtual teams research: 10 years, 10 themes, and 10 opportunities. *Journal of Management, 41*(5), 1313–1337. This is the best review I've seen with a focus on virtual teams, a discussion of the history, development, and current research, as well as future research suggestions. A great place to start for information on virtual teams.

**Jackson, S. E., & Joshi, A.** (2011). Work team diversity. In Zedeck, S. (Ed.), *APA handbook of industrial and organizational psychology, vol. 1: Building and developing the organization* (pp. 651–686). Washington, DC: American Psychological Association.

http://dx.doi.org/10.1037/12169-020. A great chapter on the importance of diversity in work teams. This article takes the reader from the very basic to the somewhat complex issues involved in this area.

**Ilgen, D. R., Hollenbeck, J. R., Johnson, M., & Jundt, D.** (2005). Teams in organizations: From input-process-output models to IMOI models. *Annual Review of Psychology, 56,* 517–543. This review chapter portrays teams as complex, dynamic systems and focuses on the way teams evolve over time.

**Kozlowski, S. W. J., & Ilgen, D. R.** (2006). Enhancing the effectiveness of work groups and teams. *Psychological Science in the Public Interest, 7,* 77–124. In this monograph, two teams of experts make recommendations for improving work-team effectiveness.

**Simms, A., & Nichols, T.** (2014). Social loafing: A review of the literature. *Journal of Management Policy and Practice, 15,* 58–67. An interesting look at the over 100 years of social-loafing research. The paper discusses both causes and outcomes while proposing research propositions for future research.

**Sundstrom, E., McIntyre, M., Halfhill, T., & Richards, H.** (2000). Work groups: From the Hawthorne Studies to work teams of the 1990s and beyond. *Group Dynamics: Theory, Research, and Practice, 4*(1), 44–67. This excellent review and discussion of work teams is a good place to start for those interested in this area.

# Leadership

Photo: Jeff Kowalsky/Bloomberg/Getty Images

# LEARNING OBJECTIVES

This chapter should help you understand:

- What leadership is and how the effectiveness of leaders is evaluated
- The various types of power and how they are employed by leaders
- The major elements of the various leadership theories
- The historical development of leadership research and conceptualization
- How to distinguish between leader traits and behaviors
- What kinds of contingencies affect leadership processes
- The most influential theories about leadership over the past few decades, such as implicit, transformational, authentic, and servant leadership theories
- The differences between transformational and transactional leaders
- How both gender and culture affect leadership processes
- The role of leader and subordinate emotions in organizational effectiveness

David Paul Morris/Bloomberg/Getty Images

**A CLOSER LOOK**
What qualities contribute to the success of a leader like Mark Zuckerberg, who founded Facebook while still in college and has helped it become one of the most valuable companies in the world?

Certainly, the use of the term *leadership* is not limited to academic circles. We are fascinated by leadership—in government, in the community, in the boardroom, on the football field, and on the shop floor. Leadership is an important dimension along which people are evaluated in all walks of life. Leadership is an especially hot topic during political elections. We heard a great deal about the leadership style and qualities of Barack Obama versus Mitt Romney during the U.S. presidential campaign of 2012. The leadership qualities of these two men were a central focus of campaign advertising and constantly debated on news shows.

Defining leadership is no simple matter. Most business professionals would consider Jack Welch, Mary Barra (shown in the photo that opens this chapter), Jeff Bezos, Bill Gates, and the late Steve Jobs to be outstanding leaders, but their personalities and circumstances certainly differed considerably. Have you had the good fortune to spend time with a really terrific leader? What was this person like? If this person was your boss, was he or she able to motivate you to work hard and remain committed to the company? As this last question implies, leadership is intricately linked to other topics in organizational psychology such as work motivation and job attitudes.

Many of us have also known people who seemed to be terrible leaders. These individuals most likely had poor relationships with others, were not respected or trusted, and seemed unable to identify the best way to get work done. Although at times it might seem easy to classify people as good or bad leaders, we'll see in this chapter that the issue is more complex than that.

We will spend considerable time discussing leadership theories and the research that has been conducted about leadership—much of which provides a foundation for the application of leadership theories to organizations. A recent survey of 10 top-tier journals uncovered 752 articles focused on leadership since 2000—indeed, the study of leadership is very popular and continues to grow (Dinh et al., 2014). After our discussion of leadership theories in this chapter, we will turn, in Chapter 14, to a discussion of organizational development techniques and discover how the leadership theories presented in this chapter are applied to organizations.

## WHAT IS LEADERSHIP?

Among the many different definitions of leadership, the one I prefer is this: Leadership is a social process through which an individual intentionally exerts influence over others to structure their behaviors and relationships. There are good leaders and bad leaders; merely being given the responsibility and status of a leader doesn't make a person a good leader. Rather, effective leadership is a function of the outcomes produced by those who are being led, usually operationalized as the successful long-term performance of the leader's work group or subordinates. The core of leadership, then, is influence over others, and this is typically linked to relationship building. To understand this influence, we need to examine the issue of power in organizations.

## THEORIES

Power is defined as an individual's potential influence over the attitudes and behaviors of one or more other individuals (Yukl, 2002). It is a resource that leaders can use to exert influence over their followers or subordinates. Although power is often viewed as something inherently negative, organizations could not survive without power as the basis of influence (Steers, Porter, & Bigley, 1996). John French and Bertram Raven (1958) developed the most often cited and discussed typology of power in the literature. This typology identifies five major bases of power (see **Table 13.1**), each of which has the potential to play an important role in the leadership and dynamics of an organization.

The first base, *legitimate power,* is the power bestowed on an individual by the organization. This is what we think of when we talk about authority. When we question whether a particular employee has the authority to make an important decision, we are asking whether the organization has provided this person with the legitimate power to make that decision. We can certainly think of individuals who, based on the

**leadership**
A social process through which an individual intentionally exerts influence over others to structure their behaviors and relationships.

**effective leadership**
Usually operationalized as the successful long-term performance of the leader's work group or subordinates.

**power**
An individual's potential influence over the attitudes and behavior of one or more other individuals.

| **TABLE 13.1** | Bases of Power |
|---|---|
| Legitimate power | Conferred on a person by the organization |
| Reward power | Exists when an individual controls the reward of others |
| Coercive power | Exists when an individual controls the punishment of others |
| Expert power | Held by those who have specific expertise or proficiencies |
| Referent power | Gained when one is shown respect and admiration by others |

Source: French & Raven (1958)

nature of their job titles and responsibilities, have legitimate power. However, they do not necessarily use that power—or use it in effective ways. Some individuals think that all they need to be successful and respected leaders is the legitimate power provided by the company, but as we will soon see, a good deal more than this is required for successful leadership.

The second base, *reward power,* is simply the power that results from controlling the rewards or outcomes that others strive for. Parents have almost unlimited reward power over their kids because they control access to the candy, iPads and video games, and Build-a-Bear paraphernalia that children covet. In organizations, the person who makes decisions about employees' raises, promotions, and assignments is said to have reward power. The other side of this coin, however, is the third base: *coercive power.* People with coercive power have control over punishments, which they often use to get others to do what they want. The manager who consistently intimidates employees by arousing fear in them and insinuating that if they don't produce at a particular level, they will be written up, forced to work additional hours, or transferred to a less desirable position is someone who manages through coercion.

*Expert power,* the fourth base, is associated with an employee's special knowledge or proficiency, but it is not limited to those at the top of an organizational hierarchy. Consider computer technicians, for instance. They're not at the top of the organizational structure, but they have a great deal of expert power that is essential for the functioning of the organization. Without their knowledge, the organization could be crippled. Expert power at lower levels of the organization sometimes balances the legitimate power at upper levels (Steers et al., 1996).

The fifth base, *referent power,* is power gained through respect or admiration. Though strongly related to reputation and status, referent power can be obtained by anyone in the organization, regardless of hierarchical position. For example, an employee who is not high up in the organization and thus has low legitimate reward and coercive power may nevertheless have a high level of referent power because she is a well-respected team player who always seems to say and do the right things and is considerate of others' needs and perspectives.

Power certainly plays a role in the classroom. A recent study of 555 undergraduates revealed that when professors operate and behave in accordance with what the

www.dilbert.com    scottadams@aol.com

© 2002 United Feature Syndicate, Inc.    7/27/02

**A CLOSER LOOK**

Think of a time when a boss or leader has taken this approach with you. How did it make you feel? Why wasn't it successful?

authors call "prosocial bases of power"—reward, reference, and expert—students perceive that the professors understand them and so relate to them better (Finn, 2012). More negative perceptions emerge when students perceive that professors behave in accordance with "antisocial bases of power"—legitimate and coercive.

In the remaining sections of this chapter, I will trace the historical development of various leadership theories and summarize the empirical evidence for and against these theories. Before we get started, however, think about the successful leaders you've encountered and consider their similarities and differences. You may be able to identify some similarities, such as being conscientious and having good people skills (although I can think of successful leaders whom I didn't like very much and who didn't have good people skills), but I'm quite certain you can also identify many differences in style, approach, beliefs, values, vision, and behaviors among those effective leaders. In short, there isn't one "best" way to lead. As we proceed with our review of the leadership research, this fact will become clear to you. Indeed, the complexity of effective leadership is what makes studying, predicting, and understanding it both interesting and challenging.

## Trait Theories

The first systematic study of leadership began in the 1930s with the development of **trait theories**, which focus on identifying the individual characteristics that make people good leaders. The central question posed by such research concerned what effective leaders had in common. Was it intelligence? Was it a domineering personality? Was it aggressiveness? This trait approach to leadership, sometimes called the *great man/great woman theory*, dominated leadership research into the 1950s. During this beginning phase, the research was largely atheoretical (House & Aditya, 1997), based mostly on commonsense notions of leadership and social interactions. Numerous individual characteristics were studied, including gender, dominance, intelligence, appearance, physical energy, need for power, and need for achievement. In 1948, a seminal review was published by R. M. Stogdill, who uncovered studies in which traits such as intelligence and dominance were significantly related

**trait theories**
Leadership theories that focus on identifying the individual characteristics that make people good leaders; sometimes called the *great man/great woman theories*.

to leader effectiveness. However, the overall results were not very supportive of these relationships, and there didn't appear to be much consistency in the findings. Scholars concluded that there were few, if any, universal traits that predicted leadership (Stogdill, 1948).

Interest in traits waned in the mid-20th century as a result of reviews like Stogdill's, but interest in their potential role in leadership has reemerged in the last 30 years. One review concluded that factors such as intelligence, dominance, and masculine orientation were consistent predictors not of effective leadership but of the type of person who tends to emerge as a leader in small groups (Lord, DeVader, & Alliger, 1986). That is, in groups without an assigned leader, men who are viewed as more intelligent and dominant than others tend to take on the leadership role. In other studies, David Kenny and his colleagues demonstrated that behavioral flexibility—the extent to which an individual is willing and able to consider what behaviors and approaches might work best in a particular situation—is a very useful predictor of who emerges as a leader in small groups (Kenny & Zaccaro, 1983; Zaccaro, Foti, & Kenny, 1991). Situational variability will play a role in many of the contingency theories that we discuss later in this chapter, where researchers study the influence of a leader's treatment of different individuals within a group or organization.

One study found that individuals high on dominance, intelligence, and self-efficacy were more likely to emerge as leaders than those with other personality trait patterns (Smith & Foti, 1998). Stogdill himself concluded in 1974 that his earlier paper might have drawn too negative a conclusion regarding the role of traits in leadership. Thus, it appears that traits play a larger role in leadership processes than was believed in the 1950s.

Some researchers have focused specifically on the Big Five traits. A meta-analysis of more than 70 studies found that the Big Five traits accounted for 53% of the variance in leader emergence and 39% in leader effectiveness. In particular, extraversion and conscientiousness appeared to be the most important and consistent predictors (Judge, Bono, Ilies, & Gerhardt, 2002). More recent research has begun teasing apart the effects of the Big Five on leadership outcomes. For instance, one study of military personnel in Singapore found that extraversion plays an important role in **leadership self-efficacy (LSE)**, the perceived ability of an individual to successfully accomplish leadership tasks (Ng, Ang, & Chan, 2008). Individuals high on extraversion (i.e., being sociable and assertive) tend to rate highly on leadership self-efficacy scales, which often results in their being effective leaders. A recent laboratory study also found support for these links (Big Five → LSE → leader behaviors/effectiveness). The researchers argue that the Big Five characteristics appear to be more distal leadership traits (i.e., farther from proper leadership behavior in the variable chain) and that distal leadership, in turn, influences motivation constructs like LSE and goal orientation, which impact directly on effectiveness (Hendricks & Payne, 2007). Thus, whereas the Big

**leadership self-efficacy (LSE)**
The perceived capabilities of an individual to successfully accomplish leadership tasks.

**TECHNICAL TIP**

Recall from Chapter 6 that the Big Five model is a popular and validated classification scheme in which personality is described in terms of five broad dimensions: openness, conscientiousness, extraversion, agreeableness, and neuroticism (OCEAN).

Five characteristics and other traits may not always have a direct effect on leader effectiveness, they often have substantial indirect effects through other constructs like self-efficacy.

## Behavior Theories

After concluding that no specific traits could consistently predict effective leadership, researchers in the 1950s took a new direction. Now the emphasis was on leader *behaviors*. Indeed, the rationale for behavior theories was that if traits aren't particularly useful in helping us understand the leadership process and what makes a good leader, perhaps we should begin to look at what leaders actually *do*. Much of the research in this area was conducted at The Ohio State University, the University of Michigan, and the University of Iowa. The Iowa studies, led by Kurt Lewin, examined three types of leadership styles: authoritarian, democratic, and laissez-faire. They revealed that most subordinates prefer democratic leaders but that there isn't much of a relationship between leader style and subordinate behaviors. The conclusions of the Ohio State and Michigan studies were very similar; I focus here on the former because Ohio State was the location of the most extensive research program ever conducted on leader behaviors.

The Ohio State studies gathered self-reports of leader behaviors using a survey called the Leader Opinion Questionnaire (LOQ), as well as observations and ratings of leader behaviors using a questionnaire called the Leader Behavior Descriptive Questionnaire (LBDQ). The LBDQ items were rated on a five-point scale ranging from "Never" to "Always." After hundreds of different leader behaviors were identified and many dimensions examined, they were categorized in terms of two major dimensions (Fleishman & Harris, 1962). The first dimension, initiating structure, refers to behaviors through which leaders define the roles both they and their subordinates play in achieving the group's formal goals. Examples of initiating-structure behaviors include assigning specific tasks to subordinates, planning ahead for the next job to be done, pushing for higher production by setting difficult goals, defining procedures, and so on.

The second dimension, consideration, concerns the extent to which leaders act in a supportive way and show concern and respect for their subordinates. Examples of consideration behaviors include emphasizing participative decision making, forging two-way communication, and working to establish a favorable rapport with subordinates. Interestingly, the University of Michigan studies identified two very similar dimensions: *task-oriented behaviors* and *relationship-oriented behaviors*. The terms from the two sets of studies (*initiating structure/task-oriented* and *consideration/relationship-oriented*) are often used interchangeably.

The consideration and initiating-structure dimensions of the LBDQ are shown in **Table 13.2**, along with 10 behavior statements related to each. Consideration is clearly reflected in such statements as "Does little things to make it pleasant to be a member of the group." Indicative of initiating structure are statements like "Lets group members know what is expected of them." One thing to keep in mind is that leaders are not necessarily one or the other; for instance, a leader can be either high or low on

**behavior theories** Leadership theories that focus on identifying what leaders actually do, in the hope that this approach will provide a better understanding of leadership processes.

**initiating structure** Behaviors through which leaders define their own and their subordinates' roles in achieving the group's formal goals.

**consideration** The extent to which leaders act in a supportive way and show concern and respect for their subordinates.

**TABLE 13.2** Items from the Leadership Behavior Description Questionnaire (LBDQ)

| My Leader/Boss: | Never 1 | 2 | 3 | 4 | Always 5 |
|---|---|---|---|---|---|

**Consideration**

1. Is friendly and approachable.
2. Does little things to make it pleasant to be a member of the group.
3. Puts suggestions made by the group into operation.
4. Treats all group members as his or her equals.
5. Gives advance notice of changes.
6. Keeps to him- or herself. (R)*
7. Looks out for the personal welfare of group members.
8. Is willing to make changes.
9. Refuses to explain his or her actions. (R)
10. Acts without consulting the group. (R)

**Initiating Structure**

1. Lets group members know what is expected of them.
2. Encourages the use of uniform procedures.
3. Tries out his or her ideas in the group.
4. Makes his or her attitudes clear to the group.
5. Decides what shall be done and how it will be done.
6. Assigns group members to particular tasks.
7. Makes sure that his or her part in the group is understood by group members.
8. Schedules the work to be done.
9. Maintains definite standards of performance.
10. Asks that group members follow standard rules and regulations.

*(R) signifies that the item is reverse-scored so that the favorability of the item lines up with the rest.

Source: Stogdill, R. M. (1963). *Manual for the Leader Behavior Description Questionnaire–Form XII: An experimental revision.* Columbus, OH: Bureau of Business Research, The Ohio State University.

both initiating structure and consideration. In fact, there tends to be a small positive correlation between the two dimensions.

Can you think of a boss you've worked with who was very directive in terms of deadlines and goals but also supportive in his or her interactions with employees? If so, then you have an example of a supervisor who is high on both facets of leadership behaviors. Of course, there are other leaders who have been known to lean fairly far in one direction or the other. For instance, Generals George Patton and Omar Bradley were both extremely successful and respected military leaders during

World War II, but Patton was low on consideration and high on initiating structure, whereas Bradley was high on consideration and relatively low on initiating structure. In short, these were leaders in the same field at the same time who attained impressive goals in very different ways.

The most important contribution of the behavioral approach to leadership has been the classification of leader behaviors in terms of the two broad dimensions just discussed. Unfortunately, specific findings have been inconsistent. For instance, some studies have found a negative correlation between consideration behaviors and leader effectiveness, whereas others have found a positive correlation (for a review, see Bass, 1985). Most of this research was conducted in the 1960s and 1970s, but more recent studies have continued to examine leader behaviors and started to clarify important relationships.

Judge, Piccolo, and Ilies (2004) examined the relationships between both consideration and initiating structure and a set of leadership effectiveness indicators via a meta-analysis. In arguing that these leadership behaviors are important and should not be viewed as relevant only to the history of leadership, they reported correlations from .22 to .78 between these behaviors and constructs such as follower job satisfaction, follower motivation, leader performance, and leader effectiveness. A 2008 study has expanded our knowledge base in this area. Supervisors' ratings of almost 400 mid-level leaders' consideration behaviors more strongly affected performance ratings than did the supervisors' ratings of initiating-structure behaviors (Zimmerman, Mount, & Goff, 2008). The authors reasoned that supervisors may weight consideration behaviors so heavily because they understand the role that interpersonal skills play in effective leadership.

Two recent papers have continued to flesh out our understanding of consideration and initiating structure. Across two studies involving almost 1,000 participants in various occupations, researchers found that exhibiting too little *or* too much initiating structure had negative effects on subordinate's trust in the supervisor, job satisfaction, affective organizational commitment, and display of organizational citizenship behaviors (OCBs) (Lambert, Tepper, Carr, Holt, & Barelka, 2012). Interestingly, there was a more linear relationship between these outcome variables and consideration behaviors. That is, consideration had a positive effect on the outcomes and the positive effect continued even at very high levels of consideration behaviors. The only exception to this was for trust in the supervisor; in this case, the results indicate that too much consideration can reduce the level of trust that subordinates have for their supervisors.

A second paper composed of two studies found that (1) consideration was a stronger predictor of interpersonal justice (the extent to which people are treated with respect and politeness) than was initiating structure, (2) counterproductive work behaviors (CWBs) were highest when supervisors were low on consideration and high on initiating structure, and (3) with respect to initiating structure, the lowest levels of CWBs emerged for those whose leaders demonstrated a moderate level of initiating structure as opposed to high or low levels (Holtz & Harold, 2013). These two recent papers provide strong evidence that leader behaviors are impactful and that consideration and initiating structure are both important with differential effects on different outcome variables.

Another very intriguing approach to traits and behaviors has been presented recently. Researchers have proposed an integrated trait–behavioral model of leadership effectiveness (DeRue, Nahrgang, Wellman, & Humphrey, 2011). Their meta-analysis found that leader traits associated with task competence were related to task-oriented leader behaviors, which had an effect on performance-related leadership outcomes. On the other hand, interpersonal attributes of leaders were related to relationship-oriented behaviors, which had an effect on affect-based criteria like satisfaction with the leader. This approach is likely to get more research attention as leadership researchers continue working to better understand this important process. Indeed, as we'll see when we discuss leader–member exchange theory and other contemporary approaches, much of the current research has focused on the intersection between outcomes and relationships.

As with trait theory, no one set of behaviors has emerged as being consistently predictive of effective leadership across a series of studies. This inconsistency may be due to the use of several different measures of leader behaviors (Schriesheim, House, & Kerr, 1976), the use of questionnaires that relied on participants' recall of behaviors, and a chief focus on lower-level managers (House & Aditya, 1997). It may also be due to the impact of situational variables on the leadership process; this is where the journey takes us next—to contingency theories.

## Contingency Theories

Because researchers were unable to discover a specific set of traits or behaviors that predicted effective leadership, they began to consider the role of the situation. In the 1960s, contingency theories grew out of this new approach to the study of leadership. Contingency theories differ from both trait and behavioral theories by formally taking into account situational or contextual variables. The central question, in other words, is whether leadership is contingent on the context or situation in which it takes place. We now turn to a discussion of three of the best-known contingency theories: Fiedler's contingency theory, path–goal theory, and leader–member exchange (LMX) theory.

**contingency theories**
Leadership theories that differ from both trait and behavioral theories by formally taking into account situational or contextual variables.

**Fiedler's Contingency Theory** In 1967, Fred Fiedler published his contingency theory of leader effectiveness, which maintains that effective leadership is a joint function of the characteristics of the leader and the features of the situation. Specifically, he argued that task-oriented leaders are best suited for some situations and that relationship-oriented leaders are best suited for others. This was the first theory to consider how leader characteristics (i.e., traits and behaviors) might interact with situational variables to determine leader effectiveness. Given that leadership research to this point was dominated by trait and behavioral theories, it was a groundbreaking approach.

Fiedler's theory is described in terms of *situational favorability,* or the extent to which the leader perceives that she has control of the situation. Thus, the situation is deemed favorable (i.e., controllable by the leader) if the leader has a positive relationship with subordinates, if the subordinates' tasks are well defined, and if the leader has the power to make important decisions.

The degree of situational favorability matches up with *leader style* or orientation, which can be measured by the *least preferred coworker (LPC)* scale. On this scale, which contains a list of bipolar adjectives, the leader is asked to describe the single worst coworker that he or she has ever encountered.

According to Fiedler, rather than measuring a leader's attitudes directly, the LPC scale requires that we infer the leader's investment in task accomplishment through his or her reactions to a coworker who gets in the way of accomplishments. For example, if a leader gave the LPC a very negative rating, we would infer that the rating reflected the leader's frustration or anger (Ayman, Chemers, & Fiedler, 1995). We would also conclude that the leader is task-oriented, meaning that the leader prefers to work toward goals by structuring and controlling tasks. Alternatively, if the leader rated the LPC in favorable terms, the leader would be considered person-oriented, meaning that the leader prefers to reach group goals by working closely with people on an interpersonal basis. Many researchers have criticized the definition of this construct, noting that it has changed considerably with the development of the theory and at times has seemed rather unstable (Hosking & Schriesheim, 1978). Fiedler maintains that task-oriented leaders perform best in situations of high and low control, whereas relationship-oriented leaders perform best in situations of moderate control. The empirical results have been mixed, with support for some of the relationships and no support for others (House & Aditya, 1997).

So in the final analysis, despite the many criticisms of Fiedler's theory, it was the first leadership approach to consider *both* situational and individual factors; it should thus be considered an important historical contribution to the development of the field.

In an interesting twist, a meta-analysis found support for an extension of Fiedler's contingency theory called cognitive resource theory, which focuses on intelligence as an important element of leadership. Fiedler (1995) argued, consistent with his contingency theory, that the effect of leader intelligence on leader success was contingent on other variables. In a meta-analysis, researchers found support for this contingency approach by showing that intelligence had a moderately positive effect on leadership success when leaders were under low stress but had no effect on leadership success when leaders were under high stress (Judge, Colbert, & Ilies, 2004). This supports Fiedler's theory that in stressful situations, an individual uses intelligence to deal with the stress, making that individual unavailable for leadership; meanwhile, the stress distracts the individual from the tasks at hand.

**Path–Goal Theory** Given that leadership is the process of motivating subordinates, an effective leader is one who adopts whatever approach is most likely to accomplish this goal. With this in mind, we turn to the path–goal theory of leader effectiveness (House, 1971). This theory emerged from a historical context in which

> **TECHNICAL TIP**
>
> In Chapter 2, we defined a construct as an abstract quality that is not observable and is difficult to measure. In contingency theory, what is the LPC construct? How would you define it? Remember also that construct validity is the extent to which an instrument measures what it is intended to measure. Does the LPC have construct validity?

results regarding leader behaviors on work group performance and subordinate satisfaction were very inconsistent and in which a cognitive emphasis was inherent in the popular motivational theories of the day. In particular, the path–goal theory arose out of the motivational concepts related to the expectancy theory of Victor Vroom (1964; see also Chapter 9). As you may recall, expectancy theory maintains that individuals are motivated to exhibit particular behaviors if they expect positive outcomes from doing so and if they value those outcomes. According to path–goal theory, leaders will be effective to the extent that they provide subordinates with what they need to increase their motivation to perform.

The path–goal theory specifies a number of situational moderators that influence the relationship between leadership behaviors and their effectiveness. It also identifies four kinds of leader behaviors: *directive leader behaviors, achievement-oriented leader behaviors, supportive leader behaviors,* and *participative leader behaviors* (House, 1996). These categories are presented and defined in **Table 13.3**. It is interesting to note that directive leader behavior is analogous to initiating-structure behavior (task orientation), while supportive leader behavior is akin to consideration behavior (relationship orientation). Leader behaviors are predicted to have direct effects on subordinates' expectancies and values (as moderated by both subordinate and environmental characteristics), and subordinates' perceptions regarding these expectancies and values affect their satisfaction, effort, and performance (as would be predicted by expectancy theory).

A meta-analysis of these studies found support for the basic propositions related to directive behaviors, task characteristics, and employee satisfaction; however, the results for predicting performance, as well as those involving supportive behaviors as predictors, were much less consistent (Schriesheim & Neider, 1996). Reviews and critical evaluations of the theory and its accompanying research indicate that the theory has not been well tested, owing to methodological problems such as poor measures of the constructs, lack of attention to intermediate variables (i.e., subordinate expectancies and perceptions of values), and lack of control regarding other relevant variables (House, 1996; Schriesheim & Neider, 1996). Recent work has lent support to the basic notion that leader behaviors affect

| TABLE 13.3 Path–Goal Theory: Leader Behaviors | |
|---|---|
| Directive leader behaviors | Provide structure by clarifying subordinates' performance goals and clarifying standards used to evaluate subordinates. |
| Achievement-oriented leader behaviors | Stress personal accomplishments and encourage performance excellence. |
| Supportive leader behaviors | Focus on interpersonal relations and provide psychological and emotional support for subordinates. |
| Participative leader behaviors | Encourage subordinates to take an active role through mentoring, guidance, and coaching. |

subordinate satisfaction and performance and that this relationship is moderated by the situation or context (see Sarin & O'Connor, 2009; Sims, Faraj, & Yun, 2009).

**Leader–Member Exchange Theory** We have talked about leadership as being based on behaviors, traits, and now interactions between the individual and the situation. Researchers have also begun to view leadership as a reciprocal interaction between two parties (Lord, 2000). **Leader–member exchange (LMX) theory**, for instance, is a theory about work dyads that focuses on the relationships between subordinates and leaders rather than on leader behaviors or traits. A precursor to LMX, developed in the 1970s, was called vertical dyad linkage (VDL) theory (Dansereau, Graen, & Haga, 1975). A major premise of VDL theory that has carried over to LMX is the notion that leaders have different relationships with different subordinates. Whereas both trait- and behavior-based theories assume that leaders use the same style or orientation (called average leadership style) with all their subordinates, LMX suggests that their styles vary across subordinates. This results in subordinates being placed or classified in the in-group or the out-group. Subordinates in the in-group tend to have good relationships with their leaders based on mutual trust, shared responsibility, and support; those in the out-group do not experience particularly strong relationships with their supervisors and tend to be treated in a more task-oriented fashion (Yukl, 2002).

According to LMX theory, the quality of the leader–subordinate relationship is predictive of individual-, group-, and organizational-level outcomes (Gerstner & Day, 1997). According to a meta-analysis of about 80 LMX studies, the quality of LMX relationships was significantly related to such outcomes as subordinate performance ratings, job satisfaction, organizational commitment, role clarity, role conflict, and turnover intentions. (In the case of the latter two outcomes, the relationship was negative.)

In the early part of the previous decade, researchers began teasing out the effects of LMX on performance-related factors (Hofmann, Morgeson, & Gerras, 2003). For example, one study, which replicated earlier work, found positive LMX relationships to be related to favorable performance ratings (see Chapter 5) if the members of the dyad communicated frequently (Kacmar, Witt, Zivnuska, & Gully, 2003). A study of 193 Israeli workers found that favorable LMX relationships predicted employee energy levels and the level of creative work (Atwater & Carmeli, 2009). In a survey of 181 nurses across seven hospitals of a large healthcare system, job satisfaction was found to mediate the relationship between LMX and turnover. An unfavorable relationship was associated with job dissatisfaction, which was related to high turnover levels (Han & Jekel, 2011).

Additional studies have focused specifically on LMX in work teams (see our discussion of teams in Chapter 12). One study argued that the variability in LMX

**leader–member exchange (LMX) theory**
A theory about work dyads that focuses on the relationships between subordinates and leaders rather than on leader behaviors or traits.

It's simple—you can't have an in-crowd unless you leave somebody out of it—without uncool, there is no cool. So basically, you're nothing without me. HA!

Suzie would later win a Nobel Prize for her Theory of Special Social Relativity.

Betsy Streeter/Cartoonstock

**A CLOSER LOOK**
How might a leader's in-group or out-group treatment of a subordinate influence individual, group, and organizational outcomes? How might a member's status affect his or her performance?

*within* a work group may have a negative effect on outcomes because team members perceive that the equality principle has been violated if team members receive different levels of respect, trust, and tangible resources (Hooper & Martin, 2008). In a sample of over 400 employees across various jobs, the authors found that perceptions of LMX variability related to more team conflict, which was related to lower levels of job satisfaction and employee well-being.

Other work has focused on the idea of LMX differentiation within individual work teams. A study that resulted in similar findings as Hooper and Martin's work surveyed over 4,000 employees across 384 departments of a large supermarket chain in an attempt to better understand the role of LMX in affecting team turnover (Nishii & Mayer, 2009). Among the most interesting findings was that turnover was highest when the leader developed very strong LMX relationships with *only some* of the team members, which the authors referred to as high *LMX differentiation;* this certainly suggests that how managers treat and interact differentially with their team members has huge organizational implications. Perhaps leaders need to be careful about developing relationships of different quality with team members; however, as we'll see next, there may be some mitigating factors to consider.

A more recent study reports results that qualify those of Nishii and Mayer (2009). In a study of 125 small project teams composed of engineering students, the authors found support for their idea that LMX differentiation would have a positive effect on performance at later time periods (Naidoo, Scherbaum, Goldstein, & Graen, 2011). The researchers argued that LMX differentiation is a result of leaders knowing and understanding their team members; in other words, over time, as leaders recognize the strengths, abilities, and weaknesses of their team members, they learn to treat them differently (e.g., in assignment of tasks varying in difficulty/importance or in how they choose to motivate them), which results in improved performance over time. Recent research composed of a laboratory study and a field study concluded that member-related constructs like performance, locus of control, and self-efficacy are important determinants of LMX quality (Henson & Beehr, 2013).

In the most comprehensive meta-analysis to date on LMX (Dulebohn, Bommer, Liden, Brouer, & Ferris, 2012) consisting of almost 250 studies, many previous findings were corroborated and new findings established. One of the major conclusions of this massive review is that leader behaviors and perceptions explained the most variance in LMX. The authors concluded that LMX quality is more strongly influenced by leaders than followers. In particular, LMX quality is substantially influenced by transformational leadership (which considers how a leader motivates followers to higher levels of achievement; this theory is discussed in detail later in the chapter), leader's expectations of follower's success, and the use of contingent reward behavior. As a result of leaders engaging in these behaviors, followers are encouraged and reciprocate by putting in extra effort, such as exhibiting OCBs, which strengthens the LMX relationship. More research is necessary to tease apart the various dimensions of transformational leadership; whereas the data indicate that individual consideration, idealized influence, and other relations-oriented elements of transformational leadership are related to LMX, other elements such as inspirational motivation and intellectual stimulation may not be.

A second major conclusion from this meta-analysis is that LMX serves as a major mediator of many antecedent → outcome relationships. For instance, the majority of the variance in behavioral (e.g., turnover intentions), attitudinal (e.g., job satisfaction), and perceptual (e.g., procedural justice) outcomes accounted for by antecedents like positive affectivity, contingent rewards, and transformational leadership is mediated by LMX. The researchers concluded that it is the quality of the LMX relationship that determines the key outcomes and that LMX is central to understanding the relationships between these important antecedents and outcomes (Dulebohn et al., 2012). These studies on performance-related factors, intragroup dynamics, and other aspects of the leader–subordinate relationship suggest the potential importance and breadth of LMX effects.

## Contemporary Theories

Several leadership theories developed over the past few decades have captured the attention of leadership researchers and practitioners alike. We have discussed the fertile ground of LMX research; in this section, I will talk about four other theories that should continue to produce scholarly work in the coming years: implicit, transformational, authentic, and servant leadership theories.

**Implicit Leadership Theory** A very different approach to leadership was developed by Robert Lord and his colleagues (Lord, Foti, & DeVader, 1984; Lord & Maher, 1991) at the University of Akron. This approach—known as **implicit leadership theory (ILT)**—emphasizes subordinates' perceptions of leader behaviors, in contrast to the theories we've previously discussed, which maintain that leaders affect the performance of subordinates through their own behaviors, traits, charismatic qualities, and ability to structure situations and define roles (Lord, 2000). Specifically, ILT views leadership as the outcome of a perceptual process involving both leaders and subordinates. Lord and Maher (1991) actually define leadership in terms of whether one is perceived by others as a leader. In his more recent work, Lord defines leadership as a process through which the leader changes the way followers envision themselves (Lord & Brown, 2004).

> **implicit leadership theory (ILT)** A leadership theory that views leadership as the outcome of a perceptual process involving both leaders and subordinates.

The central idea here is that we all hold implicit beliefs about the personal qualities and behaviors of leaders. These beliefs develop over time and are influenced by experience and socialization. The word **prototype** is sometimes used to refer to one's mental representation of a leader. (My own prototype of a leader, for instance, is someone who is intelligent, has excellent communication skills, is committed to the work that needs to be done and to the people who do it, and knows how to motivate employees.) Lord and his colleagues (1984) have demonstrated in experimental studies that when people observe someone behaving in a way that is consistent with their prototype for an effective leader, they conclude that this person is an effective leader. The implication is that leadership effectiveness may be more about followers' perceptions than about leaders' actions. In an interesting study that connects LMX to ILT, it was shown that employees whose ILT did not match their manager's ILT reported being in a lower-quality LMX relationship (Epitropaki & Martin, 2005).

> **prototype** One's mental representation of something or someone, such as a leader.

Other research (Phillips & Lord, 1981) has demonstrated that people develop global impressions of leader effectiveness based on the extent to which a particular leader matches their prototype. Even more important, however, is the finding that people use that global impression to describe the leader and to recall leader behaviors and traits—and that in doing so, they often make errors. An example is presented in **Figure 13.1**, which concerns my perceptions of my boss, Jared. My experience with Jared's behaviors is evaluated in light of my effective leader prototype (Box A); I have decided that Jared is an effective leader (Box C) because he matches up with salient parts (Box B) of that prototype (i.e., intelligent, excellent communication skills, committed). Now, suppose that I'm asked to rate Jared on whether he is a *self-starter* or on any other dimension of his behavior that I have not observed. I decide that because Jared is an effective leader, and because being a self-starter is part of my effective leader prototype, Jared himself must also be a self-starter (Box D) even though I haven't directly observed this.

The process I've just described is akin to the cart pulling the horse: Jared's behaviors are not driving my ratings of him; rather, my global impression of him as an effective leader colors my ratings of him on other, unobserved dimensions. The implications of this process are fairly serious: When subordinates are asked to rate their leaders on scales such as the LBDQ, we can't be sure whether they are providing valid ratings of their leaders' behaviors. Perhaps they are relying instead on their general impression of their leader as effective or ineffective based on their leadership prototype and how well the leader seems to match that prototype—or, worse, only a few dimensions of that prototype. Lord's work on ILT has been at the center of leadership research over the past three decades and clearly raises many important issues for future research to consider. His more recent work has demonstrated that

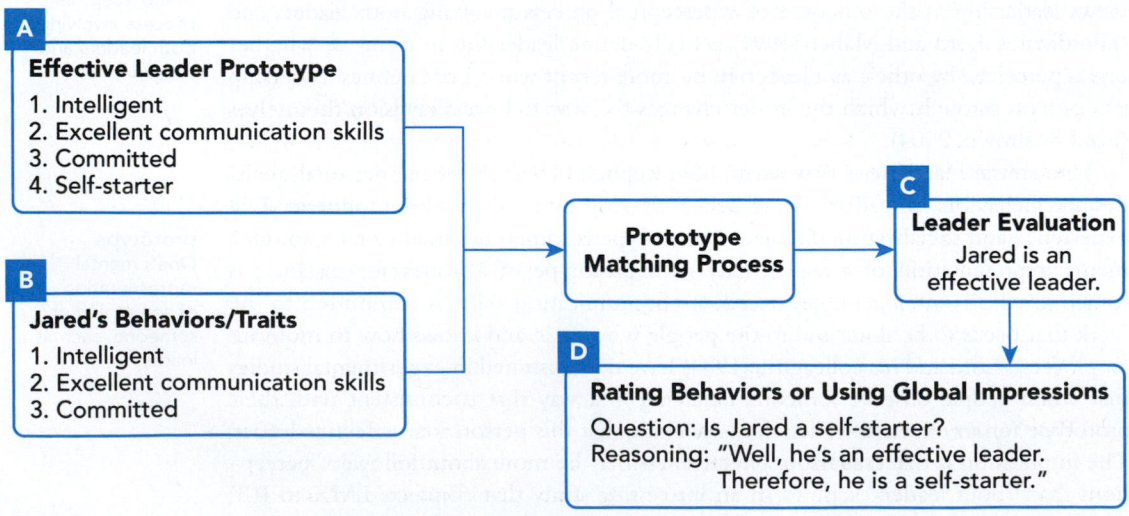

**A**

**Effective Leader Prototype**
1. Intelligent
2. Excellent communication skills
3. Committed
4. Self-starter

**B**

**Jared's Behaviors/Traits**
1. Intelligent
2. Excellent communication skills
3. Committed

**Prototype Matching Process**

**C**

**Leader Evaluation**
Jared is an effective leader.

**D**

**Rating Behaviors or Using Global Impressions**
Question: Is Jared a self-starter?
Reasoning: "Well, he's an effective leader. Therefore, he is a self-starter."

**FIGURE 13.1** Implicit Leadership Theory and Leadership Ratings

leader characteristics transfer from old leaders to similar new leaders, but when the new leader is not similar to an old leader, people rely on the general leadership prototype (Ritter & Lord, 2007). A recent review identifies the concern regarding the prototype driving our "memories," and thus our evaluations of leaders, as a very serious issue that needs to be addressed via measurement or statistical control or correction (Junker & van Dick, 2014). If subordinates don't take proactive steps to be aware of prototypes and to account for them, they may find that their leaders are favorably evaluated because of something people thought they did that fit their prototype, but really was never done.

A slightly different wrinkle has been added to this by focusing not only on how subordinates view their leaders as compared to a prototype but also on the role played by subordinates' own views of themselves along a leader prototype scale. A series of studies looking at the perceptions of over 700 employees found that the more subordinates' perceptions of their leader matched their leader prototype, the more they respected the leader and the more effective they perceived him or her to be; these studies also found that this relationship between leader prototype matching and favorable evaluation of the leader was moderated by subordinates' perception of how much they themselves possessed these prototypical leadership qualities (van Quaquebeke, van Knippenberg, & Brodbeck, 2011). For instance, the relationship between leadership prototype matching and the evaluation of the leader's effectiveness was stronger when the subordinate viewed him- or herself as possessing prototypical leadership qualities. The researchers argue that these findings demonstrate how central and important the leadership prototype is to an individual's self-concept. Another extension of ILT work is a new emphasis on followers and the role they play in the leadership process. A broad theory of followership has recently been articulated that proposes many conceptual and methodological issues to consider and provides suggestions for future research to enhance our understanding of the role of followers in leadership (Uhl-Bien, Riggio, Lowe, & Carsten, 2014).

ILT has been applied to the issues of gender and race as well. Let's look at an example of each. In four studies, researchers examined whether being White was part of the U.S. business leader prototype and found convincing support that participants, regardless of race, tended to assume profiled leaders to be White (Rosette, Leonardelli, & Phillips, 2008). Furthermore, they also found that White leaders were evaluated more favorably than were African American leaders regardless of the race of the study participant. These results are consistent with ILT, where prototypical leaders are predicted to be evaluated more favorably.

In a laboratory investigation that examined the role of gender in leader perceptions (Hall, Workman, & Marchioro, 1998), several groups, each consisting of two men and two women, were assigned to work on either a masculine-typed or feminine-typed task. Each group member provided leader ratings of every other group member. Overall, men were rated higher on leadership scales than were women; they were also more likely to emerge as leaders. Specifically, men emerged as leaders in about 70% of the groups. The relationship of gender to leadership ratings was also moderated by task type, such that the differences between males and females on leadership

© Steve Hix/Somos Images/Corbis

**A CLOSER LOOK**
What does ILT tell us about perceptions of men's versus women's abilities as leaders?

**transformational leadership**
A form of leadership in which the interaction of leader and follower raises both to higher levels of motivation and morality than they would achieve individually.

**transactional leadership**
A form of leadership in which the relationship between leader and follower is based chiefly on exchanges, with an emphasis on contingent reinforcement.

dimensions were greatest when the groups were working on a masculine-typed task. Because the issue of gender is so important in the workplace, we will discuss it in more detail later; it is worth noting here, however, that participants in a recent survey rated "an ideal U.S. president" as more similar to male than female candidates and higher in masculinity than femininity (Powell & Butterfield, 2011).

**Transformational Leadership Theory**
A major paradigm shift occurred in the leadership work of the mid-1970s, resulting in a class of theories referred to as the *new leadership theories* (House & Aditya, 1997). These theories have the following four characteristics in common: (1) they explain how leaders can take organizations to new heights; (2) they explain how certain leaders are able to achieve extraordinary levels of motivation, commitment, dedication, and so on; (3) they stress emotionally appealing behaviors such as empowering, developing a vision, and role modeling for their subordinates; and (4) they encourage increased follower self-esteem and satisfaction, as well as identification with the leader's values and vision (House & Aditya, 1997).

One of the best known of these leadership theories is transformational leadership, in which the interaction of leader and follower raises both to higher levels of motivation and morality than they would achieve individually (Bass, 1985). In effect, transformational leaders attempt to motivate subordinates to transcend their self-interest and achieve more than they think is possible. Both the leader and follower are thus *transformed,* or changed, in some noticeable and important way.

Transformational leadership is distinguished from transactional leadership, in which the relationship between leader and follower is based on exchanges and not much more (Bass, 1985; Bass & Steidlmeier, 1999). For instance, leaders who are more transactional than transformational tend to tell their subordinates what is expected of them and what they will get if they meet these expectations rather than emphasizing how the subordinates can grow and develop within the organization. In short, transactional leaders operate on the basis of *contingent reinforcement,* rewarding subordinates for specific behaviors. In real life, all leaders are partly transformational and partly transactional; thus, for example, when I speak of a "transformational leader," I am referring to a leader who tends to be more transformational than transactional.

Transformational leadership can be described in terms of four main components (Bass & Steidlmeier, 1999). The first of these, *idealized influence,* refers to the charisma brought to a relationship by a leader who arouses in the follower a strong desire to identify with or emulate the leader. Leaders who provide the second component, *inspirational motivation,* give followers challenges and a reason to engage in shared goals.

Their inspirational appeal focuses on the best in people, such as harmony, charity, and good works (Bass & Steidlmeier, 1999). The third component, *intellectual stimulation,* refers to the process through which transformational leaders increase follower awareness of problems from a new perspective. This approach helps followers to think critically and to approach problems with an open and flexible mind, thus encouraging creative problem solving. Finally, *individualized consideration* is what leaders share with followers when they treat each as an individual, providing support, encouragement, and growth experiences to all.

Overall, transformational leaders concentrate their efforts on long-term goals, develop and articulate a vision to share, inspire followers to enthusiastically pursue that vision, and coach followers to take greater responsibility for their own and others' development. They go the extra mile and do more than just *motivate* their followers; they *inspire* them.

Research has connected transformational leadership to important organizational outcomes like job satisfaction, organizational commitment, and work group performance (House & Aditya, 1997). A meta-analysis has demonstrated that the four main transformational behaviors—idealized influence, inspirational motivation, intellectual stimulation, and individualized consideration—are significantly correlated with leadership effectiveness (Lowe, Kroeck, & Sivasubramaniam, 1996). Transformational leadership results in a high level of subordinate motivation and commitment, in addition to well-above-average performance (House & Aditya, 1997). Of course, elements of transactional leadership are important, too, such as reinforcing subordinates based on their performance. Thus, transformational leaders are more successful if they exhibit some transactional behavior as well, but transactional leadership alone is typically not so successful (Bass, 1985). It has been shown that in military platoons under stressful situations, the best performance resulted from platoon leaders and sergeants who exhibited transactional contingent reward and transformational behaviors (Bass, Avolio, Jung, & Berson, 2003).

Research on transformational leadership continues at a blistering clip. Let's look at a few examples. First, because transformational leadership is believed to bring followers to a higher level of commitment to and identification with the leader and organization, it seems reasonable to expect that it will influence OCBs. Recall from Chapter 4 that OCBs are behaviors that seem to go above and beyond the call of duty—though not necessarily included in one's job description, they tend to be in the best interest of both the organization and one's coworkers. In one study of bankers in Korea, researchers found that transformational leadership worked through justice perceptions to affect OCBs directed at one's supervisor and coworkers (Cho & Dansereau, 2010). For instance, when a leader showed individualized consideration toward followers, those followers perceived the leader as being interpersonally just and proceeded to help the leader through OCBs. A very interesting study was conducted with Israeli kibbutz teachers, who tend to be more collectivistic in their perspective, with a focus on maintaining the group (*allocentrism*), and teachers from an urban location, who tend to be more individualistic, with a focus on individual goals (*idocentrism*) (Nahum-Shani, & Somech, 2011).

The researchers found the relationship between transformational leadership and OCBs to be positive and moderated by allocentrism, such that teachers expressing charisma were also rated as more altruistic by their school principals; this relationship was stronger when teachers were allocentric.

Second, a team of authors have suggested that transformational leadership can actually result in two conflicting outcomes: dependence on the leader or empowered self-direction (Kark, Shamir, & Chen, 2003). These scholars propose that transformational leadership can lead to such a strong personal identification with the leader that the followers become dependent on him or her. On the other hand, transformational leadership can also lead to social identification with coworkers and the organization, resulting in an increase in self-efficacy and self-esteem. In their study of Israeli mid-level managers, they found empirical support for these theoretical relationships.

In a very intriguing study of 152 CEOs and over 400 top management team members, researchers demonstrated that the transformational leadership of the CEOs directly impacted the behaviors of top management team members (e.g., risk-taking propensity, collaborative behavior, information exchange), which in turn had an effect on corporate entrepreneurship regarding product innovation and strategic activities (Ling, Simsek, Lubatkin, & Veiga, 2008). This study draws very clear implications for organizations and shows an effect of transformational leadership that goes beyond laboratory studies and theoretical posturing to produce real-world, bottom-line effects. Some studies have also begun examining transformational leadership in teams and have shown positive effects on team functioning.

Another study (Schaubroeck, Lam, & Cha, 2007) found this positive transformational leadership–team performance relationship to be strengthened when the team was high on collectivism (i.e., high on shared goals and cohesiveness) and power distance (i.e., having great respect for authority and viewing status differences as legitimate). Because this study's participants were financial services employees in either Hong Kong or the United States, however, the results likely have cultural implications; Western cultures like the United States tend to be low on collectivism and power distance, whereas Eastern cultures like Hong Kong tend to be high on both of these dimensions.

Of course, like most constructs we talk about in this book, there are likely boundary conditions around transformational leadership. That is, human behavior is complex, and thus transformational leadership may not be a strong determinant of positive organizational outcomes all the time. There may be situations where transformational leadership does not significantly improve organizational outcomes and potentially may detract from them. A recent study of 200 Chinese employees speaks directly to this issue. The researchers were interested in exploring boundary conditions and found that, among other things, when team members already perceived they were in a closely knit, cohesive work group, transformational leadership as measured by OCBs didn't matter that much. Specifically, when team members did not initially identify with their team as a cohesive group, transformational leadership improved their mindset and led to increased levels of OCBs, but if members did initially feel high identity with their team, then transformational leadership didn't lead to increased levels of OCBs (Li, Chiaburu, Kirkman, & Xie, 2013). There are other findings in this study that also suggest boundary conditions for transformational leadership. I want to reiterate that there are few absolutes in I/O psychology. Even though positive leadership behaviors usually have positive effects, almost nothing has positive influences all the time.

**Authentic and Servant Leadership** There are two other approaches to leadership that are, at some level, related to transformational leadership and are getting a good deal of research and practical attention. First, authentic leadership describes individuals who have "achieved high levels of authenticity in that they know who they are, what they believe and value, and they act upon those values and beliefs while transparently interacting with others" (Avolio, Gardner, Walumbwa, Luthans, & May, 2004, p. 802). In a recent review of the existing authentic leadership literature, the authors uncovered 91 published papers on the topic with most of the empirical work happening after 2005 (Gardner, Cogliser, Davis, & Dickens, 2011). Some of this recent work has demonstrated positive relationships among authentic leadership, authentic followership, need satisfaction, and performance among Belgian service employees (Leroy, Anseel, Gardner, & Sels, 2012). Other recent research has shown that authentic leadership encourages creativity among Portuguese employees (Rego, Sousa, Marques, & e Cunha, 2012). However, most of the research to this point has been theoretical and focused on identifying how authentic leadership differs from other types of leadership or leadership theories—for instance, authentic leadership differs from transformational leadership in that authentic leadership does not necessarily include a charismatic component. The 2011 comprehensive review by Gardner et al. sketches out a future research agenda that includes things like the pursuit of stronger theory building and the expansion of the nomological network for authentic leadership. Studies based on this research agenda will likely provide a great deal more information about how those who lead with their own genuine and unique styles can be successful and effective leaders. This promises to be a very exciting and energizing new avenue for leadership research.

Another new and exciting direction for leadership research is the notion of servant leadership, which was introduced by Greenleaf (2002) and is defined as placing the needs of subordinates before one's own and focusing efforts on helping subordinates to grow into their potential so as to achieve career success. In a comprehensive conceptual review of servant leadership, van Dierendonck (2010) distilled this concept into six important dimensions: (1) empowering and developing people, (2) humility, (3) authenticity, (4) interpersonal acceptance, (5) providing direction, and (6) stewardship. It's interesting to note that one major distinction drawn between transformational and servant leadership is that servant leadership is primarily focused on the growth and development of the individual and transformational leadership is focused on the organization—for the transformational leader, the growth and development of the employee is important only in so far as it leads to favorable organizational outcomes (performance, return on investment, profit, etc.). Further, as I noted before, inherent in transformational leadership is the potential for narcissism and negative long-term

**authentic leadership** Leading through one's own personal, genuine style that engenders trust in followers and builds relationships.

**servant leadership** Leading through personal integrity and driven by a desire to serve other people.

## PRACTITIONER FORUM

Nancy Warner

### Jamen Graves

*PhD, 1999, I/O Psychology, Alliant International (formerly California School of Professional Psychology)*
*Senior Partner, Korn/Ferry International*

As you can see from this chapter, organizational researchers have been trying for a long time to answer the question: "What is leadership?" Similarly, organizations have invested considerable resources to define and operationalize leadership in a manner that fits their strategy and culture. After many years of consulting with organizations of all shapes and sizes, I have seen all types of leadership models. In fact, there are probably as many leadership models as there are organizations. While we could argue that some models are better than others, they have rarely clarified what leadership looks like at each critical level in the organization.

There are many benefits associated with building leadership models, such as giving clarity and priority to particular sets of personal, interpersonal, and organizational competencies that are seen as critical to driving business success. Yet a drawback of these models is that they are based on the assumption that leadership is similar at each level of the organization. Not surprisingly, leaders at each level struggle to put these models into practice. For example, I recall hearing a group of employees from a large financial company respond to the new leadership model by saying, "We get that strategic agility is important to our company, but what does this mean for us?"

Organizations are gradually shifting their models away from a one-size-fits-all approach to a level-specific one. Competencies are moving from broad definitions to specific behavioral indicators. I recently partnered with a large healthcare organization to help define leadership requirements at three different levels. Using the Lominger competency framework, we used three criteria to differentiate leadership expectations at the manager, director, and executive levels. The criteria were time, values, and skills. We found that as the company's leaders moved from one level to the next, they spent their time on very different activities, specific values shifted, and the skills required also changed. For example, as leaders move up to higher levels, they must learn to spend more time developing others and empowering them as opposed to doing the work for them. They must also value success as a result of their team's accomplishments as opposed to viewing success in terms of their individual contributions.

These are not easy transitions to make, yet organizations that can help align and stratify leadership expectations by level are reaping great benefits. Not only can they maximize business performance, they can also attract leaders who are better suited to particular levels and improve how they engage, develop, and retain them.

### Applying Your Knowledge

1. What theories discussed thus far in this chapter would help inform the concept of different leadership skills being required for different leadership levels?

2. How does the latest research on LMX, ILT, and transformational, authentic, and servant leadership align with the leadership model described here?

3. How does the leadership model described by Graves relate to what we know about situational factors in leadership outcomes?

outcomes for the subordinates and the organization. Servant leadership has a very different flavor because the emphasis is clearly on treating others with humility and there is no self-centered, charismatic element to it. Similarly, whereas there is some substantial overlap between authentic and servant leadership, authentic leadership is centered on being true to oneself and servant leadership is centered on serving, growing, and developing others.

An interesting study of over 200 hairstylists and 470 customers focused on the effectiveness of servant leadership on performance in a customer service context (Chen, Zhu, & Shou, 2015). The researchers argued that because servant leadership is centered on serving others, they would expect servant leadership to predict customer service above and beyond transformational leadership. They found that manager's servant leadership did predict high service quality, customer-focused citizenship behavior, and customer-oriented prosocial behavior that was delivered by hair stylists even when controlling for transformational leadership. In other words, a manager who exhibits behaviors consistent with servant leaders tends to have hair stylists who, as reported by their clients, work hard to provide the clients with positive outcomes such as high service quality.

# NEW DIRECTIONS IN LEADERSHIP RESEARCH

Now that we have discussed the various leadership theories at length, I will take a closer look at the impact of gender issues on leadership—a topic with significant implications for the effectiveness of organizations. After that, we will consider the influence of culture on leadership and the role of emotions in leadership, with a look at a new area of research on the dark triad.

## Gender and Leadership

Certainly, we are all aware of the changing nature of our workforce. Women and minorities are currently being employed at rates far greater than this country has ever seen before. Six out of every 10 women age 16 and over were labor-force participants in 2007; they made up 47% of the labor force in 2014. Overall, 57% of women participate in the labor force and the unemployment rate is about equal across sexes (6.1% vs. 6.3%—women vs. men) (U.S. Department of Labor, 2014).

About 50% of all high-paying management, professional, and related occupations were held by women in 2014. However, this percentage varies a great deal across different industries. For instance, 35% of financial managers are women whereas 48% of medical and health managers are women (U.S. Department of Labor, 2014).

The **glass ceiling** refers to a situation in which qualified individuals are prevented from truly achieving all that they can because of some form of discrimination. The federal government created the Glass Ceiling Commission in 1991 to study the barriers preventing women from rising to the top of the corporate ladder. Its report at that time indicated that although women made up 43% of executive, administrative, and management workers, they held only 3% to 5% of the top executive positions. More recent data paint a still alarming picture. Only 14.2% of CEOs of S&P 500 companies were women in 2015 (Egan, 2015). Only 5% of executive positions nationally are currently held by women (Pew Research Center, 2015). Progress has been made in some fields. For the first time in history more than 100 women were serving in the U.S. Congress in 2014—20 senators and 84 representatives; however, that is still only 20% and 19% respectively. Women make up over 40% of college faculty but

**glass ceiling**
Refers to a situation in which qualified individuals are prevented from truly achieving all that they can because of some form of discrimination.

only 26% of college presidents (Cook, 2012); and although about 33% of lawyers in the United States are women, only a shade under 20% are partners (American Bar Association, 2013). These data are not limited to the United States. For instance, women in Ireland are not achieving leadership roles in organizations at the same rate as their male counterparts. A series of interviews of 30 female managers in Ireland identified two major individual barriers: (1) a woman's current career stage and (2) a family's current life-cycle stage (Cross, 2010). The women interviewed also noted that pregnancy leave often renders women forgotten: They are no longer visible to the organization and seem to get passed over or have their role minimized.

In 2008, Hillary Clinton ran a very strong campaign in the Democratic primaries, coming closer than any woman before her to becoming a major political party's candidate for president of the United States. During this time, she noted that her campaign was "making cracks" in the glass ceiling. However, four years later, in the run-up to the 2012 presidential election, only one woman, Minnesota congresswoman Michele Bachmann, declared herself a candidate, and she did not make it very far in the primary process. As I write this, Ms. Clinton looks to be the favorite to win the Democratic nomination for the 2016 U.S. presidential race—clearly the role of women in politics does seem to be evolving, even if at a rather slow pace. Indeed, even as women continue to make progress in the workforce and in leadership positions, there is still a long way to go.

Alice Eagly has been a leader in bringing issues of gender to the forefront of leadership studies. In a series of meta-analyses, she and her colleagues identified the important variables involved in linking gender to leadership and summarized the big picture. For instance, they looked at the role of gender in leadership style and found consistent (albeit small) differences between men and women, including the fact that women are more participative and interpersonally oriented than men (Eagly & Johnson, 1990). Their results also demonstrated that in situations that were congenial to a particular gender—such that the characteristics of the situation matched well with gender roles (e.g., women in the role of head nurse and men in the role of construction manager)—both men and women leaders tended to be task-oriented. This last finding is consistent with Eagly's work on gender role theory. The authors concluded from their extensive review that women tend to lose authority or legitimate power if they employ feminine (participative and interpersonally oriented) styles of leadership in male-dominated roles (Eagly & Johnson, 1990).

Another meta-analysis looking at the role of gender in leadership effectiveness (Eagly, Karau, & Makhijani, 1995) asked two very important questions: (1) Are leaders of one gender more effective than leaders of the other gender? (2) Do situations or contexts affect the likelihood that leaders of one gender or the other will be more effective? Again based on gender role theory, these researchers predicted that men would be more effective—or at least *perceived* to be more effective—than women in leadership roles that have been defined in masculine terms, or what are now termed *agentic roles,* and women would be perceived as more effective in feminine roles, or what are now termed *communal roles.* In other words, they anticipated that gender congeniality would moderate the relationship between gender and leader effectiveness.

Some interesting results emerged. First, women and men did not differ overall in terms of their perceived effectiveness as leaders. Second, gender congeniality did moderate the gender/leader effectiveness relationship: Male leaders were perceived as more effective in agentic contexts, and female leaders were perceived as more effective in communal contexts (Eagly et al., 1995). This last finding is especially interesting; it suggests that both men and women are unlikely to be perceived as effective leaders in situations that are not traditionally viewed as gender-congruent. Of course, considering that leadership tends to be defined in masculine terms, women are already at a disadvantage in many leadership situations: In order to behave in a way that is consistent with prototypical leadership (e.g., being aggressive and directive), they must behave in contrast to their gender roles (e.g., being nurturing, supportive, and participative). Thus, women are criticized for not being "leader-like" due to their feminine characteristics—but when they adjust and take on more masculine traits in order to be viewed as "leader-like," they are criticized for not being true to their femininity. This conflict, or "double bind" as it's called, is at the root of the stress and struggles faced by many women in leadership positions today. Highly communal female leaders are criticized for not being agentic enough, but highly agentic female leaders are criticized for lacking communion (Carli & Eagly, 2011). In their comprehensive review, Carli and Eagly concluded that the gender gap in leadership cannot be explained by inherent differences between the genders in traits or ability. Rather, the differences are likely due to greater domestic responsibilities for women, women's time spent away from paid work, and gender stereotypes and discrimination. Although we have seen many positive changes in recent years, there is still much to do to make leadership equally available to both genders.

Of course, the position of leader has traditionally been viewed by the general public as being a male role, so the fact that women have been hindered in obtaining and being successful in leadership positions has more to do with stereotypes about leadership than about women's actual ability to lead. A recent meta-analysis by Koenig and her colleagues summarized over 200 effects and concluded that stereotypes of leaders are "decidedly masculine" (Koenig, Eagly, Mitchell, & Ristikari, 2011). This is consistent with Lord's work on ILT, discussed earlier in the chapter. In fact, one study speaks directly to this issue. Following from Lord's work on implicit leadership theory, researchers asked whether gender stereotypes bias leadership perceptions during encoding (i.e., processing and storage of behaviors) rather than just at the point at which the target's behaviors are compared with his or her leadership prototype. In a series of studies, it was found that participants were less likely to encode task-based

Wade Payne/AP Photo

**A CLOSER LOOK**
Pat Summitt is the all-time winningest coach in NCAA basketball history for either men or women. In 38 years, she never had a losing season, and in 2012 she was awarded the Presidential Medal of Freedom. How do women like Pat Summitt impact the perception of women as leaders?

(or masculine) leadership traits when the leader was female rather than male (Scott & Brown, 2006). In other words, people store behaviors as being indicative of different traits, depending on the gender of the leader. Furthermore, task-based behaviors tend to be more typically linked with favorable leadership traits when exhibited by men than when exhibited by women.

Using gender role theory as a background, Eagly and Karau predicted that men would emerge as leaders in contexts or situations that were consistent with male gender roles and that women would emerge as leaders in contexts or situations that were consistent with female gender roles. An extensive meta-analysis of the existing literature supported their predictions: Men emerged more often as leaders in task-oriented situations, whereas women emerged more often as leaders in socially oriented situations (Eagly & Karau, 1991). Another study found that women high on dominance (an empirically identified leader trait) were more likely to emerge as a leader in a laboratory setting with a male partner when provided with a female leader role model. However, even women high on dominance as a personality trait tended not to emerge as leaders when experiencing a male leader model (Carbonell & Castro, 2008).

Another line of research has used identical and fraternal twins to demonstrate that only about 30% of the variance in leadership occupancy (i.e., the extent to which individuals have held leadership positions) in both males and females could be accounted for by genetic factors; almost 70% was due to environmental factors (Arvey, Rotundo, Johnson, Zhang, & McGue, 2006; Arvey, Zhang, Avolio, & Kreuger, 2007). The researchers conclude that most of the variance in leadership ratings and leadership occupancy appears attributable to work, broader life events, and other yet undiscovered factors. This suggests that learning how to lead is a very reasonable goal for both males and females who aspire to be future leaders—perhaps leaders are not born but made! Obviously, the social context and our experiences with others impact our leadership behaviors and successes.

Some have argued over the years for the "feminine advantage" perspective on leadership effectiveness (Yukl, 2002). The notion is that because women are more adept at being inclusive, interpersonally sensitive, and nurturing than are men, they should be better leaders. Vecchio (2002) argues convincingly against this perspective by citing a good deal of research that did not find these differences between the genders. However, a meta-analysis of leadership behaviors across genders found that female leaders tended to exhibit higher levels of transformational leadership behaviors and transactional contingent reward behaviors than did male leaders, who tended to exhibit higher levels of the typically less effective transactional behaviors than did female leaders (Eagly, Johannesen-Schmidt, & van Engen, 2003). Although these differences were generally small, they were statistically significant; there were also small statistical differences between genders on leadership outcomes such as effectiveness, with females performing better than males. Obviously, Vecchio's analysis and Eagly and her colleagues' review lead to different conclusions, suggesting the need for additional research and better conceptual development (for a review, see Eagly, 2007).

## Culture and Leadership

Although cultural issues were ignored by leadership researchers for many years, they have since become the focus of research (Dickson, Hanges, & Lord, 2000) due to the global economy and the increased diversification of organizations. Some scholars have referred to the interest in cross-cultural leadership as an "explosion" in the field (Dickson, Den Hartog, & Mitchelson, 2003). Indeed, Robert House and his colleagues have proposed a theory of cross-cultural leadership maintaining that expected, accepted, and effective leader behavior varies by culture (House & Aditya, 1997). According to these authors, what a particular culture values in its leaders is based on the implicit leadership theory endorsed by that culture. This idea is, of course, an extension of Lord's work on ILT (Lord, 2000; Lord et al., 1984; Lord & Maher, 1991).

An interesting study demonstrated that leadership prototypes develop through different processes in individualistic versus collectivistic cultures (Ensari & Murphy, 2003). Ideas along these lines constitute one focus of the ongoing Global Leadership and Organizational Behavior Effectiveness (GLOBE) research project, which involves 61 countries and more than 200 researchers led by House. These researchers argue that although some leader behaviors or traits are universally accepted and effective, there are many others for which acceptance and effectiveness are more culture specific (House & Aditya, 1997). GLOBE researchers argue that future research from the GLOBE project should show with increasing frequency the many leadership effects or processes that are moderated by culture (Dickson et al., 2003). Some recent work has begun to systematically address these issues. In a large and comprehensive review of the GLOBE project, the authors reported many interesting results from the 20 years of work (Dorfman, Javidan, Hanges, Dastmalchian, & House, 2012). For instance, executives tend to lead in a way that is consistent with the leadership prototypes that are pervasive in their culture. This means that culture (as measured by leadership prototypes) has a very strong effect on leadership styles and behaviors. On the other hand, the authors report that some leader behaviors are universal—for example, charismatic/value-based leadership is universally effective regardless of culture. Finally, effective leaders are identified by the extent to which their behaviors match the cultural expectations for leader behavior—it is the fit between expectations and behavior that really determines whether leaders are perceived as effective.

It is likely that many other traits and behaviors vary across cultures. One study demonstrates just such expected differences (Gerstner & Day, 1994). When these researchers administered a survey measuring 59 leadership traits to a sample of international and American graduate students (the international sample consisted of students from China, France, Germany, Honduras, India, Japan, and Taiwan), they found that the traits seen as most characteristic of business leaders varied across cultures. This result suggests that leadership prototypes also vary across cultures. For instance, the five most prototypical traits identified by Japanese participants were *disciplined, intelligent, trustworthy, educated,* and *responsible;* those identified by U.S. participants were *persistent, industrious, goal-oriented, determined* and *had good verbal skills.* In short, there are clear differences between these two cultures in terms of what they view as prototypical

© moodboard/Corbis

**A CLOSER LOOK**
How much overlap
is there between
what Western and
Eastern cultures
consider important
leadership traits?

leadership. As noted above, the extent to which the leader's behaviors match what is prototypical for his or her culture is important in determining perceptions of effectiveness.

A recent study has extended these ideas a step further by demonstrating that leaders' global experiences impact their ability to think strategically. This isn't terribly surprising as strategic thinking reaps the benefits from multiple and diverse relationships, conversations, ideas, and experiences. What is more intriguing is that the relationship between global experiences and strategic thinking was moderated by the cultural distance between the leader's own culture and the culture of his or her experiences. In other words, leaders whose international experiences took place in cultures that were very different from their own culture were better strategic thinkers (Dragoni et al., 2014). For years I've encouraged undergraduates to participate in study-abroad programs. I think this study provides additional support for my encouragement because it shows clearly the value of experiencing culturally-distant cultures.

Research looking at attitudes and perceptions across 21 countries found that self-ratings of leadership characteristics were more apt to relate to both peer and subordinate ratings in cultures characterized by high assertiveness (Atwater, Wang, Smither, & Fleenor, 2009). Other findings of this study also suggest that self-awareness is really important and may explain differences in leader effectiveness across cultures. Another important cultural variable, power distance—the extent to which an individual or culture sees power and authority as hierarchical or egalitarian—has been examined in terms of leadership. A study of employees in the United States and China found that transformational leadership was more positively linked to procedural justice when employees were lower on power distance (Kirkman, Chen, Farh, Chen, & Lowe, 2009). The effects of transformational leadership also impacted the frequency of OCBs through perceptions of justice and power distance.

The authors of this study concluded that there are reliable differences in leadership perceptions across cultures. The implication is that we need to understand these and other differences much more thoroughly if we are to comprehend the true nature of leadership processes. Indeed, a heightened awareness of such differences may help employees understand their coworkers better and may help organizations understand their employees better as the workplace continues to become more diverse and global in nature. Eagly and Chin argue that we have compartmentalized diversity constructs from the leadership literature (Eagly & Chin, 2010). By this they mean that our leadership theories have developed with little regard for diversity issues and that when we do consider diversity issues, we do so separately from the leadership theory per se—there isn't much integration. They strongly encourage researchers to consider

## I/O TODAY

### Romance of Leadership: How much do leaders really matter?

CEO compensation has been a topic of intense public discussion and debate in recent years. This debate usually takes the form of the question: Are CEOs paid too much for what they do? While CEOs and company owners have historically been well compensated, the gap between CEO pay and the pay of the average employee has widened dramatically.

A 2014 *New Yorker* article noted that in 1950, CEOs were typically paid about 20 times that of the average worker in their company (Cassidy, 2014). Today, this ratio is closer to 200 times that of the average worker, and in some organizations, it's even higher (Tim Cook, CEO of Apple, is estimated to earn 6,258 times that of the average Apple employee, after accounting for stock options and other benefits). A number of critics have suggested that this disparity in pay is problematic: The widening gap between average workers and CEOs might be one reason why there is a shrinking middle class and why minimum wage is not a "livable wage" for some families. So, why are CEOs paid so well?

Psychologists James R. Meindl and Sanford B. Ehrlich suggested a phenomenon known as *the romance of leadership (ROL)*—the idea that we attribute to leaders far too much credit for their organization's successes and failures (1987). Although this theory was first proposed 30 years ago, it certainly can be applied to many situations today. Consider, for example, the success of Apple under Steve Jobs. While Jobs was known as a charismatic and skillful leader, there were likely other contributors to his success, including having a talented team of developers and emerging at the right time to take advantage of other technological and cultural developments, among other factors.

ROL doesn't suggest that leaders are not important, or that researchers shouldn't study influential individuals. But ROL does serve as a good reminder that followers matter, too; over the past few decades, I/O psychologists have also examined how follower behaviors, beliefs, and personality affect whether a leader is likely to be successful.

Schyns and colleagues (2007) noted that romance of leadership may heavily influence which leaders are apt to be seen as charismatic. Similarly, Kulich and colleagues (2007) noted that ROL works differently for men and women leaders, such that a company's financial performance is more likely to be associated with the success of a male leader than with the success of a female leader. ROL theories might also have implications for how leaders should manage their public image, especially as leaders are increasingly called on to engage with the public and the media.

As researchers devise more sophisticated methods for research (such as experience sampling methods and multilevel modeling), they can also examine how leadership changes over time. If a leader has done well for a certain period of time, perhaps his or her mistakes are more likely to be overlooked or forgiven. Researchers may also be guilty of any number of mistakes in how they assess leaders, including halo effect or leniency. In the end, it is important to recognize that while leaders can have important effects on the success of an organization, they are only one piece of the puzzle of organizational performance.

#### Discussion Questions

1. What are some examples of impediments that might prevent a leader from having an influence over the bottom line of a company? Are there any organizational structures or situations that might make a leader obsolete?

2. Consider the issue of CEO pay. Do you believe that CEOs today are compensated fairly? If not, how might we address this problem? What would be the possible results of limiting CEO pay?

#### References

Cassidy, J. (2014, March 31). Forces of divergence: Is surging inequality endemic to capitalism? *The New Yorker*. Retrieved from http://www.newyorker.com/magazine/2014/03/31/forces-of-divergence

Kulich, C., Ryan, M. K., & Haslam, A. S. (2007). Where is the romance for women leaders? The effects of gender on leadership attributions and performance-based pay. *Applied Psychology, 4,* 582–601.

Meindl, J. R., & Ehrlich, S. B. (1987). The romance of leadership and the evaluation of organizational performance. *The Academy of Management Journal, 30,* 91–109.

Schyns, B., Felfe, J., & Blank, H. (2007). Is charisma hyper-romanticism? Empirical evidence from new data and meta-analysis. *Applied Psychology, 4,* 505–527.

#### Additional Readings

Bligh, M. C., Kohles, J. C., & Pillai, R. (2011). Romancing leadership: Past, present, and future. *Leadership Quarterly, 22,* 1058–1077.

how leadership theories can incorporate gender, race, ethnicity, culture, and sexual orientation. Furthermore, they propose that researchers should draw on the research and theory that has addressed these diversity issues and build new leadership theories that truly consider these issues as mainstream and important—or alter existing ones to incorporate them.

## Emotions and Leadership

Mood, emotions, and affect have become hot topics in I/O psychology in recent years. Accordingly, leadership researchers have begun to examine the role of emotions in the leadership process. For instance, research has begun drawing links between transformational leaders' emotional expressions and various outcomes. One study showed clearly that transformational leaders express more positive emotions than do less transformational leaders and that these positive emotions have a direct effect on followers' moods. Furthermore, both leaders' emotions and followers' moods had positive effects on leader effectiveness and the perceived attractiveness of the leader (Bono & Ilies, 2006).

A second area where emotions and leadership are being connected involves **emotional intelligence (EI)**, or the ability to assess and manage one's own emotions as well as understand those of others. Emotional intelligence and cognitive ability are often identified as key variables in determining leader effectiveness. A recent study demonstrated that an element of EI, empathy (the ability to understand and identify with another's feelings), plays a central role in affecting leadership perceptions as well as both relational and task-based leadership behaviors (Kellett, Humphrey, & Sleeth, 2006). These results suggest that emotionally intelligent leaders create a bond with their followers because the followers feel valued and understood.

The link between EI and organizational outcomes has been investigated in a recent study of South Korean employees in which it was argued that EI worked through transformational leadership in affecting leader effectiveness (Hur, van den Berg & Wilderom, 2011). The researchers concluded that leaders high in EI are more effective leaders because they exhibit more transformational behaviors. Here, we see a very clear integration of the interplay of affective variables (EI) with leader behaviors from the theory of transformational leadership in an Eastern culture; this research is a great example of how a few of the major elements in this chapter can be combined in one research program.

In another review and analysis, the authors noted the likely importance of EI in leadership but also pointed out that the evaluation data on the effectiveness of training programs teaching emotional/social skills are weak and inconclusive (Riggio & Lee, 2007). More sophisticated research is necessary to provide more direction regarding how to best develop leaders' emotional skills.

Of course, there is a flipside to the influence of emotions as well—that is, negative emotions or traits can often co-occur with poor leadership. In recent years the notion of the "dark triad" has garnered a great deal of attention and is composed of three personality traits which tend to be reflected in unfeeling and manipulative behavior. *Psychopathy* is the more formal and technical term that describes individuals who are

**emotional intelligence (EI)**
The ability, capacity, or skill to identify and manage one's own emotions and understand the emotions of others.

antisocial, impulsive, and low on empathy. *Narcissism* is also characterized by a lack of empathy and is defined by characteristics of entitlement, grandiosity, and selfishness. *Machiavellianism* describes individuals who are callous, cold, manipulative, and exploitative (Paulhus & Williams, 2002). The research on the dark triad focuses on high levels of these personality factors, but at the subclinical level. This means that individuals are high on these traits, but their symptomatology is such that they would not be diagnosed with any kind of personality disorder. Obviously, there is a sense of negativity associated with all of these personality traits. Although these traits are correlated, they are also clearly independent of each other. Paulhus and Williams provide us with some insight and clarity on the issues: "To varying degrees, all three entail a socially malevolent character with behavior tendencies toward self-promotion, emotional coldness, duplicity, and aggressiveness," (p. 557). Think about a good leader who you have worked for, and I'm quite certain you wouldn't describe him or her in that light.

Before we talk about some recent research linking the dark triad to leadership, let's get a little more general background about the dark triad. A very simple but interesting study found that individuals who scored high on the dark triad traits also expressed more interest in sensational or risky phenomena and reported taking great pleasure in others' misfortune, which is described by the German term *Schadenfreude*. Past research tell us that individuals who score high on the dark triad traits exhibit "dark" behaviors like hyper-competitiveness and a lack of empathy. More recent findings tell us that these individuals also take joy in the suffering of others and have an interest in "dark" pastimes (James, Kavanagh, Jonason, Chonody, & Scrutton, 2014).

How do the dark triad traits relate to leadership? In a recent study of over 400 students and organizational employees, researchers found that individuals high on dark triad traits also reported more frequent use of "hard tactics," such as the threat of punishment, manipulation of people, and manipulation of situations (Jonason, Slomski, & Partyka, 2012). It is interesting to note that men scored higher on the dark triad traits than women did, and men also reported greater use of hard tactics. In fact, the use of hard tactics served to fully mediate the relationship between gender and hard tactics. In other words, the difference between men and women in the use of hard tactics is explained through their differences in dark triad traits. The authors argue that dark triad traits facilitate workplace influence through the use of forceful and aggressive hard tactics. They wonder aloud whether these dark triad traits, which lead to hard tactics, help or hinder individuals in climbing the corporate ladder and ascending to important leadership positions. Another question not directly raised by this paper is whether men ascend more frequently to leadership positions than women in part because of their dark triad traits and hard tactics. This seems like an exciting and fruitful area for future research.

Another new line of research has introduced the idea of *arrogant leadership,* which differs from narcissism in that arrogance is a narrower term, focused on specific behaviors, and not a personality construct reflected in a clinical or subclinical personality disorder (Johnson et al., 2010). Workplace arrogance consists of the exaggeration of the leaders' self-importance, which results in the disparagement of their colleagues.

In a series of studies, Johnson and his team defined the construct and it's nomological network. They developed and validated a scale that is now being used in current research studies. Some of the things we know about arrogant leaders from this research include: (1) arrogance is correlated with dominance, anger, and superiority; (2) arrogance is negatively related to work performance; and (3) high levels of arrogance are associated with low self-esteem and low cognitive ability. It's very interesting that arrogant leaders also tend to be low on cognitive ability, perhaps suggesting that low-cognitive-ability leaders try to compensate by appearing confident and superior. The research, however, suggests that this ploy doesn't work, as arrogant leaders are liked and respected less than other, less arrogant leaders. This is another new area of leadership research that will likely gather more attention in future years.

## Summary

This chapter provided an overview of leadership, with an emphasis on the theoretical and empirical work done in the field. I began by defining leadership and demonstrating how the concept of power and its different types relate to leadership processes. I then emphasized that leaders use different types of power in different situations and that some leaders rely on some types of power more than other types.

Next, I presented the major theories of leadership, with an eye toward tracing their historical development. My rationale here was to show that history provides clues about how our thinking on leadership has evolved and become more sophisticated as researchers sought out new approaches that explained or resolved the deficiencies of past work. I described trait theories as the first real systematic approach to leadership, explaining that because no traits consistently emerged as necessary to be a good leader, this approach was largely abandoned (albeit revived later) in favor of research on leadership behaviors. The latter approach has revealed that some effective leaders exhibit mostly consideration behaviors, whereas others exhibit mostly initiating-structure behaviors, though researchers failed to identify behaviors that consistently predicted effective leadership. Taking a different direction, I then considered research on situational and individual moderators, as well as contingencies. In particular, I presented Fiedler's theory as an important novel approach that eventually came under criticism—with the result that leadership advocates began looking elsewhere for a theoretical orientation. Fiedler's theory, however, did provide a basis for path–goal theory, which built on expectancy theory and focused on the leader's goal of motivating subordinates. This discussion of contingency theory finally led us to leader–member exchange (LMX) theory, which seeks to understand the many variables at work in the reciprocal leader–subordinate relationship.

In a later section, I spent considerable time discussing four contemporary theories—implicit leadership theory (ILT), transformational leadership theory, authentic leadership theory, and servant leadership theory—that have great potential to help us understand leadership processes. I also noted that the perspective on leadership taken by both LMX and ILT is very different from that of more traditional theories. At the conclusion of the chapter, I described three cutting-edge issues in leadership that promise to be relevant in the 21st century—gender, culture, and emotions (including a discussion of the emerging study of dark triad traits). These issues merit further study, as an understanding of their impact on leadership processes promises to enhance organizational practice.

## Key Terms

authentic leadership (p. 451)
behavior theories (p. 437)
consideration (p. 437)
contingency theories (p. 440)
effective leadership (p. 433)
emotional intelligence (EI) (p. 460)
glass ceiling (p. 453)
implicit leadership theory (ILT)
  (p. 445)
initiating structure (p. 437)

leader–member exchange (LMX)
  theory (p. 443)
leadership (p. 433)
leadership self-efficacy (LSE) (p. 436)
power (p. 433)
prototype (p. 445)
servant leadership (p. 451)
trait theories (p. 435)
transactional leadership (p. 448)
transformational leadership (p. 448)

## TAKING IT TO THE FIELD

Leadership is a topic that has generated considerable interest. There are plenty of pop psychology and management books on leadership, and not all of them offer useful advice. Sophie Konig is the founder of KoniGames, a company that designs and manufactures children's games. Her company has recently experienced an uptick in turnover, and during some of the exit interviews, departing employees have complained about the "lack of leadership" in the company. She has turned to you for ideas on how to improve leadership at KoniGames and what she, as a female leader, can do to improve her relationship with her subordinates.

Hi again—

Thank you so much for being willing to help me! KoniGames has gone through a lot of changes over the past year. When we were a small company (under 100 employees), I knew each and every employee by name. The company has over 500 employees now, and I am finding that my previous approach to leadership is not working as well these days.

I've been reading a book that argues women tend not to be respected as leaders. In order to prove our leadership, women must be more aggressive and more demanding of our followers to show that we have what it takes to lead. The book recommends that I set harder goals, speak loudly and firmly, and avoid being polite and friendly with employees. The book suggests that being too friendly makes you seem like a doormat, so female leaders should demand that followers do as they're told, or they won't have a job for long. This will be a big change for me—I was used to being pretty friendly with my employees, but it's clear that this approach is not working anymore.

What do you think? What would you suggest?

Sophie

## Critical Thinking Questions

1. The theories of transformational and transactional leadership suggest two very different ways to lead. Is one of these approaches universally more effective than the other, or do both approaches work equally well in certain situations? How could you use both? What would that theory look like?

2. Based on what you read in this chapter, how has the role of gender in leadership changed over the past few decades? How do you think gender will factor into leadership in the future? How about race—what do you expect to see happen in that domain and why?

3. The trait theory of leadership suggests that certain individual characteristics make people more effective leaders. Based on this perspective, do you believe that leaders are "born" or "made"?

4. The chapter talked a great deal about leadership perceptions. Why are leadership perceptions so important? Where do relationships fit into this puzzle?

5. Consider the traits described by the "dark triad." If we don't typically consider these to be positive personality traits, what are some reasons that people who display them are able to achieve leadership positions? What can followers and other leaders within an organization do to prevent leaders with dark triad traits from moving up in an organization? Should they prevent this movement?

## Application Questions

1. Consider each of the bases of power. How might a college instructor demonstrate each of these? How do you react when instructors use these types of power?

2. One aspect of LMX theory that researchers are beginning to explore is the varying quality of relationships within a team. Research demonstrates that when leaders have very strong relationships with only a few team members, it leads to turnover. Have you ever experienced something like this? Were you one of the favorites or one of the "outsiders"? What effect did this have on you?

3. Imagine you have a friend who is interested in becoming more transformational in her leadership style. What behaviors would you suggest she increase in order to become more transformational?

4. Consider some examples of famous female leaders. What are some ways in which female leaders are treated differently from male leaders (by the media as well as by peers and followers)?

5. Consider servant leadership. What might be some behaviors a leader could engage in that would indicate s/he was a servant leader? Why do you believe servant leadership is such a popular approach right now?

## Suggested Readings

**Van Dierendonk, D.** (2011). Servant leadership: A review and synthesis. *Journal of Management, 37*(4), 1228–1261. This paper provides a nice historical look at the servant–leader construct as well as a thoughtful integration of the literature with suggestions for future research.

**Eagly, A. H., & Chin, J. L.** (2010). Diversity and leadership in a changing world. *American Psychologist, 65*(3), 216–224. This paper provides great insight into leadership and the role diversity plays. Eagly is a dynamic leader in this field, and she draws on her career's work to present a foundation and a look to the future.

**House, R. J., & Aditya, R. N.** (1997). The social scientific study of leadership: Quo vadis? *Journal of Management, 23*(3), 409–473. A great review of leadership theories—and one that presents relevant research on each theory.

**Dorfman, P., Javidan, M., Hanges, P., Dastmalchian, A., & House, R.** (2012). GLOBE: A twenty year journey into the intriguing world of culture and leadership. *Journal of World Business, 47*, 504–518. This article summarizes the work of the GLOBE project and provides a fascinating story of the research and its conclusions.

**Dulebohn, J. H., Bommer, W. H., Liden, R. C., Brouer, R. L., & Ferris, G. R.** (2012). A meta-analysis of antecedents and consequences of leader-member exchange: Integrating the past with an eye toward the future. *Journal of Management, 38*(6), 1715–1759. A great overview of LMX theory and research, and a complete assessment of the research findings.

**Steers, R. M., Porter, L. M., & Bigley, G. A.** (1996). *Motivation and leadership at work* (6th ed.). New York: McGraw-Hill. This easy read covers all the major theories in the areas of both motivation and leadership.

CHAPTER

# 14

# Organizational Theory and Development

Photo: Stewart Cohen/The Image Bank/Getty Images

## LEARNING OBJECTIVES

This chapter should help you understand:

- The various organizational theories and how they have developed
- The differences between bureaucratic theory and Scientific Management
- How Theory X differs from Theory Y
- How open-system theory provides a useful framework for thinking about organizations
- What organizational development is and why it is so important for the long-term success of organizations
- The basic premises on which organizational change is based
- The major principles of many organizational development interventions, as well as some benefits of each
- Some of the specifics concerning organizational development interventions, such as total quality management and gainsharing
- Technostructural interventions such as reengineering
- How culture-change interventions and knowledge-management interventions can act to transform organizations profoundly

What do you think about the company you work for? Is it a good company? Is it a company for which you expect to work for a long time, or is it just serving your needs right now? If your company is a good one to work for, what is it that makes it good? Is it financially successful? Does it treat its employees with respect and dignity? Do employees have input into the company's direction? I think these are all good questions, and the answers say a great deal about the organization that employs you.

In 2015, Apple topped the list of the most admired companies in the world for the fourth straight year ("World's Most Admired Companies," updated annually). Over the course of the past decade, Google has been at or near the top of *Fortune* magazine's list of 100 best companies to work for ("100 Best Companies to Work For," updated annually). Wegmans Food Markets, a leader in grocery stores, has also been consistently ranked high on this list. What do these companies have in common that allows them to be so successful—not only economically and competitively but also from the perspective of employees and applicants? In addition to providing employee-centered benefits such as medical benefits, fitness centers, onsite stores, profit sharing, and elder-care assistance (as we have discussed in earlier chapters), companies like these emphasize the culture or environment in which their employees work.

One theme throughout this text has been that, given the changes confronting the world of work (e.g., downsizing, empowerment, global competition, diversity), organizations need to be forward-looking. Indeed, to remain competitive economically, attractive to applicants, and valued by employees, organizations today must be willing and able to alter their environment—a move that sometimes necessitates a complete change of direction. As a reflection of the need to change, this chapter discusses organizational theories that are used to categorize, analyze, and improve organizations, with a focus on how organizations behave and what techniques they can use to operate more effectively and efficiently to compete in this ever-changing and increasingly competitive business environment.

# ORGANIZATIONAL THEORY

**Organizational theory** can be defined as a set of propositions that explains or predicts how groups and individuals behave in varying organizational structures and circumstances (Shafritz, Ott, & Jang, 2011). It is not a stretch to say that much of how the world behaves is relevant to the study of organizational theory. From our various community associations to our local churches, from government agencies to local and national charities to the workplace, organizational theory can help explain and predict behaviors that take place in many aspects of our lives. In order to explain the structure and functioning of organizations, I discuss organizational theory specifically in the context of the last category, the workplace. *Classical organizational theory*—one of three major organizational approaches—is important in this context.

**organizational theory**
A set of propositions that explains or predicts how groups and individuals behave in varying organizational structures and circumstances.

## Classical Organizational Theory

Some scholars have argued that organizational theory has its roots in ancient or medieval times, but the formal study of organizational theory appears to have begun when factories became popular in Great Britain in the 1700s (Shafritz, Ott, & Yang, 2015). Classical organizational theory, the first type of organizational theory to develop, has four basic tenets (Shafritz et al., 2015):

- Organizations exist for economic reasons and to accomplish productivity goals.
- Scientific analysis will identify the one best way to organize for production.
- Specialization and the division of labor maximize production.
- Both people and organizations act in accordance with rational economic principles.

With the building of large, complex factories came a multitude of new and sophisticated problems managers had to handle. To be successful in this new economy, industrial and mechanical engineers needed to organize production systems to keep the machines busy and work flowing. Toward this end, workers were viewed as merely part of the mix—as interchangeable cogs in an organization-wide machine. In fact, a common argument was that organizations should work like machines, with people and technology as their components. The four preceding tenets helped maintain this focus.

Two particular developments occurred within classical organizational theory: Scientific Management and bureaucracy. We will consider each in turn.

**Scientific Management** In the late 1800s and early 1900s, Frederick Taylor provided a framework that he believed would be useful in structuring organizations. From the perspective of this framework, which he called *Scientific Management*, the organization is a machine—a pragmatic machine whose focus is simply to run more effectively. The Scientific Management school conducted time and motion studies and analyzed temperature, illumination, and other conditions of work, all the while looking at the effects of these conditions on productivity and efficiency. Taylorism, as this approach was sometimes called, had as its premise the notion that there is one best way to get the job done. Accordingly, its tactics were quite simple: Conduct studies that gather data indicating what the fastest and most efficient method is, then implement that method. In short, Taylorism maintained that factory workers would be much more productive if their work was designed scientifically. In the early 1900s, this notion became a movement; sweeping through our nation's factories, it had a profound—almost revolutionary—effect on the business field (Shafritz et al., 2015).

Scientific Management can be summarized in terms of four principles (Taylor, 1916/1996). First, management gathers data from the workers, who are in the best position to understand the job duties and tasks. These data are analyzed and reduced to laws and rules, which are applied to workers' jobs in the form of detailed procedures and how-to explanations. Second, workers are selected carefully—or, as Taylor put it, "scientifically"—and then trained so that they become more efficient than ever before. Third, scientific selection, data collection, and training are combined to enhance efficiency. Taylor argued that these processes must be brought together because science and workers are not a "natural combination." Finally, the work itself is redistributed, with management taking over tasks previously left to subordinates (e.g., factory workers). Taylor emphasized that cooperation and genuine sharing of the labor were important if the overall process was to work (see Wagner-Tsukamoto, 2007).

In one of his last addresses before he died in 1915, Taylor gave an example of how Scientific Management, when applied to the "science of shoveling," had worked at Bethlehem Steel (Taylor, 1916/1996). Taylor noticed that there was great variability in the loads that men placed on their shovels; he proceeded to scientifically study this process by paying a couple of employees to shovel for a specified period of time with varying loads. What he found was that efficiency—that is, amount shoveled in a specified amount of time—varied as a function of the size of the shovel load (see **Figure 14.1**). The employees started with a 38.5-pound load, using increasingly smaller loads as testing continued. As the loads got smaller, efficiency improved, due largely to the employees' greater strength and energy. However, at about 20 pounds, efficiency began to decrease. The optimum shovel load turned out to be about 20.5 pounds—the weight at which the most ore or coal could be moved in a fixed amount of time. Taylor then developed shovels with a maximum capacity of 21 pounds

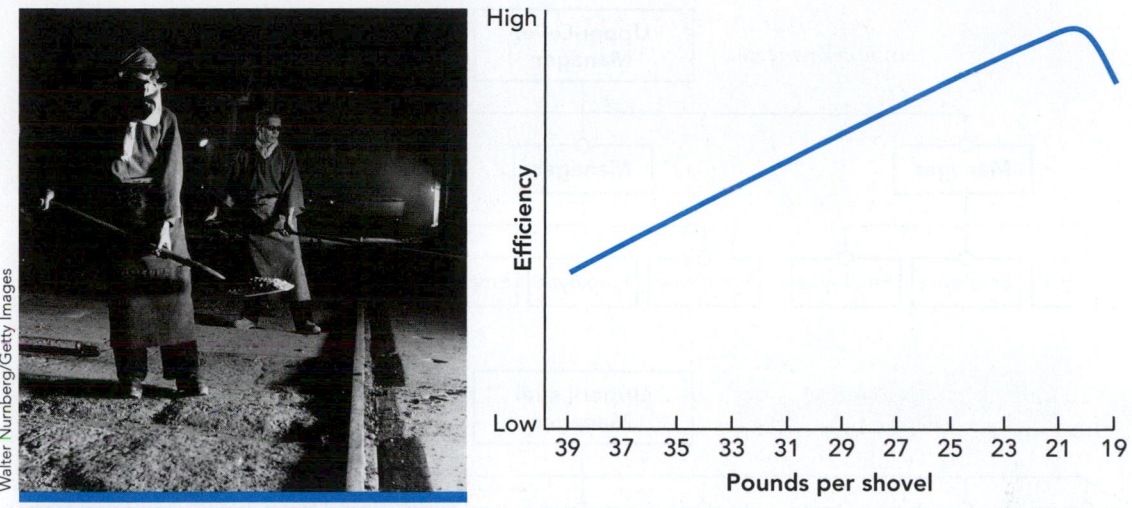

Efficiency

High

Low

39  37  35  33  31  29  27  25  23  21  19

**Pounds per shovel**

Walter Nurnberg/Getty Images

**FIGURE 14.1**   An Example of Taylorism

and taught employees how to use them. The use of these new shovels resulted in an almost immediate increase in efficiency: Each shoveler's daily yield of coal went from 16 tons to 59 tons!

**Bureaucracy**   Max Weber was a German sociologist who studied organizations in the late 1800s and early 1900s. Specifically, he analyzed historically large and efficient organizations such as the Egyptian empire, the Prussian army, and the Roman Catholic Church (Wagner & Hollenbeck, 1998). Weber used these careful analyses to develop the notion of *bureaucracy,* which, in his view, described the structure, organization, and operation of many efficient organizations. Let's consider four major features of a bureaucratic organization.

First, each job in a bureaucratic organization is a specialized position with its own set of responsibilities and duties. Weber called this idea **division of labor**—a rather simple approach in which employees are narrowly trained to do only the particular tasks and duties assigned to their jobs. Dividing up tasks in this manner allows the organization to take advantage of individuals' particular strengths, thus avoiding the problems that result from asking people to perform tasks requiring skills they don't have. Of course, one potential difficulty in bureaucracies involves the coordination of various tasks handled by various employees. In other words, it is good that each employee has his or her particular task to do, but it can be difficult to coordinate the many tasks done by all employees while at the same time ensuring a particular outcome or end product for the organization.

Second, bureaucracies tend to be top-down pyramidal organizations, like the one shown in the top panel of **Figure 14.2**. At every level of the organization (except for the very top), employees report to a person one level up in the chain of command.

**division of labor**
An approach whereby each job in a bureaucratic organization is a specialized position with its own set of responsibilities and duties.

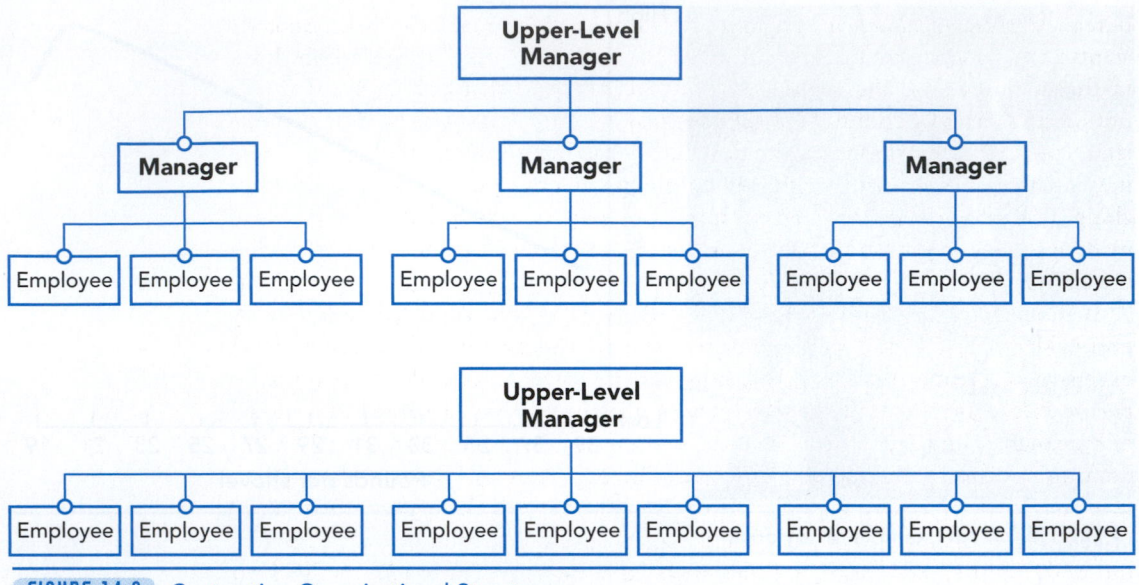

**FIGURE 14.2** Contrasting Organizational Structures

According to Weber, this hierarchical system of supervision is necessary if the division of labor is to be beneficial.

Third, bureaucracies rely on the principle of **delegation of authority**, an approach whereby supervisors, rather than trying to do everything themselves, assign particular tasks to separate employees and hold them responsible for completing these tasks. We have all experienced managers who are incapable of delegating; these managers—often called **micro-managers**—try to take charge of everything that goes on in the organization rather than holding employees responsible for individual tasks.

Finally, bureaucracies are characterized by a **span of control**. This feature, which is related to the chain-of-command idea, refers to the number of subordinates who report to a given supervisor. As you might imagine, the goal for organizations is to find just the right span of control. If the span of control is too large, supervisors are unable to effectively manage the many subordinates; if it is too small, there is an over-abundance of supervisors managing too few employees. Historically, the optimal span of control has varied considerably across companies, but the trend in the late 20th and early 21st centuries has been toward larger spans of control as a result of smaller numbers of middle-level managers (see Chapter 1). A comparison of the top and bottom panels in Figure 14.2 shows what happens to the span of control when layoffs or organizational restructuring results in the reduction of middle-level management, as happened dramatically in the United States during the 1990s and has happened again with the recent recession.

In a classic text on the psychology of organizations, Daniel Katz and Robert Kahn (1978) emphasized two additional issues that are important to Weberian

**delegation of authority**
An approach whereby supervisors assign particular tasks to separate employees and hold them responsible for completing these tasks.

**micro-managers**
Managers who, instead of delegating individual tasks to employees, try to take charge of all tasks.

**span of control**
The number of subordinates who report to a given supervisor.

bureaucracy: *standardization of tasks* and *centralized decision making*. Task standardization is analogous to Taylor's notion of the "one best way" to get a job done, in that it pertains to the training of employees toward that end. Related to the notion of a chain of command is the idea that decision making should be centralized. I noted earlier that it can be difficult to coordinate the many tasks done by individual employees while at the same time moving the work of the organization along. This becomes easier in a bureaucratic system, in which major decisions are made by one or more individuals who are centralized under one command, as in the military.

It is no secret that bureaucracies today are viewed with skepticism and perhaps even disdain. The U.S. government and even universities are often described as excessively bureaucratic. Here, too, however, we need to consider the historical period in question—specifically, the context in which Weber developed his model of bureaucracy and Taylor developed the concept of Scientific Management. At this point in the late 19th and early 20th centuries, there were no theories of organizations and no reliable format or framework to follow in developing an organization or improving organizational functioning. The industrial revolution had begun in the 18th century, and large factories came into their own throughout the 19th century. During these early years, there was little or no sense of how industrial organizations should be run, and disorder and chaos were prevalent. Indeed, Scientific Management and bureaucracies were developed to provide these directionless organizations with formal, orderly, and efficient functioning. Both of these approaches proved to be very helpful at the time.

In more modern times, however, theorists have begun to argue that bureaucratic structures are ineffective for organizations operating in rapidly changing environments, such as the medical field. For instance, in 2014 an Ebola outbreak originated in Guinea, West Africa, and became the world's largest Ebola epidemic, claiming more than 11,300 lives over a two-year period (CBS/Associated Press, 2016).

**A CLOSER LOOK**

The military uses a central decision-making body reflective of a bureaucratic system. What are the benefits and drawbacks to bureaucratic systems?

Bureaucracy played a significant role in creating and exacerbating many of the errors that were responsible for delays in getting proper medical treatment for those in need. For instance, because of red tape attributed to the World Health Organization (WHO) and various governments, chlorine delivered to sites where it was needed was expired, protective gear needed by the medical personnel went missing, approval for boots and buckets was delayed, and the approval for the building of clinics stalled (Associated Press, 2015). According to Dr. Irwain Redlener, director of the National Center for Disaster Preparedness at Columbia University in New York, if WHO had

## I/O TODAY

### Holacracy: Managing Work Without Managers

In March of 2015, Tony Hsieh, the CEO of Zappos, sent a startling announcement to his employees: He was eliminating managers, and anyone who did not want to work under this new structure could take a severance package and leave. About 14% of employees took the severance. This major change in Zappos' structure turned the idea of bureaucracy on its ear and helped to generate quite a bit of attention around the new concept of *holacracy.*

Holacracy is an organizational structure where authority and decision-making responsibilities are distributed throughout self-organized teams (as opposed to a manager taking responsibility for decisions). Instead of job descriptions, employees' places in the company are defined by roles, which describe what their goals are, what organizational domains they are associated with, and what ongoing activities they should be performing. These roles are organized into circles (and an individual may be part of several circles), with each circle having a clearly defined purpose.

Each circle is self-organized and follows a structured process for making decisions that allows all members to propose ideas, amend those ideas, and raise objections. Circles also hold regular tactical meetings to discuss progress and data, as well as governance meetings to discuss and adapt roles to meet the needs of the organization. While the governance process is quite rigid and rule-based, advocates of holacracy emphasize that this underlying structure allows individual workers a great deal of autonomy. As long as they are filling the duties of their roles and keeping their circle updated, employees can accomplish the work however they like (though permission may still be required for use of expenses and resources). Arguably, having roles instead of job descriptions allows employees to more quickly adapt their behaviors to changing circumstances. Because circles can self-organize, they can adjust their goals and the behaviors they need to enact to achieve them.

Zappos is not the only organization to embrace a holacratic approach—Precision Nutrition, the David Allen Company, and Medium are other notable examples. These organizations are generally positive about their experiences, indicating that they are able to grow their business without adding bureaucracy, and many employees feel more ownership and pride in their work. As with any new approach, however, holacracy has earned its fair share of detractors. Critics suggest that despite supporters' claims, holacracies are still hierarchical and continue to rely on managers (just without the job title). They also suggest that this structure can prevent people from understanding the big picture of what is going on in an organization. In addition, it is not clear where the customer fits into holacracy, and how their needs will be clearly addressed (Denning, 2014).

Although organizations have met initial success with holacracy, its long-term viability is not clear. However, given the push for organizations to become more nimble to address changing marketplaces and globalization, holacracy may gain traction over the next few years.

#### Discussion Questions

1. What are some benefits and drawbacks to less hierarchical organization where leadership is not always clear? What organizational characteristics might suggest a less top-down structure, such as holacracy, would be successful?
2. If you had to choose between working in a holacracy or in a more traditional bureaucratic organization, which might you choose? Why?

#### References

Denning, S. (2014, January 15). Making sense of Zappos and Holacracy. *Forbes.* Retrieved from http://www.forbes.com/sites/stevedenning/2014/01/15/making-sense-of-zappos-and-holacracy/

#### Additional Readings

This paper offers a brief explanation of holacracy, including several short case studies: http://www.holacracy.org/whitepaper.

responded sooner and declared an international emergency, and if a stronger response had been initiated by WHO, thousands of lives would have been saved (Associated Press, 2015).

Weber himself warned that work in a bureaucracy can be so simplified and unchallenging that workers might become dissatisfied and unmotivated, resulting in lower productivity overall (Wagner & Hollenbeck, 1998). Some recent work has demonstrated the complexities involved in changing a bureaucracy into a different type of organization (Hopfl, 2006; Josserand, Teo, & Clegg, 2006). Arguably, it was these basic criticisms of both bureaucracy and Scientific Management that led to the development of alternative theories of organizations.

## Humanistic Theory

The human relations movement resulted, in part, from a reaction to the rigidity of classical organizational theory. Factors that were not even remotely associated with the classical approach to organizations—such as employees' motives, goals, and aspirations—were emphasized by those in the human relations movement (Katz & Kahn, 1978). The relationship between supervisor and subordinate has been especially important in the humanistic theory of organizations, which explains organizational success in terms of employee motivation and the interpersonal relationships that emerge within the organization.

Perhaps the best example of humanistic theory is Douglas McGregor's (1960) work on Theory X and Theory Y. McGregor argued that managers' beliefs and assumptions about their employees determine how they behave toward those employees. Managers' behaviors, of course, affect employees' attitudes and behaviors, which in turn affect managers' attitudes, beliefs, and behaviors (see Chapters 10 and 13 for more details). This cycle is illustrated in **Figure 14.3**, which clearly shows the importance of the

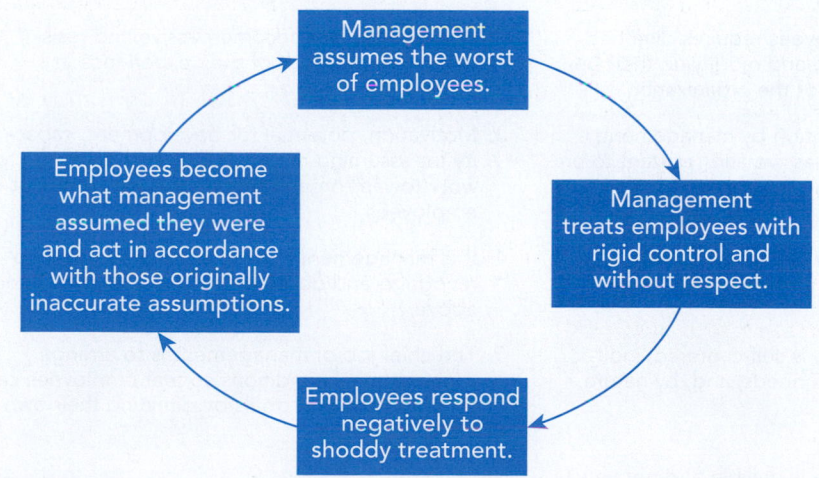

**FIGURE 14.3** Self-Fulfilling Theory X Cycle

interaction between employees and management. This interaction often involves a *self-fulfilling prophecy* in which employees, over time, learn to act and believe in ways consistent with how managers think they act and believe—even if this wasn't the case initially.

According to McGregor, employees were traditionally viewed as lazy, interested only in what's best for themselves, inherently uninterested in work, lacking in ambition, and not very intelligent. Management's job, therefore, was to control and direct employees in order to make economic profits. Without a firm hand, it was thought, employees would be passive and unresponsive to the organization's needs. This perspective is what McGregor refers to as *Theory X;* he argues that it was the most prevalent set of beliefs about employees from the birth of industry until the mid-1900s.

In order for organizations to develop and become truly effective, a different approach was needed—and, according to McGregor, this had to start with management's view of employees. McGregor did not dispute the notion that employees lacked ambition and were somewhat lazy, but he argued that they had developed these behaviors because of the way they were treated by managers, whose behaviors in turn stemmed from their preconceived notions about employees. So, again, we see the vicious cycle depicted in Figure 14.3. McGregor proposed *Theory Y* as a new perspective necessary for improving both employees and organizations.

**Table 14.1** presents the assumptions and responsibilities of management under both Theory X and Theory Y. The differences are clear: Compared with Theory X,

## TABLE 14.1  Theory X and Theory Y

| Theory X | Theory Y |
|---|---|
| 1. Management is responsible for the economic well-being of the organization. | 1. Management is responsible for the economic well-being of the organization. |
| 2. Management of employees requires directing, controlling, motivating, and modifying their behavior to fit the needs of the organization. | 2. Employees have become passive and resistant only as a result of their experience in organizations. |
| 3. Without active intervention by management, employees would be passive and resistant to organizational needs. | 3. Motivation, potential for development, capacity for assuming responsibility, and readiness to work toward organizational goals are inherent in employees. |
| 4. The average employee is lazy, works as little as possible, lacks ambition, and dislikes responsibility. | 4. It is management's job to allow employees to recognize and develop the characteristics listed above. |
| 5. The average employee is self-centered, indifferent to organizational needs, and, by nature, resistant to change. | 5. The chief job of management is to arrange organizational conditions so that employees can achieve their own goals by directing their own efforts. |
| 6. The average employee is gullible and not very bright. | |

Theory Y takes a much more humanistic and developmental orientation, emphasizing not only the inherent goodness, capacity, and potential of employees but also their readiness to develop those inherent characteristics. Theory Y also emphasizes management's responsibility for nurturing those qualities and providing employees with opportunities to develop their inherently positive characteristics in the workplace (McGregor, 1957).

Throughout this text, we have talked about many "new" concepts in management, including empowerment, participation, self-managed work teams, transformational leadership, self-assessment, and organizational citizenship behavior. If you think back to our discussion of these and other developments in I/O psychology, you can see that they are all consistent with the human relations movement—or what McGregor called the *Theory Y approach* to organizational management. Most of McGregor's work was done in the late 1950s and early 1960s, but it has taken on great importance since it first came on the scene, shaping to a considerable degree the approach taken by many successful organizations worldwide.

Recent theoretical work in this area emphasizes learning and ethics (Rosanas, 2008). The learning that happens between people in organizations is central to the relationships that form and the effectiveness that follows. Furthermore, it is argued that decisions made in organizations ought to be evaluated along a series of dimensions (e.g., effectiveness, distinctive competence, and identification with the organization) in which ethics plays a central role. Thinking along these lines is consistent with the traditional humanistic approach—and also extends it.

## Open-System Theory

It is important to recognize that organizations are not always well-defined by the purposes for which they were developed. On the contrary, organizations develop and change over time as a result of both internal and external forces. This is the basic premise of Katz and Kahn's (1978) *open-system theory* of organizations (see **Figure 14.4**). The three key elements of open-system theory are inputs, throughputs, and outputs. *Inputs* are transformed during the *throughputs* stage into *outputs*, which

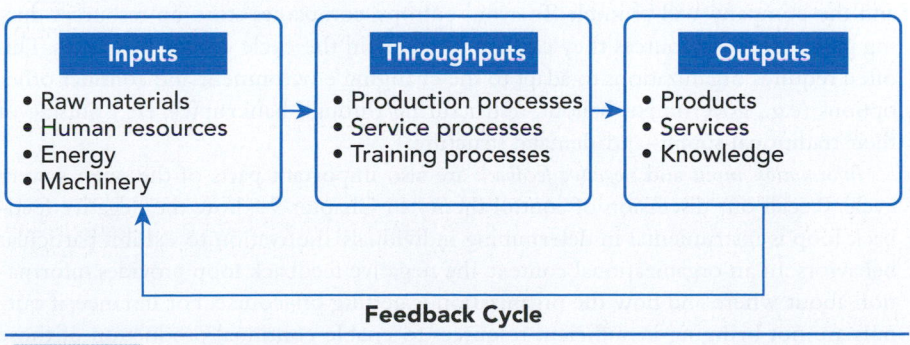

**FIGURE 14.4**  The Cycle of Open-System Theory

in turn are brought back into the process as additional inputs—and thus the process continues.

For example, a car manufacturer that uses production processes to transform raw materials into automobiles is, in effect, using throughputs to transform inputs into outputs. The outputs (automobiles) are then sold for money, which is reinvested as inputs into the system—and transformation or production continues. Katz and Kahn (1978) point out that organizations thrive only as long as there is a continuous flow of energy from the external environment into the system and a continuous export of products out of the system. This simple principle is at the heart of several disciplines, including economics, psychology, and biology. And, indeed, Katz and Kahn developed their theory based on the principles of biology that define all living things as open systems.

Plants and animals, for instance, both give to and take from the environment in which they exist—and well-run organizations operate in a very similar way. In our car manufacturer scenario, for example, the organization would be headed toward eventual death if the automobiles stopped bringing in money and production was negatively affected. In fact, this is exactly the position that the big three American car manufacturers found themselves in a couple of years ago. The declining economy and rising oil prices reduced profits and led to budget cuts and layoffs at all three. Eventually, General Motors and Chrysler filed for bankruptcy in 2009. This was followed by a government bailout to try to revive the struggling automotive industry, which seemed to be on more solid footing in 2012 than it had been a few years earlier.

**Table 14.2** presents the 10 characteristics of open systems as presented by Katz and Kahn (1978). We've already discussed inputs, throughputs, outputs, and the cyclic nature of the process, but there are other important characteristics of open systems, too—such as *negative entropy*. Entropy is a principle in many branches of science positing that all forms of organization move toward disorganization or death (Katz & Kahn, 1978), whereas the principle of negative entropy suggests that organizations must avoid this movement toward death by continuing to import energy from outside the system. Thus, for example, our car manufacturer must continue to transform raw materials (inputs) into cars (outputs)—for if this cycle is broken, entropy will follow and the company will crumble. To avoid entropy, companies store up resources during good times—resources they can use to maintain the cycle during bad times. This often requires organizations to adapt to the changing environment and consider other options (e.g., government bailout, restructuring through bankruptcy, etc.) outside of their traditional supply-and-demand structure.

*Information input* and *negative feedback* are also important parts of the open-system cycle. Recall our discussion of control theory in Chapter 9—how the negative feedback loop is instrumental in determining individuals' motivation to exhibit particular behaviors. In an organizational context, the negative feedback loop provides information about where and how the organization is getting off-course. For instance, if outputs are not bringing in sufficient resources to enable continual production of those outputs, changes need to be made at the input or throughput stage.

| **TABLE 14.2**   Characteristics of Open Systems | |
|---|---|
| Importation of energy | Energy is brought in from the external environment for use by the system. |
| The throughput | That energy is transformed. |
| The output | A product or service is exported. |
| Systems as cycles | The pattern of importation of energy and exportation of products and services continues. |
| Negative entropy | The tendency of all systems to move eventually toward death is reversed. |
| Information input and negative feedback | Information input and negative feedback allow the system to correct or adjust its course. |
| The steady state | Surviving open systems are characterized by a balance in energy exchange. |
| Differentiation | Open systems move toward more specialized functions. |
| Integration and coordination | Bringing the system together as a unified process is necessary for the system to continue. |
| Equifinality | There are many ways within the system to get to the same conclusion or endpoint. |

The last characteristic I'll mention here is *equifinality,* the notion that a system can reach the same end state in different ways. In other words, there isn't just one way to achieve a particular outcome. Note that this is inconsistent with the basic premise of Scientific Management that there is "one best way" to do everything. The idea of equifinality reflects the human element in organizations, providing more flexibility and allowing for more creativity in their development and operations. Given this human element, the only stable aspect of organizations and the environment they interact with is that they change—a lot and often! Thus, being limited to "one best way" tends not to result in effective organizations.

# ORGANIZATIONAL DEVELOPMENT

Organizational development is not an easy topic to explain, but let's start with this definition: **Organizational development (OD)** is a planned, organization-wide effort to increase organizational effectiveness through behavioral science knowledge and technology (Beckhard, 1969). Many argue that OD is really about promoting positive humanistic changes in organizations; that is, it's as much about helping the people in an organization as it is about helping make the organization

**organizational development (OD)**
A planned, organization-wide effort to increase organizational effectiveness through behavioral science knowledge and technology.

more productive (Church, Waclawski, & Siegal, 1999). But some newer thinking in this area is starting to broaden OD interventions (Marshak & Grant, 2008) to include other less traditional approaches, which we will discuss later in the chapter. OD programs share some important characteristics among themselves. In particular, they tend to do the following:

- Involve the total organization
- Be supported (and initiated) by top management
- Entail a diagnosis of the organization, as well as an implementation plan
- Be long-term processes
- Focus on changing attitudes, behaviors, and performance of groups/teams
- Emphasize the importance of goals, objectives, and planning

These characteristics explain what OD is; what OD *isn't* is a short-term patch to hide an organizational problem. In fact, when OD fails, it is often because the characteristics just listed have been ignored in favor of superficial changes that have very little impact on the organization's effectiveness and result in greater stress and lower morale at the company. If anything, bad OD programs take organizations back a few steps rather than moving them forward. New CEOs are frequently expected by their boards to immediately initiate successful organizational change efforts, but these efforts are rarely successful because changing organizations is such a complex endeavor (Greiner, Cummings, & Bhambri, 2003), especially for new leaders. For instance, Andrea Jung was made CEO of Avon Products in 1999, but her tenure didn't end well; she was removed from the CEO position in 2011. Her first few years were very successful, but in 2005 stock prices were tumbling and there was a strong push to restructure and to make some serious organizational changes. Under her leadership, Avon attempted to make those changes; however, after about five more years, it became clear that the change efforts weren't working, and the organization decided to try some new leadership (Lublin & Karp, 2011).

## Why Organizations Need Organizational Development

Organizations embark upon OD interventions for many reasons, but much of the time it is because of changes in an organization's operating environment. Like everything else we've covered in this book, organizational practices and programs operate not in a vacuum but, rather, in a context that affects those practices and programs. Whether social, technical, economic, or political in nature, sometimes environmental changes necessitate development of the organization to make it more effective. The key to meeting these challenges is utilizing the knowledge, expertise, and commitment of individuals to enhance organizational effectiveness (Wirtenberg, Lipsky, Abrams, Conway, & Slepian, 2007)—this is where OD comes into the picture. Can you think of any creatures—or technologies, for that matter—durable enough to survive without adapting to new environments? Certainly, humans and computers have evolved. In order for organizations to survive, they, too, must be adaptable enough to change over time.

In a thought-provoking and very readable analysis of management in the 21st century, Michael Hitt (2000) discusses changes over the previous 15 to 20 years, changes to come in the next 20 to 30 years, and the accompanying challenges that organizations now face. In fact, this section of the chapter is partly based on this fascinating article. We often hear about how much things have changed in recent years. Here is an incredible example: In 1990, use of the Internet was limited to scientific exchanges and some government correspondence—and that's all. A decade later, almost 1 billion people were communicating and conducting business on the Internet. When I started my job at the University of Akron in 1989, I had some access to an archaic e-mail system from a computer lab in our department but no access at all from my office, and I had very little idea what the Internet was. Now, my 10-year-old nephew uses the mouse like he was born with it in his hand, my 17-year-old son uses the Internet routinely for school projects and through the state's "technology in the classroom" initiative he uses it in his classes regularly throughout the school day, and my 22-year-old son serves as my computer consultant!

Hitt (2000) argues that the competitive landscape of the 21st century will be characterized by substantial and sporadic changes. He focuses on two major changes in this landscape that successful companies will need to navigate through organizational development. The first one concerns the technological revolution and the knowledge explosion that accompanies it; according to one estimate, due to incredible advances in medicine, communications, and technology, we double our knowledge every 50 years.

The second change concerns globalization, which has become the norm for successful organizations as additional countries become more active in the world economy, as different economies and markets develop, and as new economic rules and alliances emerge. One rapid change that we've explored has to do with the increasing diversity of the workforce—in terms of age, gender, race, ethnicity, and mental and physical disability. Because today's workforce is so different from that of previous generations, organizations need to make adjustments in the way they operate. In fact, the most competitive firms are likely to be those that use this incredible diversity to increase knowledge, creativity, and overall effectiveness. Organizations have to find ways to turn this diversity into a 21st-century advantage. (Recall Chapter 11, in which we examined family-friendly policies in the context of diversity.)

We have talked historically about the "Fortune 500"; we are beginning now to focus more on the "Global 500"—companies that are active across the globe, not just in the United States. Companies that aren't ready to make the changes necessitated by the technological revolution and globalization can quickly lose their competitive advantage. For instance, IBM and Apple were the undeniable leaders in the business and home computer industries in the 1980s and 1990s. However, by the early 2000s IBM was losing money on its PCs even though it had introduced personal computers years before. IBM was forced to sell its computer division to Lenovo in 2004. To IBM's credit, they repurposed themselves as a result of the changes in the industry and competition—even though the repurposing came late and after some considerable struggles. IBM now sees itself as an "innovation company" that focuses on analytics and providing clients with valuable insights from the analysis of "big data" (Manu, 2012). To take another example, The Gap has seen huge sales declines in recent years; some of the reasons include poor retail plans and designs as well as stores that are too large given the e-commerce boom (Gorenstein, 2011). They, too, are responding with serious organizational changes, including a reduction of their brand stores in North America and an increased focus on their Gap Outlet and Gap Factory stores and their online channels in efforts to rebuild their brand (Gap Inc., 2015).

One result of the technological revolution is the incredible speed with which products become obsolete. Technology changes so quickly that last year's cutting-edge product, which seemed to secure the future of one company, is completely replaced by this year's cutting-edge product, which may be developed and manufactured by a different company. If the first company is not prepared to keep pace, it can be left behind (as happened to Borders and Tower Records) and lose its competitive advantage to other companies (Amazon and Apple) that are more prepared and willing to change with the environment. The rise and fall of the dot-coms (i.e., Internet companies such as E-Toys.com, Pets.com, and CDWorld.com) exemplify this rapid change. When they were launched, these companies seemed to be market leaders with a long future; less than one year later, most of them had ceased to exist.

As for how to deal with these many fast-paced changes in the workplace, Hitt (2000) makes a few interesting suggestions. First, managers need to adopt new forms of managerial thinking that are global in orientation and allow for strategic flexibility, as well as new organizational structures. Similarly, managers have to be able to operate and thrive in environments characterized by ambiguity and uncertainty because the changes occurring in these environments are neither predictable nor amenable to deliberate step-by-step procedures. Second, organizations must have highly developed human capital. Indeed, well-trained and highly skilled employees are essential if companies are to maintain a competitive edge. Achieving this goal, of course, requires careful and thorough recruitment, selection, placement, training, and development of employees.

Finally, an emphasis on continuous learning and knowledge dissemination throughout the organization is what will set successful companies apart from those that don't survive. It's not enough for only a few employees to continue to learn; new knowledge needs to be shared throughout all levels of the organization. (We'll revisit this point later in the chapter.) In addition, Greiner and his colleagues (2003) emphasize the match among a CEO's orientation, organizational flexibility, characteristics of the team members, and the organization's change history as important to successful organizational development.

Some companies on the cutting edge actually try to stockpile employees with a vast array of knowledge and skills because they recognize that, as things change, what these individuals have to offer will become especially valuable. The ability to "think outside the box" is also important; in other words, employees and managers must be capable of coming up with creative and novel ideas. Sometimes the old ways and old approaches don't work anymore; to stay ahead, companies need to be flexible and innovative.

Let's talk a bit about innovation, which we can define as the process of developing new ideas, methods, or products. An interesting example of innovation comes from the largest consumer products company in the world, Procter and Gamble (P&G). In what it calls the biggest innovation in laundry in 25 years, P&G developed Tide Pods, which are palm-size detergent tablets to be tossed into the washing machine with no fuss or mess (Anderson, 2012). Only about 15% to 20% of all new products are successful, but P&G's rate is about 50%. Innovations like the Tide Pod can take years to refine and can cost as much as the entire first year's sales. Indeed, innovation is both important and risky; of course, you can argue that not innovating may be the riskier alternative (see Borders, Tower Records, etc.).

As a world leader in innovation, P&G spends billions of dollars on product testing. It has 25 facilities worldwide where employees watch consumers use its products (Anderson, 2012). About 50 P&G researchers work at the Beckett Ridge Innovation Center outside Cincinnati, where they watch and videotape 20,000 people per year wash dishes, wash clothes, change diapers, and so on. The 3,000-square-foot grocery store and 2,000-square-foot mock house are instrumental in the testing process and so important for innovation. Once the testing of Tide Pods was complete and the product tweaked, P&G spent $150 million on the marketing campaign before rolling it out to stores in February 2012. P&G forecasted $300 million in sales in the first year. Of course, those sales alone wouldn't cover the cost of the innovation, but if the product is successful for a few years, then the sales will more than offset the costs. The company's 2014 annual report shows that Tide Pods have grown to more than 7% of their laundry detergent business (Proctor & Gamble, 2014). They were also ranked as the #1 leader in the 2013 New Product Pacesetters list (nonfood products category). Innovation is incredibly important for companies that want to remain leaders or major players in their industries.

A recent empirical study examined the roles of transformational leadership and climate for excellence in affecting team innovation (Eisenbeiss, van Knippenberg, & Boerner, 2008). The authors studied 33 research and development teams and found that transformational leadership was

© Richard Levine/Alamy

**A CLOSER LOOK**
What practices help companies like P&G achieve a high rate of successful innovation, as exemplified by products like Tide Pods, despite the high research and development costs and potential risk of failure?

**TECHNICAL TIP**

*You will recall from the last chapter that transformational leadership describes situations in which a leader inspires exceptional performance from followers, and the leader–follower dyad together achieves more than either could alone.*

positively related to the extent to which team members perceived that there was support for innovation. When team members felt supported, they were more likely to be innovative as long as the team was focused on performance and the normative climate was one of excellence. This study suggests that team innovation is related to team-level beliefs and perceptions and leadership behaviors, but the relationships are complex ones.

Hitt (2000) concludes by saying that "[m]anagement in the new millennium must build an organization that is constantly being transformed. It must develop and respond continuously to new technologies, new markets, new businesses, and new people in the form of employees and customers" (p. 15). A recent analysis agrees with Hitt, but goes even one step further and talks about *organizational ambidexterity,* which refers to the ability of an organization to compete in both mature markets, where control and small gains are valued, and new markets, where flexibility and experimentation are necessary for large improvements (O'Reilly & Tushman, 2008). Organizational development and change are the means by which we can accomplish both of these.

Some recent work has articulated variables and processes necessary for such successful change. A study of employees from two companies—one in the automotive parts industry and the other in financial services—found that the effectiveness of managerial influence tactics was affected by leader–member exchange (LMX) (see Chapter 13 for a more detailed discussion of LMX; Furst & Cable, 2008). In particular, when employees experience high LMX, they tend not to be resistant to change tactics by the supervisor. Researchers also found that employees interpret change tactics on the part of others based on the attributions they make for the others' behaviors. In other words, employees in a positive relationship with their manager may attribute sanctions to situational factors rather than to the manager and, thus, exhibit low resistance to the change effort.

In-depth interviews of employees at all levels of a hospital found that participants emphasized three categories of variables as important to their subjective experience of change: emotional/attitudinal issues, process issues, and outcome issues (Jones et al., 2008). Participants emphasized the importance of positive attitudes toward change but warned of communication problems and conflict while noting the importance of planning and recognizing both positive and negative outcomes. A more recent study found that employees' affective experiences during phase 1 of an organizational change impacted their commitment and behavioral responses to that change during phase 2, about a year later (Seo et al., 2012). Other researchers demonstrate the importance of coping in the change process. They argue that knowing how employees appraise organizational change efforts (e.g., attitudes and cognitive evaluations) is not enough; knowing about the coping strategies used and emotional reactions is also important (Fugate, Kinicki, & Prussia, 2008).

## Models of Organizational Change

Organizational development interventions are focused on making changes in organizations. To understand how organizations change, we must understand three basic elements of the process. First, the **change agent** (sometimes called the *interventionist*)

**change agent**
The individual who initiates the change process in an organization; also called the *interventionist.*

is the individual who initiates the change process. This person is usually external to the organization, such as an organizational consultant; less often it is someone internal to the organization. On the whole, however, this person is significantly involved in diagnosing and classifying the organization's problems so as to define what changes need to be made.

As the recipient of the *change effort,* the **client** is also central to the process. This effort is most likely to have an effect if the client is receptive to it; thus, the client needs to be kept abreast of whatever ideas are being considered by the change agent. The client may be a particular individual, a work team, or perhaps the entire organization.

A key concept for organizational change that involves both the change agent and the client is called **resistance to change**, which has traditionally been defined as the state in which clients create or choose unreasonable obstacles or barriers, intent on preventing or sinking the change (Ford, Ford, & D'Amelio, 2008). The argument has always been that clients or the recipients of the change effort have to be open and willing to change or the change effort will fail—resistance to change will lead to an unsuccessful change effort.

Rather than placing all the blame on the recipients, some recent scholars take a different view, arguing that the change agent may also contribute to resistance to change through his or her attitudes, behaviors, or inaction (Ford et al., 2008). The authors also suggest that resistance to change might be a self-serving perception of change agents who are looking to blame others for ineffective change efforts; they further propose that resistance to change could be a positive thing (as healthy dissent is in other situations) that leads to altered change efforts and eventual success. They argue for a revision in how we think of resistance to change and a broader, more flexible understanding of what is involved in resistance to organizational change with the goal of improving the effectiveness of change efforts.

Finally, the **intervention** is the program or initiative suggested or implemented by the change agent. An intervention consists of sequenced activities intended to help an organization increase its effectiveness (Cummings & Worley, 2005). As such, it intentionally disrupts the status quo in its attempt to change the organization. Some recent work has taken a slightly different approach and shown that career management is important during organizational change efforts (Lips–Wiersma & Hall, 2007). Furthermore, the researchers argue from their data that individuals take more responsibility for their career development during times of organizational change. They refer to the interdependence of the employee and the organization as an "organizational dance" in which there is reciprocal influence on the career development process.

There are two well-established models of organizational change, both of which stem from the early work of Kurt Lewin. Let's consider each in turn.

**client**
The recipient of an organizational change effort in an organization.

**resistance to change**
The characteristic of some individuals who so prefer to keep things the way they are that they intentionally or otherwise work to make change more difficult and less successful.

**intervention**
The program or initiative that is suggested or implemented by the change agent in an organizational change effort.

mediaphotos/iStock/Getty Images

**A CLOSER LOOK**
We often think of resistance to change as an obstacle to overcome, but can such resistance actually be a positive and productive stance to take?

**A CLOSER LOOK**

Kurt Lewin was one of the leaders of early applied psychology involving organizational leadership and change. How has Lewin's work impacted organizational change theories and interventions?

**Lewin's Change Model** Lewin is considered a pioneer of I/O psychology because of his interest in organizational change, as well as his work on group processes and leadership. He characterized change as a matter of modifying those forces that are acting to keep things stable (Lewin, 1951). Any behavioral situation, according to Lewin, is characterized both by forces operating to maintain stability or equilibrium and by forces pushing for change. Stability results when the former win out over the latter. Lewin suggested that for planned change to occur in organizations with the least amount of tension and resistance, it is best to try to modify the forces that are maintaining the status quo rather than dramatically increasing the forces for change.

The three steps in his change process are depicted in the top panel of **Figure 14.5**. In the first of these steps, known as *unfreezing,* the forces maintaining the status quo are broken down, and the system is opened up for change. This step is often accomplished by demonstrating that the behaviors and outcomes prevalent in the organization are not consistent with the organization's goals and objectives. Once the organization has been opened up for change, the second step of the process, *moving,* begins. At this point, real organizational change begins to happen, as reflected in the new attitudes, values, and behaviors that result from the intervention. During the final step, called *refreezing,* the changes that were implemented become stabilized, and the organization reaches a new level of equilibrium.

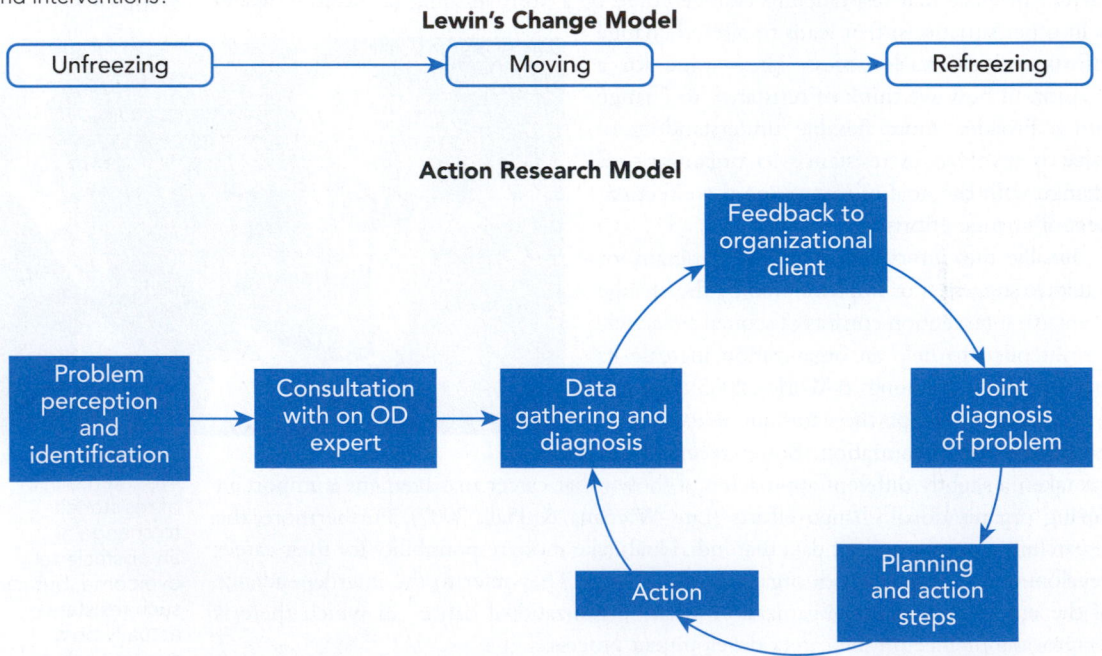

**Lewin's Change Model**

Unfreezing → Moving → Refreezing

**Action Research Model**

Problem perception and identification → Consultation with on OD expert → Data gathering and diagnosis → Feedback to organizational client → Joint diagnosis of problem → Planning and action steps → Action → (back to Data gathering and diagnosis)

**FIGURE 14.5** Change Models

Organizational policies, norms, and structures are used to support these changes, resulting in a new sense of stability. This basic three-step model, though still perceived as a major factor in organizational change processes, has been developed and enhanced by other theorists, resulting in more steps but holding to the basic premises of Lewin's early work.

**Action Research Model** In the 1940s, Lewin developed a second model of organizational change—the *action research model*. In this case, he was motivated by what he viewed as social problems that needed to be addressed from both a methodological and social perspective. Toward this end, he called for social scientists to take a more active role by combining theory building with research on real-world practical problems. Lewin died before he was able to fully develop and expand his ideas for action research, but others have followed his lead.

The major characteristic of the action research model is its cyclical nature. Initial research about the organization is the foundation on which subsequent action is built. The results of this action, in turn, provide information that can be used to guide further action—and the cyclical process continues. The various steps in the action research model are presented in the bottom panel of Figure 14.5. Here, we can clearly see a research orientation with multiple data-gathering and problem-diagnosis stages. Lewin's idea was that research informs practice—a central theme of his model. He conceived of a process whereby I/O psychologists could attain a deeper understanding of an organizational phenomenon through cycles of fact finding and taking action (Dickens & Watkins, 1999).

A recent study at the Danish Lego Company applied action research to organizational change and sensemaking, which is what employees do to gain a better understanding of their workplace (Luscher & Lewis, 2008). This process usually involves the search for information and a process of questioning that leads employees to gain a better understanding of both the problem and potential solutions. This study uncovered and demonstrated a process that makes use of paradoxes to enhance openness to organizational change among managers. This process may prove helpful to managers in understanding organizational change and how to push through the various constraints to successful change interventions.

**sensemaking**
The process whereby employees exert effort to interpret and understand work-related events.

## Organizational Development Interventions

Effective interventions can be described as those that (1) fit the needs of the organization, (2) are based on causal knowledge of intended outcomes, and (3) transfer change-management competence to organization members (Cummings & Worley, 2005). The first criterion suggests that not all interventions are right for all organizations. Indeed, an intervention is more likely to succeed if it fits with what organization members believe and perceive to be appropriate—and if they are committed to being a part of it and its eventual success.

The second criterion implies that because interventions usually have goal- or objective-based outcomes, the interventions themselves must be based on the knowledge that these outcomes will reasonably result from them. Of course, we don't always know with certainty that a particular intervention will work—especially given the complexity of human behavior in both our personal lives and our work lives.

As for the last criterion, which implies that organizational members should be better able to carry out planned change activities on their own following an intervention (Cummings & Worley, 2005), OD interventions are developed and implemented in such a way that they eventually become part of the organization's routine and thus become less driven by the OD consultant. In fact, one sign that an OD intervention has succeeded is that the OD consultant becomes more and more expendable with the passage of time. (This point needs qualifying, of course, because in situations in which new opportunities for change have developed, the further expertise of OD consultants is necessary.)

There are many different OD interventions available, and numerous experts have proposed categorical schemes for how to organize them. However, I will focus on seven of the most popular interventions here.

**Survey Feedback** One widely used intervention strategy involves the systematic collection of data via organizational surveys. These data are then summarized, analyzed, fed back to people employed by the organization, and used as a basis for planning, with the outcome being a framework for organizational changes. The steps involved in survey feedback are rather simple:

- Top management supports and actively participates in the survey process.
- An anonymous survey is administered to organization members, tapping their attitudes, perceptions, and beliefs.
- Survey results are compiled by department, plant, or demographic segment.
- The consultant provides feedback to organizational members in the form of a data compilation and summary.
- Managers, task forces, and other employees meet with the consultant to identify potential changes for implementation.

I myself have been involved in many survey feedback programs while doing work for various organizations. For instance, I did some survey work for a provider of clinical and behavioral services—a mental health clinic. I met with the chair of the task force that was charged with gathering information from employees in order to evaluate the company's strengths and weaknesses. After a couple of meetings with this individual and other task force members, I developed a 140-item survey that measured employees' levels of job satisfaction, levels of trust in management, levels of stress and tension, attitudes toward the team emphasis, beliefs about organizational citizenship behaviors (OCBs), and so on. Demographic data such as gender, age, experience, and education were also gathered.

After surveying about 200 employees, I compiled the data and presented the task force with a detailed written report of my findings; in addition, I made an onsite oral presentation to the task force members. All employees had access to the complete

**TECHNICAL TIP**

*In Chapter 2, we talked a good bit about different methods for collecting data, such as self-administered questionnaires. Typically, these questionnaires or surveys are administered to a subset of employees (a sample) and valuable data about attitudes, opinions, desires, or beliefs are obtained.*

report, as well as to a memo that I had written directly to the employees summarizing the data. Finally, I made a series of recommendations based on the data that I thought would enhance the effectiveness, morale, and productivity of this particular organization. Some of my recommendations were implemented, and I was hired two years later to develop and conduct a follow-up survey. This survey revealed that, although some employees still had concerns, the organization overall had experienced sizable improvements in the targeted areas as a result of this OD intervention.

**Team Building**  As you may recall, we discussed the organizational role played by teams in Chapter 12. Here, we're concerned specifically with team building, a technique used by organizations to develop teams or to enhance the effectiveness of existing teams. Most of the experts in this area assume that in order for work groups or teams to be successful, the members must collaborate and be interdependent. One of the best parallel examples of team building is the process through which sports teams develop. Whether they're involved in Little League, high school, college, or professional sports, team members must learn how to pool their individual abilities, coordinate their individual efforts, strive for agreed-upon goals, and establish a uniform set of work patterns and structures to maximize team performance (Forsyth, 1999). Specifically, team-building interventions focus on the following objectives:

team building
A technique used by organizations to develop teams or to enhance the effectiveness of existing teams.

- Clarifying role expectations and responsibilities among team members
- Improving supervisor–subordinate relations
- Improving problem solving, decision making, and planning by team members
- Reducing conflict among team members
- Developing a vision, mission, or set of goals
- Building cohesion and unity within the team

Team building is an extremely popular OD intervention and has been used in a variety of industries, such as hotel management, manufacturing, urban transit, health, and sports (Salas, Rozell, Mullen, & Driskell, 1999). Despite widespread practitioner enthusiasm for the effectiveness of team building, there has been little in the way of well-controlled research. Nevertheless, one meta-analysis that reviewed the studies that do exist found strong support for the impact of team building on team performance (Svyantek, Goodman, Benz, & Gard, 1999). This review also took an applied perspective and examined the role played by different organizational characteristics in affecting the relationship between team building and team performance. The results indicated that team building had a stronger impact on team performance when (1) it was initiated to correct existing problems; (2) it was combined with other OD interventions; (3) the intervention was strongly supported by members of the organization, including the immediate team supervisor; (4) it was

Gail Burton/AP Photo

**A CLOSER LOOK**
How is team building in sports similar to team building in other organizations?

implemented in a participative management climate; and (5) performance was measured at the group level.

*Outdoor experiential training (OET)* is a newer approach to team building that makes use of the outdoors and entails various physical and mental exercises, as well as group activities. A recent study found that outdoor management training (a version of OET) had a positive effect on self-efficacy, leadership motivation, and emotional intelligence (Kass & Grandzol, 2012).

**total quality management (TQM)**
An initiative that focuses on employee involvement in the control of quality in organizations; also called *continuous improvement* or *quality management*.

**Total Quality Management** Total quality management (TQM)—also called *continuous improvement* or *quality management*—focuses on employee involvement in the control of quality in organizations. Many organizations have implemented a quality initiative in which all of the organization's activities concentrate on the quality of products made or services provided. This emphasis on quality was spearheaded by the work of W. Edwards Deming and Joseph M. Juran, who presented their ideas to U.S. companies during World War II. However, their ideas were much better received by the Japanese than by Americans (Cummings & Worley, 2005). As Japanese companies became increasingly formidable in their competition with American companies (especially in the automobile industry), American executives began to take notice and, eventually, Deming's ideas were also well received in the United States.

In fact, they are now so popular that the U.S. government gives an award to companies that best meet the ideals of the TQM movement—namely, the Malcolm Baldrige National Quality Award. The criteria used for the Baldrige Award are (1) the extent to which quality values are communicated throughout the organization, (2) the organization's ability to meet customer needs, (3) the extent and caliber of the approaches used to monitor the quality of goods and services produced, (4) the effective use of data supporting the TQM system, and (5) the extent to which the full potential of employees has been utilized (Tata, Prasad, & Thorn, 1999). TQM has become a vast enterprise, including consulting firms that specialize in quality work; nationwide training programs on the basic principles of TQM; and numerous national associations, including the American Society for Quality and the Association for Quality and Participation.

TQM interventions are typically conducted in a series of stages. They begin, like many of the other programs discussed throughout this book, with the support of top management. This means that senior management must receive training on what TQM is, how it operates, and what their responsibilities are. During the second stage, employees are trained in quality methods such as *statistical process control*—a technique proposed by Deming that focuses on identifying problems reflective of a low-quality product or service.

An empirical investigation found that individual differences among those involved in the TQM effort predicted its success. In particular, employees' trust in colleagues, commitment to the organization, and higher-order-need strength were more strongly related to the effectiveness of TQM than were situational variables. Given that participants' individual differences important to the TQM process have received very little research attention, these findings suggest that we need a stronger conceptual understanding of how these and other variables operate in this context (Coyle-Shapiro & Morrow, 2003). A recent study built a conceptual understanding around person–organization (P–O) fit and argued that the components of P–O fit (which is similar to person–environment [P–E] fit, discussed in Chapter 7) should be important antecedents of one's receptivity and orientation toward TQM. These researchers found that individuals' attitudes toward TQM were at their highest when both the organization and the individual valued putting the organization first (self-transcendence) and working toward goals (goal-orientedness) (Ertürk, 2012). In an attempt to advance what we know about this process, one study of six semiconductor plants in Malaysia demonstrated that TQM practices resulted in employees' feelings of empowerment and high levels of job involvement (Boon, Arumugam, Safa, & Bakar, 2007).

Steve Vidler/Superstock

**A CLOSER LOOK**
Because Disney is so highly regarded for its customer service, it is often used as a benchmark by other companies looking to improve their customer service. What part of the TQM process does benchmarking reflect and why is it important?

The third, or active, stage involves the actual implementation of TQM processes and procedures. At this time, employees identify not only areas in which their department or division excels but also deviations from quality standards (i.e., error). The potential causes of these deviations, or *output variations,* are examined, corrected, and brought within the range of acceptable quality.

The fourth stage in the process is a self-comparison analysis whereby the organization compares its effectiveness to that of competitors that set the benchmarks for the industry. For instance, an organization attempting to improve its customer service is likely to compare its performance to Disney's benchmarks because Disney is widely recognized as a world leader in customer service (Cummings & Worley, 2005). Then, during the final stage of the process, rewards are linked to the achievement of the TQM intervention's goals. This, of course, is the main point of the whole process. Because the focus is on developing or employing a work process that produces high-quality goods and services that are as good as or better than those produced by the competition, the rewards are linked to processes that achieve those results. In the airline industry, for example, these processes would include being on time most often, having the lowest rate of lost luggage, having the fewest customer complaints, and having the smallest percentage of canceled flights.

One criticism of TQM is that it is so rational and technical in its approach that it ignores the importance of social-political conditions and the consequences of change (Knights & McCabe, 2002). A recent review was critical of the level of rigor of the research projects designed to evaluate the effectiveness of TQM initiatives (Wayhan & Balderson, 2007). However, the authors noted that more recent studies have been more sophisticated and rigorous and that they have demonstrated a link between

TQM initiatives and the firm's financial performance. A recent study of 223 CEOs of Taiwanese high-tech companies found that TQM was related to organizational learning and that both TQM and learning had positive effects on innovation performance (Hung, Lien, Wu, & Kuo, 2011).

**gainsharing**
An OD intervention that involves paying employees a bonus based on improvements in productivity.

**Gainsharing** Gainsharing is an OD intervention that involves paying employees a bonus based on improvements in productivity. This approach to increasing employee participation and benefits while also improving organizational productivity was first documented in 1935 by the Nunn-Bush Shoe Company of Milwaukee. One of the most frequently used varieties of gainsharing—the Scanlon Plan—was developed a few years later by Joseph Scanlon of the Empire Steel and Tin Plate Company of Cleveland (Gowen, 1991). The use of gainsharing continued to grow quickly after that; in fact, many contemporary organizations, such as General Electric, DuPont, Whole Foods, and General Motors, have instituted some form of gainsharing. In 1990, about 47% of American companies used some form of variable pay program; that number increased to 91% in 2014 (Aon Hewitt, 2014).

Gainsharing plans have as their basic premise a link between pay and performance—the assumption being that this link will lead to increased employee involvement and job satisfaction, as well as improved productivity and self-management. Although there are a few different types of gainsharing plans, and even these are sometimes altered to be organization-specific, most such plans have the following components in common. The first is a *suggestion system* that encourages employees to think about ways to improve productivity and then share those ideas. The second is an election of *department teams* composed of nonmanagement employees who are charged with overseeing the formal procedures used in considering, evaluating, and implementing the employees' suggestions. The third is a *review board* composed of both management and nonmanagement employees whose purpose is to improve communication between the two groups and allow management to answer questions posed by nonmanagement. By means of this review board, the two groups can educate each other about how the "other half" lives and what issues are important to them. Finally, all gainsharing plans are based on a formula that generates a *bonus pool* of dollars that are then distributed among employees.

In essence, gainsharing revolves around two factors that we've discussed at length throughout this text: participation and justice. Gainsharing programs create a sense of justice, or fairness, by distributing "gains" equally between the employer and employees. One study found that both distributive justice and procedural justice were correlated with gainsharing satisfaction across two different gainsharing organizations. Gainsharing is successful when employees have favorable reactions to it because these reactions lead to organizational commitment and trust in management, which results in greater effort and performance (Coyle-Shapiro, Morrow, Richardson, & Dunn, 2002). Indeed, the role of trust in organizational change was highlighted in one article that placed it at the center of organizational change processes (Morgan & Zeffane, 2003).

Finally, one study found that individuals opted for pay alternatives that, although more risky, had a greater potential payoff—one tied to individual rather than group performance (Kuhn & Yockey, 2003). Another study argues that the value of employee suggestions declines quickly over time and that, therefore, maintaining a stream of new suggestions is important (Arthur & Huntley, 2005).

**Technostructural Interventions** OD interventions that focus on the technology and structure of organizations have increased in popularity as organizations have become more and more focused on effectiveness, efficiency, and productivity. One basic technostructural intervention has to do with the structural design of organizations, which determines how the work of an organization progresses throughout the various layers of the organization. Some OD practitioners alter this structural design to meet particular needs or goals of an organization and its employees. The most basic version—the *functional* organizational design—is structured according to the various functions of the employees.

**Figure 14.6** provides an example of this design. Notice that the president/CEO has a number of employees (all vice presidents, or VPs) immediately below him or her and that each of these, in turn, is responsible for a particular function within the organization. For instance, someone is in charge of the manufacturing process, and someone else is in charge of marketing. The responsibilities for these different functions are independently held by various employees. Although this structure prevents duplication of labor by locating employees who are doing the same or similar jobs in the same department, it can also result in departments that become very limited

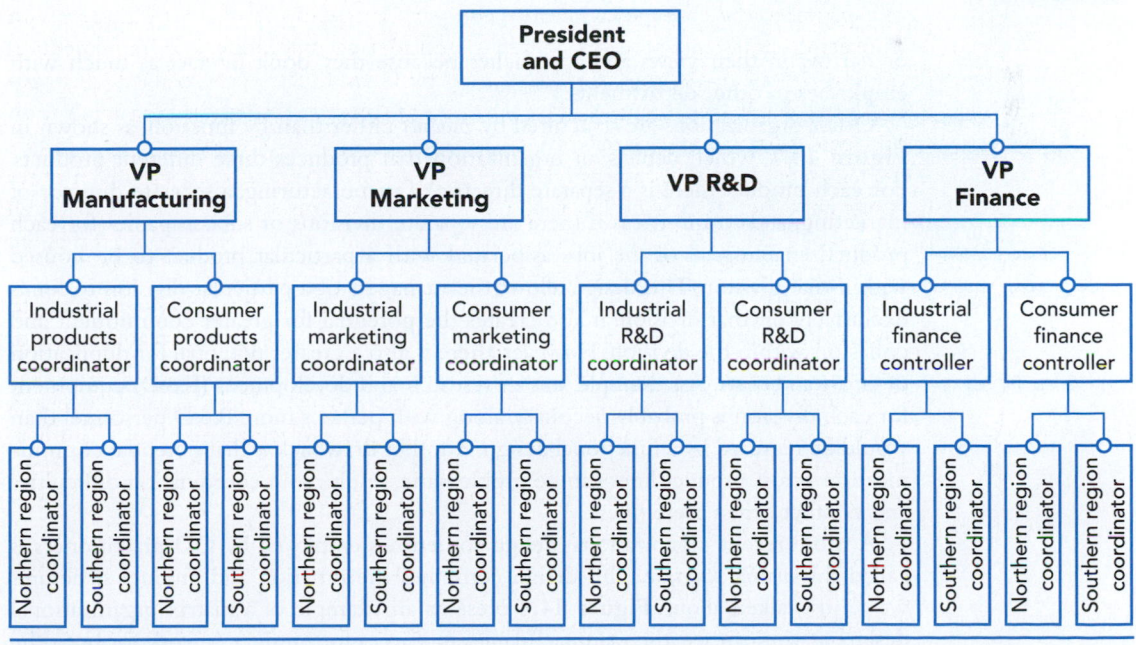

**FIGURE 14.6** Functional Organizational Design

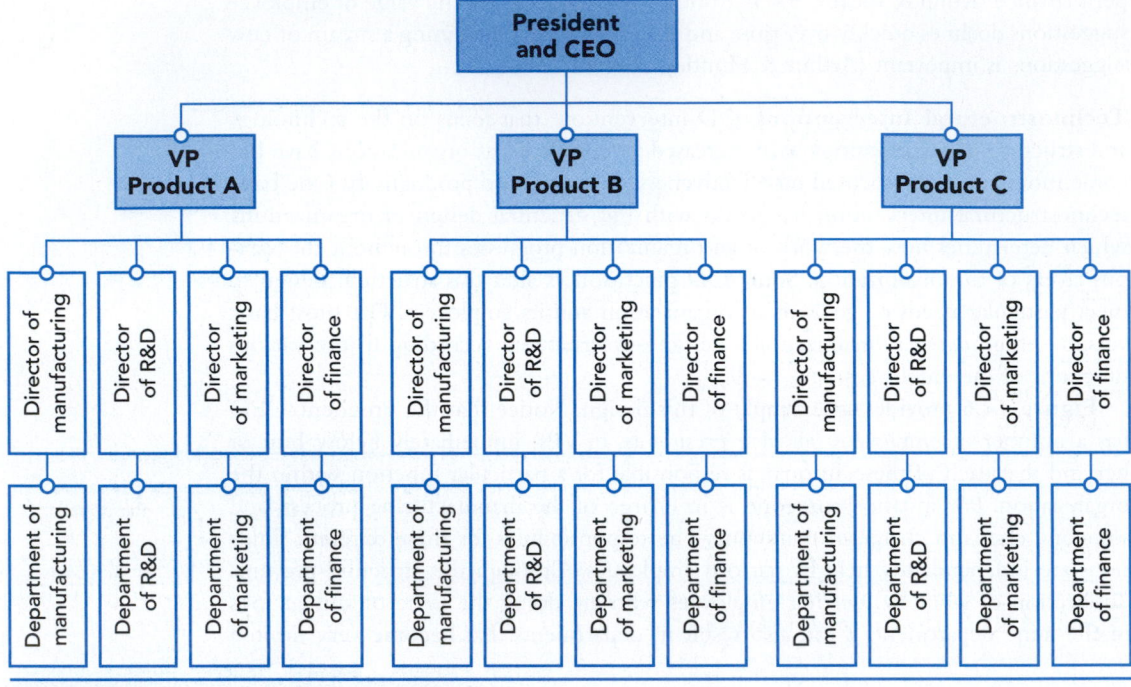

**FIGURE 14.7** Product-Based Organizational Design

or narrow in their views and approaches because they don't interact as much with employees in other departments.

Other organizations are structured by *product* rather than by function, as shown in **Figure 14.7**, which depicts an organization that produces three different products. For each product there is a separate director of manufacturing, a separate director of marketing, and so on. It's as if there are separate divisions or subcompanies for each product, enabling all of the jobs associated with a particular product to be housed within one division. This design allows the managers of a particular division to focus exclusively on that division; it also creates the potential for greater commitment and cohesion within the division. However, there is also a greater potential for duplication of effort and costs. For example, similar research and development (R&D) equipment for each division is probably necessary, along with perhaps more R&D personnel than would be required by a functional design. Another drawback is that potential communication across product lines can be problematic, resulting in coordination difficulties and conflict across these lines.

A more recent organizational design sometimes employed by OD practitioners is called the *matrix structure*. This design combines the function and product structures we've just talked about. **Figure 14.8** presents an example of a matrix organizational design; as you can see, the manufacturing employees for product A work for both the VP of manufacturing and the product A coordinator. In effect, the employees have two

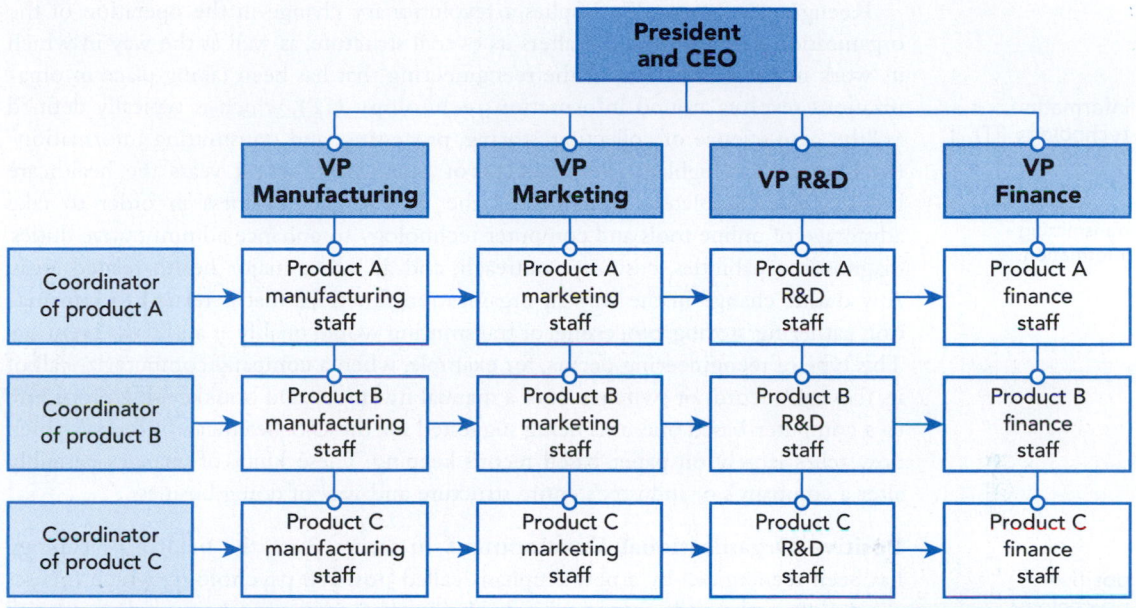

**FIGURE 14.8** Matrix Organizational Design

bosses; but this also means that the bosses—in this case, the VP of manufacturing and the product A coordinator—have to work together as supervisors because neither has ultimate authority. Reading across Figure 14.8 demonstrates product-based authority; reading down demonstrates functional-based authority. Certainly, this structure is more complex than either of the other two structures that combine to form this matrix. One advantage of this approach is that it encourages communication and cooperation between managers, thereby maintaining consistency across product lines and across functional departments. However, given its complexity, a matrix structure can be very difficult to introduce, especially in the absence of a preexisting supportive culture.

The last technostructural intervention we will consider is **reengineering**, also known as *business process redesign,* which involves the fundamental rethinking and redesign of business processes to improve critical performance as measured by cost, quality, service, and speed (Hammer & Champy, 1993). There are four elements of reengineering. First is the *fundamental* element, an examination of what the company does and why. Second is the *radical* element, a willingness to make crucial and far-reaching organizational changes rather than merely superficial changes. Third is the *dramatic* element, which focuses on making striking performance improvements rather than slight performance improvements. The last element is the idea that the reengineering intervention is centered on the *processes* of the organization, not just the tasks, jobs, or structures (Beugré, 1998). A recent study found that the communication aspects of the redesign process were especially important for the success of a reengineering effort (Kock, Danesh, & Komiak, 2008).

**reengineering**
The fundamental rethinking and redesign of business processes to improve critical performance as measured by cost, quality, service, and speed; also called *business process redesign.*

Reengineering generally implies a revolutionary change in the operation of the organization. The organization alters its overall structure, as well as the way in which its work is structured. Most of the reengineering that has been taking place in organizations revolves around **information technology (IT)**, which is typically defined as "the new science of collecting, storing, processing, and transmitting information" (McDonagh & Coghlan, 1999, p. 41). For instance, in recent years the healthcare industry has completely reengineered the way it does business in order to take advantage of online tools and computer technology to enhance administrative duties, diagnostic capabilities, customer outreach, and all other major health-related areas. Any drastic change in the way an organization functions that is related to information gathering, storing, processing, or transmitting would qualify as an IT intervention. This type of reengineering occurs, for example, when a company computerizes all of its files and records or switches from a manual inventory and bookkeeping procedure to a computer-based one, as is being suggested for the U.S. healthcare industry, which now relies largely on paper-based record keeping. These kinds of changes certainly alter a company's or industry's entire structure and way of doing business.

**Positive Organizational Development** In recent years, the field of psychology has been reenergized by a new emphasis called **positive psychology**, which focuses on the strengths and virtues of individuals rather than on their weaknesses and impairments. The assumption of positive psychology is that individuals want to be productive and lead meaningful and enriching lives. Researchers at universities like the University of Pennsylvania and the University of Michigan have been leading the way in studying positive experiences regarding the domains of love, work, and play (Positive Psychology Center, 2007).

As an offshoot of research and theorizing, positive psychology has spawned positive organizational behaviors and positive organizational scholarship (Luthans & Youssef, 2007). The notion is rather simple: Organizations can benefit from scholarship focused on positive organizational practices and behaviors. Furthermore, tools can be used by and techniques can be taught to organizational members that will allow them to be effective positive organizational change agents. This approach has become so popular in recent years that a special issue of the *Journal of Organizational Behavior* was dedicated to positive organizational behavior/scholarship in 2008. The University of Michigan's Ross School of Business has a Center for Positive Organizations (http://positiveorgs.bus.umich.edu/), and there are several conferences devoted to positive organizational research. Positive organizational scholarship focuses on emotional intelligence, creativity, wisdom, work engagement, humor, self-efficacy, optimism, hope, and resilience and how these can help individuals meet organizational demands and foster performance (Bakker & Schaufeli, 2008).

Stemming from the positive psychology movement is a newer OD technique called **appreciative inquiry (AI)**, which engages employees by focusing on positive messages, the best of what the employees have to offer, and the affirmation of past and present strengths and successes. Developed by researchers at Case Western University, it uses the art of asking questions to search for the best in people, organizations, and the world around them (Egan & Lancaster, 2005). Organizations, such as Verizon,

Avon, the U.S. Navy, and John Deere, have been identified as employing AI in their OD efforts (Egan & Lancaster, 2005).

The process is defined by four stages. First, questioning is used in *discovery* to determine the strengths of the organization and its people. Second, in the *dream* stage, the information gathered at discovery is analyzed and elaborated upon to arrive at a vision statement or focused intent. Third, this information is used to *design* innovative ways to identify where the organization should be going. Finally, the design of the future company is sustained or maintained in the *destiny* stage. The distinctive characteristic of this approach is its unyielding emphasis on positive elements, traits, experiences, and possibilities. AI is not about fixing the problems; it's about building from strengths.

Let's talk briefly about AI at American Express as an illustration of the process (for a more detailed discussion, see Giglio, Michalcova, & Yates, 2007). The CEO believed that the core values of American Express had carried the company through hard times and that reengineering employees around a "refreshed" set of core organizational values would lead them successfully into the future. American Express used the four stages I just described to change the organization. For instance, in the discovery stage, it began the process of reengaging key leaders and employees by asking participants to recall moments of peak performance, to recount when they were most proud of working for American Express, and to describe what they expected the ideal future to look like for the company.

The leaders of this intervention argue that AI promoted a sense of ownership and rallied people around a common set of core values (Giglio et al., 2007). They were amazed that leadership groups around the world identified the same core values, cultural variables, and relevant solutions—culture did not seem to be a barrier to coming together around the future of American Express. Finally, they argue that the AI approach—focusing on stories of success, integrity, and responsibility—led to growth in these values and, therefore, to a strengthening of the corporate culture (Giglio et al., 2007).

AI has grown in popularity to the point that there are multiple national centers, magazines and periodicals, and hundreds of books dedicated to explaining the AI process and how it can improve organizations. I expect that AI will continue to grow as a popular and effective OD technique—in fact, some have suggested it as the ideal technique for the current state of the world.

**Organizational Transformation** To this point, we have discussed organizational development in a somewhat traditional way. Now, however, we turn to the work of Jerry Porras, a leader in the OD field, who draws a distinction between OD and what he says is at the cutting edge of OD—namely, organizational transformation (Porras & Silvers, 1991).

Organizational transformation refers to any intervention primarily directed toward creating a new vision for an organization and changing its beliefs, purpose, and mission. OD, by contrast, focuses more on work-setting variables that are mismatched with the organization's desires (although some would say that organizational transformation is OD at a deeper level). Porras himself suggests that organizational transformation is an approach that will continue to grow in popularity as more upper-level executives recognize the need for and potential benefit of profound shifts in the vision and direction of their organizations (Porras & Silvers, 1991). Such shifts are indeed

**organizational transformation**
A term that refers to any intervention primarily directed toward creating a new vision for an organization and changing its beliefs, purpose, and mission.

## PRACTITIONER FORUM

Laura Heft

**Laura Heft**

*PhD, 1999, I/O Psychology,*
*University of Missouri, St. Louis*
*Director, Human Resources*
*Edward Jones*

One of the keys to implementing a solution that delivers sustainable results is to take a "systems" approach to the intervention. The work of organization development includes attacking a problem holistically by designing an intervention (or series of interventions) aimed at addressing the multiple factors that influence the organization's ability to perform (e.g., work process, culture, talent, structure). An example is provided below.

In an important area of our business, sluggish results, changing market conditions, and opportunities to leverage new social media technologies required a change in our strategy. The process began with the establishment of a senior-level task force to diagnose and analyze the root cause. After the problem and the contributing factors were deeply understood, a new leader was brought in to develop a vision for the future and put it into action.

The change was substantial and required a complete reengineering of the area. In order to implement the new strategy, changes were needed in how the work was done (new processes and job redesign), where the work was done (move from centralized to decentralized, geographically dispersed work), and by whom (new skills sets and expertise were required to do the work).

The existing employees in the area were evaluated and then assigned to new roles or redeployed to other jobs in the firm. As the change was being implemented, the impact on employees was monitored through the administration of an employee survey, which was subsequently repeated at relevant intervals. The senior leader took responsibility for the results of the survey

and developed action plans to respond to issues that emerged.

Another part of the change intervention included team development meetings with the senior leadership team. These meetings were designed to help the team come together to identify new objectives for the work, clarify roles, and develop guidelines on how the team was going to communicate and work together (i.e., establishing a new culture). Within six months, this new area was beginning to see results.

Frequently, large-scale organizational changes are not proactively managed and, as a result, are not successful. Leaders are often reluctant to tackle the complexity and scope of the entire integrated system and instead opt for addressing only part of the solution. The early success of this intervention is most likely attributable to the "systems" approach taken to align the work, talent, goals, and culture in an integrated way to execute on the strategy.

### Applying Your Knowledge

1. How does the "systems" approach implemented by Edward Jones align with open-system theory, discussed earlier in the chapter? Use Figure 14.4 to diagram the change implemented at Edward Jones to solve this problem.

2. What role did leadership play in implementing change? Do you think it's possible to implement large-scale change without strong centralized leadership?

3. How did this change plan try to account for resistance to change? How important do you think accounting for such resistance is to implementing a successful change strategy? Why?

becoming commonplace in today's organizations as they find themselves in the center of a changing world that is becoming more knowledge-intensive, fast-paced, global, and dynamic (Karakas, 2009).

Organizational transformation usually results from a serious jolt to a company that prompts the CEO and other senior executives to change their business strategy and, with that, their mission and vision for the company. At the forefront of many attempts at organizational transformation is culture change, the alteration of a pattern of beliefs, values, norms, and expectations shared by organizational members. The culture of an organization evolves historically, stemming directly from the leaders, and often founders, of a company. Several companies are famous for their organizational cultures; examples include Disney, Nordstrom, IBM, and Apple. In some cases, the culture is so much a part of the company that it can't be changed.

In fact, there are experts who believe that culture change, in general, is too difficult and never very likely to be successful. Others, however, recognize its difficulty but embrace its potential and believe in its usefulness. Although an organization's culture can be instrumental in a company's success (as is true of the companies just mentioned), it can also be detrimental, leading companies to attempt to change the ineffective culture. Finally, because of the complexities involved, culture change itself can lead to many unintended consequences, such as behavioral compliance and cultural erosion (Harris & Ogbonna, 2002). In the last decade, large investment banks have served as a good example of this idea: They made some changes that were quite risky (various types of mortgages to "unqualified" people) and resulted, in part, in the market crash of 2008 and serious consequences for customers and the organizations themselves.

T. G. Cummings and C. G. Worley (2005) present an excellent list of the determinants of successful culture change. First, the organization and change agent must develop a clear vision of the new strategy, as well as of the shared values, attitudes, and action steps needed to make it a reality. Second, as with any organizational intervention, culture change is likely to succeed only with support from top management; in fact, this is especially the case with culture change. Third, senior executives not only have to support the culture-change efforts but also must live by them. Instead of just paying lip service to the changes in attitudes and behaviors, these executives need to implement them, believe in them, and demonstrate their complete alignment with them in their day-to-day activities. Fourth, the supportive systems of the organization must be intricately involved in the financial and control systems, and management systems must provide the support and resources necessary to give the culture change an opportunity for success.

The fifth determinant of culture change has to do with issues of selection. Because it is important that new hires be socialized into the new culture rather than into the culture that is being left behind, consideration should be given to hiring employees (especially at higher levels) based on their match to or consistency with the new shared values, beliefs, and behaviors. Furthermore, employees who don't fit with the new culture should be let go. Senior employees who prefer the old culture and don't see the need or opportunity for change are often leaders in the resistance against change—a situation that is very detrimental to the change process. Karakas (2009) says it very well: "Too many of the problems in societies today stem from management that is ill prepared to deal with the chaos and complexity of today's world. We suffer from the lack of new managers equipped with new roles, qualifications, capacities, and skills" (p. 17). The worst oil spill in history took place in 2010 when an explosion on the Deepwater Horizon oil drilling rig claimed the lives of 11 employees and sent oil spewing into the sea for 87 days. Some argue that this catastrophe was exacerbated because BP was not prepared to deal with such a potentially catastrophic accident.

**culture change**
The alteration of a pattern of beliefs, values, norms, and expectations shared by organizational members.

Various analyses of the accident have pointed to three contributing causes: the riskiness of oil drilling, regulatory challenges, and human and organizational factors (Tilcsik & Cleafield, 2015). The human errors (such as only seeing what one wanted to see and misinterpreting the results of critical safety tests) took place within a culture that was totally focused on minimizing costs and preventing injuries rather than preventing catastrophe. Organizational change and transformation are key to preparing managers, organizations, and employees to be better equipped.

A second approach to organizational transformation that has taken companies by storm is **knowledge management**—a method in which organizations enhance their operations through attempts to generate, transform, disseminate, and use knowledge (Geisler, 2007). Although there is widespread belief in the effectiveness of knowledge management and its close cousin, *learning organizations,* these concepts have just begun to be tested and written about in recent years. For instance, a recent study supported the idea that how individuals in an organization allocate attention to various problems is important and that the overlap between an employee's expertise and the expertise needed to solve a given problem explains why some problems receive more attention than others (Haas, Criscuolo, & George, 2015). Technology companies have focused resources in this area and have developed many, many software products focused on knowledge management and learning initiatives (e.g., Capterra, http://www.capterra.com/knowledge-management-software/). Recent studies have begun to look at the role of social technology (such as social media) in knowledge management and learning. McKinsey's Global Institute, for example, has published a report that focuses on the use of social technology to improve business and knowledge management (McKinsey Global Institute, 2012). Experts agree that learning organizations tend to be characterized by (1) an organizational structure that facilitates learning, (2) a sophisticated information system that allows companies to manage knowledge for a competitive advantage, (3) a human resources system that promotes and rewards employees for continuous learning and knowledge management, (4) a strong organizational culture that fosters openness and creativity, and (5) supportive leaders who are active participants in learning and knowledge management (Cummings & Worley, 2005).

As Lew Platt, former CEO of Hewlett-Packard (HP), put it: "Successful companies of the 21st century will be those who do the best jobs of capturing, storing, and leveraging what their employees know" (quoted in Martiny, 1998, p. 71). In 1996, Hewlett-Packard (HP) embarked on a knowledge-management initiative that was designed to deliver more value to customers, bring more intellectual capital to solutions, and create an enthusiastic environment about knowledge sharing. The HP credo for this initiative was to make "the knowledge of the few, the knowledge of the many" (Martiny, 1998, p. 72). Knowledge management has been successfully integrated into the business strategy of HP and many other organizations as well (HP Knowledge Management, 2014). Its importance at General Electric, for example, is attested to by the fact that knowledge management was one of three business processes for which former CEO Jack Welsh took personal responsibility (Stewart, 2000).

**knowledge management**
A method in which organizations enhance their operations through attempts to develop, disseminate, and use knowledge.

A CLOSER LOOK
Labeling their employees "knowledge assets" is not a characteristic of a learning organization. What are the five characteristics of learning organizations?

Knowledge management has become such an integral part of organizations that many companies have created a new position—that of "chief knowledge officer," who is responsible for spearheading knowledge and learning initiatives. Most large companies have chosen to invest in knowledge management in the last 10–15 years. The list of companies in *KMWorld*'s list of 100 companies that matter most in knowledge management, as indicated by the tools they offer to their customers, includes industry leaders like Apple, HP, IBM, Oracle, and Hyland (McKellar, 2015). Microsoft argues that productivity has been increased due to knowledge management because it saves time while maintaining quality and predictability (Hainey, 2015). Even the United States Agency for International Development (USAID) argues that knowledge is one of the most important assets for addressing global health challenges and they suggest that the management of knowledge will impact the health, social, and economic status of the entire world (K4Health, 2016).

According to John Peetz, the former chief knowledge officer at Ernst & Young, knowledge management was one of four core work processes at that company: sell work, do work, manage people, and manage knowledge. Among his job duties was evangelizing about the importance of sharing knowledge, as well as managing and backing projects that found, published, and distributed knowledge throughout the firm (Stewart, 1998). Although it appears clear to organizations that managing and sharing knowledge are important to maintaining a competitive edge, one successful and respected management guru, Jeffrey Pfeffer, suggests that organizations need to go one step beyond knowledge management. Pfeffer argues that knowing what to do is not enough; organizations must also put that knowledge to good use. In short, truly successful and cutting-edge organizations must work to bridge the knowing–doing gap (Pfeffer & Sutton, 2013).

Recently, knowledge management has been linked to innovation, which is of paramount importance to all organizations (du Plessis, 2007). Knowledge management provides the tools and processes to ensure that knowledge is both available and accessible for use in the creation of new knowledge. Others argue that tacit knowledge—know-how acquired through experience that is hard to communicate to others—is intricately linked to innovation and leads to competitive advantage (Seidler-de Alwis & Hartmann, 2008).

Learning companies that have a handle on knowledge can respond faster and more effectively to the chaos and dynamics of current organizations, markets, and industries. It is widely believed that organizational culture plays an important role in the learning and innovation process and multiple recent studies have explored these links. One empirical study interviewed 451 CEOs of Spanish organizations and found a positive effect of organizational culture on organizational learning; organizational learning, in turn, had a positive effect on technical innovation (Sanz-Valle, Naranjo-Valencia, Jiménez-Jiménez, & Perez-Caballero, 2011). Specifically, the authors found that organizational learning mediated the relationship between organizational culture and technical innovation. A more recent study of HR directors, technology management directors, and CEOs from a variety of industries in Spain found that knowledge-oriented leadership impacted knowledge-management practices, which has a positive effect on innovation (Donate & Sánchez de Pablo, 2015). The implication of this work is that through the use of knowledge development and management practices companies can increase their product innovation. Another recent study was able to connect knowledge management to interpersonal processes at work, which in turn improved innovation (Fu, 2015). Taking a slightly different approach, a recent study found that when companies in similar industries exist in close geographical proximity to each other (e.g., the Research Triangle in North Carolina) there is more learning and sharing of information, resulting in improved innovation (Lai, Hsu, Lin, Chen, & Lin, 2014).

## Summary

This chapter presents information about two related organizational topics: organizational theory and organizational development. These were defined and discussed in terms of their importance to the effectiveness of organizations. I then presented three organizational theories: classical organizational theory, with its emphasis on Scientific Management and bureaucracy, and the more recent approaches known as humanistic theory and open-system theory.

Before discussing various techniques of organizational development, I spent considerable time highlighting reasons why companies, if they are to be successful, must pursue OD. I also presented examples of companies that have succeeded in part because of OD, as well as examples of companies that did not succeed owing to a lack of flexibility and willingness to change. In this context, I provided a detailed discussion of Lewin's general change model and the more well-developed action research model.

Next, I considered some of the most frequently used OD interventions, such as survey feedback, team building, total quality management, and gainsharing; empirical support was cited, along with a description of their potential benefits and disadvantages. I also introduced more recently conceived OD interventions such as reengineering, information technology, and appreciative inquiry. Finally, I discussed organizational transformation in the context of interventions that profoundly change the nature of the organization. Here, I discussed the role of culture change and knowledge management specifically as determinants of organizational innovation.

## Key Terms

appreciative inquiry (AI) (p. 496)

change agent (p. 484)

client (p. 485)

culture change (p. 499)

delegation of authority (p. 472)

division of labor (p. 471)

gainsharing (p. 492)

information technology (IT) (p. 496)

intervention (p. 485)

knowledge management (p. 500)

micro-managers (p. 472)

organizational development (OD) (p. 479)

organizational theory (p. 469)

organizational transformation (p. 497)

positive psychology (p. 496)

reengineering (p. 495)

resistance to change (p. 485)

sensemaking (p. 487)

span of control (p. 472)

team building (p. 489)

total quality management (TQM) (p. 490)

## TAKING IT TO THE FIELD

Organizational development is an area that seems straightforward at first; however, each intervention requires a number of steps that can become quite complex, especially for large organizations. Gavin McBride, the CEO of Arianda Software, has asked for your help in implementing an intervention in his own I/O firm. Read through the information he has provided, and answer his questions.

Hello—

Thanks for being willing to help Arianda Software with our project. I think we really need to make some changes to serve our customers better.

Here at Arianda we pride ourselves on the excellent customer service we offer to companies that buy our software products. At our customer service center, knowledgeable consultants walk clients through problems, either online or over the phone. In the past, we put out a new version of our software every few years. Now, we can send companies updates on almost a weekly basis. Troubleshooting instructions typically change with each update, and our staff needs to stay on top of these changes so they can help our customers. We need an efficient, reliable system to deliver the important information for each update to our consultants, when they need them.

I've been hearing a lot about knowledge management and learning organizations. To help me decide what direction to go in, I'd love your thoughts on the following questions:

1. What is knowledge management, and would this help us with our problem?
2. What might be some tools that we could use to implement an effective knowledge-management system? What steps would you suggest we take to determine how best to craft this system?

*(continued)*

3. What steps would we need to take to implement this major culture change in our organization?

I look forward to your response. This seems promising, but I want to make sure that I don't jump onto a fad that won't actually solve our problem.

Best,
Gavin

## Critical Thinking Questions

1. The similar-sounding concepts of organizational change, organizational development, and organizational transformation are all discussed in the chapter. How do these three concepts differ? How are they similar?

2. Frederick Taylor's concept of Scientific Management was one of the earliest theories in the history of I/O psychology. Since then, how have organizational theories developed from the foundation laid by Scientific Management? To what extent do later theories draw on or diverge from the concepts of Scientific Management?

3. This chapter provides a number of different organizational structures or designs that companies might adopt (e.g., hierarchical, matrix, functional organizational designs, holacracy). Choose two organizational structures/designs to compare. How are these two types of organizational structures different? What are the advantages and disadvantages of each? If you were designing an organization, which would you select and why?

4. Total quality management (TQM) is one type of organizational development intervention discussed in the chapter. It is widely used and believed to be highly effective. What makes TQM so effective? How do the components of TQM influence or enhance organizations?

5. One approach to organizational change—appreciative inquiry (AI)—is becoming increasingly popular in a wide variety of organizations. This approach incorporates the input and perspectives of not only managers and organizational leaders but also employees throughout the organization. Drawing on concepts you have learned throughout the book, what do you think some outcomes of this employee participation might be? In other words, when given the chance to provide their input in organizational change initiatives, how might individual employees benefit?

## Application Questions

1. Think of a time when you had to deal with a bureaucracy. What did you need to do? Did you see any reason for that bureaucracy's existence?

2. Have you ever been in an organization that was undergoing an organizational development intervention? What happened? How did employees react?

**3.** Consider an organization where you have worked. Do you think this organization was a "learning organization"? Why or why not?

**4.** Consider positive organizational development. Do you believe people should spend more time focusing on using their strengths or addressing their weaknesses? Why?

**5.** Imagine you work for a company that uses gainsharing. Do you think you would like it? Why or why not?

## Suggested Readings

**Bakker, A. B., & Schaufeli, W. B.** (2008). Positive organizational behavior: Engaged employees in flourishing organizations. *Journal of Organizational Behavior, 29*, 147–154. This article is the introduction to the journal's special issue on positive organizational behavior. The entire journal issue is fascinating stuff.

**Cummings, T., & Worley, C.** (2014). *Organization development and change.* Cengage learning. This book is an extremely readable overview of organizational change and OD.

**Easterby-Smith, M., & Lyles, M. A.** (2011). *Handbook of organizational learning and knowledge management* (2nd ed.). West Sussex, UK: Wiley. A thorough discussion of the recent work focused on learning and knowledge management in organizations. This compilation is current and very informative.

**Hitt, M. A.** (2000). The new frontier: Transformation of management for the new millennium. *Organizational Dynamics, 28*(3), 7–17. This stimulating review of issues confronting organizations includes suggestions from an expert about how to approach such issues in the 21st century.

**Katz, D., & Kahn, R. L.** (1978). *The social psychology of organizations* (2nd ed.). New York: Wiley. Though not an easy read, this classic text is still recognized as the authority on organizational topics such as change, development, power, structure, and groups.

**Luthans, F., & Youssef, C. M.** (2007). Emerging positive organizational behavior. *Journal of Management, 33,* 321–349. This is a terrific introduction and review of the whole positive organizational behavior movement.

# Glossary

**360-degree feedback** A method of performance appraisal in which multiple raters at various levels of the organization evaluate a target employee and the employee is provided with feedback from these multiple sources

**active learning** Resources and activities, such as practice, problem solving, written communication, and verbal interactions, intended to improve analysis and synthesis of information

**actual criterion** Our best real-world representative of the ultimate criterion, which we develop to reflect or overlap with the ultimate criterion as much as possible

**adverse impact** The most accepted operationalization of discrimination, defined in the EEOC Guidelines as the "80% rule of thumb"; a selection battery exhibits adverse impact (i.e., discriminates) against a group if the selection rate for that group is less than 80% of the selection rate for the group with the highest selection rate

**affective commitment** Emotional attachment to an organization, characterized by a strong belief in and acceptance of the organization's goals and values, a willingness to exert effort on behalf of the organization, and a strong desire to remain a part of the organization

**affective disposition** The tendency to respond to classes of environmental stimuli in predetermined, affect-based ways

**affirmative action (AA)** A practice employed in many organizations to increase the number of minorities or protected class members in targeted jobs

**appreciative inquiry (AI)** The art and practice of using questions to help an organization enhance its positive potential

**archival research** Research relying on secondary data sets that were collected either for general or specific purposes identified by an individual or organization

**Army Alpha and Army Beta** Mental ability tests developed by I/O psychologists during World War I that were used to select and classify army personnel

**assessment center (AC)** An approach or method in which multiple raters (*assessors*) evaluate applicants or incumbents (*assessees*) on a standardized set of predictors (*exercises*)

**attitude** The degree of positive or negative feeling or belief a person has toward a particular person, place, or thing

**attribute** A dimension along which individuals can be measured and along which they vary

**authentic leadership** Leading through one's own personal, genuine style that engenders trust in followers and builds relationships

**BARS** A performance appraisal format that uses behavioral descriptors for evaluation

**base rate** The percentage of current employees who are successful on the job

**behavior description interview** An interviewing technique that relies on candidates sharing examples of past behaviors related to tasks required for the new job

**behavior theories** Leadership theories that focus on identifying what leaders actually do, in the hope that this approach will provide a better understanding of leadership processes

**biodata** Personal history information obtained through a biographical information blank (BIB) that asks respondents about their attitudes, hobbies, experiences, and so on

**biographical information** In the context of selection, any information that is descriptive of an individual's personal history

**bona fide occupational qualification (BFOQ)** A characteristic, such as one's gender, religion, or national origin, that is required or necessary to effectively do the job

**brainstorming** A technique in which all members of a group generate potential solutions without fear of having their suggestions criticized by other members

**burnout** A condition that occurs when employees become so stressed that they experience emotional exhaustion, depersonalization, and a sense of reduced personal accomplishment

**case studies** Examinations of a single individual, group, company, or society

**causal inference** A conclusion, drawn from research data, about the likelihood of a causal relationship between two variables

**central tendency** The tendency to use only the midpoint of the scale in rating one's employees

**change agent** The individual who initiates the change process in an organization; also called the *interventionist*

**clerical ability** A specific cognitive ability, relevant for jobs such as secretary, administrative assistant, and bookkeeper, involving a focus on both perceptual speed and accuracy in processing verbal and numerical data

**client** The recipient of an organizational change effort in an organization

**coaching** One-on-one collaborative relationship in which an individual provides performance-related guidance to an employee

**coefficient of determination** The percentage of variance in a criterion that is accounted for by a predictor

**cohesion** The strength of members' motivation to maintain membership in a group and of the links or bonds that have developed among the members

**Common-Metric Questionnaire (CMQ)** A worker-oriented job analysis instrument that attempts to improve the generalizability of worker-oriented approaches through the use of items focused on slightly less general work behaviors

**comparable worth** A doctrine maintaining that jobs of equal (or comparable) worth to the organization should be compensated equally

**compensable factors** Dimensions or factors that are used to rate jobs, indicating that employees are compensated based on these factors; examples include effort, skill, responsibility, and working conditions

**competencies** The skills, behaviors, and capabilities that allow employees to perform specific functions

**composite criterion** A weighted combination of multiple criteria that results in a single index of performance

**computer adaptive testing** The process through which computer technology is used to identify easier and harder questions for applicants that eventually estimate their true ability level

**concurrent validity** The extent to which a test predicts a criterion that is measured at the same time that the test is conducted

**consideration** The extent to which leaders act in a supportive way and show concern and respect for their subordinates

**construct validity** The extent to which a test measures the underlying construct that it was intended to measure

**construct** An abstract quality, such as intelligence or motivation, that is not observable and is difficult to measure

**content validity** The degree to which a test or predictor covers a representative sample of the quality being assessed

**context** The social-psychological climate in which performance appraisal takes place

**contextual performance** Activities performed by employees that help to maintain the broader organizational, social, and psychological environment in which the technical core operates

**contingency theories** Leadership theories that differ from both trait and behavioral theories by formally taking into account situational or contextual variables

**continuance commitment** Attachment to an organization as a function of what the employee has invested in it; also called *sunk-costs commitment*

**continuous learning** Directed and long-term effort to learn; stems from an intense desire to acquire knowledge and improve results and from participation in activities that facilitate learning

**convergent validity** The degree to which a measure of the construct in which we are interested is related to measures of other, similar constructs

**coping** Efforts that help people manage or reduce stress

**correlation coefficient (r)** A statistic that measures the strength and direction of the relationship between two variables

**counterproductive work behaviors (CWBs)** Any behaviors that bring, or are intended to bring, harm to an organization, its employees, or its stakeholders

**criteria** Evaluative standards that can be used as yardsticks for measuring an employee's success or failure

**criterion contamination** A condition in which things measured by the actual criterion are not part of the ultimate criterion

**criterion deficiency** A condition in which dimensions in the ultimate measure are not part of or are not captured by the actual measure

**critical incidents** Examples of job performance used in behaviorally anchored rating scales or job-analytic approaches

**culture change** The alteration of a pattern of beliefs, values, norms, and expectations shared by organizational members

**cybervetting** The use of social media as part of background investigations used to make employee selection decisions

**deduction** An approach to science in which we start with theory and propositions and then collect data to test those propositions—working from theory to data

**delegation of authority** An approach whereby supervisors assign particular tasks to separate employees and hold them responsible for completing these tasks

**dependent variable** The variable of interest, or what we design experiments to assess

**Dictionary of Occupational Titles (DOT)** A tool developed by the Department of Labor in the 1930s that has been used to classify occupations and jobs, consisting of narrative descriptions of tasks, duties, and working conditions of about 12,000 jobs

**disparate impact cases** Cases involving employment procedures that apparently unintentionally discriminate against or unfairly affect a minority group

**disparate treatment cases** Cases involving discrimination that results from intentional differential treatment or behavior

**dissertation** A unique piece of scholarly research that is usually the last hurdle before obtaining a PhD

**distributed practice** Training in which the practice is divided into segments, usually with rest periods in between

**distributional errors** Rating errors, such as severity, central tendency, and leniency, that result from a mismatch between actual rating distributions and expected rating distributions

**divergent validity** The degree to which a measure of the construct in which we are interested is unrelated to measures of other, dissimilar constructs

**division of labor** An approach whereby each job in a bureaucratic organization is a specialized position with its own set of responsibilities and duties

**dual-earner couple** A couple in which both members are employed and maintain a family life

**dynamic criteria** Measures reflecting performance levels that change over time

**effective leadership** Usually operationalized as the successful long-term performance of the leader's work group or subordinates

**emotion regulation** The ways in which individuals monitor their emotions and the expression of those emotions

**emotional intelligence (EI)** The ability, capacity, or skill to identify and manage one's own emotions and understand the emotions of others

**emotional labor** The effort, planning, and control required by employees to express organizationally desired emotions during interpersonal interactions

**emotion-focused coping** A coping style that involves cognitive, or thought-related, strategies that minimize the emotional effects of stress-inducing events

**employment at-will** A common law doctrine stating that employers and employees have the right to initiate and terminate the employment relationship at any time, for any reason or for no reason at all

**element** In job analysis, the smallest unit of work activity

**equity sensitivity** An individual difference indicating the extent to which people are affected by overreward or underreward situations

**essential functions** Tasks that are significant and meaningful aspects of the job

**expatriates** Employees who are temporarily working and residing in a foreign country

**expectancy** An individual's belief about the likelihood of achieving a desired performance level when exerting a certain amount of effort

**experience sampling methodology (ESM)** A technique that allows researchers to obtain repeated real-time reports of phenomena such as moods and emotions through the use of technology such as smartphones and other mobile devices

**experimental methods** Research procedures that are distinguished by random assignment of participants to conditions and the manipulation of independent variables

**external validity** The extent to which the results obtained in an experiment generalize to other people, settings, and times

**extraneous variable** Anything other than the independent variable that can contaminate our results or be thought of as an alternative to our causal explanation; also called a *confounding* variable

**feedback environment (FE)** The contextual aspects of the day-to-day supervisor–subordinate and coworker–coworker feedback process

**feedback orientation (FO)** An individual's overall receptivity to feedback

**field experiment** An approach to research that employs the random assignment and manipulation of an experiment, but does so outside the laboratory

**Frame of Reference (FOR) Training** A type of training designed to enhance raters' observational and categorization skills so that all raters share a common view and understanding of performance levels to improve rater accuracy

**free riding** A situation that occurs when employees do less than their share of the work but still share equally in the rewards

**Functional Job Analysis (FJA)** A highly structured task-oriented approach developed by Sidney Fine in which data are obtained about what tasks a worker does and how those tasks are performed

**gainsharing** An OD intervention that involves paying employees a bonus based on improvements in productivity

**glass ceiling** Refers to a situation in which qualified individuals are prevented from truly achieving all that they can because of some form of discrimination

**group tests** Tests in which many applicants can be tested at one time

**groupthink** A mode of thinking that individuals engage in when the desire to agree becomes so dominant in a cohesive group that it tends to override the realistic appraisal of alternative courses of action

**growth need strength** The extent to which individuals value higher-order needs or desire to fulfill them

**halo** The rating error that results from either (1) a rater's tendency to use his or her global evaluation of a ratee in making dimension-specific ratings for that ratee or (2) a rater's unwillingness to discriminate between independent dimensions of a ratee's performance

**human capital** The education, training, and experiences of individual employees that provide value to organizations

**hypothesis** A tentative statement about the relationship between two or more variables

**implicit leadership theory (ILT)** A leadership theory that views leadership as the outcome of a perceptual process involving both leaders and subordinates

**in-basket** An individual exercise in which assessees are asked to act as a manager in a particular company with certain issues or ideas that need to be considered and responded to

**incumbents** Employees who are currently occupying the job of interest

**independent variable** A variable that is systematically manipulated by the experimenter or, at the least, measured by the experimenter as an antecedent to other variables

**individual tests** Tests that are administered to one person at a time

**induction** An approach to science that consists of working from data to theory

**industrial/organizational (I/O) psychology** The application of psychological principles and theories to the workplace

**information technology (IT)** The science of collecting, storing, processing, and transmitting information

**informed consent** Participants signifying (usually in writing) their willingness and desire to participate in a particular research study after being provided with important and relevant information about the risks, procedures, and benefits of such participation

**initiating structure** Behaviors through which leaders define their own and their subordinates' roles in achieving the group's formal goals

**instrumentality** The perceived relationship between the performance of a particular behavior and the likelihood that a certain outcome will result from that behavior

**instructional design** A set of events that facilitate training through their impact on trainees

**integrity tests** Tests used in an attempt to predict whether an employee will engage in counterproductive or dishonest work-related behaviors such as cheating, stealing, or sabotage; also called honesty tests

**internal consistency** An indication of the extent to which individual test items seem to be measuring the same thing

**internal validity** The extent to which we can draw causal inferences about our variables

**interrater reliability** The extent to which multiple raters or judges agree on ratings made about a particular person, thing, or behavior

**intervention** The program or initiative that is suggested or implemented by the change agent in an organizational change effort

**interviews** Procedures designed to predict future performance based on an applicant's oral responses to a series of oral questions

**job** A collection of positions similar enough to one another to share a common job title

**job analysis** The process of defining a job in terms of its component tasks or duties and the knowledge or skills required to perform them

**job crafting** The process through which employees are allowed to customize, modify, and craft their own job with respect to tasks, responsibilities, and processes

**job description** As an outcome of job analysis, a written statement of what jobholders actually do, how they do it, and why they do it

**Job Element Method (JEM)** A worker-oriented approach to job analysis that was designed to identify the characteristics of superior workers in a particular job

**job enrichment** The process of increasing the motivating potential of jobs, often by strengthening the key motivating characteristics identified by job characteristics theory

**job evaluation** As an outcome of job analysis, a technique that attempts to determine the value or worth of particular jobs to organizations so that salaries can be set accordingly

**job involvement** The extent to which employees are cognitively engaged in their jobs

**job satisfaction** A pleasurable, positive emotional state resulting from the cognitive appraisal of one's job or job experiences

**job specifications** An outcome of job analysis delineating the KSAOs deemed necessary to perform a job; often called job specs

**knowledge management** A method in which organizations enhance their operations through attempts to develop, disseminate, and use knowledge

**KSAOs** The knowledge, skills, abilities, and other characteristics that are required for successful job performance

**leaderless group discussion (LGD)** A group exercise designed to tap managerial attributes that requires the interaction of a small group of individuals

**leader–member exchange (LMX) theory** A theory about work dyads that focuses on the relationships between subordinates and leaders rather than on leader behaviors or traits

**leadership self-efficacy (LSE)** The perceived capabilities of an individual to successfully accomplish leadership tasks

**leadership** A social process through which an individual intentionally exerts influence over others to structure their behaviors and relationships

**learning** The relatively permanent change in behavior that occurs as a result of experience or practice

**leniency** The rating error that results when (1) the mean of one's ratings across ratees is higher than the mean of all ratees across all raters or (2) the mean of one's ratings is higher than the midpoint of the scale

**manipulation** The systematic control, variation, or application of independent variables to different groups of participants

**massed practice** Training in which all the practice takes place at one time, without breaks

**mean** The arithmetic average of a group of scores, typically the most useful measure of central tendency

**measurement** The assignment of numbers to objects or events using rules in such a way as to represent specified attributes of the objects

**mechanical ability** A specific cognitive ability involving a focus on mechanical relations, recognition of tools used for various purposes, and sometimes actual mechanical skills

**median** The score in the middle of the distribution

**mental model** An organized knowledge structure that helps an individual make sense of the world around him or her

**meta-analysis** A methodology that is used to conduct quantitative literature reviews

**micro-managers** Managers who, instead of delegating individual tasks to employees, try to take charge of all tasks

**mindguard** A member of a cohesive group whose job it is to protect the group from outside information that is inconsistent with the group's views

**mode** The most frequent single score in a distribution

**multiple cutoff approach** A noncompensatory model of employee selection in which "passing scores," or cutoffs, are set on each predictor

**multiple hurdle approach** A rendition of the multiple cutoff approach in which the predictors are administered in a predetermined order and applicants are measured on the next predictor only if they scored above the cutoff on the previous predictor

**multiple regression** A statistical technique that, when used in the selection context, allows us to estimate how well a series of predictors forecasts a performance criterion

**multiteam systems** Tightly coupled teams that work on collective goals

**need** A force that organizes perceptions, beliefs, cognitions, and actions, giving rise to behaviors that reduce the force and bring about a steady state

**normal distribution** A mathematically based distribution depicted as a bell-shaped curve, in which most of the observations cluster around the mean and there are few extreme observations

**normative commitment** Attachment to an organization that reflects one's obligation to continue employment with the organization; also called *moral commitment*

**norms** Shared expectations about appropriate ways of responding in a group

**objective criteria** Performance measures that are based on counting rather than on subjective judgments or evaluations; sometimes called *hard* or *nonjudgmental criteria*

**observational methods** Research procedures that make use of data gathered from observation of behaviors and processes in order to describe a relationship or pattern of relationships

**organizational behavior management (OBM)** The application of the principles of behavioral psychology to the study and control of individual and group behavior within organizational settings

**organizational commitment (OC)** The psychological attachment that binds an employee to the organization

**organizational development (OD)** A planned, organization-wide effort to increase organizational effectiveness through behavioral science knowledge and technology

**organizational justice** The study of people's perceptions of fairness in organizational contexts

**organizational psychology** The systematic study of dispositional and situational variables that influence the behaviors and experiences of individuals and groups at work

**organizational theory** A set of propositions that explains or predicts how groups and individuals behave in varying organizational structures and circumstances

**organizational transformation** A term that refers to any intervention primarily directed toward creating a new vision for an organization and changing its beliefs, purpose, and mission

**organization-based self-esteem (OBSE)** A measure of how valuable employees view themselves as organization members

**organization-motivated aggression** Attempts by someone inside or outside the organization to cause injury or to be destructive as a result of some organizational factor

**organization-motivated violence** The negative effects on people or property that result from organization-motivated aggression

**overlearning** The process of giving trainees continued practice even after they have appeared to master the behavior, resulting in high levels of learning

**paper-and-pencil tests** Frequently used tests in which individuals respond to questions in a test booklet or mark answers on computer sheets to be scanned

**parallel forms reliability** The extent to which two independent forms of a test are equivalent measures of the same construct; sometimes called *equivalent forms reliability* or *coefficient of equivalence*

**parental leave** A program offered by organizations that enables employees to combine work and family responsibilities related to child rearing

**perceived behavioral control** An individual's belief about how easy or difficult performance of a behavior is likely to be

**perceived organizational support (POS)** Employees' global beliefs concerning the extent to which the organization values and cares about them

**performance tests** Tests that require the manipulation of an object or a piece of equipment

**performance** Actual on-the-job behaviors that are relevant to the organization's goals

**personality tests** Tests in which numbers are systematically assigned to individuals' characteristics

**person–environment (PE) fit** The agreement or match between an individual's KSAOs and values and the demands of a job and characteristics of an organization

**point system** The most common approach to job evaluation, which involves estimating the value of jobs based on points assigned to various predetermined dimensions

**position** An individual's place in the organization defined by the tasks performed

**Position Analysis Questionnaire (PAQ)** A widely used job analysis instrument that focuses on general work behaviors

**positive psychology** The scientific study of the strengths and virtues of individuals and institutions

**power test** A test with no fixed time limits and relatively difficult items

**power** An individual's potential influence over the attitudes and behavior of one or more other individuals

**predictive validity** The extent to which test scores obtained at one point in time predict criteria obtained in the future

**problem-focused coping** A coping style that involves behaviors or actions targeted toward solving or handling the stress-inducing problem itself

**process loss** Any nonmotivational element of a group situation that detracts from the group's performance

**prototype** One's mental representation of something or someone, such as a leader

**psychological contract** An employee's idiosyncratic beliefs about the terms and conditions of the reciprocal agreement with his or her employer

**psychomotor tests** Tests that measure both the speed and the accuracy of motor and sensory coordination

**quasi-experiment** A research design that resembles an experimental design but does not include random assignment

**random assignment** The procedure by which research participants, once selected, are assigned to conditions such that each one has an equally likely chance of being assigned to each condition

**range** The simplest measure of dispersion, reflecting the spread of scores from the lowest to the highest

**Rater Error Training (RET)** A type of training originally developed to reduce rater errors by focusing on describing errors like halo to raters and showing them how to avoid making such errors

**readiness** Possessing the background characteristics and necessary level of interest that make learning possible

**realistic job preview (RJP)** During an employment interview, the presentation of an accurate glimpse of what the job would be like

**reasonable accommodations** Changes or exceptions made by an employer that allow qualified disabled individuals to successfully do a job

**recruitment** The process of encouraging potentially qualified applicants to seek employment with a particular company

**reengineering** The fundamental rethinking and redesign of business processes to improve critical performance as measured by cost, quality, service, and speed; also called *business process redesign*

**reliability** The consistency or stability of a measure

**resistance to change** The characteristic of some individuals who so prefer to keep things the way they are that they intentionally or otherwise work to make change more difficult and less successful

**role ambiguity** A situation that results when role expectations are unclear and employees are thus not sure what is expected of them

**role conflict** A situation that results when role expectations are inconsistent, as when a supervisor sends employees mixed messages about their roles

**role differentiation** The process by which a group or organization establishes distinct roles for various members of the group or organization

**role** A set of behaviors expected of a person who occupies a particular position in a group

**science** A process or method for generating a body of knowledge

**scientist/practitioner model** An approach used to train I/O psychologists maintaining that because I/O psychologists are both generators and consumers of knowledge, training must be focused on both theory and application

**selection battery** A set of predictors, or tests, that are used to make employee hiring decisions

**selection ratio** The number of job openings divided by the number of applicants

**self-efficacy expectations** Individuals' perceptions of their ability to successfully complete a task or attain a goal

**self-managed work team (SMWT)** A work team that is responsible for monitoring and controlling the overall process or product, as well as for doling out specific tasks to team members

**self-regulation** The manner in which individuals monitor their own behaviors and make adjustments to those behaviors in the pursuit of goals

**sensemaking** The process whereby employees exert effort to interpret and understand work-related events

**servant leadership** Leading through personal integrity and driven by a desire to serve other people

**severity** The tendency to use only the low end of the scale or to give consistently lower ratings to one's employees than other raters do

**sexual harassment** Behaviors such as unwelcome sexual advances, requests for sexual favors, and other conduct of a sexual nature, submission to or rejection of which affects one's job or creates an offensive work environment

**shared mental models** Organized structures combining the knowledge, beliefs, and understandings of two or more individuals that help coordinate their efforts

**situational interview** An interviewing technique that relies on candidates sharing responses or intentions about job-related dilemmas or situations proposed to them with respect to the new job

**situational judgment tests (SJTs)** Paper-and-pencil test or video vignette that provides hypothetical scenarios for candidates to respond to by choosing the best alternative

**situational specificity** The belief that test validities are specific to particular situations

**social loafing** The reduction in individual effort that occurs when people work in groups instead of alone

**span of control** The number of subordinates who report to a given supervisor

**spatial ability** A specific cognitive ability involving a focus on geometric relations, such as visualizing objects and rotating them spatially to form a particular pattern

**speed test** A test containing relatively easy items with a short time limit in which individuals must complete as many items as they can

**standard deviation** A measure of dispersion that is calculated as the square root of the variance

**statistic** An efficient device for summarizing in a single number the values, characteristics, or scores describing a series of cases

**strains** Undesirable personal outcomes resulting from the combined stressful experiences of various life domains

**strategic job analysis** An approach to job analysis that considers the status of jobs as they currently exist but also factors in how jobs are likely to change in the future as a result of anticipated organizational or industry changes

**stressor** Any disruptive event or force that pushes a psychological or physical function beyond its range of stability, producing a strain within the individual

**subject matter experts (SMEs)** Individuals who participate in job analyses as a result of their expertise

**subjective criteria** Performance measures that are based on the judgments or evaluations of others rather than on objective measures such as counting; sometimes called *soft* or *judgmental criteria*

**subjective norm** An individual's perception of the social pressures to perform or not perform a particular behavior

**sucker effect** An outcome that occurs when group members become concerned that their coworkers are holding back, at which point they reduce their own efforts to the level they believe is being exhibited by their coworkers

**surveys** A data collection technique that involves selecting a sample of respondents and administering some type of questionnaire

**synthetic validity** Validity that is inferred based on the links between job components and KSAOs

**task** A work activity that is performed to achieve a specific objective

**Task Inventory Approach** Task-oriented approach which uses task statements generated by experts familiar with the job in question

**task performance** The work-related activities performed by employees that contribute to the technical core of the organization

**task-oriented** Referring to approaches to job analysis that focus on describing the various tasks that are performed on the job

**taskwork** Activities, behaviors, or actions that involve the task-oriented aspects of work

**team building** A technique used by organizations to develop teams or to enhance the effectiveness of existing teams

**teamwork** Activities, behaviors, or actions that involve the process-oriented aspects of work

**telework** Working arrangements in which employees enjoy flexibility in work hours and/or location

**test** A systematic procedure for observing behavior and describing it with the aid of numerical scales or fixed categories

**test–retest reliability** The stability of a test over time; often called a coefficient of stability

**theory** A set of interrelated constructs (concepts), definitions, and propositions that present a systematic view of a phenomenon by specifying relations among variables, with the purpose of explaining and predicting the phenomenon

**total quality management (TQM)** An initiative that focuses on employee involvement in the control of quality in organizations; also called *continuous improvement* or *quality management*

**training** The formal procedures that a company utilizes to facilitate learning so that the resultant behavior contributes to the attainment of the company's goals and objectives

**trait theories** Leadership theories that focus on identifying the individual characteristics that make people good leaders; sometimes called the *great man/great woman theories*

**transactional leadership** A form of leadership in which the relationship between leader and follower is based chiefly on exchanges, with an emphasis on contingent reinforcement

**transformational leadership** A form of leadership in which the interaction of leader and follower raises both to higher levels of motivation and morality than they would achieve individually

**true halo** Halo that results from accurate intercorrelations among performance dimensions rather than from rating error

**ultimate criterion** A theoretical construct encompassing all performance aspects that define success on the job

**underemployment** When a worker is in a job that, by some standard, is inferior or below his or her capacity or ability

**undue hardship** An accommodation for the disabled that would result in significant difficulty or expense given the employer's size and financial resources

**unobtrusive naturalistic observation** An observational technique whereby the researcher unobtrusively and objectively observes individuals but does not try to blend in with them

**upward appraisal ratings** Ratings provided by individuals whose status, in an organizational-hierarchy sense, is below that of the ratees

**utility** The degree to which a selection battery is useful and cost efficient

**valence (value)** The expected level of satisfaction to be derived from some outcome

**validity coefficient (r)** A correlation that serves as an index of the relationship between a predictor and a criterion, used by selection researchers and practitioners as evidence that a particular test is a valid predictor of a performance criterion

**validity generalization (VG)** A statistical approach used to demonstrate that test validities do not vary across situations

**validity shrinkage** A statistical phenomenon reflecting the likelihood that a given selection battery will demonstrate lower validity when employed with a different sample

**variance** A useful measure of dispersion reflecting the sum of the squared differences between each score and the mean of the group divided by the number of total scores

**work centrality** The degree of importance that work holds in one's life

**work group** An interdependent collection of individuals who share responsibility for specific outcomes for their organizations

**work motivation** A force that drives people to behave in a way that energizes, directs, and sustains their work behavior

**work sample tests** Tests that attempt to duplicate performance criteria measures and use them as predictors, thus forming miniature replicas of the job

**workaholic** An individual whose high drive to work and high job involvement become so intense that they result in work–life imbalance issues

**worker-oriented** Referring to approaches to job analysis that examine broad human behaviors involved in work activities

**work–family conflict (WFC)** A model of work–family relations in which work and family demands are incompatible

**work–family enrichment** A model of work–family relations in which positive attitudes and behaviors are believed to carry over from one domain to the other

# References

**100 Best Companies to Work For.** (2016). *Fortune.* Retrieved March 6, 2016, from http://fortune.com/best-companies/

**AARP.** (2015, June). 2015 report: Caregiving in the U.S. Retrieved from http://www.aarp.org/content/dam/aarp/ppi/2015/caregiving-in-the-united-states-2015-report-revised.pdf

**Aberson, C. L.** (2003). Support for race-based affirmative action: Self-interest and procedural justice. *Journal of Applied Social Psychology, 33*(6), 1212–1225.

**Adams, J. S.** (1965). Inequity in social exchange. In L. Berkowitz (Ed.), *Advances in experimental psychology* (Vol. 2, pp. 267–299). New York: Academic Press.

**Aguinis, H., & Kraiger, K.** (2009). Benefits of training and development for individuals and teams, organizations, and society. *Annual Review of Psychology, 60*(1), 451–474.

**Aidman, E., Chadunow, C., Johnson, K., & Reece, J.** (2015). Real-time driver drowsiness feedback improves driver alertness and self-reported driving performance. *Accident Analysis & Prevention, 81,* 8–13.

**Ajzen, I., & Fishbein, M.** (1980). *Understanding attitudes and predicting social behavior.* Englewood Cliffs, NJ: Prentice-Hall.

**Ajzen, I., & Fishbein, M.** (2005). The influence of attitudes on behavior. In D. Albarracín, B. T. Johnson, & M. P. Zanna (Eds.), *The handbook of attitudes* (pp. 173–221). Mahwah, NJ: Erlbaum.

**Ajzen, I., & Madden, T. J.** (1986). Prediction of goal-directed behavior: The role of intention, perceived control, and prior behavior. *Journal of Experimental Social Psychology, 22,* 453–474.

**Allen, D. G., Biggane, J. E., Pitts, M., Otondo, R., & Van Scotter, J.** (2013). Reactions to recruitment web sites: Visual and verbal attention, attraction, and intentions to pursue employment. *Journal of Business and Psychology, 28*(3), 263–285.

**Allen, N. J., & Meyer, J. P.** (1996). Affective, continuance, and normative commitment to the organization: An examination of construct validity. *Journal of Vocational Behavior, 49,* 252–276.

**Allen, R. S., & White, C. S.** (2002). Equity sensitivity theory: A test of responses to two types of under-reward situations. *Journal of Managerial Issues, 14*(4), 435–451.

**Allen, T. D., Facteau, J. D., & Facteau, C. L.** (2004). Structured interviewing for OCB: Construct validity, faking, and the effects of question type. *Human Performance, 17*(1), 1–24.

**Allen, T. D., Golden, T. D., & Shockley, K. M.** (2015). How effective is telecommuting? Assessing the status of our scientific findings. *Psychological Science in the Public Interest, 16*(2), 40–68.

**Alliger, G. M., & Dwight, S. A.** (2000). A meta-analytic investigation of the susceptibility of integrity tests to faking and coaching. *Educational and Psychological Measurement, 60*(1), 59–72.

**Alliger, G. M., & Janak, E. A.** (1989). Kirkpatrick's levels of training criteria: Thirty years later. *Personnel Psychology, 42,* 331–342.

**Alliger, G. M., Tannenbaum, S. I., Bennett, W., Jr., Traver, H., & Shotland, A.** (1997). A meta-analysis of the relations among training criteria. *Personnel Psychology, 50,* 341–358.

**Allworth, E., & Hesketh, B.** (2000). Job requirements biodata as a predictor of performance in customer service roles. *International Journal of Selection and Assessment, 83*(3), 137–147.

**Ambient Insight Research.** (2015). The 2014–2019 US Mobile Learning market. Retrieved December 9, 2015, from http://www.ambientinsight.com/Reports/MobileLearning.aspx#section5

**Ambrose, M. L., & Kulik, C. T.** (1999). Old friends, new faces: Motivation research in the 1990s. *Journal of Management, 2*(3), 231–292.

**America in 2050: Even older and more diverse.** (2012). MSNBC. Retrieved March 13, 2012, from http://www.msnbc.msn.com/id/26186087/ns/us_news-life/t/america-even-older-more-diverse/

**American Bar Association.** (2013). A current glance at women in the law. *American Bar Association.* Retrieved August 19, 2015, from http://www.americanbar.org/dam/aba/marketing/women/current_glance_statistics_feb2013.authcheckdam.pdf

**American Civil Liberties Union.** (2015). Non-discrimination laws: State by state information [Map]. Retrieved on November 16, 2015, from https://www.aclu.org/map/non-discrimination-laws-state-state-information-map

**American Psychological Association.** (2009). *Publication manual of the American Psychological Association* (6th ed.). Washington, DC: Author.

**American Psychological Association.** (2010). *Ethical principles of psychologists and code of conduct: Including 2010 amendments.* Washington, DC: Author. http://www.apa.org/ethics/code/

**American Psychological Association.** (2015). About behavior analysis. Washington, DC: Author. http://www.apadivisions.org/division-25/about/index.aspx

**American Society for Training and Development.** (2011). *State of the industry: ASTD's annual review of trends in workplace learning and performance.* Alexandria, VA: Author.

**Anderson, M.** (2012, March 4). From idea to store shelf: A new product is born. *Yahoo! News.* Retrieved from http://news.yahoo.com/idea-store-sehlf-product-born-174428924.html

**Anderson, N., Potočnik, K., & Zhou, J.** (2014). Innovation and creativity in organizations a state-of-the-science review, prospective commentary, and guiding framework. *Journal of Management, 40*(5), 1297–1333.

**Andressen, P., Konradt, U, & Neck, C. P.** (2012). The relation between self-leadership and transformational leadership: Competing models and the moderating role of virtuality. *Journal of Leadership & Organizational Studies, 19,* 68–82.

**Antecol, H., & Cobb-Clark, D.** (2003). Does sexual harassment training change attitudes? A view from the federal level. *Social Science Quarterly, 84,* 826–842.

**Aon Hewitt.** (2014, August 27). New Aon Hewitt survey shows 2014 variable pay spending spikes to record-high level. Retrieved March 6, 2016, from http://aon.mediaroom.com/New-Aon-Hewitt-Survey-Shows-2014-Variable-Pay-Spending-Spikes-to-Record-High-Level

**Arthur, J. B., & Huntley, C. L.** (2005). Ramping up the organizational learning curve: Assessing the impact of deliberate learning on organizational performance under gain-sharing. *Academy of Management Journal, 48,* 1159–1170.

**Arthur, W., Jr., Bennett, W., Jr., Edens, P. S., & Bell, S. T.** (2003). Effectiveness of training in organizations: A meta-analysis of design and evaluation features. *Journal of Applied Psychology, 88*(2), 234–245.

**Arthur, W., Jr., Day, E. A., McNelly, T. L., & Edens, P. S.** (2003). A meta-analysis of the criterion-related validity of assessment center dimensions. *Personnel Psychology, 56*(1), 125–154.

**Arthur Jr., W., Doverspike, D., Muños, G. J., Taylor, J. E., & Carr, A. E.** (2014). The use of mobile devices in high-stakes remotely delivered assessments and testing. *International Journal of Selection and Assessment, 22,* 113–123.

**Arthur, W., Jr., Glaze, R. M., Villado, A. J., & Taylor, J. E.** (2010). The magnitude and extent of cheating and response distortion effects on unproctored Internet-based tests of cognitive ability and personality. *International Journal of Selection and Assessment, 18*(1), 1–16.

**Artz, B.** (2010). The impact of union experience on job satisfaction. *Industrial Relations, 49,* 387–405.

**Artz, B.** (2012). Does this impact of union experience on job satisfaction differ by gender? *Industrial and Labor Relations Review, 65,* 225–243.

**Arvey, R. D., & Begalla, M. E.** (1975). Analyzing the homemaker job using the Position Analysis Questionnaire (PAQ). *Journal of Applied Psychology, 60,* 513–517.

**Arvey, R. D., Bouchard, T. J. J., Segal, N. L., & Abraham, L. M.** (1989). Job satisfaction: Environmental and genetic components. *Journal of Applied Psychology, 74*(2), 187–192.

**Arvey, R. D., Rotundo, M., Johnson, W., Zhang, Z., & McGue, M.** (2006). The determinants of leadership role occupancy: Genetic and personality factors. *Leadership Quarterly, 17,* 1–20.

**Arvey, R. D., Zhang, Z., Avolio, B. J., & Kreuger, R. F.** (2007). Developmental and genetic determinants of leadership role occupancy among women. *Journal of Applied Psychology, 92,* 693–706.

**Ash, R. A., & Edgell, S. L.** (1975). A note on the readability of the Position Analysis Questionnaire (PAQ). *Journal of Applied Psychology, 60,* 765–766.

**Ashmos, D. P., & Nathan, M. L.** (2002). Team sense-making: A mental model for navigating uncharted territories. *Journal of Managerial Issues, 14*(2), 198–217.

**Associated Press.** (2015, September 15). How bureaucracy, bungling hurt Ebola response. Retrieved March 6, 2016, from http://www.cbsnews.com/news/bureaucracy-bungling-hurt-ebola-response/

**Atwater, L. E., & Carmeli, A.** (2009). Leader–member exchange, feelings of energy, and involvement in creative work. *The Leadership Quarterly, 20,* 264–275.

**Atwater, L. E., Daldman, D. A., Atwater, D., & Cartier, P.** (2000). An upward feedback field experiment: Supervisors' cynicism, reactions, and commitment to subordinates. *Personnel Psychology, 53,* 275–297.

**Atwater, L. E., Wang, M., Smither, J. W., & Fleenor, J. W.** (2009). Are cultural characteristics associated with the relationship between self and others' ratings of leadership? *Journal of Applied Psychology, 94*(4), 876–886.

**Austin, J. T., & Davies, S. A.** (2000). History of industrial-organizational psychology. In A. E. Kazdin (Ed.), *Encyclopedia of psychology* (Vol. 4, pp. 252–255). Oxford, UK: Oxford University Press.

**Austin, J. T., & Villanova, P. D.** (1992). The criterion problem: 1917–1992. *Journal of Applied Psychology, 77,* 836–874.

**Austin, J. T., Villanova, P. D., & Hindman, H. G.** (1995). Legal requirements and technical guidelines involved in implementing performance appraisal systems. In G. R. Ferris & M. R. Buckley (Eds.), *Human resource management: Perspectives, context, functions, and outcomes* (pp. 271–288). Boston: Allyn & Bacon.

**Avery, D. R., & McKay, P. F.** (2006). Target practice: An organizational impression management approach to attracting minority and female job applicants. *Personnel Psychology, 59,* 157–187.

**Avolio, B, J., Gardner, W. L., Walumbwa, F. O., Luthans, F., & May, D. R.** (2004). Unlocking the mask: A look at the process by which authentic leaders impact followers attitudes and behaviors. *The Leadership Quarterly, 15,* 801–823.

**Axonify.** (n.d.). *Pep Boys case study*. Retrieved June 25, 2015, from http://www.axonify.com/wp-content/uploads/2012/08/PepBoys_CaseStudy-Final.pdf

**Ayman, R., Chemers, M. M., & Fiedler, F.** (1995). The contingency model of leadership effectiveness: Its level of analysis. *Leadership Quarterly, 6*(2), 147–167.

**Aziz, A., & Zickar, M. J.** (2006). A cluster analysis investigation of workaholism as a syndrome. *Journal of Occupational Health Psychology, 11,* 52–62.

**Babbie, E.** (1998). *The practice of social research.* Belmont, CA: Wadsworth.

**Bakker, A. B. & Demerouti, E.** (2007). The job-demands resources model: State of the art. *Journal of Managerial Psychology, 22,* 309–328.

**Bakker, A. B., Demerouti, E., & Dollard, M. F.** (2008). How job demands affect partners' experience of exhaustion: Integrating work–family conflict and crossover theory. *Journal of Applied Psychology, 93,* 901–911.

**Bakker, A. B., Demerouti, E., Oerlemans, W., & Sonnetag, S.** (2013). Workaholism and daily recovery: A day reconstruction study of leisure activities. *Journal of Organizational Behavior, 34,* 87–107.

**Bakker, A. B., & Schaufeli, W. B.** (2008). Positive organizational behavior: Engaged employees in flourishing organizations. *Journal of Organizational Behavior, 29,* 147–154.

**Balducci, C., Cecchin, M., Fraccaroli, F., & Schaufeli, W. B.** (2012). Exploring the relationship between workaholism and workplace aggressive behaviour: The role of job-related emotion. *Personality and Individual Differences, 53*(5), 629–634.

**Baldwin, T. P., & Ford, J. K.** (1988). Transfer of training: A review and directions for future research. *Personnel Psychology, 41,* 63–105.

**Baltes, B. B., & Heydens-Gahir, H. A.** (2003). Reduction of work–family conflict through the use of selection, optimization, and compensation behaviors. *Journal of Applied Psychology, 88*(6), 1005–1018.

**Bandura, A.** (1986). *Social foundations of thought and action.* Englewood Cliffs, NJ: Prentice-Hall.

**Bandura, A., & Locke, E. A.** (2003). Negative self-efficacy and goal effects revisited. *Journal of Applied Psychology, 88*(1), 87–99.

**Bardsley, J. J., & Rhodes, S. R.** (1996). Using the Steers–Rhodes (1984) framework to identify correlates of employee lateness. *Journal of Business and Psychology, 10*(3), 351–365.

**Barger, P., & Grandey, A.** (2006). "Service with a smile" and encounter satisfaction: Emotional contagion and appraisal mechanisms. *Academy of Management Journal, 49,* 1229–1238.

**Barrett, G. V., Caldwell, M. S., & Alexander, R. A.** (1985). The concept of dynamic criteria: A critical reanalysis. *Personnel Psychology, 38*(1), 93–97.

**Barrett, G. V., & Kernan, M. C.** (1988). Performance appraisal and terminations: A review of court decisions since Brito v. Zia with implications for personnel practices. *Personnel Psychology, 40*(3), 489–503.

**Barrick, M. R., Mount, M. K., & Judge, T. A.** (2001). Personality and performance at the beginning of the new millennium: What do we know and where do we go next? *International Journal of Selection & Assessment, 9*(1/2), 9–30.

**Barrick, M. R., Stewart, G. L., Neubert, M. J., & Mount, M. K.** (1998). Relating member ability and personality to work-team processes and team effectiveness. *Journal of Applied Psychology, 83*(3), 377–391.

**Bass, B. M.** (1985). *Leadership and performance beyond expectations.* New York: Free Press.

**Bass, B. M., Avolio, B. J., Jung, D. I., & Berson, Y.** (2003). Predicting unit performance by assessing transformational and transactional leadership. *Journal of Applied Psychology, 88*(2), 207–218.

**Bass, B. M., & Steidlmeier, P.** (1999). Ethics, character, and authentic transformational leadership behavior. *Leadership Quarterly, 10*(2), 181–217.

**Bauer, T. N., & Erdogan, B.** (2011). Organizational socialization: The effective onboarding of new employees. In S. Zedeck (Ed.), *APA handbook of industrial and organizational psychology,* Vol 3 (pp. 51–64). Washington, DC: American Psychological Association.

**Beal, D. J., Trougakos, J. P., Weiss, H. M., & Green, S. G.** (2006). Episodic processes in emotional labor: Perceptions of affective delivery and regulation strategies. *Journal of Applied Psychology, 91*(5), 1053–1065.

**Beaty, J. C., Nye, C. D., Borneman, M. J., Kantrowitz, T. M., Drasgow, F., & Grauer, E.** (2011). Proctored versus unproctored Internet tests: Are unproctored noncognitive tests as predictive of job performance? *International Journal of Selection and Assessment, 19*(1), 1–10.

**Beckhard, R.** (1969). *Organization development: Strategies and models.* Reading, MA: Addison-Wesley.

**Bell, B. S., & Kozlowski, S. W. J.** (2002). Adaptive guidance: Enhancing self-regulation, knowledge, and

performance in technology-based training. *Personnel Psychology, 55*(2), 267–306.

**Bell, S. T.** (2007). Deep-level composition variables as predictors of team performance: A meta-analysis. *Journal of Applied Psychology, 92,* 595–615.

**Bennis, W., & Biederman, P. W.** (1997). *Organizing genius: The secrets of creative collaboration.* Reading, MA: Addison-Wesley.

**Berdahl, J. L., & Aquino, K.** (2009). Sexual behavior at work: Fun or folly? *Journal of Applied Psychology, 94,* 34–47.

**Berg, J. M., Wrzesniewski, A., & Dutton, J. E.** (2010). Perceiving and responding to challenges in job crafting at different ranks: When proactivity requires adaptivity. *Journal of Organizational Behavior, 31,* 158-186.

**Bergeron, D. M., Shipp, A. J., Rosen, B., & Furst, S. A.** (2013). Organizational citizenship behavior and career outcomes: The cost of being a good citizen. *Journal of Management, 39(4),* 958–984.

**Berkelaar, B. L., & Buzzanell, P.** (2015). Online employment screening and digital career capital: Exploring employers' use of online information for personnel selection. *Management Communication Quarterly, 29*(1), 84–113.

**Berkley, R. A., & Watt, A. H.** (2006). Impact of same-sex harassment and gender-role. *Employee Responsibilities and Rights Journal, 18,* 3–19.

**Bernardin, H. J.** (1978). Effects of rater training on leniency and halo errors in student ratings of instructors. *Journal of Applied Psychology, 63*(3), 301–308.

**Bernardin, H. J., & Beatty, R. W.** (1984). *Performance appraisal: Assessing human behavior at work.* Boston: Kent.

**Bernardin, H. J., & Buckley, M. R.** (1981). Strategies in rater training. *Academy of Management Review, 6,* 205–212.

**Bernardin, H. J., Cooke, D. K., & Villanova, P. D.** (2000). Conscientiousness and agreeableness as predictors of rating leniency. *Journal of Applied Psychology, 85*(2), 232–236.

**Bernardin, H. J., Orban, J., & Carlyle, J.** (1981). Performance ratings as a function of trust in appraisal and rater individual differences. Paper presented at the 41st annual meeting of the Academy of Management, San Diego, CA.

**Bernardin, H. J., & Pence, E. C.** (1980). Effects of rater training: Creating new response sets and decreasing accuracy. *Journal of Applied Psychology, 65,* 60–66.

**Bernardin, H. J., Tyler, C. L., & Villanova, P.** (2009). Rating level and accuracy as a function of rater personality. *International Journal of Selection and Assessment, 17*(3), 300–310.

**Bernardin, H. J., & Villanova, P.** (2005). Research streams in rater self-efficacy. *Group & Organization Management, 30*(1), 61–88.

**Berry, C. M., Sackett, P. R., & Wiemann, S.** (2007). A review of recent developments in integrity test research. *Personnel Psychology, 60*(2), 271–301.

**Berry, G. R.** (2011). Enhancing effectiveness on virtual teams: Understanding why traditional team skills are insufficient. *Journal of Business Communication, 48*(2), 186–206.

**Bersin, J.** (2013, February 17). Big data in human resources: Talent analytics (people analytics) comes of age. *Forbes.* Retrieved from http://www.forbes.com/sites/joshbersin/2013/02/17/bigdata-in-human-resources-talent-analytics-comes-of-age/

**Bertua, C., Anderson, N., & Salgado, J. F.** (2005). The predictive validity of cognitive ability tests: A UK meta-analysis. *Journal of Occupational and Organizational Psychology, 78*(3), 387–409.

**Beugré, C. D.** (1998). Implementing business process reengineering: The role of organizational justice. *Journal of Applied Behavioral Science, 34*(3), 347–360.

**Bhagat, R. S., Allie, S. M., & Ford, D. L., Jr.** (1995). Coping with stressful life events: An empirical analysis. In R. Crandall & P. L. Perrewé (Eds.), *Occupational stress: A handbook* (pp. 93–112). Washington, DC: Taylor & Francis.

**Biddle, D. A.** (2010). Should employers rely on local validation studies or validity generalization (VG) to support the use of employment tests in Title VII situations? *Public Personnel Management, 39*(4), 307–326.

**Biles, P. D.** (1999). *OSHA workplace violence prevention guidelines.* Paper presented at the Work, Stress, and Health '99: Organization of Work in a Global Economy conference. Abstract retrieved April 9, 2009, from the American Psychological Association, Public Interest Directorate website: http://www.apa.org/pi/wpo/niosh/abstract12.html

**Björk, B., Welling, P., Laakso, M., Majlender, P., Hedlund, T., & Guǒnason, G.** (2010). Open access to the scientific journal literature: Situation 2009. *PLoS ONE, 5*(6). Retrieved from http://journals.plos.org/plosone/article?id=10.1371/journal.pone.0011273

**Blackmore, E. R., Stansfield, S. A., Weller, I., Munce, S., Zagorski, B. M., & Stewart, D. E.** (2007). Major depressive episodes and work stress: Results from a national population survey. *American Journal of Public Health, 97,* 2088–2093.

**Blake, R.** (2006, July 24). Employee retention: What employee turnover really costs your company. Retrieved April 21, 2009, from http://archive.managernewz.com/2006/0724.html

**Blakely, C. L., Andrews, M. C., & Moorman, R. H.** (2005). The moderating effects of equity sensitivity on the relationship between organizational justice and organizational citizenship behaviors. *Journal of Business Psychology, 20*(2), 259–273.

**Blakely, G. L., Blakely, E. H., & Moorman, R. H.** (1998). The effects of training on perceptions of sexual harassment allegations. *Journal of Applied Social Psychology, 28*(1), 71–83.

**Blanding, M.** (2015, January 26). Workplace stress responsible for up to $190B in annual U.S. healthcare costs. Retrieved November 19, 2015, from http://www.forbes.com/sites/hbsworkingknowledge/2015/01/26/workplace-stress-responsible-for-up-to-190-billion-in-annual-u-s-heathcare-costs/

**Blau, G.** (1994). Developing and testing a taxonomy of lateness behavior. *Journal of Applied Psychology, 79*(6), 959–970.

**Blau, G.** (1999). Testing the longitudinal impact of work variables and performance appraisal satisfaction on subsequent overall job satisfaction. *Human Relations, 52*(8), 1099–1113.

**Bliese, P. D., & Britt, T. W.** (2001). Social support, group consensus, and stressor–strain relationships: Social context matters. *Journal of Organizational Behavior, 22,* 425–436.

**Bloom, A. J., Yorges, S. L., & Ruhl, A. J.** (2000). Enhancing student motivation: Extensions from job enrichment theory and practice. *Teaching of Psychology, 27*(2), 135–137.

**Blum, M. L., & Naylor, J. C.** (1968). *Industrial psychology.* New York: Harper & Row.

**Blume, B. D., Ford, J. K., Baldwin, T. T., & Huang, J. L.** (2010). Transfer of training: A meta-analytic review. *Journal of Management, 36*(4), 1065–1105.

**Bolino, M. C., & Turnley, W. H.** (2005). The personal costs of citizenship behavior: The relationship between individual initiative and role overload, job stress, and work–family conflict. *Journal of Applied Psychology, 90*(4), 740–748.

**Bolino, M. C., Turnley, W. H., & Bloodgood, J. M.** (2002). Citizenship behavior and the creation of social capital in organizations. *Academy of Management Review, 27*(4), 505–522.

**Bolino, M. C., Turnley, W. H., & Niehoff, B. P.** (2004). The other side of the story: Reexamining prevailing assumptions about organizational citizenship behavior. *Human Resource Management Review, 14*(2), 229–246.

**Boller, S.** (2012). "Make it social: How we use Twitter as a learning tool." Bottom-Line Performance. Retrieved August 15, 2012, from http://www.bottomlineperformance.com/make-it-social-how-we-use-twitter-as-a-learning-tool/

**Bond, J. T., & Galinsky, E.** (2006, November). *What workplace flexibility is available to entry-level, hourly employees?* Retrieved April 8, 2009, from the Families and Work Institute website: http://familiesandwork.org/site/research/reports/brief3.pdf

**Bono, J. E., & Colbert, A. E.** (2005). Understanding responses to multi-source feedback: The role of core self-evaluations. *Personnel Psychology, 58*(1), 171–203.

**Bono, J. E., & Ilies, R.** (2006). Charisma, positive emotions and mood contagion. *Leadership Quarterly, 17,* 317–334.

**Bono, J. E., Foldes, H. J., Vinson, G., & Muros, J. P.** (2007). Workplace emotions: The role of supervision and leadership. *Journal of Applied Psychology, 92*(5), 1357–1367.

**Boon, O. K., Arumugam, V., Safa, M. S., & Bakar, N. A.** (2007). HRM and TQM: Association with job involvement. *Personnel Review, 36,* 939–962.

**Borman, W. C.** (2004). The concept of organizational citizenship. *Current Directions in Psychological Science, 13,* 238–241.

**Borman, W. C.** (2010). Cognitive processes related to forced-choice, ideal point responses: Dragsow, Chernyshenko, and Stark got it right! *Industrial and Organizational Psychology, 3*(04), 504–506.

**Borman, W. C., Buck, D. E., Hanson, M. A., Motowidlo, S. J., Stark, S., & Drasgow, F.** (2001). An examination of the comparative reliability, validity, and accuracy of performance ratings made using computerized adaptive rating scales. *Journal of Applied Psychology, 86*(5), 965–973.

**Borman, W. C., Hanson, M. A., & Hedge, J. W.** (1997). Personnel selection. *Annual Review of Psychology, 48,* 299–337.

**Borman, W. C., & Motowidlo, S. J.** (1997). Task performance and contextual performance: The meaning for personnel selection research. *Human Performance, 10*(2), 99–109.

**Boudreau, J. W., & Ramstad, P. M.** (2003). Strategic industrial and organizational psychology and the role of utility analysis models. In W. C. Borman, D. R. Ilgen, and R. Klimoski (Eds.), *Handbook of psychology: Vol. 12. Industrial and organizational psychology* (pp. 193–221). New York: Wiley.

**Bowling Green State University, Department of Psychology.** (2009). *Job descriptive index.* Reprinted with permission of Bowling Green State University, Department of Psychology, Bowling Green, OH, 43403.

**Boye, M. W., & Jones, J. W.** (1997). Organizational culture and employee counterproductivity. In R. A. Giacalone & J. Greenberg (Eds.), *Antisocial behavior in organizations* (pp. 172–184). Thousand Oaks, CA: Sage.

**Bozer, G., Joo, B. K., & Santora, J. C.** (2015). Executive coaching: Does coach–coachee matching based on similarity really matter? *Consulting Psychology Journal: Practice and Research, 67*(3), 218–233.

**Brannick, M. T., Levine, E. L., & Morgeson, F. P.** (2007). *Job and work analysis: Methods, research, and applications for human resource management* (2nd ed.). Los Angeles: Sage.

**Bray, D. W., Campbell, R. J., & Grant, D. L.** (1974). *Formative years in business: A long-term AT&T study of managerial lives.* New York: Wiley.

**Breaugh, J. A., Greising, L. A., Taggart, J. W., & Chen, H.** (2003). The relationship of recruiting sources and pre-hire outcomes: Examination of field ratios and applicant quality. *Journal of Applied Social Psychology, 33*(11), 2267–2287.

**Brennan v. Prince William Hospital Corp.,** 503 F.2d 282 (4th Cir. 1974).

**Brockner, J.** (1988). *Self-esteem at work*. Lexington, MA: Lexington Books.

**Brockner, J., Wiesenfeld, B. M., & Martin, C. L.** (1995). Decision frame, procedural justice, and survivors' reactions to job layoffs. *Organizational Behavior and Human Decision Processes, 63,* 59–68.

**Brodbeck, F. C., Kerschreiter, R., Mojzisch, A., Frey, D., & Schulz-Hardt, S.** (2002). The dissemination of critical, unshared information in decision-making groups: The effects of prediscussion dissent. *European Journal of Social Psychology, 32,* 35–56.

**Brody, H. M., & Grodan, A.** (2010). The effect of the fair pay act on disparate-impact cases. *Employment Relations Today.* doi:10.1002/ert.20276

**Brown, J.** (2002). Training needs assessment: A must for developing an effective training program. *Public Personnel Management, 31*(4), 569–578.

**Brown, M., & Benson, J.** (2003). Rated to exhaustion? Reactions to performance appraisal processes. *Industrial Relations Journal, 34,* 67–81.

**Bruck, C. S., Allen, T. D., & Spector, P. E.** (2002). The relation between work–family conflict and job satisfaction: A finer-grained analysis. *Journal of Vocational Behavior, 60*(3), 336–353.

**Brunelli, M.** (1999, November 4). How Harley-Davidson uses cross-functional teams. *Purchasing, 127,* 144.

**Bruppacher, H. R., Alam, S. K., LeBlanc, V. A., Latter, D., Laik, V. N., Savoldelli, G. L., Mazer, C. D., Kurrek, M. M., & Joo, H. S.** (2010). Simulation-based training improves physicians' performance in patient care in high-stakes clinical setting of cardiac surgery. *Anesthesiology, 112*(4), 985–992.

**Brutus, S.** (2010). Words versus numbers: A theoretical exploration of giving and receiving narrative comments in performance appraisal. *Human Resource Management Review, 20*(2), 144–157.

**Brutus, S., Fletcher, C., & Baldry, C.** (2009). The influence of independent self-construal on rater self-efficacy in performance appraisal. *The International Journal of Human Resource Management, 20*(9), 1999–2011.

**Buchannan, N. T., Settles, I. H., Hall, A. T., & O'Connor, R. C.** (2014). A review of organizational strategies for reducing sexual harassment: Insights from the U.S. military. *Journal of Social Issues, 70*(4), 687–702.

**Budworth, M.-H., Latham, G. P., & Manroop, L.** (2015). Looking forward to performance improvement: A field test of the FeedForward Interview for performance management. *Human Resource Management, 54,* 45–54.

**Burgess, J. R. D., & Russell, J. E. A.** (2003). The effectiveness of distance learning initiatives in organizations. *Journal of Vocational Behavior, 63*(2), 289–303.

**Burnett, J. R., & Motowidlo, S. J.** (1998). Relations between different sources of information in the structured selection interview. *Personnel Psychology, 51,* 964–983.

**Burwell v. Hobby Lobby Stores, Inc.,** 573 U.S. 1 (2014).

**Cable, D. M., Gino, F., & Staats, B. R.** (2013, March 19). Reinventing employee onboarding. *MIT Sloan Management Review, 54*(3), 23–28.

**Cable, D. M., & Turban, D. B.** (2003). The value of organizational reputation in the recruitment context: A brand-equity perspective. *Journal of Applied Social Psychology, 33*(11), 2244–2266.

**Cadsby, C. B., Song, F., & Tapon, F.** (2007). Sorting and incentive effects of pay for performance: An experimental investigation. *Academy of Management Journal, 50,* 387–405.

**Camara, W. J., & Kimmel, E. W.** (2005). *Choosing students: Higher education admissions tools for the 21st century.* Mahwah, NJ: Erlbaum.

**Campbell Interest and Skill Survey (CISS).** (n.d.). Retrieved October 10, 2006, from http://www.pearsonassessments.com/tests/ciss.htm

**Campbell, J. P.** (1990). Modeling the performance prediction problem in industrial and organizational psychology. In M. Dunnette & L. M. Hough (Eds.), *Handbook of industrial and organizational psychology* (2nd ed., Vol. 1, pp. 687–732). Palo Alto, CA: Consulting Psychologists Press.

**Campbell, J. P., Gasser, M. B., & Oswald, F. L.** (1996). The substantive nature of job performance variability. In K. R. Murphy (Ed.), *Individual differences and behavior in organizations* (pp. 258–299). San Francisco: Jossey-Bass.

**Campbell, J. P., McCloy, R. A., Oppler, S. H., & Sager, C. E.** (1993). A theory of performance. In N. Schmitt & W. C. Borman (Eds.), *Personnel selection in organizations* (pp. 35–70). San Francisco: Jossey-Bass.

**Campbell, J. P., McHenry, J. J., & Wise, L. L.** (1990). Modeling performance in a population of jobs. *Personnel Psychology, 43,* 313–333.

**Carbonell, J. L., & Castro, Y.** (2008). The impact of a leader model on high dominant women's self-selection for leadership. *Sex Roles, 58,* 776–783.

**Carless, S., & De Paola, C.** (2000). The measurement of cohesion in work teams. *Small Groups Research, 31*(1), 71–88.

**Carli, L. L., & Eagly, A. H.** (2011). Gender and leadership. *The Sage Handbook of Leadership,* 103–117.

**Carlson, D. S., Grzywacz, J. G., Ferguson, M., Hunter, E. M., Clinch, C. R., & Arcury, T. A.** (2011). Health and turnover of working mothers after childbirth via the work–family interface: An analysis across time. *Journal of Applied Psychology, 96*(5), 1045–1054.

**Carmeli, A., & Josman, Z. E.** (2006). The relationship among emotional intelligence, task performance, and organizational citizenship behaviors. *Human Performance, 19*(4), 403–419.

**Carpal tunnel syndrome reaching epidemic proportions.** (2005, January 18). Retrieved April 21, 2009, from *Medical News Today* website: http://www.medical-newstoday.com/articles/19014.php

**Carrns, A.** (2010, December 5). Training in trouble. *The Boston Globe.* Retrieved December 11, 2015, from http://www.boston.com/jobs/news/articles/2010/12/05/companies_question_value_of_diversity_training/?page=1

**Cartwright, S., & Cooper, C. L.** (1997). *Managing workplace stress.* Thousand Oaks, CA: Sage.

**Carver, C. S., & Scheier, M. F.** (1998). *On the self-regulation of behavior.* Cambridge, UK: Cambridge University Press.

**Cascio, W. F.** (1995). Whither industrial and organizational psychology in a changing world of work? *American Psychologist, 50*(11), 928–939.

**Cascio, W. F.** (2003). *Managing human resources: Productivity, quality of work life, profits* (6th ed.). New York: McGraw-Hill.

**Cascio, W. F., & Aguinis, H.** (2010). *Applied psychology in human resource management* (7th ed.). Upper Saddle River, NJ: Prentice-Hall.

**Casler, K., Bickel, L., & Hackett, E. (2013).** Separate but equal? A comparison of participants and data gathered via Amazon's MTurk, social media, and face-to-face behavioral testing. *Computers in Human Behavior, 29,* 2156–2160.

**Casper, W., Wayne, J. H., & Manegold, J. G.** (2013). Who will we recruit? Targeting deep- and surface-level diversity with human resource policy advertising. *Human Resource Management, 52*(3), 311–332.

**Cassidy, J.** (2014, March 31). Forces of divergence: Is surging inequality endemic to capitalism? *The New Yorker.* Retrieved from http://www.newyorker.com/magazine/2014/03/31/forces-of-divergence

**Catanzaro, D.** (1997). Course enrichment and the job characteristics model. *Teaching of Psychology, 24*(2) 85–87.

**Caterpillar Global Mining.** (2011). Finding technology solutions to combat operator fatigue. *Viewpoint: Perspectives on Modern Mining, 2.*

**Cavanaugh, M. A., Boswell, W. R., Roehling, M. V., & Boudreau, J. W.** (2000). An empirical examination of self-reported work stress among U.S. managers. *Journal of Applied Psychology, 85*(11), 65–74.

**Cawley, B. D., Keeping, L. M., & Levy, P. E.** (1998). Participation in the performance appraisal process and employee reactions: A meta-analytic review of field investigations. *Journal of Applied Psychology, 83*(4), 615–633.

**CBS/Associated Press.** (2016, January 14). WHO declares official end to Ebola outbreak in West Africa. Retrieved March 6, 2016, from http://www.cbsnews.com/news/who-declares-official-end-to-ebola-outbreak-in-west-africa

**Centers for Disease Control and Prevention.** (2014). Occupational violence. The National Institute for Occupational Safety and Health (NIOSH). Retrieved April 11, 2016, from http://www.cdc.gov/niosh/topics/violence/

**Centers for Disease Control and Prevention.** (2015, November 30). Heart disease fact sheet. Retrieved January 11, 2016, from http://www.cdc.gov/dhdsp/data_statistics/fact_sheets/fs_heart_disease.htm

**Chamorro-Premuzic, T., & Furnham, A.** (2008). Personality, intelligence and approaches to learning as predictors of academic performance. *Personality and Individual Differences, 44,* 1596–1603.

**Chan, D., & Schmitt, N.** (2002). Situational judgment and job performance. *Human Performance, 15*(3), 233–254.

Chang, A., Bordia, P., & Duck, J. (2003). Punctuated equilibrium and linear progression: Toward a new understanding of group development. *Academy of Management Journal, 46*(1), 106–117.

Chavez, C. I., & Weisinger, J. Y. (2008). Beyond diversity training: A social infusion for cultural inclusion. *Human Resource Management, 47*(2), 331–350.

Chen, B. X. (2014, August 10). Simplifying the bull: How Picasso helps to teach Apple's style. *The New York Times.* Retrieved December 11, 2015, from http://www.nytimes.com/2014/08/11/technology/-inside-apples-internal-training-program-.html?_r=0

Chen, G., Goddard, T. G., & Casper, W. J. (2004). Examination of the relationships among general and work-specific self-evaluations, work-related control beliefs, and job attitudes. *Applied Psychology: An International Review, 53*(3), 349–370.

Chen, G., Ployhart, R. E., Thomas, H. C., Anderson, N., & Bliese, P. D. (2011). The power of momentum: A new model of dynamic relationships between job satisfaction and turnover intentions. *The Academy of Management Journal, 54,* 159–181.

Chen, Z., Zhu, J., & Zhou, M. (2015). How does a servant leader fuel the service fire? A multilevel model of servant leadership, individual self identity, group competition climate, and customer service performance. *Journal of Applied Psychology, 100*(2), 511–521.

Cheng, Y., & Stockdale, M. S. (2003). The validity of the three-component model of organizational commitment in a Chinese context. *Journal of Vocational Behavior, 62*(3), 465–489.

Chiaburu, D. S., Oh, I. S., Berry, C. M., Li, N., & Gardner, R. G. (2011). The five-factor model of personality traits and organizational citizenship behaviors: A meta-analysis. *Journal of Applied Psychology, 96*(6), 1140–1166.

Cho, J., & Dansereau, F. (2010). Are transformational leaders fair? A multi-level study of transformational leadership, justice perceptions, and organizational citizenship behaviors. *The Leadership Quarterly, 21,* 409–421.

Choi, J. N., & Sy, T. (2010). Group-level organizational citizenship behavior: Effects of demographic faultlines and conflict in small work groups. *Journal of Organizational Behavior, 31,* 1032–1054.

Choi, S., & Rainey, H. G. (2010). Managing diversity in U.S. federal agencies: Effects of diversity and diversity

management on employee perceptions of organizational performance. *Public Administration Review, 70*(1), 109–121.

Chory, R. M., & Westerman, C. Y. K. (2009). Feedback and fairness: The relationship between negative performance feedback and organizational justice. *Western Journal of Communication, 73*(2), 157–181.

Christensen, L. B. (1994). *Experimental methodology.* Boston: Allyn & Bacon.

Christian, M. S., Edwards, B. D., & Bradley, J. C. (2010). Situational judgment tests: Constructs assessed and a meta-analysis of their criterion-related validities. *Personnel Psychology, 63,* 83–117.

Christian, M. S., & Ellis, A. P. J. (2011). Examining the effects of sleep deprivation on workplace deviance: A self regulatory perspective. *Academy of Management Journal, 54,* 913–934.

Church, A. H., Waclawski, J., & Siegal, W. (1999). Will the real O.D. practitioner please stand up? A call for change in the field. *Organization Development Journal, 17*(2), 49–59.

Circadian. (2005). Absenteeism: A bottom line killer. [White paper]. Retrieved from: http://www.workforceinstitute.org/wp-content/themes/revolution/docs/Absenteeism-Bottom-Line.pdf

Claes, R., & Heymans, M. (2008). HR professionals' views on work motivation and retention of older workers: A focus group study. *Career Development International, 13(2),* 95–111.

Clarke, N. (2002). Job/work environment factors influencing training transfer within a human service agency: Some indicative support for Baldwin and Ford's transfer climate construct. *International Journal of Training and Development, 6*(3), 146–162.

Cleverly v. Western Electric, 594 F.2d 638 (8th Cir. 1979).

Cober, R. T., Brown, D. J., Blumental, A. J., Doverspike, D., & Levy, P. E. (2000). The quest for the qualified job surfer: It's time the public sector catches the wage. *Public Personnel Management, 29*(4), 479–496.

Cober, R. T., Brown, D. J., Keeping, L. M., & Levy, P. E. (2004). Recruitment on the net: How do organizational web site characteristics influence applicant attraction? *Journal of Management, 30*(5), 623–646.

Cober, R. T., Brown, D. J., Levy, P. E., Cober, A. B., & Keeping, L. M. (2003). Organizational web sites: Web site content and style as determinants of organizational attraction. *International Journal of Selection and Assessment, 11*(2/3), 158–169.

**Cohen, D. B., Aamodt, M. G., & Dunleavy, E. M.** (2010). *Technical advisory committee report on best practices in adverse impact analyses.* Washington, DC: Center for Corporate Equality.

**Cohen, S. G.** (1994). Designing effective self-managing work teams. In M. M. Beyerlein & D. A. Johnson (Eds.), *Advances in interdisciplinary studies of work teams* (Vol. 1, pp. 67–102). Greenwich, CT: JAI Press.

**Cohen, S. G., & Bailey, D.** (1997). What makes teams work: Group effectiveness research from the shop floor to the executive suite. *Journal of Management, 23,* 239–290.

**Cole, M. S., Bedeian, A. G., & Feild, H. S.** (2006). The measurement equivalence of web-based and paper-and-pencil measures of transformational leadership. *Organizational Research Methods, 9*(3), 339–369.

**Collins, C. J., & Stevens, C. K.** (2002). The relationship between early recruitment-related activities and the application decisions of new labor-market entrants: A brand equity approach to recruitment. *Journal of Applied Psychology, 87*(6), 1121–1133.

**Collins, J. M., & Schmidt, F. L.** (1993). Personality, integrity, and white collar crime: A construct validity study. *Personnel Psychology, 46,* 295–311.

**Connelly, R., DeGraff, D. S., & Willis, R. A.** (2004). *Kids at work: The value of employer-sponsored on-site child care centers.* WE Upjohn Institute.

**Conway, N., & Briner, R.** (2012). Investigating the effect of collective organizational commitment on unit-level performance and absence. *Journal of Occupational and Organizational Psychology, 85,* 472–486.

**Conte, J. M., Dean, M. A., Ringenbach, K. L., Moran, S. K., & Landy, F. J.** (2005). The relationship between work attitudes and job analysis ratings: Do rating scale type and task discretion matter? *Human Performance, 18*(1), 1–21.

**Cook, B. J.** (2012). The American college president study: Key findings and takeaways. *American Council on Education.* Retrieved August 19, 2015, from http://www.acenet.edu/the-presidency/columns-and-features/Pages/The-American-College-President-Study.aspx

**Cook, T. D., & Campbell, D. T.** (1979). *Quasi-experimentation: Design and analysis issues for field settings.* Boston: Houghton Mifflin.

**Corbett, C., & Hill, C.** (2012). Graduating to a pay gap: The earnings of women and men one year after college graduation. Retrieved from http://www.aauw.org/research/graduating-to-a-pay-gap/

**Cordes, C. L., & Dougherty, T. W.** (1993). A review and an integration of research on job burnout. *Academy of Management Review, 18*(4), 621–656.

**Cortina, J. M., Goldstein, N. B., Payne, S. C., Davison, H. K., & Gilliland, S. W.** (2000). The incremental validity of interview scores over and above cognitive ability and conscientiousness scores. *Personnel Psychology, 53*(2), 325–351.

**Cota, A. A., Evans, C. R., Dion, K. L., Kilik, L., & Longman, R. S.** (1995). The structure of group cohesion. *Personality and Social Psychology Bulletin, 21*(6), 572–580.

**Cote, S., & Morgan, L. M.** (2002). A longitudinal analysis of the association between emotion regulation, job satisfaction, and intentions to quit. *Journal of Organizational Behavior, 23*(8), 947–962.

**Cotti, C. D., Haley, M. R., & Miller, L. A.** (2014). Workplace flexibilities, job satisfaction and union membership in the US workforce. *British Journal of Industrial Relations, 52,* 403–425.

**Coyle-Shapiro, J. A.-M., & Morrow, P. C.** (2003). The role of individual differences in employee adoption of TQM orientation. *Journal of Vocational Behavior, 62*(2), 320–340.

**Coyle-Shapiro, J. A.-M., Morrow, P. C., Richardson, R., & Dunn, S.** (2002). Using profit sharing to enhance employee attitudes: A longitudinal examination of the effects on trust and commitment. *Human Resource Management, 41*(4), 423–439.

**Cronshaw, S. F.** (2012). Functional Job Analysis. In M. A. Wislon, W. Bennet, S. G. Gibson, & G. M. Alliger (Eds.). *The Handbook of Work Analysis: Methods, Systems, Applications, and Science of Work Measurement in Organizations* (265–279). New York: Routledge.

**Cropanzano, R., Slaughter, J. E., & Bachiochi, P. D.** (2005). Organizational justice and black applicants' reactions to affirmative action. *Journal of Applied Psychology, 90*(6), 1168–1184.

**Cross, C.** (2010). Barriers to the executive suite: Evidence from Ireland. *Leadership and Organization Development Journal, 31*(2), 104–119.

**Crump, M. J. C., McDonnell, J. V., & Gureckis, T. M.** (2013). Evaluating Amazon's Mechanical Turk as a tool for experimental behavioral research. *PLoS ONE* 8(3):e57410. doi:10.1371/journal.pone.0057410

**Crute, S.** (2007, November & December). *Caring for the caregiver*. Retrieved April 19, 2009, from http://www.aarpmagazine.org/family/caregiving/caring_for_the_caregiver.html

**Cucina, J. M., Vasilopoulos, N. L., & Sehgal, K. G.** (2005). Personality-based job analysis and the self-serving bias. *Journal of Business and Psychology, 20*(2), 275–290.

**Cummings, T. G., & Worley, C. G.** (2005). *Organization development and change* (8th ed.). Cincinnati, OH: South-Western.

**Curtis, A. B., Darvey, R. D., & Ravden, D.** (2005). Sources of political distortions in performance appraisals: Appraisal purpose and rater accountability. *Group and Organizational Management, 30*(1), 42–60.

**Dahling, J. J., Chau, S. L., & O'Malley, A.** (2012). Correlates and consequences of feedback orientation in organizations. *Journal of Management, 38*, 530–545.

**Dalal, R. S.** (2005). A meta-analysis of the relationship between organizational citizenship behavior and counterproductive work behavior. *Journal of Applied Psychology, 90*(6), 1241–1255.

**Dansereau, F., Graen, G. B., & Haga, W.** (1975). A vertical dyad linkage approach to leadership in formal organizations. *Organizational Behavior and Human Performance, 13*, 46–78.

**Davis, R. S.** (2013). Unionization and work attitudes: How union commitment influences public sector jobs. *Public Administration Review, 73*, 74–84.

**Day, D. V., Sin, H., & Chen, T. T.** (2004). Assessing the burdens of leadership: Effects of formal leadership roles on individual performance over time. *Personnel Psychology, 57*(3), 573–605.

**De Haan, E., Duckworth, A., Birch, D., & Jones, C.** (2013). Executive coaching outcome research: The contribution of common factors such as relationship, personality match, and self-efficacy. *Consulting Psychology Journal: Practice and Research, 65*(1), 40–57.

**Deadrick, D. L., Bennett, N., & Russell, C. J.** (1997). Using hierarchical linear modeling to examine dynamic performance criteria over time. *Journal of Management, 23*(6), 745–757.

**Deadrick, D. L., & Madigan, R. M.** (1990). Dynamic criteria revisited: A longitudinal study of performance stability and predictive validity. *Personnel Psychology, 43*, 717–744.

**Debnath, S. C., Lee, B. B., & Tandon, S.** (2015). Fifty years and going strong: What makes Behaviorally Anchored Rating Scales so perennial as an appraisal method? *International Journal of Business and Social Science, 6*, 16–25.

**Deci, E. L.** (1975). *Intrinsic motivation*. New York: Plenum Press.

**Deci, E. L., & Ryan, R. M.** (2000). The "what" and "why" of goal pursuits: Human needs and the self-determination of behavior. *Psychological Inquiry, 11*(4), 227–268.

**De Cuyper, N., De Witte, H., Vander Elst, T., & Handaja, Y.** (2010). Objective threat of unemployment and situational uncertainty during a restructuring: Associations with perceived job insecurity and strain. *Journal of Business and Psychology, 25*(1), 75–85.

**Deloitte.** (2014). It's official: Forced ranking is dead. *The Wall Street Journal, U.S. Edition*. Retrieved October 20, 2015, from http://deloitte.wsj.com/cio/2014/06/10/its-official-forced-ranking-is-dead/

**Demerouti, E., Bakker, A. B., Nachreiner, F., & Schaufeli, W. B.** (2001). The job demands–resources model of burnout. *Journal of Applied Psychology, 86*(3), 499–512.

**DeNavas-Walt, C., & D. Proctor, B. D.** (2014). U.S. Census Bureau, Current Population Reports P60-249, Income and Poverty in the United States: 2013, U.S. Government Printing Office, Washington, DC, Table A-4.

**den Hartog, D. N., Boselie, R., & Paauwe, J.** (2004). Performance management: A model and research agenda. *Applied Psychology: An International Review, 53*(4), 556–569.

**DeNisi, A. S., & Kluger, A. N.** (2000). Feedback effectiveness: Can 360-degree appraisals be improved? *Academy of Management Executive, 14*(1), 129–139.

**DeNisi, A. S., & Pritchard, R. D.** (2006). Performance appraisal, performance management, and improving individual performance: A motivational framework. *Management and Organizational Review, 2*, 253–277.

**Denning, S.** (2014, January 15). Making sense of Zappos and Holacracy. *Forbes.* Retrieved from http://www.forbes.com/sites/stevedenning/2014/01/15/making-sense-of-zappos-and-holacracy/

**DeRue, D. S., Nahrgang, J. D., Wellman, N., & Humphrey, S. E.** (2011). Trait and behavioral theories of leadership: An integration and meta-analytic test of their relative validity. *Personnel Psychology, 64,* 7–52.

**DeShon, R. P., & Gillespie, J. Z.** (2005). A motivated action account theory of goal orientation. *Journal of Applied Psychology, 90,* 1096–1127.

**Diaz v. Pan American World Airways, Inc.,** 442. F.2d 385 (5th Cir. 1971).

**Dickens, L., & Watkins, K.** (1999). Action research: Rethinking Lewin. *Management Learning, 300*(2), 127–140.

**Dickinson, A. M.** (1989). The detrimental effects of extrinsic reinforcement on "intrinsic motivation." *The Behavior Analyst, 12,* 1–15.

**Dickson, M. W., Den Hartog, D. N., & Mitchelson, J. K.** (2003). Research on leadership in a cross-cultural context: Making progress, and raising new questions. *Leadership Quarterly, 14,* 729–768.

**Dickson, M. W., Hanges, P. J., & Lord, R. G.** (2000). Trends, developments and gaps in cross-cultural research on leadership. In W. Mobley (Ed.), *Advances in global leadership* (Vol. 2, pp. 2–22). Stamford, CT: JAI Press.

**Diefendorff, J. M., Croyle, M. H., & Gosserand, R. H.** (2005). The dimensionality and antecedents of emotional labor strategies. *Journal of Vocational Behavior, 66*(2), 339–357.

**Diefendorff, J. M., & Gosserand, R. H.** (2003). Understanding the emotional labor process: A control theory perspective. *Journal of Organizational Behavior, 24*(8), 945–959.

**Diefendorff, J. M., & Lord, R. G.** (2003). The volitional and strategic effects of planning on task performance and goal commitment. *Human Performance, 16*(4), 365–387.

**Dimotakis, N., Scott, B. A., & Koopman, J.** (2011). An experience sampling investigation of workplace interactions, affective states, and employee well-being. *Journal of Organizational Behavior, 32*(4), 572–588.

**Dinh, J. E., Lord, R. G., Gardner, W. L., Meuser, J. D., Liden, R. C., & Hu, J.** (2014).

Leadership theory and research in the new millennium: Current theoretical trends and changing perspectives. *The Leadership Quarterly, 25*(1), 36–62.

**Dishman, L.** (2014). Can performance be quantified? Wearable tech in the office. Retrieved October 26, 2015, from http://www.fastcompany.com/3023793/dialed/can-performance-be-quantified-wearable-tech-in-the-office

**DiversityInc.** (2015). The 2015 DiversityInc top 50 companies for diversity. Retrieved December 11, 2015, from http://www.diversityinc.com/the-diversityinc-top-50-companies-for-diversity-2015/

**Dobbins, G. H., Cardy, R. K., & Platz-Vieno, S. J.** (1990). A contingency approach to appraisal satisfaction: An initial investigation of the joint effects of organizational variables and appraisal characteristics. *Journal of Management, 16,* 619–632.

**Dodd, Stevens introduce landmark bill to provide paid leave for workers**. (2007, June 21). Retrieved April 20, 2009, from http://dodd.senate.gov/?q=node/3953

**Donate, M. J., & Sánchez de Pablo, J. D.** (2015). The role of knowledge-oriented leadership in knowledge management practices and innovation. *Journal of Business Research, 68,* 360–370.

**Donnelly, D. P., & Quirin, J. J.** (2006). An extension of Lee and Mitchell's unfolding model of voluntary turnover. *Journal of Organizational Behavior, 27,* 59–77.

**Donovan, J. J., Dwight, S. A., & Schneider, D.** (2014). The impact of applicant faking on selection measures, hiring decisions, and employee performance. *Journal of Business and Psychology, 29*(3), 479–493.

**Donovan, J. J., & Radosevich, D. J.** (1999). A meta-analytic review of the distribution of practice effect: Now you see it, now you don't. *Journal of Applied Psychology, 84*(5), 795–805.

**Donovan, M. A., Drasgow, F., & Munson, L. J.** (1998). The Perceptions of Fair Interpersonal Treatment scale: Development and validation of a measure of interpersonal treatment in the workplace. *Journal of Applied Psychology, 83*(5), 683–692.

**Doran, G.T.** (1981). There's a SMART way to write management goals and objectives. *Management Review, 70* (11), 35–36.

**Dorfman, P., Javidan, M., Hanges, P., Dastmalchian, A., & House, R.** (2012). GLOBE:

A twenty year journey into the intriguing world of culture and leadership. *Journal of World Business, 47,* 504–518.

Douglas, S. C., Kiewitz, C., Martinko, M. J., Harvey, P., Kim, Y., & Chun, J. U. (2008). Cognitions, emotions, and evaluations: An elaboration likelihood model for workplace aggression. *Academy of Management Review, 33,* 425–451.

Doverspike, D., Cober, A. B., & Arthur, W., Jr. (2004). Multi-aptitude test batteries. In J. C. Thomas (Ed.), *Comprehensive handbook of psychological assessment* (Vol. 4, pp. 21–34). Hoboken, NJ: Wiley.

Doverspike, D., & O'Malley, A. (2006, February). When generations collide. *International Public Management Association for Human Resources News, 1,* 5–6.

Dragoni, L., Oh, I. S., Tesluk, P. E., Moore, O. A., VanKatwyk, P., & Hazucha, J. (2014). Developing leaders' strategic thinking through global work experiences: The moderating role of cultural distance. *Journal of Applied Psychology, 99*(5), 867–882.

Drasgow, F., Chernyshenko, O. S., & Stark, S. (2010). 75 years after Likert: Thurstone was right! *Industrial and Organizational Psychology, 3*(4), 465–476.

du Plessis, M. (2007). The role of knowledge management in innovation. *Journal of Knowledge Management, 11,* 20–29.

Duarte, N. T., Goodson, J. R., & Klich, N. R. (1993). How do I like thee? Let me appraise the ways. *Journal of Organizational Behavior, 14*(3), 239–249.

Dulebohn, J. H., Bommer, W. H., Liden, R. C., Brouer, R. L., & Ferris, G. R. (2012). A meta-analysis of antecedents and consequences of leader-member exchange: Integrating the past with an eye toward the future. *Journal of Management, 38*(6), 1715–1759.

Duncan, T. S. (1995). Death in the office—Workplace homicides. *Law Enforcement Bulletin, 64*(4), 20–25.

Dunford, B. B., & Devine, D. J. (1998). Employment at-will and employee discharge: A justice perspective on legal action following termination. *Personnel Psychology, 51,* 903–934.

Dunham, R. B., & Herman, J. B. (1975). Development of a female Faces Scale for measuring job satisfaction. *Journal of Applied Psychology, 60*(5), 629–631.

Dunlop, P. D., & Lee, K. (2004). Workplace deviance, organizational citizenship behavior, and business

unit performance: The bad apples do spoil the whole barrel. *Journal of Organizational Behavior, 25*(1), 67–80.

Dunnette, M. D. (1962). Personnel management. *Annual Review of Psychology, 13,* 285–314.

Dupré, K. E., & Barling, J. (2006). Predicting and preventing supervisory workplace aggression. *Journal of Occupational Health Psychology, 11,* 13–26.

Eagly, A. H. (2007). Female leadership advantage and disadvantage: Resolving the contradictions. *Psychology of Women Quarterly, 31,* 1–12.

Eagly, A. H., & Chin, J. (2010). Diversity and leadership in a changing world. *American Psychologist, 65,* 216–224.

Eagly, A. H., Johannesen-Schmidt, M. C., & van Engen, M. L. (2003). Transformational, transactional, and laissez-faire leadership styles: A meta-analysis comparing women and men. *Psychological Bulletin, 129*(4), 569–591.

Eagly, A. H., & Johnson, B. T. (1990). Gender and leadership style: A meta-analysis. *Psychological Bulletin, 108*(2), 233–256.

Eagly, A. H., & Karau, S. J. (1991). Gender and the emergence of leaders. *Journal of Personality and Social Psychology, 60*(5), 685–710.

Eagly, A. H., Karau, S. J., & Makhijani, M. G. (1995). Gender and the effectiveness of leaders: A meta-analysis. *Psychological Bulletin, 117*(1), 125–145.

Eatough, E. M., Chang, C., Miloslavic, S. A., & Johnson, R. E. (2011). The relationship of role stressors with organizational citizenship behavior: A meta-analysis. *Journal of Applied Psychology, 96*(3), 619–632.

Educational Testing Service. (2007). *Adaptive tests.* Retrieved March 19, 2008, from http://www.ets.org

Edwards, J. C., Rust, K. G., McKinley, W., & Moon, G. (2003). Business ideologies and perceived breach of contract during downsizing: The role of the ideology of employee self-reliance. *Journal of Organizational Behavior, 24*(1), 1–23.

EEOC v. Abercrombie & Fitch, 575 U.S. 1 (2015).

EEOC v. Atlas Paper Box Co., 868 F.2d 1487 (6th Cir. 1989).

EEOC v. Univ. of Texas Health Science Center at San Antonio, 710 F.2d 1091 (5th Cir. 1983).

**Egan, M.** (2015, March 24). Still missing: Female business leaders. CNN Money. Retrieved August 19, 2015, from http://money.cnn.com/2015/03/24/investing/female-ceo-pipeline-leadership/

**Egan, T. M., & Lancaster, C. M.** (2005). Comparing appreciative inquiry to action research: OD practitioner perspectives. *Organization Development Journal, 23,* 29–49.

**Eisenbeiss, S. A., van Knippenberg, D., & Boerner, S.** (2008). Transformational leadership and team innovation: Integrating team climate principles. *Journal of Applied Psychology, 93*(6), 1438–1446.

**Elfenbein, H. A.** (2008). Emotion in organizations: A review and theoretical integration in stages. *The Academy of Management Annals, 1,* 315–386.

**Eliason, M., & Storrie, D.** (2009). Does job loss shorten life? *Journal of Human Resources, 44*(2), 277–302.

**Elicker, J. D., Foust, M. S., O'Malley, A. L., & Levy, P. E.** (2008). Employee lateness behavior: The role of lateness climate and individual lateness attitude. *Human Performance, 21*(4), 427–441.

**Elicker, J. D., Levy, P. E., & Hall, R. J.** (2006). The role of leader–member exchange in the performance appraisal process. *Journal of Management, 32*(4), 531–551.

**Elst, T. V., De Cuyper, N., & De Witte, H.** (2011). The role of perceived control in the relationship between job insecurity and psychosocial outcomes: Moderator or mediator? *Stress and Health, 27*(3), e215–e227.

**Engle, E. M., & Lord, R. G.** (1997). Implicit theories, self-schemas, and leader–member exchange. *Academy of Management Journal, 40*(4), 988–1010.

**Ensari, N., & Murphy, S. E.** (2003). Cross-cultural variations in leadership perceptions and attribution of charisma to the leader. *Organizational Behavior and Human Decision Processes, 92*(1–2), 52–66.

**Epitropaki, O., & Martin, R.** (2005). From ideal to real: A longitudinal study of the role of implicit leadership theories on leader–member exchanges and employee outcomes. *Journal of Applied Psychology, 90*(4), 659–676.

**Equal Employment Opportunity Commission.** (2002a, December 2). *EEOC updates guidance on national origin discrimination.* Retrieved March 30, 2009, from http://www.eeoc.gov/press/12-2-02.html

**Equal Employment Opportunity Commission.** (2004, September 2). *Discriminatory practices.* Retrieved April 20, 2009, from http://www.eeoc.gov/abouteeo/overview_practices.html

**Equal Employment Opportunity Commission.** (2005, March 21). *The ADA: Your employment rights as an individual with a disability.* Retrieved April 20, 2009, from http://www.eeoc.gov/facts/ada18.html

**Equal Employment Opportunity Commission.** (2007, February 2). *Sexual harassment.* Retrieved March 30, 2009, from http://www.eeoc.gov/types/harassment.html

**Equal Employment Opportunity Commission.** (2009a, March 11). *Age discrimination.* Retrieved March 30, 2009, from http://www.eeoc.gov/types/age.html

**Equal Employment Opportunity Commission.** (2009b, March 11). *National origin discrimination.* Retrieved March 30, 2009, from http://www.eeoc.gov/origin/index.html

**Equal Employment Opportunity Commission.** (2009c, March 11). *National origin-based charges FY 1997–FY 2007.* Retrieved March 30, 2009, from http://www.eeoc.gov/stats/origin.html

**Equal Employment Opportunity Commission.** (2009d, March 11). *Pregnancy discrimination.* Retrieved March 30, 2009, from http://www.eeoc.gov/types/pregnancy.html

**Equal Employment Opportunity Commission.** (2009e, March 11). *Religious discrimination.* Retrieved March 30, 2009, from http://www.eeoc.gov/types/religion.html

**Erickson, R. J., Nichols, L., & Ritter, C.** (2000). Family influences on absenteeism: Testing an expanded process model. *Journal of Vocational Behavior, 57,* 246–272.

**Ertürk, A.** (2012). The role of person-organization fit in TQM: Influence of values and value congruence on TQM orientation/quality management and practices, edited by Dr. Kim-Song Ng. Retrieved on March 18, 2016, from http://www.intechopen.com/books/quality-management-and-practices/the-role-of-person-organization-fit-in-tqm-influence-of-values-and-value-congruence-on-tqm-orientat

**Ethridge v. State of Alabama,** 847 F.Supp. 903, 906-07 (M.D. Ala.1993).

**Evanoff, E., Zeringue, A., Franzblau, A., & Dale, A. M.** (2014). Using job-title-based physical exposures from O★NET in an epidemiological study of carpal tunnel syndrome. *Human Factors, 56,* 166–177.

**Evans, C. R., & Dion, K. L.** (1991). Group cohesion and performance: A meta-analysis. *Small Group Research, 22*(2), 175–186.

**Evans, D. C.** (2003). A comparison of the other-directed stigmatization produced by legal and illegal forms of affirmative action. *Journal of Applied Psychology, 88*(1), 121–130.

**Families and Work Institute.** (2007). *When work works: Making work "work."* Retrieved December 9, 2008, from http://familiesandwork.org/site/research/reports/3wbooklet.pdf

**Family Caregiver Alliance.** (2012) Selected caregiver statistics. Retrieved February 15, 2016, from https://www.caregiver.org/selected-caregiver-statistics

**Fang, H.-M, & Chang, W.-C.** (2014). The effects of member familiarity, task results visibility, and perceived coworker loafing on technology supported team performance: Social loafing effect perspective. *Asia Pacific Management Review, 19,* 361–373.

**Farnham, A.** (February 5, 2014). 20 fastest growing occupations. *ABC News.* Retrieved February 22, 2016, from http://abcnews.go.com/Business/americas-20-fastest-growing-jobs-surprise/story?id=22364716

**Farr, J. L., & Tippins, N. T.** (2013). *Handbook of employee selection.* New York: Routledge.

**Feder, J., & Levine, L.** (2010). *Pay equity legislation.* Washington, DC: Congressional Research Service. Retrieved July 11, 2012, from http://digitalcommons.ilr.cornell.edu/key_workplace/763

**Federal Aviation Administration.** (2012). Fair Treatment of Experienced Pilots Act (the age 65 law): Information, questions and answers. Retrieved November 30, 2015, from https://www.faa.gov/other_visit/aviation_industry/airline_operators/airline_safety/info/all_infos/media/age65_qa.pdf

**Fehr, R., Yam, K. C. S., & Dang, C.** (2015). Moralized leadership: The construction and consequences of ethical leader perceptions. *Academy of Management Review, 40*(2), 182–209.

**Ferguson, M., & Barry, B.** (2011). I know what you did: The effects of interpersonal deviance on bystanders. *Journal of Occupational Health Psychology, 16(1),* 80–94.

**Ferris, G. R., Munyon, T. P., Basik, K., & Buckley, M. R.** (2008). The performance evaluation context: Social, emotional, cognitive, political, and relationship components. *Human Resource Management Review, 18,* 146–163.

**Ferris, P. A.** (2009). The role of the consulting psychologist in the prevention, detection, and correction of bullying and mobbing in the workplace. *Consulting Psychology Journal: Practice and Research, 61*(3), 169–189.

**Fiedler, F. E.** (1967). *A theory of leadership effectiveness.* New York: McGraw-Hill.

**Fiedler, F. E.** (1995). Cognitive resources and leadership performance. *Applied Psychology: An International Review, 44*(1), 5–28.

**Findley, H. M., Giles, W. F., & Mossholder, K. W.** (2000). Performance appraisal process and system facets: Relationships with contextual performance. *Journal of Applied Psychology, 85*(4), 634–640.

**Fine, S., & Gottleib-Litvin, Y.** (2013). Justifying counterproductive work behaviors and an integrity-based conditional reasoning test: Back to the drawing board? *International Journal of Selection and Assessment, 21,* 328–333.

**Finn, A. N.** (2012). Teacher use of prosocial and antisocial power bases and students' perceived instructor understanding and misunderstanding in the college classroom. *Communication Education, 61*(1), 67–79.

**Fishbein, M., & Ajzen, I.** (1975). *Belief, attitude, intention and behavior: An introduction to theory and research.* Reading, MA: Addison-Wesley.

**Fisher v. University of Texas at Austin,** 631 F.3d 213 (5th Cir. 2011).

**Fisher, C. D.** (2000). Mood and emotions while working: Missing pieces of job satisfaction? *Journal of Organizational Behavior, 21,* 185–202.

**Fisher, C. D.** (2003). Why do lay people believe that satisfaction and performance are correlated? Possible sources of a commonsense theory. *Journal of Organizational Behavior, 24,* 753–777.

**Fitzpatrick, L.** (2010). Why do women still earn less than men? Retrieved December 29, 2010, from http://www.time.com/time/printout/0,8816,1983,185,00.html

**Flanagan, D. P., & Kaufman, A. S.** (2009). *Essentials of WISC-IV assessment.* Hoboken, NJ: Wiley.

**Fleishman, E. A., & Harris, E. F.** (1962). Patterns of leadership behavior related to employee grievances and turnover. *Personnel Psychology, 15,* 43–56.

**Fletcher, C., and Baldry, C.** (2015). Multi-source feedback systems: A research perspective. In I. T. Robertson and C. L. Cooper (Eds.), *Personnel psychology and human resources management: A reader for students and practitioners.* John Wiley & Sons.

**Flynn, F. J., & Schaumberg, R. L.** (2012). When feeling bad leads to feeling good: Guilt-proneness and affective organizational commitment. *Journal of Applied Psychology, 97,* 124–133.

**Folger, R., Konovsky, M., & Cropanzano, R.** (1992). A due process metaphor for performance appraisal. In B. Staw and L. Cummings (Eds.), *Research in organizational behavior* (Vol. 14, pp. 129–177). Greenwich, CT: JAI Press.

**Ford, J. D., Ford, L. W., & D'Amelio, A.** (2008). Resistance to change: The rest of the story. *Academy of Management Review, 33,* 362–377.

**Ford, M. T., Heinen, B. A., & Langkamer, K. L.** (2007). Work and family satisfaction and conflict: A meta-analysis of cross-domain relations. *Journal of Applied Psychology, 92,* 57–80.

**Forsyth, D.** (1999). *Group dynamics* (3rd ed.). Belmont, CA: Brooks/Cole.

**Foust, M. S., Elicker, J. D., & Levy, P. E.** (2006). Development and validation of a measure of an individual's lateness attitude. *Journal of Vocational Behavior, 69,* 119–133.

**Franklin, Gringer & Cohen, P. C.** (n.d.). *Key provisions of the Family and Medical Leave Act of 1993.* Retrieved March 30, 2009, from http://www.franklinringer.com/news-articles/labor-employment-law/key-provisions-of-the-family-medical-leave-act-of-1993/

**Freifeld, L.** (2013, November 29). Mobile learning is gaining momentum. *Training Magazine.* Retrieved October 8, 2015, from http://www.trainingmag.com/content/mobile-learning-gaining-momentum

**Freifeld, L.** (2015, February 10). Training magazine ranks 2015 top 125 organizations. *Training.* Retrieved July 25, 2015, from http://www.trainingmag.com/training-magazine-ranks-2015-top-125-organizations

**French, J., & Raven, B. H.** (1958). The bases of social power. In D. Cartwright (Ed.), *Studies of social power* (pp. 607–623). Ann Arbor, MI: Institute for Social Research.

**Fugate, M., Kinicki, A. J., & Prussia, G. E.** (2008). Employee coping with organizational change: An examination of alternative theoretical perspectives and models. *Personnel Psychology, 61,* 1–36.

**Fugate, M., Kinicki, A. J., & Scheck, C. L.** (2002). Coping with an organizational merger over four stages. *Personnel Psychology, 55*(4), 905–928.

**Fullagar, C. J., & Egleston, D. O.** (2008). Norming and performing: Using microworlds to understand the relationship between team cohesiveness and performance. *Journal of Applied Social Psychology, 38,* 2574–2593.

**Fulmer, R. M., Stumpf, S. A., & Bleak, J.** (2009). The strategic development of high potential leaders. *Strategy & Leadership, 37*(3), 17–22.

**Fulton, L. V., Ivanitskaya, L. V., Bastian, N. D., Erofeev, D. A., & Mendez, F. A.** (2013). Frequent deadlines: Evaluating the effect of learner control on healthcare executives' performance in online training. *Learning and Instruction, 23,* 24–32.

**Fu, N.** (2015). The role of relational resources in the knowledge management capability and innovation of professional service firms. *Human Relations, 68,* 731–764.

**Furst, S. A., & Cable, D. M.** (2008). Employee resistance to organizational change: Managerial influence tactics and leader–member exchange. *Journal of Applied Psychology, 93,* 453–462.

**Gabriel, A. S., Daniels, M. A., Diefendorff, J. M., & Greguras, G. J.** (2015). Emotional labor actors: A latent profile analysis of emotional labor strategies. *Journal of Applied Psychology, 100,* 863–879.

**Gabriel, A. S., Frantz, N. B., Levy, P. E., & Hilliard, A. W.** (2014). The supervisor feedback environment is empowering, but not all of the time: Feedback orientation as a critical moderator. *Journal of Occupational and Organizational Psychology, 87*(3), 487–506.

**Gagné, M., & Deci, E. L.** (2005). Self-determination theory and work motivation. *Journal of Organizational Behavior, 26,* 331–362.

**Gagné, R. M., Briggs, L. J., & Wager, W. W.** (1992). *Principles of instructional design* (4th ed.). Fort Worth, TX: Harcourt Brace Jovanovich.

**Gajendran, R. S., Harrison, D. A., & Delaney-Klinger, K.** (2015). Are telecommuters remotely good citizens? Unpacking telecommuting's effects on performance via i-deals and job resources. *Personnel Psychology*, 68(2), 353–393.

**Gammon, A. R., Griffith, R. L., & Kung, M.** (2011). *How do real applicants who are fakers compare to nonfakers?* Paper presented at the annual meeting of the Society for Industrial and Organizational Psychology, Chicago, IL.

**Gap Inc.** (2015, June 15). Gap Inc. announces strategic initiatives to increase productivity and profitability of namesake brand. Retrieved March 6, 2016, from http://www.gapinc.com/content/gapinc/html/media/pressrelease/2015/med_pr_gps_gap_61515.html

**Gardner, W. L., Cogliser, C. C., Davis, K. M., & Dickens, M. P.** (2011). Authentic leadership: A review of the literature and research agenda. *The Leadership Quarterly, 22*(6), 1120–1145.

**Gardner, D., & Diedrick, D. L.** (2009). Underprediction of performance for U.S. minorities using cognitive abilities measures. *Equal Opportunities International, 27*(50), 455–464.

**Garfield, M. J., & Dennis, A. R.** (2012). Toward an integrated model of group development: Disruption of routines by technology-induced change. *Journal of Management Information Systems, 29,* 43–86.

**Garofano, C. M., & Salas, E.** (2005). What influences continuous employee development decisions? *Human Resource Management Review, 15*(4), 281–304.

**Gatewood, R. D., & Feild, H. S.** (2001). *Human resource selection* (5th ed.). Fort Worth, TX: Harcourt College.

**Gatewood, R. D., Feild, H. S., & Barrick, M.** (2007). *Human resource selection* (6th ed.). Fort Worth, TX: Harcourt College.

**Gatewood, R. D., Feild, H. S., & Barrick, M.** (2011). *Human resource selection* (7th ed.). Mason, OH: South-Western, Cengage Learning.

**Gaugler, B. B., Rosenthal, D. B., Thornton, G. C., III, & Bentson, C.** (1987). Meta-analysis of assessment center validity. *Journal of Applied Psychology,* 72(3), 493–511.

**Geisler, E.** (2007). A typology of knowledge management: Strategic groups and role behavior in organizations. *Journal of Knowledge Management, 11,* 84–96.

**Gellatly, I. R.** (1995). How important are dispositional factors as determinants of job satisfaction? Implications for job design and other personnel programs. *Journal of Applied Psychology, 72*(3), 366–373.

**Gellatly, I. R., Meyer, J. P., & Luchak, A. A.** (2006). Combined effects of the three commitment components on focal and discretionary behaviors: A test of Meyer and Herscovitch's propositions. *Journal of Vocational Behavior, 69*(2), 331–345.

**Gerhart, B.** (1987). How important are dispositional factors as determinants of job satisfaction? Implications for job design and other personnel programs. *Journal of Applied Psychology, 72*(3), 366–373.

**Gersick, C. J. G.** (1989). Making time: Predictable transitions in task groups. *Academy of Management Journal, 32,* 274–309.

**Gerstner, C. R., & Day, D. V.** (1994). Cross-cultural comparison of leadership prototypes. *Leadership Quarterly, 5*(2), 121–134.

**Gerstner, C. R., & Day, D. V.** (1997). Meta-analytic review of leader–member exchange theory: Correlates and construct issues. *Journal of Applied Psychology, 82*(6), 827–844.

**Giacalone, R. A., & Greenberg, G.** (1997). *Antisocial behavior in organizations.* Thousand Oaks, CA: Sage.

**Giangreco, A., Carugati A., & Sebastiano, A.** (2010). Are we doing the right thing? Food for thought on training evaluation and its context. *Personnel Review, 39*(2), 162–177.

**Giglio, G., Michalcova, S., & Yates, C.** (2007). Instilling a culture of winning at American Express. *Organizational Development Journal, 25,* 33–37.

**Gilbreth, L. M.** (1914). *The psychology of management: The function of the mind in determining, teaching and installing methods of least waste.* Sturgis & Walton Company.

**Gill, H., Meyer, J. P., Lee, K., Shin, K. H., & Yoon, C. Y.** (2011). Affective and continuance commitment and their relations with deviant workplace behaviors in Korea. *Asia Pacific Journal of Management, 28*(3), 595–607.

**Gillespie, I., Rose, D. S., & Robinson, G. N.** (2006). *Narrative comments in 360 degree feedback: Who says what?* Paper presented at the 21st Annual Conference of the Society for Industrial and Organizational Psychology, Dallas, TX.

**Gilmer, B. V. H.** (1981). The early development of industrial-organizational psychology. In J. A. Sgro (Ed.),

*Virginia Tech Symposium on Applied Behavioral Science* (Vol. 1, pp. 3–16). Lexington, MA: Lexington Books.

**Gilson, L. L., Maynard, M. T., Jones Young, N. C., Vartiainen, M., & Hakonen, M.** (2015). Virtual teams research: 10 years, 10 themes, and 10 opportunities. *Journal of Management, 41*(5), 1313–1337.

**Gino, F., Schweitzer, M. E., Mead, N. L., & Ariely, D.** (2011). Unable to resist temptation: How self-control depletion promotes unethical behavior. *Organizational Behavior and Human Decision Processes, 115,* 191–203.

**Giumetti, G. W., Schroeder, A. N. & Switzer, F. S.** (2015). Forced distribution rating systems: When does "Rank and Yank" lead to adverse impact? *Journal of Applied Psychology, 100,* 180–193.

**Goffin, R. D., Jelley, R. B., & Wagner, S. H.** (2003). Is halo helpful? Effects of inducing halo on performance rating accuracy. *Social Behavior and Personality, 31*(6), 625–636.

**Goh, J., Pfeffer, J., & Zenios, S. A.** (2015). The relationship between workplace stressors and mortality and health costs in the United States. *Management Science.* doi:http://dx.doi.org/10.1287/mnsc.2014.2115

**Goldberg, C. B., & Waldman, D. A.** (2000). Modeling employee absenteeism: Testing alternative measures and mediated effects based on job satisfaction. *Journal of Organizational Behavior, 21,* 665–676.

**Golden, T. D.** (2006). Avoiding depletion in virtual work: Telework and the intervening impact of work exhaustion on commitment and turnover intentions. *Journal of Vocational Behavior, 69,* 176–187.

**Golden, T. D., Barnes-Farrell, J. L., & Mascharka, P. B.** (2009). Implications of virtual management for subordinate performance appraisals: A pair of simulation studies. *Journal of Applied Social Psychology, 39*(7), 1589–1608.

**Golden, T., & Gajendran, R. S.** (2014, January). (When) does telecommuting improve performance? The moderating role of work characteristics. *Academy of Management Proceedings* (Vol. 2014, No. 1, p. 15656). Academy of Management.

**Golden, T. D., Veiga, J. F., & Simsek, Z.** (2006). Telecommuting's differential impact on work–family conflict: Is there no place like home? *Journal of Applied Psychology, 91*(6), 1340–1350.

**Goldman, B. M., Gutek, B. A., Stein, J. H., & Lewis, K.** (2006). Employment discrimination in organizations: Antecedents and consequences. *Journal of Management, 32,* 786–830.

**Goldman-Mellor, S. J., Saxton, K. B., & Catalano, R. C.** (2010). Economic contraction and mental health: A review of the evidence, 1990–2009. *International Journal of Mental Health, 39*(2), 6–31.

**Goldring, E. B., Mavrogordato, M., & Haynes, K. T.** (2015). Multisource principal evaluation data: Principals' orientations and reactions to teacher feedback regarding their leadership effectiveness. *Educational Administration Quarterly, 51,* 572–599.

**Goldstein, H. W., Zedeck, S., & Goldstein, I. L.** (2002). Is this your final answer? *Human Performance, 15*(1–2), 123–142.

**Goldstein, I. L., & Ford, J. K.** (2002). *Training in organizations: Needs assessment, development, and evaluation* (4th ed.). Belmont, CA: Wadsworth.

**Gollwitzer, P. M., & Sheeran, P.** (2006). Implementation intentions and goal achievement: A meta-analysis of effects and processes. *Advances in Experimental Social Psychology, 38,* 69–120.

**Gonzalez, G.** (2004). Elder care resources offer comfort to workers. *Business Insurance, 38*(13), 11–12.

**Goodman, P. S., & Dabbish, L. A.** (2011). Methodological issues in measuring group learning. *Small Group Research, 42*(4), 379–404.

**Goren, H., Kurzban, R., & Rapoport, A.** (2003). Social loafing vs. social enhancement: Public goods provisioning in real-time with irrevocable commitments. *Organizational Behavior and Human Decision Processes, 90*(2), 277–290.

**Gorenstein, P.** (2011, October 14). The Gap slashes stores: What went wrong and how they can fix it. *The Daily Ticker.*

**Gould, K. E.** (2005). The corporate university: A model for sustaining an expert workforce in the human services. *Behavior Modification, 29*(3), 508–520.

**Gowan, M. A., Riordan, C. M., & Gatewood, R. D.** (1999). Test of a model of coping with involuntary job loss following a company closing. *Journal of Applied Psychology, 84*(1), 75–86.

**Gowen, C. R., III.** (1991). Gain-sharing programs: An overview of history and research. *Journal of Organizational Behavior Management, 11*(2), 77–99.

**Grandey, A. A., & Brauburger, A. L.** (2002). The emotion regulation behind the customer service smile. In R. G. Lord, R. J. Klimoski, & R. Kanfer (Eds.), *Emotions in the workplace: Understanding the structure and role of emotions in organizational behavior* (pp. 260–294). San Francisco: Jossey-Bass.

**Grandey, A. A., Fisk, G. M., Mattila, A. S., Jansen, K. J., & Sideman, L. A.** (2005). Is "service with a smile" enough? Authenticity of positive displays during service encounters. *Organizational Behavior and Human Decision Processes, 96,* 38–55.

**Grant, A. M.** (2008). The significance of task significance: Job performance effects, relational mechanisms, and boundary conditions. *Journal of Applied Psychology, 93*(1), 108–124.

**Grant, A. M., Fried, Y., Parker, S. K., & Frese, M.** (2010). Putting job design in context: Introduction to the special issue. *Journal of Organizational Behavior, 31,* 145–157.

**Gratz v. Bollinger,** 539 U.S. 244 (2003).

**Green, C., & Heywood, J. S.** (2008). Does performance pay increase job satisfaction? *Economica, 75*(300), 710–728.

**Greenhaus, J. H., & Powell, G. N.** (2006). When work and family are allies: A theory of work–family enrichment. *Academy of Management Review, 31*(1), 72–92.

**Greenleaf, R. K.** (2002). *Servant leadership: A journey into the nature of legitimate power and greatness* (25th anniversary ed.). Mahwah, NJ: Paulist Press.

**Greenwald, J.** (2001, June 18). Rank and fire. *Time, 157,* 38–40.

**Gregory, J. B., & Levy, P. E.** (2010). Employee coaching relationships: Enhancing construct clarity and measurement. *Coaching: An International Journal of Theory, Research and Practice, 3*(2), 109–123.

**Greiner, L., Cummings, T., & Bhambri, A.** (2003). When new CEOs succeed and fail: 4-H theory of strategic transformation. *Organizational Dynamics, 32*(1), 1–16.

**Gray, T. G., Hood, G., & Farrell, T.** (2015). The development and production of a novel smartphone app to collect day-to-day feedback from doctors-in-training and their trainers. *BMJ Innovation, 1,* 25–32.

**Griffeth, R. W., Hom, P. W., & Gaertner, S.** (2000). A meta-analysis of antecedents and correlates of employee turnover: Update, moderator tests, and research implications for the next millennium. *Journal of Management, 26*(3), 463–488.

**Griffith, R. L., & Converse, P. D.** (2011). The rules of evidence and the prevalence of applicant faking. In M. Ziegler, C. McCann, & R. Roberts (Eds.), *New perspectives on faking in personality assessments.* Oxford, UK: Oxford University Press.

**Griggs v. Duke Power,** 401 U.S. 424 (1971).

**Grindle, A. C., Dickinson, A. M., & Boettcher, W.** (2000). Behavioral safety research in manufacturing settings: A review of the literature. *Journal of Organizational Behavior Management, 20*(1), 29–68.

**Gross, J.** (1998). Antecedent- and response-focused emotion regulation: Divergent consequences for experience, expression, and physiology. *Journal of Personality and Social Psychology, 74*(1), 224–237.

**Grote, D.** (2005). *Forced ranking: Making performance management work.* Boston, MA: Harvard Business School Press.

**Grunberg, L., Anderson-Connolly, R., & Greenberg, E. S.** (2000). Surviving layoffs: The effects of organizational commitment and job performance. *Work and Occupations, 27*(1), 7–31.

**Grutter v. Bollinger,** 539 U.S. 306 (2003).

**Grzywacz, J. G., Almeida, D. M., & McDonald, D.** (2002). Work–family spillover and daily reports of work and family stress in the adult labor-force. *Family Relations, 51,* 28–36.

**Grzywacz, J. G., Arcury, T. A., Márin, A., Carrillo, L., Burke, B., Coates, M. L., & Quandt, S. A.** (2007). Work–family conflict: Experiences and health implications among immigrant Latinos. *Journal of Applied Psychology, 92,* 1119–1130.

**Guay, R. P., Choi, D., Oh, I. S., Mitchell, M. S., Mount, M., & Shin, K. H.** (2016). Why people harm the organization and its members: Relationships among personality, organizational commitment, and workplace deviance. *Human Performance, 29*(1), 1–15.

**Gully, S. M., Payne, S. C., Koles, K. L. K., & Whiteman, J.-A. K.** (2002). The impact of error training and individual differences on training outcomes: An attribute–treatment interaction perspective. *Journal of Applied Psychology, 87*(1), 143–155.

Gutek, B. A., & Koss, M. P. (1993). Changed women and changed organizations: Consequences of and coping with sexual harassment. *Journal of Vocational Behavior, 42,* 28–48.

Gutman, A. (2000). *EEO law and personnel practices* (2nd ed.). Thousand Oaks, CA: Sage.

Gutman, A. (2003). The Grutter, Gratz, & Costa rulings. *Industrial-Organizational Psychologist, 41*(2), 117–127.

Gutman, A., & Dunleavy, E. (2007). The Supreme Court ruling in Parents v. Seattle School District: Sending Grutter and Gratz back to school. *The Industrial-Organizational Psychologist, 45*(2), 41–49.

Haas, M. R., Criscuolo, P., & George, G. (2015). Which problems to solve? Online knowledge sharing and attention allocation in organizations. *Academy of Management Journal, 58*(3), 680–711.

Hackett, R. D., Bycio, P., & Hausdorf, P. A. (1994). Further assessments of Meyer and Allen's (1991) three-component model of organizational commitment. *Journal of Applied Psychology, 79,* 15–23.

Hackett, R. D., & Guion, R. M. (1985). A reevaluation of the absenteeism–job satisfaction relationship. *Organizational Behavior and Human Decision Processes, 35,* 340–381.

Hackman, J. R., & Oldham, G. R. (1976). The job characteristics model. *Organizational Behavior and Human Decision Processes, 16,* 256.

Hackman, J. R., & Oldham, G. R. (1980). *Work redesign.* Upper Saddle River, NJ: Pearson.

Hahn, C. (2007). Day care: An office affair. *Bloomberg Business.* Retrieved February 15, 2016, from http://www.businessweek.com/debateroom/archives/2007/04/day_care_an_office_affair.html

Hainey, I. (2015, November 15). Knowledge management is power for companies. *The National.* Retrieved March 6, 2016, from http://www.thenational.ae/business/the-life/knowledge-management-is-power-for-companies

Halbesleben, J. R. B., Harvey, J., & Bolino, M. C. (2009). Too engaged? A conservation of resources view of the relationship between work engagement and work interference with family. *Journal of Applied Psychology, 94*(6), 1452–1465.

Hall, R. J., Workman, J. W., & Marchioro, C. A. (1998). Sex, task, and behavioral flexibility effects on leadership perceptions. *Organizational Behavior and Human Decision Processes, 74*(1), 1–32.

Hallett, M. B., & Gilbert, L. A. (1997). Variables differentiating university women considering role-sharing and conventional dual-career marriages. *Journal of Vocational Behavior, 50,* 308–322.

Halzack, S. (2013). PNC staffers have back up child- and elder-care options. *The Washington Post.* Retrieved February 15, 2016, from https://www.washingtonpost.com/business/capitalbusiness/pnc-staffers-have-backup-child--and-elder-care-options/2013/05/02/1bd126c6-b271-11e2-9a98-4be1688d7d84_story.html

Hammer, L. B., Cullen, J. C., Neal, M. B., Sinclair, R. R., & Shafiro, M. V. (2005). The longitudinal effects of work–family conflict and positive spillover on depressive symptoms among dual-earner couples. *Journal of Occupational Health Psychology, 10*(2), 138–154.

Hammer, L. B., Kossek, E. E., Anger, W. K., Bodner, T., & Zimmerman, K. L. (2011). Clarifying work–family intervention processes: The roles of work–family conflict and family-supportive supervisor behaviors. *Journal of Applied Psychology, 96*(1), 134.

Hammer, L. B., Kossek, E. E., Yragui, N. L., Bodner, T. E., & Hanson, G. C. (2008). Development and validation of a multidimensional measure of family supportive supervisor behaviors (FSSB). *Journal of Management, 35*(4), 837–856.

Hammer, M., & Champy, J. (1993). *Reengineering the corporation: A manifesto for business revolution.* New York: HarperCollins.

Han, G., & Jekel, M. (2011). The mediating role of job satisfaction between leader–member exchange and turnover intentions. *Journal of Nursing Management, 19,* 41–49.

Hanover, J. M. B., & Cellar, D. F. (1998). Environmental factors and the effectiveness of workforce diversity training. *Human Resource Development Quarterly, 9*(2), 105–124.

Harris, L. C., & Ogbonna, E. (2002). The unintended consequences of culture interventions: A study of unexpected outcomes. *British Journal of Management, 13*(1), 31–49.

Harris, M. M., & Hollman, K. D. (n.d.). Tip-topics: The top trends in I-O psychology: A graduate student perspective. Retrieved February 22, 2016, from http://www.siop.org/tip/Apr13/19_TipTopics.aspx

Harrison, D. A., Kravitz, D. A., Mayer, D. M., Leslie, L. M., & Lev-Arey, D. (2006). Understanding attitudes toward affirmative action programs in employment: Summary and meta-analysis of 35 years of research. *Journal of Applied Psychology, 91*(3), 1013–1036.

Harrison, D. A., Newman, D. A., & Roth, P. L. (2006). How important are job attitudes? Meta-analytic comparisons of integrative behavioral outcomes and time sequences. *Academy of Management Journal, 40,* 305–325.

Harrop, P., Hayward, J., Das, R., & Holland, G. (2015). *Wearable technology 2015–2025: Technologies, markets, forecasts.* IDTechEx.

Harvey, P., Summers, J. K., & Martinko, M. J. (2010). Attributional influences on the outcome–aggression relationship: A review and extension of past research. *International Journal of Organization Theory and Behavior, 13*(2), 174–201.

Harvey, R. J. (1991). Job analysis. In M. D. Dunnette & L. M. Hough (Eds.), *Handbook of industrial and organizational psychology* (2nd ed., Vol. 2, pp. 71–163). Palo Alto, CA: Consulting Psychologists Press.

Harvey, R. J. (1993). *Research monograph: Development of the Common-Metric Questionnaire (CMQ).* Retrieved April 22, 2009, from Personnel Systems & Technologies Corporation website: http://www.pstc.com/documents/monograph.pdf

Harvey, R. J. (2010). Motor oil or snake oil: Synthetic validity is a tool not a panacea. *Industrial and Organizational Psychology, 3(3),* 351–355.

Hatala, J. P., & Fleming, P. R. (2007). Making transfer climate visible: Utilizing social network analysis to facilitate the transfer of training. *Human Resource Development Review, 6*(1), 33–63.

Hattrup, K., O'Connell, M. S., & Wingate, P. H. (1998). Prediction of multidimensional criteria: Distinguishing task and contextual performance. *Human Performance, 11*(4), 305–319.

Hauenstein, N. M. A. (1998). Training raters to increase the accuracy of appraisals and the usefulness of feedback. In J. W. Smither (Ed.), *Performance appraisal: State of the art in practice* (pp. 404–442). San Francisco: Jossey-Bass.

Hedge, J. W., & Borman, W. C. (1995). Changing conceptions and practices in performance appraisal. In A. Howard (Ed.), *The changing nature of work* (pp. 451–482). San Francisco: Jossey-Bass.

Hedge, J. W., & Teachout, M. S. (2000). Exploring the concept of acceptability as a criterion for evaluating performance measures. *Group and Organizational Management, 25*(1), 22–44.

Hegewisch, A., & Hartmann, H. (2014, September). *The gender wage gap: 2013: Differences by race and ethnicity.* Retrieved from http://www.iwpr.org/initiatives/pay-equity-and-discrimination/#publications

Hendricks, J. W., & Payne, S. C. (2007). Beyond the Big Five: Leader goal orientation as a predictor of leadership effectiveness. *Human Performance, 20,* 317–343.

Hennessy, D. A. (2008). The impact of commuter stress on workplace aggression. *Journal of Applied Social Psychology, 38*(9), 2315–2335.

Henningsen, D. D, Henningsen, M. L. M., Eden, J., & Cruz, M. G. (2006). Examining the symptoms of groupthink and retrospective sensemaking. *Small Group Research, 37,* 36–64.

Hensel, J. M., Ruiz, C., Finney, C., & Dewa, C. S. (2015). Meta-analysis of risk factors for secondary traumatic stress in therapeutic work with trauma victims. *Journal of Traumatic Stress, 28*(2), 83–91.

Henson, J. A., & Beehr, T. A. (2013). Subordinates' performance and personality as predictors of leader rated leader-member exchange. *Academy of Management Proceedings, No. 1l.*

Hermelin, E., Lievens, F., & Robertson, I. T. (2007). The validity of assessment centres for the prediction of supervisory performance ratings. *International Journal of Selection and Assessment, 15*(4), 405–411.

Herold, D. M., Davis, W., Fedor, D. B., & Parsons, C. K. (2002). Dispositional influences on transfer of learning in multistage training programs. *Personnel Psychology, 55*(4), 851–869.

Hershcovis, M. S., Turner, N., Barling, J., Arnold, K. A., Dupré, K. E., Inness, M., . . . Sivanathan, N. (2007). Predicting workplace aggression: a meta-analysis. *Journal of Applied Psychology, 92*(1), 228.

Hertel, G., Geister, S., & Konradt, U. (2005). Managing virtual teams: A review of current empirical research. *Human Resource Management Review, 15,* 69–95.

Herzberg, F., Mausner, B., & Snyderman, B. (1959). *The motivation to work*. New York: Wiley.

Heslin, P. A., & VandeWalle, D. (2011). Performance appraisal procedural justice: The role of a manager's implicit person theory. *Journal of Management, 37*(6), 1694–1718.

Heslin, P. A., Vandewalle, D., & Latham, G. P. (2006). Keen to help? Managers' implicit person theories and their subsequent employee coaching. *Personnel Psychology, 59,* 871–902.

Highhouse, S. (1999). The brief history of personnel counseling in industrial-organizational psychology. *Journal of Vocational Behavior, 55*(3), 318–336.

Highhouse, S., Hoffman, J. R., Greve, E. M., & Collins, A. E. (2002). Persuasive impact of organizational value statements in a recruitment context. *Journal of Applied Social Psychology, 32,* 1737–1755.

Hill, R., Tranby, E., Kelly, E., & Moen, P. (2013). Relieving the time squeeze? Effects of a white collar workplace change on parents. *Journal of Marriage and Family, 75,* 1014–1029.

Hirschfeld, R. R., & Feild, H. S. (2000). Work centrality and work alienation: Distinct aspects of a general commitment to work. *Journal of Organizational Behavior, 21,* 789–800.

Hitt, M. A. (2000). The new frontier: Transformation of management for the new millennium. *Organizational Dynamics, 28*(3), 7–17.

Hobfoll, S. E., & Shirom, A. (2000). Conservation of resources theory: Applications to stress and management in the workplace. In: R. T. Golembiewsik (ed.), *Handbook of Organization Behavior* (pp. 57–81). New York: Dekker.

Hoch, J. E., & Kozlowski, S. W. J. (2012). Leading virtual teams: Hierarchical leadership, structural supports, and shared team leadership. *Journal of Applied Psychology, 99,* 390–403.

Hoch, J. E., & Kozlowski, S. W. (2014). Leading virtual teams: Hierarchical leadership, structural supports, and shared team leadership. *Journal of Applied Psychology, 99*(3), 390.

Hochschild, A. R. (1983). *The managed heart: Commercialization of human feeling.* Berkeley: University of California Press.

Hochwarter, W. A., Witt, L. A., & Kacmar, K. M. (2000). Perceptions of organizational politics as a moderator of the relationship between conscientiousness and job performance. *Journal of Applied Psychology, 85*(3), 472–478.

Hodgkinson, G. P., & Healey, M. P. (2008). Cognition in organizations. *Annual Review of Psychology, 59,* 387–417.

Hoffman, B. J., Blair, C. A., Meriac, J. P., & Woehr, D. J. (2007). Expanding the criterion domain? A quantitative review of the OCB literature. *Journal of Applied Psychology, 92*(2), 555–566.

Hoffman, B. J., Lance, C. E., Bynum, B., & Gentry, W. A. (2010). Rater source effects are alive and well after all. *Personnel Psychology, 63,* 119–151.

Hoffnung, M., & Williams, M. A. (2013). Balancing act: Career and family during college-educated women's 30s. *Sex roles, 68*(5-6), 321–334.

Hofmann, D. A., Jacobs, R., & Baratta, J. E. (1993). Dynamic criteria and the measurement of change. *Journal of Applied Psychology, 78,* 194–204.

Hofmann, D. A., Morgeson, F. P., & Gerras, S. J. (2003). Climate as a moderator of the relationship between leader–member exchange and content specific citizenship: Safety climate as an exemplar. *Journal of Applied Psychology, 88*(1), 170–178.

Hofmann, W., & Patel, P. V. (2015). SurveySignal: A convenient solution for experience sampling research using participants' own smartphones. *Social Science Computer Review, 33,* 235–253.

Hogan, J., Barrett, P., & Hogan, R. (2007). Personality measurement, faking, and employment selection. *Journal of Applied Psychology, 92*(5), 1270–1285.

Hogan, R., & Hogan, J. (1995). *Hogan Personality Inventory manual* (2nd ed.). Tulsa, OK: Hogan Assessment Systems.

Holladay, C. L., & Quinones, M. A. (2008). The influence of training focus and trainer characteristics on diversity training effectiveness. *Academy of Management Learning & Education, 7*(3), 343–354.

Hollenbeck, J. R., Beersma, B., & Schouten, M. E. (2012). Beyond team types and taxonomies: A dimensional scaling conceptualization for a team description. *Academy of Management Review, 37,* 82–106.

Holman, D. J., Axtell, C. M., Sprigg, C. A., Totterdell, P., & Wall, T. D. (2010). The mediating role of job characteristics in job redesign interventions: A serendipitous quasi-experiment. *Journal of Organizational Behavior, 31,* 84–105.

Holtom, B. C., Lee, T. W., & Tidd, S. T. (2002). The relationship between work status congruence and work-related attitudes and behaviors. *Journal of Applied Psychology, 87*(5), 903–915.

Holton, E. F., Coco, M. L., Lowe, J. L., & Dutsch, J. V. (2006). Blended delivery strategies for competency-based training. *Advances in Developing Human Resources, 8*(2), 210–228.

Hom, P. W., & Griffeth, R. W. (1991). Structural equations modeling test of a turnover theory: Cross-sectional and longitudinal analyses. *Journal of Applied Psychology, 76*(3), 350–366.

Holtz, B. C., & Harold, C. M. (2013). Effects of leadership consideration and structure on employee perceptions of justice and counterproductive work behavior. *Journal of Organizational Behavior, 34,* 492–519.

Hong, Y., Wyer, R. S., & Fong, C. P. S. (2008). Chinese working in groups: Effort dispensability versus normative influence. *Asian Journal of Social Psychology, 11*(3), 187–195.

Hooper, D. T., & Martin, R. (2008). Beyond personal leader–member exchange (LMX) quality: The effects of perceived LMX variability on employee reactions. *Leadership Quarterly, 19,* 20–30.

Hopfl, H. M. (2006). Post-bureaucracy and Weber's "modern" bureaucrat. *Journal of Organizational Change Management, 19,* 8–21.

Hornung, S., Rousseau, D. M., Glaser, J., Angerer, P., & Weigl, M. (2010). Beyond top-down and bottom–up work redesign: Customizing job content through idiosyncratic deals. *Journal of Organizational Behavior, 31,* 187–215.

Horwitz, S. K., & Horwitz, I. B. (2007). The effects of team diversity on team outcomes: A meta-analytic review of team demography. *Journal of Management, 33,* 987–1015.

Hosking, D. M., & Schriesheim, C. A. (1978). Improving leadership effectiveness: The leader match concept—A book review. *Administrative Science Quarterly, 23,* 496–505.

Hough, L. (1998). Personality at work: Issues and evidence. In M. Hakel (Ed.), *Beyond multiple choice:*

*Evaluating alternatives to traditional testing for selection* (pp. 131–159). Hillsdale, NJ: Erlbaum.

House, R. J. (1971). A path-goal theory of leader effectiveness. *Administrative Science Quarterly, 16,* 321–338.

House, R. J. (1996). Path-goal theory of leadership: Lessons, legacy, and a reformulated theory. *Leadership Quarterly, 7*(3), 323–352.

House, R. J., & Aditya, R. N. (1997). The social scientific study of leadership: Quo vadis? *Journal of Management, 23*(3), 409–473.

Howard, J. L., & Frink, D. D. (1996). The effects of organizational restructure on employee satisfaction. *Group and Organization Management, 21*(3), 278–303.

HP Knowledge Management. (2014). Find knowledge and insights across your enterprise: The HP Knowledge Management solution. Hewlett-Packard. Retrieved March 6, 2016, from http://www8.hp.com/h20195/v2/GetPDF.aspx/4AA5-9191ENW.pdf

Huang, X., Rode, J. C., & Schroeder, R. G. (2011). Organizational structure and continuous improvement and learning: Moderating effects of cultural endorsement of participative leadership. *Journal of International Business Studies, 42,* 103–120.

Huffcutt, A. I., Culbertson, S. S., & Weyhrauch, W. S. (2014). Moving forward indirectly: Reanalyzing the validity of employment interviews with indirect range restriction methodology. *International Journal of Selection and Assessment, 22,* 297–309.

Hülsheger, U. R., Lang, J. W., Schewe, A. F., & Zijlstra, F. R. (2015). When regulating emotions at work pays off: A diary and an intervention study on emotion regulation and customer tips in service jobs. *Journal of Applied Psychology, 100*(2), 263.

Humphrey, S. E., Hollenbeck, J. R., Meyer, C. J., & Ilgen, D. R. (2011). Personality configurations in self-managed teams: A natural experiment on the effects of maximizing and minimizing variance in traits. *Journal of Applied Social Psychology, 41*(7), 1701–1732.

Humphrey, S. E., Morgeson, F. P., & Mannor, M. J. (2009). Developing a theory of the strategic core of teams: A role composition model of team performance. *Journal of Applied Psychology, 94,* 48–61.

Humphrey, S. E., Nahrgang, J. D., & Morgeson, F. P. (2007). Integrating motivational, social, and contextual work design features: A meta-analytic summary and theoretical extension of the work design literature. *Journal of Applied Psychology, 92,* 1332–1356.

**Hung, R. Y. Y., Lien, B. Y., Wu, C., & Kuo, Y.** (2011). The impact of TQM and organizational learning on innovation performance in the high-tech industry. *International Business Review, 20*(2), 213–225.

**Hunt, C. M., Davidson, M. J., Fielden, S. L., & Hoel, H.** (2010). Reviewing sexual harassment in the workplace—an intervention model. *Personnel Review, 39*(5), 655–673.

**Hunter, J. E., & Hunter, R. F.** (1984). Validity and utility of alternative predictors of job performance. *Psychological Bulletin, 96*(1), 72–98.

**Hunter, J. E., & Schmidt, F. L.** (1990). *Methods of meta-analysis: Correcting error and bias in research findings.* Thousand Oaks, CA: Sage.

**Hur, Y., van den Berg, P. T., & Wilderom, C. P. M.** (2011). Transformational leadership as a mediator between emotional intelligence and team outcomes. *The Leadership Quarterly, 22*(4), 591–603.

**Hurtz, G. M., & Donovan, J. J.** (2000). Personality and job performance: The Big Five revisited. *Journal of Applied Psychology, 85*(6), 869–879.

**Ianiro, P.M., & Kauffeld, S.** (2014). Take care what you bring with you: How coaches' mood and interpersonal behavior affect coaching success. *Consulting Psychology Journal: Practice and Research, 66*(3), 231–257.

**Ilgen, D. R., Fisher, C. D., & Taylor, M. S.** (1979). Consequences of individual feedback on behavior in organizations. *Journal of Applied Psychology, 64,* 349–371.

**Ilies, R., & Judge, T. A.** (2003). On the heritability of job satisfaction: The mediating role of personality. *Journal of Applied Psychology, 88*(4), 750–759.

**Ilies, R., Judge, T. A., Wagner, D. T.** (2010). The influence of cognitive and affective reactions to feedback on subsequent goals. *European Psychologist, 15,* 121–131.

**Ilies, R., Peng, A. C., Savani, K., & Dimotakis, N.** (2013). Guilty and helpful: An emotion-based reparatory model of voluntary work behavior. *Journal of Applied Psychology, 98(6),* 1051–1059.

**Institute for Women's Policy Research.** (2015, March). Fact sheet: The gender wage gap: 2014. *IWPR #C430.*

**International Coach Federation.** (2015). Need coaching? Retrieved December 11, 2015, from http://coachfederation.org/need/?navItemNumber=501

**Jackson, S. E., & Joshi, A.** (2011). Work team diversity. In Zedeck, S. (Ed.), *APA handbook of industrial and organizational psychology, vol. 1: Building and developing the organization* (pp.651–686). Washington, DC: American Psychological Association. http://dx.doi.org/10.1037/12169-020

**Jackson, S. E., & Schuler, R. S.** (2000). *Managing human resources: A partnership perspective* (7th ed.). Cincinnati, OH: South-Western.

**James, S., Kavanagh, P. S., Jonason, P. K., Chonody, J. M., & Scrutton, H. E.** (2014). The Dark Triad, schadenfreude, and sensational interests: Dark personalities, dark emotions, and dark behaviors. *Personality and Individual Differences, 68,* 211–216.

**Janis, I. L.** (1972). *Victims of groupthink.* Boston: Houghton Mifflin.

**Janis, I. L.** (1982). *Groupthink.* Boston: Houghton Mifflin.

**Janis, I. L., & Mann, L.** (1977). *Decision making: A psychological analysis of conflict, choice, and commitment.* New York: Free Press.

**Jawahar, I. M., Stone, T. H., & Kisamore, J. L.** (2007). Role conflict and burnout: The direct and moderating effects of political skill and perceived organizational support on burnout dimensions. *International Journal of Stress Management, 14,* 142–159.

**Jayson, S.** (2012, October 24). Burnout up among employees. *USA Today.*

**Jehanzeb, K., Rasheed, A., & Rasheed, M. F.** (2013). Organizational commitment and turnover intentions: Impact of employee's training in private sector of Saudi Arabia. *International Journal of Business and Management, 8*(8), 79.

**Jex, S. M., Bliese, P. D., Buzzell, S., & Primeau, J.** (2001). The impact of self-efficacy on stressor–strain relations: Coping style as an explanatory mechanism. *Journal of Applied Psychology, 86*(3), 401–409.

**Johns, T., & Gratton, L.** (2013). The third wave of virtual work. *Harvard Business Review, 91*(1), 66–73.

**Johnson, J. W., Steel, P., Scherbaum, C. A., Hoffman, C. C., Jeanneret, P. R., & Foster, J.**

(2010). Validation is like motor oil: Synthetic is better. *Industrial and Organizational Psychology, 3*(3), 305–328.

Johnson, R. J., Chang, C. H., & Lord, R. G. (2006). Moving from cognition to action. *Psychological Bulletin, 132,* 381–415.

Johnson, S. K., Bettenhausen, K., & Gibbons, E. (2009). Realities of working in virtual teams: Affective and attitudinal outcomes of computer-mediated communication. *Small Group Research, 40*(6), 623–649.

Jonason, P. K., Slomski, S., & Partyka, J. (2012). The Dark Triad at work: How toxic employees get their way. *Personality and Individual Differences, 52,* 449–453.

Jones, L., Watson, B., Hobman, E., Bordia, P., Gallois, C., & Callan, V. J. (2008). Employee perceptions of organizational change: Impact of hierarchical level. *Leadership & Organization Development Journal, 29,* 294–316.

Jones, M. D., Sliter, M., & Sinclair, R. R. (2015). Overload, and cutbacks, and freezes, Oh my! The relative effects of the recession-related stressors on employee strain and job satisfaction. *Stress and Health.* doi:10.1002/smi.2657

Joni, S.-N. (2004). *The third opinion: How successful leaders use outside insight to create superior results.* New York: Portfolio/Penguin.

Joseph, D. L., Jin, J., Newman, D. A., & O'Boyle, E. H. (2015). Why does self-reported emotional intelligence predict job performance? A meta-analytic investigation of mixed EI. *Journal of Applied Psychology, 100,* 298–342.

Josserand, E., Teo, S., & Clegg, S. (2006). From bureaucratic to post-bureaucratic: The difficulties of transition. *Journal of Organizational Change Management, 19,* 54–64.

Judge, T. A., Bono, J. E., Erez, A., & Locke, E. A. (2005). Core self-evaluations and job and life satisfaction: The role of self-concordance and goal attainment. *Journal of Applied Psychology, 90,* 257–268.

Judge, T. A., Bono, J. E., Ilies, R., & Gerhardt, M. W. (2002). Personality and leadership: A qualitative and quantitative review. *Journal of Applied Psychology, 87*(4), 765–780.

Judge, T. A., Bono, J. E., & Locke, E. A. (2000). Personality and job satisfaction: The mediating role of job characteristics. *Journal of Applied Psychology, 85*(2), 237–249.

Judge, T. A., Colbert, A. E., & Ilies, R. (2004). Intelligence and leadership: A quantitative review and test of theoretical propositions. *Journal of Applied Psychology, 89*(3), 542–552.

Judge, T. A., & Hulin, C. L. (1993). Job satisfaction as a reflection of disposition: A multiple-source causal analysis. *Organizational Behavior and Human Decision Processes, 56,* 388–421.

Judge, T. A., Locke, E. A., Durham, C. C., & Kluger, A. N. (1998). Disposition effects on job and life satisfaction: The role of core evaluations. *Journal of Applied Psychology, 83*(1), 17–34.

Judge, T. A., Piccolo, R. E., & Ilies, R. (2004). The forgotten ones? The validity of consideration and initiating structure in leadership research. *Journal of Applied Psychology, 89*(1), 36–51.

Judge, T. A., Piccolo, R. F., Podsakoff, N. P, Shaw, J. C., & Rich, B. L. (2010). The relationship between pay and job satisfaction: A meta-analysis. *Journal of Vocational Behavior, 77,* 157–167.

Judge, T. A., Scott, B. A., & Ilies, R. (2006). Hostility, job attitudes, and workplace deviance. *Journal of Applied Psychology, 91,* 126–138.

Judge, T. A., Simon, L. S., Hurst, C., & Kelley, K. (2014). What I experienced yesterday is who I am today: Relationship of work motivations and behaviors to within-individual variation in the five factor model of personality. *Journal of Applied Psychology, 99,* 199–221.

Judge, T. A., Thoresen, C. J., Bono, J. E., & Patton, G. K. (2001). The job satisfaction–job performance relationship: A qualitative and quantitative review. *Journal of Applied Psychology, 127,* 376–407.

Jung, D. I., & Sosik, J. J. (1999). Effects of group characteristics on work group performance: A longitudinal investigation. *Group Dynamics: Theory, Research, and Practice, 3*(4), 279–290.

Junker, N. M., & van Dick, R. (2014). Implicit theories in organizational settings: A systematic review and research agenda of implicit leadership and followership theories. *The Leadership Quarterly, 25*(6), 1154–1173.

**K4Health.** (2016). Knowledge management for global health. Johns Hopkins University. Retrieved March 6, 2016, from https://www.k4health.org/topics/knowledge-management

**Kacmar, K. M., Witt, L. A., Zivnuska, S., & Gully, S. M.** (2003). The interactive effect of leader–member exchange and communication frequency on performance ratings. *Journal of Applied Psychology, 88*(4), 764–772.

**Kanfer, R.** (1990). Motivation theory and industrial and organizational psychology. In M. Dunnette & L. Hough (Eds.), *Handbook of industrial and organizational psychology* (2nd ed., Vol. 1., pp. 75–170). Palo Alto, CA: Consulting Psychologists Press.

**Kantrowitz, T. M., & Dainis, A. M.** (2014). How secure are unproctored pre-employment tests? Analysis of inconsistent test scores. *Journal of Business and Psychology, 29*(4), 605–616.

**Karakas, F.** (2009). New paradigms in organization development: Positivity, spirituality, and complexity. *Organization Development Journal, 27*(1), 11–26.

**Karasek, R.** (1990). Lower health risk with increased job control among white-collar workers. *Journal of Organizational Behaviour, 11,* 171–185.

**Karau, S. J., & Hart, J. W.** (1998). Group cohesiveness and social loafing: Effects of a social interaction manipulation on individual motivation within groups. *Group Dynamics: Theory, Research, and Practice, 2*(3), 185–191.

**Karau, S. J., & Williams, K. D.** (1993). Social loafing: A meta-analytic review and theoretical integration. *Journal of Personality and Social Psychology, 26,* 377–384.

**Karau, S. J., & Williams, K. D.** (1997). The effects of group cohesiveness on social loafing and social compensation. *Group Dynamics: Theory, Research, and Practice, 1,* 156–168.

**Karim, M. N., Kaminsky, S. E., & Behrend, T. S.** (2014). Cheating, reactions, and performance in remotely proctored testing: An exploratory experimental study. *Journal of Business and Psychology, 29*(4), 555–572.

**Kark, R., Shamir, B., & Chen, G.** (2003). The two faces of transformational leadership: Empowerment and dependency. *Journal of Applied Psychology, 88*(2), 246–255.

**Kass, D., & Grandzol, C.** (2012). Evaluating the value-added impact of outdoor management training for leadership development in an MBA program. *Journal of Experiential Education, 35*(3), 429–446.

**Kate, N. T.** (1998). Two careers, one marriage. *American Demographics, 20*(4), 28.

**Kath, L. M., Swody, C. A., Magley, V. J., Bunk, J. A., & Gallus, J. A.** (2009). Cross-level, three-way interactions among work-group climate, gender, and frequency of harassment on morale and withdrawal outcomes of sexual harassment. *Journal of Occupational and Organizational Psychology, 82,* 159–182.

**Katz, D., & Kahn, R. L.** (1978). *The social psychology of organizations* (2nd ed.). New York: Wiley.

**Katzell, R. A., & Austin, J. T.** (1992). From then to now: The development of industrial-organizational psychology in the United States. *Journal of Applied Psychology, 77*(6), 803–835.

**Kauffeld, S., & Lehmann-Willenbrock, N.** (2009). Sales training: Effects of spaced practice on training transfer. *Journal of European Industrial Training, 34*(1), 23–37.

**Kaufman, A. S.** (1994). *Intelligent testing with the WISC-III.* New York: Wiley.

**Keeping, L. M., & Levy, P. E.** (2000). Performance appraisal reactions: Measurement, modeling, and method bias. *Journal of Applied Psychology, 85*(5), 708–723.

**Keller, A. C., & Semmer, N. K.** (2013). Changes in situational and dispositional factors as predictors of job satisfaction. *Journal of Vocational Behavior, 83,* 88–98.

**Kellett, J. B., Humphrey, R. H., & Sleeth, R. G.** (2006). Empathy and the emergence of task and relations leaders. *Leadership Quarterly, 17,* 146–162.

**Kenny, D. A., & Zaccaro, S. J.** (1983). An estimate of the variance due to traits in leadership. *Journal of Applied Psychology, 68*(4), 678–685.

**Kenworthy, J., & Wong, A.** (2005). Developing managerial effectiveness: Assessing and comparing the impact of developmental programmes using a management simulation or management game. *Developments in Business Simulations and Experiential Learning, 32,* 164–175.

**Kerlinger, F. N.** (1986). *Foundations of behavioral research* (3rd ed.). Fort Worth, TX: Holt, Rinehart and Winston.

**Kerr, N. L., & Tindale, R. S.** (2004). Group performance and decision making. *Annual Review of Psychology, 55,* 623–655.

**Khanna, C., Medsker, G. J., & Ginter, R.** (2013). 2012 income and employment survey results for the Society for Industrial and Organizational Psychology.

*Human Resources Research Organization (HumRRO).* Retrieved on March 21, 2016, from http://www.siop.org/2012SIOPIncomeSurvey.pdf

**Kickul, J., Lester, S. W., & Finkl, J.** (2002). Promise breaking during radical organizational change: Do justice interventions make a difference? *Journal of Organizational Behavior, 23,* 469–488.

**Kinicki, A. J., McKee-Ryan, F. M., Schriesheim, C. A., & Carson, K. P.** (2002). Assessing the construct validity of the Job Descriptive Index: A review and meta-analysis. *Journal of Applied Psychology, 87*(1), 14–32.

**Kirkman, B. L., Chen, G., Farh, J., Chen, Z. X., & Lowe, K. B.** (2009). Individual power distance orientation and follower reactions to transformational leaders: A cross-level, cross-cultural examination. *Academy of Management Journal, 52*(4), 744–764.

**Kirkman, B. L., & Mathieu, J. E.** (2005). The dimensions and antecedents of team virtuality. *Journal of Management, 31,* 700–718.

**Kirkman, B. L., & Rosen, B.** (1999). Beyond self-management: Antecedents and consequences of team empowerment. *Academy of Management Journal, 42*(1), 58–74.

**Kirkpatrick, D. L.** (1976). Evaluation of training. In R. L. Craig (Ed.), *Training and development handbook* (pp. 18–27). New York: McGraw-Hill.

**Kish-Gephart, J. J., Harrison, D. A., & Treviño, L. K.** (2010). Bad apples, bad cases, and bad barrels: Meta-analytic evidence about sources of unethical decisions at work. *Journal of Applied Psychology, 95*(1), 1–31.

**Klein, H. J., Molloy, J. C., & Cooper, J. T.** (2009). Conceptual foundations: Construct definitions and theoretical representations of workplace commitments. In H. J. Klein, T. E. Becker, & J. P. Meyer (Eds.), *Commitment in organizations: Accumulated wisdom and new directions.* New York: Routledge/Taylor & Francis.

**Kluger, A. N., & DeNisi, A.** (1996). The effects of feedback interventions on performance: A historical review, a meta-analysis, and a preliminary Feedback Intervention Theory. *Psychological Bulletin, 119,* 254–284.

**Kluger, A. N., & Nir, D.** (2010). The Feedforward Interview. *Human Resource Management Review, 20*(3), 235–246.

**Knights, D., & McCabe, D.** (2002). A road less travelled: Beyond managerialist, critical and processual

approaches to total quality management. *Journal of Organizational Change Management, 15*(3), 235–254.

**Kock, N., Danesh, A., & Komiak, P.** (2008). A discussion and test of a communication flow optimization approach for business process redesign. *Knowledge and Process Management, 15,* 72–85.

**Koenig, A. M., Eagly, A. H., Mitchell, A. A., & Ristikari, T.** (2011). Are leader stereotypes masculine? A meta-analysis of three research paradigms. *Psychological Bulletin, 137*(4), 616–642.

**Koltko-Rivera, M. E.** (2006). Rediscovering the later version of Maslow's hierarchy of needs: Self-transcendence and opportunities for theory, research, and unification. *Review of General Psychology, 10,* 302–317.

**Komar, S., Brown, D. J., Komar, J., & Robie, C.** (2008). Faking and the validity of conscientiousness: A Monte Carlo investigation. *Journal of Applied Psychology, 93,* 140–154.

**Konovsky, M. A., & Cropanzano, R.** (1991). Perceived fairness of employee drug testing as a predictor of employee attitudes and job performance. *Journal of Applied Psychology, 76,* 698–707.

**Koppes, L. L.** (1997). American female pioneers of industrial and organizational psychology during the early years. *Journal of Applied Psychology, 82*(4), 500–515.

**Koppes, L. L.** (Ed.). (2007). *Historical perspectives in industrial and organizational psychology.* Mahwah, NJ: Erlbaum.

**Koppes, L. L., & Pickren, W.** (2007). Industrial and organizational psychology: An evolving science and practice. In L. L. Koppes (Ed.), *Historical perspectives in industrial and organizational psychology* (pp. 3–36). Mahwah, NJ: Erlbaum.

**Kossek, E. E., & Nichol, V.** (1992). The effects of on-site child care on employee attitudes and performance. *Personnel Psychology, 45,* 485–509.

**Kossek, E. E., & Ozeki, C.** (1998). Work–family conflict, policies, and the job-life satisfaction relationship: A review and directions for organizational behavior–human resources research. *Journal of Applied Psychology, 83*(2), 139–149.

**Kossek, E. E., Ruderman, M. N., Braddy, P. W., & Hannum, K. M.** (2012). Work–nonwork boundary management profiles: A person-centered approach. *Journal of Vocational Behavior, 81*(1), 112–128.

**Kotsou, I., Nelis, D., Gregoire, J., & Mikolajczak, M.** (2011). Emotional plasticity. *Journal of Applied Psychology, 96*(4), 827–839.

**Kraiger, K., Ford, J. K., & Salas, E.** (1993). Application of cognitive, skill-based, and affective theories of learning outcomes to new methods of training evaluating. *Journal of Applied Psychology, 78*(2), 311–328.

**Kreiner, G. E., Hollensbe, E. C., & Sheep, M. L.** (2009). Balancing borders and bridges: Negotiating the work–home interface via boundary work tactics. *Academy of Management Journal, 52*(4), 704–730.

**Kristof-Brown, A. L., Zimmerman, R. D., & Johnson, E.** (2005). Consequences of individuals' fit at work: A meta-analysis of person–job, person–organization, person–group, and person–supervisor fit. *Personnel Psychology, 58*, 281–342.

**Kruger, J., & Dunning, D.** (1999). Unskilled and unaware of it: how difficulties in recognizing one's own incompetence lead to inflated self-assessments. *Journal of personality and social psychology, 77*(6), 1121.

**Kuhn, K. M., & Yockey, M. D.** (2003). Variable pay as a risky choice: Determinants of the relative attractiveness of incentive plans. *Organizational Behavior and Human Decision Processes, 90*(2), 323–341.

**Kulich, C., Ryan, M. K., & Haslam, A. S.** (2007). Where is the romance for women leaders? The effects of gender on leadership attributions and performance-based pay. *Applied Psychology: An International Review, 4,* 582–601.

**Kulik, C. T., Pepper, M. B., Roberson, L., & Parker, S. K.** (2007). The rich get richer: Predicting participation in voluntary diversity training. *Journal of Organizational Behavior, 28*(6), 753–769.

**Kulik, C. T., & Roberson, L.** (2008). Diversity initiative effectiveness: What organizations can (and cannot) expect from diversity recruitment, diversity training, and formal mentoring programs. In A. P. Brief (Ed.), *Diversity at work* (pp. 265–317). Cambridge, UK: Cambridge University Press.

**Kuncel, N. R., Hezlett, S. A., & Ones, D. S.** (2001). A comprehensive meta-analysis of the predictive validity of the Graduate Record Examinations: Implications for graduate student selection and performance. *Psychological Bulletin, 127*(1), 162–181.

**Kuncel, N. R., Hezlett, S. A., & Ones, D. S.** (2004). Academic performance, career potential, creativity, and job performance: Can one construct predict them all? *Journal of Personality and Social Psychology, 86*(1), 148–161.

**Kuncel, N. R., Ones, D. S., & Sackett, P. R.** (2010). Individual differences as predictors of work, educational and broad life outcomes. *Personality and Individual Differences, 49*, 331–336.

**Kunin, T.** (1955). The construction of a new type of attitude measure. *Personnel Psychology, 8,* 65–77.

**Kunin, T.** (1998). The construction of a new type of attitude measure. *Personnel Psychology, 51,* 823–824.

**Kurtessis, J. N., Eisenberger, R., Ford, M. T., Buffardi, L. C., Stewart, K. A., & Adis, C. S.** (2015). Perceived organizational support: A meta-analytic evaluation of organizational support theory. *Journal of Management,* March 2015.

**Kurtzberg, T. R., Naquin, C. E., & Belkin, L. Y.** (2005). Electronic performance appraisals: The effects of e-mail communication on peer ratings in actual and simulated environments. *Organizational Behavior and Human Decision Processes, 98*(2), 216–226.

**Lachance-Grzela, M., & Bouchard, G.** (2010). Why do women do the lion's share of housework? A decade of research. *Sex roles, 63*(11–12), 767–780.

**Lai, Y.-L., Hsu, M.-S., Lin, F.-J., Chen, Y.-M., & Lin, Y.-H.** (2014). The effects of industry cluster knowledge management on innovation performance. *Journal of Business Research, 67,* 734–739.

**Lambert, L. S., Tepper, B. J., Carr, J. C., Holt, D. T., & Barelke, A. J.** (2012). Forgotten but not gone: An examination of fit between consideration and initiating structure needed and received. *Journal of Applied Psychology, 97*(5), 913–930.

**Landers, R. N., & Behrend, T. S.** (2015). An inconvenient truth: Arbitrary distinctions between organizations, Mechanical Turk, and other convenience samples. *Industrial and Organizational Psychology, 8*(2), 142–164.

**Landy, F. J., & Farr, J. L.** (1980). Performance rating. *Psychological Bulletin, 87,* 72–107.

**Lang, J. W. B., Kersting, M., Hülsheger, U. R., & Lang, J.** (2010). General mental ability, narrower cognitive abilities, and job performance: The perspective of the nested-factors model of cognitive abilities. *Personnel Psychology, 63*, 595–640.

**Langfred, C. W.** (2000). Work group design and autonomy: A field study of the interaction between task interdependence and group autonomy. *Small Group Research, 31*(1), 54–70.

**Langfred, C. W.** (2007). The downside of self-management: A longitudinal study of the effects of conflict on trust, autonomy, and task interdependence in self-managing teams. *Academy of Management Journal, 50,* 885–900.

**Lapierre, L. M., & Allen, T. D.** (2006). Work-supportive family, family-supportive supervision, use of organizational benefits, and problem-focused coping: Implications for work–family conflict and employee well-being. *Journal of Occupational Health Psychology, 11,* 169–181.

**Lardner, J.** (2002, March). Why should anyone believe you? *Business 2.0.*

**Larson, J. R., Jr., Christensen, C., Franz, T. M., & Abbott, A. S.** (1998). Diagnosing groups: The pooling, management, and impact of shared and unshared case information in team-based medical decision making. *Journal of Personality and Social Psychology, 75,* 93–108.

**Larson, J. R., Jr., Foster-Fishman, P. G., & Franz, T. M.** (1998). Leadership style and the discussion of shared and unshared information in decision-making groups. *Personality and Social Psychology Bulletin, 24*(5), 482–495.

**Laschinger, H. K. S., & Nosko, A.** (2015). Exposure to workplace bullying and post-traumatic stress disorder symptomology: The role of protective psychological resources. *Journal of Nursing Management, 23,* 252–262.

**Latham, G. P.** (1988). Human resource training and development. *Annual Review of Psychology, 39,* 545–582.

**Latham, G. P., & Saari, L. M.** (1979). The application of social learning theory to training supervisors through behavior modeling. *Journal of Applied Psychology, 64,* 239–246.

**Lau, V. C. S., Au, W. T., & Ho, J. M. C.** (2003). A qualitative and quantitative review of antecedents of counterproductive behavior in organizations. *Journal of Business and Psychology, 18*(1), 73–99.

**Lauby, S.** (2010). How job seekers may use social media in the future. Retrieved July 23, 2011, from http://mashable.com/2010/10/11/job-seekers-social-media-future/

**Lawler, E. E.** (2001). *Organizing for high performance.* San Francisco: Jossey-Bass.

**Lawler, E. E., & Porter, L. W.** (1967). The effects of performance on job satisfaction. *Industrial Relations, 7,* 20–28.

**Lawson, R. B., & Shen, Z.** (1998). *Organizational psychology: Foundations and applications.* New York: Oxford University Press.

**LeBlanc, M. M., & Barling, J.** (2004). Workplace aggression. *Current Directions in Psychological Science, 13*(1), 9–12.

**LeBlanc, M. M., & Kelloway, E. K.** (2002). Predictors and outcomes of workplace violence and aggression. *Journal of Applied Psychology, 87*(3), 444–453.

**LeBreton, J. M., Scherer, K. T., & James, L. R.** (2014). Corrections for criterion reliability in validity generalization: A false prophet in a land of suspended judgment. *Industrial and Organizational Psychology, 7,* 478–500.

**Ledbetter v. Goodyear Tire & Rubber Co.,** 550 U.S. 618 (2007).

**Lee, R. T., Brotheridge, C. M., & Lovell, B. L.** (2010). Tenderness and steadiness: Relating job and interpersonal demands and resources with burnout and physical symptoms of stress in Canadian physicians. *Journal of Applied Social Psychology, 49*(9), 2319–2342.

**Lee, T.** (2013, December 13). Best Buy ends flexible work program for its corporate employees. *Minneapolis Star Tribune.* Retrieved from http://www.startribune.com/no-13-best-buy-ends-flexible-work-program-for-its-corporate-employees/195156871/?refer=y

**Lee, T. H., Gerhart, B., Weller, I., & Trevor, C. O.** (2008). Understanding voluntary turnover: Path-specific job satisfaction effects and the importance of unsolicited job offers. *Academy of Management Journal, 51,* 651–671.

**Lee, T. W., Mitchell, T. R., Holtom, B. C., McDaniel, L. S., & Hill, J. W.** (1999). The unfolding model of voluntary turnover: A replication and extension. *Academy of Management Journal, 42*(4), 450–462.

**LePine, J. A., Piccolo, R. F., Jackson, C. L., Mathieu, J. E., & Saul, J. R.** (2008). A meta-analysis of teamwork processes: Tests of a multidimensional model and relationships with team effectiveness criteria. *Personnel Psychology, 61,* 273–307.

Leroy, H., Anseel, F., Gardner, W. L., & Sels, L. (2012). Authentic leadership, authentic followership, basic need satisfaction, and work role performance: A cross-level study. *Journal of Management.* doi:10.1177/0149206312457822

Leslie, L. M., Mayer, D. M., & Kravitz, D. A. (2014). The stigma of affirmative action: a stereotyping-based theory and meta-analytic test of the consequences for performance. *Academy of Management Journal, 57*(4), 964–989.

Leung, D. Y. P., & Kember, D. (2005). Comparability of data gathered from evaluation questionnaires on paper and through the Internet. *Research in Higher Education, 46*(5), 571–591.

Levy, P. E., Cavanaugh, C. M., Frantz, N. B., Borden, L. A., & Roberts, A. (in press). Revising the social context of performance management: Performance Appraisal effectiveness. In D. S. Ones, N. Anderson, C. Viswesvaran, & H. K. Sinangil (Eds.), *Handbook of industrial, work and organizational (IWO) psychology*, 2nd Edition. Thousand Oaks, CA: Sage.

Levy, P. E., & Steelman, L. A. (1997). Performance appraisal for team-based organizations: A prototypical multiple rater system. In M. Beyerlein, D. Johnson, & S. Beyerlein (Eds.), *Advances in interdisciplinary studies of work teams: Vol. 4. Team implementations issues* (pp. 141–165). Greenwich, CT: JAI Press.

Levy, P. E., & Williams, J. R. (2004). The social context of performance appraisal: A review and framework for the future. *Journal of Management, 30*(6), 881–905.

Lewin, K. (1951). *Field theory in social science.* New York: Harper.

Lewin, K., Dembo, T., Festinger, L., & Sears, P. (1944). Level of aspiration. In J. M. Hunt (Ed.), *Personality and the behavior disorders* (Vol. 1, pp. 333–378). New York: Ronald.

Lewis-Duarte, M., & Bligh, M.C. (2012). Agents of influence: Exploring the usage, timing and outcomes of executive coaching tactics. *Leadership & Organization Development Journal, 33*(3), 255–281.

Li, N., Chiaburu, D. S., Kirkman, B. L., & Xie, Z. (2013). Spotlight on the followers: An examination of moderators of relationships between transformational leadership and subordinates' citizenship and taking charge. *Personnel Psychology, 66,* 225–260.

Li, N., Liang, J., & Crant, J. M. (2010). The role of proactive personality in job satisfaction and organizational citizenship behavior: A relational perspective. *Journal of Applied Psychology, 95,* 395–404.

Liao, H., & Rupp, D. (2005). The impact of justice climate and justice orientation on work outcomes: A cross-level multifoci framework. *Journal of Applied Psychology, 90,* 242–256.

Lichtenberger, E. O., Mather, N., Kaufman, N. L., & Kaufman, A. S. (2012). Essentials of assessment report writing (Vol. 22). Hoboken, NJ: Wiley.

Lievens, F., & Anseel, F. (2004). Confirmatory factor analysis and invariance of an organizational citizenship behaviour measure across samples in a Dutch-speaking context. *Journal of Occupational and Organizational Psychology, 77*(3), 299–306.

Lievens, F., & Highhouse, S. (2003). The relation of instrumental and symbolic attributes to a company's attractiveness as an employer. *Personnel Psychology, 56*(1), 75–102.

Lievens, F., Ones, D. S., & Dilchert, S. (2009). Personality scale validities increase throughout medical school. *Journal of Applied Psychology, 94*(6), 1514–1535.

Lievens, F., Sanchez, J. I., Bartram, D., & Brown, A. (2010). Lack of consensus among competency ratings of the same occupation: Noise or substance? *Journal of Applied Psychology, 95*(3), 562–571.

Linderbaum, B. G., & Levy, P. E. (2007). *The development and validation of the Feedback Orientation Scale.* Paper presented at the 22nd annual meeting of the Society for Industrial and Organizational Psychology, New York.

Linderbaum, B. G., & Levy, P. E. (2010). The development and validation of the feedback orientation scale. *Journal of Management, 36*(6), 1372–1405.

Ling, Y., Simsek, Z., Lubatkin, M. H., & Veiga, J. F. (2008). Transformational leadership's role in promoting corporate entrepreneurship: Examining the CEO–TMT interface. *Academy of Management Journal, 51*(3), 557–576.

Lipp, D. (2013). "DISNEY U: How Disney University develops the world's most engaged, loyal, and customer-centric employees," *McGraw-Hill.* Retrieved December 11, 2015, from https://trainingmag.com/content/inside-disney-u

Lips-Wiersma, M., & Hall, D. T. (2007). Organizational career development is not dead: A case study on managing the new career during organizational change. *Journal of Organizational Behavior, 28,* 771–792.

**Little, L. M., Kluemper, D., Nelson, D. L., & Ward, A.** (2013). More than happy to help? Customer-focused emotion management strategies. *Personnel Psychology, 66*(1), 261–286.

**Liu, Y., Ferris, G. R., Xu, J., Weitz, B. A., & Perrewe, P. L.** (2014). When ingratiation backfires: The role of political skill in the ingratiation–internship performance relationship. *Academy of Management Learning & Education, 13,* 569–586.

**Locke, E. A.** (1976). The nature and causes of job satisfaction. In M. D. Dunnette (Ed.), *Handbook of industrial and organizational psychology* (pp. 1297–1349). Chicago: Rand McNally.

**Locke, E. A.** (1990). *A theory of goal setting and task performance.* Englewood Cliffs, NJ: Prentice-Hall.

**Locke, E. A., & Latham, G. P.** (2002). Building a practically useful theory of goal setting and task motivation: A 35-year odyssey. *American Psychologist, 57*(9), 705–717.

**Locke, E. A., & Latham, G. P.** (2006). New directions in goal-setting theory. *Current Directions in Psychological Science, 15,* 265–268.

**Lofquist, L. H., & Dawis, R. V.** (1969). *Adjustment to work: A psychological view of man's problems in a word-oriented society.* New York: Appleton-Century-Crofts.

**Loher, B. T., Noe, R. A., Moeler, N. L., & Fitzgerald, M. P.** (1985). A meta-analysis of the relation of job characteristics to job satisfaction. *Journal of Applied Psychology, 70*(2), 280–289.

**Loi, R., Hang-yue, N., & Foley, S.** (2006). Linking employees' justice perceptions to organizational commitment and intention to leave: The mediating role of perceived organizational support. *Journal of Occupational and Organizational Psychology, 79,* 101–120.

**London, M., & Smither, J. W.** (2002). Feedback orientation, feedback culture, and the longitudinal performance management process. *Human Resource Management Review, 12*(1), 81.

**Longenecker, C. O., Sims, H. P., Jr., & Gioia, D. A.** (1987). Behind the mask: The politics of employee appraisal. *Academy of Management Executive, 1,* 183–193.

**Lopez, E. M., & Greenhaus, J. H.** (1978). Self-esteem, race, and job satisfaction. *Journal of Vocational Behavior, 13,* 75–83.

**Lord, R. G.** (2000). Leadership. In A. E. Kazdin (Ed.), *Encyclopedia of psychology* (Vol. 3, pp. 775–786). Washington, DC: American Psychological Association.

**Lord, R. G., & Brown, D. J.** (2004). *Leadership processes and follower self-identity.* Mahwah, NJ: Erlbaum.

**Lord, R. G., DeVader, C. L., & Alliger, G. M.** (1986). A meta-analysis of the relation between personality traits and leadership perceptions: An application of validity generalization procedures. *Journal of Applied Psychology, 71*(3), 402–410.

**Lord, R. G., Foti, R. J., & DeVader, C. L.** (1984). A test of leadership categorization theory: Internal structure, information processing, and leadership perceptions. *Organizational Behavior and Human Performance, 34,* 343–378.

**Lord, R. G., & Levy, P. E.** (1994). Moving from cognition to action: A control theory *perspective. Applied Psychology, 43*(3), 335–367.

**Lord, R. G., & Maher, K. J.** (1991). *Leadership and information processing: Linking perception and performance.* Boston: Unwin Hyman.

**Lothaller, H., Mikula, G., & Schoebi, D.** (2009). What contributes to the (im) balanced division of family work between the sexes? *Swiss Journal of Psychology, 68*(3), 143–152.

**Lowe, G. S.** (1987). *Women in the administrative revolution: The feminization of clerical work.* Oxford, UK: Polity Press.

**Lowe, K. B., Kroeck, K. G., & Sivasubramaniam, N.** (1996). Effectiveness correlates of transformational and transactional leadership: A meta-analytic review of the MLQ. *Leadership Quarterly, 7,* 385–425.

**Lowery, C. M., Beadles, N. A. I., & Krilowicz, T. J.** (2002). Note on the relationships among job satisfaction, organizational commitment, and organizational citizenship behavior. *Psychological Reports, 91*(2), 607–617.

**Lowman, R. L., Kantor, J., & Perloff, R.** (2007). A history of I-O psychology educational programs in the United States. In L. L. Koppes (Ed.), *Historical perspectives in industrial and organizational psychology* (pp. 111–138). Mahwah, NJ: Erlbaum.

**Lublin, J., & Karp, H.** (2011, December 14). Avon replacing Andrea Jung as CEO. *The Wall Street Journal.*

**Ludwig, T. D., & Geller, E. S.** (1997). Assigned versus participative goal setting and response generalization: Managing injury control among professional pizza deliverers. *Journal of Applied Psychology, 82*(2), 253–261.

**Ludwig, T. D., & Geller, E. S.** (2000). Intervening to improve the safety of delivery drivers: A systematic behavioral approach. *Journal of Organizational Behavior Management, 19*(4), 1–124.

**Luksyte, A., Spitzmueller, C., & Maynard, D. C.** (2011). Why do overqualified incumbents deviate? Examining multiple mediators. *Journal of Occupational Health Psychology, 16*(3), 279.

**Luscher, L. S., & Lewis, M. W.** (2008). Organizational change and managerial sense-making: Working through paradox. *Academy of Management Journal, 51,* 221–240.

**Luthans, F., & Youssef, C. M.** (2007). Emerging positive organizational behavior. *Journal of Management, 33,* 321–349.

**Lynch, S.** (2015, February 23) Why your workplace might be killing you. *Stanford Graduate School of Business.* Retrieved February 15, 2016, from https://www.gsb.stanford.edu/insights/why-your-workplace-might-be-killing-you

**Machan, D.** (1999). A dyed-in-the-wool skeptic. *Forbes, 163*(1), 96–98.

**Mael, F. A.** (1991). A conceptual rationale for the domain and attributes of biodata items. *Personnel Psychology, 44,* 763–792.

**Malos, S. B.** (1998). Current legal issues in performance appraisal. In J. W. Smither (Ed.), *Performance appraisal: State of the art in practice* (pp. 49–94). San Francisco: Jossey-Bass.

**Manu, M. A.** (2012). *Disruptive business: Desire, innovation and the re-design of business.* Gower Publishing, Ltd.

**Marique, G., & Stinglhamber, F.** (2011). Identification to proximal targets and affective organizational commitment: The mediating role of organizational identification. *Journal of Personnel Psychology, 10*(3), 107–117.

**Marriott International.** (n.d.). *Corporate diversity.* Retrieved April 1, 2009, from http://www.marriott.com/corporateinfo/culture/Diversity.mi

**Marshak, R. J., & Grant, D.** (2008). Organizational discourse and new organization

development practices. *British Journal of Management, 19*(Suppl. 1), S7–S19.

**Martin v. PGA Tour, Inc.,** 994 F. Supp. 12452 (D.Or 1998).

**Martin, R., Guillaume, Y., Thomas, G., Lee, A., & Epitropaki, O.** (2016). Leader-member exchange (LMX) and performance: A meta-analytic review. *Personnel Psychology, 69*(1), 67–121.

**Martinko, M. J., & Zellars, K. L.** (1998). Toward a theory of workplace violence and aggression: A cognitive appraisal perspective. In R. W. Griffin, A. O'Leary-Kelly, & J. M. Collins (Eds.), *Dysfunctional behavior in organizations: Violent and deviant behavior* (pp. 1–42). Stamford, CT: JAI Press.

**Martins, L. L., Eddleston, K. A., & Veiga, J. F. J.** (2002). Moderators of the relationship between work–family conflict and career satisfaction. *Academy of Management Journal, 45*(2), 399–409.

**Martins, L. L., & Shalley, C. E.** (2011). Creativity in virtual work: Effects of demographic differences. *Small Group Research, 42*(5), 536–561.

**Martiny, M.** (1998). Knowledge management at HP consulting. *Organizational Dynamics, 27*(2), 71–77.

**Maslach, C.** (2003). Job burnout: New directions in research and intervention. *Current Directions in Psychological Science, 12*(5), 189–192.

**Masterson, S. S., Lewis, K., Goldman, B. M., & Taylor, M. S.** (2000). Integrating justice and social exchange: The differing effects of fair procedures and treatment on work relations. *Academy of Management Journal, 43*(4), 738–748.

**Mathieu, J. E., Heffner, T. S., Goodwin, G. F., Salas, E., & Cannon-Bowers, J. A.** (2000). The influence of shared mental models on team process and performance. *Journal of Applied Psychology, 85*(2), 273–283.

**Mathieu, J. E., Marks, M. A., & Zaccaro, S. J.** (2001). Multi-team systems. In N. Anderson, D. Ones, H. K. Sinangil, & C. Viswesvaran (Eds.), *International handbook of work and organizational psychology* (pp. 289–313). London: Sage.

**Mathieu, J. E. & Rapp, T. L.** (2009). Laying the foundation for successful team performance trajectories: The roles of team charters and performance strategies. *Journal of Applied Psychology, 94*(1), 90–103.

Mathieu. J. E., Tannenbaum, S. I., Kukenberger, M. R., Donsbach, J. S., & Alliger, G. M. (2015). Team role experience and orientation: A measure and tests of construct validity. *Group & Organization Management, 40*, 6–34.

Mathieu, J. E., & Zajac, D. M. (1990). A review and meta-analysis of the antecedents, correlates, and consequences of organizational commitment. *Journal of Applied Psychology, 108*(2), 171–194.

Mathiowetz, V., Rogers, S. L., Dowe-Keval, M., Donahoe, L., & Rennels, C. (1986). The Purdue Pegboard: Norms for 14- to 19-year-olds. *American Journal of Occupational Therapy, 3*, 174–179.

Matos, K., & Gallinsky, E. (2012). 2012 national study of employers. *Families and Work Institute.*

Matyszczyk, C. (2015, May 12). Woman allegedly fired for deleting iPhone app that monitored her 24/7. *CNET.* Retrieved October 26, 2015, from http://www.cnet.com/news/woman-allegedly-fired-for-deleting-iphone-app-that-monitored-her-24-hrs-a-day/

Maurer, T. J., Mitchell, D. R. D., & Barbeite, F. G. (2002). Predictors of attitudes toward a 360-degree feedback system and involvement in post-feedback management development activity. *Journal of Occupational and Organizational Psychology, 75*(1), 87–107.

Maurath, D. (2014). A critical incident for big data. *The Industrial Organizational Psychologist, 51,* 16–27. Retrieved from http://www.siop.org/tip/jan14/513feat.pdf

Mayer, R. C., & Davis, J. H. (1999). The effect of the performance appraisal system on trust for management: A field quasi-experiment. *Journal of Applied Psychology, 84*(1), 123–136.

Maysent, M., & Spera, S. (1995). Coping with job loss and career stress: Effectiveness of stress management training with outplaced employees. In L. R. Murphy, J. J. Hurrell, Jr., S. L. Sauter, & G. P. Keita (Eds.), *Job stress interventions* (pp. 159–170). Washington, DC: American Psychological Association.

McCann, M. A. (2006). *The Wonderlic test for the NFL draft: Linking stereotype threat and the law.* Retrieved March 24, 2008, from http://ssrn.com/abstract=934307

McKellar, H. (2015, March 1). KMWorld 100 companies that matter in knowledge management. *KM World.* Retrieved March 6, 2016, from http://www.kmworld.com/Articles/Editorial/Features/KMWorld-100-COMPANIES-That-Matter-in-Knowledge-Management-102189.aspx

McKinsey Global Institute. (2012). The social economy: Unlocking value and productivity through social technologies. Washington, DC: McKinsey & Co.

McLellan, L. (2015). Wearable technology creates new legal problems. The Legal Intelligencer. Retrieved October 26, 2015, from http://www.thelegalintelligencer.com/id=1202729164562/Wearable-Technology-Creates-New-Legal-Problems?slreturn=20150915095728

McCormick, E. J. (1976). Job and task analysis. In M. D. Dunnette (Ed.), *Handbook of industrial and organizational psychology* (pp. 651–696). Chicago: Rand McNally.

McCormick, E. J. (1979). *Job analysis: Methods and applications.* New York: AMACOM.

McCormick, E. J., Jeanneret, P. R., & Mecham, R. C. (1972). A study of characteristics and job dimensions as based on the Position Analysis Questionnaire (PAQ). *Journal of Applied Psychology, 56,* 347–368.

McCrae, R. R., & Terracciano, A. (2005). Universal features of personality traits from the observer's perspective: Data from 50 cultures. *Journal of Personality and Social Psychology, 88*(3), 547–561.

McDaniel, M. A., Morgeson, F. P., Finnegan, E. B., Campion, M. A., & Braverman, E. P. (2001). Use of situational judgment tests to predict job performance: A clarification of the literature. *Journal of Applied Psychology, 86*(4), 730–740.

McDaniel, M. A., Whetzel, D. L., Schmidt, F. L., & Maurer, S. D. (1994). The validity of employment interviews: A comprehensive review and meta-analysis. *Journal of Applied Psychology, 79*(4), 599–616.

McDonagh, J., & Coghlan, D. (1999). Can O.D. help solve the IT dilemma? O.D. in IT-related change. *Organization Development Journal, 17*(4), 41–48.

McEntire, L. E., Dailey, L. R., Osburn, H. K., & Mumford, M. D. (2006). Innovations in job analysis: Development and application of metrics to analyze job data. *Human Resource Management Review, 16*(3), 310–323.

McGehee, W., & Thayer, P. W. (1961). *Training in business and industry.* New York: Wiley.

McGonagle, A. K., Fisher, G. G., Barnes-Farrell, J. L., & Grosch, J. W. (2015). Individual and work factors related to perceived work ability and labor force outcomes. *Journal of Applied Psychology, 100*(2), 376–398.

McGregor, D. M. (1957). The human side of enterprise. *Management Review, 46,* 22–28.

McGregor, D. M. (1960). *The human side of enterprise.* New York: McGraw-Hill.

McHenry, J. J., Hough, L. M., Toquam, J. L., Hanson, M. A., & Ashworth, S. (1990). Project A validity results: The relationship between predictor and criterion domains. *Personnel Psychology, 43,* 336–354.

McIntyre, R. M., & Salas, E. (1995). Measuring and managing for team performance: Emerging principles from complex team environments. In R. A. Guzzo & E. Salas (Eds.), *Team effectiveness and decision making in organizations* (pp. 9–45). San Francisco: Jossey-Bass.

McKay, P. F., & Avery, D. R. (2006). What has race got to do with it? Unraveling the role of racioethnicity in job seekers' reactions to site visits. *Personnel Psychology, 59,* 395–429.

McKee-Ryan, F. M., & Harvey, J. (2011). "I have a job, but . . .": A review of underemployment. *Journal of Management, 37*(4), 962–996.

McKee-Ryan, F. M., Virick, M. Prussia, G. E., Harvey, J., & Lilly, J. D. (2009). Life after the layoff: Getting a job worth keeping. *Journal of Organizational Behavior, 30,* 561–580.

McKinley, W., Zhao, J., & Rust, K. G. (2000). A sociocognitive interpretation of organizational downsizing. *Academy of Management Reviews, 25*(1), 227–243.

Medvedeff, M., Gregory, J. B., & Levy, P. E. (2008). How attributes of the feedback message affect subsequent feedback seeking: The interactive effects of feedback sign and type. *Psycholgica Belgica, 48* (2&3), 109–125.

Meier, L. L., & Spector, P. E. (2013). Reciprocal effects of work stressors and counterproductive work behavior: A five wave longitudinal study. *Journal of Applied Psychology, 98,* 529–539.

Meindl, J. R., & Ehrlich, S. B. (1987). The romance of leadership and the evaluation of organizational performance. *The Academy of Management Journal, 30,* 91–109.

Melchers, K. G., & Annen, H. (2010). Officer selection for the Swiss armed forces: An evaluation of validity and fairness issues. *Swiss Journal of Psychology, 69*(2), 105–115.

Melchior, M., Caspi, A., Milne, B. J., Danese, A., Poulton, R., & Moffitt, T. E. (2007). Work stress precipitates depression and anxiety in young working men and women. *Psychological Medicine, 37,* 1119–1129.

Melzer, H., Bebbington, P., Brugha, T., Jenkins, R., McManus, S., & Stansfeld, S. (2010). Job insecurity, socio-economic circumstances, and depression. *Psychological Medicine, 40,* 1401–1407.

Meriac, J. P., Gorman, C. A., & Macan, T. (2015). Seeing the forest but missing the trees: The role of judgments in performance management. *Industrial and Organizational Psychology, 8,* 102–108. doi:10.1017/iop.2015.6

Meriac, J. P., Hoffman, B. J., Woehr, D. J., & Fleisher, S. (2008). Further evidence for the validity of assessment center dimensions: A meta-analysis of the incremental criterion-related validity of dimension ratings. *Journal of Applied Psychology, 93*(5), 1042–1052.

Meritor Savings Bank v. Vinson, 477 U.S. 57 (1986).

Mero, N. P., Guidice, R. M., & Anna, A. L. (2006). The interacting effects of accountability and individual differences on rater response to a performance-rating task. *Journal of Applied Social Psychology, 36*(4), 795–819.

Mero, N. P., Guidice, R. M., & Brownlee, A. L. (2007). Accountability in a performance appraisal context: The effect of audience and form of accounting on rater response and behavior. *Journal of Management, 33*(2), 223–252.

Mero, N. P., & Motowidlo, S. J. (1995). Effects of rater accountability on the accuracy and the favorability of performance ratings. *Journal of Applied Psychology, 80,* 517–524.

Mesmer-Magnus, J. R., & DeChurch, L. A. (2009). Information sharing and team performance: A meta analysis. *Journal of Applied Psychology, 94*(2), 535–546.

Mesmer-Magnus, J. R., & Viswesvaran, C. (2010). The role of pre-training interventions in learning: A meta-analysis and integrative review. *Human Resource Management Review, 20,* 261–282.

MetLife Mature Market Institute. (2006, July). *The MetLife caregiving cost study: Productivity losses to U.S. business.* Retrieved April 8, 2009, from http://www.metlife.com/assets/cao/mmi/publications/studies/MMIStudies-Caregiver-Cost-Study.pdf

Meyer, A. (1992). Getting to the heart of sexual harassment. *HR Magazine, 37,* 82–84.

Meyer, H. H. (1991). A solution for the performance appraisal feedback enigma. *Academy of Management Executive, 5,* 68–76.

Meyer, J. P., & Allen, N. J. (1997). *Commitment in the workplace: Theory, research, and application.* Thousand Oaks, CA: Sage.

Meyer, J. P., & Herscovitch, L. (2001). Commitment in the workplace: Toward a general model. *Human Resource Management Review, 11*(3), 299–326.

Meyer, J. P., Stanley, D. J., Herscovitch, L., & Topolnytsky, L. (2002). Affective, continuance, and normative commitment to the organization: A meta-analysis of antecedents, correlates, and consequences. *Journal of Vocational Behavior, 61*(1), 20–52.

Meyer, J. P., Stanley, L. J., & Parfyonova, N. M. (2012). Employee commitment in context: The nature and implication of commitment profiles. *Journal of Vocational Behavior, 80*(1), 1–16.

Miller, C. C. (2015, May 15). Mounting evidence of advantages for children of working mothers. *The New York Times.* Retrieved February 15, 2016, from http://www.nytimes.com/2015/05/17/upshot/mounting-evidence-of-some-advantages-for-children-of-working-mothers.html?_r=0

Miles, S. R., Cromer, L. D., & Narayan, A. (2015). Applying equity theory to students' perceptions of research participation requirements. *Teaching of Psychology, 42*(4), 349–356.

Milkovich, G. T., & Newman, J. M. (1984). *Compensation.* Plano, TX: Business Publications.

Miller, D. L. (2001). Reexamining teamwork KSAs and team performance. *Small Group Research, 32*(6), 745–766.

Mitchell, T. R., Holtom, B. C., Lee, T. W., Sablynski, C. J., & Erez, M. (2001). Why people stay: Using job embeddedness to predict voluntary turnover. *Academy of Management Journal, 44*(6), 1102–1121.

Moen, P., Kelly, E., & Hill, R. (2011). Does enhancing work-time control and flexibility reduce turnover? A naturally occurring experiment. *Social Problems, 58,* 69–98.

Mohsen, A., & Nguyen, T. T. (1999). Succeeding with self-managed work teams. *Industrial Management, 41*(4), 24–28.

Mol, S. T., Born, M. P., & van der Molen, H. T. (2005). Developing criteria for expatriate effectiveness: Time to jump off the adjustment bandwagon. *International Journal of Intercultural Relations, 29*(3), 339–353.

Moore, J. L., Dickson-Deane, C., & Galyen, K. (2011). e-Learning, online learning, and distance learning environments: Are they the same? *The Internet and Higher Education, 14*(2), 129–135.

Moran, C. M., Diefendorff, J. M., Kim, T. Y., & Liu, Z. Q. (2012). A profile approach to self-determination theory motivations at work. *Journal of Vocational Behavior, 81,* 354–363.

Moran, R. T., Abramson, N. R., & Moran, S. V. (2014). *Managing cultural differences.* New York: Routledge.

Moravec, M., Juliff, R., & Hesler, K. (1995). Partnerships help a company manage performance. *Personnel Journal, 74*(1), 104–107.

Morgan, D. E., & Zeffane, R. (2003). Employee involvement, organizational change and trust in management. *International Journal of Human Resource Management, 14*(1), 55–75.

Morgan, R. B., & Casper, W. J. (2000). Examining the factor structure of participant reactions to training: A multidimensional approach. *Human Resource Development Quarterly, 11*(3), 301–317.

Morgeson, F. P., Campion, M. A., Dipboye, R. L., Hollenbeck, J. R., Murphy, K., & Schmitt, N. (2007). Reconsidering the use of personality tests in personnel selection contexts. *Personnel Psychology, 60*(3), 683–729.

Morgeson, F. P., Delaney-Klinger, K., Mayfield, M. S., Ferrara, P., & Campion, M. (2004). Self-presentation processes in job analysis: A field experiment investigating inflation in abilities, tasks, and competencies. *Journal of Applied Psychology, 89*(4), 674–686.

Morgeson, F. P., & Humphrey, S. E. (2006). The Work Design Questionnaire (WDQ): Developing and validating a comprehensive measure for assessing job design and the nature of work. *Journal of Applied Psychology, 91*(6), 1321–1339.

Morgeson, F. P., Reider, M. H., & Campion, M. A. (2005). Selecting individuals in team settings:

The importance of social skills, personality characteristics, and teamwork knowledge. *Personnel Psychology, 58,* 583–611.

**Morris, J. A., & Feldman, D. C.** (1996). The dimensions, antecedents, and consequences of emotional labor. *Academy of Management Review, 21*(4), 986–1010.

**Motowidlo, S. J., Borman, W. C., & Schmit, M. J.** (1997). A theory of individual differences in task and contextual performance. *Human Performance, 10*(2), 71–83.

**Mount, M. K., Oh, I., & Burns, M.** (2008). Incremental validity of perceptual speed and accuracy over general mental ability. *Personnel Psychology, 61,* 113–139.

**Mowday, R. T.** (1991). Equity theory predictions of behavior in organizations. In R. M. Steers and L. W. Porter (Eds.), *Motivation and work behavior* (5th ed., pp. 111–130). New York: McGraw-Hill.

**Mowday, R. T., Steers, R. M., & Porter, L. W.** (1979). The measurement of organizational commitment. *Journal of Vocational Behavior, 14,* 224–247.

**Mullen, B., & Copper, C.** (1994). The relation between group cohesiveness and performance: An integration. *Psychological Bulletin, 115,* 210–227.

**Mulrine, A.** (2008, May 15). The army trains a skeptics corps to battle groupthink. Retrieved April 19, 2009, from *U.S. News & World Report* website: http://www.usnews.com/articles/news/world/2008/05/15/thearmy-trains-a-skeptics-corps-to-battle-groupthink.html

**Mumford, T. V., Van Iddekinge, C. H., Morgeson, F. P., & Campion, M. A.** (2008). The team role test: Development and validation of a team role knowledge situational judgment test. *Journal of Applied Psychology, 93,* 250–267.

**Munsterberg, H.** (1913). *Psychology and industrial efficiency.* Boston: Houghton Mifflin.

**Murphy, K. R.** (2003). *Validity generalization: A critical review.* Mahwah, NJ: Erlbaum.

**Murphy, K. R., & Cleveland, J. N.** (1995). *Understanding performance appraisal: Social, organizational and goal-based perspectives.* Thousand Oaks, CA: Sage.

**Murphy, K. R., & Jako, B.** (1989). Under what conditions are observed intercorrelations greater than or smaller than true intercorrelations? *Journal of Applied Psychology, 74,* 827–830.

**Murphy, K. R., & Reynolds, D. H.** (1988). Does true halo affect observed halo? *Journal of Applied Psychology, 73,* 235–238.

**Nahum-Shani, I., & Somech, A.** (2011). Leadership, OCB and individual differences: Idiocentrism and allocentrism as moderators of the relationship between transformational and transactional leadership and OCB. *The Leadership Quarterly, 22,* 353–366.

**Naidoo, L. J., Scherbaum, C. A., Goldstein, H. W., & Graen, G. B.** (2011). A longitudinal examination of the effects of LMX, ability, and differentiation on team performance. *Journal of Business and Psychology, 26,* 347–357.

**National Alliance for Caregiving.** (2015, August). Caregiver profile: The typical caregiver. Retrieved February 15, 2016, from http://www.caregiving.org/wp-content/uploads/2015/05/Caregiving-in-the-US-2015_Typical_CGProfile.pdf

**National Coalition to Protect Family Leave (NCPFL).** (n.d.). *Improvements to the FMLA regulations are urgently needed—Protect FMLA by clarifying "medical leave" provisions.* Retrieved March 30, 2009, from http://www.protectfamilyleave.org/about/issue.cfm

**National Committee on Pay Equity.** (n.d.). *Handling the arguments against pay equity.* Retrieved from http://www.pay-equity.org/info-opposition.html

**National Women's Law Center.** (2014). *The Lilly Ledbetter Fair Pay Act five years later—A law that works* [White paper]. Retrieved from http://www.nwlc.org/resource/lilly-ledbetter-act-five-years-later-law-works

**Neuman, J. H., & Baron, R. A.** (1998). Workplace violence and workplace aggression: Evidence concerning specific forms, potential causes, and preferred targets. *Journal of Management, 24*(3), 391–419.

**Ng, K., Ang, S., & Chan, K.** (2008). Personality and leader effectiveness: A moderated mediation model of leadership self-efficacy, job demands, and job autonomy. *Journal of Applied Psychology, 93,* 733–743.

**Ng, T. W. H., Eby, L. T., Sorensen, K. L., & Feldman, D. C.** (2005). Predictors of objective and subjective career success: A meta-analysis. *Personnel Psychology, 58,* 367–408.

**Ng, T. W. H., & Feldman, D. C.** (2012). Breaches of past promises, current job alternatives, and promises of future idiosyncratic deals: Three-way interaction effects on organizational commitment. *Human Relations, 65*(11), 1463–1486.

Ng, T. W. H., & Feldman, D. C. (2015). Idiosyncratic deals and voice behavior. *Journal of Management, 41*(3), 893–928.

Ng, T. W. H., Feldman, D. C., & Lam. S. S. K. (2010). Psychological contract breaches, organizational commitment, and innovation-related behaviors: A latent growth curve modeling approach. *Journal of Applied Psychology, 95*(4), 744–751.

Ng, T. W. H., Sorensen, K. L., & Feldman, D. C. (2007). Dimensions, antecedents, and consequences of workaholism: A conceptual integration and extension. *Journal of Organizational Behavior, 28,* 111–136.

Ng, T. W. H., Sorenson, K. L., & Yim, F. H. (2009). Does the job satisfaction–job performance relationship vary across cultures? *Journal of Cross-Cultural Psychology, 40,* 761–796.

Nichols, M. (2003). A theory for eLearning. *Educational Technology & Society, 6*(2), 1–10.

Nielsen, T. M., Hrivnak, G. A., & Shaw, M. (2009). Organizational citizenship behavior and performance: A meta-analysis of group-level research. *Small Group Research, 40*(5), 555–577.

Nijstad, B. A., Stroebe, W., & Lodewijkx, H. F. M. (2003). Production blocking and idea generation: Does blocking interfere with cognitive processes? *Journal of Experimental Social Psychology, 39*(6), 531–548.

Nishii, L. H., & Mayer, D. M. (2009). Do inclusive leaders help reduce turnover in diverse groups? The moderating role of leader-member exchange in the diversity to turnover relationship. *Journal of Applied Psychology, 94,* 1412–1426.

Noonan, L. E., & Sulsky, L. M. (2001). Impact of frame-of-reference and behavioral observational training on alternative training effectiveness criteria in a Canadian military sample. *Human Performance, 14*(1), 3–26.

Norris-Watts, C., & Levy, P. E. (2004). The mediating role of affective commitment in the relation of the feedback environment to work outcomes. *Journal of Vocational Behavior, 65*(3), 351–365.

Northwestern National Life Employee Benefits Division. (1993). *Fear and violence in the workplace:*

*A survey documenting the experience of American workers.* Minneapolis, MN: Northwestern National Life Insurance.

Nurudeen, S. M., Kwakye, G., Berry, W. R., Chaikof, E. L., Lillemoe, K. D., & Millham, F., . . . Haynes, A. B. (2015). Can 360-Degree reviews help surgeons? Evaluation of multisource feedback for surgeons in a multi-institutional quality improvement project. *Journal of the American College of Surgeons,* 837–844.

O'Boyle, E. H., Forsyth, D. R., & O'Boyle, E. H. (2011). Bad apples or bad barrels: An examination of group- and organizational-level effects in the study of counterproductive work behavior. *Group and Organization Management, 36*(1), 39–69.

O'Driscoll, M. P., Poelmans, S., Spector, P. E., Kalliath, T., Allen, T. D., Cooper, C. L., . . . Sanchez, J. I. (2003) Family-responsive interventions, perceived organizational and supervisor support, work–family conflict, and psychological strain. *International Journal of Stress Management, 10*(4), 326–344.

O'Leary-Kelly, A. M., Griffin, R. W., & Glew, D. J. (1996). Organization-motivated aggression: A research framework. *Academy of Management Review, 21*(1), 225–253.

O'Neill, T. A., Allen, N. J., & Hastings, S. E. (2013). Examining the "pros" and "cons" of team conflict: A team-level meta-analysis of task, relationship, and process conflict. *Human Performance, 26,* 236–260.

O'Neill, B. S., & Mone, M. A. (1998). Investigating equity sensitivity as a moderator of relations between self-efficacy and workplace attitudes. *Journal of Applied Psychology, 83*(5), 805–816.

Occupational Information Network. (2009, January 13). *O*NET—Beyond information—Intelligence.* Retrieved March 5, 2009, from http://www.doleta.gov/programs/onet/

Oh, I. S., Wang, G., & Mount, M. K. (2011). Validity of observer ratings of the five-factor model of personality traits: A meta-analysis. *Journal of Applied Psychology, 96*(4), 762.

Oldham, G. R., & Hackman, J. R. (2010). Not what it was and not what it will be: The future of job design research. *Journal of Organizational Behavior, 31,* 463–479.

**O'Neill, T.** (2012). Canadian scholars working to bridge the perceived scientist-practitioner gap. *The Industrial-Organizational Psychologist, 49,* 63–66.

**Ones, D. S., Dilchert, S., Viswesvaran, C., & Judge, T. A.** (2007). In support of personality assessment in organization settings. *Personnel Psychology, 60*(4), 995–1027.

**Openshaw, E., & Greenspun, H.** (2014, February 20). The digitised employee—can wearable technology help create a healthier, more productive workforce? *Financial Times.* Retrieved October 20, 2015, from http://www.ft.com/intl/cms/s/0/3b8cb4ca-9a6b-11e3-8e06-00144feab7de.html#axzz3odtf1HKO

**O'Reilly, C. A., III, & Tushman, M. L.** (2008). Ambidexterity as a dynamic capability: Resolving the innovator's dilemma. *Research in Organizational Behavior, 28,* 185–206.

**Ortman, J. M., Velkoff, V. A., & Hogan, H.** (2014). An aging nation: the older population in the United States. *Washington, DC: US Census Bureau,* 25-1140.

**Orvis, K. A., Fisher, S. L., & Wasserman, M. E.** (2009). Power to the people: Using learner control to improve trainee reactions and learning in web-based instruction environments. *Journal of Applied Psychology, 94*(4), 960–971.

**Ostroff, C., & Atwater, L. E.** (2003). Does whom you work with matter? Effects of referent group gender and age composition on managers' compensation. *Journal of Applied Psychology, 88*(4), 725–740.

**The Oxford Group.** (2013). Blended learning—current use, challenges, and best practice. The Oxford Group.


**Paolacci, G., & Chandler, J.** (2014). Inside the Turk: Understanding Mechanical Turk as a participant pool. *Current Directions in Psychological Science, 23,* 184–188.

**Parents v. Seattle School District,** 127 S. Ct. 2738 (2007).

**Park, J., & Wentling, T.** (2007). Factors associated with transfer of training in workplace e-learning. *Journal of Workplace Learning, 19*(5), 311–329.

**Park, W.** (2000). A comprehensive empirical investigation of the relationships among variables in the groupthink model. *Journal of Organizational Behavior, 21,* 873–887.

**Parker, K. & Patten, E.** (2013). The sandwich generation. *Pew Research Center Social and Demographic Trends.* Retrieved February 15, 2016, from http://www.pewsocialtrends.org/2013/01/30/the-sandwich-generation/

**Parsons, H. M.** (1974). What happened at Hawthorne? New evidence suggests the Hawthorne effect resulted from operant reinforcement contingencies. *Science, 183*(4128), 922–932.

**Patel, H., Pettitt, M., & Wilson, J. R.** (2012). Factors of collaborative working: A framework for a collaboration model. *Applied Ergonomics, 43,* 1–26.

**Paulhus, D. L., & Williams, K. M.** (2002). The dark triad of personality: Narcissism, machiavellianism, and psychopathy. *Journal of Research in Personality, 36,* 556–563.

**Paullay, I. M., Alliger, G. M., & Stone-Romero, E. F.** (1994). Construct validation of two instruments designed to measure job involvement and work centrality. *Journal of Applied Psychology, 7*(92), 224–228.

**Paulsen, N., Callan, V. J., Grice, T. A., Rooney, D., Gallois, C., Jones, E., . . . Bordia, P.** (2005). Job uncertainty and personal control during downsizing: A comparison of survivors and victims. *Human Relations, 58,* 463–496.

**Payne, R. L.** (2000). Eupsychian management and the millennium. *Journal of Managerial Psychology, 15*(3), 219–226.

**Pedhazur, E. J., & Schmelkin, L. P.** (1991). *Measurement, design, and analysis: An integrated approach* (2nd ed.). Hillsdale, NJ: Erlbaum.

**Peebles, K. A.** (2012). Negligent hiring and the information age: How state legislatures can save employers from inevitable liability. *William & Mary Law Review, 35,* 1396–1433.

**Peek-Asa, C., Casteel, C., Allareddy, V., Nocera, M., Goldmacher, S., O'Hagan, E., . . . Harrison, R.** (2007). Workplace violence prevention programs in hospital emergency departments. *Journal of Occupational and Environmental Medicine, 49,* 756–63.

**Perez, L. M., Jones, J., Englert, D. R., & Sachau, D.** (2010). Secondary traumatic stress and burnout among law enforcement investigators exposed to disturbing media images. *Journal of Police and Criminal Psychology, 25,* 113–124.

**Perretti, F., & Negro, G.** (2007). Mixing genres and matching people: A study in innovation and team composition in Hollywood. *Journal of Organizational Behavior, 28,* 563–586.

Perry-Jenkins, M., Repetti, R. L., & Crouter, A. C. (2000). Work and family in the 1990s. *Journal of Marriage and the Family, 62,* 981–998.

Peterson, M. H., Griffith, R. L, & Converse, P. D. (2009). Examining the role of applicant faking in hiring decisions: Percentage of fakers hired and hiring discrepancies in single- and multiple-predictor selection. *Journal of Business and Psychology, 24,* 373–386.

Peterson, M. H., Griffith, R. L., Isaacson, J. A., Oson, M. H., Griffith, R. L., Isa (2011). Applicant faking, social desirability, and the prediction of counterproductive work behaviors. *Human Performance, 24,* 270–290.

Petit v. City of Chicago, 352 F.3d 1111 (7th Cir. 2003).

Petrou, P., Demerouti, E., Peeters, M. C. W., Schaufeli, W. B., & Hetland, J. (2012). Crafting a job on a daily basis: Contextual correlates and the link to work engagement. *Journal of Organizational Behavior, 33,* 1120–1141.

Pew Research Center. (2015, January). Women and Leadership: Public says women are equally qualified, but barriers persist. Washington, DC: Pew Research Center.

Pfeffer, J., & Sutton, R. I. (2013). *The knowing-doing gap: How smart companies turn knowledge into action.* Cambridge, MA: Harvard Business Press.

Phillips, J. S., & Lord, R. G. (1981). Causal attributions and perceptions of leadership. *Organizational Behavior and Human Performance, 28,* 143–163.

Pichler, S., Varma, A., Michel, J. S., & Levy, P. E. (2015). Leader-Member Exchange, group- and individual-level procedural justice and reactions to performance appraisals. *Human Resource Management, 54,* 1–13.

Piedmont, R. L. (1998). *The revised NEO Personality Inventory: Clinical and research applications.* New York: Plenum Press.

Pierce, J. L., Gardner, D. G., Cummings, L. L., & Dunham, R. B. (1989). Organization-based self-esteem: Construct definition, measurement, and validation. *Academy of Management Journal, 32*(3), 622–648.

Pinder, C. C. (1984). *Work motivation: Theories, issues and applications.* Dallas, TX: Scott, Foresman.

Pinder, C. C. (1998). *Work motivation in organizational behavior.* Upper Saddle River, NJ: Prentice-Hall.

Pinder, C. C. (2008). *Work motivation in organizational behavior.* Upper Saddle River, NJ: Psychology Press.

Piotrowski, C. (2014). Mapping the research domain of I/O psychology: A content analysis of dissertations. *Psychology and Education, 51*(3–4), 26–29.

Ployhart, R. E. (2006). Staffing in the 21st century: New challenges and strategic opportunities. *Journal of Management, 32,* 868–897.

Ployhart, R. E., & MacKenzie, W. I., Jr. (2011). Situational judgment tests: A critical review and agenda for the future. In S. Zedeck (Ed.), *APA handbook of industrial and organizational psychology Volume 2, Selecting and developing members for the organization* (pp. 237–252). Washington, DC: APA.

Podsakoff, N. P., Whiting, S. W., Podsakoff, P. M., & Blume, B. D. (2009). Individual- and organizational- level consequences of organizational citizenship behaviors: A meta-analysis. *Journal of Applied Psychology, 94*(1), 122–141.

Podsakoff, N. P., Whiting, S. W., Podsakoff, P. M., & Mishra, P. (2011). Effects of organizational citizenship behaviors in selection decisions in employment interviews. *Journal of Applied Psychology, 96*(2), 310–326.

Poon, J. M. (2012). Distributive justice, procedural justice, affective commitment, and turnover intention: A mediation–moderation framework. *Journal of Applied Social Psychology, 42*(6), 1505–1532.

Popovich, P. M., Scherbaum, C. A., Scherbaum, K. L., & Polinko, N. (2003). The assessment of attitudes toward individuals with disabilities in the workplace. *Journal of Psychology, 137*(2), 163–177.

Popper, K. (1959). *The logic of scientific discovery.* New York: Basic Books.

Porras, J. I., & Silvers, R. C. (1991). Organization development and transformation. *Annual Review of Psychology, 42,* 51–78.

Porter, C. O. L. H., Hollenbeck, J. R., Ilgen, D. R., Ellis, A. P. J., West, B. J., & Moon, H. (2003). Backing up behaviors in teams: The role of personality and legitimacy of need. *Journal of Applied Psychology, 88*(3), 391–403.

Positive Psychology Center. (2007). *Positive psychology center.* Retrieved April 17, 2009, from http://www.ppc.sas.upenn.edu/

Posthuma, R. A. (2002). Employee selection procedures and the business necessity defense. *Applied HRM Research, 7*(1–2), 53–63.

**Powdthavee, N.** (2011). Anticipation, free rider problems, and adaptation to trade unions: Re-examining the curious case of dissatisfied union members. *Industrial and Labor Relations Review, 64,* 1000–1019.

**Powell, G. N., & Butterfield, D. A.** (2011). Sex, gender, and the US presidency: Ready for a female president? *Gender in Management: An International Journal, 28*(6), 394–407.

**Powers, D. E.** (2004). Validity of Graduate Record Examinations (GRE) general test scores for admissions to colleges of veterinary medicine. *Journal of Applied Psychology, 89*(2), 208–219.

**Preston, J.** (2011). Social media history becomes a new job hurdle. Retrieved July 24, 2011, from http://www.nytimes.com/2011/07/21/technology/social-media-history-becomes-a-new-job-hurdle.html

**Primoff, E. S., & Eyde, L. D.** (1988). Job element analysis. In S. Gael (Ed.), *The job analysis handbook for business, industry, and government* (Vol. 2, pp. 807–824). New York: Wiley.

**Prince, C., & Stewart, J.** (2002). Corporate universities: An analytical framework. *Journal of Management Development, 21*(10), 794–811.

**Prindle, M.** (2010). Enron Ethics—The Culture of Enron. Business.MattPrindle.com. Retrieved October 8, 2015, from http://business.mattprindle.com/leadership-skills/enron-ethics-the-culture-of-enron/

**Privacy Rights Clearinghouse.** (2015). Fact sheet 7: Workplace privacy and employee monitoring. Retrieved October 26, 2015, from https://www.privacyrights.org/workplace-privacy-and-employee-monitoring

**PR Newswire.** (2015, November 17). As work-life balance becomes top priority, more Americans voluntarily seek part-time work, RecruitiFi survey finds. *PR Newswire.* Retrieved February 15, 2016, from http://www.prnewswire.com/news-releases/as-work-life-balance-becomes-top-priority-more-americans-voluntarily-seek-part-time-work-recruitifi-survey-finds-300179936.html

**Probst, T. M.** (2000). Wedded to the job: Moderating effects of job involvement on the consequences of job insecurity. *Journal of Occupational Health Psychology, 5*(1), 63–73.

**Proctor & Gamble.** (2014). P&G 2014 annual report. Retrieved March 6, 2016, from http://www.pginvestor.com/interactive/lookandfeel/4004124/PG_Annual_Report_2014.pdf

**Pyburn, K. M., Ployhart, R. E., & Kravitz, D. A.** (2008). The diversity-validity dilemma: Overview and legal context. *Personnel Psychology, 61,* 143–151.

**Psychological Corporation.** (1979). *Revised manual for the Minnesota Clerical Test.* San Antonio, TX: Author.

**Psychological Corporation.** (1980). *The Bennett Mechanical Comprehension Test manual.* San Antonio, TX: Author.

**Pulakos, E. D.** (1984). A comparison of rater training programs: Error training and accuracy training. *Journal of Applied Psychology, 69,* 581–588.

**Pulakos, E. D.** (1986). The development of training programs to increase accuracy. *Organizational Behavior and Human Decision Processes, 38,* 76–91.

**Qiao, J. X.** (2008). Corporate universities in China: Processes, issues, and challenges. *Journal of Workplace Learning, 21*(2), 166–174.

**Rackspace.** (April, 2014). The human cloud at work: A study into the impact of wearable technologies in the workplace. *Rackspace US, Inc.* Accessed October 20, 2015, from https://www.rackspace.co.uk/sites/default/files/Human%20Cloud%20at%20Work.pdf

**Rademakers, M.** (2005). Corporate universities: Driving force of knowledge innovation. *The Journal of Workplace Learning, 17*(1/2), 130–136.

**Raes, E., Kyndt, E., Decuyper, S., Van den Bossche, P. & Dochy, F.** (2014). An exploratory study of group development and team learning. *Human Resource Development Quarterly, 26,* 5–30.

**Rapp, A. A., Bachrach, D. G., & Rapp, T. L.** (2013). The influence of time management skill on the curvilinear relationship between organizational citizenship behavior and task performance. *Journal of Applied Psychology, 98*(4), 668–677.

**Ree, J. M., Earles, J. A., & Teachout, M. S.** (1994). Predicting job performance: Not much more than g. *Journal of Applied Psychology, 79*(4), 518–524.

**Rego, A., & Cunha, M. P.** (2010). Organisational justice and citizenship behaviors: A study in the Portuguese cultural context. *Applied Psychology: An International Review, 59*(3), 404–430.

Rego, A., Sousa, F., Marques, C., & e Cunha, M. P. (2012). Authentic leadership promoting employees' psychological capital and creativity. *Journal of Business Research, 65,* 429–437.

Reilly, R. R., & McGourty, J. (1998). Performance appraisal in team settings. In J. W. Smither (Ed.), *Performance appraisal: State of the art in practice* (pp. 244–277). San Francisco: Jossey-Bass.

Reiter-Palmon, R., Brown, M., Sandall, D. L., Buboltz, C., & Nimps, T. (2006). Development of an O*NET web-based job analysis and its implementation in the U.S. Navy: Lessons learned. *Human Resource Management Review, 16,* 294–309.

Renko, M., Kroeck, K. G., & Bullough, A. (2011). Expectancy theory and nascent entrepreneurship. *Small Business Economics.* doi:10.1007/s11187-011-9354-3

Rennie, J. (2007, January 22). *Stressed with work? Blame office politics.* Retrieved April 21, 2009, from http://www.eveningtimes.co.uk/news/display.Var.1137551.0.stressed_with_work_blame_office_politics.php

Rhoades, L., & Eisenberger, R. (2002). Perceived organizational support: A review of the literature. *Journal of Applied Psychology, 87*(4), 698–714.

Ricci v. DeStefano, 129 S. Ct. 2658, 557 U.S. 557, 174 L. Ed. 2d 490 (2009).

Riggio, R. E., & Lee, J. (2007). Emotional and interpersonal competencies and leader development. *Human Resource Management Review, 17,* 418–426.

Riketta, M. (2002). Attitudinal organizational commitment and job performance: A meta-analysis. *Journal of Organizational Behavior, 23*(3), 257–266.

Riordan, D. & Riordan, M. (2013). Guarding against groupthink in the professional work environment: A checklist. *Journal of Academic and Business Ethics, 7,* 1.

Ritter, B. A., & Lord, R. G. (2007). The impact of previous leaders on the evaluation of new leaders: An alternative to prototype matching. *Journal of Applied Psychology, 92,* 1683–1695.

Robbins, R. D. (2014). The class of 2014 by the numbers. Retrieved from http://features.thecrimson.com/2014/senior-survey/

Roberson, L., Kulik, C. T., & Pepper, M. B. (2009). Individual and environmental factors influencing the use of transfer strategies after diversity training. *Group & Organization Management, 34*(1), 67–89.

Robinson, S. L. (1996). Trust and breach of the psychological contract. *Administrative Science Quarterly,* 574–599.

Roch, S. G., & O'Sullivan, B. J. (2003). Frame of reference rater training issues: Recall, time and behavior observation training. *International Journal of Training and Development, 7*(2), 93–107.

Roch, S. G., Woehr, D. J., Mishra, V., & Kieszczynska, U. (2012). Rater training revisited: An updated meta-analytic review of frame-of-reference training. *Journal of Occupational and Organizational Psychology, 85,* 370–395. doi:10.1111/j.2044-8325.2011.02045.x

Rockstuhl, T., Dulebohn, J. H., Ang, S., & Shore, L. M. (2012). Leader–member exchange (LMX) and culture: A meta-analysis of correlates of LMX across 23 countries. *Journal of Applied Psychology, 97*(6), 1097–1130.

Rode, J. C., Mooney, C. H., Arthaud-Day, M. L., Near, J. P., Baldwin, T. T., Rubin, R. S., & Bommer, W. H. (2007). Emotional intelligence and individual performance: Evidence of direct and moderated effects. *Journal of Organizational Behavior, 28*(4), 399–421.

Rodgers, R., & Hunter, J. E. (1991). Impact of management by objectives on organizational productivity. *Journal of Applied Psychology, 76*(2), 322–336.

Roehling, M. V., & Wright, P. (2004). Organizationally sensible v. legal-centric responses to the eroding employment at-will doctrine. *Employee Responsibilities and Rights Journal, 16*(2), 89–103.

Roethlisberger, F. J., & Dickson, W. J. (1939). *Management and the worker.* Cambridge, MA: Harvard University Press.

Rogelberg, S. G., & Gill, P. M. (2004). The growth of industrial and organizational psychology: Quick facts. *The Industrial-Organizational Psychologist, 42*(1), 25–27.

Rojon, C., McDowall, A., & Saunders, M. N. K. (2015). The relationships between traditional selection assessment and workplace performance criteria specificity: A comparative meta-analysis. *Human Performance, 28(1),* 1–25.

Rooney v. Koch Air, LLC., 410 F.3d 376 (U.S. App. 2005).

**Roppolo, L. P., Heymann, R., Pepe, P., Wagner, J., Commons, B., Miller, R., Allen, E., Horne, L., Wainscott, M. P., & Idris, A. H.** (2011). A randomized controlled trial comparing traditional training in cardiopulmonary resuscitation (CPR) to self-directed CPR learning in first year medical students: The two-person CPR study. *Resuscitation, 82*(3), 319–325.

**Rosanas, J. M.** (2008). Beyond economic criteria: A humanistic approach to organizational survival. *Journal of Business Ethics, 78,* 447–462.

**Rose, A., Timm, H., Pogson, C., Gonzalez, J., Appel, E., & Kolb, N. (**2010). *Developing a cybervetting strategy for law enforcement: A special report.* Defense Personnel Security Research Center (PERSEREC). Washington, DC: U. S. Department of Defense.

**Rosen, C. C., Chang, C. H., Johnson, R. E., & Levy, P. E.** (2009). Perceptions of the organizational context and psychological contract breach: Assessing competing perspectives. *Organizational Behavior and Human Decision Processes, 108,* 202–217.

**Rosen, C. C., & Hochwarter, W. A.** (2014). Looking back and falling further behind: The moderating role of rumination on the relationship between organizational politics and employee attitudes, well-being, and performance. *Organizational Behavior and Human Decision Processes, 124,* 177–189.

**Rosen, C. C., & Levy, P. E.** (2013). Stresses, swaps, and skill: An investigation of the psychological dynamics that relate work politics to employee performance. *Human Performance, 26*(1), 44–65.

**Rosenthal, R.** (1991). *Meta-analytic procedures for social research* (rev. ed.). Thousand Oaks, CA: Sage.

**Rosette, A. S., Leonardelli, G. J., & Phillips, K. W.** (2008). The White standard: Racial bias in leader categorization. *Journal of Applied Psychology, 93,* 758–777.

**Ross, W. E., Huang, K. H., & Jones, G. H.** (2014). Executive onboarding: Ensuring the success of the newly hired department chair. *Academic Medicine, 89*(5), 728–733.

**Roth, P. L., Bobko, P., & Mabon, H.** (2002). Utility analysis: A review and analysis at the turn of the century. In N. Anderson, D. S. Ones, C. Viswesvaran, & H. K. Sinangil (Eds.), *Handbook of industrial, work and organizational psychology: Vol. 1. Personnel psychology* (pp. 383–384). Thousand Oaks, CA: Sage.

**Roth, P. L., Bobko, P., & McFarland, L. A.** (2005). A meta-analysis of work sample test validity: Updating and integrating some classic literature. *Personnel Psychology, 58*(4), 1009–1037.

**Roth, P. L., Bobko, P., & Switzer, F. S., III.** (2006). Modeling the behavior of the 4/5ths rule for determining adverse impact: Reasons for caution. *Journal of Applied Psychology, 91*(3), 507–522.

**Rotundo, M., & Sackett, P. R.** (2002). The relative importance of task, citizenship, and counterproductive performance to global ratings of job performance: A policy-capturing approach. *Journal of Applied Psychology, 87*(1), 66–80.

**Rounds. J., Armstrong, P. I., Liao, H. Y., Lewis, P., & Rivkin, D.** (2008). *Second generation occupational interest profiles for the O\*NET system: Summary.* Raleigh, NC: National Center for O\*NET Development. Retrieved July 11, 2012, from http://www.onetcenter.org/dl_files/SecondOIP_Summary.pdf

**Rousseau, D. M.** (2001). Idiosyncratic deals: Flexibility vs. fairness? *Organizational Dynamics, 29,* 260–271.

**Rubin, R. S., Dierdorff, E. C., & Bachrach, D. G.** (2013). Boundaries of citizenship behavior: Curvilinearity and context in the citizenship and task performance relationship. *Personnel Psychology, 66,* 377–406.

**Rudisill, J. R., & Edwards, J. M.** (2002). Coping with job transitions. *Consulting Psychology Journal: Practice and Research, 54*(1), 55–64.

**Rutkowski, K. A., & Steelman, L. A.** (2005). Testing a path model for antecedents of accountability. *Journal of Management Development, 24*(5), 473–486.

**Ryan, R. M., & Deci, E. L.** (2000). Self-determination theory and the facilitation of intrinsic motivation, social development, and well-being. *American Psychologist, 55*(1), 68–78.

**Rynes, S. L., & Cable, D. M.** (2003). Recruitment research in the twenty-first century. In W. C. Borman, D. R. Ilgen, & R. Klimoski (Eds.), *Handbook of psychology: Vol. 12. Industrial and organizational psychology* (pp. 55–76). New York: Wiley.

**Rynes, S. L., Gerhart, B., & Parks, L.** (2005). Personnel psychology: Performance evaluation and pay for performance. *Annual Review of Psychology, 56,* 571–600.

**Rynes, S. L., & Rosen, B.** (1995). A field survey of factors affecting the adoption and perceived success of diversity training. *Personnel Psychology, 48,* 247–270.

Saal, F. E., Downey, R. G., & Lahey, M. A. (1980). Rating the ratings: Assessing the quality of rating data. *Psychological Bulletin, 88,* 413–428.

Sablynski, C. J., Lee, T. W., Mitchell, T. R., Burton, J. P., & Holtom, B. C. (2002). Turnover: An integration of Lee and Mitchell's unfolding model and job embeddedness construct with Hulin's withdrawal construct. In J. M. Brett & F. Drasgow (Eds.), *The psychology of work: Theoretically based empirical research* (pp. 189–203). Mahwah, NJ: Erlbaum.

Sachau, D. A. (2007). Resurrecting the motivation-hygiene theory: Herzberg and the positive psychology movement. *Human Resource Development Review, 6,* 377–393.

Sackett, P. R. (1994). *The content and process of the research enterprise within industrial and organizational psychology.* Presidential address presented at the 9th Annual Conference of the Society for Industrial and Organizational Psychology, Nashville, TN.

Sackett, P. R., & Laczo, R. M. (2003). Job and work analysis. In W. C. Borman, D. R. Ilgen, & R. J. Klimoski (Eds.), *Handbook of psychology: Industrial and organizational psychology* (Vol. 12, pp. 21–37). New York: Wiley.

Sagie, A. (1998). Employee absenteeism, organizational commitment, and job satisfaction: Another look. *Journal of Vocational Behavior, 52,* 156–171.

Sahibzada, K., Hammer, L. B., Neal, M. B., & Kuang, D. C. (2005). The moderating effects of work–family role combinations and work–family organizational culture on the relationship between family-friendly workplace supports and job satisfaction. *Journal of Family Issues, 26*(6), 820–839.

Saks, A. M., & Burke, L. A. (2012). An investigation into the relationship between training evaluation and the transfer of training. *International Journal of Training and Development, 16*(2), 118–127.

Salas, E., Rozell, D., Mullen, B., & Driskell, J. E. (1999). The effect of team building on performance: An integration. *Small Group Research, 30*(3), 309–329.

Salgado, J. F. (2002). The Big Five personality dimensions and counterproductive behaviors. *International Journal of Selection and Assessment, 10*(1–2), 117–125.

Salgado, J. F., & Anderson, N. (2003). Validity generalization of GMA tests across countries in the European community. *European Journal of Work and Organizational Psychology, 12*(1), 1–17.

Salgado, J. F., Anderson, N., Moscoso, S., Bertua, C., de Fruyt, F., & Rolland, J. P. (2003). A meta-analytic study of general mental ability validity for different occupations in the European community. *Journal of Applied Psychology, 88*(6), 1068–1081.

Sanchez, J. I., & Levine, E. L. (2009). What is (or should be) the difference between competency modeling and traditional job analysis? *Human Resource Management Review, 19,* 53–63.

Sanchez, R. J., Truxillo, D. M., & Bauer, T. N. (2000). Development and examination of an expectancy-based measure of test-taking motivation. *Journal of Applied Psychology, 85*(5), 739–750.

Sanz-Valle, R., Naranjo-Valencia, J. C., Jiménez-Jiménez, D., & Perez-Caballero, L. (2011). Linking organizational learning with technical innovation and organizational culture. *Journal of Knowledge Management, 15*(6), 997–1015.

Sarin, S., & O'Connor, G. C. (2009). First among equals: The effect of team leader characteristics on the internal dynamics of cross-functional product development teams. *Journal of Product Innovation Management, 26*(2), 188–205.

Schappe, S. P. (1998). Understanding employee job satisfaction: The importance of procedural and distributive justice. *Journal of Business and Psychology, 12*(4), 493–503.

Schaubroeck, J., Lam, S. S. K., & Cha, S. E. (2007). Embracing transformational leadership: Team values and the impact of leader behavior on team performance. *Journal of Applied Psychology, 92,* 1020–1030.

Scheer, L. K., Kumar, N., & Steenkamp, J.-B. E. M. (2003). Reactions to perceived inequity in U.S. and Dutch interorganizational relationships. *Academy of Management Journal, 46*(3), 303–316.

Schein, E. H. (1980). *Organizational psychology* (3rd ed.). Englewood Cliffs, NJ: Prentice-Hall.

Schilling, M. S., Oeser, N., & Schaub, C. (2007). How effective are decision analyses? Assessing decision process and group alignment effects. *Decision Analysis, 4*(4), 227–242.

Schippmann, J. S., Ash, R. A., Batjtsta, M., Carr, L., Eyde, L. D., Hesketh, B., . . . Sanchez, J. I. (2000). The practice of competency modeling. *Personnel Psychology, 53,* 703–740.

**Schleicher, D. J., Day, D. V., Mayes, B. T., & Riggio, R. E.** (2002). A new frame for frame-of-reference training: Enhancing the construct validity of assessment centers. *Journal of Applied Psychology, 87*(4), 735–746.

**Schmidt, F. L., & Hunter, J. E.** (1998). The validity and utility of selection methods in personnel psychology: Practical and theoretical implications of 85 years of research findings. *Psychological Bulletin, 124*(2), 262–274.

**Schmidt, F. L., & Kaplan, L. B.** (1971). Composite vs. multiple criteria: A review and resolution of the controversy. *Personnel Psychology, 24,* 419–434.

**Schmidt, F. L., & Oh, I.** (2010) Can synthetic validity methods achieve discriminant validity? *Industrial and Organizational Psychology, 3*(3), 344–350.

**Schmitt, N., Gooding, R. Z., Noe, R. A., & Kirsch, M.** (1984). Meta-analyses of validity studies published between 1964 and 1982 and the investigation of study characteristics. *Personnel Psychology, 37,* 407–422.

**Schneider, R. J., Goff, M., Anderson, S., & Borman, W. C.** (2003). Computerized adaptive rating scales for measuring managerial performance. *International Journal of Selection and Assessment, 11*(2/3), 237–246.

**Schriesheim, C. A., House, R. J., & Kerr, C.** (1976). Leader initiating structure: A reconciliation of discrepant research results and some empirical tests. *Organizational Behavior and Human Performance, 15*(2), 297–321.

**Schriesheim, C. A., & Neider, L. L.** (1996). Path-goal leadership theory: The long and winding road. *Leadership Quarterly, 7*(3), 317–321.

**Schroeders, U., & Wilhelm, U.** (2010). Testing reasoning ability with handheld computers, notebooks and paper and pencil. *European Journal of Psychological Assessment, 26*(4), 284–292.

**Schuerger, J. M.** (1995). Career assessment and the Sixteen Personality Factor Questionnaire. *Journal of Career Assessment, 3*(2), 157–175.

**Schwartz, J.** (1990, November 5). How safe is your job? *Newsweek, 5,* 44–47.

**Schyns, B., Felfe, J., & Blank, H.** (2007). Is charisma hyper-romanticism? Empirical evidence from new data and meta-analysis. *Applied Psychology: An International Review, 4,* 505–527.

**Scotch, R. K.** (2014). Models of disability and the Americans with Disabilities Act. *Berkeley Journal of Employment & Labor Law, 21*(1), 213–222.

**Scott, K. A. & Brown, D. J.** (2006). Female first, leader second? Gender bias in the encoding of leadership behavior. *Organizational Behavior and Human Decision Processes, 101,* 130–242.

**Scott, K. D., & Taylor, G. S.** (1985). An examination of conflicting findings on the relationship between job satisfaction and absenteeism: A meta-analysis. *Academy of Management Journal, 28*(3), 599–612.

**Scott, W. D.** (1903). *The theory of advertising.* Boston: Small, Maynard.

**Searle, B. J.** (2008). Does personal initiative training work as a stress management intervention? *Journal of Occupational Health Psychology, 13,* 259–270.

**Seaward, M. R.** (1999). The sandwich generation copes with elder care. *Benefits Quarterly, 15*(2), 41–48.

**Seidler-de Alwis, R., & Hartmann, E.** (2008). The use of tacit knowledge within innovative companies: Knowledge management in innovative enterprises. *Journal of Knowledge Management, 12,* 133–147.

**Seijts, G. H., & Kyei-Poku, I.** (2010). The role of situational interviews in fostering positive reactions to selection decisions. *Applied Psychology: An International Review, 59*(30), 431–453.

**Seldon, S., & Orenstein, J.** (2011). Government e-recruiting web sites: The influence of e-recruitment content and usability on recruiting and hiring outcomes in US state governments. *International Journal of Selection and Assessment, 19*(1), 31–40.

**Semadar, A., Robins, G., & Ferris, G. R.** (2006). Comparing the validity of multiple social effectiveness constructs in the prediction of managerial job performance. *Journal of Organizational Behavior, 27*(4), 443–461.

**Semeijn, J. H., Van der Heijden, B. I. J. M., & Van der Lee, A.** (2014). Multisource ratings of managerial competencies and their predictive value for managerial and organizational effectiveness. *Human Resource Management, 53,* 773–794.

**Senécal, J., Loughead, T. M., & Bloom, G. A.** (2008). A season-long team-building intervention program: Examining the effect of team goal setting on cohesion. *Journal of Sport & Exercise Psychology, 30*(2), 186–199.

**Senge, P. M.** (2006). *The leader's new work: Building learning organizations.* San Francisco: Jossey-Bass.

Seo, M.-G., Taylor, M. S., Hill, N. S., Zhang, X., Tesluk, P. E., & Lorinkova, N. M. (2012). The role of affect and leadership during organizational change. *Personnel Psychology, 65,* 121–165.

Shafritz, J. M., Ott, J. S., & Jang, Y. S. (2011). *Classics of organizational theory* (Vol. 7). Belmont, CA: Wadsworth.

Shafritz, J. M., Ott, J., & Jang, Y. S. (2015). *Classics of organization theory* (Vol. 8). Cengage Learning.

Sheldon, O. J., Dunning, D., & Ames, D. R. (2014). Emotionally unskilled, unaware, and uninterested in learning more: Reactions to feedback about deficits in emotional intelligence. *Journal of Applied Psychology, 99,* 125–137.

Shore, L. M., Tetrick, L. E., Shore, T. H., & Barksdale, K. (2000). Construct validity of measures of Becker's side bet theory. *Journal of Vocational Behavior, 57,* 428–444.

Silverman, S. B. (1991). Individual development through performance appraisal. In K. N. Wexley (Ed.), *Developing human resources* (Vol. 5, pp. 120–151). Washington, DC: Bureau of National Affairs.

Silzer, R., & Parson, C. (2015). Practice in I-O psychology: Trends in professional membership, activities, development, and representation (2008–2015). *The Industrial-Organizational Psychologist, 53*(1), https://social.hse.ru/data/2015/07/24/1085812209/TIP-1506.pdf#page=172

Simons, T., & Roberson, Q. (2003). Why managers should care about fairness: The effects of aggregate justice perceptions on organizational outcomes. *Journal of Applied Psychology, 88*(3), 432–443.

Sims, H. P., Jr., Faraj, S., & Yun, S. (2009). When should a leader be directive or empowering? How to develop your own situational theory of leadership. *Business Horizons, 52*(2), 149–158.

Singh, P. (2008). Job analysis for a changing workplace. *Human Resource Management Review, 18,* 87–99.

Sitzmann, T. (2011). A meta-analytic examination of the instructional effectiveness of computer-based simulation games. *Personnel Psychology, 64,* 489–528.

Slaughter, J. E., Sinar, E. F., & Bachiochi, P. D. (2002). Black applications' reactions to affirmative action plans: Effects of plan content and previous experience with discrimination. *Journal of Applied Psychology, 87*(2), 333–344.

Sleek, S., Michel, A., & Mikulak, A. (2014). Workplace diversity initiatives may mask discrimination. Association for Psychological Sciences. Retrieved December 11, 2015, from http://www.psychologicalscience.org/index.php/news/minds-business/workplace-diversity-initiatives-may-mask-discrimination.html

Smith, A. (2012). EEOC hearing highlights pregnancy and caregiver discrimination. Retrieved March 13, 2012, from http://www.shrm.org/LegalIssues/FederalResources/Pages/EEOCHearingPDA.aspx

Smith, J. A., & Foti, R. J. (1998). A pattern approach to the study of leader emergence. *Leadership Quarterly, 9*(2), 147–160.

Smith, P. C., & Kendall, L. M. (1963). Retranslation of expectations: An approach to the construction of unambiguous anchors for rating scales. *Journal of Applied Psychology, 47,* 149–155.

Smith, P. C., Kendall, L. M., & Hulin, C. L. (1969). *Measurement of satisfaction in work and retirement.* Chicago: Rand McNally.

Smither, J. W., London, M., Flautt, R., Vargas, Y., & Kucine, I. (2003). Can working with an executive coach improve multisource feedback ratings over time? A quasi-experimental field study. *Personnel Psychology, 56*(1), 23–44.

Snell, A. F., Sydell, E. J., & Lueke, S. B. (1999). Towards a theory of applicant faking: Integrating studies of deception. *Human Resource Management Review, 9*(2), 219–242.

Snider, B. (2013). Hiring discrimination may be OK with a BFOQ. FindLaw, June 3, 2013. Retrieved from http://blogs.findlaw.com/free_enterprise/2013/06/hiring-discrimination-may-be-ok-with-a-bfoq.html

Society for Human Resource Management. (2014). Total financial impact of employee absences across the United States, China, Australia, Europe, India, and Mexico. [White paper]. Retrieved from: http://www.shrm.org/Research/SurveyFindings/Documents/Total%20Financial%20Impact%20of%20Employee%20Absences%20Report.pdf

Society for Industrial and Organizational Psychology. (n.d.). *Graduate training programs in industrial-organizational psychology and related fields.* Retrieved October 6, 2006, from http://www.siop.org/GTP/

Society for Industrial and Organizational Psychology. (1999). *Guidelines for education and training at the doctoral level in industrial-organizational psychology.*

Retrieved October 11, 2006, from http://www.siop.org/PhDGuidelines98.aspx

**Society for Industrial and Organizational Psychology.** (2006). *Building better organizations.* Retrieved March 2, 2009, from http://www.siop.org/visibilitybrochure/siopbrochure.aspx

**Society for Industrial and Organizational Psychology.** (2015). SIOP announces top 10 workplace trends for 2016. Retrieved February 22, 2016, from http://www.siop.org/article_view.aspx?article=1467

**Somech, A., & Drach-Zahavy, A.** (2007). Strategies for coping with work–family conflict: The distinctive relationships of gender role ideology. *Journal of Occupational Health Psychology, 12,* 1–19.

**Somers, M. J.** (2009). The combined influence of affective, continuance and normative commitment on employee withdrawal. *Journal of Vocational Behavior, 74*(1), 75–81.

**Somers, M. J.** (2010). Patterns of attachment to organizations: Commitment profiles and work outcomes. *Journal of Occupational and Organizational Psychology, 83*(2), 443–453.

**Song, L. J., Huang, G., Peng, K. Z., Law, K. S., Wong, C., & Chen, Z.** (2010). The differential effects of general mental ability and emotional intelligence on academic performance and social interactions. *Intelligence, 38*(1), 137–143.

**Sonnentag, S., Binnewies, C., & Mojza, E. J.** (2010). Staying well and engaged when demands are high: The role of psychological detachment. *Journal of Applied Psychology, 95*(5), 965–976.

**Spector, P. E.** (1997). The role of frustration in antisocial behavior at work. In R. A. Giacalone & J. Greenberg (Eds.), *Antisocial behavior in organizations* (pp. 1–17). Thousand Oaks, CA: Sage.

**Spector, P. E., Bauer, J. A., & Fox, S.** (2010). Measurement artifacts in the assessment of counterproductive work behavior and organizational citizenship behavior: Do we know what we think we know? *Journal of Applied Psychology, 95*(4), 781–790.

**Spector, P. E., & Fox, S.** (2010). Counterproductive work behaviors and organizational citizenship behavior: Are they opposite forms of active behavior? *Applied Psychology: An International Review, 59*(1), 21–39.

**Spector, P. E., Fox, S., Penney, L. M, Bruursema, K., Goh, A., & Kessler, S.** (2006). The dimensionality of counterproductivity: Are all counterproductive behaviors created equal? *Journal of Vocational Behavior, 68*(3), 446–460.

**Spector, P. E., & Jex, S. M.** (1991). Relations of job characteristics from multiple data sources with employee affect, absence, turnover intentions, and health. *Journal of Applied Psychology, 76,* 46–53.

**Spies, R. A., Carlson, J. F. & Geisinger, J. F.** (2010). *The Eighteenth Mental Measurements Yearbook.* Lincoln, NE: Buros Institute of Mental Measurements.

**Spink, K. S., Wilson, K. S., & Odnokon, P.** (2010). Examining the relationship between cohesion and return to team in elite athletes. *Psychology of Sport and Exercise, 11,* 6–11.

**Spool, M. D.** (1978). Training programs for observers of behavior: A review. *Personnel Psychology, 31*(4), 853–888.

**Srivastava, A., Locke, E. A., Judge, T. A., & Adams, J. W.** (2010). Core self-evaluations as causes of satisfaction: The mediating role of seeking task complexity. *Journal of Vocational Behavior, 77,* 255–265.

**Stajkovic, A. D., & Luthans, F.** (1997). A meta-analysis of the effects of organizational behavior modification on task performance. *Academy of Management Journal, 40*(5), 1122–1149.

**Stanley, L., Vandenberghe, C., Vandenberg, R., & Bentein, K.** (2013). Commitment profiles and employee turnover. *Journal of Vocational Behavior, 82*(3), 176–187.

**Stanton, J. M., & Rogelberg, S. G.** (2001). Using Internet/intranet web pages to collect organizational research data. *Organizational Research Methods, 4*(3), 200–217.

**Stanton, J. M., Sinar, E. F., Balzer, W. K., Julian, A. L., Thoresen, P., Aziz, S., . . . Smith, P. C.** (2002). Development of a compact measure of job satisfaction: The abridged Job Descriptive Index. *Educational and Psychological Measurement, 62*(1), 173–191.

**Staw, B. M., & Cohen-Charash, Y.** (2005). The dispositional approach to job satisfaction: More than a mirage, but not yet an oasis. *Journal of Organizational Behavior, 26,* 59–78.

**Staw, B. M., & Ross, J.** (1985). Stability in the midst of change: A dispositional approach to job attitudes. *Journal of Applied Psychology, 7*(3), 469–480.

**Steel, R. P., & Rentsch, J. R.** (1997). The dispositional model of job attitudes revisited: Findings of a 10-year study. *Journal of Applied Psychology, 82*(6), 873–879.

**Steel, R. P., Rentsch, J. R., & Van Scotter, J. R.** (2007). Timeframes and absence frameworks: A test of Steers and Rhodes' (1978) model of attendance. *Journal of Management, 33,* 180–195.

**Steele-Johnson, D., Beauregard, R. S., Hoover, P. B., & Schmidt, A. M.** (2000). Goal orientation and task demand effects on motivation, affect, and performance. *Journal of Applied Psychology, 85*(5), 724–738.

**Steele-Johnson, D., Osburn, H. G., & Pieper, K. F.** (2000). A review and extension of current models of dynamic criteria. *International Journal of Selection and Assessment, 8*(3), 110–136.

**Steelman, L. A., Levy, P. E., & Snell, A. F.** (2004). The feedback environment scale (FES): Construct definition, measurement, and validation. *Education and Psychological Measurement, 64*(1), 165–184.

**Steers, R. M., Mowday, R. T., & Shapiro, D. L.** (2004). Introduction to special topic forum: The future of work motivation theory. *Academy of Management Review, 29*(3), 379–387.

**Steers, R. M., Porter, L. M., & Bigley, G. A.** (1996). *Motivation and leadership at work* (6th ed.). New York: McGraw-Hill.

**Steers, R. M., & Rhodes, S. R.** (1978). Major influences on employee attendance: A process model. *Journal of Applied Psychology, 63*(4), 391–407.

**Steiner, I. D.** (1972). *Group processes and productivity.* New York: Academic Press.

**Stevens, M. J., & Campion, M. A.** (1999). Staffing work teams: Development and validation of a selection test for teamwork settings. *Journal of Management, 25*(2), 207–228.

**Stevens, G. W.** (2012). A critical review of the science and practice of competency modeling. *Human Resource Development Review* 12, 86–107.

**Stevens, S.** (1968, August 30). Measurement, statistics, and the schemapiric view. *Science, 161,* 849–856.

**Stewart, G. L.** (2006). A meta-analytic investigation of relationships between team design features and team performance. *Journal of Management, 32,* 29–55.

**Stewart, T. A.** (1998, January 12). The leading edge: Is this job really necessary? *Fortune, 137*(1), 154–157.

**Stewart, T. A.** (2000, October 2). The house that knowledge built. *Fortune, 142*(7), 278–279.

**Stogdill, R. M.** (1948). Personal factors associated with leadership: A survey of the literature. *Journal of Psychology, 25,* 35–71.

**Stogdill, R. M.** (1963). *Manual for the Leader Behavior Description Questionnaire–Form XII: An experimental revision.* Columbus, OH: Bureau of Business Research, Ohio State University.

**Stogdill, R. M.** (1974). *Handbook of leadership: A survey of theory and research.* New York: Free Press.

**Stokes, G. S., & Cooper, L. A.** (1994). Selection using biodata: Old notions revisited. In G. S. Stokes, M. M. Mumford, & W. A. Owens (Eds.), *Biodata handbook: Theory, research, and use of biographical information in selection and performance prediction* (pp. 311–350). Palo Alto, CA: Consulting Psychologists Press.

**Strong, E. K.** (1927). Vocational interest test. *Educational Record, 8,* 107–121.

**Strully, K. W.** (2009). Job loss and health in the US labor market. *Demography, 46*(2), 221–246.

**Sulsky, L. M., & Day, D. V.** (1994). Effects of frame-of-reference training and cognitive categorization: An empirical investigation of rater memory issues. *Journal of Applied Psychology, 79,* 535–543.

**Sulzer-Azaroff, B., Loafman, B., Merante, R. J., & Hlavacek, A. C.** (1990). Improving occupational safety in a large industrial plant: A systematic replication. *Journal of Organizational Behavior Management, 11*(1), 99–120.

**Sundstrom, E., DeMeuse, K. P., & Futrell, D.** (1990). Work teams: Applications and effectiveness. *American Psychologist, 45,* 120–133.

**Sundstrom, E., McIntyre, M., Halfhill, T., & Richards, H.** (2000). Work groups: From the Hawthorne Studies to work teams of the 1990s and beyond. *Group Dynamics: Theory, Research, and Practice, 4*(1), 44–67.

**Svyantek, D. J., Goodman, S. A., Benz, L. L., Gard, J. A.** (1999). The relationship between organizational characteristics and team building success. *Journal of Business and Psychology, 14*(2), 265–283.

**Sweeney, P. D., & McFarlin, D. B.** (1993). Workers' evaluations of the "ends" and the "means": An examination of four models of distributive and procedural justice. *Organizational Behavior and Human Decision Processes, 55,* 23–40.

Tang, T. L., & Ibrahim, A. H. S. (1998). Antecedents of organizational citizenship behavior revisited: Public personnel in the United States and in the Middle East. *Public Personnel Management, 27*(4), 529–550.

Tata, J. (2002). The influence of managerial accounts on employees' reactions to negative feedback. *Group and Organization Management, 27*(4), 480–503.

Tata, J., Prasad, S., & Thorn, R. (1999). The influence of organizational structure on the effectiveness of TQM programs. *Journal of Managerial Issues, 11*(4), 440–453.

Taylor, F. M. (1996). The principles of scientific management. In J. M. Shafritz & J. S. Ott (Eds.), *Classics of organization theory* (4th ed., pp. 66–79). Belmont, CA: Wadsworth. (Reprinted from *Bulletin of the Taylor Society*, 1916).

Taylor, H. C., & Russell, T. (1939). The relationship of validity coefficients to the practical effectiveness of tests in selection: Discussion and tables. *Journal of Applied Psychology, 23,* 565–578.

Tetrick, L. E., Miles, R. L., Marcil, L., & Van Dosen, C. M. (1994). Child-care difficulties and the impact on concentration, stress, and productivity among single and nonsingle mothers and fathers. In G. P. Keita & J. J. Hurrell, Jr. (Eds.), *Job stress in a changing workforce: Investigating gender, diversity, and family issues* (pp. 229–239). Washington, DC: American Psychological Association.

Thau, S., & Mitchell, M. S. (2010). Self-gain or self-regulation impairment? Tests of competing explanations of the supervisor abuse and employee deviance relationship through perceptions of distributive justice. *Journal of Applied Psychology, 95*(6), 1009–1031.

Theorell, T., & Karasek, R. A. (1996). Current issues relating to psychosocial job strain and cardiovascular disease research. *Journal of Occupational Health Psychology, 1*(1), 9–26.

*The Whistle* (Georgia Tech newspaper). (1991). Coca-Cola CEO's secret formula for success: Vision, confidence and luck. Retrieved on February 15, 2016, from Mark Turner Dot Net, http://www.markturner.net/wp-content/uploads/2015/05/Whistle-Brian_Dyson-Georgia_Tech_Commencement_Sept_1991-p3.pdf

Thomas, A., Palmer, J. K., & Feldman, J. M. (2009). Examination and measurement of halo via curvilinear regression: A new approach to halo. *Journal of Applied Social Psychology, 39,* 350–358.

Thorndike, R. L. (1949). *Personnel selection.* New York: Wiley.

Thurston, P.W., & McNall, L. (2010). Justice perceptions of performance appraisal practices. *Journal of Managerial Psychology, 25*(3), 201–228.

Tilcsik, A. & Cleafield, C. (2015). Five years after the Deepwater Horizon oil spill, we are closer than ever to catastrophe. *The Guardian.* Retrieved March 18, 2016, from http://www.theguardian.com/sustainable-business/2015/apr/17/deepwater-horizon-oil-spill-catastrophe-five-years

Tims, M., Bakker, A. B., & Derks, D. (2012). Daily job crafting and the self-efficacy-performance relationship. *Journal of Managerial Psychology, 29*(5), 490–507.

Tippins, N. T., Beaty, J., Gibson, W. M., Pearlman, K., Segall, D. O., & Shepherd, W. (2006). Unproctored Internet testing in employment settings. *Personnel Psychology, 59,* 189–225.

Tobin, T. J. (2001). Organizational determinants of violence in the workplace. *Aggression and Violent Behavior, 6,* 91–102.

Toffler, A. (1980). *The third wave.* New York: Morrow.

Tolman, E. C. (1932). *Purposive behavior in animals and men.* New York: Century.

Tremaine, D. W. (2015). HR legal concerns surrounding wearables. Retrieved October 26, 2015, from http://www.privsecblog.com/2015/07/articles/surveillance/hr-legal-concerns-surrounding-wearables/

Tuckman, B. W. (1965). Developmental sequences in small groups. *Psychological Bulletin, 63,* 384–399.

Tuckman, B. W., & Jensen, M. A. C. (1977). Stages of small group development revisited. *Group and Organizational Studies, 2,* 419–427.

Uhl-Bien, M., Riggio, R. E., Lowe, K. B., & Carsten, M. K. (2014). Followership theory: A review and research agenda. *The Leadership Quarterly, 25*(1), 83–104.

U.S. Bureau of Labor Statistics. (2008). *Economic news release: Mass layoffs summary.* Retrieved December 9, 2008, from http://www.bls.gov/news.release/mslo.nr0.htm

U. S. Bureau of Labor Statistics. (2010). Employment situation summary. Released January 8.

2010, for December 2009. Retrieved February 15, 2016, from http://www.bls.gov/news.release/empsit.nr0.htm

**U.S. Bureau of Labor Statistics.** (2011). Employment loss and the 2007–09 recession: An overview. Retrieved February 15, 2016, from http://www.bls.gov/mlr/2011/04/art1full.pdf

**U.S. Bureau of Labor Statistics.** (2013). Fact sheet: Workplace homicides from shootings, January 2013. Retrieved March 7, 2016, from http://www.bls.gov/iif/oshwc/cfoi/osar0016.htm

**U. S. Bureau of Labor Statistics.** (2014). *Share of labor force projected to rise for people age 55 and over and fall for younger age groups.* Retrieved December 11, 2015, from http://www.bls.gov/opub/ted/2014/ted_20140124.htm

**U.S. Bureau of Labor Statistics.** (2015). *Employment characteristics of families—2014.* Retrieved February 15, 2016, from http://www.bls.gov/news.release/pdf/famee.pdf

**U.S. Department of Justice, FBI.** (2002). Workplace violence: Issues in response. U.S. Department of Justice, Federal Bureau of Investigation.

**U.S. Department of Labor.** (2015, September 4). The cost of doing nothing: The price we all pay without paid leave policies to support America's 21st century working families. Retrieved February 15, 2016, from https://www.dol.gov/featured/paidleave/cost-of-doing-nothing-report.pdf

**U.S. Department of Labor.** (n.d.). *Federal vs. state family and medical leave laws.* Retrieved March 30, 2009, from http://www.dol.gov/esa/programs/whd/state/fmla/index.htm

**U.S. Department of Labor.** (2009). *The Family and Medical Leave Act of 1993.* Retrieved May 1, 2009, from http://www.dol.gov/esa/whd/regs/statutes/fmla.htm#SEC_2_FINDINGS_AND_PURPOSES

**U.S. Department of Labor.** (2014). *In-demand, higher paying occupations (2010–2020).* Retrieved August 17, 2015, from http://www.dol.gov/wb/stats/idoccupations.htm

**U.S. News & World Report.** (2016). U.S. News career rankings: Science: Industrial psychologist. Retrieved on February 22, 2016, from http://money.usnews.com/careers/best-jobs/industrial-psychologist

**Uggerslev, K. L., Fassina, N. E., Kraichy, D.** (2012). Recruiting through the stages: a meta-analytic test of predictors of applicant attraction at different stages of the recruiting process. *Personnel Psychology, 65,* 597–660.

**Uggerslev, K. L., & Sulsky, L. M.** (2008). Using frame-of-reference training to understand the implications of rater idiosyncrasy for rating accuracy. *Journal of Applied Psychology, 93,* 711–719.

**Van Dierendonck, D.** (2010). Servant leadership: A review and synthesis. *Journal of Management, 37*(4), 1228–1261.

**van Dierendonck, D., Schaufeli, W. B., & Buunk, B. P.** (2001). Burnout and inequity among human service professionals: A longitudinal study. *Journal of Occupational Health Psychology, 6*(1), 43–52.

**Van Eerde, W., & Thierry, H.** (1996). Vroom's expectancy models and work-related criteria. *Journal of Applied Psychology, 81*(5), 575–586.

**Van Ginkel, W. P., Tindale, R. S., & van Knippenberg, D.** (2009). Team reflexivity, development of shared task representations, and the use of distributed information in group decision making. *Group Dynamics: Theory, Research, and Practice, 13*(4), 265–280.

**Van Ginkel, W. P., & van Knippenberg, D.** (2009). Knowledge about distribution of information and group decision making: When and why does it work? *Organizational Behavior and Human Decision Processes, 108*(2), 218–229.

**Van Hooft, E. A. J., & Born, M. P.** (2012). Intentional response distortion on personality tests: Using eye-tracking to understand response processes when faking. *Journal of Applied Psychology, 97,* 301–316.

**Van Iddekinge, C. H., & Ployhart, R. E.** (2008). Developments in the criterion-related validation of selection procedures: A critical review and recommendations for practice. *Personnel Psychology, 61,* 871–925.

**Van Iddekinge, C. H., Roth, P. L., Raymark, P. H., Odle-Dusseau, H. N.** (2012). The criterion-related validity of integrity tests: An updated meta-analysis. *Journal of Applied Psychology, 97,* 499–530.

**van Quaquebeke, N., van Knippenberg, D., & Brodbeck, F. C.** (2011). More than meets the eye: The role of subordinates' self-perceptions in leader categorization processes. *The Leadership Quarterly, 22,* 367–382.

**Van Rooy, D. L., & Viswesvaran, C.** (2004). Emotional intelligence: A meta-analytic investigation of predictive validity and nomological net. *Journal of Vocational Behavior, 65*(1), 71–95.

**Van Wijhe, C. I., Peeters, M. C. W., & Schaufeli, W. B.** (2014). Enough is enough: Cognitive antecedents of workaholism and its aftermath. *Human Resource Management, 53*(1), 157–177.

**Van Yperen, N. W., & Janssen, O.** (2002). Fatigued and dissatisfied or fatigued but satisfied? Goal orientations and responses to high job demands. *Academy of Management Journal, 45*(6), 1161–1171.

**Vancouver, J. B., More, K. M., & Yoder, R. J.** (2008). Self-efficacy and resource allocation: Support for a nonmonotonic, discontinuous model. *Journal of Applied Psychology, 93,* 35–47.

**Vandenberghe, C., Bentein, K., & Stinglhamber, F.** (2004). Affective commitment to the organization, supervisor, and work group: Antecedents and outcomes. *Journal of Vocational Behavior, 64,* 47–71.

**Vecchio, R. P.** (2002). Leadership and gender advantage. *Leadership Quarterly, 13*(6), 643–671.

**Veiga, J. F., Golden, T. D., & Dechant, K.** (2004). Why managers bend the rules. *Academy of Management Executive, 18*(2), 84–90.

**Velada, R., Caetano, A., Michel, J. W., Lyons, B. D., & Kavanaugh, M. J.** (2007). The effects of training design, individual characteristics, and work environment on transfer of training. *International Journal of Training and Development, 11*(4), 282–294.

**Villanova, P. D., Bernardin, H. J., Dahmus, S. A., & Sims, R. L.** (1993). Rater leniency and performance appraisal discomfort. *Educational and Psychological Measurement, 53*(3), 789–799.

**Vinchur, A. J., & Koppes, L. L.** (2007). Early contributors to the science and practice of industrial psychology. In L. L. Koppes (Ed.), *Historical perspectives in industrial and organizational psychology* (pp. 37–60). Mahwah, NJ: Erlbaum.

**Vinchur, A. J., Shippmann, J. S., Switzer, F. S., III, & Roth, P. L.** (1998). A meta-analytic review of predictors of job performance for salespeople. *Journal of Applied Psychology, 83*(4), 586–597.

**Vroom, V.** (1964). *Work and motivation.* New York: Wiley.

**Wagner, J. A., & Hollenbeck, J. R.** (1998). *Organizational behavior: Securing competitive advantage.* Upper Saddle River, NJ: Prentice-Hall.

**Wagner-Tsukamoto, S.** (2007). An institutional economic reconstruction of scientific management: On the lost theoretical logic of Taylorism. *Academy of Management Review, 32,* 105–117.

**Walczyk, J. J., Mahoney, K. T., Doverspike, D., & Griffith-Ross, D. A.** (2009). Cognitive lie detection: Response time and consistency of answers as cues to deception. *Journal of Business and Psychology, 24,* 33–49.

**Walker, H. J., Feild, H. S., Bernerth, J. B., & Becton, J. B.** (2014). Diversity cues on recruitment websites: Investigating the effects on job seekers' information processing. *Journal of Applied Psychology, 97*(1), 214–224.

**Wamslet, P. T., Natali, M. W., & Campbell, J. P.** (2012). Only incumbent raters in O*NET? Oh yes! Oh no! *International Journal of Selection and Assessment, 20,* 283–296.

**Wanberg, C. R., Kanfer, R., Hamann, D. J., & Zhang, Z.** (2015). Age and reemployment success after job loss: An integrative model and meta-analysis. *Psychological Bulletin.*

**Wang, M., Burlacu, G., Truxillo, D., James, K., & Yao, X.** (2015). Age differences in feedback reactions: The roles of employee feedback orientation on social awareness and utility. *Journal of Applied Psychology, 100,* 1296–1308.

**Wang, G. G., & Wilcox, D.** (2006). Training evaluation: Knowing more than is practiced. *Advances in Developing Human Resources, 8*(4), 528–539.

**Wang, M., Liu, S., Zhan, Y., & Shi, J.** (2010). Daily work–family conflict and alcohol use: Testing the cross-level moderation effects of peer drinking norms and social support. *Journal of Applied Psychology, 95*(2), 377–386.

**Warr, P.** (1999). Well-being and the workplace. In D. Kahneman, E. Diener, & N. Schwartz (Eds.), *Well-being: The foundations of hedonic psychology* (pp. 392–412). New York: Russell Sage Foundation.

**Warr, P.** (2007a). Searching for happiness at work. *The Psychologist, 20*(12), 726–729.

**Warr, P. B.** (2011). Jobs and job-holders: Two sources of happiness and unhappiness. In I. Boniwell, S. A.

David, and A. C. Ayers (Eds.), *The Oxford handbook of happiness* (pp. 733–750). Oxford, England: Oxford University Press.

**Wassell, J. T.** (2009). Workplace violence intervention effectiveness: A systematic literature review. *Safety Science, 47*(8), 1049–1055.

**Wayhan, V. B., & Balderson, E. L.** (2007). TQM and financial performance: What has empirical research discovered? *Total Quality Management, 18,* 403–412.

**Wayne, S. J., & Liden, R. C.** (1995). Effects of impression management on performance ratings: A longitudinal study. *Academy of Management Journal, 38*(1), 232–260.

**Weber, J.** (2004, June 15). *More jobs—And more layoffs.* Retrieved April 8, 2009, from the *Business Week Online* website: http://www.businessweek.com/bwdaily/dnflash/jun2004/nf20040615_5695_db035.htm

**Webster, J. R., Beehr, T. A., & Love, K.** (2011). Extending the challenge-hindrance model of occupational stress: The role of appraisal. *Journal of Vocational Behavior, 79,* 505–516.

**Wegge, J., & Haslam, S. A.** (2005). Improving work motivation and performance in brainstorming groups: The effects of three group goal-setting strategies. *European Journal of Work and Organizational Psychology, 14*(4), 400–430.

**Welsh, E. T., Wanberg, C. R., Brown, K. G., & Simmering, M. J.** (2003). E-learning: Emerging uses, empirical results and future directions. *International Journal of Training and Development, 7*(4), 245–258.

**Weng, Q., & McElroy, J. C.** (2012). Organizational career growth, affective occupational commitment and turnover intentions. *Journal of Vocational Behavior, 80*(2), 256–265.

**Werner, J. M., & Bolino, M. C.** (1997). Explaining U.S. courts of appeal decisions involving performance appraisal: Accuracy, fairness, and validation. *Personnel Psychology, 50,* 1–24.

**Wesolowski, M. A., & Mossholder, K. W.** (1997). Relational demography in supervisor–subordinate dyads: Impact on subordinate job satisfaction, burnout, and perceived procedural justice. *Journal of Organizational Behavior, 18,* 351–362.

**Westman, M., Hobfoll, S. E., Chen, S., Davidson, O. B., & Laski, S.** (2004). Organizational stress through the lens of conservation of resources

(COR) theory. *Research in occupational stress and well-being, 4,* 167–220.

**Wexley, K. N., & Klimoski, R.** (1984). Performance appraisal: An update. In K. Rowland & G. Ferris (Eds.), *Research in personnel and human resources* (Vol. 2, pp. 35–79). Greenwich, CT: JAI Press.

**Wexley, K. N., & Latham, G. P.** (2002). *Developing and training human resources in organizations* (3rd ed.). Upper Saddle River, NJ: Prentice-Hall.

**Wexley, K. N., & Silverman, S. B.** (1993). *Working scared: Achieving success in trying times.* San Francisco: Jossey-Bass.

**Whetten, D. A., & Cameron, K. S.** (2002). *Developing management skills* (5th ed.). Upper Saddle River, NJ: Pearson Education.

**Whitaker, B. G.** (2007). Internet-based attitude assessment: Does gender affect measurement equivalence? *Computers in Human Behavior, 23,* 1183–1194.

**Whitaker, B. G., Dahling, J. J., & Levy, P. E.** (2007). The development of a feedback environment and role clarity model of job performance. *Journal of Management, 33*(4), 570–591.

**Whitney, D. J., Diaz, J., Mineghino, M. E., & Powers, K.** (1999). Perceptions of overt and personality-based integrity tests. *International Journal of Selection & Assessment, 7*(1), 35–45.

**Wiesenfeld, B. M., Brockner, J., & Martin, C.** (1999). A self-affirmation analysis of survivors' reactions to unfair organizational downsizings. *Journal of Experimental Social Psychology, 35,* 441–460.

**Wiesenfeld, B. M., Brockner, J., & Thibault, V.** (2000). Procedural fairness, managers' self-esteem, and managerial behaviors following a layoff. *Organizational Behavior and Human Decision Processes, 83*(1), 1–32.

**Wilder, D. A., Austin, J., & Casella, S.** (2009). Applying behavior analysis in organizations: Organizational behavior management. *Psychological Services, 6(3),* 202–211.

**Williams, M. L., McDaniel, M. A., & Nguyen, N. T.** (2006). A meta-analysis of the antecedents and consequences of pay level satisfaction. *Journal of Applied Psychology, 91,* 392–413.

**Williamson, I. O., Lepak, D. P., & King, J.** (2003). The effect of company recruitment web site orientation on individuals' perceptions of organizational attractiveness. *Journal of Vocational Behavior, 63*(2), 242–263.

**Wilson, C.** (2004, July). *How to heal work force cuts.* Credit Union Executive Newsletter, 7.

**Wilson, H. J.** (2013). Wearables in the workplace. *Harvard Business Journal.* Retrieved October 20, 2015, from https://hbr.org/2013/09/wearables-in-the-work-place

**Wirtenberg, J., Lipsky, D., Abrams, L., Conway, M., & Slepian, J.** (2007). The future of organization development: Enabling sustainable business performance through people. *Organization Development Journal, 25,* 11–22.

**Wonderlic, E. F.** (1984). *Wonderlic Personnel Test manual.* Northfield, IL: Wonderlic & Associates.

**Wong, K. F. E., & Kwong, J.Y.Y.** (2007). Effects of rater goals on rating patterns: Evidence from an experimental field study. *Journal of Applied Psychology, 92*(2), 577–585.

**Woods, S., Poole, R., & Zibarras, L.** (2012). Employee absence and organizational commitment. *Journal of Personnel Psychology, 11*(4), 199–203.

**Work Options Group.** (2006). *Employers expand elder-care benefits.* Retrieved December 10, 2008, from http://www.workoptionsgroup.com/wsj_article.html

**World's Most Admired Companies.** (2016). Retrieved March 7, 2016, from http://fortune.com/worlds-most-admired-companies/

**Wright, T. A., & Bonett, D. G.** (2007). Job satisfaction and psychological well-being as nonadditive predictors of workplace turnover. *Journal of Management, 33*(2), 141–160.

**Wu, L. Z., Zhang, H., Chiu, R. K., Kwan, H. K., & He, X.** (2014). Hostile attribution bias and negative reciprocity beliefs exacerbate incivility's effects on interpersonal deviance. *Journal of Business Ethics, 120*(2), 189–199.

**Yen, H. C., Tuan, H. L., & Liao, C. H.** (2011). Investigating the influence of motivation on students' conceptual learning outcomes in web-based vs. classroom-based science teaching contexts. *Research in Science Education, 41,* 211–224.

**Yu, J. H., Albaum, G., & Swenson, M.** (2003). Is a central tendency error inherent in the use of semantic

differential scales in different cultures? *International Journal of Market Research, 45*(2), 213–228.

**Yu, K. Y. T.** (2014). Person–organization fit effects on organizational attraction: A test of an expectations-based model. *Organizational Behavior and Human Decision Processes, 124,* 75–94.

**Yuan, Y. C., Fulk, J., Monge, P. R., & Contractor, N.** (2010). Expertise directory development, shared task interdependence, and strength of communication network ties as multilevel predictors of transactive memory work groups. *Communication Research, 37*(1), 20–47.

**Yukl, G. A.** (2002). *Leadership in organizations* (5th ed.). Upper Saddle River, NJ: Prentice-Hall.

**Yum, B. S., Roh, J. H., Ryu, J. C., Won, J. U., Kim, C .N, Lee, J. E., & Kim, K. Y.** (2006). Symptoms of PTSD according to individual and work environment characteristics of Korean railroad drivers with experience of person-under-the-train accidents. *Journal of Psychosomatic Research, 61,* 691–697.

**Yun, G. J., Donahue, L. M., Dudley, N. M., & McFarland, L. A.** (2005). Rater personality, rating format, and social context: Implications for performance appraisal ratings. *International Journal of Selection and Assessment, 13*(2), 97–107.

**Zaccaro, S. J.** (1984). Social loafing: The role of task attractiveness. *Personality and Social Psychology Bulletin, 10*(1), 99–106.

**Zaccaro, S. J., & Bader, P.** (2003). E-leadership and the challenges of leading e-teams: Minimizing the bad and maximizing the good. *Organizational Dynamics, 31*(4), 377–387.

**Zaccaro, S. J., Foti, R. J., & Kenny, D. A.** (1991). Self-monitoring and trait-based variance in leadership: An investigation of leader flexibility across multiple group situations. *Journal of Applied Psychology, 76*(2), 308–315.

**Zaccaro, S. J., Marks, M., & DeChurch, L. A.** (2012). Multiteam systems: An introduction. In S. J. Zaccaro, M. A. Marks, & L. A. DeChurch (Eds.), *Multiteam systems: An organizational form for dynamic and complex environments.* New York: Taylor & Francis.

**Zaitzow, B. H., & Fields, C. B.** (1996). Using archival data sets. In F. T. L. Leong & J. T. Austin

(Eds.), *The psychology research handbook* (pp. 251–261). Thousand Oaks, CA: Sage.

Zammuto, R. F., Griffith, T. L., Majchrzak, A., Dougherty, D. J., & Faraj, S. (2007). Information technology and the changing fabric of organization. *Organization Science, 18*(5), 749–762.

Zapata-Phelan, C. P., Colquitt, J. A., Scott, B. A., & Livingston, B. (2009). Procedural justice, interactional justice, and task performance: The mediating role of intrinsic motivation. *Organizational Behavior and Human Decision Processes, 108*, 93–105.

Zapf, D. (2002). Emotion work and psychological well-being: A review of the literature and some conceptual considerations. *Human Resource Management Review, 12*(2), 237–268.

Zellars, K. L., & Perrewé, P. L. (2001). Affective personality and the content of emotional social support: Coping in organizations. *Journal of Applied Psychology, 86*(3), 459–467.

Zhao, H., Seibert, S. E., & Lumpkin, G. T. (2010). The relationship of personality to entrepreneurial intentions and performance: A meta-analytic review. *Journal of Management, 36*(2), 381–404.

Zimmerman, R. D., Mount, M., & Goff, M. (2008). Multisource feedback and leaders' goal performance: Moderating effects of rating purpose, rater perspective, and performance dimension. *International Journal of Selection and Assessment, 16*(2), 121–133.

# Name Index

Thomas, C., 234, 273
Thomas, H. C., 335
Thompson, J., 291
Thoresen, C. J., 332
Thorn, R., 490
Thorndike, R. L., 102
Thornton, G. C., III, 185
Thurston, P. W., 152
Tidd, S. T., 322
Tims, M., 310
Tindale, R. S., 403, 407, 409, 412
Tippins, N. T., 170, 172, 174
Tobin, T. J., 391
Toffler, A., 267
Tolman, E., 296
Topolnytsky, L., 338
Toquam, J. L., 177
Totterdell, P., 289
Tranby, E., 292
Traver, H., 269
Tremaine, D. W., 159
Treviño, L. K., 21
Trevor, C. O., 337
Trougakos, J. P., 49, 354
Truxillo, D. M., 157, 299
Tuan, H. L., 262
Tuckman, B., 403, 404, 405, 406
Turban, D. B., 203
Turnley, W. H., 116, 119
Tushman, M. L., 484

**U**

Uggerslev, K. L., 145, 206
Uhl-Bien, M., 447

**V**

van den Berg, P. T., 460
Van den bossche, 406
Van der Heijden, B. I. J. M., 130
Van der Lee, A., 130
van der Molen, H. T., 117
van Dick, R., 447
van Dierendonck, D., 294, 451
Van Dosen, C. M., 378
Van Eerde, W., 298
van Engen, M. L., 456
Van Ginkel, W. P., 412
Van Hooft, F. A. J., 181
Van Iddekinge, C. H., 183, 195, 208, 426
van Knippenberg, D., 412, 447, 483

van Quaquebeke, N., 447
Van Rooy, D. L., 177
Van Scotter, J. R., 204, 335
Van Wijhe, C. I., 351
Van Yperen, N. W., 301
Vancouver, J. B., 301
Vandenberg, R., 348
Vandenberghe, C., 345, 348
Vander Elst, T., 387
Vandewalle, D., 152, 264
Vargas, Y., 264
Vartiainen, M., 424, 425
Vasilopoulos, N. L., 83
Vecchio, R. P., 456
Veiga, J. F., 145, 372, 375, 450
Velada, R., 254
Velkoff, V. A., 379
Villado, A. J., 172
Villanova, P. D., 108, 111, 142, 151, 157
Vinchur, A. J., 12, 191, 195
Vinson, M., 49, 234
Virick, M., 385
Visweswaran, C., 177, 179, 256
Vroom, V., 296, 297, 298, 442

**W**

Waar, P., 368
Waclawski, J., 480
Wager, W. W., 249
Wagner, D. T., 148
Wagner, J. A., 471, 475
Wagner, S. H., 141
Wagner-Tsukamoto, S., 470
Walczyk, J. J., 183
Waldman, D. A., 334
Walker, H. J., 206
Wall, T. D., 289
Walumbwa, F. O., 451
Wamslet, P. T., 84
Wanberg, C. R., 20, 262
Wang, G. G., 249, 268
Wang, M., 157, 371, 458
Ward, A., 353
Warr, P., 369, 387, 388
Wassell, J. T., 393
Wasserman, M. E., 262
Watkins, K., 487
Watt, A. H., 234
Wayhan, V. B., 491
Wayne, J. H., 205

Wayne, S. J., 150
Weber, J., 384
Weber, M., 471, 472, 473
Webster, J. R., 365
Wechsler, D., 171
Wegge, J., 300
Weigl, M., 310
Weisinger, J. Y., 276
Weiss, H. M., 49, 354
Welch, J., 432
Welle, B., 329
Weller, I., 337
Wellman, N., 440
Welsh, E. T., 262
Welsh, J., 500
Weng, Q., 346
Wentling, T., 262
Werner, J., 158
Wesolowski, M. A., 325
Westerman, C. Y. K., 152
Westman, M., 363
Wexley, K. N., 148, 250, 251, 252, 254, 258, 259, 266, 363
Whetten, D. A., 264
Whetzel, D. L., 192
Whitaker, B. G., 154, 156, 328
White, C. S., 295
Whiteman, J.-A. K., 253
Whiting, S. W., 116
Whitney, D. J., 182
Wiemann, S., 183
Wiesenfeld, B. M., 385, 386
Wilcox, D., 249, 268
Wilder, D. A., 305
Wilderom, C. P. M., 460
Wilhelm, U., 171
Williams, J. R., 119, 127, 130, 146
Williams, K. D., 407
Williams, L. M., 461
Williams, M. L., 294
Williamson, I. O., 204
Wilson, C., 384, 385
Wilson, H. J., 159
Wilson, J. R., 415
Wilson, K. S., 403
Wingate, P. H., 116
Wirtenberg, J., 480
Wise, L. L., 109
Witt, L. A., 149, 150, 443
Woehr, D. J., 115, 185
Won, J. U., 366

# Subject Index

Note: Page numbers followed by f indicate figures; those followed by t indicate tables.